XINJIANG

Studies of Central Asia and the Caucasus

Books in this series are published in association with the Central Asia–Caucasus Institute of the Johns Hopkins University's Paul H. Nitze School of Advanced International Studies, under the editorship of S. Frederick Starr.

XINJIANG

CHINA'S MUSLIM BORDERLAND

S. FREDERICK STARR, EDITOR

M.E.Sharpe
Armonk, New York
London, England

Library of Congress Cataloging-in-Publication Data

Xinjiang : China's Muslim borderland / edited by S. Frederick Starr.
    p. cm.—(Studies of Central Asia and the Caucasus)
Includes bibliographical references and index.
ISBN 0-7656-1317-4 (alk. paper); ISBN 0-7656-1318-2 (pbk.)
1. Xinjiang Uygur Zizhiqu (China) I. Starr, S. Frederick. II. Series.

DS793.S62 X5632 2004
951'.—dc21   2003011518

Printed in the United States of America

The paper used in this publication meets the minimum requirements of
American National Standard for Information Sciences
Permanence of Paper for Printed Library Materials,
ANSI Z 39.48-1984.

BM (c)   10   9   8   7   6   5   4   3   2
BM (p)   10   9   8   7   6   5   4   3   2

Contents

List of Tables and Illustrative Materials

Figures

Boxes

Illustrations

Illustrations by Liang Xi

Photographs

Photographs follow page 24.

Photographs by Stanley Toops

List of Acronyms

AFV	armored fighting vehicle
APC	armored personnel carrier
CIA	Central Intelligence Agency
CMC	Central Military Commission
CCP	Chinese Communist Party
CNPC	Chinese National Petroleum Company
ETIM	Eastern Turkistan Islamic Movement
ETNC	East Turkistan National Congress
ETLO	Eastern Turkistan Liberation Organization
ETR	Eastern Turkistan Republic
FIEs	foreign-invested enterprises
GDP	gross domestic product
GMD	Guomindang
IFV	infantry fighting vehicle
INA	Ili National Army
ITHRA	International Taklimakan Human Rights Association
ISI	Inter-Services Intelligence
LAC	Line of Actual Control
MAC	Military Affairs Commission
MBT	main battle tank
MRL	multiple rocket launcher
MUCD	military unit cover designation
NBS	National Bureau of Statistics
NGOs	nongovernmental organizations
NSA	National Security Agency
NSC	National Security Council
PAPF	People's Armed Police Force
PLA	People's Liberation Army
PRC	People's Republic of China
RFA	Radio Free Asia
SAM	surface-to-air missile
SCO	Shanghai Cooperation Organization
SIGINT	signal intelligence

TRACECA   Transport Corridor Europe Caucasus Asia, a Programme
           of the European Commission
UKY   Uyghur kompyutér yéziqi
XMD   Xinjiang Military District
XMR   Xinjiang Military Region
XPCC   Xinjiang Production and Construction Corps (Xinjiang
           shengchan jianshe bingtuan)
XRC   Xinjiang Revolutionary Committee
XUAR   Xinjiang Uyghur Autonomous Region

Note on Transliteration

In this volume, we employ Hanyu Pinyin for the transliteration of Chinese, and a modified Library of Congress system for Russian. There is no universally recognized system for romanizing modern Uyghur from its modified Arabic script. We have decided not to use the People's Republic of China's (PRC) old Roman-based script (*yéngi yéziq*) for two reasons: It contains odd characters and diacritical marks not in the Roman alphabet, and it has been largely abandoned in the PRC itself since 1984. Instead, for Uyghur names and terms, we use a relatively new system, Uyghur kompyutér yéziqi (UKY), which is coming into increasing use on the Internet.[1] Its conventions are essentially the same as those in general use for romanizing Turkic languages (as in Henry G. Schwarz's *Uyghur-English Dictionary,* or Reinhard F. Hahn's *Spoken Uyghur*[2]), with a few modifications to limit the number of unfamiliar diacritics and ease the typing of Uyghur on computer keyboards. The modifications are as follows:

Usual Transliteration	UKY	Example Using UKY
ç	ch	chapan
ä	e	erkin
e	é	éyiq
ğ	gh	ghalip
ñ	ng	ming
š	sh	sheher

In the UKY system, "q" is pronounced as a hard "k" in the back of the throat, and "x" is pronounced like the "ch" in "Bach." This differs from how these letters are pronounced in Pinyin and the old PRC Uyghur romanization system, but it accords with Turkological usage.

The spellings used for names of Xinjiang places and historical personages vary greatly in the literature. Here, we attempt to use spellings that will be most familiar to readers, even when they are at odds with modern Uyghur or Chinese pronunciation. Thus, for example, we use "Kashgar," not "Qeshqer," "Kaxgar," or "Kashi," for the city in the southwest corner of the Xinjiang region. In addition, we use the Mandarin Chinese name for the city of "Yining" rather than the Uyghur name "Gulja."

Notes

1. "Uyghur Kompyuter Yeziqi," http://misiram\n.com/uth\ghurlar/til_yeziq/uly_elipbe.ht (accessed 6 June 2002). This site contains a chart of the transcription system in modified Arabic and Roman scripts.
2. Henry G. Schwarz, *An Uyghur-English Dictionary* (Bellingham: Center for East Asian Studies, Western Washington University, 1992); and Reinhard F. Hahn, *Spoken Uyghur* (Seattle: University of Washington Press, 1991).

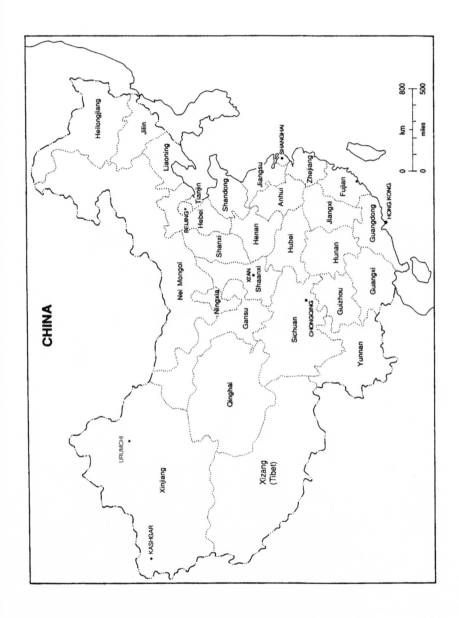

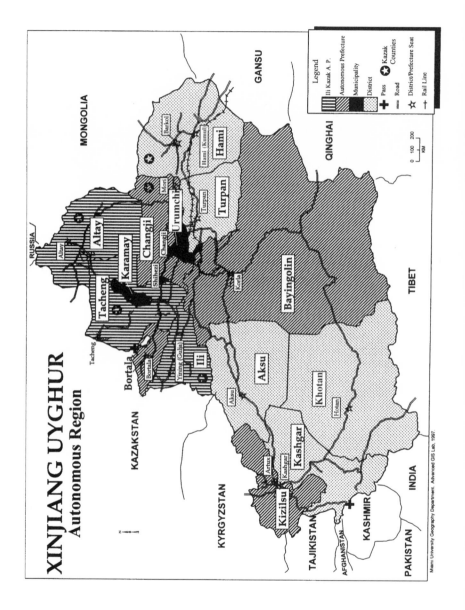

XINJIANG UYGHUR
Autonomous Region

Legend

Ili Kazak A. P.
Autonomous Prefecture
Municipality
District

Pass
Road

Kazak Counties

District/Prefecture Seat
Rail Line

0 100 200
KM

MONGOLIA

RUSSIA

KAZAKSTAN

KYRGYZSTAN

TAJIKISTAN

AFGHANISTAN

KASHMIR

PAKISTAN

INDIA

TIBET

QINGHAI

GANSU

Altay

Tacheng

Karamay

Changji

Urumchi

Hami

Turpan

Bayingolin

Aksu

Khotan

Kashgar

Kizilsu

Ili

Bortala

Barköl

Hami (Kumul)

Mori

Turpan

Korla

Shihezi

Changji

Altay

Tacheng

Bortala

Yining (Gulja)

Aksu

Hotan

Kashgar

Artux

Miami University Geography Department. Advanced GIS Lab, 1997.

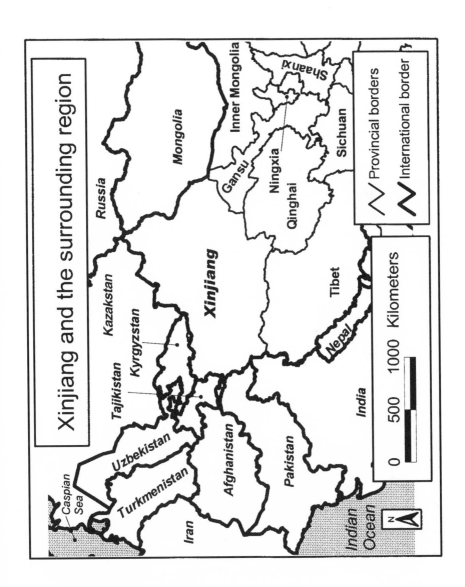

Xinjiang and the surrounding region

XINJIANG

1

Introduction

S. Frederick Starr

If Xinjiang's only claim to fame were that it is China's largest province and a sixth of its land area, if it only had the highest per capita gross domestic product (GDP) of any province outside the booming coast, or if it could only boast of being home to China's nuclear test facilities and of having the country's largest oil reserves, this book would never have been written.

But Xinjiang is also the one province of China with a substantial population that is both Turkic and Muslim. In recent years, it has witnessed a vigorous Muslim revival and has been the scene of a protracted struggle for greater autonomy and even independence. Beijing officials and Western observers concur that some of the province's Turkic inhabitants have mounted thousands of shows of resistance and committed a smaller but still significant number of violent and even terrorist acts. They speak with either pride or dismay of equally confrontational countermeasures by the Chinese authorities. All this takes place in a territory that borders eight other countries, three of them nuclear powers and five of them largely Muslim. It is these aspects of Xinjiang today that evoke the world's concern and that gave rise to this book.

Xinjiang is remote from most major world centers. Its western and southern borders are closer to Baghdad or New Delhi than to Beijing. Trains from Xinjiang's capital of Urumchi take several days to reach the capital of its northern neighbor, Russia, while its southern neighbors, Afghanistan, Pakistan, and India, are as yet unreachable from Urumchi by direct rail. Its remoteness has surrounded Xinjiang with an aura of exoticism. The nineteenth-century Russian explorer Nikolay Przhevalsky, the hero of Finnish independence C. G. Mannerheim, and the great American newsman Harrison Salisbury were but three out of scores of visitors from both the West and the East who made their way there precisely because of its remoteness and difference from all their usual points of reference.[1]

More recently, Xinjiang has entered the consciousness of the West because of the stunning Buddhist paintings that survive in cave sanctuaries near several of the ancient oasis centers along the southern rim of the

Taklimakan Desert. These 1,500-year-old masterpieces attest to the region's character as a cultural transmitter, receiving, processing, and sending out once more the most diverse cultural and religious impulses. Embodying as they do one of Buddhism's most creative moments, and in a land whose people today are overwhelmingly Muslim, they also remind us of the historical discontinuities to which so open a territory gives rise. Xinjiang's remoteness and discontinuities, along with the clear evidence of high cultural attainment in the countless towns that have flourished and decayed in its territory, leave visitors from Europe, Japan, the United States, and South Korea pondering vague questions that they can scarcely frame, let alone answer.

And yet, it is this seemingly remote land that Owen Lattimore, writing in 1950, characterizes as "[t]he Pivot of Asia" and "a new center of gravity . . . in the world."[2] Even if this claim may strike some as exaggerated, four developments occurring in the late twentieth century combine to give Lattimore's assertion a new plausibility today.

First, the onset of Deng Xiaoping's reforms in the late 1970s released Xinjiang from the quasi-military rule that had existed since the Communist takeover in 1949 and, to a considerable degree, over the century and a half before that as well. As a result, its capital at Urumchi has emerged as one of China's boom towns, exuding that special kind of glittering prosperity that sudden wealth from oil and gas creates everywhere. Calla Wiemer provides evidence in chapter 6 that Xinjiang's economy remains among the most state-centered of all China's provinces, but the reforms have nonetheless emboldened leaders in Beijing and Xinjiang itself to dream dreams and undertake grand schemes that would have been unthinkable earlier.

Second, the opening after 1987 of China's western border ended Xinjiang's forty-year isolation from its neighbors and allowed the renewal of trade and contact with the rest of Central Asia that were as old as the fabled Silk Road. Sean R. Roberts in chapter 8 documents some of the dynamics of this new interaction and indicates both the possibilities it opens to Turkic peoples in Xinjiang and the government's efforts to direct these into acceptable channels. He also reminds us that more open borders have unleashed new economic and social forces in Xinjiang that fit uneasily with the neat template of development that Beijing has imposed on the territory.

Third, the collapse of the Soviet Union and the establishment of independent states by Turkic and Iranian (e.g., Tajik) neighbors created a model of political sovereignty and cultural autonomy that entices and inspires many Turkic Uyghurs in Xinjiang. Why is it, they ask, that peoples that are poorer than us, and whose histories are far shorter than ours, enjoy self-rule while we do not? Even those who stop short of calling for independence take inspiration from the new sovereign states immediately to their west.

And fourth, the defeat of the Soviet Union's Red Army by Muslim arms in Afghanistan, the renewal of Islam in post-Communist Central Asia, and the emergence of well-funded radical Islamic movements in both of these regions have inspired many of Xinjiang's Muslims to redefine their aspirations in religious terms. A few returned to deeper forms of piety. Far more embraced Islam precisely because it is what sets them apart from their Han Chinese rulers. Shifting between policies of encouragement to minority peoples and cultures and outright repression, Beijing appears at a loss over how to handle this powerful and unpredictable force.

In the autumn of 2001, the war against terrorism exploded into this rapidly changing environment. Officials and observers in Beijing and many other world capitals urgently asked whether Xinjiang would now become a new locus of terrorist activity and of the Muslim extremism that many terrorists espoused. Immediately, sharp disagreements emerged. Some, notably the Chinese government in Beijing, claimed that this had already occurred and that the pathology had to be routed out with whatever force was necessary to accomplish the job. Others, including émigré Uyghur activists in many countries and many foreign observers, vehemently denied it. Still others insisted that the very term "terrorism" masked the real issue, which was whether Xinjiang's non–Han Chinese peoples had any right to self-rule.

Unfortunately, nearly all these overheated exchanges demonstrated with appalling clarity that the internal life of Xinjiang today remains largely a terra incognita to outsiders. Acknowledging this, foreign embassies in Beijing rushed to send out staffers to gauge the situation on the ground. Leading news media dispatched reporters and film crews to Urumchi, Kashgar, or Ili with orders to "get the story." But the mass of reports that flowed back from these efforts only deepened the confusion. Is this due to the fact that available data on Xinjiang are incomplete or inaccurate? Or is it that the evidence is available but is contradictory or inconclusive? Or, finally, do the conflicting analyses arise from the fact that conscious or unconscious biases distort the vision of even the most conscientious observers?

The authors of this book launched their collaborative effort in 1998, well before the current explosion of interest in Xinjiang. Many of them had already been studying and writing about Xinjiang for decades. They set as their task to draw a three-dimensional portrait of Xinjiang, with no concern over whether the resulting picture would support or cast doubt on existing views on the subject. They were acutely aware of the paucity of data on many key points, and equally conscious of the perverse way in which authoritative bodies of evidence can contradict each other. Looming over both of these difficulties, however, was their appreciation, which deepened as the work progressed, of the manner in which the same events or information can support strikingly different conclusions, depending on the vantage point of the observer. Bluntly, there is hardly any "fact" concerning Xinjiang that is so solid, no source of information that is so independent, and no analysis based on such overwhelming evidence that someone does not hotly contest its validity or meaning.

This contentiousness begins with the very name of the region. When Manchu rulers of Beijing declared this land to the west a part of their Qing empire, they began referring to it by what they obviously considered a fitting name: "Xinjiang," meaning "new territory" or "new frontier." While some Uyghur writers have claimed this name came into use only in the 1880s, James A. Millward finds references to it before 1800, when it supplanted the ancient Han dynasty term "western regions." But whenever it arose, no one at the time contested the accuracy or appropriateness of this name. But since 1949, China's Communist government has vehemently denied that Xinjiang was new to China in the 1760s and, as Gardner Bovingdon recounts in chapter 14, has assembled (or, depending on one's perspective, concocted) a history of Chinese rule there dating back two millennia. Many local Turkic people, however, are equally adamant in their view that the region was their ancestral homeland and the continuous seat of their culture from deep antiquity down to the most recent times, when China usurped it.

In a 1955 effort to win over Turkic speakers in the territory, Mao Zedong's government affixed to Xinjiang the sonorous title of the "Xinjiang Uyghur Autonomous Region." In practice, the administration there was neither Uyghur nor truly autonomous. But as Dru C. Gladney argues in chapter 4, the official use of this resonant title strengthened, or even created, a sense of regionwide Uyghur identity and solidarity, as well as the expectation among many Uyghurs that Xinjiang should be really autonomous and not in name only. No one in Beijing is prepared to counter this current of opinion by giving Xinjiang a new name that proclaims what the Chinese Communist Party holds to be its ancient identity as part of China. But such expectations arouse deep concern in Beijing, which responds by banning all public references to "Eastern Turkistan," the official name of two independent states established there briefly in the 1930s and 1940s, as well as the name "Uyghuristan" that some ethnic separatists favor today.

Conflicting vantage points may sharpen the controversies that swirl around Xinjiang, but their origins go far deeper than current polemics. In spite of its seeming remoteness, Xinjiang, like the rest of Central Asia, is arguably one of the most complex zones of cultural interaction on earth. Situated astride the great trade routes connecting China, the Middle East, Europe, and the Indian subcontinent, it has been a kind of cultural blotter for influences from each of these great civilizations. The fields of archaeology, linguistics, religion, technology, art, politics, and economics all confirm this truth. For millennia before 1877, when the German traveler and scholar Ferdinand von Richthoven coined the term "Silk Road,"[3] Xinjiang was defined by its unique position along multiple cultural fault lines. This makes the territory the pivot of more than Asia and imparts to it, and to the rest of Central Asia as well, a centrality that neither remoteness nor isolation can gainsay.

International Ties and Centrifugal Forces

Over the millennia, these foreign contacts have set a bewildering array of attractive models before the peoples of Xinjiang for their own development. While it is an exaggeration to say that external influences have defined Xinjiang, it is hard to find another region on which such diverse external cultural forces have been so consistently exerted. Together, these act like external gravitational fields, pulling Xinjiang in different directions and away from whatever inward cultural moorings it may have. The physical analogy is not exact, since the force is coming from outside rather than from within, yet the result is to create something akin to powerful centrifugal tendencies within Xinjiang.

Asia alone has pulled Xinjiang in three quite different directions. For most of their history, the settled oases of the Tarim basin have felt the impact of nomadic peoples to their north. Coming in a seemingly endless succession, these mounted and well-armed groups have invariably arrived as floating bands of marauders and booty-seekers. The successful ones eventually settled in the region, often creating significant cultures. Once settled, they had to face the business of rule, which invariably opened opportunities to the oasis dwellers. The newcomers' need for basic provisions also gave rise to reciprocal trade relations and to cultural interaction with the indigenous peoples.

A second and far more organized form of influence has come from the historic territory of China. To be sure, several of the dynasties that exerted the most powerful influence on Xinjiang, notably the Mongols and Manchus, had themselves emerged as leaders of settled states only after they conquered Beijing. But beginning as early as the Han and Tang times, China proper has exerted a powerful gravitational force on Xinjiang. Persisting over two millennia, this reached a crescendo during the period of Qing rule in the eighteenth and early nineteenth centuries and again under Communist rule after 1949. The new course that China adopted as a result of Deng's reforms in the

1970s has brought in its wake unprecedented pressures on Xinjiang to merge its fate with the evolving Chinese model of market development. As described by Gladney, Wiemer, and Linda Benson (chapter 7), the range and depth of China's impact since Deng have been enormous by any measure, rivaling or surpassing the Maoist changes, the Great Leap Forward, and the Cultural Revolution.

By comparison with China's steady impact through the centuries, the gravitational pull of the Indian subcontinent has been more focused chronologically. This third form of Asian influence peaked during the first millennium, during which time Buddhism became a decisive presence in nearly all the major urban centers in Xinjiang. Even after the rise of Islam, trade with Kashmir, Rajasthan, and beyond remained important for Xinjiang. More recently, Xinjiang, like the neighboring province of Tibet, has felt the impact of Sino-Indian tensions. Beijing's perception of a threat from India also gave rise to China's, and hence Xinjiang's, enduring strategic link with Pakistan. The fact that China has recently undertaken to construct a major port for Pakistan at Gwadar on the Arabian Sea that will serve the entire Indus basin, Central Asia, and Xinjiang suggests that a new age of intensive interaction with the India-Pakistan region is dawning in Xinjiang. How deeply this will affect the territory remains to be seen. One thing is certain, however: Such ties with the south will bring new influences, as has already happened as Pakistani traders attempted in the 1990s to disseminate their understanding of Islam and of an Islamic state.

Trade also provided a moving conveyer belt for Xinjiang's interaction with the Middle East and the heartland of Central Asia. Until quite recently, however, far more contact has been with the larger Persian world (including the great oasis centers of the Ferghana region and Bactria) than with the more remote Arabs farther west. Such trade brought the Persians' dualistic religions, Zoroastrianism and then Manichaeanism, and also the Syrian-Persian branch of Christianity known as Nestorianism, as well as pockets of Judaism. From the outset, Xinjiang's Islam had a strong Persian and Central Asian–Persian cast, especially with its cult of saints and the popularity of mystical Sufi brotherhoods. Like most Persian and Turkic speakers in Central Asia but unlike Persians in Iran, Xinjiang's Turkic Muslims remained Sunni even after the Saffavids adopted Shiism as the Iranian national faith in the sixteenth century. Only a small community of Tajik Ismailis in the far southwest adhere to the Shiia branch of Islam, along with some others in Tajikistan and Afghanistan. Today, Beijing insists that Xinjiang is, and always has been, solidly within the Chinese orbit, but with ideas and models flowing in from as far away as Turkey and the Arab world, this contention must at the very least be broadened.

The links with Iran and Central Asia brought Xinjiang both learning (astronomy, mathematics, medicine, and so on) and statecraft. But with the interesting exception of the Karakhanids in the tenth and eleventh centuries and, briefly, of the mercurial Yaqub Bey from Kokand, who attempted in the nineteenth century to rule the region from a base in Kashgar, all of these proved to be geographically limited and ultimately ephemeral. Attempts to organize Xinjiang politically from the west have been even less successful than those from the north and east.

Some contemporary Uyghur intellectuals in Xinjiang and in the large Uyghur émigré communities in Kazakstan, Kyrgyzstan, Turkey, Europe, and the United States speak enthusiastically of their regions' historic links with Europe. As Millward and Peter C. Perdue show in chapter 2, their effort to claim the famed "mummies" from the Taklimakan Desert as both Uyghur and European (on account of their sandy hair and plaid clothing) is doubly disingenuous. Yet, the larger point is well taken. In Han times, Xinjiang's trade extended to the Roman Empire and in Tang times to Byzantium and Western Europe. Then, from the eighteenth through the twentieth century, it was Russia that embodied Europe to the people of Xinjiang. Great Britain, operating from bases in its Indian empire, played a secondary but by no means negligible role. Long before the Soviet Union attempted to detach parts of Xinjiang from China during the 1960s, Russia provided new models in statecraft, economy, and culture for the region. Even the first movement of Islamic reform—the Jaddids—was brought to Xinjiang a century ago by secular and pro-Western Muslim Tatars from the upper Volga region of Russia.

This is not the place to debate the Europeanness of Marxism or the extent to which Chinese Communism is Marxist. Yet, it cannot be denied that the very idea of a "Uyghur Autonomous Region" traces directly to formulae that Joseph Stalin first applied in Soviet-ruled Central Asia in his effort to solve ethnic and national problems there. True, down to 1949, Mao, unlike Stalin, conceived this to include the right of secession and even thereafter permitted a greater degree of minority self-rule. But whatever their differences, both of these owe an ironic debt to notions of national self-determination prevalent in Europe at the time Vladimir Lenin was seizing power in Moscow, which were most effectively articulated by U.S. president Woodrow Wilson. The difference, of course, is that while the negotiators at Versailles saw national self-determination as a strategic ideal, Lenin and Mao perceived it merely as a tactic. Be that as it may, since the fall of the Soviet Union, a new Russia has reestablished good relations with China and hence with Xinjiang, as a result of which it may once more play the role of Xinjiang's most European neighbor, in short, of a Western model on its doorstep.

Over the centuries, these very diverse cultural zones surrounding Xinjiang have exerted a powerful and persistent gravitational force in virtually every field of endeavor. The fact that none of them has ever prevailed attests to Xinjiang's peculiar location at the junction of different civilizations. It has always been a kind of cartilage, cushion, or buffer, a zone of transition rather than a fortress marking the end of one sharply defined political or cultural zone and the start of another. Past efforts to change this essential character have never succeeded.

The implications of this situation bear emphasis. In spite of the fact that Xinjiang is a single political entity within today's China, with all its borders with foreign neighbors except India now carefully delineated, Xinjiang has never been a single territory in the past and is not really one today. As Stanley W. Toops points out in chapters 9 and 10 on demography and ecology, the vast, centrally placed, and uninhabited Taklimakan Desert transforms Xinjiang geographically into a kind of doughnut, with a large separate appendage beyond the Tian Shan to the north. Such a configuration denies to Xinjiang a single central habitation area that can serve as a receiving point and transformer for all the influences flowing in from abroad. Thus, Xinjiang's very geography reinforces the centripetal tendencies created by vigorous cultural zones beyond its borders.

Notwithstanding this, the two most powerful forces from beyond Xinjiang's borders today both act with nearly equal force on all the region's parts. To the extent that their impact falls unequally across Xinjiang, the relevant distinction is not between geographic zones but between urban and rural dwellers and between Han Chinese and ethnic minorities. These forces are, first, the assimilationist pressures enshrined in current Chinese economic and social policies and, second, the diverse economic and social transformations that flow from the global revolutions in communications and trade. Though closely related, the two differ in significant ways.

China's reforming economy provides the most immediate model for development in Xinjiang. Beijing's "Develop the West" (*xibu da kaifa*) campaign announced in 2001 will eventually pump some $12 billion into Xinjiang's economic infrastructure. Because these projects pertain mainly to communications, transportation, large-scale industry, and energy development, they fall comfortably within normal definitions of modernization, albeit with a Chinese face. And to the extent that these projects integrate Xinjiang more closely with the world beyond its borders, they can be seen as part of the larger process of globalization. China's entry into the World Trade Organization in 2000 further underscores its engagement with globalization. Yet, unlike China's prosperous coastal zone, which benefits richly from direct international investment, most of the capital for the Develop the West campaign in Xinjiang will come from elsewhere within China.[4] True, projects in gas and oil have received investments from beyond China, but even these are shaped and firmly controlled by Chinese entities. To the extent this pattern continues, it is fair to say that globalization in Xinjiang will have a strong Chinese cast and will serve the goal of assimilation into the People's Republic of China (PRC) as much or more than the goal of global integration. This underscores the thesis that the past two decades mark a fundamental shift in the long-term evolution of Xinjiang.

Two other foreign influences today affect the entirety of Xinjiang rather than one or more of its parts. The Turkey of Atatürk—nationalistic, modernizing, and staunchly secular—has long intrigued some Uyghur intellectuals, the more so because the population is largely Turkic. And as noted earlier, the establishment of sovereign states in the formerly Soviet-ruled sector of Central Asia also creates a seductive and subversive Turkic model of future development for people in Xinjiang, and especially for those alienated from Chinese policies. Simultaneously, new forms of political Islam arising from the Mediterranean to Indonesia insinuate themselves into the consciousness of Xinjiang's Muslim populace as surely as did the Sufi orders a half millennium ago. These currents parallel a general revival of Islam that has occurred throughout Central Asia, which many Muslims of Xinjiang greet all the more warmly because it gives them a sense of participating in a global movement rather than a purely regional development. Both of these currents—Turkic secularism and revival Islam—appear as alternatives to assimilation and global integration in the forms that Beijing is promoting.

Thus, it appears that all the main forces acting on the internal life of the territory today arise from developments occurring beyond Xinjiang's borders or at least gain strength and legitimacy from such developments abroad. However unprecedented the changes taking place in Xinjiang today, the overall process manifests the combination of international links and centrifugal tendencies that has characterized Xinjiang through the millennia.

Centripetal Forces in Xinjiang

The picture of Xinjiang presented so far is of a territory and culture acted on by others but not one capable of generating political, economic, and cultural energies of its own. But it cannot be denied that a variety of centripetal forces have also operated in Xinjiang down through the centuries. To some extent, these have been the natural consequences of distance and isolation. As Justin Rudelson shows,[5] each of Xinjiang's major oases constituted a kind of microculture, self-governing on a day-to-day basis and with its own distinctive economic and social features. Even if Xinjiang lacked a single large and densely populated central region that could serve as a gestation point for a larger territorial identity, it had a half-dozen important oases and other centers, each of which was a kind of laboratory where that function could be played out in microcosm. This may have retarded the development of state-based identities stretching across the region, but it had the important effect of strengthening the oases' ability to adapt selectively what came to them from abroad rather than to adopt such imported ideas and practices wholesale.

In this way, geography endowed Xinjiang's peoples with one of their most valuable traits, namely, their capacity to resist external pressures over time. These defensive skills underlie most of the centripetal forces and movements that have been generated on the territory of Xinjiang through the centuries.

The expectation that the huge and diverse territory of Xinjiang, or even a large part of it, should constitute a single political entity is a modern invention. Nonetheless, a number of significant states have arisen within this region. Many of them have comprised territory extending across Xinjiang's borders. Thus, the Karakhanids, the earliest Turkic Muslim state whose tenth- and eleventh-century rule extended deep into Afghanistan and to the borders of modern Iran, had their capitals in what is now western Xinjiang and northeastern Kyrgyzstan. Others confined their rule to Xinjiang, basing their power in either the Tarim basin south of the Tian Shan, as did the Uyghurs in the first millennium, or north of the Tian Shan, as did the seventeenth-century Zunghars.

Besides collecting taxes to pay for the maintenance of irrigation systems, the chief task of any inner Asian state was to provide security to the inhabitants of a given territory. This could be accomplished through passive or active means. The former called for a negotiated agreement with a powerful neighbor that exchanged money for noninterference or even protection against third parties. The latter meant forming and maintaining an army capable of resisting invading forces. The immense potency of their mounted and massed bowmen gave nomadic armies an inherent advantage over nearly any oasis army. This turned the oasis dwellers into deal makers and masters of diplomatic manipulation rather than fighters. It strengthened defensive skills and subtle arts of resistance among them. Even the nomadic Zunghars, once they achieved power, had to master these skills in order to garner allies in their steady resistance to the growing Qing power in the region.

Even after the establishment of Qing rule in Xinjiang during the 1760s, the old skills of defense and resistance surfaced whenever the central government's forces in the region flagged. The ambitious Yaqub Beg entered Kashgar from Kokand in present-day Uzbekistan in 1864 to take advantage of precisely such a situation. Once installed in Kashgar, however, he revealed during his thirteen-year rule the same skills at local mobilization and deal making that had sustained so many of his oasis predecessors.

Much the same occurred as Guomindang Chinese rule eroded during the 1930s and 1940s. Two "Eastern Turkistan Republics" arose in rapid succession, the first in Kashgar and the second in the Kazak territory north of the Tian Shan. Intensive maneuvering enabled the first to survive from 1931 to 1934 and the second from 1944 to 1949. It is tempting to dismiss these abortive states or Yaqub Bey's brief rule in the previous century as mere adventures. But it is clear that Mao took them seriously, detecting in them the presence of powerful centripetal energies that could seriously undermine Communist rule from Beijing. It is for this reason that Mao eventually conceded the title "Xinjiang Autonomous Region."

In doing so, Mao nourished one of the most serious centripetal movements in Xinjiang's long history: the rise of pan-Uyghur identity. Nabijan Tursun argues that this was taking root as early as the end of the nineteenth century, thanks to the influence of Russian orientalists on Uyghur travelers in tsarist lands. As he and Millward show in chapter 3, the idea of a pan-Uyghur identity gained strength under the Sheng Shicai warlord regime and the second Eastern Turkistan Republic. It was Sheng who, directly imitating the Soviet Union, designated "Uyghur" as the kind of national category Stalin had instituted elsewhere in Central Asia for Kyrgyz, Uzbeks, Tajiks, and so on.

Both destructive and constructive developments in Xinjiang today feed the Uyghur movement, which responds with a mixture of reactive and assertive moves. On the negative side, some Uyghur intellectuals responded to the reassertion of rule from Beijing much the way German intellectuals did to Napoléon Bonaparte's conquest of the many German principalities and his destruction of local institutions, namely, by defiantly asserting a single national identity. True, in the Tarim basin there was little resistance to the Communist takeover, and in the north the Communist victory elicited as much confusion as resistance. Thus, it may be an exaggeration to say that "China called forth the Uyghur people," just as it is to claim that "France called forth the German people." Yet, each claim has an element of truth.

On the other side, it is undeniable that China's educational policies since 1949 have enormously expanded the ranks of the Turkic urban intelligentsia in Xinjiang. As Benson shows in chapter 7, Uyghurs and other Turkic peoples advanced in many fields but also encountered impediments as well.

Whether or not they considered themselves Uyghur prior to their encounters with the Han Chinese establishment in Xinjiang, many came to think of themselves as Uyghur thereafter. By such a process that directly recalls what took place earlier in the Soviet republics of Central Asia, the ethnic and national policies of a Communist state that favored class over ethnicity or nationality fostered the development, if not the creation, of new ethnic consciousnesses in Xinjiang.[6]

Beyond these factors, one cannot minimize the role of improved communications and transportation in strengthening a regionwide consciousness among Xinjiang's Turkic peoples. The ability to travel easily by truck, bus, or railroad enables people of modest means to form contacts with Turkic speakers hundreds of miles from home. Radio and television broadcasts in the Uyghur language and improved telephone connections also facilitate interaction over distances. In the mid-twentieth century, the American political scientist Karl Deutsch argued that one can detect the bases of political communities in the emerging patterns of communications. He therefore counted telephone calls and first-class mail within various regions and between those regions and their neighbors. Such an exercise in Xinjiang would doubtless reveal not only an expanding base of political community among the Turkic peoples of Xinjiang but also a possible growing rift between them and the Han Chinese who dwell among them.

Taken together, these very different developments have fueled an unprecedented growth of national consciousness among the Uyghur Turks of Xinjiang, which in turn gives rise to a centripetal force that is different in kind and strength from any that had existed in Xinjiang's past.

The social base of this new consciousness does not correspond precisely to the borders of Xinjiang. The northern Kazaks remain somewhat aloof from it, Uyghur ethnic consciousness is less pronounced in areas near China proper, and some of the most ardent Uyghur nationalists are in emigration. Acknowledging this, it is fair to say that this new centripetal force comes closer to embracing the entire territory of Xinjiang than any current or past movement.

The Chinese government is acutely aware of this development and has designed its policies to undercut or minimize it. Beijing has based its approach to regional governance on principles of standardization, centralization, and assimilation. It thus recalls the French model of colonial rule more than the British system, with its emphasis on the co-optation of local elites. Given this, it was probably inevitable that this new Uyghur consciousness would clash with policies of the PRC in many areas. Many Uyghurs, especially younger urban males, have reacted to Beijing's top-down style of rule with covert and overt shows of resistance. Some support ecological causes, programs to prevent and treat AIDS, or even antialcohol campaigns, as described by Toops (chapter 10), Jay Dautcher (chapter 11), and Rudelson and William Jankowiak (chapter 12). Many others, with an eye to their own and their children's advancement in China's expanding economy, have chosen to make their peace with the new reality. These practical men and women, probably a majority among Xinjiang's minorities, are mastering the Chinese language and the modern skills necessary to thrive in a competitive world and are preserving their Turkic or Muslim identity in the private realms of their lives.

The level of civil discord increased during the 1990s. Chinese government sources enumerate almost daily incidents of violence, while an as-yet unreleased study by the RAND Corporation is said to have listed 3,000 instances of civil violence for the year 2000 alone.[7] Particularly bloody confrontations occurred at the town of Baren in 1990 and in Ili in 1997. The government was quick to blame these outbreaks on "separatists" (*fenlie zhuyi zhe*, which Chinese government translators insist on rendering clumsily as "splittists"), Muslim radicals, or terrorists and designed its indelicately named "Strike Hard, Maximum Pressure" campaign explicitly to counter them. It has condemned hundreds of men and women to death by shooting, used torture to extract confessions, jailed thousands, and stripped many others of the right to work or to practice Islam—all in the name of quelling "splittism," religious extremism, and terrorism. But it is always difficult to prove such charges, let alone to determine with any precision the actual motives of the accused, as opposed to those imputed to them by others. Yet, the discontent and resistance continue. Whether it manifests itself in published polemics, religion, civic activism, or violence, the new Uyghur consciousness is a fact of life in Xinjiang today and arguably the most significant centripetal force in the long history of the territory.

Perception and Analysis

Xinjiang's long history involving innumerable peoples, religions, and cultures; its complex web of foreign links; and its intricate interethnic relationships pose a stupendous challenge for anyone seeking to understand the region's past or present. The evidence on which any serious conclusions must be grounded is sprinkled through largely untranslated texts in Uyghur, Chinese, Japanese, and Russian, not to mention Persian, Chaghatay, Türki, and even more exotic tongues.

China has issued quantities of useful statistical data that must be consulted but sometimes treated with caution, if not cold skepticism. Strict controls arising from acute political sensitivities make it all but impossible for social scientists to conduct the kinds of field research, interviews, and surveys in Xinjiang that would be the norm for rigorous study elsewhere.

It is no wonder that so many foreign students, Chinese analysts, and even natives of the region resort to hoary generalities and self-serving clichés when they seek to "explain" Xinjiang. Lacking authoritative evidence on its internal life, they find it convenient to focus instead on Xinjiang either as a tableau of exotica or as a crude geopolitical problem. Peter Hopkirk's engaging *Foreign Devils along the Silk Road* is a masterful example of both tendencies. Essential to all such treatments is a recitation of Xinjiang's role in the "Great Game" of imperial competition. Coined by British civil servants more than a century ago, the notion of a Great Game gained new life as Central Asia reemerged in the consciousness of the international public following the collapse of the Soviet Union.

Beginning about 1970, the challenge of Xinjiang's remoteness and "otherness" began to attract a fresh generation of scholars in the West. Meanwhile, historians, economists, demographers, and even military experts began poring through the rich published sources, including important data issued in China. Their subject is less the Great Game than the ball over which it was, and is, fought. In the process, they began to appreciate Xinjiang's development from the inside out rather than from the outside in.

Far less attention, however, has been devoted to understanding the precise nature of China's interests and concerns in Xinjiang and its policies toward the territory. The opaqueness of Beijing's political processes only partly explains this neglect. Thus, the scale of Xinjiang's energy resources is no secret, nor is the presence at Lop Nor of China's sole nuclear and missile test range. How, if at all, do these affect Beijing's policy toward Xinjiang? The problem remains largely unstudied. In the same context, how does the fact that Xinjiang ranks thirteenth among thirty-one provinces in per capita GDP influence China's approach to this volatile territory? Even as these issues are neglected, considerable research has been devoted to the central institutions of the PRC and to governmental and social institutions at the village and township levels. Only recently have scholars launched a comprehensive study of how China rules its provinces, and this has yet to treat Xinjiang.[8]

In some quarters, the inattention to China's interests in Xinjiang traces to political correctness. Not without justice, Xinjiang's Turkic peoples have been cast in the role of victims of Chinese policy. If one accepts this, then to dwell on the concerns of Beijing would seem as heartless as to focus on Paris rather than the Algerians, London rather than the Irish, Moscow rather than the Chechens, or Washington rather than the American Indians.

Easily overlooked amid this exercise in victimology is the fact that Beijing's approach has included as many carrots as sticks. Large-scale affirmative action policies and some 700 major projects designed to boost Xinjiang's economy from 2002 to 2007 are but two of many examples of Beijing's commitment to Develop the West. But if such examples of proactive policies from Beijing warrant attention, so do the limits of Beijing's power to act. From the Qing era in the late eighteenth century down to the 1970s, successive governments in Beijing have actively promoted the immigration of Han Chinese to Xinjiang. Since China's economic reforms, though, such emigration has been due less to governmental pressure or support and more to impoverished Han peasants from the hinterland who set out for the west in search of a better life. This does not mean that the government does not in the end welcome this mass movement of Han people and see it as a step toward China's achieving its manifest destiny in Xinjiang. But one must still question whether Beijing, if faced with large-scale ethnic conflict, would be either willing or able to concentrate the force necessary to limit or stop this movement. Since in-migration by Han Chinese is clearly the chief cause of ethnic tension in Xinjiang today, not to mention of strain on water resources and the environment, the question is far from academic.

Notwithstanding this caveat, it is clear that in the early twenty-first century the single most consequential determinant of conditions on the ground in Urumchi, Kashgar, Ili, or Turpan is the attitudes and policies of the Chinese government. Such policies extend over many fields and ministries, including defense, internal affairs, social services, education, transportation, and energy. While usually coordinated with one another at the declarative level, the various parts of the Chinese government, like those of other large countries, are far from coherent at the operational level. For better or worse, though, they provide the institutional context against which all Turkic and Muslim aspirations in the region are set.

Why Is Xinjiang Important?

The entire population of Xinjiang is less than 2 percent of China's total of almost 1.3 billion people. Xinjiang's indigenous Turkic and Muslim population numbers only about 8 million, barely six-tenths of 1 percent of China's population. Compared to the world's other Turkic peoples, this equals only a half of Iran's Turkic population, a third of Uzbekistan's, and a ninth of Turkey's. Moreover, Xinjiang's Muslims constitute a mere two-fifths of all Muslims in China. Altogether, they are a third as numerous as Muslims in Afghanistan, and barely a twentieth of the Muslim populations of either Pakistan or India.

Against this background, one may well be tempted to dismiss Xinjiang as a minor perturbation on the world scene. But such a conclusion would be wrong on several counts. Within all of Central Asia, including Afghanistan, the Turkic and Muslim population of Xinjiang is second in size only to Uzbekistan's. Roughly equal to the Turkic population of Kazakstan, it is double the populations of neighboring Kyrgyzstan or Tajikistan, and also of Turkmenistan and Azerbaijan.

Of course, size alone is no measure of a people's impact on world affairs. Uyghurs in Xinjiang are four times more numerous than the entire Palestinian population of the West Bank and ten times more numerous than the population of Chechnya. The Turkic Tatar people of the upper Volga region in Russia are fewer in number than all the Uyghurs, but for a century they exerted a decisive influence on Muslims throughout the Middle East and Central Asia through their efforts to reform Islam.

Besides these considerations, the situation in Xinjiang today is important because China's government considers it to be so. Its Develop the West campaign is an essential element of Beijing's overall strategy of national advancement. Both the aggressive name and brutal tactics of its Strike Hard, Maximum Pressure campaign attest to the seriousness with which Beijing views the threats posed by separatists, Islamists, and terrorists. China's initiative in setting up the Shanghai Cooperation Organization in 1999 is a manifestation of its positive efforts to develop a stable regional environment for economic development in Xinjiang, as well as of its negative fears that the same three forces might assail Xinjiang from beyond its western border. The same pairing of hopes and fears lies at the heart of China's bold steps to foster regional transport and of its unprecedented pressure on Kazakstan and Kyrgyzstan to outlaw Uyghur activism even by their own citizens. It also underlies China's commitment to invest $9.5 billion in Kazakstan's Uzen oil field—the largest overseas investment in China's history—and its readiness to participate actively in the post–September 11 war on terrorism.

To acknowledge Xinjiang's importance to Beijing is not to assume that a preoccupation with that region's fate drives every aspect of Chinese policy. Precisely this assumption has led to serious errors of fact and interpretation. Every traveler to Xinjiang returns with tales of the ubiquitous presence of the People's Liberation Army (PLA). So universal has been this conviction that when visitors fail to see Chinese soldiers at every crossroad, they take it as clear evidence of the PLA's cleverness in hiding its huge encampments just out of sight. Against this, careful research by Yitzhak Shichor included in chapter 5 proves that both the number and quality of PLA forces in Xinjiang are modest at best. In other words, Beijing perceives the threat posed by Xinjiang to be of a lower order than its concerns over Taiwan and the coastal zone and has downgraded its military presence there accordingly.

A further error that easily arises from the correct recognition of Xinjiang's importance to Beijing concerns the sources of the separatist and Islamist currents it seeks to extirpate. Many observers, including senior officials in Beijing, assume that these tendencies have arisen from either cultural or ethnic diehards among the local Uyghurs, who pine for a past that never was, or from the efforts of subversive forces from abroad, whether from Afghanistan, Pakistan, Turkey, or Saudi Arabia or from Uyghur émigrés in the neighboring states of Central Asia. Such an assumption excludes from consideration what is arguably the main driver of movements for self-rule and separatism, namely, Chinese policies themselves. Gladney's review of Chinese policies of development and control in chapter 4 advances precisely this thesis, as does Benson's analysis of educational policy in chapter 7 and Toops's discussion of ecology in chapter 10. Nor should one think that the intent of the policies in question is crudely repressive. Quite the contrary, the dissemination of literacy and basic education described by Benson has as its clear purpose to develop a modern, skilled, and ethnically assimilated labor force. Similarly, Wiemer's careful study of Xinjiang's economy in chapter 6 offers a picture of remarkably successful development and even proposes that Xinjiang has unique assets that might help it to weather the critical next phases of that process. Likewise, Roberts in chapter 8 credits the vast expansion of trans-border contacts in recent years directly to Beijing's commendable economic opening to its neighbors.

In each of these cases, the prime motivating force is Beijing's own drive to transform the Chinese economy and society rather than more narrow concerns that are specific to Xinjiang. In each case, too, the government's own program for change has generated what might be called its own social antibodies in the form of frustrations over barriers to economic and social advancement, strengthened ethnic identities among non-Han peoples, strivings for self-rule or independence, demands for control over historic territories being degraded by primitive forms of development, and calls for religious assertiveness.

However obvious and inevitable these responses to Chinese policy may seem, there is no reason to believe that planners in Beijing either expected or anticipated them. This is not to minimize or deny the many instances of the Chinese government acting in Xinjiang with deliberate brutality and of its calculated intent of repressing or destroying Turkic or Muslim customs and practices. But in addition to this, the story of Chinese policy in Xinjiang is filled with unintended consequences.

As was suggested earlier, these can arise from many sources. One ministry might carry out its mission without the slightest awareness or concern for the way its projects might affect the work of another ministry only blocks away in Beijing. Did those responsible for improving Xinjiang's highways and for freeing Uyghurs to trade with other parts of China conceive the possibility that they might be creating superefficient channels for the spread of AIDS, as discussed by Dautcher in chapter 11 and by Rudelson and Jankowiak in chapter 12? Did those who conceived the famed Karakoram Highway to Pakistan have any sense that it might facilitate broadened contact with radical Islamists in Pakistan and Afghanistan, as described by Graham E. Fuller and Jonathan N. Lipman in chapter 13?

Most analyses of the current predicament in Xinjiang, whether positive or negative, simply assume intentionality on the part of Beijing. By so doing, they may miss an important element of the story, namely, the ways in which Beijing finds itself unexpectedly confronted by the unintended consequences of its own actions. But the assumption of intentionality has a yet darker side, for it easily slips into the view that Chinese policy in Xinjiang is nothing less than a deliberate conspiracy against ethnic and cultural minorities there. As we have seen, in some general sense and even in some specific instances, this may be true. But, to repeat, the story may be far more complex in reality.

These thoughts bear directly on how one views the new rail line from Urumchi to Kashgar that the state railroad system opened in 1999 to much fanfare. Toops in chapter 9 convincingly argues that for more than a century the main Han immigrants to Xinjiang have spread along newly opened roads and rail lines. He suggests that the new railroads in Xinjiang will invite emigrants from the Chinese heartland as surely as new rail lines in Siberia or the western United States invited emigrants from western Russia or the U.S. East Coast. Is this the result of a conspiracy? If so, one can scarcely imagine engaging Chinese authorities in a dialogue about the social consequences of the new routes and the ways they may possibly undermine regional stability. To the extent that it is not, a door might be open to discussing in a Chinese context a global problem arising from the free movement of peoples that has led to both progress and conflict elsewhere.

A further reason for which Xinjiang warrants informed attention is that everything happening in that territory today affects the entire region. Economic and social development is taking place throughout the broader Central Asian region of which Xinjiang is a part, bringing intended and unintended consequences in its wake. Ethnic identities are strengthening at the same time as regional communication and trade are expanding. Incomes are polarizing, creating new elites and new underclasses whose members number in the tens of millions. Various forms of radicalism and extremism are also on the rise. If Chinese policy in Xinjiang successfully addresses these vast challenges, the province will become an attractive model for others. To the extent that it fails, Xinjiang, due to its large population and economy, could pull down the vast adjoining region with it. As Roberts notes in chapter 8, China's neighbors to the west are already concerned that uncontrolled Han migration into Xinjiang may carry over to their own region, bringing with it the ethnic conflicts that are already evident within Xinjiang.

As was noted at the outset, this is a region surrounded by nuclear powers, several of which have existed in a state of mutual enmity for generations. Whether out of disinterest, ignorance, or a misplaced respect for Chinese sovereignty and sensibilities, the international community may choose to ignore Xinjiang. If it does so, it will, to an equal extent, be closing its eyes to the fate of several hundred million people in ten countries and of international security in a particularly delicate and important region.

Xinjiang's Future

This volume will doubtless challenge the reader, as it has the authors, to speculate about Xinjiang's future. A convenient way to engage in such speculations is to develop alternative scenarios. Xinjiang's unique combination of assets and problems demands that such scenarios, if they are to have any links with reality, must range from extremely positive to grimly negative.

One cannot exclude a peaceful and evolutionary scenario, in which each party comes gradually to acknowledge the concerns of the others and, through a process of trial and error, finds a path to mutual accommodation. Such a scenario would include the steady integration of Xinjiang with both China and the surrounding region, and, through such a process, the preservation of key elements of local societies and cultures. This happy outcome would transform Xinjiang into an attractive model for the development of all the multiethnic societies on its periphery.

On the other extreme, less sanguine scenarios are at least as likely to unfold. These would entail a steady rise in social tension, with hardening positions in Beijing and among Uyghurs steadily eating away at all middle ground between them. This would in turn thwart further economic development and foster the belief among all parties that sharpened conflict carries no opportunity cost, in short, that saving face and preserving honor at any cost are preferable to any visible alternative. The resulting confrontation is bound to impinge on Xinjiang's neighbors and undermine their security in ways to which the international community could not close its eyes.

One thing can be said with absolute certainty: The choice between these extreme outcomes, or any other conceivable scenarios, will be determined above all by what happens in Beijing. If, on the one hand, China evolves into a more open system, unified but with a degree of decentralization and devolution that is now absent, the first scenario will be not only possible but likely. If, on the other hand, the rigid crust of the Communist system continues to hold, it will encourage officialdom to persist in its current project of repression, which in turn will quicken the growth of national consciousness among Uyghurs and other Turkic groups, forge common ties among them, and radicalize the growing number of men and women who, through education and industry, are joining their growing middle class. But this bleak scenario will not end there. Such a system in China would itself grow increasingly brittle, until a crisis causes it to crack at its seams, opening the historical stage to a new set of scenarios, the nature of which cannot be foreseen from today's vantage point.

"The Xinjiang Project"

Such an exercise with a crystal ball is endlessly intriguing. Many in both China and the West who claim an interest in Xinjiang's fate have engaged in it, producing results that range from interesting to preposterous to irresponsible. And if in the end the future is unknowable, it is nonetheless valuable for those engaged with policy making at the national or international level not to shy away from building such hypotheses about Xinjiang. If it produces no other result, the contemplation of alternative scenarios encourages time-bound leaders and policy makers to appreciate more keenly the broad range of possible courses of actions that may in fact exist.

But that is not the purpose of this book. The goal of the present volume is instead to present a three-dimensional picture of the current situation in Xinjiang, drawing on the best research available in the social sciences, including geography, anthropology, sociology, religious studies, and economics. Furthermore, it seeks to elucidate the present in terms of Xinjiang's entire relevant past, as analyzed by modern historians. In other words, to paraphrase the historian Heinrich von Treitschke's admonition to historians to find out *"Wie es eigentlich gewesen war"* (How it actually happened), the aim of this book is to try to assay what is actually happening in Xinjiang.

Several years ago, the Sinologist Robert Oxnam and I traveled the length of Xinjiang with a small group from the Asia Society. In the present environment, when it is assumed that interest in the region began only after September 11, 2001, it is worth stressing again that this expedition took place during the summer of 1998. Over cigars in the courtyard of the former Russian consulate in Kashgar, we regretted the absence of a modern and comprehensive overview of Xinjiang and resolved to produce such a volume.

The timing could not have been better. Over the previous two decades, a strong cadre of younger scholars interested in Xinjiang had sprung up in the

West, mainly in the United States. They know all the relevant languages, whether Uyghur, Mandarin, Russian, or more arcane tongues, ancient and modern. Moreover, they all bring solid grounding in their disciplines, as well as considerable field experience. Thanks to these men and women, an impressive bibliography of dissertations and monographs was already at hand. It is no exaggeration to say that these studies constitute the most solid contribution of twentieth-century Western scholarship to the study of any part of Central Asia.

No sooner did the best of this group assemble for a first meeting in Baltimore than the question arose of including scholars from the PRC. The case for doing so was compelling. Han Chinese and Uyghur scholars had by then built up a solid body of fundamental research, often based on documents and materials unavailable in the West. Members of "the Xinjiang Project" (such was the name that had arisen spontaneously among the participants) respect these researchers as colleagues and often as personal friends. Yet, they recognized the exceptional delicacy of the task they had set before themselves and the possible difficulties this would pose to participants from China. In light of this, they decided to confine the team to those Western scholars with a proven record of fundamental research.

The Xinjiang Project was conceived as a two-part exercise. The first, embodied in this volume, was designed to provide educated nonspecialists in many countries with an authoritative introduction to the territory and its people, past and present. The intent was to avoid polemics over that many-headed hydra, "the Xinjiang question," and to present the evidence as fairly and dispassionately as possible. The authors very much hope that readers in the PRC will understand that they approached their work as independent scholars and have neither sought nor received instructions from governmental officials of any country.

From this, it should be clear that this volume was definitely not conceived as a policy monograph, nor was it designed to make or imply recommendations on future policy to any government or institution. Those tasks were carefully set aside and assigned to a second and entirely separate work, to be drafted by Graham E. Fuller and me, that will discuss the geopolitical implications of the research, draw explicit conclusions, and offer policy recommendations for national governments and international bodies.

It is worth noting what this volume does not cover. Much as they would like to have done so, the authors have not focused on the personalities and opaque internal governmental processes in Beijing that shape China's policies in Xinjiang. Nor have they ferreted out details on the personnel and internal organization of all the many domestic and foreign-based groups and movements dedicated to change in Xinjiang. And while offering tentative evidence of foreign support for Islamist activities in Xinjiang, they had no access to the intelligence reports of various countries that might provide concrete details. More important, the volume has little to say about nuclear testing, energy and mineral wealth, the many nongovernmental organizations, pre-Islamic religions, and so on. It barely touches on the arts in Xinjiang today, or the important realm of popular culture, even though both might offer valuable insights on the overall social conditions. And while several authors comment briefly on the important distinctions between different oases, towns, and regions, their main concern has been with Xinjiang as a whole rather than with its parts. Finally, this study dwells mainly with the attitudes and actions of Xinjiang's indigenous peoples rather than with the rapidly expanding population of Han immigrants who are transforming and redefining the territory. And even among them, it dwells more on the Uyghurs than the Kazaks, Hui, Kyrgyz, Tajiks, or Uzbeks.

This work was planned as a single volume, to be read sequentially. All authors read and critiqued each other's contributions. Several editorial meetings were held and hundreds of e-mails exchanged in an effort to identify and address, but not to eliminate, differences of interpretation. On March 27, 2002, the Central Asia–Caucasus Institute of Johns Hopkins University's Nitze School of Advanced International Studies organized a pair of open meetings in Washington, D.C., at which large and knowledgeable audiences reviewed and commented on the main findings, after which the authors carried out further drafting and revisions.

The Xinjiang Project would not have been possible without the generous and steadfast support of the Henry Luce Foundation of New York. Terrill E. Lautz, the vice president of that foundation and its program director for Asia, is himself a highly qualified student of China; his colleague, Helena Kolenda, the program officer for Asia, also brings years of firsthand experience in the field. Their deft guidance, intelligent advice, and notable patience helped make the Xinjiang Project a rewarding experience for all participants. On behalf of my colleagues, I warmly thank them both.

Credit for the photographs included with this volume goes to colleague Stanley W. Toops. No brief collection of illustrations can embrace so complex a place as Xinjiang. Toops's fine photographs do more than hint at its diversity and texture.

Turpan oasis, ruins of Idiqot Sheher (Karakocho), one of hundreds of ancient towns scattered across Xinjiang that figure in Uyghur-Han debates over history.

The Karakoram Mountains at Ghez. The best route to Pakistan, Afghanistan, and beyond is via the Karakoram Highway that traverses this branch of the Himalayas.

Stanley Toops

A Kazak yurt. While most Kazaks have now been urbanized, this yurt attests to the continuing practice of nomadic herding among a minority of Xinjiang's Kazaks and Kyrgyz.

Stanley Toops

While this venerable Uyghur from Kashgar seems to recall an earlier time, high Uyghur birthrates make young people more fitting symbols of Uyghur life today.

Stanley Toops

Uyghur farmers like these from Turpan oasis will suffer as aquifers are exhausted by Han in-migration and extensive agricultural practices.

Stanley Toops

Making traditional caps in Kucha. The Turkic people of Xinjiang claim a disproportionately small number of jobs in modern manufacturing there, as compared with Han Chinese.

Stanley Toops

A Kazak spring fair in Yining, where such traditional fairs coexist with modern industry and trade brought to the region by Han immigrants from central China and the coastal provinces.

Stanley Toops

The Idgah Mosque at Kashgar has long been a symbol of Uyghur identity.

Chairman Mao, shown towering above festivities marking fifty years since the "liberation" of Xinjiang, still dominates Kashgar's central square, if not its backstreets and traditional alleys.

Entrance to Kashgar's famed Sunday Bazaar, with signage carefully ordered in Uyghur, Chinese, English, and Russian.

Part I

Historical Background

2

Political and Cultural History of the Xinjiang Region through the Late Nineteenth Century

James A. Millward and Peter C. Perdue

The History of a Crossroads Region

Nationalism is about people, land, and the relationship between them. Nationalistic projects seek to define a special relationship between a unique people and a particular piece of the earth's surface. Even though there is nothing predestined or metaphysical about the shapes of countries on the map, nation-states and ethnic groups tend to treat this territory as iconic—the connection between a people and its place is felt to be sacred and can inspire feats of courage, acts of violence, and works of art. Many histories have been written to claim, bulwark, legitimate, or attack a certain relationship of peoples to their places.

The fit between nationalistic claims and historical reality is often imperfect at best, far-fetched at worst, so that few if any modern nations can truthfully claim an unproblematic relationship between territory and population over time through history. Japan is often cited as a "homogeneous" nation, but the second largest of its four main islands, Hokkaido, was as recently as the late nineteenth century inhabited mainly by Ainu, a people culturally, linguistically, and physically unlike the Japanese to the south who colonized and, ultimately, replaced them.

Thus, to survey political and cultural developments in "Xinjiang" from prehistoric to modern times, as this chapter will do, is a somewhat problematic exercise from the start. The territorial unit now known as Xinjiang has had its current shape, as a single unit, for a relatively short period: since the Qing empire annexed and began to administer it in 1760. Before then, although a certain cultural, geographic, and strategic logic often joined parts of northern and southern Xinjiang, the whole region now embraced by the borders of the "Xinjiang Uyghur Autonomous Region" (or, on separatist maps, "East Turkistan") rarely constituted a unified political entity; rather, parts were controlled either by separate rulers in the oases of southern Xinjiang or by outside forces based to the north, northwest, east, or south.

Anyone seeking to come to grips with Xinjiang faces another vexing problem. Thanks to the region's long history and its division and control by groups speaking many different languages, the same places may bear many names. A single town may have an ancient name, as well as medieval, modern, Indo-European, Chinese, Turkic, Mongolian, Persian, a Chinese rendition of Turko-Mongolian, a Persian rendition of Chinese, a Franco-Italian rendition of all the above (thanks to Marco Polo and the Jesuits), an English spelling based on transliterations of Russian transliterations of all the above, and so forth. Simply to reconcile the place-names used by the travelers Zhang Qian, Xuan Zang, and Marco Polo has spawned a major scholarly industry in both Europe and China.[1] Worse, both Chinese and Islamic sources use city names to indicate whole regions with unspecified boundaries. Then, too, specialists on Central Asian history use one or the other term depending on the time period under consideration, blithely assuming that their readers know, for example, that Turpan, Turfan, Tulufan, Jushi, Hezhou, Huozhou, Khocho, Karakhoja, Kara Khota, Jiaohe, and Gaochang, are all more or less the same place.

In modern and contemporary history, moreover, the use of certain place-names, and the definitions assigned to them, has political significance. "East Turkistan," once a rather vague geographic designation for northern Xinjiang, not always including the Kashgar area, was in the twentieth century used as a national name by separatist Turkic peoples from Xinjiang and their western supporters; for this reason, it is anathema to China. Many Turko-Mongolian names for cities in Xinjiang in use during the Qing dynasty were abandoned in the late Qing and Republican periods in favor of old Han dynasty Chinese names, only to be restored under a more multiculturally minded People's Republic of China (PRC). Moreover, the Chinese name "Xinjiang" is itself new, dating from sometime in the late eighteenth century and achieving currency as a political label only with provincehood in 1884. Thus, such phrases as "Xinjiang in the medieval period," though we will use them below for convenience, are anachronistic. Because it means "new frontier" or "new territory," this name is itself politically charged.

To alleviate some of these problems, we will for convenience generally use the names most common in the literature on modern Xinjiang. However, because the names and controversy over them are part of the history, some reference to alternative and historical names also will be necessary.

When it comes to references to China, however, the opposite problem arises: terminological unity where there should be diversity. Though much cultural and institutional continuity links the states ruling in northern China from the second century BCE to the present, to refer to them universally as "China" is a gross simplification. This is a simplification that Chinese sources through history have embraced and continue to embrace in theory (though without any single national term equivalent to "China" until the twentieth century) and that is part of the national mythology of China today. However, the political formations of the Romans, Charlemagne, the Hapsburgs, Mussolini, and the European Union can be said to share a cultural and institutional tradition, but they are not all "Rome." Thus, here we refer to the polities occupying north China by their dynastic names, as old Chinese sources generally do.

This chapter, then, examines the political developments in the region now known as Xinjiang over a long period during which there was no unit with the current geographic, political, or ethnic shape of Xinjiang. But while demarcations of territory and definitions of people have fluctuated, there have been some constants that have endured more than two millennia: the role of the region as a crossroads between civilizations and the region's position as a zone of contact and interaction between nomadic and agricultural economies. This is more than the history of a part of China, then, though it has often been written that way. Rather, this story involves outside powers and influences from India, Persia, and Central and Inner Asia, as well as from China. Only since the Qing conquest in the mid-eighteenth century has the Xinjiang region maintained more or less its current dimensions and has been largely ruled from China. The second part of this chapter covers the Qing conquest and administration of Xinjiang. Chapter 3 then takes up Xinjiang's twentieth-century history.

The Role of the Physical Landscape

Today's Xinjiang Uyghur[2] Autonomous Region, the largest of China's political units, covers an area of 1.6 million square kilometers, one-sixth of China's total area and three times the size of France. Located in the far northwest of China, Xinjiang is bounded on the northeast by Mongolia, on the north by Russia, on the west by Kazakstan, Kyrgyzstan, and Tajikistan, and on the south by Afghanistan, Pakistan, and India. To the east and south, Xinjiang borders on the Chinese regions and provinces of Tibet, Qinghai, and Gansu. Chapter 10 provides a more detailed exploration of Xinjiang's geography; here, we will simply highlight those physical aspects of the region that have most influenced its history.

Xinjiang consists of three basins, surrounded and divided by mountain ranges. The Tarim basin, defined by the Kunlun Shan, the Pamirs, and the

Tian Shan and rimmed to the east and north by the Tarim River, comprises southern Xinjiang (Nanjiang or Altishahr). At the center of this basin lies the 327,000-square-kilometer Taklimakan Desert, a mostly uninhabitable and impassible arid waste of shifting sand dunes—now of interest for its oil deposits. Around the desert rim lies a chain of fertile oases, watered by the Khotan, Yarkand, Aksu, and other rivers flowing from the mountains.

The Tarim basin and particularly Kashgar, Yarkand, and Khotan on its southern rim have historically enjoyed close contacts with northern India, northern Afghanistan (Bactria), the Ferghana valley, and Transoxiana (the region between the Amu and Syr Rivers in Central Asia). Transoxiana and Kashgaria have often been ruled as a unit by nomad states based in the north, with closer cultural and commercial links across the Pamirs than these imposing mountains would suggest. Even today, the Uzbek and Uyghur languages are extremely close and were once referred to as dialects of a single language (Türki), also spoken in parts of Afghanistan, Tajikistan, and Kyrgyzstan.

The Tarim basin is bounded on the east by the low Quruq Mountains and Bostan (Baghrash) Lake. Beyond these lies the Turpan (Turfan) basin or Depression, whose lowest point, 154 meters below sea level at Ayding Lake, is the second lowest point on the earth. East of Turpan, the flat, cobbly desert continues past Hami and southeast between the slopes of the Tian Shan and Altun Shan ranges, defining what is known as the Gansu or Hexi ("west of the [Yellow] River") Corridor; this in turn runs into the Gobi Desert. The Turpan basin also communicates with northern Xinjiang via a break in the Tian Shan range where today the city of Urumchi is located. As will be seen later on, due to these eastward and northward connections, the history of the Turpan basin has often been distinct from that of the oases farther west. Mongolia-, China-, or Tibet-based powers have often fought over Turpan; the region has also enjoyed independent rule.

Northern Xinjiang (Beijiang) centers on the Zungharian basin, and the term "Zungharia" is often used for northern Xinjiang as a whole (a usage that is followed in this volume). Though a desert lies in the interior of this basin as well, overall the Zungharian environment is less harsh than that of the Tarim basin. Its steppes and mountain slopes have traditionally supported nomadic herdsmen and permanent camps of nomad empires. Today, Chinese settlers have converted much of this pasture to farmland. To the west of the Zungharian basin, and separated from it by a spur of the Tian Shan, the Ili (Yili) River valley opens up westward into the Seven Rivers region (Semirechye or Yettisu) of Kazakstan. Unlike the more northern and drier parts of Zungharia, the Ili valley is well watered and through the centuries has provided both grassland for pastoral nomads and in recent times prime farmland. The Ili region has, through history, generally formed a single unit together with the basins of the Talas, Chu, and Semirechye Rivers; from here, nomad powers dominated both the western Tarim basin and Transoxiana, the heartland of western Turkistan (now divided among Uzbekistan, Tajikistan, and Kyrgyzstan). In the late nineteenth century, the Qing empire and Russia contested ownership of this fertile Ili region.

Human life in Xinjiang, then, is conditioned by its rivers, whose location determines where farming and large settlements are possible, and by its mountains and deserts, whose orientation encourages east-west communications along the series of oasis towns on the edge of the Tarim or along routes following the north slopes of the Tian Shan and permits north-south communication only through occasional passes through the Tian Shan. Southern Xinjiang itself, while a source of agricultural produce and an important trade route, is not well suited to horse rearing. This has contributed to a pattern whereby the Tarim basin has tended to be dominated by outside powers, particularly nomad groups based in Zungharia.

Xinjiang as a Cultural and Commercial Crossroads

Much of the recent fascination with what in the nineteenth century became known as the "Silk Road" has focused on the oases of the Tarim basin. Starting in the late nineteenth century, Aurel Stein, Albert Van Le Coq, the Japanese prince Otani, Sven Hedin, and other explorer-archaeologists traveled to the Tarim basin, Turpan, and Dunhuang farther east where they discovered (and often carted off) evidence of ancient and medieval links between Indic, Sinic, and—thanks to Alexander's outposts in Afghanistan—Mediterranean civilizations. As Buddhism spread from north India into Central Asia and by the first or second century CE into China, its iconography reflected these Hellenic influences in such elements as the modeling of hair or drapery of garments on Buddhist statuary. These features can be seen in the similarities between the enormous carved Buddhas and cave complexes at Bamiyan (now destroyed) in central Afghanistan and those of the Mogao, Yungang, and Longmen grottos in north China, as well as in countless other artifacts. The string of oases across the Tarim became a conduit for religious pilgrims from across Central Asia, with Khotan and Kucha serving as major scholastic centers. The centuries-long process by which Buddhism entered China resulted not only from the journeys of well-known Chinese pilgrims Fa Xian and Xuan Zang but also from the labors of multilingual monks such as the Kuchean translator Kumarajiva, as well as from the activities of traders. Manichaeism and Christianity, too, entered China across Xinjiang by similar mechanisms, as did Islam in several waves somewhat later.

Material goods and technologies, too, were exchanged over the desert routes through Turkistan. Silk is the most famous commodity, but other items and techniques moved with the caravans and armies as well, some destined to have great impact. Paper making came from China to Central Asia in the eighth century via Tang Chinese captives taken by Arab armies, and thence to the Mediterranean and Western Europe. Cotton and grape wine passed from Central Asia and Xinjiang into China, as did instruments that would make up the "Chinese" classical music ensemble (e.g., the pipa or Chinese lute and yangqin or hammered dulcimer). From Persia and Central Asia, Ming China borrowed Islamic astronomical and calendrical methods, as well as the cobalt glazes of the characteristic blue-and-white Ming ware. The Central Asian Timurids took techniques and motifs from Chinese painting, which thenceforth entered the repertoire of Persian (also known as Mughal) miniatures found from Delhi to Istanbul.

Space prohibits further detailing here of Xinjiang's position as an ancient cultural and commercial conduit; readers may find the story engagingly told in other recent works, which also provide entrée into the vast literature on the subject.[3] It is worth stressing, however, that these east-west commercial and religious contacts have continued since prehistoric times both because and in spite of the political and military flux that brought parts of Xinjiang under the control of one empire or another; these exchanges did not decline in importance in modern times. Central Asians and Russians acquired Chinese rhubarb and tea via entrepôts in Kashgar and Ili in increasing amounts from the eighteenth to the nineteenth century. By the late nineteenth and early twentieth centuries, Russia had become the major customer for Xinjiang's cotton. Today, the products of China's manufacturing sector move through Xinjiang into Pakistan, the new states of Central Asia, and Russia. Ideas have continued to travel as well: In the nineteenth and early twentieth centuries, Xinjiang's Muslims were exposed to new intellectual trends emanating from Bukhara, Istanbul, and Kazan in Russia.

Traditional Patterns of Rule in Xinjiang

The mountains, basins, steppes, and oases that characterize Xinjiang's geography have exercised an important influence on the region's history. Most notable has been the tendency for outside powers, and particularly nomadic peoples based north of the Tian Shan, to exercise direct or indirect control of the oases of the Tarim basin and Turpan area. Several of those northern nomadic groups formed polities powerful enough to challenge states in north China, setting up a pattern of conflict across the "Great Wall Line." Owen Lattimore, Sechin Jagchid, and Thomas J. Barfield have all offered theories regarding the mechanism and causes of that enduring interaction.[4] Xinjiang repeatedly became a sideshow to these conflicts because the nomadic powers needed both its grazing grounds in Zungharia and the agricultural products, manufactures, and trade revenues from the Tarim basin and Turpan. Chinese-based powers, when facing threats from the north, often expanded the conflict westward to cut off the nomads' access to these necessities.

A similar pattern links modern Xinjiang with the agricultural regions west of the Pamirs and Tian Shan in Transoxiana and the Ferghana valley. Nomadic powers coming out of Mongolia tended to split into eastern and western polities; their western division was often based in Semirechye (the broad Seven Rivers region adjoining the western slope of the Ala Tau and Zungharia ranges in Kazakstan), the Ili valley, or near Issyk Kul in Kyrgyzstan. From there, they conquered and attempted to control Transoxiana to the west and the Tarim basin to the east—both relatively fertile agricultural areas that could supply grain, manufactures, and tax revenues to the steppe power. However, it proved difficult to hold both the Tarim and Transoxiana from this steppe base. If the nomad power did not itself split, then Transoxiana often fell to other powers based either in Persia or farther west on the steppe.

The political history of the Xinjiang region, then, was shaped by the north-south dynamic of northern nomadic powers ruling or raiding agrarian societies to the south; Xinjiang lies at the intersection of two geostrategic circuits in which this dynamic played out, one encompassing China, Mongolia, Zungharia, and the Urumchi-Turpan area and the Tarim basin, the other taking in Zungharia, the Tarim basin, and Transoxiana.

Prehistory

There has always been close economic and political interaction between herders and farmers in the Xinjiang region, so much so that it is not always accurate to distinguish sharply between them. This close relationship begins with some of the earliest evidence of human habitation in the region. Consider the woman buried in Qewrighul near Loulan in the early second millennium BCE, whose well-preserved remains have gained her the popular name "Beauty of Loulan." She was wrapped in a shawl of woven sheep's wool and interred with a winnowing basket and grains of wheat, thus demonstrating the interpenetration of economies based on animal husbandry and agriculture in Xinjiang 4,000 years ago, a relationship borne out by other archaeological evidence as well. Both the early herders (eventually nomadic pastoralists) and farmers in the region were probably Indo-Europeans—that is, speakers of one offshoot or another of the Indo-European language family—and had "Caucasoid" skull types.[5]

The Saka (Ch. Sai) were one Indo-European group that made an early appearance on the Xinjiang stage. More a generic term than a name for a specific state or ethnic group, the Saka were part of a cultural continuum of Iranian-speaking nomads that extended across Siberia and the Central Eurasian steppe lands from Xinjiang to the Black Sea. Like the closely related Scythians, the Saka employed chariots in battle, sacrificed horses, and buried their dead in mound tombs called kurgans; royal kurgans were furnished with rich inventories of metal objects and often decorated with the dynamic animal imagery known as "animal style." In Xinjiang, Saka sites have been identified dating from around 650 through the latter half of the first millennium BCE in Tashkurghan (west of Kashgar, in the Pamirs), in Ili, and even near Toksun, south of the Tian Shan. This latter site, dated to between the fifth and second centuries BCE, yielded a statuette of a kneeling warrior wearing a tall conical hat coming to a curved point—headwear well known in classical Greek, Roman, and Near Eastern sources as a "Phrygian cap" after the steppe invaders who sported it. An identical hat, fashioned from felt and dating to around 1000 BCE, was found in a tomb near Cherchen, an agricultural town on the southern rim of the Tarim basin. Once again, we see evidence of the interpenetration of nomadic and settled peoples in Xinjiang from earliest times.[6]

Chinese sources of the second century BCE mention another group of early Xinjiang people, the Yuezhi (Yueh-chih), who inhabited the region around Dunhuang and the Gansu Corridor for millennia. When they were attacked in the second century BCE by the Xiongnu, then the ascendant nomadic power in Mongolia, some Yuezhi moved into Qinghai, others may have trickled into the Tarim basin, while the main branch of the Yuezhi ruling clan migrated first to the upper Ili valley and then, when attacked again, to the Amu (Oxus) River. There they formed an empire known as the Kushan that ultimately took control of the Hellenic states of Bactria and exercised political influence over the Tarim basin during the first century CE.[7] Most scholars agree that the Yuezhi may be equated to the speakers of Tokharian who much later (the latter half of the first millennium CE) left textual records in the Kucha, Karashahr, and Turpan areas. The linguistic connection between the nomadic Yuezhi and later agrarians of the Tarim and Turpan basins is another indication of the close interrelationship between nomadic and sedentary peoples in Xinjiang.[8]

The popular media have recently "discovered" the Xinjiang mummies excavated at sites in the Taklimakan and misleadingly called them "Europeans." Never mind that European and Chinese scholars have known about the Caucasoid mummies for at least a century. More important, neither the ancient people preserved as mummies nor any of their ancestors had ever been to Europe. The original speakers of Indo-European languages probably lived on the steppes north of the Black Sea; from there, branches migrated over time both east and west. Judging by linguistic evidence, the Tokharian and Saka (Iranian) speakers were among the earliest to take leave of the ur-Indo-European population. If they were indeed Tokharian speakers, the Yuezhi must have come east very early, even before the inhabitants of Europe spoke Indo-European languages.[9] Some scholars have even suggested that the original home of the Indo-Europeans was itself much farther east than the Black Sea steppe. If so, by the logic of the mummy-hyping documentary producers, Europeans are actually Asians!

The Classical Period

The dynamic relationship between the Mongolia-Zungharia steppe, southern Xinjiang, and north China took its classic form after the Xiongnu (Hsiung-nu), a confederation of Altaic-speaking tribes, formed an empire encompassing Mongolia, northwest China, and Zungharia.[10] They took control of southeastern Xinjiang in the first half of the second century BCE, when they defeated and dispersed the Yuezhi. The Xiongnu then established a headquarters south of the Tian Shan, levying taxes and conscripting labor from Loulan and other Tarim basin cities.

Farther east, the Han dynasty had for decades been paying tribute to the Xiongnu to keep them at bay. Frustrated with this appeasement policy, the Han court dispatched Zhang Qian to the Yuezhi in Bactria to enlist their aid against the Xiongnu (139 BCE); though it garnered useful intelligence, the mission failed. So, after some seventy years spent sending silk and princesses off to the nomads and suffering raids anyway, the Han court attempted to "cut off the right arm of the Xiongnu" by driving them militarily from Turpan and the Tarim basin. Around 120 BCE, the Han penetrated the Gansu Corridor as far as Lop Nor and established military agricultural colonies (*tuntian*) there. For the next sixty years, as Xiongnu and Han forces struggled over the Tarim basin, the region's small city-states did what they could to weather the geopolitical storm, with much pragmatic shifting of alliance.

The Xiongnu valued the Tarim and Turpan oases for their agricultural products, manpower, and tax revenue. The Han, by contrast, were fighting for strategic position, not economic gain. The campaigns were bloody. Han generals massacred local populations, staged coups, set up puppet monarchs, and forcibly relocated one city's inhabitants.[11] After around 60 BCE, the Han made an effort to establish themselves more firmly south of the Tian Shan, replacing the Xiongnu protectorate with its own protector general (*duhu*). After the Han succeeded in dividing the Xiongnu confederation into northern and southern factions (57 BCE), it could rely less on expensive military campaigns and more on fixed military agricultural colonies in southern Xinjiang, though sporadic fighting continued.

Overall, between 162 BCE (when the Xiongnu established their headquarters south of the Tian Shan) and 150 CE (after which neither Han nor Xiongnu enjoyed any influence in the south), the Xiongnu controlled Turpan and the Tarim basin for some 70 years, while the Han held sway there for about 125 years. The rest of the 310 years of Han engagement with the region may be characterized as an inconclusive tug-of-war, despite some spectacular though short-lived Han military achievements. The Han partially garrisoned the region with their military farms, but the Xiongnu, too, maintained a constant administrative center in southern Xinjiang continuously for a century (longer than the Han protectorate general that eventually displaced it). Moreover, the Han never had a foothold in Zungharia, which was occupied for this whole period by the Xiongnu and the Wusun, another nomad group.

Thus, the often-repeated assertion that all Xinjiang was Chinese during the Han dynasty is an oversimplification arising from later historians' selective reading of a rather mixed record. In this case, historians have proven more powerful than armies.

More important for us, however, is the pattern established by the Han-Xiongnu rivalry over Xinjiang: A nomadic power in the north exploited Turpan and the Tarim basin as an agricultural base, and the China-based power, in order to weaken its nomad adversary, vied for control of southern Xinjiang. Later states based in China would again attempt to "cut off the right arm" of Inner Asian rivals by projecting power into Xinjiang.

The Middle Period

The situation in Xinjiang from the period following the final decline of the Xiongnu and the fall of the Han (221 CE) to the sixth century is poorly documented. The archaeological record includes coins and administrative and religious documents that suggest the Kushan empire influenced and even controlled the southern Tarim basin for some of this time. However, there are also indications of lingering Chinese or at least Chinese-style agricultural settlements, notably one at Niya. The larger principalities of the Tarim were ruled by local monarchs. Buddhism was an important presence, especially in Khotan and Kucha.

Beginning in the mid-fourth century, a new nomad confederation, the Ruanruan, arose in Mongolia and re-created an empire as vast as that of the Xiongnu, eventually taking Zungharia and collecting heavy tributes from the oasis cities south of the Tian Shan. A century later, under assault from the northern China-based Wei dynasty, the Ruanruan allowed control of the Tarim to fall to the Hephthalites, a nomad empire composed of Xiongnu fragments with some Iranian elements.[12] The Hephthalites invaded the Tarim city-states from their base in Transoxiana and by the first years of the sixth century were sending embassies to the Wei dynasty in northern and north-western China. Like their predecessors, the Hephthalites interfered mini-mally in the affairs of the Tarim cities after subduing them, contenting themselves with the extraction of tributes. The Hephthalites remained over-lords of southern Xinjiang until around 560, when they in turn were shat-tered by the newest steppe empire to ride out of Mongolia: the Kök Türk (Ch. Tujue). Meanwhile, powers based in Tibet and in the west, from Arabia to western Turkistan, entered into a new geopolitical struggle that would eventually engulf the oases of southern Xinjiang.[13]

First, the Türks. The Kök Türks are not to be confused with the Turks of modern Turkey—though the latter claim the former as ancestors. The Türks who formed their steppe empire, or khanate, from the mid-sixth century were a tribe under Ruanruan rulership, spoke the same languages, and dif-fered little from them physically—that is, they looked Mongol. The Türks overthrew the Ruanruan; soon thereafter (583), their empire divided into western and eastern khanates. The western Türks ruled Zungharia, the Ferghana valley, parts of Afghanistan, northern India, and the western Tarim basin. They enjoyed diplomatic relations with Byzantium and warred with the Sassanid dynasty of Persia. For their part, the eastern Türks were closely enmeshed with Chinese states.

China-based powers involved themselves closely in Türk politics and with Xinjiang, starting with the reunifying of the Sui dynasty (581–618), which encouraged Türk factionalism and established footholds in Hami (Yiwu) and at Ruoqiang (Shanshan) and Qiemo in the southern Tarim. These policies continued under its successor, the Tang dynasty (618–906). The Tang dy-nasty, like its Han dynasty predecessor, endeavored to weaken the nomad empire to its north through diplomatic and military means. Unlike the Han, however, the Tang royal house was closely associated with northern peoples. In fact, medieval Chinese aristocracy, including the Li family who founded the Tang, had intermarried with families of nomadic conquerors in north China, and Turkic and Sinic cultural elements were to some degree blended in this dynasty, with members of the Tang court riding horses, speaking Turkic in preference to Chinese, and playing polo (even their women). One Tang prince chose to live in a yurt and offered visiting guests chunks of roast mutton. For this and other reasons, the Tang was one of imperial China's most open and cosmopolitan periods.

This "Turkicness" of the Tang may in part explain its success vis-à-vis the

Türk empire, whose eastern branch it virtually annexed. The Tang then mobilized its Türk allies in the 630s and 640s to conquer or awe into submission the Indo-European oasis states in Turpan and the Tarim basin, who, in alliance with the western Türks, had controlled Silk Road trade. The Tang ruled over the Tarim indirectly, ultimately establishing a protectorate generalship first at Turpan and then at Kucha. This office and the four western garrisons at Kucha, Karashahr (Yanqi), Kashgar, and Khotan supervised native rulers in the Tarim city-states. Chinese political and cultural influence in the eastern part of Xinjiang was great during this period, but demographically the Tang conquest marked not the Sinicization but rather the beginnings of the Turkicization of southern Xinjiang. This was especially so in the still Indo-European cities of Kucha and Turpan where Turkic troops allied with the Tang moved in force.

As during the Han period, to say that Xinjiang was "Chinese territory" during the Tang period oversimplifies a politically complex and fluid situation involving the Türks, Tibet, and the Arabs, as well as the Tang.[14] The Tang reached its greatest territorial extent in Central Asia in 657, having subdued the western Türks with protectorate generalships in western Zungharia, Transoxiana, Kabul, and even in eastern Persia. At this brief historical moment, Tang suzerainty extended thinly over Samarkand, Bukhara, Herat, and right up to the frontiers of the expanding Arab empire. Five years later, however, Transoxiana was in rebellion; soon after that, the western Türks were again autonomous, and real Tang influence was restricted to lands east of the Pamirs and south of the Tian Shan, with the exception of an outpost in Beshbaliq (Beiting), in the vicinity of modern Urumchi.

Tang lost ground in southern Xinjiang as well, with Tibet taking the southern Tarim oases from 670 until the 690s. Even after the Tang reentered the Tarim in 693, its position remained tenuous, constantly under threat from either Türks in the north or Tibetans in the south. Though the Tang continued to project some influence west to Transoxiana, Ferghana, the Pamir, and north India, this depended on the allegiance to the Tang of key Türk tribes.

Tang's last great Central Asian adventure lasted from 730 to 751, when it once again took on western Türk tribes to consolidate control of Zungharia and the Tarim and challenged Tibet's control of Pamir trade routes. In fifteen years of campaigns, Gao Xianzhi, a Korean general within Tang service, fought in the Pamirs and intervened in hostilities between Ferghana and Tashkent. Gao's army ultimately accepted the submission of the king of Tashkent but then executed him and looted the city. The king's son fled to the Arabs in Samarkand, who sent an army against Gao. Türk tribes again swelled the forces on each side, and the Tang and Arab armies faced off in the famous Battle of Talas (751). Unfortunately for Gao, his Türks turned against him. Still, this battle is not as important as is sometimes implied, for the Arabs did not advance. What really marked the end of the Tang forward posture in Central Asia was the An Lushan rebellion in the Chinese heartland (755–763), which forced a full retreat of Tang forces from Xinjiang. For a full thousand years from this date, that is, until the Qing dynasty, no power based in China would again rule Xinjiang.

Historical claims figure large in today's political disputes over Xinjiang. Because of this, it is worthwhile toting up the years of Tang supremacy in Xinjiang, however reductionist that may be. From their first active efforts in the region in the 630s to the 755 An Lushan rebellion, the Tang enjoyed a total of about 100 years of relatively firm sovereignty over the Tarim city-states. This century was divided into two periods by a two-decade spell of Tibetan rule, frequently disturbed by Türk and Tibetan attacks. Also during this period, Tang controlled Zungharia for about 20 years—something the Han dynasty had never accomplished. To be sure, the rest of the time Tang could occasionally claim the "submission" of western Türk tribal leaders based north of the Tian Shan, and when these chiefs were not actively attacking Tang interests, this alliance can be said to have had some military and political substance. But it must be added that except for the eastern-most Tang garrisons in the Turpan region,[15] there were few Chinese settlers in Xinjiang during the Tang period. Tang rule remained indirect, leaving local monarchs in place. It was, more-over, largely the Türk soldiers and non-Chinese commanders like Gao Xianzhi who accomplished Tang expansion into Central Asia. Indeed, no premodern agrarian empire could have extended its power over such a great distance without relying on indigenous elites, nomad auxiliaries, and quasi-autonomous generals.

As noted earlier, here again we see the pattern of control of the Tarim basin by outside powers, this time with Tibet as a contender along with nomads north of the Tian Shan and a China-based power. As during the Han-Xiongnu struggle, the political and military fate of Xinjiang during the middle period was again linked to the rivalries between great powers in China and on the steppes and mountains of Inner Asia.

More than that, however, from the events outlined earlier we may note that the Xinjiang region also fell within another circuit of interstate power relations. The Kushan and Hephthalite empires both extended influence from Afghanistan and Transoxiana into the Tarim basin. The Arabs, too, came close to doing so. Tibet and Tang warred over control of the Pamir and Karakoram Passes, because they provided important links to north Afghanistan, India, Persia, and Transoxiana. Turkic powers based in Zungharia, the

Talas valley, or the Issyk Kul area vied to hold both the western Tarim (Kashgar) and Ferghana. Hence, struggles along three enduring frontier regions—the Sino-Mongolian, the Sino-Tibetan (Qinghai), and the Pamir–Tian Shan—shaped the political fate of Xinjiang and particularly of the Tarim and Turpan basins.

The Uyghurs and the Karakhanids

The Uyghurs, the next major conquering power on the Xinjiang scene, originated, like many of their predecessors, in the Mongolian core lands of the Orkhon River valley. The tribes known by the term "Uyghur" had formerly been components of the Türk empire or khanate. With other tribes, the Uyghurs overthrew the Türk ruling house and in 744 established an empire of their own based in central Mongolia that eventually extended into northwest China, Zungharia, and at times as far west as the Ferghana valley. The Uyghurs helped the Tang militarily against the An Lushan rebellion and the Tibetans but extracted a heavy price for their aid: They sacked the Chinese city of Loyang and charged the Tang extortionate prices for the horses they supplied them.

In 840, the Uyghur khaghanate was itself destroyed and its tribes scattered by a massive attack by the Kyrgyz (Qirghiz), moving south from Tuva. After this diaspora, the main group of Uyghur tribes resettled in lands straddling the Tian Shan in what is now Urumchi and Turpan but was then known as Beshbaliq and Khocho.

The Uyghurs thus began primarily as Turko-Mongolian steppe nomads, though they built a capital city and some were even farmers before they sedentarized in Xinjiang. They were not Muslims. On the contrary, their khan, Bögü, converted to Manichaeanism. Later, their state in the Turpan area embraced Buddhism and tolerated Christianity among its urban population but opposed Islam. The Mongolian Uyghurs intermarried with the high-nosed, bearded Iranian and other Indo-European peoples who had made up the indigenous population of the Tarim basin before the arrival of Turkic groups (of whom the Uyghurs were but one of many). Therefore, while they are certainly *among* the genetic ancestors of today's Uyghurs, the Uyghurs of the Uyghur empire are not their only ancestors. Moreover, some cultural distance separates the originally nomadic, Manichaean, and Buddhist Uyghurs of Khocho and Beshbaliq from the sedentary agriculturalist Muslim Uyghurs of the Tarim basin and Turpan area in modern times. The latter were, in fact, not known as "Uyghur" until the late nineteenth and early twentieth centuries.

The Uyghur state initially fit the classic paradigm we have seen frequently in Xinjiang's history: a Turko-Mongolian nomadic power in the north ruling Indo-European oasis agriculturalists indirectly across the Tian Shan. However, the Uyghurs were not rude barbarians. Their capital at Khocho was a busy center that maintained ties with Soghdia, India, and China. Over time, these contacts led to a blending of political, economic, and cultural influences, as well as of the peoples themselves. Under their rulers, now styled *iduqqut* (sacred majesty), the Uyghurs of the Khocho state enjoyed good relations with China-based states of the Tang, the Five Dynasties, Song, Liao, and Jin, with whom they, and the ubiquitous Soghdian merchants, traded pastoral, agricultural, and mineral products. Rich Uyghur patrons supported Manichaeanism, Buddhism, and Christianity (Nestorianism) and paid for the creation of famous frescoes at Bezeklik (Turpan area) and Kizil (Kucha area). A warm climate and runoff from the Tian Shan allowed Khocho to grow double crops of grain and a wide variety of fruits and vegetables. Cotton had been grown in the region for centuries, and as this fiber was not yet prevalent in China, cotton cloth was among the Uyghur exports to the east. Grapes, then as now, were a local specialty, and the Khocho government collected wine as tax in kind.[16]

The dynasty of Uyghur kings based in the Kucha-Urumchi-Turpan-Hami area from the ninth through the thirteenth century proved longer-lived than any other power in the region, before or since. Indeed, the ruins of Khocho (Ch. Gaochang) may still be seen today near Turpan. Though Uyghuristan (as later Islamic sources would call it)[17] was not able to resist new powers arising to the east, it proved adept at accommodating to them. In the 1130s, the Uyghur iduqqut accepted the Kara Khitai (Western Liao) as overlord. In 1209, the Uyghur state submitted promptly to the rising Mongol empire, thus ensuring its own continued local authority into the 1370s, when it was finally destroyed and incorporated by the Chaghataid Mongols (on the Kara Khitai and Chaghataids, see the discussion later in this chapter). Even as vassals, however, the Uyghurs provided Genghis (Chinggis) Khan's empire with literate officials and a writing system and thus exercised an important cultural influence on the Mongol state.[18]

To the west of the Khocho-Beshbaliq Uyghur polity, a confederation emerged from the Karluk, Yaghma, and other Turkic tribes that had migrated west during the era of the Uyghur empire in Mongolia. The royal clans of the Karluks and confederated tribes occupied the former western Türk capital of Balasaghun on the Chu River (near Issyk Kul in modern Kyrgyzstan) and called themselves "khan," the highest Turko-Mongolian ruling title. In Islamic sources, they thus came to be known as the "khanal kings" or "house of the khans." Modern scholars call them the Karakhanids (ca. 840–1211).[19]

In addition to the Semirechye area of modern Kazakstan and Kyrgyzstan, the Karakhanid realm ultimately included the western Tarim basin (including Khotan, which it conquered around 1000) and Transoxiana. Once again, then, the region we now know as Xinjiang was from the ninth through the twelfth century divided into separate spheres, two of which included lands not part of Xinjiang today. The Uyghur state lay in the northeast, controlling the northern Tarim cities east of Kucha as well as Beshbaliq; the Karakhanids were to the west; and the southeastern Tarim was ruled, together with Qinghai and parts of the Gansu Corridor, by a Tibetan state known as the Tangut (Ch. Xixia).

It was the Karakhanids who linked the western Tarim basin to the Islamic world of Transoxiana and parts west, and under their rule the Turks and much of Xinjiang's population became Muslims. The conversion of the Turks to Islam was an event of world-historical significance, for the Karakhanids went on to destroy the Samanid dynasty (1000) and assume control of firmly Muslim Transoxiana; they would be only the first of a series of Turkic ruling dynasties in Central Asia and the Middle East.

From the perspective of modern Uyghur nationalism, however, the discrete histories of the Karakhanids and the Uyghur Khocho state present a problem. While the modern Uyghur people take their name from the Uyghur empire and Khocho state (Uyghuristan), they trace their religion to the Karakhanids. Today, many Uyghur and some Han Chinese scholars have embraced an alternate view of the origins of the Karakhanids that resolves this problem. The exact tribal composition of the Karakhanids and their relation to the Kök Türks and the Uyghurs are far from clear. This permits some scholars to argue, with some justification, that the Karakhanids ruling in Kashgar were not Karluks but Yaghmas, who were linked to the prediaspora Uyghur khanal house.[20] In this way, then, both the Uyghur polity centered on Khocho *and* the Karakhanid dynasty can be considered "Uyghur" because the ancestry of their ruling houses may be traced to the Orkhon-based Uyghur khanate. The present-day significance of this is clear. This interpretation deftly eliminates any contradiction between Uyghurs' namesakes, with their rich cultural heritage focused on eastern Xinjiang, and Karakhanid Islamizers of Xinjiang: Both are genealogically "Uyghur."

Of course, a dispassionate observer would consider it obvious that both Karakhanid and Uyghur states and their peoples are among the "ancestors" of the modern Uyghurs, simply because they were there and played an important role in the region's history. Still, such is the symbolic importance of names, genealogy, and simple national narratives that it makes for a more satisfying national story to attribute Islamic conversion to "Uyghurs" as well.

The Kara Khitay and the Mongols

The now-familiar drama of overlords displacing overlords played itself out again with the arrival in Xinjiang of another ruling dynasty, the Kara Khitay (Black Khitay). The Khitay or Khitan (Qidan) were Mongol speakers[21] who had ruled in north China as the Liao dynasty from 907 to 1125. Their name, incidentally, became the Turkic term for China; Islamic and Russian sources introduced the name to medieval and early modern Europe, where it became "Cathay." It is still used in Uyghur to mean "China" and "Chinese," though the PRC has attempted to ban the usage, which Han Chinese consider derogatory.

In the late 1120s, the Jin dynasty destroyed the Khitan state. One member of the Khitan royal clan, Yelü Dashi, fled to Mongolia, where he gathered followers from among the raw tribesmen, and then went west to Beshbaliq, where he collected more adherents and accepted the submission of the Uyghurs. He then moved farther west, taking Balasaghun, Kashgar, Khotan, and eventually Samarkand and Transoxiana from the Karakhanid rulers. By 1141, Yelü Dashi ruled as a *gurkhan* (khan of khans or overlord) over both the Uyghur and Karakhanid empires, a territory that extended from the Amu River in the west to the Tangut lands and eastern Mongolia in the east, and from Siberia to Balkh (northern Afghanistan) and Khotan in the south. The Islamic state of Khwarazm, on the Aral Sea, paid tribute, even though it was not entirely subordinated to the Kara Khitay.

The Kara Khitay poses a challenge to anyone wishing to ascribe simple historical identities to Central Asian states. Because of the Kara Khitay background as rulers of north China for two centuries, Yelü Dashi brought with him knowledge of Chinese governing practices and institutions. Perhaps because of this Chinese background, unlike the Türks and Karakhanids, the Kara Khitay did not subdivide the empire into eastern and western divisions or dole out appanages to its princes.[22] At the same time, neither did Yelü Dashi institute a centralized Chinese-style empire in Central Eurasia. On the contrary, Kara Khitay governance of its vassal countries remained indirect to the extreme. Local rulers, including the Uyghur iduqquts and Karakhanid khans, enjoyed almost complete autonomy as long as they paid their taxes and tributes. Moreover, although Yelü Dashi was educated in Chinese, it is doubtful whether many of the ruling Khitans actually spoke the language. And although the Kara Khitay state (like that of the Uyghurs in Khocho) used Chinese for some administrative and prestige purposes, it also employed Persian, Uyghur, and the native Khitan language and script. Kara Khitay armies included Khitan, Turkic, Mongol, Tangut, and perhaps Tungus (Jurchen) soldiers; in its administrative retinue were Chinese and Uyghurs.

The state ruled over Iranian- and remaining Tokharian-speaking peoples throughout the settled regions of western and eastern Turkistan. Like the Mongols who would follow them, then, the Kara Khitay were a multiethnic polity rather than a particular national or ethnic group.[23]

Even though the Kara Khitay introduced few changes at the local level, local elites chafed against the oppressive tributes levied on them. By the end of the twelfth century, unrest broke out throughout the Tarim basin, Zungharia, and Transoxiana. In Khocho in 1209, the Uyghurs rebelled and their iduqqut pledged loyalty to Genghis Khan, who had just unified the tribes in Mongolia; Genghis honored the iduqqut as his "fifth son," initiating a special relationship between the Uyghurs and the growing Mongol empire.[24]

Genghis's last adversary on the path to consolidating his control over Mongolia had been the Naiman tribe. After he defeated it in 1208, Küchlük, a Naiman prince, fled west, managed to rally followers, and by 1211 effectively usurped control of the Kara Khitay state while its gurkhan was preoccupied fighting in Transoxiana. Küchlük, a former Christian and Buddhist convert, paved the way for the Mongols to conquer Xinjiang by reversing the Kara Khitay's liberal religious policy. After Küchlük's merciless anti-Muslim pogroms, when the Mongols rode into Xinjiang between 1216 and 1218, the Muslim inhabitants of the Tarim basin welcomed them as liberators. Of course, the Buddhist Uyghurs in Turpan remained staunch Mongol allies as well.

The Mongol Period

Before his death in 1227, Genghis Khan divided his vast empire among his sons. Jochi, the eldest, received western central Eurasia, where Jochi's own son Batu would later carve out the khanate of the Golden Horde. The second son, Chaghatai, was granted the territories of the Kara Khitay empire, with a capital in Almaliq (in modern Ili), and the band of oases extending from Samarkand to Turpan—that is, what Persian sources by this time called "Turkistan." The lands of Genghis's designated successor as Great Khan, Ögödei, included central Siberia and northern Zungharia, with main pastures on the Imil and Irtysh Rivers near modern Tarbagatay (Tacheng or Chuguchak). By custom, the youngest son, Tolui, was "prince of the hearth" and was given the Mongol homelands centered on modern Mongolia, as well as the bulk of Genghis's army.

This arrangement, though neat in appearance, sowed the seeds of centuries of instability, particularly on the territory of the former Kara Khitay empire. It was an easy matter to control the oases of Transoxiana and southern Xinjiang from the Chagatai base in the Ili valley. However, the Great

Khans farther east held the right to install and remove rulers, and they were the ones who controlled the revenues from these Muslim and Uyghur cities. The Uyghur kingdom remained subject to the Great Khans in Beijing until the start of the fourteenth century, as did Khotan formally until 1375.[25] Another built-in source of tension arose from the fact that while Ögödei inherited the superior position of Great Khan, it was Tolui who occupied the symbolically important Orkhon valley lands—where Ögödei would in fact build the Mongol imperial capital of Karakoram. This gave rise to ongoing conflict between the Ögödeids and Toluids (successors of Ögödei and Tolui, respectively) over the Great Khanship. Likewise, the other branches of the Mongol ruling house challenged the Chaghataids for control of the Tarim basin and Transoxiana. Moreover, there would be constant tension between those Mongols who remained in Mongolia and those ruling from China.

All of this ensured that events in Xinjiang and even Transoxiana would be linked to the stormy politics of the Mongol imperial center to the east and that the politico-military fate of the region would again be implicated in the struggles between powers in north China and Mongolia as during the Han-Xiongnu and the Tang-Türk rivalries. To the west, the rich cities of Transoxiana, in theory part of the Chaghataid legacy, would sometimes be ruled together with the Tarim and Zungharia and at other times fall under the control of local Mongol and Turkic strongmen. Khans based in Xinjiang would repeatedly raid Afghanistan and northern India. Generally speaking, the fratricidal struggles and opportunistic alliances of the Mongols and Turks ensured a long and bewilderingly complex epoch of flux throughout Xinjiang and neighboring areas from the thirteenth through the seventeenth century.

The details of the political and military narrative of this period need not concern us here. A word should be said, however, about the place of Uyghuristan under Mongol rule, the fate of the Uyghur dynasty, and the extent to which Xinjiang may be said to have been controlled from China during the Mongol period. The Uyghur state centered in the modern Turpan and Urumchi area escaped destruction during the initial Mongol conquests by joining Genghis early (1209) and providing military forces to the Mongol campaigns when required. Uyghurs held high offices in the Mongol empire. In the late thirteenth century, however, this eastern part of Xinjiang again became a front in the conflict between a China-based power (the Great Khan Khubilai, a Toluid) and the steppe-based power (Ögödeids and Chaghataids). Wars and raids arising from this conflict devastated the irrigation infrastructure of the Turpan region, and the Uyghur ruling house eventually fled east to China and Khubilai's protection.[26] This victory by Khaidu (an Ögödeid, succeeded after his death in 1301 by the Chaghataids) over

Khubilai marked a turning point: The steppe-based Chaghataid khans broke free of interference from their cousins in Mongolia and China.

Both Chinese and Western modern sources often state that during the Yuan (Mongol) period, "Chinese" rule extended deep into Central Asia.[27] As is clear from the previous account, however, starting with Genghis's death in 1227 and certainly after the death of Ögödei in 1241, there was no unified Mongol empire but rather four distinct and competing khanates. Though the Toluid Great Khans, who ruled north China, also claimed overlordship over the Tarim basin, the Ögödeids and Chaghataids contested this claim and by the early fourteenth century effectively excluded the China-based Toluids from the Xinjiang region. Therefore, to state that Yuan dynasty China controlled Xinjiang is inaccurate; the most one can say is that the Mongol Great Khanal house, based first in Mongolia and then in north China, exercised some influence over southern Xinjiang during the thirteenth century but lost that influence thereafter.

Another major geohistorical watershed was crossed in the 1330s when the Chaghataid khan Tarmashirin converted to Islam. This alienated the Buddhist, Christian, and shamanist nomads of Issyk Kul and the Ili area, who rebelled against him and shifted their allegiance to a new khan in the east. This split of the Chaghatai khanate left one line of Islamic, western Chaghataids in Transoxiana (where they soon became little more than figurehead khans under Turkic strongmen, including Tamerlane) and another branch ruling over the Tarim basin and the former Uyghuristan (the Turpan area) from what now came to be called "Moghulistan," a geographic unit that included Zungharia and part of modern Kazakstan and Kyrgyzstan. With this severing of Xinjiang from Transoxiana in 1333–1334, Xinjiang began to take its modern shape.

Moghuls: The Muslim Chaghataids

"Moghul" (Mughal) is the Persian version of the word "Mongol." Though it has come to be used for the dynasty of Turko-Mongolian Muslim rulers in India, "Moghul" refers more precisely to the Chaghataids who reigned (and occasionally ruled) over Xinjiang and Transoxiana from the fourteenth to the seventeenth century. During this period, they, too, like the Turks before them, became Muslims, and Islam now penetrated the worlds of both nomadic tribesmen and oasis dwellers, including the formerly Buddhist Uyghur kingdom in the Turpan area. When a new wave of Mongols (the Zunghars) came onto the scene in the seventeenth century, the Tarim basin they conquered had become fully Muslim.

During these three centuries, the Moghul Chaghataid khans often reigned only in name. In practice, power over northern and southern Xinjiang was with few exceptions dispersed among concurrent rulers in several oases, with non-Chaghataids running things behind the scenes. One such group of kingmakers was the Dughlat clan, rich landowners throughout Moghulistan and the Tarim basin who served as amirs (princes) under the Chaghataid khans and whose succession they manipulated. Another such group was the Sufi masters of the Naqshbandi order, who began in the late sixteenth century to gain increasing influence, culminating in their monopolization of secular power in the Tarim basin in the latter half of the seventeenth century.

The Moghul period in Xinjiang is also marked by a quickening of commercial exchanges with China. From the early 1400s, despite intermittent war at the frontier, trade and other cultural exchanges passed regularly between the Ming dynasty and the Timurid capitals of Samarkand and Herat, as well as the Tarim oases and other Central Asian areas. It was the Ming practice to channel foreign traders into diplomatic protocols and refer to them as tributaries; some Chinese authors have tried to use these Ming rhetorical devices to argue that Chaghataids accepted Ming suzerainty, but this is nonsense—not least because those same princes were frequently at war with the Ming over Hami and Turpan. Rather, the bottlenecks to trade imposed by the Ming state and its requirement that merchants have official status handed rulers in Xinjiang a lucrative opportunity. While playing along with Ming pretensions of universal superiority, they coolly contracted out the right to organize "embassies"—in reality, trade caravans—to the highest merchant bidders.[28]

The most significant development of the fourteenth through the seventeenth century in the Xinjiang area was its continued Islamization. It was the Sufis, or Islamic mystics, who did the most to spread Islam among the Turkic and Mongol nomads in Xinjiang as well as on the Qipchaq (Kazak) steppe. Close spiritual and marital links with rulers, large endowments, and a tight network structure provided support for the activities of Sufi orders both west and east of the Pamirs. Through magical healing and surviving trials by fire and other miracles, the Sufi missionaries won nomads over to Islam and also secured their military support for secular purposes.

The Sufi order most prominent in Xinjiang, and especially in Kashgaria, was a branch of the Naqshbandiyya descended from Ahmad Kasani (1461–1562), a spiritual master generally known as Makhdum-i A'zam. The Makhdumzada Khojas, as this order is known, became active in the Tarim basin in the late sixteenth century, led by one of Makhdum-i A'zam's younger sons, Ishaq Wali (d. 1599). Besides successfully proselytizing among Kyrgyz tribes, Ishaq made the Chaghataid ruler of the western Tarim basin his disciple. Ishaq's followers became known as the Ishaqis or Ishaqiyya. A short time later, Khoja Muhammad Yusuf (d. 1653), a descendent of Makhdum-i A'zam through the patriarch's eldest son, also came east. He preached in the Tarim basin, Uyghuristan, and western China, until he was poisoned by Ishaqis jealous of his success. After this, disciples under Khoja Yusuf's son Khoja Afaq (Apaq; d. 1694) carried on his work. Their branch of the Makhdumzada Naqshbandis in Xinjiang came to be known as the Afaqis, and the Afaqiyya Khoja Afaq's *mazar* (tomb) complex still stands in the Kashgar suburbs (see chapter 13).

The Ishaqiyya and Afaqiyya became bitter rivals, with the former established in Yarkand and the latter in Kashgar. This factional enmity, though mainly devoid of theological content, would continue until the mid-nineteenth century. In the 1670s, the Ishaqis and the Chaghataid khan in Yarkand managed to drive Khoja Afaq from Kashgar. He sought redress for the loss of "his country" with none other than the Fifth Dalai Lama, then a forceful, expansionist ruler leading the reformist Gelugpa or Yellow Hat school of Tibetan Buddhism to supremacy over other schools and over the Tibetan kings. The Dalai Lama then played the Mongol card, precipitating the conquest of the Tarim basin by yet another Mongol power, the Zunghars. The chain of imperial conquests thus set in motion would completely reshape the dynamic of Inner Asian history and Xinjiang's place in it.[29]

From Empires to Nations in Central Eurasia

From the previous survey, it is clear that until the eighteenth century no Chinese dynasty had continuously controlled for any length of time or governed in any thoroughgoing way the entire territory that is modern Xinjiang. The Han and Tang dynasties had settled the Turpan area and established isolated garrisons elsewhere. The Mongol Yuan in theory briefly kept all of China and Central Eurasia under one khan, though the fault lines of this empire are all too visible. Current Chinese claims that Xinjiang has been part of China "for 5,000 years" have only rhetoric on their side.

Viewed from this long perspective, the Qing conquest of and consolidation of rule in Xinjiang in 1759 is a relatively recent event in Chinese imperial history. Yet, China's control of Xinjiang does not have to be ancient to be significant. The imperial conquest established the mechanisms of control and the cast of mind that have characterized Chinese attitudes toward Xinjiang ever since. The non-Han peoples of the region have had to respond to Qing, and ultimately Chinese, dominance for over two centuries.

Xinjiang's modern political situation is a consequence of global trends that began in the sixteenth century. This was the era when Europeans "discovered" the New World and competed for control there. It was also the time when three dynamic Asian empires converged in continental Eurasia, and specifically in Xinjiang. As the Russians, Manchus, and Zunghars spread their power into the center of the continent, the peoples of Xinjiang found themselves under inescapable external pressure.

The Russians came first. After the Cossacks defeated the khan of Siberia in 1582, they moved rapidly east, establishing fortresses on riverbanks. By 1649, they had reached the Pacific coast, lured eastward by furs, or "soft gold." Since the Middle Ages, the Muscovite state needed fur revenues, and to the tsars, Siberia looked like El Dorado. The hunting peoples of the Siberian forests offered no resistance to Russian demands for "tribute," so the Cossacks faced no serious resistance until they reached Manchuria, where they encountered a formidable rival.

Nurhachi (1559–1626), the founder of the Qing state, had begun in the late sixteenth century to wage war against the other tribes of Manchuria, extracting tribute from them in the form of furs and the valuable ginseng root. He also used pressure on the Koreans and the Chinese in southern Manchuria to build up his resources. In 1616, he declared himself the ruler of a new dynasty, the Latter Jin, controlling most of Manchuria. By 1644, his successors had taken Beijing, and over the next four decades their Qing dynasty would conquer all of China. Russians and Manchus first came into conflict in the 1650s, after the Russians founded the fortress of Albazin. When the powerful Manchu army twice destroyed the fortress, the Russians accepted the need to negotiate. The Nerchinsk Treaty of 1689, negotiated by Jesuit intermediaries, stabilized the Manchu-Muscovy frontier by providing for border demarcation, control of populations on both sides, and regularized trade relations. By eliminating the autonomy of the peoples in the borderlands, the two empires aimed to divide the steppe between them. The partition reached at Nerchinsk in 1689 lasted for 300 years, until the collapse of the Soviet Union.

A third power, however, contested this Sino-Russian division of the steppe. In the late sixteenth century, the Oirats or western Mongols (Wei-la, E-lu-te, Wei-lu-te, Wei-la-te, Ölöd, Eleuth, and so on) also began to unify themselves against their Qing and Mongol rivals to the east. Among these western Mongols, the Zunghar (Junghar, Jegün Ghar, Dzunghar, or Zhun-ga-er) tribe came to dominate. The Zunghar leader Batur Hungtaiji (r. 1634–1653) took charge of the confederation just as the Manchus took Beijing, the Russians arrived in the Pacific, and the feud between the Ishaqi and Afaqi Khojas began to heat up in the Tarim basin. Although Batur looked for support from Russia, he found his main allies to the south, in Tibet, where the Buddhist lamas often allied themselves with Mongol powers. In 1578, the eastern Mongolian Altan Khan had given the title "Dalai Lama" to the head of the dominant Gelugpa faction of the Tibetan church. Most of the Mongols converted to Tibetan Buddhism, and many Tibetan lamas joined the khans as clerical personnel and advisers—just as Uyghurs had earlier joined Genghis Khan's growing state. The Dalai Lama pronounced Altan a reincarnation of Khubilai, which added to his luster.

Because he was not descended from Genghis Khan, Batur Hungtaiji could never take the khan title himself. Indeed, several western Mongol tribes rejected his authority and broke away from the Zunghar confederation. One group moved south to Qinghai and another, the Torghuts, went as far west as the Volga River. In a Great Assembly (*khuriltai*) in 1640, nearly all the Mongols gathered together with the Tibetan lamas to form a loose confederation that agreed on a common law code and peaceful settlement of disputes. This confederation nearly fell apart after the death of Batur, but in 1670 Batur's nephew, Galdan, armed with a khanal title that the Dalai Lama had granted him, returned to Zungharia from a lamasery in Tibet to take charge of the khanate. Thanks to the importance of his Buddhist connection, Galdan no longer needed a hereditary link to Genghis Khan.

Under Galdan (r. 1670–1697), the Zunghars created a true state. Still, the Zunghar khans had far fewer resources to build their state and far weaker control over their allies than did the Russians and Chinese over theirs. Hence, the Dalai Lama's call to restore Afaq Khoja to power in the Tarim basin came as an important opportunity for this growing empire. Between 1678 and 1680, the Zunghars took control of the Tarim basin and the Turpan area, setting up the Afaqi Khojas as local authorities. From that date until the mid-eighteenth century, the Zunghar state was the predominant power in Xinjiang. It depended for its survival on a precarious combination of Mongol pastoralists, Tibetan clerics, and oasis cultivators. At the same time, it mobilized its forces to expand westward against the Kazaks, north against the Russians, and east against the Khalkha Mongols. Because the Zunghars also looked to these same neighbors as sources of agricultural products, artisans, metal weaponry, salt, and textiles, they engaged in complex dances of negotiation as well as war.

The geostrategic situation had now taken a familiar form, with a Mongol power threatening a China-based state. In attempting to expand from Zungharia into eastern Mongolia, Galdan challenged the power of the formidable Kangxi emperor of the Qing dynasty (r. 1662–1722), who personally led a merciless series of campaigns designed to extinguish him. In 1690, Kangxi's troops held off Galdan at the Battle of Ulan Butong, 350 kilometers north of Beijing, but Galdan escaped capture with the aid of clever Tibetan negotiators. The furious Qing emperor vowed to exterminate Galdan and his Zunghars "down to the roots." In 1696, his armies finally crushed

Galdan at the Battle of Jaomodo, in the middle of the steppe near Ulaanbaatar in modern Mongolia. Galdan died the next year, probably poisoned by his remaining followers, just when the relentless emperor had set off on another personal campaign against him.

Although the main conflicts took place in Mongolia, Xinjiang was an important strategic resource for both sides. Kangxi feared that Galdan would succeed in rallying the Muslim population of the oases against the Qing, so much so that he seems to have believed that Galdan would convert to Islam! This is not as improbable as it sounds, for the Naqshbandi missionaries had made some inroads among the Oirats, and previous Turko-Mongolian rulers in Zungharia had all sooner or later converted. Even if Galdan did not become Muslim, the Turkic peasants and merchants of southern Xinjiang provided a great deal to the Zunghar state he headed. Galdan promoted mining in Xinjiang and searched for iron ore, as well as saltpetre and nitre to make gunpowder. He learned the technology of fine steel making from Xinjiang merchants in contact with Persia. He sent emissaries across Central Eurasia in search of supplies, obtaining cannons from the Russians; horses, oxen, and sheep from nomads; and other artisanal products from the Tarim basin oases. To support his military campaigns, he forced the oasis peoples to deliver taxes in kind and labor. Each year, one-third of the settled male population had to serve his army. Only the easternmost oasis of Hami escaped Zunghar exactions, when its ruler captured Galdan's fourteen-year-old son and placed his territory under Qing protection.

Galdan's nephew, Tsewang Rabdan, took control of the Zunghar state in 1697 and ruled until his death in 1727. The Zunghars tried to expand their power during this period, drawing on their control of the Tarim basin and fending off Qing efforts to weaken them. They failed to capture Hami in 1715 but beat off an ambitious Qing attempt to conquer Urumchi (the old Beshbaliq area). The main scene of Zunghar-Qing competition then shifted south from Mongolia to Qinghai (Kokonor or Amdo) and Tibet, as the Qing attempted to cut the close ties between the lamas and the Zunghar state. After the Zunghars intervened in a succession crisis in Lhasa and looted the city, the Qing sent an invasion force to Lhasa in 1720 so as to ensure that the new Dalai Lama would not back the Zunghars. Following his death in 1722, the Kangxi emperor's wishes to destroy the Zunghar state remained unfulfilled, but he could look with satisfaction on the extension of Qing power into Qinghai and expanded Qing influence in Tibet.

Xinjiang's fabled riches also stimulated the greed of the Russians. Peter the Great (1685–1725), whose motto was "gold is the heart of the state," sent a military expedition into the heart of Zunghar territory in search of gold. The Zunghar army repelled the Russian army, inflicting great losses.

The effort would have failed anyway, as Xinjiang gold turned out to be a will-of-the-wisp.

The Yongzheng emperor (r. 1723–1735) continued the great Qing enterprise of smashing the Zunghars, but with considerably less success. At first, due to his general concern for institutional reform and cost cutting, he cut back frontier garrisons and tried to stabilize the border. As had been the case many times in the past, Turpan was caught in a tug-of-war between the two empires. Tsewang Rabdan tried to move the Turpan people north, while the Qing tried to move them south. Turpan proved more of a strategic burden to the Qing than an asset, because its grain supplies were too small to support both a military garrison and the civilian population, but it needed to be defended against Zunghar attack. Echoing the decision of his predecessor during the standoff between Khaidu and Khubilai, in 1733 the *beg* (a local headman) of Turpan led nearly all of his people into northwest China. They lived there near the Anxi garrison for two decades in the squalor of a refugee camp.

Continual raids provoked the Yongzheng emperor into approving an ambitious expedition in 1731 to drive off the Zunghar troops and even take Urumchi. The army succeeded in pushing back the Zunghars but failed to occupy Urumchi. At the same time, the Qing's most loyal but incompetent general, Furdan, marched a large force into far western Mongolia—straight into an ambush. Furdan suffered the worst defeat of Qing arms until the nineteenth century.

Both sides needed a rest. Negotiations established a truce and a demarcation line between Qing and Zunghar that held for twenty years, but no definite peace. After spending a huge sum fighting the Zunghars, Yongzheng, like his father before him, had still failed to break their hold in Xinjiang.

The Qianlong emperor (r. 1736–1796) made peace with the Zunghars and allowed them regular trading relations and periodic tribute missions to Beijing. Galdan Tsering (r. 1727–1745), Tsewang Rabdan's successor as leader of the Zunghars, enthusiastically promoted the trade at the officially approved border post of Suzhou in western Gansu. Here, the Zunghars could trade animals, furs, medicinal products, and dried grapes for brocades, tea, rhubarb, and silver. The Qing goal was to "transform" the fierce nomad warriors into peaceful traders with the lure of profit while at the same time maintaining strict controls over the trade. Beijing limited the size and frequency of missions and strictly prohibited Chinese exports of gunpowder, metals, or weaponry. This border trade grew much faster than the Qing expected, however, and even began to drain silver from the Chinese interior. The Zunghars drove huge herds of animals to the border, pressuring local officials to allow them to exceed the official limits on trade. While the Qing sought to weaken the Zunghars militarily, the Zunghars' goal was to earn silver that would strengthen their state.

The truce opened up new opportunities for some people. Many Mongols and Muslim, Turkic-speaking inhabitants of the Tarim basin and the Turpan area—today's Uyghurs—fled Zunghar oppression to seek a better life under the Qing. On the Qing side, this frontier trade stimulated new cooperation between officials and merchants, an arrangement called "merchant management under overall official supervision." In the late nineteenth century, the Qing government would form similar joint ventures to promote industrialization. In this manner, frontier contacts with different peoples stimulated the Chinese bureaucracy to develop new institutions. Xinjiang's irritating challenges to imperial control, like the sand in an oyster, often produced pearls of institutional reform.

One other trade route crossing Xinjiang was also vital to the Zunghar state: the "boiled tea" trade with Tibet. For the Buddhist Zunghars, carrying tea to Tibet had more religious than economic value. It allowed them to continue their links with the clerics of Lhasa and their Mongol coreligionists and to present rich gifts to the Dalai Lama. Because these trade missions passed through Xining in Qinghai, they required Qing approval. This the Qing grudgingly granted, to avoid alienating the Mongols of Kokonor and to show generosity toward their ally in Tibet. Still, the Qianlong emperor always had in the back of his mind the same goal as his ancestors: extermination of the rival state in Central Eurasia.

The Qing-Zunghar trade was a product of a special situation, when the two powers were still evenly balanced. Trading relations served strategic interests for both sides, but neither side favored free trade. Merchants worked with state officials under close supervision and found ways to make profits, but their exchanges also served state power. Xinjiang's trade, never free of political intervention, has flourished only when it benefited the security of the state.

Crushing the Zunghar State

After Galdan Tsering's death in 1745, the Zunghar leadership once again fell into disarray, as two rival princes, Dawaci and Amursana, struggled to become khan. In 1754, after being defeated by Dawaci, Amursana made the fatal decision to call in Qing aid. The Qianlong emperor was ready to pounce. Over the objections of many of his ministers, he sent a large army to Zungharia, which quickly ousted Dawaci and put Amursana on the throne at Ili. Qianlong, however, intended to divide the former Zunghar state into four separate units, each under a different khan, so as to weaken them. Amursana, on the other hand, claimed to be the sole khan and soon rebelled against Qing control, stimulating revolts all over Xinjiang. The Qing army, taken by surprise, had to march again to Ili in 1756. This time it pursued Amursana and his scattered followers into the most distant hills, and even into Kazak territory. Amursana eventually escaped to Russia, where he died of smallpox. After prolonged haggling with the Russians, Qianlong eventually secured Amursana's body, to be triumphantly displayed in Beijing.

To secure victory after the prolonged conflict with the Zunghars, Qianlong was willing to put heavy pressure on subject peasantry in China and on Mongol allies. A Mongol prince, Chingunjav, even launched a short-lived rebellion as a result. Nor did Qianlong shrink from ruthless tactics, including ethnocide. At one point, he ordered the massacre of all able-bodied Zunghars captured in battle and the enslavement of all their women and children, so as to obliterate their identity as a people. By the end of the campaigns, the entire Zunghar population of nearly 1 million people had disappeared, victims of massacre, disease, or flight. Roughly 30 percent died in battle, 40 percent died of smallpox, 20 percent fled to the Russians and Kazaks, and the rest vanished into the steppe.[30]

Eliminating the Zunghars still did not ensure Manchus control of Xinjiang. Where would the Qing armies stop? They freed an influential Afaqi Khoja, Burhan ad-Din (Uyg. Burhanuddin; Ma. Bulanidun), from Zunghar captivity and installed him in Kashgar. But just as with Amursana, the Khojas had different goals than the Qing. When Amursana rebelled, Burhan and his brother, Khoja Jihan, began raiding other towns in the Tarim basin. Qing troops confronted and defeated Burhan in Kucha in 1756, but Qing forces were too small to maintain control and Amursana was still their main target. Meanwhile, Emin Khoja, the ruler of Turpan, offered his support to the Qing army. In 1758, the Qing forces besieged and captured Kucha, but Khoja Jihan eluded them. They also took Aksu but nearly starved while besieging Yarkand early in 1759. When Kashgar finally fell later in the year, and a frightened sultan of the Pamirs handed over the severed heads of Burhan ad-Din and Khoja Jihan to the Qing commander, the Qianlong emperor thought he could celebrate victory. But in 1765 the town of Uch Turpan (Ush) refused to pay its dues, forcing the Qing to send yet another expedition. Only then did the oasis cities abandon their resistance to Qing rule. The Kazaks, who had originally supported Amursana, also now entered into trade relations and sent an ambassador to the Qing emperor. Finally, it seemed, all the peoples of Zungharia and the Tarim basin recognized the hegemony of the Qing emperor.

The definitive conquest of Xinjiang reinforced Qing boasts of success.

Large stone steles credited the emperor with superhuman insight. Clearly, he knew that Heaven was on his side. Qianlong counted the three military expeditions to Xinjiang among the most glorious of the "Ten Great Campaigns" of his reign. By exterminating the Zunghars, subduing the Tarim basin (Altishahr), and bringing peace to the Central Eurasian borders, he could claim to have found the final solution for the security of the Inner Asian frontier, a solution no previous ruler had ever attained. The immediate costs to the natives of Xinjiang were indeed high—massacre, devastation, and control by an imperial power—but this was nothing new. What was novel was the way the Qing consolidated its rule in Zungharia and the Tarim basin and created a systematic administration that it would maintain for a century and then restore for another three decades. These efforts laid the foundations for China's rule in the Xinjiang region in the twentieth century.[31]

The conquest of the Zunghars of Xinjiang also left a powerful historiographical legacy. Chinese compilers at once set out to completely dominate the written record, churning out imperially sponsored military histories, maps, and gazetteers. Each of these volumes fixed in print Beijing's official version: The conquest of Xinjiang was a Heavenly determined victory of a universal benevolent emperor over "rebels" and "bandits." Among the Mongols, however, discrepant versions survived in written and oral forms. Many Mongol nobles felt gratitude toward the Qing for eliminating their incessant quarrels and bringing them economic prosperity, even at the cost of their freedom. But even they could not accept that Heaven had determined the Qing victory. They saw it more realistically as the outcome of Mongol disunity and Qing military might. Meanwhile, a vital oral tradition preserved tales of heroic resistance to Qing rule that survived into the twentieth century. These tales attributed magical powers to Amursana and prophesied his return as the fierce Buddhist deity Mahakala riding on the great warrior horse Marakhbasi. The living memory of Chingunjav and Amursana also inspired Mongols resisting Chinese control in the twentieth century. Indeed, there is an Amursana Street in the Mongolian capital Ulaanbaatar.

Folk traditions of the Turkic peoples of Xinjiang preserve the memory of comparable historical heroes. Some have lionized the Khojas and others from the mid-eighteenth through the nineteenth century for their holy resistance to infidel Khitay invaders. One Khoja descendent, Iparhan, became a heroine to Uyghurs in modern times because of her legendary resistance to the Qianlong emperor, to whom she was married.[32]

Finally, the Zunghar-Qing wars left an important national and geopolitical legacy. The fact that the Qing conquered up to, but not beyond, the Pamirs caused subsequent generations to think of the Tarim basin and

Zungharia and Transoxiana as separate political units in a manner they had not done earlier. This began the process of leading the Turkic Muslims of Xinjiang to conceive of themselves as a group distinct from other Central Asians and Turkic speakers. Thus, Beijing's eighteenth-century conquest of Xinjiang left historical fragments that all the disparate peoples of Xinjiang could eventually reassemble to create new narratives of national unity.

The Beginnings of Modern Chinese Rule in Xinjiang

Over a period of 2,000 years, the Tarim basin was contested by a long succession of imperial powers based in Zungharia/Semirechye, China, or Tibet. Whoever ruled Xinjiang, however, held only part of it, and even then only temporarily. Scores of ruined cities in the deserts of Xinjiang testify to the impermanence of imperial dreams. Percy Shelley's "Ozymandias" would have felt at home in this harsh environment:

> I met a traveler from an antique land
> Who said: Two vast and trunkless legs of stone
> Stand in the desert. Near them, on the sand,
> Half sunk, a shattered visage lies, whose frown,
> And wrinkled lip, and sneer of cold command,
> Tell that its sculptor well those passions read,
> Which yet survive, stamped on these lifeless things,
> The hand that mocked them, and the heart that fed:
> And on the pedestal these words appear:
> "My name is Ozymandias, King of Kings:
> Look on my works, ye Mighty, and despair!"
> Nothing beside remains. Round the decay
> Of that colossal wreck, boundless and bare
> The lone and level sands stretch far away.

From our perspective in the twenty-first century, however, the Qing empire appears to have started something more permanent. By first establishing military and civil administrations and then promoting immigration and agricultural settlements, it went far toward ensuring the continued presence of China-based power in the region. It made sure that settlers, voluntary or involuntary, supported themselves under state supervision, and it worked to strengthen commercial links between Xinjiang and the Chinese interior. By creating facts on the ground, the Qing, initially at least, aimed to control Xinjiang forever.

Qing Control of Xinjiang

After Qing armies conquered Xinjiang in the mid-eighteenth century, the generals knew they had a serious problem on their hands. The armies, numbering about 25,000 men, had defeated large Mongol forces and put down uprisings all over Turkistan. They now had to govern an area of over 2 million square kilometers, larger than the seven states of California, Oregon, Washington, Nevada, Montana, Arizona, and Idaho combined, or three times the size of France. It contained about 600,000 people, including military dependents, peasant settlers, east Turkistani oasis dwellers, and nomads, scattered across an extraordinarily rugged terrain. In order to administer the territory, Qing officials drew on time-honored policies of previous China-based dynasties, but they also created striking innovations. Xinjiang's special situation, so radically different from China's interior, required new methods of rule.

Qing policies of control were built on coercion, commercial incentives, and the active promotion of colonial settlement. Military force came first. Xinjiang's administration resembled a vast military camp unlike anything else in the empire. The headquarters of the military garrison in Ili became the administrative center for the entire territory. Below the top level, however, diverse arrangements were made. Until 1884, only Ili itself and the far eastern oases of Hami, Turpan, and Urumchi had a Chinese-style civil administration. The oases of the Tarim basin were run by a bureaucracy of begs, who reported to the military and were appointed by a Qing government office known as the Ministry for Administering the Outer Provinces (Ch. Lifanyuan; Ma. tulergi golo be dasara jurgan). Mongols remained in quasi-tribal units ruled by their chiefs (*jasakhs*), likewise with Lifanyuan supervision. Military power shaded off gradually from north to south, and from east to west. Nearly 100,000 military personnel and their dependents dominated Ili, but soldiers were less evident in Turpan and Urumchi, with only a small force posted to the southwest.

The key to Qing administrative success, in the military as well as other spheres, was to make the most of their limited forces by flexibly accommodating to local interests. The empire's policy of flexibility and nonintervention contrasts sharply with the modern nation-state's programs to impose uniformity and transform local society. However, the fact that the Qing used native elites and only partially implemented the normal Chinese administrative system in Xinjiang does not mean that Xinjiang was a mere Qing protectorate or vassal state before it was made a province in 1884. From the 1760s on, Xinjiang was an integral part of the Qing empire, albeit under administrative systems unlike those in the Chinese interior (the British governed India in a similar way). Beijing applied the same flexible approach to administration in such other nonprovincial territories as Mongolia, Qinghai, Manchuria, and to a certain degree Tibet and Taiwan as well. In modern terminology, all these frontier areas might be labeled "special administrative zones," following different rules than those applied in the interior.

Provisioning the military and administrative apparatus in a poor region such as Xinjiang was a major challenge. The Qing authorities were concerned to reduce taxes from the high levels imposed by the Zunghars before them and thereby build legitimacy for their rule. At the same time, the Qing increased the size and scope of imperial administration well beyond Zunghar levels. Imperial rule in Xinjiang could thus be maintained only by increasing agricultural production. Moreover, the Qing emperors expected Xinjiang to pay for itself, without subventions from the center to support the troops. Even though it never achieved such self-sufficiency, the goal alone stimulated substantial efforts at economic development.

Then as now, investment in the region's infrastructure was shaped more by security concerns than by calculations of economic profitability. Early measures established traditional military colonies (*tuntian*, the direct ancestors of the twentieth-century *Xinjiang shengchan jianshe bingtuan*), where soldiers worked fields adjoining their garrisons. In Turpan and elsewhere in Xinjiang, abandoned garrison towns still testify to the presence of Han and Tang imperial military colonists. Now, the Qing extended this practice to the entire northern region of Xinjiang, creating a network of military colonies that vastly exceeded those of its predecessors.

It soon became apparent that this strategy of control required substantial money and resources. Exploration for water sources and steppes to raise agricultural yields required large inputs of money and labor. Soldiers working on garrison lands alone could never generate all the needed revenue. This conundrum forced the government in Beijing to introduce two major innovations: a shift from state to private landholding, to increase productivity, and the active promotion of immigration from the interior to open uncultivated lands. Officials began to encourage soldiers to move their families out to the region and guaranteed them long-term leases, or virtual ownership, of their lands. From a temporary occupation army whose soldiers rotated back home every few years, the Qing army became a force of soldier-farmers permanently settled in northern and eastern Xinjiang.[33] One vestige of this Qing military settlement still detectable today is the small Sibe (Xibo) community near Yining (Gulja), which comprises the only remaining Manchu native speakers in China. They descend from an eighteenth-century Manchu garrison force in the region. Other Mongol military settlements survive elsewhere in Xinjiang.

It was the new civilian settlers who most rapidly developed the region, however. Because migration reinforced military control, Qing officials did something they had not done elsewhere in China: They actively helped Han peasants to move to the distant Xinjiang frontier. Fearing that uprooted peasants were more likely to engage in banditry or sharp business practices that would alienate non-Chinese populations, in most frontier areas officials tried to restrain migration to frontier areas, despite China's burgeoning population. Even in Xinjiang, Chinese immigration in the eighteenth and early nineteenth centuries was channeled mostly to the sparsely populated east and north of Xinjiang, where Han would not interfere with the local Muslim population. Before the 1830s, the only Chinese settled in the Tarim basin were a few hundred merchants.

Most Chinese immigrants to Xinjiang came from the desperately poor northwest provinces of China, where peasants scratched out a bare subsistence on drought-ridden fields. By 1781, nearly 20,000 households had left the northwest for Xinjiang, bankrolled by the state. Officials paid their transport costs and gave them animals, agricultural tools, seed, housing, and tax-free lands. Organized official settlement ceased after 1781, but Han and Chinese Muslim (Hui) peasants continued to head for the frontier on their own. Xinjiang was hardly an agrarian paradise, but it had the fields, water supplies, and stable harvests that northwest China lacked. By 1800, the new settlers comprised over one-quarter of the total population of the region. But they remained concentrated in the Urumchi and Ili areas, even after 1831, when Chinese were permitted to settle permanently in the Tarim basin. The Qing state also followed a Zunghar practice in moving Muslims from the oases of southern Xinjiang to the north to farm the Ili valley. These migrants became known as farmers (*taranchis*) and for a time were treated as an ethnic group distinct from the Uyghurs of the south.

One more group ended up in Xinjiang, albeit involuntarily. These were convicts exiled to Xinjiang for serious crimes, often after receiving pardons from capital punishment. Some were high-ranking officials who had fallen into disgrace; others were murderers, thieves, rapists, tax resisters, or military deserters. They did not live together. Officials were exempted from the penal labor of the ordinary criminal, but they all shared the rigors of the frontier, at least temporarily. Among the literati class, exile was so common that it forged bonds of loyalty that influenced the officials on their return. In this way, exile in Xinjiang created networks spanning regional, cultural, and class boundaries.

Many exiled intellectuals participated in research and writing projects that produced Xinjiang's geographies and local histories, as well as reams of poetry. The forthright Imperial Commissioner Lin Zexu had touched off the Opium War of 1842 against the British by trying to ban opium imports on the south coast. After China's defeat, he was rewarded with banishment to Xinjiang. There, he made himself useful by conducting field surveys throughout the Tarim basin that contributed to further development of the hydraulic system and greater exploitation of southern Xinjiang's agricultural potential in the late nineteenth and twentieth centuries.

The presence of Han Chinese soldiers, farmers, and scholars in Xinjiang would not suffice to bind the region to the empire. The Qing rulers knew well that Xinjiang needed links with the interior, and its centrifugal places needed connections with each other. During the course of the conquest, they had put a great deal of effort into cutting off trade routes that oriented Xinjiang and Mongolia away from Beijing. They strictly controlled trade at the border with Russia and limited contacts with Tibet. They also granted authority to certain Chinese merchants to trade with compliant Kazak and Kyrgyz nomads. From these herders, the Qing obtained sheep and horses, necessary to support their garrisons, while the nomads obtained cotton cloth woven in southern Xinjiang and valuable silks from China that they could sell in Central Asia. After the mid-eighteenth century, the Qing created more commercial ties between the Chinese heartland and Xinjiang, intervening actively in the local currency and investing in stud farms, iron mines, and commercial real estate. They even found some gold.

Yet, Xinjiang's local tax base still could not support the Qing administration. The Qing practiced revenue sharing across the empire by directing tax surpluses from wealthy regions to poorer frontiers. By the 1840s, Xinjiang received annually over 4 million ounces of silver for salaries and operating costs. This specie pumped up the local monetary system but was insufficient to meet all the expenses of military administration or to pay the local begs, who collected revenues from their subjects in grain and in the local copper coin. Just as in the rest of the empire, grain, copper, and silver all circulated through the hands of peasants, merchants, and officials. The rate of exchange between copper and silver fluctuated widely, despite Qing efforts to stabilize and integrate currency zones. Xinjiang was at the extreme end of a spectrum, because of its heavy dependence on merchant taxes for revenue and the very high ratio of land taxes collected in kind (grain and locally woven cotton cloth). Copper coins were in short supply and circulated only locally. Xinjiang's mints could not meet the demand for specie. Silver from Chinese government coffers spread along the trade routes, often leaving Qing territory altogether. As commercial integration was considered vital to the security of the province, officials and merchants worked together to generate increased circulation of goods and money.

Still, the combined effect of all these military, demographic, and commercial policies was limited. They never rendered imperial rule in Xinjiang

completely secure. The troops, concentrated in Ili in the north, had difficulty supporting themselves. No emperor was prepared to pay to increase
troop strength in Xinjiang, yet outside Ili the Qing military presence was
insufficient to prevent repeated invasions of the Kashgar region by Khoja
descendents based in Kokand, invasions that at first enjoyed some local sympathy. Han immigrants, though eager to lend a hand to Qing forces to save
their own lives and property, could also spark local tension, and many were
massacred during the Kokandi invasions between the 1820s and the 1840s, as
well as during the local Muslim rebellions of the 1860s.

Thus, in the mid-nineteenth century Xinjiang remained a frontier territory, not a province, with distinct institutions and only fragile ties to the rest
of the empire. Some officials in Beijing still thought it a waste of money, a
barren wasteland of little value. Others considered it a vital buffer, a forward
defense zone against invasion from the west. Considerations of domestic and
international security were always mixed together, and there was no consensus on how to deal with the region. Bold officials repeatedly attacked the
useless expenditures on the region. Many of these skeptics came from the
prosperous lower Yangzi and saw no value in protecting remote deserts. On
the other hand, two nineteenth-century scholars, Wei Yuan and Gong Zizhen,
argued passionately for the importance of Xinjiang. Gong urged the court to
make Xinjiang a province and to fill it with migrants from the interior. He
saw it not as El Dorado but as something akin to Shangri-la, a place where
the tough climate would cure the decadent softness of the interior (Gong
never actually went there himself).

Wei and Gong's real contribution was to link discussion of Xinjiang with
the new frontier threat coming from the south coast, in the form of British
merchants selling opium. Both of them clearly linked maritime and Central
Asian frontier defense. Xinjiang thus provided a stimulus for a vigorous new
interest on the part of Chinese literati in statecraft and frontier affairs. Indeed, much of Xinjiang's nineteenth-century history prefigured China's experience with Western powers. The khan of Kokand began demanding
exemptions of customs duties for his trade in 1817, and when the Qing
refused, he supported an invasion by the Khoja Jahangir that succeeded in
slaughtering the Qing garrison in Kashgar and destabilizing other Tarim
basin cities. After an expensive campaign, Qing troops finally recaptured the
Tarim basin and took Jahangir prisoner, but they never subdued Kokand.
Eventually, in 1835, Qing negotiators agreed to allow Kokand to station a
trade representative at Kashgar and commercial agents in other oases of the
Tarim basin, and even to levy duties on trade within the empire. This was
China's first "unequal" treaty; its terms became a model for those of later
treaties signed with the British after the Opium War of 1842.[34]

Qing control over Xinjiang slipped throughout the nineteenth and early twentieth centuries, and as this occurred, the threat of domestic uprisings and foreign invasions grew. Southern Xinjiang remained the weakest part of the Qing empire. Following the 1862 Chinese Muslim uprisings in Shaanxi, Gansu, and Qinghai, Chinese and Turkic Muslims across Xinjiang revolted in 1864, cutting the region off from Qing control. Yaqub Beg, a warlord from Kokand, moved into the resulting power vacuum with his own occupying force. He succeeded in imposing his rule over the local population and creating an emirate centered in Kashgar that embraced the Tarim basin. By 1872, he managed to subjugate a new Chinese Muslim regime in Urumchi and Mongols in Korla. Meanwhile, the Russians moved into the Ili region from 1871 to 1881, claiming that the Chinese empire was unable to keep order there. In the late 1870s, armies under the command of the scholar-general Zuo Zongtang repressed the Chinese Muslim uprisings. After Yaqub Beg died and his regime crumbled in fratricidal succession struggles, Zuo's force retook the Tarim basin with little opposition. The Qing then successfully pressured the Russians to withdraw. The reconquest of Xinjiang drained the regime's coffers, but it was one of the few Qing diplomatic and military triumphs in the nineteenth century. The decision to transform Xinjiang into a province in 1884 completed the formal administrative integration of Xinjiang into the empire. Henceforth, Xinjiang would be subject to an administration modeled on that of the Chinese interior.

Of the four Central Eurasian frontier regions—Manchuria, Mongolia, Xinjiang, and Tibet—Xinjiang had always been the most restive, though after the Uch Turpan rebellion in 1765 there was no more serious trouble until the Kokandi invasions between the 1820s and the 1840s, which were restricted to the western part of the Tarim basin. These invasions, and their repression by Qing forces, were bloody and expensive affairs. But despite this Achilles' heel in the southwest of the region, Xinjiang's commerce and population both expanded through the 150 years of Qing rule. The Qing may be said to have successfully effected a transition from traditional rule by nomadic conquerors north of the Tian Shan to a new style of imperialism. This new order was based on bureaucratic rule by outside conquerors and local elites and on colonial settlement by Han Chinese immigrants. From the 1760s to the early twentieth century, the Qing laid the foundation of future Chinese rule in Xinjiang. Never secure, and never a source of profit, Xinjiang was to the Qing and remained in Chinese eyes a vital imperial possession, valued at first as a strategic buffer zone, but increasingly seen as an integral part of a new China, despite its cultural and physical distance from China proper.

3

Political History and Strategies of Control, 1884–1978

James A. Millward and Nabijan Tursun

In the 1870s, through an effective deployment of military and diplomatic means that rather surprised Russia and the Western powers, the Qing conquered Xinjiang for a second time. By 1884, when Xinjiang became a province, several things had changed since the first conquest a century earlier. The steppe was enclosed, and Inner Asia's tribal peoples were now mostly subjects of either the Russian or Qing empires. Though most imperial boundaries remained to be demarcated and were porous to determined merchants and herdsmen, nonetheless both the steppe as a No Man's Land and the freelance nomad were things of the past. The Chinese elites and intellectual classes who in a generation would press the antidynastic revolution held very different ideas regarding Xinjiang than had their eighteenth-century forebears. They regarded Xinjiang as an inalienable part of Qing—soon to be Chinese national—territory. In keeping with this shift, the Qing court, too, had come to support the more assimilationist approaches to controlling Xinjiang that had been much discussed in unofficial and semiofficial circles since the 1820s. These entailed abandoning those eighteenth-century imperial policies that permitted political diversity in the Chinese and Inner Asian empire built by Qing emperors Kangxi through Qianlong. Instead, the new thinking favored:

1. Political integration by means of Chinese-style administration in Xinjiang
2. Development of a solidly ethnic Han officialdom in Xinjiang, instead of the local Turkic *begs* (local headsmen) and princes and Manchu and Mongol military officials
3. Intensified promotion of Chinese immigration to Xinjiang and reclamation of land there
4. Cultural assimilation of a segment of the Uyghur population through Confucian education

The overarching goal or justification for all these policies was stability and economic self-sufficiency of the frontier territory. This project continues today; with the reactions it engendered it shaped the twentieth-century history of Xinjiang.

From a twenty-first-century Chinese perspective, one might say that these policies have succeeded over the long run. After all, Xinjiang is now more fully settled by loyal Chinese, more highly developed economically, and more firmly under Beijing's control than at any time in the past. But this long view obscures the fact that over the past century there have been many reversals and oscillations in China's approach to Xinjiang. Two modes predominate. The first, which has, arguably, proven relatively successful, may be characterized as pluralistic in that it allows relatively greater political and cultural autonomy to local peoples. The second is muscularly integrationist and assimilationist, and it has been disastrous from the standpoints of both the central government and the indigenous peoples.

We can see alternations between the same two policy modes during periods of rule by warlords, the Guomindang (GMD), and Communists in Xinjiang. This continuity can be traced to the fact that the tensions and trade-offs in Chinese rule of Xinjiang today remain the same as those that were obtained during the Qing: tight central control versus local autonomy; cultural assimilation versus tolerance of local ways; the desire, on the one hand, for a strong military presence and aggressive land colonization programs, versus, on the other hand, the high cost of and negative local reactions to the military presence and these settlement programs.

Turkic peoples in Xinjiang have also been hemmed in by contradictory pressures. The Russo-Soviet imperial presence in Central Asia and aspirations toward Xinjiang meant that twentieth-century Turkic nationalists often found themselves squeezed between two giant powers. Chinese governments have accused Turkic nationalists in Xinjiang of pro-Russian or pro-Soviet sympathies; tsarist and Soviet Russia have not hesitated to sacrifice Xinjiang's Turkic peoples as pawns in the larger game of Russo-Chinese relations.

All of these factors mean that Xinjiang's twentieth-century history is more complex than the narratives of either Uyghur separatist groups or the Chinese state implies. This tumultuous era sits uncomfortably with the black-and-white nationalistic assumptions of either side.[1]

Provincehood and Late Qing Policies

The Xinjiang that the Qing reconquered between 1875 and 1881 was a shattered land—particularly in the east and north, where the Qing military and Chinese agrarian presence had been greatest. Ruling institutions, government buildings, irrigation systems, bridges, roads, and cities were in ruins; former Qing personnel, including the begs, were either dead or stripped of their lands. Viewing this, field commander and future Xinjiang governor Liu Jintang lamented that "since the chaos, the old system has been entirely swept away, and to contemplate restoring it involves myriad difficulties."[2]

Initially, the territory was governed by "postpacification" reconstruction agencies staffed by Hunanese officers and men from Zuo Zongtang's army. Because they were starting from scratch and because of Zuo's grand plan for provincialization of Xinjiang, they began instituting the rudiments of Chinese-style (*junxian*) administration in the region. As in the wake of similar episodes in the past, there was an empirewide debate over what to do with Xinjiang, in which officials voiced considerable opposition to provincialization and the investment it would entail. The eminent statesman and "maritime defense" advocate Li Hongzhang was among those opposing provincial status and further outlays for what he called "useless Xinjiang" (*wuyong zhi Xinjiang*), although he favored provincehood for Taiwan, whose status was simultaneously under debate.[3] The opponents' objections were familiar: Qing forces were too weak in the area, Chinese were too few, and there was insufficient fertile land to support a full-scale junxian system or a military presence of the requisite size.[4] In the end, however, the court agreed that both Xinjiang and Taiwan should be provinces.

Xinjiang converted to provincial status in 1884. This reform should not be confused with "annexation," which happened in the mid-eighteenth century, albeit under a form of administration unlike that in China proper. Rather, at the end of the nineteenth century the weakened Manchu ruling house, in a desperate search for cost-effective solutions to secure its fraying imperial frontiers, embraced a more "Chinese" way of running the empire. With the shift to provincial status, Xinjiang would no longer be under the jurisdiction of a Manchu general in Ili, but of a Han governor (Liu Jintang) in Urumchi. Beg autonomy on the local level gave way to administration by Han county, subprefectural, and prefectural magistrates (although Turkic elders and clerks continued to fill beglike intermediary roles between the Chinese state and Turkic society). In addition, Beijing promised to fund a robust program to resettle Chinese homesteaders and criminal exiles in Xinjiang and rebuild infrastructure, in hopes of restoring agricultural production and thus boost tax revenues in the new province.

There was a cultural corollary to these reforms. Administration by the Chinese system in localities elsewhere in China depended on the cooperation of local elites trained in the Confucian classics who shared values and a more or less common spoken dialect with officials posted there from other provinces. Elites educated their sons with private instructors or in local free schools in preparation for the civil service exams. It followed that Xinjiang's elites must do likewise. As Zuo put it, "If we wish to change their peculiar customs and assimilate them to our Chinese ways (*huafeng*), we must establish free schools and make the Muslim children read [Chinese] books, recognize characters and understand spoken language."[5] The reconstruction agencies thus set up Confucian schools in both the Han and Turkic areas of Xinjiang, including some fifty schools in the Muslim cities of the Tarim basin. In each, a teacher supervised the rote learning of Confucian classics by between fifteen and twenty Uyghur boys, mostly sons of begs and other local worthies. After 1907, the number of schools was expanded, as enrollments were drawn more generally from nonelite classes of the population, and the curriculum "modernized" to include science, mathematics, physical education, and vocational subjects.

Provincialization thus entailed more than a superficial reworking of the administration. As a solution, it had emerged from long-running debates over the place and status of Xinjiang in the empire and represented a concerted state effort to Sinicize the administration, population, and economy of Xinjiang. In actual practice, however, most changes along these lines were symbolic, and Xinjiang authorities achieved few concrete results. Uyghurs not surprisingly resisted Confucian pedagogy and compulsory modern education in Chinese. Though reclassified and stripped of some of their former privileges, Turkic herdsmen continued to exercise considerable local autonomy and extract their remuneration from their communities, while Chinese officials remained powerless to govern without them.

In fiscal matters, the major problem was that the plan to reconstruct and repopulate Xinjiang depended on an initial investment from the court that never materialized. After Russia relinquished the Ili region in 1881, the weakening Qing dynasty turned from the Xinjiang crisis to growing troubles on the southern frontier, where war with France over northern Vietnam (Annam) soon broke out (1884). After this, not only did the court fail to provide promised funds for the physical reconstruction of Xinjiang's infrastructure, but in some years it even missed the regular annual budget allocation. After the debacle of the Boxer Rebellion (1900) burdened the Qing with an annual indemnity to the foreign powers, Xinjiang's annual stipend began regularly falling short by over half. To compensate, between 1887 and 1910 Xinjiang authorities levied new taxes and quadrupled land tax rates. Recent Chinese settlers began abandoning their new farms and returning home to Gansu.

The failure of the Chinese resettlement program in the late nineteenth century produced one noteworthy outcome: the filling in of southeastern and northern Xinjiang by Uyghurs. Attracted by fertile lands left empty by the wars, impoverished Uyghurs began migrating in the 1880s and 1890s from the south to the Ili area, Tabarghatai, Kur Kara Usu, Jinghe, Urumchi, and even the chain of settlements (previously almost entirely Chinese) from the capital to Qitai. Uyghurs were also migrating, some with government assistance, to the nearly vacant lands on the lower reaches of the Tarim River, the Lop Nor area, and around today's Ruoqiang. In the first years of the twentieth century, Xinjiang governor Tao Mo acknowledged both this fact and the mixed record of Chinese resettlement programs in a memorial requesting a halt to the expensive efforts to lure Chinese homesteaders from China proper. The "turbaned people [Uyghurs] have lived on the frontier for generations," he wrote. "Their bodies are acclimated to the land, and their hearts content with the work. . . . If we resettle a household [of Uyghurs], we will get a household's worth of results," implying that the same could not be said of Han settlers.[6] This is of course a startling inversion of the stereotype, common in Qing times and still today, that Chinese farmers worked harder and more successfully than Uyghurs. It is also an ironic result of the Tungan rebellion and Qing reconquest that eastern Xinjiang, the former heartland of the medieval Uyghur state, became more fully inhabited by Uyghurs than in earlier decades.[7]

Deadly Dinner Parties: Chinese Warlords in East Turkistan

The change in power of 1911–1912 in Xinjiang involved roughly the same mix of elements as in other parts of China: a handful of revolutionary activists linked to the Revolutionary Alliance (Tongmeng hui); reform-minded officers and soldiers in modernized New Army units; and members of the Brothers and Elders secret society (Gelao hui), who were numerous in Zuo's Hunanese forces and hence throughout Xinjiang, where they also ran an organized crime syndicate engaged in the cultivation and selling of opium, now a major Xinjiang crop.[8] Although the antidynastic movement thus involved primarily Han Chinese, the revolutionaries working in the Ili region enjoyed some success rallying non-Han as well as Han against the Manchu regime. Propaganda directed at Turkic peoples, for example, drew a parallel between Zuo's massacres of Muslims during the reconquest of Xinjiang and the famous massacres in Jiading and Yangzhou during the seventeenth-century Qing conquest of central China. The implication was that Zuo (although himself Han) had been doing the bloody work of the Manchus and that Muslims should make common cause with the Han to bring down their common Qing oppressors.[9]

This message may have been well received, for in early January 1912, when the New Army in Ili mutinied against the Qing authorities and Manchu garrison troops, all significant groups, including Tungans (Chinese Muslims; today's Hui nationality) and local Uyghurs, joined the uprising. In the provincial capital Urumchi, Qing loyalists managed to repress an earlier coup attempt, although many of the revolutionaries and Gelao hui members involved had escaped to southern Xinjiang, where they continued to agitate and assassinate Qing officials. Through the winter of 1912, revolutionaries in Ili fought the rump Qing forces in Urumchi, the province splitting for neither the first nor the last time along the Tian Shan divide. The Gelao hui itself became a quasi-autonomous force in the south.

Yang Zengxin

Following the abdication of the last Qing emperor and the rise to power of Yuan Shikai in Beijing, Yang Zengxin, a Yunnan native who had held posts as Urumchi circuit intendant and commissioner for judicial affairs, quietly seized control of the capital. Yuan recognized the fait accompli, appointing Yang governor of Xinjiang Province under the People's Republic of China (PRC). In seizing power, Yang relied on a coterie of Tungan officers and troops whom he had known since former postings in Gansu and Ningxia. With Yuan's support behind him and the former Qing governor of the province out of the way, Yang reached terms with the Ili revolutionaries, to whom he offered offices in the new provincial government. Over the next few years, Yang packed key positions with loyal Tungans, family members, and fellow Yunnan provincials. He further consolidated his power by co-opting his rivals, including Gelao hui members, the Ili revolutionaries, and even Uyghurs from Hami (Qumul) and Turpan who had rebelled over taxation and misrule. In each case, Yang resolved the crisis by incorporating former enemies within the government, posting them far away from their allies and power bases, and then quietly arresting and executing them.[10]

Yang's government (1912–1928) has drawn both praise and condemnation from subsequent historians. Aitchen Wu (Wu Aizhen), a Republican official in Xinjiang under Yang's successor, describes Xinjiang as an "earthly paradise" thanks to Yang's ruthless brand of Confucianist law and order. Owen Lattimore points out, approvingly, that Yang was by temperament a "competent" old-fashioned Mandarin rather than a modern Republican governor. However, Yang enjoyed far more personal power than had any governor or Ili general in Xinjiang under the Qing. Until 1928, the Republican Chinese central government existed more in theory than in practice. Yang paid lip service to Chinese authority but ran his province as an autocracy and exported its bullion to personal bank accounts in Tianjin and Manila.[11]

What today might be called Yang's "management style" is summed up by his handling of an incident early in his tenure. When Yuan sought in 1915 to make himself emperor in a restored Chinese monarchy, a group of Yunnanese officers and cadets whom Yang had installed in Urumchi wanted to join the movement opposing the restoration. Yang himself, no fan of Republicanism, supported Yuan, and his officers began plotting against him. After an elaborate charade in which Yang pretended to trust them, in February 1916 Yang invited the plotters to a New Year's party at the Ministry of Education in Urumchi. When the first toasts were drunk, Yang signaled his guards, who beheaded the plotters where they sat at the table. As the remaining guests looked on aghast, Yang finished his meal.[12] He may have imagined himself a latter-day Ban Chao, the Han dynasty general who had staged a similar dinner party ambush while conquering the Tarim basin city-states.

Yang pursued his main goal of retaining personal power by isolating the province and maintaining the ignorance of its populace. Uprisings in Hami and Turpan in 1912 had raised the specter of the Uyghur rebellion. Although he had been able to defuse these incidents through duplicity, Yang worried about Uyghur loyalty, particularly given the spread of Bolshevism and Turkic nationalism in Russian (soon to be Soviet) Central Asia. Of special concern was the new Islamic educational movement known as *usul-i jadid* (jadidism; discussed later on). Yang thus threw his political and financial support behind conservative qadis, imams, and Uyghur upper classes who opposed socialism and new education, encouraging them to close Uyghur new schools, open traditional Islamic *mektep*, and construct mosques. Yang himself choked off funding for Chinese-language modern education, forcing a return to the curriculum focused on Confucian texts. In this, he followed a policy identical to that pursued by the tsarist empire in its last years in Kazan, Bukhara, and elsewhere, namely, to attempt to quash liberal influences by bolstering qadimist ("old-ist") religious conservatives.[13]

Yang also monitored the mail, censored the press, and attempted to block the import of publications from both China and Central Asia, especially those published by revolutionary Uyghurs, such as *The Voice of the Poor* (*Kembigheller Awazi*) and *Young Uyghur* (*Yash Uyghur*). He investigated foreigners and students who returned to Xinjiang after study abroad, deported Turkish and Soviet nationals who preached new ideas, and arrested vocal advocates of development and liberalism.[14] Only later in his tenure, when forced by rampant disease and a shortage of trained official personnel, did Yang permit medical training and open the Xinjiang Academy of Politics and Law (instruction was in Russian; this institution later became Xinjiang University).

Yang could not seal off his province economically, however, due to its precarious fiscal basis and powerful tsarist and, later, Soviet economic interests there. The fall of the Qing and the end of central subsidies to Xinjiang left chronic revenue shortfalls. Yang dealt with this in part by improving the efficiency of tax collection, but mainly through printing paper money in no fewer than four local currencies throughout the province. He manipulated the exchange rates and required merchants to purchase the local scrip with specie, but Yang's administration ran chronic deficits nonetheless.[15]

As the political situation in Russia deteriorated through the 1910s, Yang managed to limit the disruption caused by a series of refugee crises involving Kazaks and White forces. Economically, however, Xinjiang remained vulnerable to events to its north and west. In the 1881 Treaty of St. Petersburg, the Qing had ceded trade rights to Russia in return for Russian withdrawal from the Ili region. Since that time, Xinjiang's exchange of raw materials for Russian manufactures had played a growing role in the provincial economy, one many times as important as the trickle of trade between Xinjiang and China proper. The Bolshevik Revolution and civil war led to an almost total cessation of this trade by 1919, leaving Xinjiang's cotton and pastoral products without a market and creating severe shortages of cloth, sugar, fuel, and industrial products. Trade with the Soviet Union revived slowly in the 1920s, and Yang concluded his own agreements with the new government, eliminating such egregiously unfair terms of the 1881 treaty as extraterritoriality and duty-free status for Russian merchants. A formal treaty between the PRC and the Soviet Union, concluded in 1924 with Yang's involvement, opened Soviet consulates in several Xinjiang cities and for the first time granted China reciprocal offices in Alma-Ata, Tashkent, Semipalatinsk, Andijan, and Zaisan—consulates that mainly represented the interests of Yang's government. Xinjiang's trade with the Soviet Union boomed, surpassing 24 million rubles in value by 1928, almost ten times the value of the province's trade with China proper. Though initially most of this was through Zungharia, the 1930 completion of the Turksib Railway brought southwestern Xinjiang relatively closer to Soviet markets through the railhead at Frunze (Bishkek).[16]

Yang proved skillful, up to a point, at balancing the many interests in Xinjiang through cronyism and surveillance. He played ethnic groups (Kazaks, Mongols, Tungans, and Uyghurs) and regional cliques

(Yunnanese, Shaanxi-Gansu, and Hunan-Hubei) against one another, affording loyal factions opportunity for personal enrichment off their jurisdictions. All the while, Yang kept an eye on everyone through a wide-ranging network of informants.

Jin Shuren

Ultimately, however, the factionalism Yang had unleashed ended his career and life. After crushing the Yunnanese clique that plotted against him in 1915–1916, Yang had redirected his patronage to a group of officials from the northwest Chinese provinces of Gansu and Shaanxi. A rival clique from Hunan and Hubei coalesced around a modernizing official named Fan Yaonan. Fan came to Xinjiang with the personal recommendation of the Chinese president Li Yuanhong, who hoped to replace Yang with Fan as the Xinjiang governor. Fan tried to speed things along by having Governor Yang shot during a banquet at the Xinjiang Academy of Politics and Law in July 1928—an apt enough end for Yang, who had ambushed his own rivals at a dinner party. Though the assassination succeeded, the coup failed when Fan was himself outmaneuvered by Jin Shuren, Yang's second in command. Jin executed Fan and his coconspirators and declared himself provincial governor, a post in which the new GMD government under Chiang Kai-shek soon recognized him, having little choice in the matter.

Jin was as autocratic as Yang but proved to be far less politically adept than his predecessor. He stoked inflation through unrestrained printing of unbacked bills, exploited government monopolies for personal profit, and levied taxes that the public resented. Moreover, he abandoned Yang's balancing act with respect to Xinjiang's diverse ethnic groups and returned to a Sinicizing approach. Whereas Yang had followed early Qing precedent in co-opting indigenous elites, Jin alienated them through such policies as a tax on livestock butchering, prohibition of the hajj, and the replacement of local officials with Han officials. His dispatching of Han deputies to govern Mongol and Kyrgyz herdsmen was bitterly resisted, and his move to eliminate the autonomous status of the *wang* or *khan* of Hami touched off a province-wide conflagration (discussed later in this chapter). In April 1933, with Tungan and Uyghur rebels threatening Urumchi, Jin fell from power in a coup staged by aggrieved Han officers, White Russians, and officers of a Chinese force from northeast China repatriated by the Soviets. He was succeeded by Sheng Shicai, a graduate of military academies in Japan and Guangdong and a veteran officer of Chiang's 1928 Northern Expedition.

Turkic Nationalist and Independence Movements

Unlike Mongolia and Tibet, Xinjiang did not declare independence from China when the Qing dynasty fell in 1911. While there was certainly resentment of Qing and Chinese rule, there was no unified leadership in place to declare or seize independence nor, arguably, any generally shared sense that a given part or all of the Xinjiang region per se should be a nation of the Turkic people in the modern sense. Attitudes and concepts regarding ethnic, national, and political identity were changing quickly, however, thanks in large part to new Islamic education policies and contact with Turkic and Islamic modernizing movements abroad.

Jadidist Education and the Uyghur Enlightenment

The first seeds of modern Turkic nationalism in Xinjiang were planted around the beginning of the twentieth century in the Kashgar and Yining (Gulja) areas. Uyghur capitalists who had traveled to Germany, Turkey, and Russia found their homeland to be backward by comparison. Deeply influenced by liberal Tatar and Turkish intellectuals, they sought to implement modern education among the Turkic peoples in Xinjiang. The most famous of these merchant-industrialists, the brothers Hüsen Musabayow (Hüseyin Musa Bay Hajji, 1844–1926) and Bawudun Musabayow (Baha al-Din Musa Bay, 1855–1928), founded a European-style school in Artush County (outside Kashgar) as early as 1885.[17] Influenced by the usul-i jadid "new method" Islamic education movement (founded by the Tartar Ismail Bey Gasprinskii [1851–1914]) and by pan-Turkism emanating from Turkey, in the first years of the twentieth century the Musabayows' educational venture hired teachers from abroad; sent Uyghur students to study in Istanbul, Kazan, and St. Petersburg; and opened other schools, including a teacher training program in Artush and a technical worker's school in association with Hüsen's modern tannery in Yining. The Musabayows also opened a publishing house in Kashgar. Returned students and graduates of the teacher's college fanned out to start schools elsewhere in Xinjiang. For example, Mesud Sabiri (1887–1952), who would later advocate Uyghur autonomy as an adviser to the GMD in Xinjiang, returned from studying medicine in Istanbul in 1915 and founded a pharmacy and eight schools, enrolling a total of 2,000 students in Yining.[18]

Besides the Artush-Kashgar area and Yining, a third important locus of jadidist education was the Turpan area, where another Uyghur trader, Mexsut (Mahsud) Muhiti (1885–1933), opened a modern Turkic-language school in Astana in 1913 after unsuccessfully lobbying Nanjing to do so. Students from the Astana school went on to foreign study, newspaper publishing, or government posts.[19]

What made these schools revolutionary was a curriculum that abandoned the traditional goals of *mektep* and *madrassah* education in favor of a new set of subjects: foreign languages, geography, history, science, mathematics, accounting, Turkic language and literature, religion, and even athletics. These reforms were not anti-Chinese in themselves; indeed, an analogous educational movement began under official auspices with the post-Boxer reforms and culminated a few years later with the New Culture movement in China. Like Chinese new education, however, jadidism in Xinjiang rejected traditional canonical learning in favor of personal and national strengthening through modern education; for this reason, religious conservatives and Governor Yang interfered with and shut down many new schools and publications.

After the success of the Bolshevik Revolution in Russia (1918) and the establishment of the ethnically defined socialist republics in former tsarist Turkistan, teachers and publications imported to Xinjiang reflected an outlook that was both influenced by communism and more strongly nationalistic. In 1921, a group known as the Organization of Workers and Farmers of Altishahr and Zungharia (Altisheher-Junghar Ishchi Dehqanlar Teshkilati)[20] convened a congress in Tashkent. In several resolutions, this congress renamed itself the Organization of Revolutionary Uyghur (Inqilawi Uyghur Itipaqi), sent representatives to Moscow for consultations, and dedicated itself to the establishment of Communist rule in Xinjiang.[21] (This event is often cited as the first use of the ethnonym "Uyghur" for the urban and agrarian Turkic population of Xinjiang, though the usage did not arise de novo. Russian academics had from the late nineteenth century posited a connection between the ninth-century Uyghur empire, the Karakhanids, and the later population of the Tarim basin, and many Uyghur traders and students in Russia had learned of and embraced this association prior to 1921).

Not all Turkic nationalists in Xinjiang accepted the Soviet model. In these same years, many upper-class and highly educated Tatars, Uzbeks, and others with Turkic-nationalist and anti-Communist beliefs fled Soviet territory for exile in Xinjiang. These liberal, nationalistic intellectuals influenced pedagogy and publishing, and Xinjiang's Turkic nationalist movement began to divide over attitudes toward communism and the Soviet Union. This division would influence the political and military developments of the 1930s and 1940s.

Rebellion

Grievances accumulated from Yang's tenure and egregious misrule by Jin sparked a conflagration in eastern Xinjiang in 1931 that soon engulfed the entire province. The wars of the early 1930s are often depicted as a continuation of the nineteenth-century rebellions based on religious difference. However, while the uprisings of the early twentieth century may share with those of the nineteenth century an ultimate cause in dissatisfaction with aspects of the colonial regime, the proximate causes, place of origin, local and outside actors, and ideological concerns were all different from those of sixty years earlier. Moreover, the factionalization and opportunism of the various rebel and opposition movements indicate that although Islam played a role, this was by no means a straightforward case of "Islam versus China" along a civilizational fault line. Nor were the rebels exclusively Uyghur.

The immediate issue that brought on the rebellion was an administrative holdover from the Qing period, Jin's effort to eliminate it, and tensions engendered by Chinese migration into eastern Xinjiang. The Manchu regime, following Mongol precedent in keeping with its Inner Asian outlook, had allowed aristocratic allies in some Mongolian and Turkic areas to maintain personal hereditary rule over their lands and peoples. Even after 1911, Shah Mexsut (Maqsud Shah), the khan or wang of Hami, continued to enjoy these feudal privileges in Hami and environs. Since Shah Mexsut spoke Chinese well and never challenged Yang's authority, the warlord left him in power, despite local uprisings in 1907 and 1912 against the khan's excessive taxation and corvée.

The continued existence of a hereditary satrapy within Xinjiang province ran counter to a centralizing trend throughout China; in non-Han frontier areas especially, both central government and local militarists had been striving to eliminate the patchwork of local indirect rule that was a legacy of the pluralist Qing imperial policy. In the case of Hami, Shah Mexsut's territory straddled the key road linking Xinjiang and China proper. Many Chinese believed, moreover, that there was much "unopened land" in the Hami and Turpan areas and that Shah Mexsut's regime limited Chinese settlement (and Urumchi's ability to tax Chinese settlers) in the area.[22] Therefore, when Shah Mexsut died in 1930, Jin abolished the khanate and put the region under county administration like the rest of Xinjiang. Though some Uyghurs may have welcomed the end of Shah Mexsut's rule, with its heavy corvée service requirement, their hopes of relief were dashed when Jin doubled their agricultural taxes in the first year and expropriated improved but fallow farmlands (officially dubbed "wasteland") to give to Han refugees fleeing war and famine in Gansu. These Chinese settlers received tools, seed, and a two-year tax holiday, while Uyghur farmers were compensated for their confiscated farmland with unirrigated ground abutting the desert. To make matters worse, the new Chinese garrison posted to Hami commandeered grain and livestock and extorted bribes.[23]

In February 1931, Chinese platoon commander Zhang Guohu decided to marry a Uyghur girl in a small village outside Hami and coerced the father into allowing the marriage. According to one account of the event, the father plotted with local Uyghurs to ambush Zhang and his men during the wedding; Zhang himself was killed by a man disguised as the bride.[24] A mob then attacked new Chinese settlers and took control of the Hami Muslim old town. After Chinese reinforcements from Urumchi drove the rebels into the hills, they came under the leadership of two of Shah Mexsut's former ministers: Xoja Niyaz Haji and Yulbars Khan.

Over the next few months, indiscriminate Chinese reprisals against Muslims turned the entire countryside of the Hami-Turpan region against the Chinese administration. Uyghurs were joined in their rebellion by Kazaks, Kyrgyz, and Tungans (Muslim Chinese). In particular, on Yulbars's invitation, a charismatic young Tungan warlord from Gansu, Ma Zhongying, intervened in the summer of 1931.

Open rebellion broke out in Turpan in late 1932 and spread throughout the province in the winter of 1932–1933. The best-known English-language accounts of this period attribute the Turpan and other oasis rebellions to lieutenants of Ma Zhongying;[25] however, more recent research in Chinese and Japanese demonstrates that even before the Hami rebellion there was already an underground organization in place in Turpan and the Tarim basin led by Turkic leaders, notably Maxmut (Mahmud) Muhiti (brother of jadidist school founder Mexsut Muhiti). With some reluctance, these figures allied with the Tungans in operations against Jin.[26]

The rebellion in early 1930s Xinjiang was not a bilateral conflict between Muslims and Chinese. Although communal and ethnic concerns were important factors, and certainly contributed to its bloody character, the reality of the rebellion was complex and multisided. In fact, besides Tungan and Uyghur fighting in concert, there were also struggles pitting Turkic against Chinese Muslims. Besides the Uyghurs and Tungans, forces arrayed against the Xinjiang provincial government included Kazaks, Kyrgyz, and other Chinese commanders and armies. Moreover, outside influence and intervention played a role: The Nationalist government dispatched "pacification commissioners" and GMD party agents and muddied the waters by extending recognition and official titles to Tungans who were themselves fighting the Xinjiang provincial government. Ultimately, it was Soviet support and military intervention on behalf of certain Chinese and Uyghur groups that proved decisive against both Tungan and Uyghur rebel movements (claims of substantial Japanese or British support of rebel groups in Xinjiang in the 1930s are exaggerated).[27] This was a time and place where ethnic, religious, and political alliances were fungible; even the White Russian troops in the employ of the Xinjiang government were by 1934 largely commanded and armed by the Soviet Union.

In northern and eastern Xinjiang, the fighting focused on Urumchi. Sheng, as Jin's military commander, held off Uyghur and Tungan besiegers first with reinforcements from Ili, including refugee White Russian troops, and later with Chinese soldiers from northeast China (Manchuria) who had fled the Japanese into Soviet territory and were repatriated to Xinjiang. In the course of his campaigns, Sheng arrested and executed thousands of people, including the famous Uyghur poet Abduhaliq Uyghur and Mexsut Muhiti (Sheng displayed the latter's head in Astana, where Mexsut Muhiti had opened his modern school).[28]

As noted earlier, the repatriated northeastern Chinese and White Russians joined with other interest groups to overthrow Jin in 1933, and Sheng took control of the Urumchi government. Vehemently anti-Japanese, Sheng enjoyed strong Soviet support. For reasons that remain unclear, but which may have involved Soviet incentives, in the summer of 1933 Xoja Niyaz, Mahmut Muhiti, and most Uyghur forces switched sides to join Sheng against the Tungan armies; Sheng promised Xoja Niyaz a position as commander in southern Xinjiang and encouraged him to advance along the north rim of the Tarim toward Kashgar. Despite Sheng's rise and alliance with the Uyghur rebels, however, the Tungans had by now taken control of much of Zungharia, thanks to an alliance of their own with Zhang Peiyuan, the Chinese commander in the Ili region.

Meanwhile, there were other foci of rebellion in southern Xinjiang. In late 1932, a faction of Tungans under Ma Zhancang proceeded along the northern rim of the Tarim basin and joined in Kucha with a Uyghur force under a secret society member named Timur Beg; together, the combined force marched on Kashgar. In the southern Tarim, a rebellion started by gold miners had come under the leadership of Muhemmed Imin Bughra and his two brothers; the three styled themselves "emirs" of a new state. Though a member of the Islamic 'ulama and teacher in a madrassah, Bughra sympathized with the modernizing, nationalistic ideas of the jadidist movement.[29] His Khotan government extended its influence westward toward Yarkand, and in July 1933 one of the Bughra brothers, along with Sabit Damolla, an internationally traveled former publisher, set up an office in Kashgar known as the Kashgar Affairs Office of the Khotan Government.

From the spring through the fall of 1933, the old Muslim city of Kashgar found itself in a position similar to that of the goat carcass in a game of bozkashi. Players struggling for control of the city included a Kyrgyz adventurer, Osman 'Ali and his mountaineers; Timur Beg and his Kuchean Uyghur force; Tungans under Ma Zhancang; and the representative of "provincial authority," Ma Shaowu. Ultimately, despite the fact that his commander Ma Zhongying was at war with Urumchi, Ma Zhancang sought refuge in the Chinese cantonment with Ma Shaowu (though ostensibly enemies, Ma Zhancang and Ma Shaowu were, after all, fellow Tungans, and Uyghur and Tungan were now on opposite sides). Next, Ma Zhancang's men ambushed Timur Beg and displayed his head on a spike in front of the Idgah Mosque. Osman 'Ali, after twice looting the city and fruitlessly attacking the well-fortified Chinese citadel, withdrew to his mountain camp.

At this point, in November 1933, Sabit stepped in to proclaim the foundation of the Eastern Turkistan Republic (ETR).[30]

The First Eastern Turkistan Republic

A month earlier, the Khotan emirate's Kashgar Affairs Office had metamorphosed into the East Turkistan Independence Association, and Uyghurs and other Central Asians with progressive and nationalistic views gravitated to it. The group borrowed the Swedish mission's printing press to print periodicals and manifestos. Its relationship with the Bughras in Khotan seems to have attenuated, although the details of this remain unclear. In any case, the ministers of the new government founded in November 1933 were drawn primarily not from Khotan but from circles associated with the jadidist enlightenment movement of the 1910s and 1920s: educators, publishers, and merchants from the Kashgar-Artush and Turpan areas. Cabinet ministers included Uzbeks, Kyrgyz, and Uyghurs.

Surprisingly, Sabit announced that the new republic's president would be Xoja Niyaz, the former vizier of the Hami khan, then allied with Sheng and physically far away. This choice involved a degree of wishful thinking: a hope that the respected hajji and noted leader of the Turpan rebellion would again change sides, this time to cast his lot with those seeking Turkic independence.

There is disagreement over the character of the new ETR government, in particular its embrace of Islam. A Chinese government white paper has ascribed this movement to "fanatical Xinjiang separatists and extremist religious elements"; likewise, the author of the only extended English-language study of the period points to Bughra's mistreatment of Christian missionaries in Khotan as evidence of the intolerance and extremism of the first ETR.[31] But as we have seen, the ETR government proclaimed in Kashgar was distinct from the Bughra emirate in Khotan. Moreover, in one of his first acts after forming the new government, Sabit assured foreigners of their safety and continued welcome in Kashgar. The historian Shinmen Yasushi argues on the basis of his analysis of the publications, mass mobilization techniques, and the ETR constitution that the new state was founded on the modernizing, reformist, and developmental ideals of the jadidist movement, while also implying a role for Islam. The constitution's first clauses announce that it will govern in accordance with shari'a, but the remainder of the document concerns such matters as modern education, libraries, and public health, as well as tax reform, debt relief, and economic growth; it outlines a democratic republic and promises elections, although it leaves the specifics of local government and representative bodies sketchy. The ethnoreligious ambiguity extends even to the name of the new government. It struck its first copper coins in the name of the Republic of Uyghuristan (Uyghurstan Jumhuriyiti); some contemporary primary sources refer to it as the "Eastern Turkistan Islamic Republic," while others, including the constitution, call it simply the "Eastern Turkistan Republic," the name which later coins and passports employed as well.[32] According to a man present at the time, after some debate the government decided on "Eastern Turkistan Republic" on the grounds that there were other Turkic peoples besides Uyghurs in Xinjiang and in the newly established government.[33]

Of course, questions regarding the identity or ideology of the ETR are mostly moot, since the new regime, which claimed to extend northeast to Aksu and southwest to Khotan, was in fact hard-pressed to maintain its foothold in Kashgar. It had next to no resources, suffered from runaway inflation, and enjoyed no international recognition but rather the active antipathy not only of the Nanjing government but also of the Soviet Union. The ETR could not even dislodge the Tungan forces holed up in the Chinese "new city."

Soviet Intervention, "Tunganistan," and the End of the ETR

Beleaguered by Tungans under Ma Zhongying and by Zhang Peiyuan's Chinese troops, Sheng appealed for further aid from the Soviets, who had many reasons to help him. Since the nineteenth century, Xinjiang was an important supplier of cotton, wool, livestock, hides, and other raw materials to Russia and the Soviet Union and a market for its manufactures. Moscow also coveted northern Xinjiang's minerals. Yang and Jin had both concluded trade deals offering favorable tariffs to the Soviet Union. Strategically, the Soviets feared Japanese influence in or annexation of Xinjiang: Japan had already annexed Manchuria and invaded Inner Mongolia; Japanese aides were rumored to have joined Ma Zhongying's camp; and Japan turned out quantities of pan-Turkic and pan-Islamic propaganda. Finally, with its own Central Asian republics only recently secured from Muslim *basmachi* guerrillas, the Soviet Union did not relish the prospect of an independent Turkic Muslim republic such as the ETR taking root in Kashgar, especially since basmachi figures from Uzbekistan and Kyrgyzstan had surfaced in the Kashgar government. Moscow thus stepped in to save the nominal Chinese government of Xinjiang.

The Soviet Union had already helped Jin by repatriating the Chinese Northeastern Salvation Army to Xinjiang. When Sheng sought assistance, Joseph Stalin responded in January 1934 with two brigades of Soviet troops, christened "Altayiiskii" and "Tarbakhataiskii."[34] With air support and chemical bombs, they quickly crushed Zhang Peiyuan's force and drove Ma Zhongying away from Urumchi to the southeast. The Tungans then retreated toward Kashgar, where Xoja Niyaz had by now arrived and assumed the position of president of the ETR. In February, the Tungan army set on Kashgar in the name of the GMD, driving Xoja Niyaz, Sabit, and the ETR government to Yengi Hissar. The Tungans who had been besieged in the Kashgar Chinese city then sacked old Kashgar, slaughtering many Uyghur civilians; one primary source estimates 4,500 dead.[35] It was thus the Tungans, or Chinese Muslims, who brought the first ETR to an end, though the Soviet Union, Sheng, and Nanjing all played an indirect role.

In their denouement, the 1930s rebellions took several more odd turns. In April 1934, Ma Zhongying personally entered Kashgar, where he delivered a speech at the Idgah Mosque, exhorting the local populace to show loyalty to Nanjing. Then three months later, after his troops had been defeated by Sheng's provincials and their Soviet reinforcements, Ma Zhongying was apparently lured into the Soviet Union to undertake military training. Xoja Niyaz and Maxmut Muhiti betrayed Sabit and other ETR ministers to Sheng. Sheng then put Xoja Niyaz and Mahmut Muhiti in charge of southern Xinjiang. Other members of the ETR government escaped to India and Afghanistan, where Muhiti himself was forced to flee in 1937 when Sheng again employed Soviet troops to suppress a Uyghur rebellion in Kashgar. He also attacked the remaining Tungans, who had set up a short-lived and rapacious regime (dubbed "Tunganistan" by outsiders) in Khotan, where they waited fruitlessly for Ma Zhongying's return. They heard from him periodically until 1937, after which, like so many others in Stalin's Soviet Union, he disappeared—one source suggests he died in the Spanish Civil War![36]

Sheng and the Soviets

From 1934 to 1941, Xinjiang was a Soviet satellite much like Outer Mongolia. In return for military aid to quell the rebellions and continued

support to keep him in power, Sheng granted the Soviets open concessions of Zungharia's mineral wealth, including oil at the Dushanzi fields
near Wusu; he also welcomed Soviet advisers into his government. Soviet
political, technical, military, and security personnel penetrated and reorganized Sheng's administration and developed his extensive and much-
feared secret police apparatus. A regiment of Soviet People's Commissariat
of Internal Affairs troops was stationed near Hami as a defense against
possible Japanese invasion.

Soviet influence was particularly strong in regard to Sheng's policies
toward Xinjiang's non-Chinese peoples and would have lasting effects.
Sheng departed from GMD ideology of "five races of China" to recognize
fourteen ethnic categories in Xinjiang: Uyghur, Taranchi (Uyghurs in Ili),
Kazak, Kyrgyz, Uzbek, Tatar, Tajik, Manchu, Sibe (Xibo), Solon, Han,
Hui (i.e., Tungan), Mongol, and Russian. This represented the first time
"Uyghur" entered official use to refer to the Türki-speaking nonnomad
population of southern Xinjiang. Some activists with Russian and Soviet
connections in the Turpan area had adopted the term in the 1920s (notably
the poet Abduhaliq "Uyghur"[37]), and as we have seen, the 1933–1934
Kashgar republic considered calling itself "Uyghuristan." Chinese governments up until Sheng's had distinguished Turki Muslims from Chinese
Muslims by referring to the former as "wrapped-head" or "turbaned Muslims" (chantou or chanhui), after the turbans some Uyghur men wore.

Sheng's administration thus adopted Stalinist nationalities policy for
Xinjiang and began implementing korenizatsiia: creating cultural associations for each of the new ethnic categories, assigning government posts
on their basis, and promoting literacy and publication in various Turkic
languages. Just as in the Soviet Union, the goal of this approach was to
undermine potential broader bases of identity, especially Turkic or Muslim, and to foster interethnic competition. Indeed, some Uyghur intellectuals objected to this, though most Xinjiang peoples seem to have accepted
the ethnic identifications.[38] With only minor changes, these categories,
and the approach underlying them, have continued as the basis for PRC
minority policy in Xinjiang up to the present.

There were some material advantages to the Soviet presence. Relative
peace and stability allowed Sheng to reform the currency and to begin
developing communications and agricultural infrastructure. Soviet investment and open trade relations spurred economic recovery, especially in
Zungharia, and helped tame province-wide inflation.

Unfortunately, Sheng also shared Stalin's fondness for purges, as he
executed between 50,000 and 100,000 political prisoners during his career. After repressing the 1937 uprising in the south with Soviet troops,

Sheng launched a series of purges against the cohort of Turkic and Tungan intellectual and political leaders who had helped him secure power. These included Xoja Niyaz, whom Sheng accused of spying for the Japanese. Later, he arrested as "Trotskyites," a group of Chinese Communists originally sent to him from Moscow and employed another group dispatched from Yan'an by Mao Zedong; Mao's brother Zemin was among this group of technical, cultural, and bureaucratic personnel.[39]

Balanced as it was between world powers, Xinjiang's situation was highly sensitive to shifts in global strategic alignments. Stalin's support for Sheng had derived in great part from the latter's position as a bulwark against Japanese westward expansion. In 1941, however, Stalin signed an antiaggression pact with Japan to protect the Soviet eastern flank in preparation for the upcoming conflict with Adolf Hitler in the west. Once Hitler invaded the Soviet Union (June 1941), Stalin could spare few resources for Sheng's Xinjiang. Moreover, when the United States joined the war in December and began funneling aid to the GMD, Sheng decided that the tide had turned against the Soviets and realigned himself with the GMD government in China. He cut off Soviet trade, kicked out Soviet personnel, and executed his Chinese Communist advisers (including Mao Zemin). Sheng became chairman of the GMD Xinjiang branch and welcomed Nationalist troops, officials, and a U.S. consulate into Urumchi. From 1942, GMD influence in the region grew.

Sheng's downfall came after he tried to change his spots a third time. Following the failure of the German army to take Stalingrad in 1943, Sheng once again sought the patronage of the Soviet Union. He arrested the GMD representatives in Xinjiang, writing to Stalin that they were Japanese spies and telling Chiang they were Communists. This time, however, Stalin refused to help, and Sheng was forced to return abjectly to the Nationalist government, which orchestrated his removal from Xinjiang in September 1944.[40]

Guomindang Government

With the arrival of the GMD, a China-based power again controlled the Xinjiang government. In the three decades since this was last the case, national and ethnic consciousness had developed greatly among the Turkic and other non-Chinese peoples in Xinjiang, shaped by jadidist ideas and the rhetoric of Sheng's Soviet-style nationalities policies and tempered in the fires of communal and ethnic warfare. GMD thinking about Xinjiang, however, had evolved little from that of the late Qing. Thus, the GMD plan for Xinjiang (never to be fully realized) involved colonization by up to 1 million Han Chinese, replacement of Turkic by ethnic Chinese officials at all administrative levels, economic integration with China proper, settlement of nomads, and enormous tax increases to pay for a standing GMD army of 100,000 Han and Tungan troops. And while Sheng's regime, tyrannical as it was, had at least paid frequent lip service to the notion of "equality of the nationalities," Wu Zhongxin, the new GMD governor, took the opportunity of his first public speech to reiterate Chiang's theory that all non-Han peoples throughout the former territory of the Qing empire were originally racially Chinese and that such categories as "Uyghur," "Kazak," and "Kyrgyz" did not exist.[41]

It was in fiscal and economic policy that the GMD government in Xinjiang proved most disastrous. Sheng's rupture of relations with the Soviet Union had dealt the region a terrible blow, cutting off both supply of manufactured goods and demand for Xinjiang's agricultural, pastoral, and extractive products. Rosy plans for economic integration with China could not fill the gap left by the loss of Xinjiang's major trade partner and source of capital investment. The GMD aggravated the underlying crisis by undisciplined minting of Xinjiang dollars, followed by an attempt to replace the Xinjiang currency, at exchange rates unfavorable to Xinjiang residents, with the Nationalist Chinese dollar—then so severely inflationary that Xinjiang authorities themselves would not accept it for the purposes of tax payment. Chinese merchants were the only beneficiaries of the currency change; meanwhile, Uyghur and other Turkic entrepreneurs were forced to pay greatly increased fees for the foreign travel permits necessary to do business in the Soviet Union.[42]

Nomadic Kazaks, many of whom were already in revolt against Sheng, found little improvement under the GMD. Starting in 1943, the Chinese government evicted nomads and settled Chinese farmers on grasslands near Jitai; Lattimore reports that GMD troops machine-gunned camps of uncooperative Kazaks, and Kazak guerillas under Osman Batur staged sporadic raids on Chinese settlements and government targets. By late 1944, when Sheng left Xinjiang, Urumchi had already lost control of northeastern Xinjiang, and revolt was spreading into the Ili valley.[43]

The Second ETR and Coalition Government

In October 1944, a rebellion against the Chinese and the GMD broke out in a small town south of Yining. This was the start of what would be known as the "Three Districts Revolution" (named after the Ili, Altay, and Tarbagatay districts that made up northern Xinjiang). Rapidly gathering supporters, and aided by Xinjiang exiles trained and repatriated at this critical moment by the Soviet Union, rebels took Yining by November. Amid massacres of Chinese, according to a U.S. consular report, the leader of the rebels, an Islamic scholar named Elihan (Ali Han) Töre, declared the formation of "the Turkistan Islam Government."[44] However, former members of this government now living outside Xinjiang deny that there was ever any hint of pan-Islamic ideology to what became the second ETR.[45]

This new ETR was soon fiercely battling GMD forces. While Osman Batur led his Kazaks against the GMD in the north, a newly organized Ili National Army (whose tunic buttons bore the Cyrillic letters "BTP," Russian for ETR) pushed southward. By September 1945, ETR and GMD troops faced each other across the Manas River, not far from Urumchi, with the former in control of Zungharia and the latter holding on in southern Xinjiang.[46]

During this crisis, the Chinese government dispatched Zhang Zhidong to Urumchi, where he replaced Wu Zhongxin as governor. Soon thereafter, the ETR leadership, apparently pressed by the Soviet Union, requested a cease-fire and entered negotiations to form a coalition government with the GMD, offering in addition to drop the name "Eastern Turkistan Republic." The sudden truce in Xinjiang arose from great power politics: In the Treaty of Friendship and Alliance signed by China and the Soviet Union in August 1945, Chiang formally consented to the territorial and railway concessions in Manchuria that the United States had promised the Soviet Union at Yalta the previous February. The Yalta terms, of course, were part of the U.S. effort to obtain Soviet entry into the war against Japan. With rich concessions in northeast China already in his hands, Mongolia's Soviet satellite status ensured, and Japan no longer a threat, Stalin chose not to overreach in Xinjiang, especially as Soviet access to northern Xinjiang's oil and minerals was already secure under the ETR government. Stalin could afford to recognize Xinjiang as constituting "the internal affairs of China."[47]

Talks to form a coalition government in Xinjiang were drawn out and difficult, and the agreement reached in July 1946 lasted only a year. Neither side lived up to the key points of the treaty: The Ili group retained its own currency and control over its military and promoted its own cause through the political activities of its party (the Union for Defense of Peace and Democracy) throughout the south, and the GMD police and military mounted a campaign of intimidation against Turkic activists and interfered in county elections in southern Xinjiang to block the election of Turkic representatives. The GMD also provided covert military aid to Osman Batur, who had broken with the Ili group once its Soviet ties became evident.

This period nonetheless saw important political developments. Zhang Zhidong, as chairman of the newly organized provincial assembly, clearly recognized the importance of ethnic issues in Xinjiang. He renounced the Han chauvinism of his predecessor, writing in 1947 that "we Chinese comprise only 5 percent of the population of Sinkiang. Why have we not turned over political power to the Uighurs and other racial groups who constitute the other 95 percent?"[48] In the formal structure of the coalition government, cabinet ministries and high-level provincial positions were apportioned among Xinjiang's various ethnicities and across political lines, with GMD and Ili partisans each holding influential posts. Zhang even offered to work toward a ratio of 30 percent Han to 70 percent non-Han in southern Xinjiang's civil service jobs. He also employed three influential Uyghurs as advisers and ministers in his government: Bughra, Masud Sabiri Bayqozi, and Eysa (Isa) Yusup Aliptékin.[49] These men were important in what became, after the cease-fire with the ETR, a political and ideological campaign for the hearts and minds of the Turkic peoples in southern Xinjiang.

Although the rebellion in Ili seemed at first to have an Islamic character, by the summer of 1946 Elihan Töre had disappeared under mysterious circumstances over the Soviet border, and the Ili group was led by Exmetjan (Ahmet jan) Qasimi, a Soviet-educated Uyghur alumnus of Sheng's prisons, who pursued a secular, socialist agenda. In the coalition with the GMD, Qasimi served as provincial vice chairman, second to Zhang, but the ETR lived on beneath the veneer of cooperation with Urumchi. It represented an "independent" state of Uyghurs, Tungans, Manchus, Mongols, and other nationalities, though it was in fact dependent on the Soviet Union. Against this model, and opposing what they saw as ethnic balkanization of the Turk people, Bughra, Sabiri, and Aliptékin promoted the idea of Türkis enjoying "autonomy" within the Chinese republic. Zhang, too, seemed to support this idea, which had resonated with the early writings of Sun Yat-sen, even though Chiang and the right wing of the GMD did not. Perhaps Zhang saw such concessions to the aspirations of non-Han peoples for self-determination as the only possible way wartime China could maintain a foothold in Xinjiang.

Thus, the enclosure of the steppe by China- and Russia-based empires, a process underway since the eighteenth century, dictated the options of Turkic nationalists in Xinjiang on the eve of the Cold War: "independence" under Soviet tutelage or "autonomy" within China. In retrospect, we may say that neither the Soviet Scylla nor the Chinese Charybdis promised real self-determination, though at the time the prospects may have seemed brighter.

When the coalition government failed, Zhang Zhidong stepped down in May 1947 to be replaced as provincial assembly chairman by Sabiri. The Ili group's propaganda organs denounced Sabiri, perhaps somewhat unfairly, as a stooge of the right-wing GMD. Nevertheless, influence of the GMD military on the Xinjiang government increased over the next two years, and Aliptékin and Bughra distanced themselves from their former colleague. Sabiri dissolved the provincial assembly and held new district elections that resulted in the creation of a bogus diarchy: where a district head or minister was Turkic, his assistants or vice minister was Han, and vice versa—with real power in the hands of the Chinese. And Xinjiang's economy, undermined by spiraling inflation, followed that of Nationalist China into a free fall.

Finally, in January 1949 Nanjing replaced Sabiri with Burhan Shehidi, a well-traveled Kazan-born Tatar with family roots in Aksu. Burhan was partially successful in stabilizing Xinjiang's finances by restoring the Xinjiang dollar. He also allowed the renewed expansion of Turkic nationalist organizations. However, besides negotiating with the Soviets to re-open full trade relations, there was little he could do about the deteriorating economy or the political situation before the victory of the Chinese Communist Party (CCP) in China once again realigned the outside forces shaping Xinjiang's fate.

Meanwhile, the ETR fared somewhat better. Insulated by its independent currency against the Chinese inflation, the three districts of northern Xinjiang enjoyed relatively good times in the latter half of the 1940s thanks to a continuing subsidy from the Urumchi government, trade with the Soviet Union, and renewed Soviet investment in mining enterprises. The government developed a regular and efficient tax system; increased elementary education and launched higher technical training programs; loaned money and seed to encourage agricultural development; and invested in medical facilities and publications in the region's five main languages, with the result that rates of typhus decreased and those of literacy increased. Even U.S. consular reports noted that the ETR regime was locally popular.[50]

Assumption of Power by the Chinese Communist Party

In the latter half of 1949, as the CCP began its final drive to victory in the civil war with the GMD, southern Xinjiang remained under GMD control, the ETR held power in the north, and Osman Batur and other Kazak groups enjoyed de facto autonomy in the mountains. Despite Stalin's misgivings about the upstart Mao Zedong, the Soviet Union supported the new People's Republic of China and ultimately reached a common understanding about the future status of Xinjiang: It was all, including the ETR, to revert to PRC rule.

Zhang Zhidong, who had joined the Communists, negotiated the surrender of the GMD commander in Xinjiang, Tao Zhiyue. Ignoring Chiang's order to fight the Communists to the bitter end, Tao began negotiating his surrender but allowed some GMD military figures, and Uyghurs closely associated with the GMD, to escape over the passes to India and Afghanistan. An American CIA agent attempted to flee via Tibet but was killed on the Tibetan border by fearful guards.[51] By mid-October 1949, units of the People's Liberation Army (PLA) under Wang Zhen moved into southern Xinjiang and assumed control with resistance only from Osman Batur and other small Kazak groups. Though the CCP occupation of Xinjiang is called a "peaceful liberation," this "banditry," as PRC sources call it, was not wiped out until 1954.

The socialist "allies" of the ETR in north Xinjiang posed a trickier challenge to the PRC than former GMD enemies in the south; the ETR had of course come to power on a wave of virulent anti-Chinese sentiment, which the ETR leaders had not hesitated to exploit but were now forced to renounce. Deng Lichun, a PRC representative, met with the ETR leadership in Yining in July 1949. Mao then invited these leaders to attend the Beijing meeting of the National People's Consultative Conference, a congress intended to demonstrate the support of China's non-Han and non-Communist groups for the CCP. Exmetjan Qasimi, Abdulkerim Abbas, Ishaq Beg (a Kyrgyz), and Luo Zhi (a Chinese) made up the Xinjiang delegation, and in late August they boarded a plane in Alma-Ata en route to Beijing. On September 3, interim ETR leader Seypidin Ezizi (Sayfudin), a Soviet-educated Uyghur from a prominent Atush family, heard from the Soviet ambassador that the plane had crashed; he informed Deng Lichun, and they kept the news secret, hurriedly dispatching Seypidin at the head of a new delegation to the meeting. PRC authorities did not officially announce the demise of the ETR leadership until December, by which time PLA forces had occupied northern Xinjiang and reorganized the Ili National Army, jailing and executing some of its officers as "pan-Turkist" or "nationalists." Seypidin officially acknowledged the PRC line that the Three Districts Revolution was a part of the Chinese revolution and that all Xinjiang fell within the PRC. He also presided over the burial of the remains of Exmetjan Qasimi and the others when they were returned to Yining.[52]

There are various theories regarding the death of the ETR leadership; the main suspects are, of course, Mao, Stalin, or even the two acting in concert. The latter scenario is favored by former members of the ETR who fled to the Soviet Union and can since 1991 publish more freely. They argue that

Exmetjan Qasimi intended to demand independence or true self-determination at the Beijing meeting. For this reason, he had become an embarrassment to Stalin, who, having secured continued Soviet access to Xinjiang's oil and other minerals in return for a loan to the fledgling PRC government, had no further need for a Zungharian client state.[53] Nevertheless, the question of the fate of the ETR leadership awaits a definitive answer.

The Consolidation of PRC Power in Xinjiang

In the early 1950s the CCP faced many challenges in extending its reach, consolidating its power, and trying to prepare China for a transition to socialism. In most places in China, the CCP's work teams enjoyed local support and some understanding of local conditions and could at least speak the local language. Xinjiang, on the other hand, was mainly terra incognita. With the exception of a few party members seconded to Xinjiang under Sheng's regime and during the United Front era of cooperation with the GMD, the CCP had no one with local experience. Though there were local Turkic Communists in Exmetjan Qasimi's Union for the Defense of Peace and Democracy in Xinjiang, they were associated with the independence-minded ETR and the Soviet Union. Thus, in Xinjiang the CCP acted cautiously at first.

After the "peaceful liberation," Xinjiang was governed by the PLA First Field Army under General Wang Zhen. Among this temporary regime's most urgent tasks was the identification and training of local Turkic cadres; the task was complicated by the fact that the loyalties of the most progressive elements among the Uyghurs were suspect for their ETR and Soviet ties. First Field Army work teams conducted mass mobilization campaigns and formed people's consultative committees to identify and promote non-Han cadres to positions of local authority. Meanwhile, it used the nationwide "three-anti" campaign (late 1951–1952) to purge Turkic leaders linked to the ETR.

Land Reform

The land reform movement in Xinjiang served similar political purposes, while simultaneously setting the stage for the collectivization of agriculture. Through public denunciations and confiscation of the property of "landlords," the CCP simultaneously recruited "activists" and undermined local elites while in theory at least improving the economic conditions of poor farmers. As elsewhere in China, land reform initially won the party some support among peasants in Xinjiang, who were given their own land to work (at least temporarily, until the implementation of larger-scale collectives a few years later). The PLA work teams carrying out the land reform also introduced new forms of local-level organization and allowed the party to recruit and install its own operatives to govern local society.

In nomadic areas, however, this process was more difficult. For one thing, in Zungharia, home for most of the Kazak herders, the PLA did not inherit the legacy of GMD control; it had, moreover, faced armed resistance to its takeover of Xinjiang from Osman Batur and other Kazak leaders. The party was therefore forced to move slowly. The concept of land reform was itself ill-adapted to the pastoral nomadic economy in which herds, not lands, were of primary economic importance and society was organized around clan structures. Whereas by 1955 some two-thirds of Xinjiang's farmers were in mutual aid teams or first-stage cooperatives (itself a slower pace of collectivization than in China proper), a year later only one-third of the region's herders belonged to mutual aid teams. It would not be until the Great Leap Forward (see the discussion later on) that frenzied campaigns forced some 72 percent of nomads into collectives; even then, many "collectives" continued to consist of the old clans under clan leaders with new socialist titles.[54]

Islam

The other target of the early 1950s campaigns in Xinjiang was the Islamic establishment. While there are Muslims throughout the PRC, only in Xinjiang did the party face a majority, non-Chinese-speaking Islamic population with a well-established clerical organization that deeply penetrated society. Although the PRC quickly instituted its own codes in place of Islamic law and substituted its own officials for the *qazi* who had handled local adjudications in the past, the new Chinese government at first permitted Islamic education and left Islamic leaders, including mosque and *mazar* (tomb) personnel, in place under the supervision of the CCP.

It was through the land reform program that the party undermined the independence of institutionalized Islam in Xinjiang. Before the CCP takeover, there were tens of thousands of rural and urban mosques and tomb complexes (mazars) of various sizes in the Tarim basin, and thousands of *axuns* (*akhunds* or imams), qazi, and other personnel. Supporting this establishment was the Islamic tithe and rents from land endowments (*waqf*); in the Kashgar area, for example, mosques and mazars held about 2 percent of arable land. The PRC followed precedents of both Qing and Chinese warlord regimes in attempting to co-opt and control it. The new government first eliminated Islamic taxes (1950–1951); then in the land reform and associated "Movement to Reduce Rents and Oppose Local

Despots," it expropriated waqf lands and thus eliminated institutional Islam's main source of revenue. The state then put clerics on its payroll and incorporated them institutionally within the Beijing-based Chinese Islamic Association. Authorities also pressured axuns into relinquishing their private wealth; many did so through large donations to support public works construction projects or the war with the United States in Korea. Though some Islamic leaders continued to enjoy high status locally, state funding for Islam was not generous. According to informants in Kashgar, in the mid-1950s worshipers risked bumping their heads into prayer hall walls because the mosques could not afford lamp oil.[55]

In addition to the formal Islamic establishment, Xinjiang's Islam had another dimension that proved less straightforward for the state to co-opt and control. As noted in the last chapter, Sufi, or *ishan*, orders had been influential in the region since the fifteenth century, at times even wielding political power. They remained active in the twentieth century (see chapter 13). Though not mutually exclusive from the Sunni Islam embraced by most Muslims in Xinjiang, Sufi practice was less institutionalized and less tied to real estate, centering instead around a revered teacher who led initiates in breathing exercises, ritual dance, music, and chanted remembrances of God. Any sort of building could house weekly prayer meetings. Visiting holy tombs was also important to ishan adherents, but these included not only the grand tombs of revered personages in Kashgar and Yarkand but also many smaller shrines, some little more than stone cairns festooned with flags, animal skulls, horns, yak tails, and the like—in continuation of the pre-Islamic Inner Asian tradition. The faithful visited shrines during festivals, gathered with neighbors, and prayed for good harvests, health, or the birth of sons.

Even while the campaigns of the early 1950s undermined the autonomy of institutionalized Islam in the Tarim basin cities, ishan groups actually experienced an explosion of popularity, opening new prayer halls and enrolling initiates in both cities and the countryside. PRC tolerance for this may reflect the limited reach of the state and party in Uyghur areas, or perhaps a recognition that popular Sufism in Xinjiang was apolitical and posed no immediate threat to Beijing's rule. In any case, the party's moderate approach to Sufi practice changed in the mid-1950s as part of a broad shift to more radical policies that would continue for twenty years.

Bingtuan State Farms

Another dimension of PRC power in Xinjiang was the Xinjiang Production Construction Corps (Xinjiang shengchan jianshe bingtuan). From its origins as an organization for the settlement and employment of 100,000 demobilized troops (including the 80,000 soldiers of the GMD Xinjiang garrison), the bingtuan was designed to promote economic development and permanent settlement of Han Chinese in Xinjiang. As such, it was the direct descendent of Qing-era state farms (see chapter 2), themselves an elaboration of Han and Tang dynasty frontier precedents. Even after it had become primarily civilian in composition, the PRC bingtuan also in theory served as Xinjiang's militia, maintaining elements of a military hierarchy and ties to the PLA. Through the mid-1970s, it was also the primary institution absorbing the hundreds of thousands of Han Chinese migrants (many recruited by the bingtuan itself from Shanghai and other crowded eastern cities), sent-down youth, and convicts dispatched to Xinjiang.

Much of Xinjiang's population growth in the 1950s through the 1970s involved migrants resettled and employed by the bingtuan. From 1954 to 1957, the bingtuan population grew from 200,000 to 300,000; by 1966, it numbered 500,000 to 600,000. During the Great Leap Forward famine years (1959–1961), the bingtuan handled over 2 million Han refugees from outside Xinjiang; it processed another 1.6 six million Chinese youth during the first stage of the Cultural Revolution (1966–1967). Though many of these new arrivals returned east when given the chance, a 1975 report claimed that some 450,000 urban youth had been settled in Xinjiang, making it one of the largest destinations for the Maoist youth rustication programs.

The demobilized soldiers and many of the later migrants joining the bingtuan were put to work in the campaign to reclaim farmland from Xinjiang's "wilderness." Their land clearing, forest cutting, dam building, canal digging, and crop planting greatly expanded the amount of land under cultivation. From around a million hectares under cultivation in 1949, Xinjiang's overall cultivated area tripled to 3.2 million hectares by 1961; some 700,000 hectares of this increase was in bingtuan lands. Most of the new farmlands were reclaimed from the steppe in Zungharia; however, although the bulk of the bingtuan expansion was in the north and east, the strategic significance of the bingtuan derives in large part from the enclaves of Han settlement it created around the Tarim basin. These new settlements brought sizeable numbers of Chinese settlers to the southern oases for the first time in history.[56]

"Autonomy"

Xinjiang is formally integrated into the PRC as an "autonomous region" comprised of "autonomous" counties, districts, and prefectures. In expanding the Chinese nation-state to incorporate the diverse peoples and far-flung lands of the Qing empire, the CCP hoped both to quell separatism in its borderlands and to avoid the Han chauvinistic assimilationism of the GMD. Toward this goal, it borrowed from the Soviet Union the concept of "nationality" (Ru. *narod*; Ch. *minzu*) and other ideological approaches to managing ethnonational differences. As noted earlier, in Xinjiang Sheng's regime and the second ETR had already implemented the Soviet-style approach and identified fourteen official "nationalities" from a more complex and fluid cultural field. The PRC maintained these categories with only minor changes and allocated political, cultural, educational, and other resources in accordance with them.

However, the Chinese Communist leadership also departed in a significant way from the Soviet model. The Soviet Union had created national republics in non-Russian areas, with the right to secede (theoretical through most of the Soviet period, but actually exercised in 1991). Mao and the CCP seemed set to follow this model, indicating in the 1930s that under a Chinese Communist regime non-Chinese areas could seek independence from China if they so wished.[57] Uyghurs at an official convention in Ili in 1951 appealed to Beijing to establish a Republic of Uyghuristan, along the lines of the Soviet Central Asian republics.[58] Once in power, however, the Chinese Communist leadership opted for a system of nominal self-rule or autonomy (*zizhi*) by non-Han peoples at local and regional levels, under overarching control of the CCP, with no right of secession.

Beginning in 1953, as sufficient numbers of trained local "minority nationality" cadres became available to fill local government positions, Chinese authorities began designating autonomous areas, starting at the bottom and gradually moving up the administrative hierarchy. Autonomous areas were assigned to Kazak, Kyrgyz, Hui (Chinese Muslim), Mongols, Tajiks, and Sibe (Xibo) groups. Notably absent from this system are any autonomous Uyghur localities, despite the fact that Uyghurs comprise the majority of the population overall and in most urban areas of Xinjiang. Xinjiang as a whole became the Xinjiang Uyghur Autonomous Region (XUAR) in 1955. Seypidin Ezizi, a Uyghur, served as chairman of the region's people's council, but ultimate authority lay in the hands of Wang Enmao, a veteran of the CCP's Long March who held top regional military and party posts.

The minority autonomy policy avoided the appearance of colonialism and kept non-Han officials in positions of visible authority in the region—as had been the norm since the GMD's forced compromise with the ETR in the coalition government of the mid-1940s. This system must have found some favor among non-Han in Xinjiang, and it arguably contributed to their general acceptance of PRC rule. But the system also aided the cause of PRC control in Xinjiang through the nested administrative system that put the majority Uyghurs in structural competition with other groups and kept real power in the hands of upper-level party officials, who were predominantly Han.[59]

Twenty Years of Maoism in Xinjiang, 1957–1978

PRC authorities in Xinjiang in the early 1950s, still consolidating their rule and eager for local support, trod carefully around the issues of Uyghur and other non-Chinese cultures. Policy watchwords were to "practice democracy" in dealings with non-Han, to avoid "great Han chauvinism" even while guarding against "local nationalism," and to avoid mechanical application of policies from eastern China to Xinjiang, instead giving due attention to "local conditions."[60] Beginning around 1956, however, shifts in the domestic Chinese political and economic situations and in the Sino-Soviet relationship converged to send China lurching to the left, as policies now known as "Maoist" replaced the more gradual, developmental model embraced by Liu Shaoqi, Deng Xiaoping, and others in the Chinese leadership. The era of "class struggle as the key link" began.

The Hundred Flowers and the Great Leap Forward

The Hundred Flowers movement (1956), that is, Mao's call for open criticism of the party—followed immediately by the anti-Rightist movement to crush those same critics—revealed a deep and broad current of discontent with Xinjiang's promised "autonomy" in actual practice. Those who spoke out criticized the bingtuan for damaging the environment; they denounced Han cadres for haughtiness, ignorance, and insensitivity toward Uyghur issues; and they demanded more real autonomy and more non-Han holding positions of real authority. Some even called for the expulsion of Chinese and the creation of a state separate from China.[61]

At the same time, PRC relations with the Soviet Union were rapidly deteriorating. Because of its historical relationship with Russia and the Soviet Union, Xinjiang was especially sensitive to the repercussions of the Sino-Soviet split, which impacted its economy, the political fortunes of non-Han cadres, and even the scripts used for its Turkic languages (no longer to be Cyrillic). As tensions with the Soviet Union grew in the late 1950s, many Turkic officials with (or without) prior associations with the ETR or Soviet Union came under attack for "local nationalism," a crime increasingly linked to "revisionism" (a coded reference to the Soviet Union). What was the anti-Rightist campaign in China was focused in Xinjiang primarily on Islamic figures and "local nationalists" and became in effect a de-Sovietizing purge of non-Han political elites, led by the nimble Seypidin, who with Wang Enmao cochaired the committee that "rectified" many of his former ETR colleagues. A CCP historian writes that this campaign labeled 1,612 cadres "local nationalists" and dispatched most to labor camps for thought reform. Some perished in these camps during the Great Leap Forward period (1959–1961); a few did not emerge until 1979.[62]

The cultural intolerance and anti-Soviet witch-hunts intensified during the next Maoist campaign, the Great Leap Forward. This utopian scheme undertook to radically accelerate collectivization of China's agrarian sector, reshape the land with massive public works projects, and decentralize industry, all relying not on material inputs but rather on political exhortation and the mobilized will of the people. The result was economic chaos and famine or near-famine conditions nationwide from 1959 to 1961.

The Great Leap in Xinjiang followed the same general trajectory as elsewhere in China. Agricultural producers' cooperatives were merged into people's communes some ten times larger, with their members partaking of communal living and eating arrangements. Local authorities proclaimed wild production targets and then disguised their failure to achieve them. As elsewhere, the Great Leap policies produced famine in Xinjiang. Zhu Peimin, a CCP historian, acknowledges several thousand deaths from starvation in Xinhe, Kucha, Aksu, Bay counties, and in the Kashgar area, including those of a thousand convicts in bingtuan prison camps.[63] Zhu might be expected to minimize the extent of the crisis; nevertheless, Xinjiang was undoubtedly better off than other Chinese provinces, from which over a million rusticated youth and refugees migrated to Xinjiang during the famine years.

One particular characteristic of Xinjiang's Great Leap was its impact in the pastoral nomadic areas where the CCP had earlier failed to replace tribal with party government or to fully implement land reform. From 1958, the CCP forced its policies through aggressively, amid a torrent of propaganda in the "Mass Education" campaign. Kazak production brigades merged with farming collectives to create huge agrarian-pastoral communes, shifting decision-making authority far from the nomads themselves. Most Kazaks were not only collectivized but partially or fully sedentarized as a result of these changes, and predictably, the disruption of the Great Leap in Kazak areas manifested itself in losses of livestock: Though figures for key years are unavailable, the annual average rates of herd increase from 1958 to 1965 were one-fourth their pre–Great Leap average.[64]

Xinjiang's status as a frontier region with a majority of non-Han inhabitants also differentiated its Great Leap experience from that of provinces to the east. By 1958, the party fully abandoned its ostensibly even-handed approach to ethnic matters of the early 1950s, when official organs condemned "great Han chauvinism" as often as "local nationalism." Such niceties were forgotten in the assimilationism of the Maoist high tide, and the party launched its Religious Reform movement, with a distinct anti-Islamic thrust. Wang Enmao spoke of the imminent "complete blending of all the nationalities" as critical to continued socialist construction in Xinjiang, implying, in other words, that assimilation was necessary to development. Meanwhile, the bingtuan embarked on a massive expansion, clearing farms and building industry on former pasturelands in northern Xinjiang. The extension of the rail line from Hami to Urumchi (completed 1962) brought more Han migrants into the area. As grain grew scarce, authorities ordered continued food shipments from the Tarim basin to support the capital and bingtuan developments in eastern Xinjiang. Xinjiang also exported grain eastward.[65]

These Great Leap policies (anti-Sovietism and antilocal nationalism; intensified CCP penetration of the former ETR territory; surging Chinese immigration; economic disruption; pastures commandeered for agriculture; and requisitions of grain from the Uyghur south to support the Han northeast) frightened and angered many people in northern Xinjiang, who were further egged on by intensive Soviet propaganda. In April through May 1962, tens of thousands of Uyghurs, Kazaks, and others fled Ili and Tarbagatay for Soviet territory, a refugee flow staunched only when several battalions of PLA and bingtuan troops sealed the border and quelled a large disturbance in Ili. The bingtuan later resettled the several depopulated border counties from which the refugees had fled and established a string of state farms worked by Chinese all along the border from Altay to Ili.[66]

The Cultural Revolution

When the disastrous results of the Great Leap became known, Mao was forced to relinquish direct leadership of the CCP to Liu Shaoqi, Deng Xiaoping, and others committed to a more gradualist program. As the PRC returned to less radical economic policies and, for a time, less strident political rhetoric, Xinjiang authorities displayed more tolerance toward non-Chinese culture and revised their statements about the projected "blending" of the nationalities. They now admitted that this fusion would only take place "after a very long historical period."[67]

Just a few years later, however, the trend again shifted, as Mao drew on his still powerful charisma and sagelike status to arouse China's youth, and many less youthful opportunists, into an attack on the CCP and government power holders themselves. Starting in 1966, thousands of radical and often violent Red Guards, heeding Mao's call to travel about the country and "attack the headquarters," took the train to Urumchi, where they formed an organization known as the Second Red Headquarters. Xinjiang's government, party, and the bingtuan leadership were dominated by the First Field Army, which had first occupied the region in 1949; Wang Enmao was a veteran of this army, and as a "local emperor" he was the prime target of the Second Red Headquarters. In response, Wang organized his own Red Guard group, the First Red Headquarters, to defend against the outsider Red Guards, their "rebel" allies in the bingtuan, and their arriviste leaders.

Available published accounts focus on Cultural Revolution activity in Urumchi, in Shihezi, and along the rail line to Hami, with some information on armed clashes in Yining, Khotan, and Kashgar. The bingtuan, its numbers swollen with politicized youths from Shanghai, played a central role in much of this turmoil. A "rebel" group under Ding Sheng emerged from the ranks to attack the bingtuan leadership for its supposedly capitalist nature and legacy of GMD service shared by many of its members. Ding's faction warred with the bingtuan militia forces and, after taking casualties in a battle in January 1967, trumpeted its cause in Beijing. The following summer, a bingtuan rebel force of 50,000 workers and 6,000 armed troops itself marched against factories, colleges, and government offices in Urumchi. Although in early 1967 Beijing called on the PLA to restore order by taking control of Xinjiang's government, economy, media, and bingtuan, armed fighting continued nevertheless, with some 1,300 violent clashes in 1967–1968. The worst of these occurred after the army itself split, and a rogue PLA unit joined rail workers and Red Guards to blockade the rail line, besiege Hami, and fight pitched battles with regular PLA troops. These factions waged their civil war in the strategic gateway to Xinjiang, cutting off communications with China proper; they were, moreover, close to the Lop Nor nuclear proving grounds, where China had just tested its first hydrogen bomb in June 1967. Reports published in Hong Kong suggested that Wang even threatened to seize the Lop Nor facility unless Mao lent his political support to restrain the Red Guards and settle the situation in Xinjiang.[68] As elsewhere in China, events in Xinjiang had spun out of control, and it must not have seemed impossible for Xinjiang to return to a situation like that from the second decade of the twentieth century to the 1930s, when central Chinese authorities lost hold of Urumchi.

Xinjiang was among the last places in the PRC to emerge from this military chaos, with armed conflict ending only in the late summer of 1968 when "revolutionary committees" reasserted central control. Wang was forced out; officers of Lin Biao's Fourth Field Army displaced the First Field Army personnel; and Lin's man Long Shujin took control of the region, promoting the radical political, economic, and cultural agendas of Lin, Mao, and Mao's wife, Jiang Qing. After Lin's failed coup, flight, and death in September 1971, however, Beijing purged Long. Over the next several years, Yang Yong and Seypidin Ezizi co-led the region, again returning to somewhat more moderate policies.

Such moderation was much needed, for the Cultural Revolution damaged Xinjiang's economy more seriously than it did that of other parts of China. Xinjiang's grain production increased hardly at all for ten years (1965–1975), while the region's population grew by over 40 percent. This rendered Xinjiang a grain-deficit region, where it had once experienced a grain surplus.[69] The severity of this economic disruption derived largely from the fact that the bingtuan, meant to spearhead production and development in the region, had instead thrown itself so zealously into politics and armed conflict. As a result of this unsettling rogue behavior, and its perennial debt, Beijing dissolved the bingtuan as an autonomous entity in 1975, putting prefectural- and regional-level agencies in charge of its manifold farms and enterprises (Beijing would resurrect the bingtuan in 1981 as a response to higher levels of Uyghur unrest).[70]

The Other Cultural Revolution in Xinjiang

Insofar as the Cultural Revolution in Xinjiang was about anything other than power struggles and Mao's lunacy, it involved Wang's attempt to prevent the extremism of the Red Guards (reflective of an increasingly radical politics in Beijing) from unleashing ethnic and communal violence or encouraging Soviet intervention. Despite his ultimate fall, Wang was largely successful in keeping the lid on, something Beijing acknowledged by affording him a relatively soft landing in Beijing (by Cultural Revolution standards) and putting him in charge of Xinjiang again in 1981.[71]

There are no detailed published accounts of events in Uyghur areas during the Cultural Revolution. However, contemporary press calls for "unity" in northern Xinjiang, a reported uprising in Yining in early 1969, and ongoing border skirmishes with Soviet troops, including a Soviet-organized "Xinjiang Minority Refugee Army," suggest that the danger of rebellion and/or Soviet involvement was real. Moreover, although the political turmoil in Urumchi was largely a Han affair, it, too, had an ethnic dimension. For example, one faction of the Second Red Headquarters planned a rally of tens of thousands of non-Han in the spring of 1968 to denounce Wang for "great Han chauvinism" (after Zhou Enlai's intervention, the bingtuan and PLA pressured the group to cancel the rally).[72] And from early 1968 until early 1970, an East Turkistan People's Revolutionary Party organized and issued publications from central and branch offices throughout Xinjiang, advocating an independent, secular, and communist ETR oriented toward the Soviet Union. This party comprised what an internal PRC publication from the 1990s calls the most serious "counter-revolutionary separatist conspiracy" since 1949.[73]

The leftward lurch of the Great Leap Forward and Cultural Revolution period and its officially sanctioned Han chauvinism undermined even the limited influence Uyghurs and other non-Han groups had enjoyed in Xinjiang's governance under the autonomy system. Most of Xinjiang's top-ranked non-Han cadres were accused of treason and purged in the Cultural Revolution, with some being secretly executed. Total numbers of "minority nationality" cadres in Xinjiang government and party positions fell by some 25 percent between 1965 and 1975, and Uyghurs were hardly represented at all in the XUAR regional government after the "revolutionary committees" took power in 1969.

Little known, but perhaps of greatest long-term significance, is the attack on non-Chinese culture and the events that took place during these years out of the capital area, in smaller cities and villages of Xinjiang where most Uyghurs live. The "Leftist" cultural program at the height of the Cultural Revolution was virulently xenophobic; Mao's wife, Jiang Qing, who for a time exercised great power, considered minority nationalities "foreign invaders and aliens" with "outlandish" songs and dances; she reportedly "despised" Xinjiang.[74] In this atmosphere, insults to and attacks on Islam and Central Asian customs were as common as they were appalling. Though we lack systematic treatments of the issue, there are anecdotal accounts of Qur'ans and other texts being burned, Islamic elders humiliated and paraded in the streets, Islamic sites closed and desecrated, pigs penned in mosques, Uyghur girls' long hair forcibly bobbed, and traditional dress prohibited (these abuses are fully in line with better-documented reports regarding Tibet). Moreover, though Red Guard rampages came to an end in 1969, official intolerance and assimilationism lasted until the late 1970s, when Deng Xiaoping's government finally restored the notion of "autonomy" for minority nationalities and dropped from the constitution the Maoist dictum that "national struggle is in the final analysis a question of class struggle."[75]

Chinese intellectuals and even politicians have openly discussed and deplored the horrors of the Cultural Revolution in Han areas, and most Chinese survivors have successfully put the era behind them, conveniently blaming the worst abuses on the disgraced Gang of Four. However, there has been little public self-reflection or self-criticism by the party and no comparable airing of the Cultural Revolution experience of non-Han peoples, on whom the onslaught on culture and identity was arguably worse than for majority Han. Discussion of such events would be near suicidal for a non-Han writer in Xinjiang today, and dangerous even for a Han. Yet, it would seem impossible to fully understand the disaffection and separatism among Uyghurs and other Xinjiang nationalities without considering the legacy of the Cultural Revolution. Certainly, the party has never regained its initial popularity of the 1950s, and its grip on the Xinjiang region, stronger than ever in material terms, is politically weakened as a result.

Part II

Chinese Policy Today

4

The Chinese Program of Development and Control, 1978–2001

Dru C. Gladney

Since the late 1990s, China's control over the region known as Xinjiang and its integration into China proper has increased dramatically. At the same time, China's response to domestic troubles within the region has increasingly come under attack. Amnesty International and the U.S. State Department have issued reports strongly condemning China for its harsh treatment of accused separatists in Xinjiang. At the same time, China openly joined the West in its war on terrorism and received President George W. Bush's public praise for its support in the campaign during his 2002 visit to Beijing. Admitting the vast economic underdevelopment of the region, China launched in 1999 a campaign to "Develop the Great Northwest," which is but the most recent of many attempts to develop the region and bring it ever more closely under Beijing's control. Four years into this campaign, problems and civil unrest remain.

This chapter examines three quite different and to some extent mutually contradictory patterns of control that the Chinese state has applied to the region since the late 1970s. Each of these is rooted in China's past, but all of them differ dramatically from what occurred during the previous decades of Chinese Communist rule over Xinjiang. The three patterns can be described as "ethnicization," "integration," and "transnationalization." The fate of these three patterns of China's recent control in the region goes far toward defining the challenges facing China's Xinjiang policy today.

Pattern One: Ethnicization—The Nationalist History of Chinese Control

Why have there been increasing tensions in Xinjiang, and what are their implications for the future of Chinese control of the region? Ethnic and cultural divisions first showed themselves following the fall of China's last empire, when Xinjiang was divided for over two decades by regional warlords with local and ethnic bases in the north, south, and west. The tendency of fault lines in Turkic and Muslim Central Asia, including Xinjiang, to follow officially designated identities might be called "ethnicization." Ethnicization has meant that the current cultural fault lines of China and Central Asia increasingly follow official designations of national identity. Hence, for Central Asia the breakup of the Soviet Union did not lead to the creation of a greater "Turkistan" or a pan-Islamic collection of states, despite the predominantly Turkic and Muslim population of the region. Rather, the breakup fell along the former Soviet border lines, which helped to establish the national majority and minority groups within those former borders. China clearly is not about to fall apart, not yet anyway. Yet, it also has serious problems with ethnic issues and in governance in the various regions, and it must solve both for other more pressing reasons. An overview of the ethnicization of Xinjiang as the beginning of China's development strategy is necessary to understand the events of the last few years. This suggests that China's age-old autonomy policy, inherited from the period of close Sino-Soviet cooperation, is in serious need of revision.

Chinese histories notwithstanding, every Uyghur firmly believes that his or her ancestors were the indigenous people of the Tarim basin, which did not become known in Chinese as "Xinjiang" ("new dominion") until the eighteenth century. Nevertheless, the official national minority identity of the present people known as "Uyghur," which have tenuous links to an ancient Uyghur kingdom, is a more recent phenomenon related to "Great Game" rivalries, Sino-Soviet geopolitical maneuverings, and Chinese nation-building. While a collection of nomadic steppe peoples known as "Uyghurs" has existed since before the eighth century, this identity was lost from the fifteenth to the twentieth century. The Uyghurs and other officially recognized minority nationalities in the region are directly affected by China's nationality policy, since China does not have a policy of recognizing separate indigenous peoples with certain rights to land. China's policy of ethnic designation specifically avoids the issue of "indigeneity" and attachment to specific places or lands, thanks to strongly held Chinese beliefs that all the lands of China have been in the hands of Chinese since the Han dynasty. Hence, all Han Chinese are as indigenous as any local ethnic group to the lands of China. Hence, China's minority policy is one of minority nationality recognition and autonomous administration, not one that designates indigenous peoples or rights. Thus, the background of Uyghur claims to the region and competing Chinese laws regarding autonomy have much to do with China's current policies in Xinjiang and local responses to them.

According to Morris Rossabi, it was not until 1760, after their defeat of the Mongolian Zungars, that the Manchu Qing dynasty exerted full and formal control over the region, establishing it as their "new dominion" (*Xinjiang*). This administration lasted barely 100 years, when it fell to the Yaqub Beg rebellion (1864–1877) and expanding Russian influence.[1] Until they encouraged major migrations of Han Chinese in the mid-nineteenth century, the Qing were mainly interested in pacifying the region by setting up military outposts that could support a vassal-state relationship. Colonization had begun with the migrations of the Han in the mid-nineteenth century but was cut short by the Yaqub Beg rebellion, the fall of the Qing empire in 1910, and the ensuing warlord era that dismembered the region until it was finally incorporated into the People's Republic of China (PRC) in 1949. Competition for the loyalties of the peoples of the oases in the Great Game played between China, Russia, and Britain further divided the Uyghurs along political, religious, and military lines. Until challenged by their incorporation into the Chinese nation-state, the people of the oases lacked any coherent sense of identity.

When China incorporated Xinjiang into an emerging nation-state, it initiated a program of delineating the so-called nations, even if these peoples did not normally see themselves as ethnic groups, nations, or nationalities. The reemergence of the label "Uyghur" that the Chinese applied to these diverse groups was arguably inappropriate, since it had last been used almost half a millennium previously to describe the largely Buddhist population of the Turpan basin. Nonetheless, when the Chinese invoked it as the appellation for the settled, meaning the Turkish-speaking Muslim oasis dwellers, the designation stuck and has never been disputed by the people themselves or the governments of the former Soviet Union or China. Indeed, Uyghurs have increasingly embraced it as a self-description. Uyghur nationalists today accept as fact that they are the lineal descendents of the people who formed the Uyghur Kingdom in seventh-century Mongolia.[2]

In discussing this ethnicization of Uyghur identity, Joseph Fletcher suggests it was a result of modern nationalism, "The Uyghur empire (ca. 760–840) once stretched as far as Kashgaria. But the idea that the Kashgarians and the inhabitants of Uyghuristan were one and the same nationality—let alone that they were all Uyghurs—is an innovation stemming largely from the needs of twentieth-century nationalism."[3]

The end of the Qing dynasty and the rise of Great Game rivalries between China, Russia, and Britain saw the region torn by competing loyalties and briefly crystallized by two short-lived and drastically different attempts at independence: the proclamations of an Eastern Turkistan Republic in Kashgar in 1933 and another in Yining (Gulja) in 1944.[4] As Linda Benson extensively documents,[5] these rebellions and attempts at self-rule did little to bridge competing political, religious, and regional differences among the Turkic Muslim people. Yet, these same peoples, beginning in 1934 and subsequently reinforced by successive Chinese Guomindang warlord administrations, became officially known as "Uyghurs." Andrew D. W. Forbes describes in exhaustive detail the sharp ethnic, religious, and political cleavages during the period from 1911 to 1949 that pitted Muslim against Chinese, Muslim against Muslim, Uyghur against Uyghur, Hui against Uyghur, Uyghur against Kazak, warlord against commoner, and Nationalist against Communist.[6] This extraordinary factionalism caused a large-scale loss of lives and the depletion of the region's resources, a tragedy that still lives in poplar memory. Indeed, many argue that it is this memory, expressed in terms of a deep-seated fear of social disorder, that helps keep the region together.

Today, despite continued regional differences among the three macroregions identified by Stanley W. Toops in chapter 9, there are nearly 9 million people across Xinjiang who regard themselves as Uyghur, out of a total population of over 16 million.[7] Many of them dream of, and some agitate for, an independent "Uyghuristan."

The Guomindang's nationality policy identified five peoples of China, dominated by the Han. They included Uyghurs under the general rubric of "Hui Muslims," which referred to all Muslim groups in China at that time. The Communists continued this policy and eventually recognized fifty-six nationalities. Uyghurs and eight other Muslim groups were split out from the general category "Hui" (which henceforth was used only with reference to Muslims who primarily spoke Chinese or did not have a separate language of their own). As a policy of ethnic control, this owed much to practices that the Soviet state had applied earlier to Central Asia. It proved to be an effective means by which the Chinese Communists could integrate the region into China.

The agency most responsible for delineating the official nationalities and overseeing the establishment of the autonomous region system is the State Ethnic Affairs Commission (Guojia Minzu Shiwu Weiyuanhui). Set up by the organic law of February 22, 1952, and with roots in the Qing dynasty's Bureau of Mongol and Manchu Affairs, the State Ethnic Affairs Commission continues to wield enormous power and influence in the border autonomous regions.[8] Indeed, the entire evolution of the officially recognized ethnic groups as *minzu* (the Chinese term that can be translated as "nationality," "ethnicity," "nation," "people," and so on) has been a subject of great debate within and outside of China, with most experts agreeing that it refers only to those fifty-six enumerated ethnic groups that receive special state recognition under the auspices of the State Ethnic Affairs Commission.[9]

Since the extension of Chinese administration and control over the region of Xinjiang is profoundly influenced by China's overall policy on nationalities, it is critical to understand the origins of that policy in the years prior to 1949. The Communist Party formulated the nationality policy of the future PRC during the 1930s for the strategic purpose of enlisting the support of peoples disgruntled both with Qing rule and with Chiang Kai-shek's nationality policy, which de-emphasized ethnic difference in favor of the unity of all peoples as members of the Chinese race. This policy took shape during the Long March from the southwest to the northwest, an arduous trek that led the Communists through the most concentrated minority areas. It was then that the Chinese Communist leaders became acutely aware of the vibrant ethnic identities of the Muslims and other peoples they encountered. The fathers of the yet-to-be-born Chinese Communist nation were faced with a stark choice between their own extermination or promising the minorities—specifically the Miao, Yi (Lolo), Tibetans, and Hui—that they would receive special treatment. The Communists set up the first Hui Muslim autonomous county in the 1930s in Tongxin, southern Ningxia, as a demonstration of their goodwill toward the Muslim Hui.

Thus, the Communists assigned a high priority to the integration of Muslims into the system of Chinese socialist control long before they moved into Xinjiang. Even before they gained control there, they had charted the pattern for ethnic control that was to have a dramatic impact on the Uyghurs and other ethnic groups in the region. That Xinjiang came to figure so prominently in the history and evolution of early Communist policy toward Muslims and nationality identification may have been strongly influenced by the fact that Chairman Mao Zedong's brother had been killed in Xinjiang in 1942, in the midst of struggles fed by interethnic and intra-Muslim factionalism.[10]

In a chapter entitled "Moslem and Marxist," Edgar Snow records several Communist encounters with militantly conservative Hui Muslims in the 1930s. He reports how Mao vehemently lectured troops of the Eighth Route Army to respect Hui customs, lest the soldiers offend them and provoke conflicts. Mao appealed to the northwest Hui to support the Communists' cause, even exhorting China's Muslims to learn from and emulate the renaissance of Turkey that occurred under Atatürk's rule.[11] Snow notes a slogan posted by Hui soldiers training under the Communist Fifteenth Army Corps, which read, "Build our own anti-Japanese Mohammedan Red Army."[12] Later party documents (*Dangshi Wenshi Ziliao*) that have come to light from the Long March reveal that until 1937 Chairman Mao explicitly promised "self-determination" to the minorities. Not only did he offer them privileges, but he also offered the right to secede from the Communist state, as Joseph Stalin had provided to Soviet minorities in his constitution of 1937. However, this right was withdrawn before 1940 and replaced with guarantees that did not go beyond limited regional "autonomy." The transition in Chinese terminology from "self-determination" (*zi zhu*) to "autonomy" (*zi zhi*) may not seem great, but for the minorities themselves it represented a major shift in policy. This shift removed whatever distinction that may have existed between Communist practice in the Soviet Union and China. Even though the right of secession was written into the constitution of the Soviet Union, the Soviet state never hesitated to denounce anyone proposing to exercise it as a "bourgeois nationalist" and hence an enemy of the state who was subject to the most severe punishment, including death. In China, no such right exists, so any individuals or groups aspiring to secede can be regarded as criminal without the nicety of having to be denounced first as bourgeois. This, along with the "antiethnic strife" law, provides a legal basis for Beijing to consider all Xinjiang activist groups pushing for independence as separatists and to execute their members.[13] As Walker Connor observes, "a request that pre-revolutionary promises be honored became counterrevolutionary and reactionary."[14]

Though the CCP promised autonomy, it quashed any illusions of separatism in the hope that by this means it would preserve "national unity." The contradiction between policies that promote ethnic autonomy and policies that promote ethnic assimilation continues to vex China's nationality policy. As June Dreyer observes, "The Communist government of China may be said to have inherited a policy of trying to facilitate the demise of nationality identities through granting self-government to minorities. It has in fact been struggling with the consequences to this day."[15]

The roots of the Chinese government's current problems over separatism must thus be traced directly back to its own early policies of recognizing ethnic aspirations. These policies contributed to, and indeed encouraged, the ethnicization of local peoples to the extent that, today, Uyghurs (and to a large degree all other ethnic nationalities) insist not only that their historical claims to the region known as "Xinjiang" are valid but also that the Communist government itself had recognized and legalized their ethnicity.

Pattern Two: Integration—The Extension of Chinese Control

After the founding of the PRC, Beijing brought Xinjiang and other minority and border areas under military control, awarded them limited autonomy, and subjected them to integrationist policies. Connor shows that the primary focus of Marxist-Leninist nationality policy and theory was on nation-building.[16] Once they had established their authority in Beijing, the Chinese Communists ceased to attach such strategic importance to obtaining the support of the minorities. Hence, they no longer considered it necessary to promise or grant full autonomy.

The general model of control and development that was laid down in the 1950s continues to this day. At the same time, there has been great discontinuity in the application of that model due to fluctuations in state policy, as occurred during the Cultural Revolution in the 1960s and 1970s and again during the move to a market economy in the 1980s and 1990s. This process follows exactly what Connor characterizes as Vladimir Lenin's three "commandments" on how a socialist state can harness nationalism:[17]

1. Prior to the assumption of power, promise to all national groups the right of self-determination (expressly including the right of secession), while proffering national equality to those who wish to remain within the state.

2. Following the assumption of power, terminate the fact—though not necessarily the fiction—of a right to secession, and begin the lengthy process of assimilation via the dialectical route of providing territorial autonomy to all compact national groups.

3. Strictly centralize the Chinese Communist Party (CCP) itself and keep it free of all nationalist proclivities.

During the early days after 1949, the Chinese Communists very effectively adhered to this formula in order to solidify their control over every aspect of national life. Even today, China, along with other highly authoritarian regimes, continues to assign an important role to nationality policy within its overall exercise of power. Claude Lefort goes so far as to argue that the concentration of power in the hands of one nationality is a fundamental characteristic of all totalitarian regimes in the modern era:

> But if the image of the people is actualized, if a party claims to identify with it and to appropriate power under the cover of this identification, then it is the very principle of the distinction between the state and society, the principle of the difference between the norms that govern the various types of relations between individuals, ways of life, beliefs and opinions, which is denied; and, at a deeper level, it is the very principle of a distinction between what belongs to the order to power, to the order of law, and to the order of knowledge which is negated. The economic, legal and cultural dimensions are, as it were, interwoven into the political. This phenomenon is characteristic of totalitarianism.[18]

Many observers have documented how political swings between the Right and the Left have brought about changes in nationality policy ever since the founding of the PRC. In Xinjiang, the changing political winds have brought about frequent and radical oscillations between poles of pluralism and ethnocentric repression. Over time, these have caused the region to suffer both from overly centralized control by the bureaucracy and army and, when the voice of Beijing becomes inaudible, from almost complete chaos. Inevitably, these shifts have had a dramatic impact on the identities of the affected nationalities and on how they express their ethnic identities. The following pages document the effects of these policies in Xinjiang, particularly since the liberalization that began in 1978.

The titular leaders of the Uyghurs in 1949 were profoundly practical people. They saw that once the Communists had defeated the Nationalists, Uyghurs had no real choice but to invite the People's Liberation Army (PLA) into Xinjiang, in what was later widely touted as a "peaceful revolution."[19] The Communists' "peaceful liberation" of Xinjiang in October 1949 and their subsequent establishment of the Xinjiang Uyghur Autonomous Region (XUAR) on October 1, 1955, seemed to perpetuate the Nationalists' policy of recognizing the Uyghurs as a minority nationality under Chinese rule. But the ongoing political uncertainties and social unrest led many of Xinjiang's Turkic peoples to conclude they had no future there. During the decade after 1953, this gave rise to large-scale migrations of Uyghurs and Kazaks from Xinjiang to Soviet Central Asia. By that date, the Uyghur population of Kazakstan, Kyrgyzstan, and Uzbekistan had reached approximately 300,000. This migration ceased only when the Sino-Soviet split led to the closing of the border in 1963. The border remained effectively sealed until the late 1980s.[20]

As Justin Rudelson and William Jankowiak document in chapter 12, China's designation of Uyghurs as a separate nationality continued to mask a very considerable regional and linguistic diversity. The term "Uyghur" was applied to many groups, among them the Loplyk and Dolans, that had very little to do with the oasis-based Turkic Muslims who became known as "Uyghurs." At the same time, Uyghur separatists today look back to the brief periods of independent self-rule under Yaqub Beg and the two Eastern Turkistan Republics, as well as to the earlier glories of the Uyghur kingdoms in Turpan and Karabalghasan, as legitimizing their claims to the region.

Today, Uyghur separatist organizations exist in at least seven cities abroad (see chapter 15). However much they may differ in their political goals and strategies for Xinjiang, they share a common vision of a continuous Uyghur claim on the region, disrupted only by Soviet and Chinese interventions. The transformation of the formerly Soviet republics of Central Asia into independent states in 1991 did much to encourage these Uyghur organizations in their hopes for an independent "Uyghuristan."

These hopes remain alive today, despite the fact that in 1996 the new Central Asian governments all signed protocols with China affirming that they would neither harbor nor support separatist groups. These protocols were reaffirmed in 1999, when Boris Yeltsin and Jiang Zemin committed the Shanghai Five nations (China, Russia, Kazakstan, Kyrgyzstan, and Tajikistan) to respect border security and suppress terrorism, drug smuggling, and separatism.[21] The policy was enforced on June 15, 1999, when Kazakstan deported to China three alleged Uyghur separatists. Several others in Kyrgyzstan and Kazakstan are awaiting extradition as of this writing.[22] When in 2001 Uzbekistan joined the Shanghai Five, now renamed the "Shanghai Cooperation Organization," it signified that the scope of this organization had grown beyond border issues to include the enhancement of national security and domestic stability.

Given the sociopolitical threats confronting the Uyghurs, it is scarcely surprising that Islam became an important, but not exclusive, cultural marker of their self-identity. The Uyghurs are Sunni Muslims, practicing Islamic traditions similar to their coreligionists elsewhere in Central Asia. As Graham E. Fuller and Jonathan N. Lipman show in chapter 13, many of them are Sufi, adhering to various branches of the Central Asian Naqshbandiyya order. However, it is also important to note that Islam was only one of several unifying markers for Uyghur identity, any one of which could come to the fore, depending on whomever Uyghurs were dealing with at any given time. This suggests that Islamic fundamentalist groups such as the Taliban in Afghanistan will have only limited appeal among Uyghurs. For example, to the Hui Muslim Chinese in Xinjiang, who number over 600,000. Uyghurs distinguish themselves as the legitimate autochthonous minority, since both share a belief in Sunni Islam. In contrast to the formerly nomadic Muslim peoples, such as the Kazaks, who number over a million, the Uyghurs might stress their attachment to the land and oasis of origin. Above all, modern Uyghurs, especially those living in larger towns and urban areas, define themselves in terms of their common reaction to Chinese efforts to influence and assimilate them.

It is understandable that Islamic traditions often become the focal point for Uyghur efforts to preserve their culture and history. A popular tradition that has resurfaced in recent years is that of the "Mashrap," gatherings where generally young Uyghurs assemble to recite poetry, sing folk or religious songs, dance, and share traditional foods. In recent years, these evening events have often become the foci for Uyghur resistance to Chinese rule.

But even if many people both within and outside the region portray the

Uyghurs as being united around separatist or Islamist causes, Uyghurs continue to be divided among themselves by religious conflicts involving competing Sufi and non-Sufi factions, territorial loyalties based on specific oases or places of origin, linguistic differences, tensions between elites and commoners, and competing political sympathies. These divided loyalties were in evidence in May 1996, when Uyghurs attacked other Uyghurs at the Imam of the Idgah Mosque in Kashgar, and in September 2002 when at least six Uyghur officials were assassinated, apparently by Uyghurs. While religious factionalism among the Uyghurs rarely erupts in violence (in contrast to the Hui),[23] it is often the case that political and regional rivalries over state policy and cooperation with the CCP lead to intense and sometimes violent divisions among them. This contested understanding of their own society, culture, politics, and history continues to influence much of the current Uyghur debate over Chinese claims to the region and separatism.

Deng Xiaoping's reforms (1978–1988) liberalized not only the economy but also the way the state regarded ethnicity. The latter dramatically affected Xinjiang and the other minority regions. The state not only extended official recognition to ethnic groups claiming the status of separate nationalities status but also directly encouraged them to advance such claims, as a means of gaining development assistance and attracting tourist dollars.

With respect to its "autonomous" status, Xinjiang falls under the same laws as other autonomous regions, prefectures, counties, and villages. Nevertheless, domestic and international factors strongly influence how these laws are applied in each of the autonomous territories. Thus, the International Campaign for Tibetan Independence and the Dalai Lama's government-in-exile shape how China's law on autonomy is applied in Tibet. In the same way, Xinjiang's proximity to the dissolving Soviet Union during 1991, the increasing importance of its oil reserves, and China's support for the war on terrorism after 2001 all influence the implementation of laws on autonomy in Xinjiang.

The Third Party plenum of 1978 repudiated former mistakes and distanced itself from previous nationality policies. A Muslim political scientist, Ma Weiliang immediately grasped the significance of this development for his coreligionists and explained how the new policy differed from the old:

> In our struggle against local nationalism in 1957, we magnified class struggle, accused some minority national cadres of attacking the party because they explained the true conditions in their regions and expressed the complaints and wishes of their people, and labeled them as local nationalists. We criticized proper national feelings, national desires, and demands as bourgeois nationalism. In 1958, we again departed from the

reality of minority nationality regions, ran counter to objective laws, advocated the so-called "reaching the sky in a single bound," . . . undermined the economy of the minority nationality regions, and created tension among the minority nationality regions. In 1962, the national conference on the work among the minority nationalities correctly summed up our experience and lessons drawn. . . . But later in 1964, under the domination of the "left" deviation, we again vigorously criticized the so-called "right capitulationism" and revisionism during the National United Front work, and refuted many of our good experiences. . . . During the Great Cultural Revolution, Lin Biao and the "gang of four" . . . artificially created large numbers of unjust, false, and wrong cases, and used the big stick of class struggle to attack and persecute many minority national cadres and the masses. They slandered minority national customs and habits and attacked both the minorities' written and spoken languages as "four old things." . . . [All this] undermined very seriously the party's policy towards the minority nationalities and the economic cultural reconstruction in their regions, and caused serious calamities. This [was] an extremely bitter experience from which we learned a lesson.[24]

The more relaxed atmosphere created by the reforms may also help explain why, as Toops indicates in chapter 9, people throughout China, and especially in Xinjiang, now consider it useful to be ethnic. In this sense, one can go as far as to say that the Chinese state reinvented ethnicity and institutionalized it for the fifty-six recognized nationalities. It is no wonder that the peoples of Xinjiang and members of all the other fifty-five recognized minority groups all welcomed the return to pluralistic policies in 1978. But what about the other 350 peoples who had never received the status of official nationalities? After the reforms, these groups all redoubled their efforts to be designated as official nationalities. But the law prevents unrecognized groups from organizing along ethnic lines, though many of them continue to try to do so informally. But in Xinjiang, as elsewhere, all forms of organizing in the name of nonrecognized ethnic groups is regarded as illegal, seditious, and a threat to national unity.

That the Chinese government still adheres to its old Stalinist cultural definition of ethnicity helps explain how local ethnic communities in Xinjiang responded to assimilative policies during the post-Deng reform period. When Beijing originally acknowledged ethnic groups and identities, it did so as a tactical and temporary move. Its strategic goal was to elicit ethnic support for the revolution. Paradoxically, the provisional measures it employed to promote this end led eventually to the hardening of ethnic boundaries and identities. And so it happened that during the economic boom of the 1980s and 1990s ethnic minorities increasingly demanded that the state recognize them—for their contribution to national unity!

Pattern Three: Transnationalization—The Limits of Chinese Control

The resurgence of a strong Uyghur ethnic identity in Xinjiang and the broadening links between Uyghurs there and the transnational Uyghur diaspora, despite China's many attempts to integrate and to some extent assimilate them, indicate the limits of Chinese control over Xinjiang. In an era of globalization, these limits on China's control extend also to the economic and political realms.

Many Uyghurs interviewed in Turpan and Kashgar argue vehemently that they constitute the autochthonous people of this region. The fact that over 99.8 percent of the Uyghur population is located in Xinjiang, whereas other Muslim peoples of China have significant populations in other provinces (notably the Hui) and outside the country (e.g., the Kazaks, Kyrgyz, and Tajiks), contributes to this important sense of belonging to the land. Although since the 1990s many Kazaks have been returning to the ancient pastoral lands in northern Xinjiang, perhaps because of the relatively poorer economic conditions in Kazakstan, there have been no known Kazak-led incidents of separatism or protest against Chinese rule in the region. By contrast, the Uyghurs continue to conceive of their ancestors as originating in Xinjiang, claiming that "it is our land, our territory," all historical evidence to the contrary notwithstanding.

The last forty years have witnessed an unprecedented sociopolitical integration of Xinjiang into the Chinese nation-state. While Xinjiang has been under Chinese political domination since the Chinese defeat of the Zunghars in 1754, until the middle of the twentieth century it was but loosely incorporated into China proper. Xinjiang's deepening incorporation into China since the 1940s is manifest in such diverse areas as communications, education, occupational shifts, and officially encouraged Han migration into the region. Between 1940 and 1982, this migration increased the Han's percentage of Xinjiang's population by a massive 2,500 percent.

Many analysts have concluded that officially supported Han migration constitutes China's primary policy instrument for assimilating its border regions.[25] This is certainly the case for Inner Mongolia, where the Mongol population now stands at a mere 14 percent. In Xinjiang, the increase of the Han population has been accompanied by the rapid growth and delineation of other non-Uyghur Muslim groups, such as the Hui (Dungans, or Chinese-speaking Muslims). Xinjiang's Hui population increased by over 520 percent between 1940 and 1982 (an average annual growth of 4.4 percent), while the Uyghur population followed a more natural biological growth rate of 1.7 percent. This dramatic increase in the Hui population led inevitably to significant tensions between the Hui and Uyghur Muslims in the region. Reflecting these tensions, many Uyghurs are quick to recall the massacre nearly a century ago of Uyghurs in Kashgar by the Hui Muslim warlord Ma Zhongying and his Hui troops.[26] The Uyghur community in exile and international Muslim groups widely believe that Chinese censuses systematically underreport the numbers of Muslims in China, which further exacerbates such tensions. Some Uyghur groups go so far as to claim, albeit with scant evidence, that China's population today includes upward of 20 million Uyghurs and nearly 50 million Muslims.[27]

China's policies of incorporation and assimilation have led to a further development of socioeconomic niches based on ethnicity. Early travelers reported little distinction in labor and education among Muslims, other than that between settled and nomadic peoples. By contrast, the 1990 census revealed vast differences in socioeconomic structure (see the occupational statistics in chapter 6). Statistics on education among Muslim minorities reported in chapter 7 indicate that policies in that field have led to the same phenomenon.

A serious shortcoming of the statistical figures on population and education in China is that they reflect only what is regarded by the state as education, namely, training in the Chinese language and the sciences. However, a high standard of traditional expertise in Persian, Arabic, Chaghatay, and the Islamic sciences continues among the elderly elite. However, Chinese policy does not consider these part of Chinese "culture," nor does it include them in enumerations of educational attainment. Although the state offers elementary and secondary education in Uyghur, it has made certain that Mandarin is the language of upward mobility in Xinjiang, as in the rest of China. In the 1950s, the government established thirteen nationality colleges throughout China, and since then it has seen to it that many Uyghurs have received training in these institutions. It is the secular intellectuals trained in these and other Chinese schools, as opposed to traditional religious elites, who are asserting political leadership in Xinjiang today.

Many Uyghurs in Urumchi point to the government's decision in 1987 to establish the Uyghur Traditional Medicine Hospital and Madrassah complex as a first step toward counterbalancing the one-sided emphasis on Han education.[28] However, most Uyghurs argue that governmental policy deliberately uses the schools to downplay their history and traditional culture and that they must therefore counteract this with their children in private.

Notwithstanding these private efforts and despite the widespread use of minority languages in the schools, the overwhelming thrust of the state's policy is to teach a centralized curriculum dominated by Han history and language. By this means it ensures that Uyghur children enter into the Chinese world and come to participate formally in the Chinese nation-state. Such a policy, aimed at inducting Uyghurs into the Han Chinese milieu, drives a wedge between the Uyghurs and their own traditions.

The increased incorporation of Xinjiang into China's political sphere has led not only to the further migration of Han and Hui into the region but also to an unprecedented opening of the rest of China to the Uyghurs. Protected by official policy, Uyghur men are heavily involved in long-distance trade throughout China. They travel freely to Tianjin and Shanghai for manufactured clothes and textiles, to Hangzhou and Suzhou for silk, and to Guangzhou and Hainan for electronic goods and motorcycles brought in from Hong Kong. Everywhere they go (especially Beijing, due to the large foreign population), they trade local currency (renminbi) for U.S. dollars. Government policy does not impede these activities, as long as they remain within the law, and even welcomes them as contributing to assimilation. But they have an important and unanticipated consequence: As Uyghurs venture outside Xinjiang, they develop a firmer sense of their own pan-Uyghur identity vis-à-vis the Han and other minorities they encounter in the course of their peregrinations throughout China.

Beijing's recent policies have also allowed Uyghurs to travel internationally. As Calla Wiemer and Sean R. Roberts demonstrate in chapters 6 and 8, respectively, the resumption of normal Sino–Central Asian relations in 1991 unleashed a surge of Uyghur trade with China's newly independent neighbors to the west. This expansion has led Uyghurs to see themselves as important players in the improved Sino–Central Asian exchanges. It has also fostered direct communication with Turkic speakers from across the border and, more important, expanded contacts with a large and often politicized Uyghur diaspora now estimated to number between 500,000 and 1 million people.

China's government-sponsored transnationalization has begun to open up Xinjiang to outside political and economic contacts. Beijing's increased involvement in the Middle East is of particular importance to Xinjiang. Because it is one of five permanent voting members in the UN Security Council and also a significant exporter of military hardware to the Middle East, the PRC has become a significant player in Middle Eastern affairs. When China's trade with most Western nations declined after the Tiananmen Square massacre in 1989, its Middle Eastern trading partners gained in importance. All of them are Muslim, as China did not open relations with Israel until 1992. China established diplomatic relations with Saudi Arabia in August 1990, increasing greatly its purchases of Saudi oil. Saudi Arabia reciprocated by canceling its long-standing diplomatic relationship with Taiwan, despite a lucrative trade between the two.

Broader considerations constrain China's opening to the Middle East. In spite of a long-term friendship with Iraq, China went along with most of the UN resolutions leading up to the 1991 war against that country, abstaining only on Resolution 678 in support of the ground war. In spite of this, China enjoys a positive reputation in the Middle East as a ready source of cheap, reliable labor and of low-grade weaponry. Following the Persian Gulf War, China increased its export of military hardware to the Middle East due, no doubt, to the need to balance its growing importation of oil from the region.[29]

Since the early 1990s, China has been a net oil importer, with its main foreign source being the Muslim Persian Gulf states.[30] Even if it succeeds in vastly increasing its imports from Russia, this dependence on the Middle East is bound to grow. Continued disappointments have diminished expectations over oil explorations in Xinjiang's Tarim basin, with the entire region yielding only 3.15 million metric tons of crude oil annually, a small fraction of China's overall output of 156 million tons in 1998. Xinjiang's oil output scarcely improved by 2002, even though over the previous decade China accounted for more than a quarter of the global increase in oil consumption. It is estimated that China will equal the United States in oil imports by 2030, and surpass Japan by 2050,[31] which will only serve to increase its dependence on the same Muslim Persian Gulf states.

China's population includes some 20 million Muslims. If Beijing mishandles its domestic Muslim problems, it runs the serious risk of alienating states that directly control the supply of its most strategic energy source. No less serious, unrest in the XUAR could readily lead to a decline in outside oil investment and revenues, thus hampering an industry of vital strategic importance to China. Such concerns may have been a primary consideration in China's early support for the U.S.-led war on terrorism in the aftermath of September 11, 2001.

The gravity of China's energy concerns can scarcely be underestimated, nor the ways in which they are likely to affect its future policy toward Xinjiang. Disappointed with the amount of proven reserves of oil and gas in Xinjiang and frustrated by the difficulties of developing its resources there, Beijing has increasingly looked elsewhere for these crucial commodities. In a flurry of trade negotiations and investments in late 1998 and early 1999, China's national petroleum company pledged more than $8 billion for oil concessions in Sudan, Venezuela, Iraq, and Kazakstan—plus $12.5 billion to lay four oil and gas pipelines (total length 13,500 kilometers) from Central Asia and Russia to China. Though China recently suspended plans for one of these pipelines, these steps nevertheless indicate its willingness to pay more than market value for secure energy supplies. According to one report, China offered as much as 30 percent above estimated value for Kazakstan's Uzen oil fields, and more than twice as much as the next highest bidder for the Venezuelan oil fields.[32] China's interest in enhancing its energy security already drives its increasing trade with Central Asia, and hence the related domestic policies affecting Xinjiang.

The interplay between China's foreign policy and its concerns over Xinjiang is not limited to the oil-rich countries or those that might invest in its domestic oil and gas industry. After the ethnic riot in February 1997 in the northwestern Xinjiang city of Yining, which led to the death of at least nine Uyghur Muslims and the arrest of several hundred more, Turkey's defense minister, Turhan Tayan, officially condemned China's handling of the issue. Beijing boldly responded by warning Turkey not to interfere in China's internal affairs. But will China be prepared to issue such a rebuke to a major supplier of oil, even when it may suspect that same supplier of encouraging Muslim activists in Xinjiang?

Muslim nations on China's borders, including the new Central Asian states, Pakistan, and Afghanistan, officially oppose the activities of Uyghur separatists. Recent agreements between the PRC and Kazakstan, Kyrgyzstan, and Tajikistan specifically prevent China's neighbors from assisting separatists on their own territory or across the border in Xinjiang. But whatever the positions of these three governments, it is possible that vocal parts of their publics may become increasingly critical of China's harsh treatment of their fellow Turkic and/or Muslim coreligionists in Xinjiang. At a popular level, the Uyghurs already receive much sympathy from their Central Asian coreligionists, and there is a continuing unofficial flow of funds and materials through China's increasingly porous borders. Thus, it is clear that concern for the situation within Xinjiang has already become a significant driver of China's foreign policy in many areas and will continue to be so in the foreseeable future.

Even if China succeeds in limiting the damage to its interests arising from religious or ethnic concerns among its neighbors to the west or from Middle Eastern countries, it must still deal with international criticism of its human rights record in Xinjiang. The World Bank loans over $3 billion a year to China, investing some $780.5 million in fifteen projects in the Xinjiang region alone. Some of that money allegedly goes to the Xinjiang Production and Construction Corps (XPCC; Xinjiang shengchan jianshe bingtuan), which human rights activist Harry Wu claimed employs prison (*laogai*) labor. At a U.S. Senate hearing on World Bank investment in Xinjiang, Assistant Treasury Secretary David A. Lipton declared that the treasury would no longer support World Bank projects associated with the XPCC. Beyond this, international organizations and companies, from the World Bank to Exxon, may not wish to subject their employees to social and political upheavals of the sort that might occur in Xinjiang, nor their investors to the risk that such upheavals entail. In this context, it is worth noting that China cancelled plans to build the oil pipeline from Kazakstan to Xinjiang and thence to internal China that was discussed earlier, citing the disinterest of outside investors and questionable market returns.

Internal developments in Xinjiang have the potential to affect Beijing's foreign policy in yet other ways. China keenly desires to participate in such international organizations as the World Trade Organization and Asia-Pacific Economic Cooperation. Unrest in Xinjiang and China's responses to it, like analogous problems with Tibet, can negatively affect these relationships.

Tibet is no longer of any major strategic or economic value to China. Yet, China's current leaders consider it important to demonstrate that they will not submit to foreign pressure to withdraw their iron hand from that region. It is worth noting that Uyghurs have begun to work closely with Tibetans abroad to exert pressure on China on international issues on behalf of both regions. The Istanbul-based Eastern Turkistan Foundation is one of many organizations committed to the establishment of an independent Uyghur homeland. In an April 7, 1997, interview, Ahmet Türköz, vice director of the foundation, reported that meetings had been taking place since 1981 between the Dalai Lama and Uyghur leaders, at the initiative of the (now deceased) Uyghur nationalist Eysa (Isa) Yusup Aliptékin.[33]

Another example of how Chinese policy in its autonomous regions can lead to the intermingling of Uyghur and Tibetan concerns involves the Unrepresented Nations and People's Organization, based in The Hague. This group originally focused solely on Tibetan issues. But its elected leader is now Erkin Aliptékin, the son of the late Uyghur nationalist.

It is extremely unlikely that the combined effect of these and other international organizations can force China to institute fundamental changes in its domestic policies. Nevertheless, it is undeniable that the threat posed by such groups and activities impairs China's ability to move with a free hand internationally or at least increases the risks. As a result, China has sought to respond rapidly, decisively, and often militarily to any domestic ethnic unrest that has the potential to constrain its actions on the international scene.

Since the breakup of the Soviet Union in 1991, China has become an important competitor for influence in Central Asia and already serves as a counterweight to Russia's waning influence there. Calling for a new interregional "Silk Route," China is constructing such a link with rails and roads.

But, as noted earlier, the increasing ethnicization of Xinjiang's neighbors in Central Asia and the resulting rise of nationalist leaders to political prominence there will mean that ancient ethnic relations and geopolitical ties extending across the borders into Xinjiang will increasingly impinge on China's policies and actions, both at home and abroad.

James P. Dorian, Brett Wigdortz, and Dru Gladney detail the growing interdependence of the entire region of which Xinjiang is a part.[34] Trade between Xinjiang and the Central Asian republics has grown rapidly, reaching $775 million in 1996, and the number of Sino-Kazak joint ventures, which now approach 200, continues to rise. Wiemer's analysis of Xinjiang's economy in chapter 6 demonstrates that foreign direct investment and international trade have begun to outpace Beijing's direct assistance to the region. This is one of the main issues raised by Uyghur separatist groups, which claim that the state is putting very little into the region compared to what it receives. In this way, the internationalization of Xinjiang's economy is giving rise to the same concerns that nationalist leaders of dependent or colonial territories in other parts of the world have always raised against their rulers.

Following the breakup of the Soviet Union, the Chinese government feared that the new independence of the neighboring states of Central Asia might inspire separatist aspirations in Xinjiang. It also worried that promoting regional trade and economic development could resurrect old links and alliances and thereby fuel ethnic separatism. True, it is now resting easier after the Central Asian states, through the Shanghai Cooperation Organization, agreed to repress local groups seeking to influence affairs in Xinjiang. But the fact that China has been able to safeguard its policy of economic development in Xinjiang only by resorting to intrusive policies directed against the freedoms of its neighbors' citizens attests to the extent to which Xinjiang is redefining the geopolitical realities in the broader region.

Uyghurs and other Muslims complain not only that the growing number of Han Chinese monopolize the best jobs and eventually take the profits back home with them but also that their presence erodes the natives' traditional way of life and denies them any significant voice in their own affairs. As the same Han traders and investors continue to expand their activities across Xinjiang's borders in the neighboring countries of Central Asia, similar complaints are already being voiced, albeit quietly and with due caution, among the Turkic peoples of Kazakstan and Kyrgyzstan.

This chapter has proposed that Chinese control of Xinjiang since 1978 has followed three quite different patterns, which were termed "ethnicization," "integration," and "transnationalization." All three patterns have coexisted and intermingled over the years and continue to influence social dynamics in the region to varying degrees. Acknowledging this, one can date the most intense period of ethnicization to the late 1970s and early 1980s, or the years of nationality recognition and support early in Deng's rule. In one sense, China has been pursuing the integration of Xinjiang with the Han heartland for nearly two millennia. However, in recent times it gained greatly in intensity and importance mainly in the period since 1991, when fears that a spirit of independence arising from the Central Asian states formed from the wreckage of the Soviet Union might spill over to Xinjiang and threaten Chinese control over the region. China, fearing that such aspirations might destabilize Xinjiang, dealt swiftly and ruthlessly with the slightest rumblings from Uyghur separatists during the mid-1990s (see Gladney, chapter 15 in this volume). Regarding transnationalization, this, too, has been a prominent feature of life in Xinjiang since the heyday of the ancient Silk Road. However, with the advent of globalization, it has become a conscious driving force in Chinese policy toward Xinjiang and has been pursued with an intensity that heretofore would have been unimaginable. Its effects can be measured by the vastly expanded travel across five open border points, the exponential expansion of telecommunications, and marked increases in both foreign and domestic direct private investment.

Whether because of these developments or in spite of them, China's fear of ethnic separatism in Xinjiang has grown over the years. Acting on these fears, it has maintained a substantial military presence there and applied whatever force it considered necessary to quell centrifugal tendencies. The number of confirmed terrorist or separatist acts reached a high point during the late 1990s. Since then it has declined, though it is unknown if this relative peace will continue.

As time goes by, the processes of transnationalization and globalization are certainly mitigating Chinese control in Xinjiang. At the same time, they bring about greater permeation of the region by state agencies and by foreign and domestic capital channeled there from Beijing. Thanks to this, Xinjiang today is without a doubt more closely integrated with the rest of China than at any previous time in its history. Chinese control of Xinjiang today is far from complete. Yet, one can conclude with certainty that China has never been as dominant there, nor its control and influence as pervasive, as at the present time.

5

The Great Wall of Steel: Military and Strategy in Xinjiang

Yitzhak Shichor

While unrelated to Xinjiang, the terrorist attack of September 11, 2001, on the United States was to have direct and immediate implications for this region.[1] Beijing, concerned for some time about the spillover of ethnoreligious terrorism from Central Asia into Xinjiang and about the growing involvement of the United States in the region, closed its border with Pakistan the next day. Roadblocks were set up along the Karakoram Highway, and tourists were refused access in the direction of the Khunjerab Pass amid increased security measures. In short, China seemed to be quickly adapting to an evolving emergency.

On September 18, a first-grade military alert was proclaimed, and various forces, including rapid reaction, fighter aircraft, air-defense missile, helicopters, and antichemical warfare units, were rushed to Xinjiang from the Lanzhou Military Region. Considered the best People's Liberation Army (PLA) outfit in Xinjiang, the Fourth Combined Arms Rapid Reaction Motorized Infantry Division quickly moved from its bases at Kuqa and Kashgar to the Sino-Afghan border. Also, a mountain field division, normally stationed along the western section of the Sino-Indian border in the Kunlun Shan and Pamirs, was moved to Tashkurghan. Convoys of troops were seen heading up the Karakoram Highway, and early-warning reconnaissance planes began patrolling Xinjiang's southern border.

A Chinese Foreign Ministry spokesman confirmed that "in order to safeguard the peace and stability of China's border areas we are fully entitled to implement security measures along our border."[2] Now perceived as justified and legitimized by the global mobilization against terrorism, Beijing used this opportunity to crack down on Uyghur "separatists" (a normal routine before public holidays, and especially China's National Day). On September 26, several dozen Muslim prisoners were publicly displayed in Kashgar and two of them were summarily executed.[3] An official spokesman argued that Uyghur separatists "have participated in terrorist activities" and "have colluded with international terrorist groups." He then added, "We hope that our fight against the East Turkistan forces will become a part of the international effort against terrorism, and [as such] it should win support and understanding."[4]

Xinjiang's security had now become intertwined with the regional and global situation. In the middle of October, Beijing reportedly moved a signal intelligence (SIGINT) unit, heretofore deployed to intercept Taiwan's telecommunications, from Fujian to Xinjiang, close to the Sino-Afghan border. While this measure could have also been used to monitor U.S. moves in the region, it supposedly reflected Beijing's readiness to help Washington in its war against the Taliban by collecting and sharing information. Indeed, at the Shanghai Asia-Pacific Economic Cooperation Summit later that month, People's Republic of China (PRC) president Jiang Zemin agreed that PLA troops in Xinjiang would provide humanitarian and other assistance to lost or injured U.S. servicemen and military aircraft and, "when necessary," special PLA forces would attack the Taliban.[5]

These developments followed one of the largest ever PLA military exercises in Xinjiang. At the end of May, the Xinjiang Military Command launched a combined armed services highland training in the Karakoram Range. It culminated in early August 2001 with a four-day live-ammunition war game held twelve miles north of Kashgar. Some 50,000 troops from the two local divisions (the Fourth from Kuqa and the Sixth from Khotan) were reportedly involved, supported by several hundred armored personnel carriers, tanks, and other military vehicles and accompanied by fighter jets and helicopters. Presided over by Fu Quanyou, PLA chief of general staff and a member of the Central Military Commission (CMC), the exercise concluded with a forty-minute parade in Kashgar. Shortly afterward, on September 14, yet another combined live-ammunition battle exercise was held at the Tian Shan and the Gobi Desert. This one was designed to prepare the paramilitary Xinjiang Production and Construction Corps (XPCC; Xinjiang shengchan jianshe bingtuan) together with the regional People's Armed Police Force (PAPF; renmin wuzhuang jingcha budui) to deal with sudden exigencies.[6]

This display of power would, at first glance, appear to reinforce the assertion by both Chinese and foreign observers that Xinjiang's "wall of steel" is of particular "strategic importance" and hence one of China's frontline military commands. As China's largest administrative unit (whose military command also covers western Tibet), Xinjiang has a longer land border (5,400 kilometers [km]) and adjoins more foreign countries (eight) than any other province of China. Furthermore, Han Chinese are still a minority of about 40 percent in this multiethnic, largely Islamic, and restive region, which is the home of China's nuclear testing and missile ranges and the location of huge and untapped energy reserves. One would assume that these characteristics, combined with Xinjiang's remoteness from the center, would call for an increased Chinese military presence there. But is this actually the case?

Let me address first the size of the military in Xinjiang. It will be possible to gain perspective on these numbers by analyzing the historical, strategic, and organizational origins of China's military profile in Xinjiang, its command structure, troop deployment, and response to security threats from the northwest (i.e., the Soviet Union) and the southwest (India). An integral component of Xinjiang's defensive capacities and one that contributes to its overall distinctiveness is its nuclear, missile range, and intelligence-collecting facilities. These themes will draw us then to age-old questions about the interaction of the military and politics in China. Concluding this overview will be an assessment of the confidence-building measures with Central Asian states that China undertook in the 1990s, the changing security climate in the region following the Afghanistan offensive, and the implications of these changes for the defense of Xinjiang.

Xinjiang's Order of Battle

Allegedly, fully a quarter of all PLA forces or, according to some "foreign experts," a million soldiers are situated in Xinjiang. These grand claims do not even include about 100,000 PAPF troops, communication units, border guards, militia, and the bingtuan's (XPCC) 14 divisions with 2.48 million "soldiers." Together, these figures imply that the overall "military" presence in Xinjiang could reach up to 3 million troops, or more than the total for the entire Chinese army![7]

Of course, this is absurd. As can be seen in table 5.1, some 220,000 PLA troops—the second lowest among China's strategic zones—are based at the Lanzhou Military Region, the largest in China and covering over 3.4 million square kilometers (sq. km). This is more than 35 percent of China's territory and includes five provinces (Shaanxi, Gansu, Ningxia, Qinghai, and Xinjiang), as well as the western part of Tibet. The density of PLA deployment in this military region is the lowest in all China, at one soldier per 15.47 sq. km, compared to 1:1.33 sq. km in the Jinan Military Region, 1:2.58 in Shenyang, and 1:3.82 in the Beijing Military Region. The Xinjiang Military District (XMD) itself (which includes western Tibet) covers over 2 million sq. km, or more than 20 percent of China's total territory and 60 percent of the area of the Lanzhou Military Region.[8] At best, fewer than half of the troops in Lanzhou region are based in Xinjiang. The *Xinjiang Yearbook* mentions 39 PLA outfits by military unit cover designation (MUCD),[9] theoretically about 100,000 troops. Yet, following Beijing's systematic demobilization and troop reduc-

Table 5.1

PLA Ground Force Deployment, 1998

Strategic (War) Zones	Military Region	Group Armies	Troops
Southeast China	Nanjing, Guangzhou	5 (1, 12, 31, 41, 42)	480,000
Northeast China	Shenyang	5 (16, 23, 39, 40, 64)	310,000
Southwest China	Chengdu	2 (13, 14)	180,000
Northwest China	Lanzhou	2 (21, 47)	220,000
North China, Capital	Beijing	6 (24, 27, 28, 38, 63, 65)	410,000
East, Strategic Reserve	Jinan	4 (20, 26, 54, 67)	240,000
Total		24	1,840,000

Sources: Adapted from www.globalsecurity.org/military/world/china/pla.htm (accessed 13 September 2002; and You Ji, *The Armed Forces of China* (St. Leonards, Australia: Allen and Unwin, 1999), p. 48.

tion since the mid-1970s,[10] and given China's policy of concentrating troops near Beijing, Xinjiang may have no more than 50,000 to 60,000 regular troops, or one soldier per 35 to 40 sq. km. Thus, in contrast to what is widely believed, PLA forces in Xinjiang are relatively few and spread very thinly.

The Lanzhou Military Region can claim only two group armies (out of twenty-four), none based in Xinjiang. Just one, Group Army Twenty-one (mostly deployed in Gansu), belongs to Category A, that is, fully trained units with modern armaments. The other, Group Army Forty-seven (mostly deployed in Shaanxi), belongs to Category B, which refers to undermanned and undertrained units with out-of-date weapons and low budgets. Such units are often engaged in production and construction and have to be trained and armed before they are capable of going into battle. Probably belonging to Group Army Forty-seven, all of Xinjiang's divisions (the Fourth, Sixth, Eighth, and Eleventh, each with 12,000 to 13,000 troops) are of this type. These, with the possible exception of the Fourth, which is a more advanced rapid reaction division, are in fact low-quality garrison divisions (*shoubeishi*), similar to regional independent divisions (*dulishi*). They are mainly responsible for border defense, protection of PLA installations, economic development, and internal security. Xinjiang's regular PLA units also include one reserve division of even lower quality (based at Shihezi), ten independent regiments (artillery and air defense, infantry, army aviation, engineering, transportation, and communication), and over ten border guard regiments, logistical support regiments, and reconnaissance units[11] (see box 5.1). Moreover, Group Army Forty-seven headquarters (MUCD 84870) is located at Lintong, Shaanxi Province, remote from Xinjiang. In sum, PLA units in Xinjiang, with few exceptions, are not only small but also professionally inferior. This is not

---

Box 5.1

Xinjiang PLA Order of Battle

- Fourth Combined Arms Rapid Reaction Motorized Infantry Division (MUCD 36101?) based at Kucha (Kuqa): Type-96 MBT, Type-88C tanks, Type-92 AFV, WZ551 IFV, two artillery regiments (former Red Army division that fought the Indians in 1962).
- Sixth Highland Motorized Infantry Division (MUCD 68220) based at Kashgar and/or Khotan.
- Eighth Motorized Infantry Division (MUCD 36146) based at Qiaziwan, Shawan, Wusu County, and Huocheng County (Korgas, Horgos); responsible for defending north Xinjiang.
- Eleventh Highland Motorized Division (MUCD 36220) based at the Karakoram Range (formerly at Urumchi; former Red Army division): Type-59 tanks, Type-891 APC.
- UI Reserve Infantry Division based at Shihezi.
- UI Armored Division, Nanjiang, newly created in the 1990s.
- Seventh People's Armed Police Division at Yining (Gulja) (MUCD 8660). Used to be a PLA infantry division stationed in Xinyuan County (Künes). In 1996, it was turned into a PAPF reserve division and suppressed the February 5, 1997, uprising in Ili and was sent afterwards to Kashgar.
- MUCD 89800, based at Malan Village Police Administrative Area (Malan cun gongan guanli qu), under the Second Artillery Corps (missiles), formerly Sixth Corps Eighteenth Division. Headquarters of the Northwest Nuclear Test Base, also known as "the Capital."
- Second Independent Field Artillery Brigade based at Urumchi: 130 mm/152 mm/100 mm guns and 122 mm MRL.
- Thirteenth Artillery Brigade (took part in the October 13, 2000, digitalized artillery command exercise; used to be a division, transferred in 1969 from Hebei).
- Urumchi Regional Air Force Command Post (formerly Ninth Air Army or Corps). It is not equipped to fight foreign invaders.
- Thirty-seventh Air Division based at Urumchi and Korla, including 109th, 110th, and 111th Air Regiments: J-7E fighters.
- Seventy-third Independent SAM-AAA Air-Defense Brigade based at Urumchi (used to be a division, transferred in 1969 from Hebei).
- First Independent Light Mechanized Infantry Regiment based at Urumchi, mainly for domestic unrest: Type-92 APC.
- Second Independent Motorized Infantry Regiment in southern Xinjiang (Shazhe? MUCD 23642?).
- Third Independent Army Aviation Regiment based at Urumchi and Korla: S-70C2, Mi17, and Mi8 armed helicopters.
- Ten or more border defense regiments (brigades?).
- Ninth Independent Motorized Engineer Regiment based at Urumchi.
- Independent Communication Regiment.
- Transportation Regiment.
- Unidentified logistical support regiments.
- Unidentified reconnaissance unit.

Sources: Adapted from www.webspawner.com/users/andrewkc/ (accessed 9 June 2001); www.china-defense.com/orbat/pla_div_list_rev34/lanzhou_mr.html (accessed 30 July 2001); and www.cmilitary.com/forums/general/messages/47911.html (accessed 23 June 2001).

Note: Some data may not reflect recent reorganizations and structural changes.

surprising. China's strategy has always been focused on the north (Beijing), on the northeast (Manchuria), and, since the end of the Sino-Soviet conflict, on the south (Taiwan)—but never on the northwest (Xinjiang).

Unlike Xinjiang's ground forces whose headquarters are located far to the east, the Lanzhou Miliary Region Ninth Air Army (or Air Corps) is based in Urumchi. In fact, since the restructuring of the mid-1980s, it has become an air force regional command post (*zhihuisuo*), an intermediate level between the air force central command in Beijing and local air units. Still, only one of the Ninth Air Army's six air divisions, the Thirty-seventh, is actually deployed in Xinjiang. At the Urumchi and Korla air bases, this division maintains three air regiments—the 109th, the 110th, and the 111th—with thirty to thirty-five aircraft each. Recently, these units have received J-7E fighters, a double-delta wing outdated aircraft based on the MiG-21. There is another air base at Kashgar and still another at Khotan.[12] Created in July 1962, the Khotan Command Post, a division-level organization, was downgraded to a maintenance field station in April 1967.[13] The Third Army Aviation Regiment (a Category A unit under Group Army Twenty-one) is also based in Xinjiang. It is equipped with U.S.-made Blackhawk S70C Sikorsky helicopters, as well as Russian-designed Mi-8 and Mi-17 and other transporters. In October 2001, following the U.S. offensive in Afghanistan, thirty WZ-9G—an armed version of an Aerospatiale Dauphine transport helicopters coproduced in Harbin—have been transferred to Kashgar for use in the border region.

These are Xinjiang's *real* fighting forces. Most of the others, including the bingtuan, the militia, and the PAPF, are auxiliaries, the main duties of which relate to internal security and construction and whose direct role in an external military confrontation is bound to be marginal, at best. To be sure, the 103,000–strong bingtuan initially absorbed some troops from the First Field Army, as well as the Guomindang (GMD) and the Ili National Army (INA; Eastern Turkistan Republic) troops. However, these were engaged almost exclusively in nonmilitary work and have over the years been largely retired. Most of the bingtuan now consists of Han civilians, migrated or sent to Xinjiang from other parts of China. Leaders and midlevel cadres are often demobilized soldiers who are at the same time reserve officers organized according to military structures and designated with military ranks. In spite of the military terminology, the bingtuan is by no means a military outfit and is not controlled by the PLA except possibly during unusual emergencies. Disbanded in April 1975 and reinstated in August 1981, the bingtuan was long known as "an army without any military funds."[14] In its December 1995 Report on the Investigative Mission to Xinjiang, the World Bank said it "was assured that the functions of this organization had no relations to the People's Liberation Army. . . . The mission found no evidence to confirm or contradict this strong assurance."[15] In fact, recently the bingtuan has been transformed into the Xinjiang Production and Construction Corps (or Group), and its former "divisions" have been renamed subgroups.

While trained and supervised by the PLA, the militia is relatively small and by no means a fighting force.[16] The same applies to the PAPF. Separated from the PLA in 1982 and subordinate, until early 1995, to the Ministry of Public Security, the PAPF is primarily responsible for internal security and border defense. In the early 1990s, significant numbers of PLA border units along the northwestern and southwestern borders of Xinjiang were transferred to the PAPF.[17] Systematically incorporating demobilized PLA troops and occasionally entire divisions and still a quasi-military unit, the PAPF is certainly not to be considered a professional military organization that can contribute significantly to Xinjiang's defense. In fact, Beijing cannot rely on either Xinjiang's military or paramilitary units to deal with serious internal problems, let alone external threats. The fact that when the Afghan crisis erupted the government immediately sent reinforcements to Xinjiang from Lanzhou and other military regions reinforces the conclusion that Xinjiang's forces are quantitatively and qualitatively inadequate to cope with emergencies.[18] This has been the case throughout premodern as well as recent Chinese history.

Military Organization and Command Structure

Over the years, the politics and economics of Xinjiang's military organization and command structure have reflected both continuities and changes in the geopolitical and ethnic environment. Fundamentally, China's military profile in Xinjiang has been determined by perceived threats from the Soviet Union (and later Russia) and, to a lesser extent, from India. Above all, Chinese military policy in Xinjiang reflects Beijing's response to Russia's changing priorities. Though Moscow had been very interested in Xinjiang and had occasionally contemplated its incorporation into the Soviet Union, Soviet leaders have always regarded northwest China as of secondary importance compared to Manchuria and the northeast. Mao Zedong never overcame his suspicion that Moscow wanted to detach Xinjiang from China and establish another Central Asian republic under its auspices, yet he was fully aware that the Soviet Union's primary interests lay in northeast China. He remembered, too, that Moscow had facilitated the Chinese Communists' bloodless takeover of Xinjiang.[19] More than anything else, it is this understanding, intertwined with China's time-honored concern to protect its capital, that has shaped China's military command structure, organization, and deployment in Xinjiang.

For many years, Xinjiang's military command was all but monopolized by the First Field Army, the unit that had "peacefully liberated" the region. Its mission was not only to complete the territorial integration of the PRC but also to frustrate perceived attempts by the United States to arouse ethnic unrest against Chinese Communism, establish an Islamic republic in Xinjiang, and seize the region's uranium mines. Nor was the latter a mere fantasy. There is a great deal of evidence, both direct and circumstantial, that the Central Intelligence Agency (CIA) distributed weapons and funds to stir unrest in Xinjiang. In the words of Linda Benson, a well-known expert on Xinjiang, "I am absolutely sure that the American government sought to organize non-Chinese ethnic groups to resist Communism, during 1949, as the Communists came to power."[20]

On August 26, 1949, two First Field Army corps began to move toward Xinjiang: the Sixth taking a northern course and the Second taking a southern course. By late September, they had completed the occupation of Gansu and Qinghai and then proceeded to Xinjiang, reaching Hami on October 13. By that time, most GMD and INA troops had already surrendered. Dealing with pockets of resistance and mop-up operations, Red Army units moved to occupy Xinjiang, with the Sixth Corps concentrating on central and northern Xinjiang and the Second Corps on the south, both supported by units of the Fifth Corps (formerly the INA). Setting out from Keriya (Yutian), a forward cavalry company reached northwest of Gêrzê, well into western Tibet, on October 30, 1950. Grouped in three divisions, former GMD troops formed a Ninth Corps, under the Twenty-second Army led by Tao Zhiyue, a former GMD commander of Xinjiang. In 1954, he became the first commander of the bingtuan that absorbed the Twenty-second Army (see box 5.2 for Xinjiang troops deployment in 1949–1950).

To some extent, troop deployment in Xinjiang today still reflects this early pattern of occupation. Thus, of the three PLA First Field Army Second Corps divisions, only one (the Fourth) has remained militarily active. By the late 1960s, it was based in Khotan with its regiments deployed along the Soviet border: the Tenth in Kashgar, the Eleventh in Yining, and the Twelfth in Tarbagatay (Tacheng). The First Cavalry Division that had reached Aksai Chin (Ladakh) was later transformed into the Eleventh Motorized Division, the other Red Army division that survives and is still based at the Karakoram Pass. The Sixth Corps Eighteenth Division became independent and was assigned to the Second Artillery Corps (missiles) to guard China's nuclear facilities at Lop Nor.[21] All other PLA units that had occupied Xinjiang, including incorporated INA and GMD troops, had been de-

Box 5.2

Xinjiang Military Region: Red Army Deployment, July 1949–October 1950

First Army:
Commander: Wang Zhen

Second Corps Headquarters: Kashgar Military Region (PLA)
Commander: Guo Peng
Political Commissar: Wang Enmao

Fourth Division: Kashgar; Tenth (Kashgar), Eleventh (Shache), and Twelfth (Jiashe) Regiments
Fifth Division: Aksu; Thirteenth (Kuqa), Fourteenth (Aksu), and Fifteenth (Khotan), Regiments, Independent Regiment (Qiemo), Independent Regiment (Altai)
Sixth Division: Yanqi; Sixteenth and Seventeenth (Yanqi) Regiments, Cavalry (Ruoqiang) Engineer Regiment (Bole)

Fifth Corps Headquarters: Yining Military Region (former INA)
Commander: Reskan Jan
Political Commissar: Saifudin

Thirteenth Division: Kashgar; Thirty-seventh (Aksu), Thirty-eighth (Kashgar), and Thirty-ninth (Khotan) Regiments
Fourteenth Division: Wusu; Fortieth (Urumchi), Forty-first (Tacheng), and Forty-second (?Urumchi) Regiments
Fifteenth Division ?
First Independent Cavalry Regiment (Altai)
Second Independent Cavalry Regiment (Xinyuan [Künes])

Sixth Corps Headquarters: Dihua Military Region (PLA)
Commander: Lou Yuanfa
Political Commissar: Gao Jinjun

Sixteenth Division: Hami; Forty-sixth (Barkol), Forty-seventh (Turfan), and Forty-eighth (Hami) Regiments
Seventeenth Division: Urumchi; Forty-ninth (Qitai), Fiftieth (Yining), and Fifty-first (Urumchi) Regiments
Eighteenth Division: Xian, later based at Malan, Lop Nur

Twenty-second Army Headquarters: Urumchi (former GMD)
Commander: Tao Zhiyue
Political Commissar: Wang Zhen

Ninth Corps Headquarters: Shule
Commander: Zhao Xiguang
Political Commissar: Zhang Zhonghan

Twenty-fifth Division: north of Wusu
Twenty-sixth Division: southwest of Urumchi
Twenty-seventh Division: north of Kuqa and east of Korla

First Cavalry Division (Independent): Yutian (former GMD)
Commander: He Jiachan

Source: Zhonggong Xinjiang Weiwuer Zizhiqu Weiyuanhui Dangshi Yanjiushi (Xinjiang-Uyghur Autonomous Region Chinese Communist Party History Research Office), comp., *Xinjiang Jiefang* (Xinjiang's liberation) (Urumchi: Xinjiang Xinhua Shudian, 1999), front map.

Table 5.2

Transformation and Deployment of XPCC Divisions in Xinjiang

No.*	Location (present)	Original Military Designation
First	Aksu	Fifth Division, PLA First Field Army Second Corps
Second	Korla	Sixth Division, PLA First Field Army Second Corps
Third	Kashgar	None
Fourth	Yining	Thirteenth Division, INA turned PLA Fifth Corps
Fifth	Hami (Bole)	Sixteenth Division, PLA First Field Army Sixth Corps
Sixth	Urumchi	Seventeenth Division, PLA First Field Army Sixth Corps
Seventh	(Changji)	Twenty-sixth Division, GMD turned PLA Twenty-second Army Ninth Corps
Eighth	Wusu (Kuitun)	Twenty-sixth Division, GMD turned PLA Twenty-second Army Ninth Corps
Ninth	Shihezi	None
Tenth	Tacheng (Hami) Altay	Eighth Division (Cavalry), GMD turned PLA Twenty-second Army

Sources: Adapted from William W. Whitson with Chen-hsia Huang, *The Chinese High Command: A History of Communist Military Politics, 1927–71* (London: Macmillan, 1973), chart A, B, map 2; and Donald H. McMillen, "Xinjiang and the Production Construction Corps: A Han Organisation in a Non-Han Region," *Australian Journal of Chinese Affairs*, no. 6 (July 1981): 74.

*By the mid-1950s, the XPCC included eleven divisions (ten agricultural and one industrial). Three agricultural divisions were added in February 2001 (at Urumchi, Hami, and Khotan).

mobilized by the mid-1950s and transformed into the agricultural and construction divisions that later became the XPCC. Reorganized over the years, they still exist today (see table 5.2).

This wholesale deactivation and demobilization provided a local elite of disciplined cadres that could be assigned to administrative, production, and public security tasks. As was later proven during the Cultural Revolution, they were loyal. Nonetheless, as fighting forces Beijing considered them the least reliable both politically and militarily. From the outset, Beijing probably had no intention of engaging these troops in battle with a professional adversary. Its overall deployment instead implied a strategy of regional defense. Indeed, most of these "local forces," including border guards, public security, PAPF troops, independent divisions, and the various bingtuan divisions, remained relatively stationary over the years, having shifted very little since their initial deployment in the early 1950s. Typical of many military systems, this stagnation reflected China's geography and backward transportation system that, in those years and to some extent even today,[22] precluded effective military mobility over long distances. True to the legacy of

China's Communist revolution and the legacy of its civil war, until the early 1980s this isolation produced a mentality of self-sufficiency (which William W. Whitson terms a "regional-defense syndrome"). This frame of mind found expression in long-term military appointments that sometimes led to narrow-mindedness and parochialism.[23]

This is underlined by the periodic reorganizations of the Xinjiang military command. Subordinate to the GMD Northwest Field Headquarters, the Xinjiang garrison before 1949 had been divided into South Xinjiang and North Xinjiang Military Districts. By the late 1940s, all of China had been divided into six large military regions (*junqu*), one of them being the Northwest Military Region. In December 1949, the Xinjiang (Provincial) Military Region (Xinjiang [sheng] junqu) was formed as one of eighteen "second-class" military regions (*erji junqu*). It handled three "third-class" military regions (*sanji junqu*): Dihua (Tihwa, renamed "Urumchi" after February 1954), where the Sixth Corps was based; Yining, the base for the Fifth Corps; and Kashgar, the base for the Second Corps. This structure existed until 1955, when the State Council reorganized the command system into twelve military regions (Shenyang, Beijing, Jinan, Nanjing, Guangzhou, Wuhan, Kunming, Chengdu, Lanzhou, Inner Mongolia, Tibet, and Xinjiang). These military regions incorporated provincial military regions (*shengjunqu*) and military subregions (*junfenqu*), based on prefectures, which then included the different garrison and guard commands (*weishu* and *jingbei*).[24]

In 1967, the Inner Mongolia and Tibet Military Regions were relegated to the status of autonomous military regions and incorporated into the Beijing and Chengdu Military Regions, respectively. Yet, the Xinjiang Military Region (XMR) still maintained its independence. Unlike other military regions whose military districts converged with subordinate provinces, the XMR was now divided into three military districts: North Xinjiang (Beijiang), East Xinjiang (Dongjiang), and South Xinjiang (Nanjiang). In 1979, the XMR was renamed the Urumchi Military Region now incorporating western Tibet and Ladakh.[25] But by this time Xinjiang's "independent" military status was near its end.

As part of the comprehensive defense reforms of 1985, the Central Command merged the eleven military regions into seven great military regions (*dajunqu*), which included Shenyang, Beijing, Jinan, Nanjing, Guangzhou, Chengdu, and Lanzhou (see map 5.1). Transformed into a district, the Urumchi Military Command was incorporated into the expanded Lanzhou Military Region. This restructuring supports the claims that by the mid-1980s the Chinese were relying on in-depth active defense against Soviet attacks in the northwest. Beijing strategists regarded Xinjiang as a vast buffer zone far away

Map 5.1   **China's Military Regions, 1986**

Source: Ngok Lee, *China's Defence Modernisation and Military Leadership* (Sydney: Australian National University Press, 1989), p. xvi.

from administrative, industrial, and military centers that could deter and—if deterrence failed—absorb a Soviet invasion. Assuming that a Soviet offensive would target China's north and northeast rather than the northwest, this doctrine was a mirror image of the Soviet strategy, as well as reflecting China's predilection for "regional defense."

Had the Chinese advocated a "forward defense" strategy, Urumchi would have been designated the command of the enlarged military region. The choice of Lanzhou implied China's growing confidence in the northwest. In the unlikely event of an invasion, Xinjiang's strategic depth would have exposed the Soviet's logistical "long tail" to Chinese counterattacks, thereby thwarting a breakthrough. Thus, a regional command center using local forces and operating at some distance from the border could hold back an enemy offensive. Even though it is subordinate to Lanzhou, the XMD is unlike other provincial military commands in that it controls *two* provincial-size military commands of its own: South Xinjiang (still incorporating western Tibet and Ladakh) and North Xinjiang.[26] These are further divided into the following military subdistricts: Aksu, Altay, Bayangolin, Bortala, Changji, Hami, Khotan, Ili, Karamay, Kashi, Kizilsu, Ngari, Tacheng, and Urumchi.[27]

These changes also reflected the fact that with the emergence of Mikhail Gorbachev in 1985 the Chinese grew less concerned over a Soviet offensive. With the perception of a reduced threat in the northwest (later underscored by the disintegration of the Soviet Union), the duties of the XMD were indeed adapted to those of a provincial military command, that is, to take care of reserve forces, militia, and border defense. Also, the army's and party's dual control of the People's Armed Forces Department (which included the militia and the newly introduced system of reserves) was transferred to local civilian party committees, even though PLA cadres still participate in the program.

Military Deployment in Xinjiang

As of 1949, three different armies were functioning in Xinjiang: the INA (about 25,000), the GMD (about 80,000), and the PLA (about 100,000), around 200,000 soldiers altogether.[28] Following the transformation of the GMD, INA, and PLA troops into the bingtuan by 1954, the number of PLA regular armed forces in Xinjiang dropped from around 110,000 to no more than 60,000.[29] By that time, China was preoccupied with economic construction based on a foreign policy of "peaceful coexistence" and on the Sino-Soviet alliance, and it by no means perceived the Soviet Union as a military threat. The main Soviet forces of the Turkistan Military District (with headquarters at Tashkent) were by now directed not against China but against Iran, with smaller concentrations along the Afghan frontier. The *entire* territory north of the 4,250-km-long Sino-Soviet border was held by no more than twenty Soviet divisions, of which less than half could have readily undertaken effective, yet unlikely, defensive or offensive operations against China's military.[30]

By the early 1960s, the strategic situation had changed dramatically. While its nuclear weapons test base was being built in Xinjiang, Beijing's relations with the two main countries bordering the region—the Soviet Union and India—had deteriorated, ultimately leading to hostilities. Perceiving this deterioration as a threat to its nuclear and military facilities in Xinjiang and to its territorial integrity, China, according to some sources, increased its regular military deployment in Xinjiang to at least three armies or, according to other sources, 500,000 troops.[31] While the figure may be exaggerated, there is no doubt that Beijing reinforced its military presence in Xinjiang in the early 1960s, if only modestly. Anticipating the crisis, in the spring of 1965 Moscow began to beef up its troops along the Chinese border. Sino-Soviet military tension climaxed in 1969. By that time, Soviet force levels along the northern Chinese border had risen dramatically. From approximately fourteen divisions in 1964, they grew to twenty-eight to thirty-four ground force divisions in 1969,[32] allegedly reaching about forty-eight divisions in the mid-1970s.

Beijing had by no means provoked this Soviet military buildup. There was no significant change in China's ground and air dispositions throughout this period, nor any forward movement from Chinese reserve concentrations in the deep interior. In a time-honored tradition, this reserve was needed to guard the capital and the industrial northeast. Moreover, Moscow doubled its military presence along the Chinese border in the latter half of the 1960s precisely when the Chinese in general, and the PLA in particular, were preoccupied with the Cultural Revolution. In those years, China was militarily inferior to the Soviet Union by any standard, definitely in terms of aircraft, missiles, and nuclear weapons. Therefore, the Soviet military upgrade was motivated less by China's actual military *capabilities* than by its military *intentions* and potentially "irresponsible" behavior, as perceived by Moscow.[33] Soviet military preparations confirm this conclusion. Crossing the Turugart Pass from Kyrgyzstan to Xinjiang, one can still see the fortified bunkers, trenches, and barbed-wire fences on the former Soviet side of the border, but none on the Chinese side.

Aware of the Soviet military advantage, the Chinese had not been tempted to move additional troops to Xinjiang, least of all from the more vulnerable north and northeast where China had a numerical military edge over the Soviets. While other northern provinces may indeed have been more heavily reinforced, there were limited redeployments in Xinjiang. Possibly, the Second Corps was activated in Xinjiang and the Ninth Air Corps (Unit 7335) was commissioned to support ground force troops, as well as to protect Red Guard organizations from Wang Enmao. In July 1969, XMR troops were estimated at no more than 85,000, much lower than other military regions at that time: Shenyang (330,000), Beijing (350,000), and Lanzhou (125,000). The only exception was Inner Mongolia (40,000).[34] This deployment strongly suggests that Beijing, in a risky move, had not prepared itself for a full-scale Soviet invasion of Xinjiang (see tables 5.3 and 5.4).

Until the mid-1970s, the backbone of China's defense system consisted of thirty-seven to thirty-eight army corps (sometimes translated as "armies"). Composed of about 40,000 to 50,000 troops each, they were mostly deployed along the coastal provinces and in the northeast, primarily around Beijing

Table 5.3

The Military Balance along the Sino-Soviet Border, 1969 and 1986
(number of divisions, millions of troops, and number of aircraft)

Deployment	1969		1986
Soviet Military Districts	Divisions	Aircraft	Divisions
Far East (HQ Khabarovsk)	12–15	1 Air Army	25
Transbaykal (HQ Chita)	8–9	1 Air Army	11
Mongolia (HQ Ulan Baator)	2–3	—	5
Siberia (HQ Novosibirsk)	—	—	5
Central Asia (HQ Alma Ata)	6–7	—	7
Total	28–34	600	53
Chinese Military Regions			
Shenyang	26	80	23
Beijing	—	—	31
Inner Mongolia	5	160	—
Lanzhou	—	—	9
Urumchi	3	54	5
Total	34	294	68

Sources: Central Intelligence Agency, "Military Forces along the Sino-Soviet Border," Intelligence Memorandum, SR IM. 70–5 (January 1970), declassified and sanitized, p. 5; and Ngok Lee, *China's Defence Modernisation and Military Leadership* (Sydney: Australian National University Press, 1989), p. 156.

Table 5.4

The Military Balance along the Sino-Soviet Border, 1970
(number of divisions, thousands of troops, and number of tanks)

Western Sector			Central and Eastern Sectors	
USSR Central, Southern, Central Asian MDs	PRC Xinjiang and Lanzhou MRs	Military Deployment	USSR Far Eastern MDs and Mongolia	PRC Beijing and Shenyang MRs
36	15	Regular Divisions	30	32
180,000	180,000	Regular Manpower	283,000	384,000
50,000	125,000	Border Troops and Militia	50,000	125,000
392,000	305,000	Total Manpower	333,000	509,000
7,000	500	Tanks	6,750	2,000

Source: International Institute for Strategic Studies, *The Military Balance, 1970–1971* (London: 1972), pp. 99, 100.

and under its direct command. The fact that there were no main force corps in the entire northwest, Xinjiang included, speaks volumes about China's military priorities. Xinjiang's defense was in the hands of regional forces that included border patrols, independent divisions and regiments, and local garrisons. In the event of an invasion, the region would have become a "front" or a "theater" where the regional commanders would take full control of all forces in the region, including air forces. Apparently more "independent" than an army corps commander, a military region commander requires central approval before he can move units under his command.[35] Thus, in terms of command authority, as well as of quantity and quality of troops, the XMR was of secondary importance, despite its so-called strategic significance.

Sino-Soviet tension, which gradually subsided after 1969, rose again in 1979 following the Soviet invasion of Afghanistan and the Chinese offensive against Vietnam. As a precaution against Soviet pressure, or even military action, a northern front was established along the Sino-Soviet border incorporating the military regions of Beijing, Shenyang, Lanzhou, and Xinjiang.[36] This could have been China's response to a Soviet military reorganization that by 1979 had established a new high command for the Far East theater of operations that controlled the military districts of the Far East, Siberia, Transbaikal, and Mongolia.[37] In the end, except for minor and local troop movements and reinforcements in the Xinjiang region, no confrontation occurred.

By the mid-1980s, the Soviets (and the Chinese) had deployed most of their troops along the central and eastern sections of the border: Moscow had forty-one divisions against China's fifty-four. However, along the western section the Soviets had deployed only twelve divisions. They faced fourteen Chinese divisions (nine in the Lanzhou Military Region and only five in the Urumchi Military Region) (see tables 5.3 and 5.4 and map 5.2). This formidable military deployment did not last long, however. By the early 1990s, the two parties had begun discussing troop reduction.

Of the countries bordering Xinjiang, the one with which troop deployment has yet to be settled is India. As soon as Xinjiang had been occupied, PLA units were sent to the Pamirs, occupying Tashkurghan, Khunjerab, Mazar, and Quanshuigou. Gaining an access to Tiber from Xinjiang, they were finally deployed in Rudok (Rutog), Aksai Chin—a territory later claimed by India. China's military presence along the border, built up gradually since the early 1950s, outweighed that of India by a big margin. By 1960, Delhi had deployed only two battalions of a locally recruited and lightly armed regular militia in Ladakh, with no supporting arms or roads leading to the western boundary sector. China not only relied on advanced roads but also had, according to Indian intelligence, over one regiment (equivalent to an

Map 5.2 **Deployment of Ground Forces on the Sino-Soviet Border**

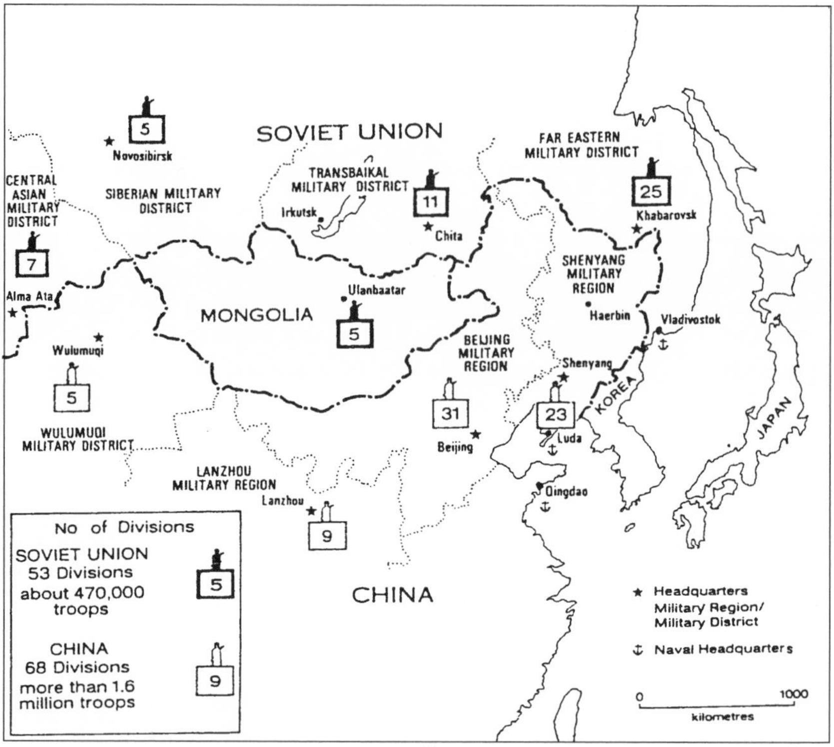

Source: Ngok Lee, *China's Defence Modernisation and Military Leadership* (Sydney: Australian National University Press, 1989), p. 156.

Indian brigade, that is, five infantry battalions) as well as supporting arms including some armor. Updating its earlier estimates, Indian military intelligence claimed at the end of 1960 that China had deployed one highly mobile and armored division in the western sector. Only in the summer of 1961 was Ladakh reinforced by another Indian battalion, still without supporting arms and still at a disadvantage compared to China. All the more so since the three Indian battalions responsible for the 300-km front line failed to construct even the elementary roads needed to support a "forward policy." At the same time, the Chinese added a number of feeder roads, relying on a much easier terrain and ample labor force and equipment.[38]

Defeated by the Chinese in the 1962 confrontation and aware of China's edge in the region, India has consistently avoided provoking China ever since.

One reason is that since 1962 the CIA had provided India with U-2 spy plane photographs of the Chinese border. In fact, since 1964 India has given permission for a U-2 detachment to be deployed at Charbatia near Cuttack on the Indian eastern coast. Its few missions supplied India with updated intelligence on Chinese deployments along the border and supplied the CIA with pictures of Lop Nor and other Xinjiang targets.[39] China has reportedly maintained this front line with the Eleventh Highland Motorized Division (MUCD 36220) based at the Karakoram Pass, which is backed by the Second Independent Motorized Infantry Regiment in southern Xinjiang.

Altogether—given Xinjiang's size, its purported strategic importance, and ethnic unrest—China's military presence in the region has been rather shallow and much less obvious in 1988 than in 1948. Still, men in uniform (soldiers, the PAPF, and public security) were definitely more numerous and visible in Xinjiang—and particularly in Urumchi—than in other parts of northwestern China.[40] Military forces are usually kept in the background so that soldiers are rarely seen. Military installations are located in inconspicuous sites, though they can be swiftly deployed in case of emergency. As none of China's neighbors represents any serious military threat today, the main role of the military in Xinjiang has more to do with internal security and production than with external defense. This, however, was not always the case.

Xinjiang's Security: The Northwestern Front

After 1949, the significance of the newly incorporated Xinjiang for China's defense diminished. The Sino-Soviet alliance considerably reduced the perceived threats from the north. Yet, even at that time, and certainly in hindsight, this detente was superficial. Unsettled borderlines and mutual mistrust survived. This implicit friction, which was to erupt later, underlined the relevance of Xinjiang, primarily its northwestern front, to China's overall national security.

Mao had been suspicious about Joseph Stalin's motives in Xinjiang from the very beginning and felt that he had been forced to compromise Chinese sovereignty over Xinjiang (and more so in Manchuria and Inner Mongolia) in order to secure Soviet military and economic aid. Sino-Soviet relations in Xinjiang were deteriorating by the late 1950s, following the repatriation of over 130,000 "Soviet nationals" and their Chinese family members to the Soviet Union, some by law, and thousands by forged certificates clandestinely distributed by the Soviet consulates in Xinjiang. This exodus caused concern in Beijing and the flow was stopped.[41]

According to Beijing, Moscow began to provoke trouble along the Sino-

Soviet border in July 1960 (precisely when the Soviet experts were withdrawn from China). Parts of the 2,250-km-long Soviet-Xinjiang frontier had never been delineated by any agreement.[42] In fact, until cross-border ethnic friction reached its climax in 1962, the Ili border had never been properly defended. In early 1962, in response to the "subversive activities" of the Soviets, China stopped issuing exit permits for Xinjiang's "Soviet" citizens. This provoked a raging Kazak demonstration in Yining (Gulja), causing PLA units to open fire. Due to this, between April 22 and the beginning of June 1962, 67,000 "Soviet" citizens illegally escaped Xinjiang to Soviet Kazakstan. As news of the Yining incident spread, it triggered similar outbreaks in other towns in Xinjiang, leading the PLA to reinforce its local garrison and to turn the border into a depopulated security zone. In July, Beijing forced the two main Soviet consulates, in Urumchi and in Yining, to close.[43]

Moscow responded by blaming China for building concentration camps in Xinjiang, persecuting Soviet citizens, and suppressing national minorities by force. China then denounced the Soviet Union for continuing its large-scale subversion in Xinjiang and distorting Xinjiang's history through the media. Throughout the 1960s, Moscow kept up a constant barrage of propaganda encouraging separatist tendencies in China and especially in Xinjiang. Beijing viewed these attempts to exploit separatism and to delegitimize Chinese sovereignty over Xinjiang as a very serious threat to China's internal stability and territorial integrity, even though they did not involve actual fighting.[44]

A year later, responding to Soviet reinforcements along the border, the escalation in Vietnam, and the prospects of a forthcoming Sino-U.S. confrontation, China announced emergency regulations for its southern and coastal provinces, as well as for Xinjiang.[45] Ethnic populations were ordered to evacuate a strip of land nearly 200 km wide along the border, which was then settled in 1966–1968 by Han farmers and bingtuan troops. As early as 1962, the XPCC had built fifty-eight state farms along the border with the Soviet Union. By the end of 1966, the bingtuan had organized 400 militia companies (*minbing lian*) and 180 core militia companies (*jigan minbing lian*), as well as special troops, tanks, cavalry, and artillery.[46] In early 1967, Beijing prohibited Soviet civilian flights over Xinjiang. These precautions proved to have been justified.

Toward the end of 1966, several thousand more Muslims fled Xinjiang into Soviet territory, driven by a new wave of political and religious persecution linked to the initial stages of the Cultural Revolution in Xinjiang, as well as by continuous Soviet exhortations.[47] Moscow was quick to exploit the deteriorating situation in the region. Doubled since January 1967,

Uyghur broadcasts from Radio Tashkent not only condemned Chinese persecution of Xinjiang's Muslim nationalities but also encouraged the Uyghurs to revolt against Chinese rule, offering them refuge. Moreover, Moscow encouraged and probably organized Kazakstan-based ethnic guerrillas to raid Xinjiang's frontier posts. According to a Xinjiang refugee leader, 5,000 such raids took place in 1966 alone. Sino-Soviet tension along the border continued, leading to several incidents in 1967. Red Guard posters seen in August claimed that Chinese troops had annihilated a Soviet cavalry unit that had allegedly invaded the Ili area.[48]

The summer 1968 Soviet invasion of Czechoslovakia and the Brezhnev doctrine that was invoked to justify Moscow's intervention in a socialist country alarmed the Chinese. The equation between Czechoslovakia and China emerged clearly in several local and central reports. Wang Enmao, the commander of the XMR, warned that his forces were "maintaining sharp vigilance, preparing for war, consolidating frontier defenses, and defending the motherland. Should the Soviet revisionists dare to attack us," he added, "we will wipe them out resolutely, thoroughly, wholly, and completely."[49] These actions and statements, underscored by Soviet troop deployments, military maneuvers along the border, and "thousands" of violent incidents, suggested that confrontation had become a real possibility.

According to Chinese protest notes, Soviet troops had begun crossing into Xinjiang in April 1969, allegedly accompanied by "several hundred" tanks and armored cars. Most of these raids took place along the border's northwestern section. Beijing complained that between June 1 and July 31 the Soviets had provoked 429 incidents along this border and also blamed the Soviets for deep intrusions by air into Chinese territory, where they built a road and military installations and moved the boundary markers. Sino-Soviet military clashes that took place on August 13 along Xinjiang's border caused both sides heavy casualties. Following these incidents, the increased tension between the two countries led the Chinese to believe that the Soviet Union was considering an all-out attack.

The Soviets blamed the Chinese for all these incidents. But after the March 2 engagement on the Ussuri River, there is every reason to believe that it was the Soviets who were largely responsible for incidents along the Sino-Soviet border, primarily in Xinjiang.[50] As mentioned earlier, the increased Soviet military presence along the border with China had been neither prompted nor followed by a similar military upgrade on the Chinese side. All the evidence suggests that the Xinjiang border clashes were a deliberate Soviet initiative. By any standard, the Chinese side was markedly inferior to the Russians. The scene of the clashes was close to main Soviet rail lines, yet remote from the Chinese transportation network. Given the Soviet military superiority, the explosive ethnic composition of this region, and its rebellious history, a Chinese provocation along this border was inconceivable.[51]

While these incidents were going on, in the summer of 1969 the Soviets created a new Central Asian Military District, probably to improve command and control of their forces along the western sector of the border with China. A series of Soviet air force moves was followed in the next few weeks by signals indicating that Moscow was seriously contemplating a surgical strike against Chinese nuclear installations, especially those in Xinjiang.[52] These threats and clashes forced Beijing to upgrade its military preparations against a possible Soviet offensive. Indeed, on August 23 the Chinese Communist Party's (CCP) Central Committee issued a directive declaring that war with the Soviet Union might break out at any time. To be sure, both sides were more concerned about the eastern section of the border than the western. In Harry Gelman's words, "the confrontation along the border between Soviet Central Asia and Xinjiang was to remain very much of a sideshow, with somewhat less at stake for both contestants, and therefore smaller forces on both sides."[53]

Aleksey Kosygin's visit to Beijing following Ho Chi Minh's funeral in September 1969 caused tension between the two countries to subside. Although no official accord was reached, the two sides agreed unofficially to withdraw their troops from the disputed border areas, to observe the existing borderline, and to avoid armed confrontations. On October 7, Beijing agreed to hold talks on the border question. China announced that it had "consistently stood for a peaceful settlement of the Sino-Soviet boundary question" and never demanded the return of the territory tsarist Russia had annexed by means of unequal treaties. On October 20, talks on the border issue opened in Beijing. For nearly ten years, while Sino-U.S. strategic relations were gradually building, Xinjiang moved to the background in China's national defense. But Beijing was still worried. In his meeting with President Richard M. Nixon on February 25, 1972, Premier Zhou Enlai warned against the Soviet Union's aggressive intentions against China. "Maybe they will try to create a Republic of Turkestan," he said. But "[i]t will not be so easy for them to enter the Sinkiang Province, and even if they come in it will be hard for them to get out. No matter what, we will make no provocations."[54] Indeed, by the late 1970s, following the Soviet invasion of Afghanistan and the Chinese offensive against Vietnam, Beijing-Moscow relations had become tense yet again.

Aware that a Soviet retaliation against China's invasion of Vietnam was possible, if unlikely, Beijing reinforced its forces in Xinjiang, put them on alert, and carried out a large-scale evacuation of civilians from border areas. But except for minor local Soviet reinforcements and troops movements opposite Xinjiang and Inner Mongolia, nothing happened. Beijing's implicit strategic alliance with Washington deterred any possible Soviet invasion.[55] Threat perceptions along Xinjiang's northwestern front declined considerably in the 1980s and 1990s. But on Xinjiang's southwestern front they increased.

Xinjiang's Security: The Southwestern Front

Long before the emergence of a Soviet threat along Xinjiang's northwestern border, Beijing had been concerned about the consolidation of Xinjiang's southwestern flank. Consciously or subconsciously, historical precedents—especially the British involvement in Xinjiang since the late nineteenth century—strengthened China's determination to secure Xinjiang's southwestern territories. This effort was launched as soon as the PLA occupied Xinjiang and moved its troops into western Tibet (Ari or Ngari) through Aksai Chin. Topographically, Aksai Chin is far more accessible to the Chinese from the north than to the Indians from the south. This was China's sole, easiest, and quickest way to reach western Tibet. Following the agreement on "the peaceful liberation of Tibet," reached in Beijing on May 23, 1951, China ordered a cavalry division to cross into Tibet. It finally set up camp in Rudok (Rutog), in an Aksai Chin territory later claimed by India.[56]

This unit literally paved the ground for what was to become the Xinjiang-Tibet (or West Tibet) Highway, used at least until the mid-1950s to supply western Tibet. Chinese frontier guards, PLA troops, and over 3,000 civilians —probably bingtuan—completed the road in October 1957. Beginning at Kargilik (Yecheng) in southwestern Xinjiang, the 1,200-km highway ended in Gar (Gaer or Gartok) in southeastern Tibet. About 180 km (or 15 percent) of the road crossed territory later claimed by India. Yet, the place was so remote that India, unable to enforce its sovereignty, preferred to keep quiet about Chinese activities there.[57] Only after Beijing revealed that it was about to complete the road connecting Xinjiang with Tibet through this territory did Delhi launch a protest. Prior to 1958, the Indians had scarcely any military deployed along the Aksai Chin border and had made no formal claim to this region.[58]

The road and the Ladakh Corridor, in general, assumed a key strategic role as the main supply and communication artery linking Xinjiang with Tibet. This is why the western part of Tibet has been wholly incorporated into the XMR, designated as the South Xinjiang Military District or Nanjiang. In his exchanges with Delhi in January 1959, Zhou insisted that Aksai Chin had always been under Chinese jurisdiction, that it belonged to southern Xinjiang's Khotan (Hetian) County, and that it was regularly patrolled by Chinese border guards. New Delhi disagreed.

Sino-Indian relations began to deteriorate in the late 1950s. By then, the road was used to shuttle troops sent to quell the Tibetan revolt. By October 1959, fighting broke out between Chinese and Indian troops. Failing to reach a settlement, India proclaimed a forward policy. Without actually attacking the Chinese, this policy was designed to block their further advance, establish India's military presence in Aksai Chin, undermine Chinese control of the disputed area, and interrupt Chinese supply lines, thereby forcing the Chinese to withdraw. This was a reckless and irrational policy that ignored earlier Chinese warnings. India's military buildup changed the regional balance and threatened Chinese army positions. India appeared to be prepared to go to war with China over Aksai Chin unless it surrendered that territory.

India's forward policy was not implemented until the end of 1961 due to its military inferiority vis-à-vis China. Increasing the number of border patrols and reconnaissance flights, Indian units began to move eastward in the winter of 1961–1962. In an attempt to cut China's transportation and communication lines, the Indians set up small outposts between, and occasionally behind, Chinese outposts on territory claimed by China. In early 1962, Western and Indian media began to anticipate an Indian military effort to drive the Chinese out of Aksai Chin. Dismissing Chinese warnings, another Indian infantry battalion was sent to Ladakh. This, too, was split into some sixty small garrisons and outposts along the western sector. In spite of India's military presence, Chinese troops were still more numerous and much better equipped.

China reacted vigorously to India's forward policy. In 1962, Beijing perceived a double-barreled threat to Xinjiang from the Soviet Union and India. PLA troops swiftly surrounded the small and isolated Indian positions and resumed the border patrols that had been unilaterally suspended in 1959. In the meantime, the PLA further improved its combat capabilities on a number of fronts, including Xinjiang, by stockpiling ammunition, weapons, gasoline, and spare parts; pooling available transport; and reducing the military's involvement in civilian production.[59] After an incident-filled summer, in September 1962, Indian troops opened fire on the Chinese, killing several. Despite this slight Chinese setback, Jawaharlal Nehru was convinced the Chinese would not attack and India was content to remain unprepared. Contrary to India's optimistic belief, China was preparing for war. Shooting broke out later that month, and on October 10 the PLA pushed back an Indian assault. Ten days later, the Chinese attacked in earnest and within forty-eight hours had smashed the Indian force. Both sides set out at once to rebuild and expand their forces. Then, on November 20–21, China unilaterally ceased hostilities and declared a cease-fire, after which it withdrew its forces from a 20-km strip along the entire front.

China's military response to India flatly contradicted Mao's doctrine of a people's war. Instead of luring the enemy into the country, the Chinese army moved boldly forward, "meeting the enemy at the gate." India's reckless self-confidence in the face of this may be traced to the fact that it had coordinated its push against China with the Soviet Union, which acted against Xinjiang at the same time.[60] India never subsequently revived its forward policy against China. In the wake of defeat, the Indian army beefed up its forces in Ladakh and opened roads to its forward positions. Yet, these were all defensive moves and at a distance from what China claimed was the border. Overall, China's tactical advantage in the western sector was so overwhelming that India could never hope to launch a successful offensive there.

Indeed, over the forty years since the war, Xinjiang's border with India in Aksai Chin has remained relatively quiet, even though it is the only section of Xinjiang's long borders that has yet to be demarcated. Negotiations to this end began in the late 1970s and gained momentum in the 1980s but have yet to result in a settlement. Meanwhile, Beijing has been consolidating its alliance with Pakistan both as a lever against India and as an insurance policy against Muslim unrest in Xinjiang.

China never considered that Pakistan posed a threat to its security, even though Pakistan shares a border with Xinjiang, joined the Western Alliance system in the 1950s, and loudly proclaimed its pan-Islamic aspirations.[61] By contrast, Pakistan grew concerned over Beijing's "aggressiveness" following the Sino-Indian border clashes in the late 1950s. Nonetheless, when Delhi rejected President Mohammad Ayub Khan's 1959 offer of a joint Indian-Pakistani defense of the subcontinent, Pakistan immediately sought an alliance with Beijing.[62]

Sino-Pakistani amity grew when the two countries settled their differences over the 450-km-long Kashmir-Xinjiang border. Talks on demarcating this border began on October 12, 1962, two days after the PLA pushed back the first Indian assault. By that time, Beijing—facing the combined effects of Muslim ethnic unrest in Xinjiang and exacerbated Soviet interference—was keenly interested in such a settlement. Concluded on February 22, 1963, the agreement gave nearly 2000 sq. km back to Pakistan. Delhi immediately dismissed the agreement, insisting that all Kashmir was under Indian sovereignty and that there was therefore no common boundary between China and Pakistan that needed to be demarcated. Ignoring India's protests, the two parties built an all-weather road connecting Gilgit to Xinjiang via the Khunjerab Pass. This Karakoram Highway served military purposes as well as political and economic ends. For this reason, the text of the agreement providing for the road, signed on October 21, 1967, was kept secret.

Massive arms transfers from Beijing and military cooperation strengthened the China-Pakistan alliance. Their respective hopes for the alliance proved to some extent contradictory. Pakistan dreamed that the alliance would enable it to express its solidarity with Xinjiang's Muslims and even support their aspirations. Beijing used the alliance as a lever to deter Islamabad from supporting these same Muslims in Xinjiang, as well as Uyghur separatists. China's hopes proved more realistic. In the end, Pakistan held back from explicitly condemning Beijing for its arbitrary treatment of Muslims in Xinjiang or from arousing them through radio broadcasts.[63] Though the effectiveness of the alliance to deter Islamic and separatist aspirations has been doubtful, China tried to replicate it in the 1990s in agreements with Kazakstan, Kyrgyzstan, and Tajikistan.

While Beijing has consistently supported Pakistan in its dispute with New Delhi over Kashmir, it has taken great care not to become militarily involved in the dispute. At the same time, China has grown concerned over the Jammu and Kashmir Liberation Front's push for Kashmiri independence and a Muslim state, knowing it could fuel Uyghur separatism in Xinjiang. For this reason, China—this time in full accord with *both* Pakistan and India—came to oppose any form of self-determination that could lead to an independent Kashmir.

Increasingly, China also came to see that the same concerns about Islamic radicalism apply equally to Pakistan itself. Pakistan, after all, is a Muslim republic that has become a base for the smuggling of religious literature (and perhaps arms as well) into Xinjiang. Beijing suspected that the Chinese-made explosives used in terrorist incidents in Xinjiang had been exported from its own territory via Pakistan to Afghanistan.[64] It also came to view Pakistan as a haven for Uyghurs who had fled there either directly from Xinjiang or indirectly, usually through Kazakstan and Kyrgyzstan, where the Pakistani consulates provided them with visas.[65] It believed that Uyghur community centers in Pakistan had given shelter to refugees who then enrolled in Islamist *madrassahs* there. One such center is "Kashgarabad," a large guest house in Islamabad run by wealthy Uyghur traders. Another is the Anwar ul-Ulum Abu Hanifa Madrassah in Rawalpindi. The principal of this establishment, Sheikh Serajuddin, had close ties with the Taliban and offered Uyghur students a safe haven on their way to Afghanistan.[66] Until the mid-1990s, Pakistan thus extended protection and support to Uyghur expatriates, including illegal immigrants. It regularly jailed these immigrants for a token few months but then allowed them to stay in the country. This, however, was the least of China's concerns.

Increasingly, Pakistan's close links with the Taliban in Afghanistan complicated its relations with China.[67] Indian intelligence often reported on the contents of interrogations of captured personnel of the Pakistan Inter-Services

Intelligence (ISI). These accounts suggest that the Pakistan army had trained Uyghurs in a camp near Mirpur across the Line of Actual Control (LAC) from India. Also, Pakistani pan-Islamic jihad groups were reportedly training Uyghurs in Baluchistan Province. A number of Pakistani militant groups such as Jamaat-e-Islami, Jamaat-e-Tablighi, and Lashkar-e-Toiba (or Tayyiba, "Army of the Faithful") backed insurgents in southern Xinjiang. Many of these received training at the Al-Badr camp at Ooji, near the Afghan-Pakistani border. Some of these active Islamic fundamentalist movements have allegedly been supported and sustained by the ISI.

Beginning in 1997, Beijing started applying pressure on Pakistan to adopt a tougher policy against the Uyghurs. Barbed-wire fences were constructed in and around the Khunjerab Pass to deter the infiltration of Muslim militants into Xinjiang.[68] Heavily dependent on China, Pakistan had little choice but to comply with China's demands. Consequently, scores of illegal Uyghur immigrants were forcibly deported to Xinjiang, Uyghur community centers were closed and "hundreds" of their Uyghur residents evicted, and Uyghur students were expelled from schools, hotels, and guest houses. Those Uyghurs who obtained Pakistani visas from Pakistan's embassies in Central Asia were now required to produce Chinese documents permitting them to proceed to any third country. China executed a Pakistani infiltrator for "fomenting trouble" in Xinjiang. Meanwhile, according to an unconfirmed Indian report, the Pakistani army shot nineteen Uyghurs who were undergoing military training in Pakistan. As such incidents mounted, China and Pakistan on October 31, 1998, signed an agreement curbing cross-border smuggling of drugs, arms, and ammunition through the Khunjerab Pass. Denied extensions of their Pakistani visas, Uyghurs who had been living in Pakistan had to leave the country. Most were detained and questioned by Chinese authorities when they crossed the Khunjerab Pass.[69] Islamabad also reassured Beijing that no religious organizations in Pakistan would be allowed to meddle in Xinjiang. Invited to visit China in June 2000, the chief of the Islamic Jamaat-e-Islami Party humbly reiterated that all Pakistani religious parties were committed to friendship with China.[70]

Nuclear and Intelligence Facilities in Xinjiang

The number of conventional Chinese forces deployed in Xinjiang is far less than previously believed, yet Xinjiang is unique among China's provinces in terms of its intelligence surveillance stations, missile impact zones, and nuclear facilities.

China's main uranium deposits are situated in Hunan, Guangdong, and Jiangxi. But as early as the 1940s, uranium was discovered in Xinjiang in

Bortala and in the Altay Shan at Koktogai. Eager to catch up with the United States, Moscow, which had exercised de facto control over this region (the Eastern Turkistan Republic) since 1944, set out to mine Xinjiang's uranium.[71]

This initiative did not go unnoticed. O. Edmund Clubb and then John Hall Paxton, the American consuls in Dihua, suspected the existence of uranium in Xinjiang already in 1943. Determined to deny the Soviets access to Xinjiang's uranium, Washington for a while toyed with the idea of a treaty with China that would have given the United States a monopoly on China's uranium. Washington was also looking for an air base in Xinjiang to be used against Soviet targets in Central Asia in the event of a third world war. Rejecting the idea, the CIA tried instead to frustrate the Soviet attempts to mine uranium in the Altay Shan and at the same time planted sonic detectors around Dihua (and perhaps also beyond the border) to monitor the progress in the Soviet atomic program at Semipalatinsk, across the border from Xinjiang in Kazakhstan. These detectors were the first to provide proof of the first Soviet atomic test at Semipalatinsk, on August 29, 1949.

By the mid-1950s, Chinese prospecting teams had discovered three rich uranium deposits in western Xinjiang (Daladi, Mengqiku'er, and Kashgar),[72] and later in southern Ili. At least three uranium mines were opened in Xinjiang. The most important is the huge mining complex No. 731 in Künes Township (Xinyuan), southeast of Yining. It belongs to the bingtuan's Seventy-second Regiment and includes a highly secret *laogai* (reform through labor camp) operation known alternatively as the Huise (Gray) Uranium Mine or the Puli Uranium Mine and worked by some 1,000 inmates. In 1962, U.S. satellites photographed another possible uranium mine at Aksu. Uranium from all the mines is apparently processed at Factory No. 734 in Ili.[73]

Assembled elsewhere, all of China's nuclear weapons were tested in Xinjiang. Construction of the nuclear weapons test base was launched in 1960 at the Huangyanggou oasis northwest of Lop Nor. The work was carried out by Xinjiang recruits consisting of former GMD troops and ordinary prisoners as well as the Second XPCC (bingtuan) Division (the former PLA Sixth Division) from Korla.[74] Known as Base 21, the Lop Nor nuclear weapons test base covers some 100,000 sq. km, over 6 percent of Xinjiang's territory, equal in size to Zhejiang Province. It has over 2,000 km of highways, an airstrip, a power plant, and an air force command post served by different types of aircraft, as well as radar and communication lines. A new town was built from scratch in 1963 to become the nuclear weapons test base headquarters (called Malan, also known as the "Capital") MUCD 89800. China's ground zero was thus ready for operations.

On October 16, 1964, the PRC triggered an atomic bomb in Xinjiang, the first of forty-five nuclear explosions.[75] Among them was the first atomic bomb dropped from the air (May 14, 1965), the first atomic bomb delivered by missile (October 27, 1966), the first hydrogen bomb dropped from the air (June 17, 1967), the first nuclear explosion in a horizontal tunnel (September 23, 1969), and the first vertical-shaft nuclear test (October 14, 1978). Most of these breakthroughs were achieved during the Cultural Revolution, although the test base could not be shielded from its effects. Invited by sympathizers at the base, Red Guard fanatics from the Harbin Military Engineering Institute began the 4,000-km journey to Lop Nor in early 1967. Meanwhile, the XMR's command received emergency orders for their arrest. Even if the test base had been secured from outside Red Guard infiltrators, it was not immune from attempts to seize power from within. These affected China's first air-dropped hydrogen bomb test on June 17, 1967.[76]

Although since 1996 China no longer conducts nuclear tests in Xinjiang, its missile range is still active and its facilities remain in place. Typical is the Northwest Nuclear Technology Institute, located in the Scientific Research District near Malan, not far from Lake Bosten. The institute used to be the primary support facility for the Lop Nor nuclear weapons test base and still maintains an archive on nuclear explosions, warfare, and weapons research bearing on testing at Lop Nor. There are indications that China had been experimenting with bacteriological weapons in Malan as early as the 1980s.[77]

China's development of intermediate and long-range missiles necessitated not only launching bases but also suitable test impact areas. In the mid-1960s, Beijing selected a number of impact areas in the depopulated western and southern parts of the Taklimakan Desert. China's first missile-carried atomic warhead was launched on October 27, 1966, by a DF-2 missile from Shuangchengzi near Jiuquan (in northern Gansu) and landed in Xinjiang, 800 km to the west. The main impact zones for conventional warheads were at Korla and Minfeng (Niya), while Lop Nor remained the impact zone for nuclear warheads.[78] In early 1967, the first measurement station was completed in the impact area and two additional impact zones were selected at the northern foot of the Kunlun Shan.[79] For some years after 1965, the CIA monitored Chinese missile telemetry, and perhaps nuclear tests as well, using sensor devices planted with Delhi's permission on the summit of Nanda Devi in the Himalayas. Also, U-2 spy aircraft continued to drop sensor devices in the vicinity of the nuclear weapons test base in Xinjiang.[80] Even today, Xinjiang is used as a missile range, for example, for test launching the DF-31.[81]

With the development of satellites, Xinjiang became integrated into the newly deployed satellite tracking, telemetry, and control network. Of the seven telemetry and control stations built in the late 1960s, one was at Kashgar (MUCD 89760).[82] In the early 1970s, it was linked by wire and then radio with the other stations and with the center, and in the late 1980s its capacity was increased. In addition, communication earth stations were constructed between 1975 and 1984 in Urumchi. By the end of 1988, a new satellite communication earth station had been built in Malan. Though these stations also transmit civilian radio and television, all of them without exception were designed and built by the military (primarily by the Commission for Science, Technology, and Industry for National Defense) and catered to military needs. In April 1984, the PLA Signal Corps opened a military satellite communication service between Beijing and Urumchi. As one report states, "The national defense communications network built by the army communications departments . . . facilitates satellite communication between the general headquarters and all the main military areas and frontier regions."[83]

Given its ethnic composition and location, Xinjiang has always been an ideal center for spying and intelligence surveillance.[84] Human intelligence operations were active in Xinjiang since well before 1949.[85] After 1949, SIGINT facilities for the collection of radio and satellite communication were set up along the Sino-Soviet border in Xinjiang (e.g., Hami).[86] In the late 1970s, China's intelligence surveillance network in Xinjiang was considerably upgraded by an ultrasecret joint venture between the U.S. National Security Agency (NSA) and the CIA, on the one hand, and the PLA on the other.[87]

The origins of this venture go back to the early 1970s, when Washington offered Beijing intelligence on Soviet troops along the border with China. Then, in September 1975, Secretary of State Henry Kissinger offered the Chinese a joint seismic and electronic facility to be established in Xinjiang in order to monitor Soviet missile bases. The issue was raised again in early 1979 during Deng Xiaoping's visit to Washington. The fall of the Shah and the loss of the two U.S. monitoring stations in Iran, as well as the Soviet invasion of Afghanistan, gave urgency to the question of a facility in Xinjiang. A few months later Beijing agreed.

Code-named CHESTNUT, two listening bases with three different radio intercept systems had been built by the fall of 1981 at Korla and Qitai. State-of-the-art American electronic equipment was reportedly provided by the CIA's Office of SIGINT Operations. Chinese SIGINT agents had reportedly been trained by the CIA in Beijing, as well as in a special computer center located in the Silicon Valley near San Francisco. This extraordinary project reflected common Sino-U.S. interests in monitoring the Soviet missile and space program and nuclear tests, as well as military and commercial flights and Soviet communications in Afghanistan. It considerably enhanced the ability of China and the United States to ferret out missile telemetry on antiballistic missile and ballistic missile tests at Sary Shagan (west of Lake Balkhash),

Tyuratam (east of the Aral Sea), Kapustin Yar (east of Volgograd), and Plesetsk (near Archangelsk), as well as the nuclear research center at Semipalatinsk.[88]

The quality of the stations' output deteriorated over time and probably became less significant after the collapse of the Soviet Union. Yet, a 1995 "Chinagate" document that a U.S. federal court forced from the Clinton administration suggests that the joint PLA-CIA operation to gather signals from Russia may not have ended with the Cold War. Operations at these two sites appear to have expanded to include Asian military communication, radar, and computer networks. It appears that the program has been continued for both military and political reasons and has become part of the worldwide Echelon System.[89] China insists that these stations were closed in the early 1990s, but sources in Taiwan allege that they still operate.[90] Two large SIGINT stations in Xinjiang—one at Dingyuanchen, used for monitoring communications in Russia and Central Asia, and one at Changji, near Urumchi, used primarily for intercepting satellite communications—were expanded in 1999–2000.[91]

Finally, around the same time the two Sino-U.S. monitoring stations were set up in Xinjiang, the two countries intensified their intelligence and operational cooperation regarding Afghanistan. Their intelligence services had established a formal working relation by 1980. The CIA bought thousands of mules from China, delivered along the Karakoram Highway to Pakistan and then to the Mujahidin in Afghanistan. Most of the weapons provided by the CIA to the Mujahidin, especially in the early stages of the war, originated in China. At an estimated $100 million a year, the Chinese delivered small arms, assault rifles, mines, antitank and antiaircraft guns, rocket launchers, and 107-mm rockets by ship to Karachi.[92] Xinjiang was also used as a base for training Afghan Mujahidin to fight the Soviet Union. With some 300 military advisers already at training facilities in Pakistan, in February 1985 the PLA opened additional training camps near Kashgar and Khotan in Xinjiang where Afghan rebels were introduced to the use of Chinese weapons, explosives, combat tactics, propaganda techniques, and espionage.[93]

The Military and Politics in Xinjiang

No sooner had they occupied Xinjiang than PLA commanders became intensively involved in the consolidation of political control over the civilian population. Peng Dehuai, the commander of the First Field Army and the Northwest Military Region, who had also been a member of the CCP's Central Committee in 1945, set the pattern. Replacing him in 1951, Wang Zhen, formerly an alternate member of the Central Committee, became both commander and political commissar of the XMR, as well as Xinjiang's ranking party secretary.[94] It was he who mobilized the military for economic growth through the establishment of the agricultural construction divisions, later known as the XPCC (bingtuan). Yet, Wang's direct involvement in Xinjiang gradually ended in 1952–1953 when Wang Enmao succeeded him.[95] Wang Enmao was by far the most influential military-cum-civilian leader in Xinjiang from the late 1940s to the 1980s, even after his removal from the region.

As Wang Zhen's deputy political commissar of the First Army and political commissar of the Second Corps, Wang Enmao took an active part in Xinjiang's "peaceful liberation." His units reached Kashgar where he soon became the top Communist official in the region with the most restive non-Han population. In 1952, Wang Enmao returned to Dihua to take over from Wang Zhen as the political commissar-cum-commander of the XMR, as well as the ranking secretary of the party's Xinjiang Committee. By 1958, Wang had a well-earned reputation for his repression and rectification policies. The full scope of his power became evident during the Cultural Revolution.

By that time, the involvement of the Xinjiang military in politics had reached its zenith. Concerned about the disruptive implications of the Cultural Revolution, Wang Enmao quickly created his own Red Guard groups. Radicals had already formed rival Red Guard gangs that had managed to infiltrate the military establishment, including both the bingtuan and some PLA units.[96] Yet, Wang Enmao was acutely aware of the Soviet threat, the explosive potential for ethnic unrest, Xinjiang's distance from the center, its nuclear facilities and scheduled tests, and its relatively small Han population (then about one-third). He was not about to permit radical Red Guards to undermine stability in this strategically sensitive region. In October 1966, he therefore unleashed an assault on the radical Red Guards, in a campaign later known as the "White Terror."

By the beginning of 1967, the situation had utterly deteriorated. On January 14, a Central Committee instruction stressed that the "spearhead of struggle may not be directed against the armed forces."[97] But then, ten days later, Mao and the combined military-civilian leadership ordered the PLA to "actively support the revolutionary Leftists." Wang not only ignored this order but also intensified pressure on the Red Guards. The most serious among a number of violent incidents, known as the "Shihezi massacre," took place on January 26, 1967, just three days after Beijing issued its order to support the Leftists. Wang's Red Guards (which included elements of the bingtuan Fourth, Seventh, and Eighth Divisions and the Twenty-third Regiment) brutally suppressed rival Red Guards. Opening fire on the "revolutionary masses," they reportedly killed 100 and injured another 500.[98] Similar confrontations occurred in the Ili-Tacheng region. Red Guard accounts later disclosed that Wang's bingtuan troops had jailed, tortured, and executed many "revolutionaries."

A number of local PLA leaders crossed the lines and joined the Red Guards. They all viewed Wang Enmao as "the real obstacle to the Great Cultural Revolution in Xinjiang." Pressure mounted on Wang to restrain his troops from suppressing the "Left." Nevertheless, even though the Cultural Revolution and military were now intertwined, Beijing could not afford chaos, least of all in Xinjiang. Thus, on January 28, two days after the Shihezi massacre, the CCP Military Affairs Commission (MAC) issued a directive underscoring war preparedness and national defense as priorities. It ordered border defense units in Xinjiang and elsewhere to carry out their primary defense and internal security missions and to postpone the Cultural Revolution "for the time being."[99] The next day, Premier Zhou "ordered the Sinkiang Military District and the production-construction corps to suspend immediately acts of hostility and to withdraw armed troops."[100] Wang was ordered to return to Beijing for "talks" with Zhou, but apparently he failed to comply.

A couple of weeks later, on February 11, the CCP Central Committee with the State Council and the MAC issued a detailed document that dealt directly with the bingtuan. It opened with an unequivocal statement, "The Production and Construction Corps of the Sinkiang Military Region is not an ordinary force of land reclamation but a productive force equipped with arms. Situated in the border area and in the front line of the struggle against revisionism and imperialism, it shoulders the heavy combat task of guarding the frontier of the mother country." The directive, designed to prevent the Red Guards and other radicals from seizing power, ordered that those who had "seized power or stolen arms and ammunition" were to be arrested and treated as counterrevolutionaries.[101]

Red Guards seized power in thirteen other provinces but not in Xinjiang, where the military continued to put down Red Guard violence and disruptions. To ensure order, a Military Control Committee was established in March 1967 in Xinjiang, and the PLA took over public security bureaus and the municipal police in Urumchi. At the same time, Wang Enmao allegedly refused to carry out Zhou's order to disband his own Red Guards. Soon, however, he and his supporters suffered a setback.

Following the Wuhan incident in the summer of 1967, Beijing ordered the main army corps to seize control of several military districts and run them directly. Xinjiang, along with a number of other provinces, was thus "reorganized." Its military region was put under the command of the Ninth Air Corps (Unit 7335) from the Lanzhou Air District. But Xinjiang's newly appointed commander, Li Chuanjun, did not assume a formal military post in Urumchi. Li's appointment was doubtless prompted by the fact that Wang had worked fifteen years to build a strong power base using local PLA units. Li's Ninth Air Corps controlled the region only on paper, and as soon as it arrived in

Xinjiang, its troops were persecuted, attacked, and "savagely beaten up."[102]

Beijing's attempts in the autumn of 1967 to settle the conflict between Unit 7335 and the bingtuan failed. In November, Mao ordered Wang Enmao to return to the capital "for training and to review mistakes committed during the Cultural Revolution."[103] Wang was not so easy a nut to crack. He continued to resist the formation of a revolutionary committee in Xinjiang, a policy that his subordinate commanders likely supported. Only in August 1968, when the violent phase of the Cultural Revolution had passed and the Red Guards dismantled, was he finally relieved of his command.

The timing of Wang's dismissal—just as Xinjiang was facing a serious Soviet threat—was odd, to say the least. It may have had less to do with Wang's "conservative" policies or with the fact that the Red Guards had criticized him for suppressing the Left and more to do with the fact that during his fifteen years in Xinjiang he had accumulated a nearly unprecedented amount of power, both military and political. This represented a challenge that Beijing leaders could no longer ignore. Whereas many senior First Field Army officers were removed in 1967 following the alleged attempt by He Long to overthrow Mao, those belonging to the Xinjiang (and Lanzhou) Military Region were hardly touched, another indication of Wang's extensive power.[104] At the same time, his dismissal even in the face of the Soviet threat is yet another indication that Xinjiang had been accorded a lower priority in Beijing's strategy.

General Long Shujin, a member of the Fourth Field Army faction and a former Hunan Military District commander, finally replaced Wang. He had survived severe Red Guard attacks during the Cultural Revolution to be named full member of the Ninth CCP Central Committee in 1969. As late as September 1968—*after* Wang's removal—he at last managed to set up the Xinjiang Revolutionary Committee (XRC), the last to be formed in China. Still, Wang's influence was not at an end. Of the seventeen XRC Standing Committee members, seven were Wang's supporters. Five were revolutionary cadres and four represented mass organizations. All four senior vice chairmen, *including* Wang, had been associated with the First Field Army—three of whom became full or alternate members of the Ninth Central Committee.[105] Wang was then transferred to Jilin Province, but thirteen years later, in 1981, Deng called him back. Deng, it turned out, needed Wang's rich experience in dealing with the region's social and political problems and therefore named him first political commissar of the Urumchi Military Region. This was a demotion, however, as he was outranked by the regional commander Xiao Quanfu, formerly of the Fourth Field Army.

By the mid-1980s, radical tendencies still survived among ranking PLA officers in the Urumchi Military Region. Two deputy commanders, Liu

Haiqing and Wang Fuzhi, had ultra-Leftist records during the Cultural Revolution. They were certainly inspired by Xiao Hua, the first political commissar of the then separate Lanzhou Military Region, who upheld the army's political-ideological work and thereby challenged Deng's emphasis on professionalism.[106] By the summer of 1985, when the Urumchi Military Region was finally incorporated into the enlarged Lanzhou Military Region, all of them had been removed and professional officers had been appointed in their stead.[107]

Since the early 1980s, several factors have caused the political role of the military in Xinjiang to decline sharply. The launch of China's post-Mao economic reforms, the collapse of the Soviet Union, and the end of Mao's revolutionary ideology changed the domestic and international landscape. Also, a new generation of professional officers has emerged, men with little political background and limited commitment to historical legacies. While the prospects of regionalism or federalism are still mentioned and debated, the likelihood that the Xinjiang military would move to separate itself from the PRC is nil. In fact, most of the conditions that formerly enabled the military to involve itself in politics, civilian affairs, and internal security have been abolished.

Xinjiang Defense: Confidence-Building Measures

Although in the early 1980s China still considered the Soviet Union its principal adversary, Beijing's emphasis on economic development at the expense of military modernization and the emergence of Gorbachev in Russia contributed to a dramatic reduction of tension.[108] Following Gorbachev's visit to China in 1989, the two parties began discussing the mutual reduction of armed forces and confidence-building measures along their border. This process accelerated after the disintegration of the Soviet Union. By 1992, the Russian military presence along the Chinese border had been sliced by over 200,000 men, 12 divisions had been disbanded, and 4,000 tanks and 350 aircraft and helicopters had been withdrawn. A five-year Sino-Russian military agreement signed in November 1993 further reduced mutual tensions.

The effect of the Soviet collapse on Xinjiang's threat perceptions has been dramatic. Initially, Beijing was concerned about the implications for China's territorial integrity. But then it realized that, suddenly, instead of facing one strong superpower Xinjiang faced four separate countries, three of which had just gained independence and could by no means be regarded as military threats. The 2,700-km-long western section of the former Soviet border was now split into four parts, the one with Russia stretching less than 55 km in the Gorno-Altay (Upper Altay) Territory. Discussions on the demarcation of this least controversial section began in February 1994. An agreement was finally ratified and entered into force on October 17, 1995.[109] In November 1997, following the demarcation of the eastern section of the border (4,195 km), the two sides agreed to proceed with the demarcation of the western section (54 km) that runs at an altitude of 2,000 to 3,000 meters above sea level. This was completed on September 10, 1998, and on November 23 Jiang Zemin and Boris Yeltsin signed the joint statement. In July 2001, Vladimir Putin and Jiang Zemin signed the Treaty on Good-Neighborly Relations, Friendship and Cooperation. The most important Beijing-Moscow agreement since 1950, it provides for increased Russian arms sales to China and the training of PLA officers at Russian military academies.[110]

Meanwhile, discussions on mutual troop reductions continued with the former Soviet republics. Inaugurating the group known as the Shanghai Five (and later the Shanghai Cooperation Organization [SCO]) on April 26, 1996, the presidents of China, Russia, Kazakstan, Kyrgyzstan, and Tajikistan signed an agreement to control armed forces within a 100-km zone along each side of the border. They also agreed to exchange information on military personnel and equipment, to limit the scope of exercises, to the presence of observers, to coordinate troop movements, and to make a staged withdrawal of forces to mutually agreed levels.[111]

The details of these levels were specified a year later when the five parties signed an agreement on arms reductions along the border, valid until December 31, 2020. The agreement stated that "the military forces deployed by both parties in the border areas will not attack each other." It also bound the parties not to "seek unilateral military superiority" and to "reduce military forces along the border areas to a minimum level commensurate with that of good-neighborly and friendly relations, making them defensive in nature." Specifically, it imposed fixed ceilings of 130,400 troops (including border guards and air and air defense forces) within the 100-km zone on each side of the border. Each of the four countries would be allowed to retain 3,900 tanks in the border zone (of which Russia would have 3,810 tanks and the rest no more than 90). The 3,900 tanks that China was permitted to keep along the border zone were far above their actual deployment. Despite earlier assurances, the treaty did not commit the Russians to withdraw forces from the border, something they had done anyway.[112]

Similarly, by the late 1990s China's perceived threat from Mongolia had been removed and the border issues settled. The process started in 1991 when Soviet troops had begun to withdraw from Mongolia. Although no information about an agreement on border demarcation is available, the Mongolian border defense administration and Xinjiang's border defense bureau held a number of meetings since the mid-1990s on border management. Delegations from the frontier forces and defense ministries of China and Mongolia signed an agreement on border defense cooperation on November 10, 1999. "Border conflict does not exist between China and Mongolia," said China's National Defense Minister Chi Haotian on this occasion.[113]

Beijing has adopted similar policies toward its other Central Asian neighbors. The first session of a working group on drafting agreements between China, Russia, Kazakstan, Kyrgyzstan, and Tajikistan convened in Beijing on April 15, 1993. Based on these discussions, on March 21, 1994, China and Kazakstan signed a preliminary border accord. A legal definition of the 1,718-km joint border demarcation was signed on April 26. The two parties began boundary survey in early August 1996, following the five-nation confidence-building border agreement signed on April 26, 1996, and President Jiang Zemin's visit to Kazakstan in early July. A "supplementary border agreement" was signed when the Chinese prime minister Li Peng visited Kazakstan in September 1997. Unresolved problems had been settled, and on July 4, 1998, the two presidents signed the border agreement that had "finally, thoroughly and irrevocably" resolved the outstanding disputes over the frontier. Ratified by the Kazak parliament on February 3, 1999, the agreement assigned about 57 percent of the 944 sq. km of the disputed territory to Kazakstan and 43 percent to China. Kazakstan thus became the first of the four Central Asian countries to settle once and for all the territorial disputes dating from Soviet times, if not before.[114]

On September 20, 1996, China and Tajikistan announced that they would step up their military cooperation with a view to achieving troop reductions and mutual disarmament in the vicinity of their common border, stretching for over 400 km. Discussions began in October 1997 and the Boundary Agreement was signed on August 13, 1999, demarcating the sections in the Karazak Pass and Markansu River. The mountainous Pamir section, where China claims a substantial part of the Badakhshan Autonomous Region, remained unresolved.[115] Nearly a year later, on July 4, 2000, the two parties agreed to speed up their border talks and to solve the border problem "without delay" on the basis of existing treaties, while maintaining the status quo in the meantime. A few days later, China agreed to provide Tajikistan with assistance valued at 5 million yuan, following discussions on bilateral military cooperation. China offered additional aid valued at 10 million yuan when President Imomali Rakhmonov visited China in May 2002. He also offered China 992 sq. km of mountainous terrain along the Sary Kol range in the eastern Murghab region of the Pamirs as part of a deal to finally set borders between the two countries. According to presidential spokesman Zafar Saidov, the area is unpopulated, is "of no great value to Tajikistan," and represents only a fraction of the territory claimed by Beijing.[116] The agreement still had to be ratified by the national parliament. It was supposed to pass without difficulty, unlike in Kyrgyzstan, where a similar agreement triggered a wave of protests and demonstrations.

China's 1,100-km border with Kyrgyzstan has apparently been settled, although Kyrgyz parliamentarians still dispute it. Drafting of the border agreement between the two countries began on April 15, 1993, and an initial settlement (covering four disputed sections) was reached on July 4, 1996. A final agreement (covering the fifth section) was reached on October 28, 1998, and was signed on August 28, 1999. Initially demanding 96 percent of the disputed territory, China finally settled for 30 percent. Yet, while the 1996 agreement had been ratified by the parliament (some say illegally), the 1999 agreement was kept secret by Kyrgyz officials. It had been signed by the president before being submitted for parliamentary discussion or ratification.[117]

Only in late May 2001 did legislators discover that according to the new agreement Kyrgyzstan would cede an additional 95,000 hectares of territory to China, bringing the total to about 125,000 hectares. Consequently, the formal border demarcation that began on June 5 was immediately suspended after parliament adopted a resolution halting the demarcation process and attempting to compel the government to renounce earlier delimitation agreements with China. Whereas members of Parliament protested that Kyrgyzstan was sacrificing its territorial integrity in order to appease Beijing, the government insisted not only that the deal was legitimate but also that Kyrgyzstan had managed to keep 70 percent of the disputed territory. As Kyrgyz foreign minister Muratbek Imanaliev declared, "The absence of a legally validated frontier causes various conflicts, confrontations and local military clashes. It is vitally important for our country to avoid such clashes."[118] Earlier, on January 6, a Chinese military delegation presented military supplies worth 5 million yuan (over $600,000) to the Kyrgyz armed forces.

President Askar Akaev also insisted that the 1999 border agreement with China was the best Kyrgyzstan could hope for and was in the country's interest. Based on this stand, the government submitted the agreement to the parliament for approval in May 2002. On May 7, President Akaev warned government ministers not to reveal details of the border agreement to opposition parliamentarians. Three parliamentary committees began reviewing the agreement on May 8 and the Legislative Assembly (the lower chamber) approved it on May 10, under heavy pressure from Akaev and his administration. Both Akaev and Prime Minister Kurmanbek Bakiev personally attended the session and asked the deputies to ratify the agreement. The ratification sparked demonstrations all over Kyrgyzstan and a wave of protests by opposition parties, which claimed that the ratification did not meet the constitutional requirement of a two-thirds majority by both chambers of parliament. After failing twice to approve the agreement, the Kyrgyzstan People's Assembly (the upper chamber) finally ratified the border agreement on May 17. This decision sparked another wave of demonstrations leading to clashes with the police and many arrests. An appeal to the Constitutional Court was rejected on May 21.[119]

China's present concern in Central Asia is not over possible military clashes or invasions of its territory, but over ethnic unrest and Islamic revivalism that could undermine Xinjiang's internal stability. Since Xinjiang "separatist" elements have received moral and rhetorical support and, much more important, material and even military assistance from outside, Xinjiang irredentism is therefore viewed not just as an internal problem but as an issue of national security. This combined internal-external security threat involves all of China's Central Asian neighbors. Since the early 1990s, Beijing has managed to expand gradually its economic, political, and military leverage over Kazakstan, Kyrgyzstan, and Pakistan, using it to urge these governments to prohibit and inhibit separatist activities and activists directed toward Xinjiang. These policies, however, could not be applied in the case of one country that contributed directly to the unrest in Central Asia in general, and in Xinjiang in particular: Afghanistan.

Until the late 1970s, Beijing did not perceive Afghanistan as a military or even religious threat. Claiming the entire Pamirs in the early 1950s, by the mid-1950s the Chinese conceded Afghanistan's right to the Wakhan Corridor. This was implied by the March 1963 Sino-Pakistani border accord that also fixed one end of the Sino-Afghani border. Negotiations on the noncontroversial, very short (30 km) border delimitation began in June 1963. Agreement was quickly reached on August 2, and the final treaty was signed on November 22. Early on, the Afghans had agreed not to allow anti-Chinese activities to be mounted on their soil. This situation was upheld until the April 1978 coup d'état that established the Democratic Republic of Afghanistan. The new Afghan regime condemned China for establishing diplomatic relations with the United States, for invading Vietnam, and for arming and training "antirevolutionary" Afghan guerrillas and refugees. The Soviet invasion of Afghanistan in late December 1979 increased Beijing's threat perception and overnight created a new front in Xinjiang.

It was this threat (and the Vietnamese invasion of Cambodia) that brought China and the United States more closely together than ever. By 1980, Washington had begun to supply China with a variety of weapons, and an agreement was reached on the establishment of two joint tracking and listening installations in Xinjiang. Xinjiang had become a base for Chinese operations against the Soviets in Afghanistan as soon as they arrived. PLA personnel provided training, arms, organization, financial support, and military advisers to the Mujahidin resistance throughout nearly the entire Soviet military presence in Afghanistan—with the active assistance and cooperation of the CIA. Until the mid-1980s, most of China's training centers for the Afghan rebels were located in Peshawar and along the Pakistani border. Since then, China trained several thousand Mujahidin in camps near Kashgar and Khotan inside Xinjiang and provided them with machine guns, rocket launchers, and surface-to-air missiles valued at an estimated $200 million to $400 million.[120]

The Soviet withdrawal from Afghanistan in 1989 and the emergence of the Islamic State of Afghanistan in April 1992 led to the normalization of Sino-Afghan relations. Yet, the factional fighting, the intensification of the civil war, and, eventually, the consolidation of the Taliban in 1996 brought new problems that directly affected the internal security of Xinjiang.[121] Reportedly, Uyghur militants had been trained by, and fought with, the Afghan Mujahidin since 1986, and Chinese officials say that the arms and explosives used against the Chinese in Xinjiang originated in Afghanistan. Funds for the Muslim resistance to Chinese rule in Xinjiang came from smuggled Afghan heroin. Although Taliban officials assured China that they did not harbor Uyghur fugitives, there is solid evidence about Uyghurs who were recruited by the Taliban while studying at the Dar ul-Ulum Sharia in Kabul and at Kabul University and who joined the fighting in the north. Contrary to the Taliban claims that it lacked outside support, 100 (some say 600) Uyghurs were reportedly helping Taliban Islamic guerrillas in Afghanistan. Tahir Yuldashev, the leader of the Islamic Movement of Uzbekistan, who had fled in early 1999 to Afghanistan, is said to have been training several hundred Muslim militants from Central Asia, including an unknown number of Uyghurs from Xinjiang.[122]

To cope with this problem, Beijing's best and only option was dialogue, rather than the use of force. Suspended in February 1993, relations with Kabul resumed in early 2000 when a Chinese embassy reopened there. In return, the Taliban handed to China thirteen Uyghur rebels who had earlier been given "political asylum" in Afghanistan. Based on its policy toward the other Central Asian countries, Beijing likewise adopted the practical and expedient policy of engagement in its relations with the Taliban. On September 11, 2001, the day of the terrorist attack on the United States, the Chinese reportedly signed a deal with Taliban officials to expand economic and technical cooperation.[123]

The defeat of the Taliban by the U.S.-led Western offensive may have solved China's Afghan problem, even as it created another, namely, a U.S. military presence in Xinjiang's backyard. This leaves one problem yet unresolved: Sino-Indian relations. In 1993 and 1996, the two sides agreed to maintain peace and tranquility, reduce tension along the LAC, and respect that border pending a definitive settlement. Adopting a number of confidence-building measures, China and India agreed, among other things, to limit the size of armed forces and weapons within the assigned zones along the LAC and to avoid large-scale military exercises. They also agreed to prohibit combat aircraft flights, opening fire, and the use of "hazardous chemicals" within 10 km of the border. Nevertheless, the precise limits, implementation, and verification mechanisms and procedures have yet to be negotiated.[124]

Notwithstanding these agreements, official Indian sources have reported nearly 200 Chinese intrusions since 1997 and around 100 in 1999 alone, mostly along the Ladakh LAC, where the PLA has reportedly been paving military roads.[125] Consistently denied by China, these reports reflect Beijing's growing concern about the resurgence of Muslim agitation in Kashmir and the possible spillover of instability into Xinjiang. By the summer of 2001, Sino-Indian border talks resumed, and the two sides started by recording their differences over the middle sector of the 4,060-km-long LAC. No real progress, however, has yet been made in the western section (Aksai Chin).[126] By the beginning of 2002, this region had become the most serious threat to Xinjiang's security and, moreover, one of the most explosive regions in the world.

Conclusion

At the dawn of the twenty-first century, Xinjiang has allegedly become more secure than ever. Its Central Asian borders have been officially pacified, reflecting friendly economic, political, and military relations with Kazakstan, Kyrgyzstan, and Tajikistan as well as a joint struggle against perceived threats of terrorism, religious extremism, and separatism. Yet, although it shares, and even leads, this struggle, Washington's intrusion into Xinjiang's backyard is causing great concern for Beijing. In fact, one of Beijing's fundamental incentives for creating the Shanghai Five and the SCO had been to exclude the United States from Central Asia, something it had warned against even before September 11. Afterward, in January 2002 Chief of the PLA General Staff Department Fu Quanyu was quoted as saying, "America is using the war on terror to gain world hegemony. Though China is relatively silent on the subject, it has made clear its worry about America's military penetration of Central Asia, specifically building air bases in Kazakstan and Kyrgyzstan and stationing troops in Tajikistan. All three border on China."[127]

Beijing is concerned less with the possibility of an all-out U.S. military invasion of Xinjiang than with the prospect of Washington using Central Asian bases for a unilateral armed interference in Xinjiang following the precedents of Kosovo, Afghanistan, and Iraq—especially if the situation in the Taiwan Strait deteriorates. In such a case, China's Xinjiang rear is by no means secured. The U.S. presence is not simply a challenge, but also an additional front. Beijing is also concerned that the United States would encourage, incite, and urge separatist movements in Xinjiang to act against China, as it did in the late 1940s. In this perspective, China's Central Asian policy has miscarried. Despite China's pressure and "leverage," local governments—notably Kazakstan, Kyrgyzstan, and Pakistan—have not only failed to deal effectively with separatist Uyghur organizations, activities, and individuals but have also ignored China's protests over their military cooperation with the United States. In fact, they seem to have welcomed the U.S. presence not only for the economic benefits it brings but also as an opportunity to diminish China's (and Russia's) long shadow.

Therefore, despite the confidence-building measures reached with its Central Asian neighbors, Beijing will remain sensitive about Xinjiang not because it maintains significant military presence there but precisely because it does not. China's military policy in Xinjiang conforms neatly to its fundamental strategy adopted since its inauguration, which can be defined as "maximum security at minimum costs." Beijing has invested a fraction of what the Soviet Union and especially the United States have invested in defense. Still, Beijing has managed to accomplish the fundamental objectives of its defense policy, primarily to guarantee China's territorial integrity against external threats and hostilities while being isolated and, moreover, involved in regional military confrontations, such as the Korean War, the Vietnam War, and the war with India. Since the early 1990s, Beijing has managed to reach agreements with nearly all its neighbors involving border settlements, troop reduction, and other confidence-building measures. Relations with India have also improved. Although this is the only part of China's border not yet settled, the perception of a threat from the south has nonetheless declined. In fact, the Islamic threat is now pushing the two countries closer to one another.

Part III

Xinjiang from Within

6

The Economy of Xinjiang

Calla Wiemer

The course of Xinjiang's economic development has been shaped by a powerful confluence of environmental and sociopolitical factors. The region is remote from heavily populated areas, and the natural environment is largely harsh and inhospitable. Well into the twentieth century, Xinjiang was crossable only by camel caravan. The journey from China's heartland took many months and was fraught with both natural and man-made perils.[1] Locals eked out a subsistence existence from the land and engaged in barter trade with passing traffic.

Remote though the location is, Xinjiang's position at the intersecting fringes of three great empires made it the prize in the "Great Game" of the late nineteenth and early twentieth centuries, sought after by the Chinese, the Russians, and the British. China maintained an uneasy hold on the region. The economy was dominated by Russia in the north and Britain in the south. Local Turkic peoples resisted subjugation and were subdued in turn, tensions ever present. Ethnic unrest continues to the present. Minority peoples have not broadly participated in the economic development of the last two decades. To achieve stable ethnic relations and maintain social stability in the future, it will be essential to involve them more fully.[2]

Vast oil and gas reserves have provided a platform for the economic development of Xinjiang under the People's Republic of China (PRC). Extraction and processing of these natural resources have demanded capital investment, both directly and in associated infrastructure, that has in turn fueled broader-based economic growth and the in-migration of labor. The strategic importance of the oil and gas industries and the substantial capital and technological requirements associated with tapping these resources have prompted central government domination over this core of Xinjiang's industry.

Even beyond its control over the exploitation of fuel resources, however, the central government continues to be involved in Xinjiang's economy to an exceptional degree. Furthermore, Beijing has historically directed the settlement of Han Chinese into the region. Through these mechanisms, the central government, in an effort to ensure stability in a frontier area, has more actively asserted its control over development in Xinjiang than in any other region.

The PRC can claim striking achievements in the development of Xinjiang's economy over the last two decades. China's gross domestic product (GDP) has reportedly grown at the phenomenal rate of 9.5 percent per year during the 1978–2000 period.[3] Xinjiang's GDP rose even faster at 10.3 percent per year.[4] More rapid population growth in Xinjiang than in the rest of China diminished the margin on a per capita basis, Xinjiang showing GDP growth per capita of 8.4 percent per year for the period versus China's 8.1 percent. Recent years, however, have not been as good for Xinjiang relative to the rest of China. In the 1990–2000 period, Xinjiang's annual per capita GDP growth was 7.8 percent, while that for China as a whole was 8.9 percent.[5]

Xinjiang's economic achievement stands out more dramatically when viewed against the wide regional variation that exists within China. On a per capita GDP basis, Xinjiang in 2000 ranked twelfth among China's thirty-one provinces and regions, with the first eleven ranking positions being held by coastal provinces.[6] Thus, by the standards of inland China, Xinjiang today is extraordinarily well off.

History of Xinjiang's Development

When the Communist government came to power in 1949, Xinjiang's economy was overwhelmingly agricultural with very little industry having been sustainably established. During the preceding century, periods of social stability had alternated with periods of tumult, economic advance with backsliding. At the time of China's incorporation into the newly founded PRC, Xinjiang, like the rest of the country, faced recovery from years of war and economic turmoil: Extensive irrigation works had been constructed in Xinjiang in the past, but these were now unmaintained; much cropland lay fallow or poorly tended and livestock herds were decimated; nascent factories had closed or been destroyed; most mining activity and oil extraction had ceased; manifold taxes strangled economic incentives; and inflation soared to such a point that a box of matches cost a million yuan.[7]

Since the Qing empire regained control of Xinjiang in the 1880s, intermittent progress in economic development had been achieved. Indeed, the late Qing was a period of notable advance: Agriculture was commercialized, handicraft industry showed healthy development with some larger mechanized factories established, and trade greatly increased under Russian and British influence.

In agriculture, Qing rulers followed a tradition of using military troops to reclaim land for farming and build irrigation works. This custom had originated with the Han dynasty 2,000 years earlier and was reactivated during the Tang (seventh to ninth century) and Yuan (thirteenth to fourteenth century) dynasties, when China again gained sway in the region. It was a practical necessity: The only way to provision an army in so remote a locale was for it to produce what it needed. The practice reached new heights during the Qing. Following the destruction of the Yaqub Beg period, the Qing launched an aggressive drive to expand cultivation. Not only were more than 50,000 demobilized troops offered incentives to stay and farm, but newcomers were attracted from the interior of China with free allotments of land, seeds, and silver tael earmarked for buying equipment and establishing homes. Overseers were stationed, one to every ten households, to guard against absconding. Prisoners sent from other provinces were also enjoined to take up farming. In 1890 alone, some 1,500 convicts arrived.[8]

Progress in agriculture supported the rise of handicrafts. Most important were carpet making, cotton and silk spinning and weaving, alcoholic beverage production, leather tanning and fashioning of goods, and jade carving. Most of this activity was small scale and unmechanized. But rapid growth in carpet exports to Britain and Russia supported factories employing hundreds and even thousands. The spinning and weaving of the region's raw cotton also became commercially viable, to the extent that cotton cloth became Xinjiang's number one export by the turn of the twentieth century. The Qing government promoted sericulture by recruiting skilled workers from other provinces to transfer technology to Xinjiang. Silk fabric, too, found ready export via British and Russian traders, although the quality of production was poor and the scale of operations modest.

Extractive industries made tentative gains under the late Qing. Up to 100,000 tons of coal were produced annually by mines in Urumchi, Hami, Ili, and Tacheng. An end to the government monopoly in jade mining gave rise to private initiatives that in turn stimulated the local carving industry.

To tap oil resources in the Dushanzi field, the Qing government enlisted the aid of Russian scientists, who drilled a single 20-meter well in 1909 and struck oil. Xinjiang's first mechanized well was put into operation, and a substantial investment was made in Russian refining equipment that was installed in Urumchi. But the anticipated returns never came. An uprising in Ili commanded the governor's attention, and, claiming there was "not enough money in the coffers" under the waning Qing dynasty to operate the well, he ordered it closed. The refining equipment was left sitting idle, and the Xinjiang oil industry quickly expired.[9]

China's defeat in the mid-nineteenth-century Opium Wars broadly opened the doors to foreign encroachment, and in Xinjiang in particular, alliances of the foreign powers with Yaqub Beg facilitated entry. Under the late Qing, the Russians controlled trade in the north, centering their activity in Ili, with consulates also in Urumchi, Tacheng, Altay, and Kashgar. The British controlled the south, directing transit from Kashgar toward the Indian subcontinent. By the turn of the twentieth century, there were about 10,000 Russian and 3,000 British traders living among the 2 million residents of Xinjiang.[10] Since foreign traders operated tax free, they were able to crowd out heavily taxed local traders and monopolize commerce in internationally traded goods. By the late nineteenth century, Russian traders had extended their networks into the Chinese interior through Xinjiang, although with the completion of the trans-Siberian railway in 1903, Xinjiang's role as an east-west transit corridor diminished. By the early twentieth century, Russia and Britain had taken control of banking and finance in Xinjiang, running the currency exchanges and issuing bank notes in rubles and pounds.

In the turmoil that surrounded the collapse of the Qing dynasty, 100,000 working people are estimated to have fled Xinjiang for other parts of Central Asia.[11] A process of recovery began in the aftermath, but development over the ensuing decades under the Nationalist regime moved in fits and starts, and it finally ended in a steep downward slide. Four distinct periods are associated with the four different warlords who ruled Xinjiang: Yang Zengxin (1911–1928), Jin Shuren (1928–1933), Sheng Shicai (1933–1942), and Zhang Zhizhong (1942–1949).

The amplitude of the economic waves associated with these four periods shows up dramatically in the agricultural data of table 6.1. Healthy recovery under Yang was followed by a severe downturn under the corrupt and profligate Jin. The enlightened and capable Sheng then turned things around again, and finally, under the stress of world war and civil war, Zhang brought the Republican era to an ignominious close.

Yang's success in reviving the Xinjiang economy under the new Republican government was grounded in policies favoring agricultural development. The main elements of his program were (1) a waterworks plan for all of Xinjiang; (2) land reclamation by the military with incentives to attract farmers; (3) rewards to local officials for achievements in land reclamation and irrigation; and (4) prohibitions against outsiders occupying and renting pasturelands to protect local herdsmen.[12] Yang also organized an effort to promote sericulture and silk spinning and weaving, with modest results. One of the most notable industrial success stories under Yang was a leather tanning business in Ili built by a Uyghur with imported German equipment that employed 200 workers at its peak.[13] Yang also oversaw efforts in minerals extraction and metallurgy, but with mixed results. Following the Russian

Table 6.1

Early Twentieth-Century Agricultural Activity

	Cultivated Land (thousand hectares)	Grain (thousand tons)	Cotton (thousand tons)	Herds (million heads)
1918	802	2,061	10.5	18.4
1933	309	695	10.6	5.4*
1942	996	1,761	14.2	19.7
1949	373**	848	5.1	10.4

Source: Wang Shuanqian, *Zou xiang 21 Shiji de Xinjiang* (Urumchi: Xinjiang People's Publishing House, 1999), pp. 51–57.
*1931 value.
**The source gives this as the realistically cultivated area, noting that most of the 1,210 thousand hectares alleged in the National Bureau of Statistics data to have been cultivated actually lay in waste.

revolution, new treaties were negotiated with the Soviet Union to confer greater economic rights on Xinjiang. However, the Soviet Union largely failed to honor these, instead reclaiming Russia's dominating role in trade and finance. Xinjiang continued to export mainly agricultural commodities and import industrial goods.

Jin's rule was rife with corruption, favoritism, lavish spending on the military, and fiscal and monetary mismanagement. Predictably, the economy foundered and after a few years was in a state of collapse.

The 1930s saw an economic rebound under the capable administration of Sheng and close ties with the Soviet Union. Sheng advanced a high-minded "Eight Point Policy" that called for "1) establishment of racial equality; 2) guarantee of religious freedom; 3) equitable distribution of agricultural and rural relief; 4) reform of government finance; 5) the cleaning up of government administration; 6) the expansion of education; 7) the promotion of self-government; and 8) the improvement of the judiciary."[14] The government undertook major initiatives in agriculture, establishing extension centers with Soviet assistance for dispersing new technology and crop varieties, providing loans to farmers to support investment, constructing waterworks projects, opening public veterinary clinics, and sponsoring reinvigorated military involvement in land reclamation. Small-scale industry flourished in cotton, silk, and wool yarns and textiles; carpets; processed foods; and leather goods. A printing industry developed and materials were published in minority languages.

A major achievement in infrastructure development during this period was the construction, with Soviet loans, of a road from Horgos via Urumchi to Hami and extending from there eastward to the Gansu Highway. This permitted motorized transport finally to replace camel caravans in linking Xinjiang with the interior of China. All armaments and equipment from the Soviets for fighting the Japanese came across this road.[15] The Soviets also participated in the renewed development of the Dushanzi oil field. By 1942, thirty-three wells were in operation and a few thousand workers were producing 7,300 tons a year. Coal mining, too, developed quickly, with production hitting 1.8 million tons in the same year. Many cities built power plants, and electrification spread widely.[16]

But as civil war and world war took their toll in the 1940s, the Zhang administration was caught in the broader national milieu of rising taxes and loose money issuance. The Eastern Turkistan Republic was established in 1944 with Soviet support, and relations between the Soviet Union and the Chinese Nationalists soured. Russian technicians departed, taking equipment with them and leaving the Dushanzi oil field to deteriorate to such a degree that by 1949 only two wells were still pumping. The drop in trade with the Soviet Union caused prices on agricultural products to fall and those on industrial goods to rise. As farmers were squeezed, waterworks fell into disrepair, fields lay fallow, and herds died off.

Between the late Qing and the fall of the Nationalist government, Xinjiang had thus gyrated through three cycles of boom and bust. With its incorporation into the PRC, the ups and downs were to continue, but now more closely integrated with national forces. The first column of table 6.2 tracks real GDP per capita through the political movements that drove economic activity in the PRC. Recovery from civil war and help from the Soviet Union launched a brief period of development in the 1950s. But the decade culminated in the overshoot of the Great Leap Forward and the Sino-Soviet rift, which Xinjiang acutely felt. Three Soviet consulates in Xinjiang were closed, and 80,000 ethnic minority people fled across the border with suspected Soviet assistance. The Great Leap Forward was followed by economic collapse and famine in the early 1960s, then another brief period of recovery. But yet another downturn soon followed with the onset of the Cultural Revolution in the late 1960s. By the mid-1970s, real GDP per capita was mired at the mid-1950s level. Only with the reform policies that began in 1978 did per capita growth take off in a sustained way.

Although per capita output did not rise over the course of two decades, growth in the aggregate took place to accommodate a more than doubling of population (shown in the third column of table 6.2). Underlying this population growth was an active government program to resettle Han Chinese into the region. The resettlement of Hans into Xinjiang helped integrate the region with the rest of China and facilitated the exercise of central

Table 6.2

PRC Output and Population, Selected Years

	(1) GDP per Capita* (mil ¥)	(2) Bingtuan GDP Share (%)	(3) Population (million persons)	(4) Han Population (million persons)	(5) Han Population Share (%)	(6) Cultivated Land (thousand hectares)
1952	170	15.1	4.65	0.33	7.1	1,543
1955	207	13.5	5.12	0.55	10.7	1,690
1960	314	24.1	6.86	1.94	28.3	3,145
1962	217	25.8	6.99	2.08	29.8	3,054
1966	305	26.3	8.38	3.10	37.0	3,330
1969	210	29.1	9.44	3.71	39.3	3,167
1971	249	31.3	10.10	4.05	40.1	3,160
1974	202	29.9	11.26	4.66	41.4	3,143
1975	229	15.3	11.55	4.78	41.4	3,147
1978	292	21.7	12.33	5.13	41.6	3,185
1980	338	22.6	12.83	5.31	41.4	3,182
1985	574	21.5	13.61	5.35	39.3	3,083
1990	810	19.9	15.29	5.75	37.6	3,087
1995	1,286	16.5	16.61	6.32	38.0	3,128
2000	1,699	16.6	18.46	7.50	40.6	3,417

*1952 constant prices.

authority. In 1955, the Han population of Xinjiang stood at just over half a million, or more than 10 percent of Xinjiang's total population (see the fourth and fifth columns of table 6.2). By 1962, the Han population was over 2 million and constituted nearly 30 percent of the total. By 1971, Hans numbered 4 million for a 40 percent share, with this share remaining roughly stable over the years since.

Along with the resettlement of Han Chinese into Xinjiang, the central government further consolidated control over the economy by establishing the centrally administered Xinjiang Production and Construction Corps (XPCC; Xinjiang shengchan jianshe bingtuan). The bingtuan originally came into existence by absorbing discharged military personnel transferring to civilian work. It has made important contributions in agriculture by bringing new land under cultivation and introducing more advanced technologies to the region. The impact of the bingtuan on farming is reflected in the sixth column of table 6.2. Cultivated acreage doubled during the 1950s largely due to the reclamation efforts of the bingtuan.

Beyond farming, the bingtuan has maintained a pervasive economic presence. Its activities range from processing agricultural commodities to producing steel, from extracting minerals to providing electricity and water, and from educating students numbering in the hundreds of thousands to conducting scientific research. The bingtuan fell into decline during the latter part of the Cultural Revolution; its output plummeted from ¥705 million in 1971 to only ¥356 million in 1975.[17] Its share in employment hit a maximum of 22.5 percent in 1967 but fell to 15.9 percent by 1977.[18] Then in 1981, the Chinese Communist Party, the State Council, and the Central Military Commission jointly issued a decision to restore it. Jurisdiction over the bingtuan lay with the Ministry of Agriculture until 1990, at which point the State Council took over direct plan supervision of it.

The era of reform and opening under Deng Xiaoping brought a devolution of economic decision making and the rise of a market system. But the transformation was less profound and sweeping in Xinjiang than in most of China. Xinjiang's large state farms were not atomized in the way the agricultural communes that prevailed elsewhere were. Nor was the dominant extractive sector so amenable to the entry of small business as manufacturing was elsewhere. Finally, Xinjiang's great distance from the coast militated against the infusion of foreign trade and investment.

The economic opening of Xinjiang owed less to governmentally planned change than to the breakup of the Soviet Union in 1991, which led to the establishment of the independent Central Asian republics on Xinjiang's border. Even before this watershed, China had experienced more than a decade of "reform and opening."[19] Prior to the reforms, all international trade had been controlled by the central plan. Provincial-level trade bureaus implemented the plan's directives to procure commodities for export and to distribute imports to end users. Reform brought a devolution of authority, which in turn spawned a proliferation of trading companies differentiated by locality, product specialty, and position in the administrative hierarchy. Progress was gradual through the first decade of reform. In 1980, the value of Xinjiang's direct trade stood at $31 million, with all of it being carried out by a single state-owned monopoly trading company. By 1991, the number of trading companies in Xinjiang had grown only to five, but the value of trade had climbed to $459 million.

The second largest trading entity in Xinjiang after the Xinjiang government is the bingtuan. In 1984, the bingtuan received the right to export its own products and import its own inputs. Prior to this, the bingtuan had provided the Xinjiang government with more than 50 percent of the region's exports.

Xinjiang's trade was largely oriented toward the eastern seaboard until 1988. In that year, the State Council, recognizing the potential of westward trade, gave Xinjiang authority to approve offices of foreign economic entities and opened the Horgos border crossing to entry from third countries. It

Table 6.3

Xinjiang Exports and Imports (in million US$)

	Exports			Imports		
	Total	Kazakstan	Kyrgyzstan	Total	Kazakstan	Kyrgyzstan
1990	335	—	—	75	—	—
1991	363	—	—	96	—	—
1992	454	173	16	297	117	15
1993	495	143	31	427	186	57
1994	576	86	28	464	163	72
1995	769	62	105	659	270	120
1996	550	41	65	854	283	35
1997	665	55	65	781	353	36
1998	808	149	166	724	351	25
1999	1,027	457	95	738	481	32
2000	1,204	449	99	1,060	791	67
2001	668	201	51	1,103	772	42

Sources: Customs General Administration of the PRC, "China Monthly Exports and Imports," December 2001, p. 15; Xinjiang Uyghur Autonomous Region Bureau of Statistics, *Xinjiang Statistical Yearbook, 2001* (Beijing: China Statistics Press, 2001), p. 625; for Kazakstan and Kyrgyzstan, Customs General Administration of the PRC printout. *Xinjiang Statistical Yearbook* data through 1998 are from the Xinjiang Office of Foreign Economic Relations and Trade (MOFTEC); for later years, from the customs administration. Customs figures for earlier years generally fall short of those from the MOFTEC, so the change in reporting source for the yearbook is not the reason for the increase in measured exports. This increase may be due in part to efforts by customs at more comprehensive statistical reporting beginning in 1998 to better capture shop trade. Customs magnitudes are attributed by province according to trade administration, rather than by origin of production or destination of use.

also approved two major capital investment projects: the construction of the northern Xinjiang railway stretching to Alashankou and the expansion of the Urumchi airport. Later that year, the Ministry of Foreign Trade authorized five cities (Yining [Gulja], Tacheng, Altay, Changji, and Kashan) to conduct direct small-scale barter trade with the Soviet Union.

Not until the breakup of the Soviet Union did cross-border trade take off. Over the following decade, trade flows were prone to wild fluctuations (see table 6.3) triggered by the changing policies and practices of the new states across the border.

The breakup of the Soviet Union in 1991 brought an initial boom in trade with the newly independent countries of Central Asia. Existing linkages to state enterprises remained active, and private trading began to flourish within a liberalized environment. Disruption of the old Soviet internal trade framework created supply vacuums that Chinese traders rushed to fill. Official records do not give a true picture of the level of this activity, because much trade went unreported in 1991 and 1992. But in 1993, the situation took a turn. Domestic production was falling off steeply in the new republics amid rising inflation. Credit lines were exhausted as payments fell into arrears. Even the delivery of bartered goods proved unreliable and tensions mounted. Rapid privatization in Kazakstan brought in new business owners who often failed to respect obligations incurred by their predecessors. The imposition of illicit fees and generalized corruption drove up the cost of trade. Relations with China became so strained that in 1994 Premier Li Peng undertook a state visit to the Central Asian republics in an effort to resolve the difficulties.

Meanwhile, Deng's "Southern Tour" of 1992 had accelerated China's opening to foreign trade and capital flows. In Xinjiang, this meant increasing autonomy at the provincial and subprovincial levels to conduct border trade, manage foreign exchange, offer tax incentives, authorize foreign travel, and approve investment projects. The number of companies conducting border trade mushroomed from 5 in 1991 to 346 in 1996. Of these, 104 were established within the bingtuan. Many of the companies operated at the enterprise or farm level. Trade was further facilitated when the number of border and internal customs checkpoints was increased to more than twenty by 1996. A pivotal event took place at the national level when the exchange rate was unified in 1994. This brought a sharp devaluation in the official Bank of China rate, which paved the way for market-based allocation of foreign currency and the elimination of export subsidies.

By the latter 1990s, border trade was becoming normalized. Cash payment supplanted barter, and the large arrears that had erupted with the dissolution of Kazakstan's state enterprises were resolved to China's satisfaction. But erratic policies and practices in Kazakstan have continued to buffet trading activity. In 2001, Kazakstan instituted new customs procedures that led to a dramatic drop in Chinese exports not only to Kazakstan but also, indirectly, to Kyrgyzstan. Whereas previously tariffs on small-scale trade had been imposed on a per truck basis, the new procedures required assessment by commodity, greatly inflating the time demands of inspection and raising the effective tax rate. The Chinese press also complained about the complete changeover of Kazakstan's customs personnel and of "serious chaotic extraction of payments at border posts and the diversion of funds."[20] But practices on the Chinese side of the border also contributed to the decline in trade. Another report in the Chinese press alludes to a domestic crackdown on black market currency trading.[21] By 2002, however, currency practices had reportedly been liberalized with traders being permitted to enter China with Renminbi, rather than having to buy it after arrival from the Bank of China.

Leading Sectors and the Role of the State

The sectoral composition of Xinjiang's economy differs markedly from that of China as a whole (see table 6.4). In 2000, the production of primary commodities accounted for a 21.1 percent share of GDP in Xinjiang, as opposed to 15.9 percent for the entire country. The production of secondary commodities, which includes the dominant extractive sector and a disproportionately large construction sector, accounted for a much smaller share of Xinjiang's GDP, at 43.0 percent versus 50.9 percent nationally. The tertiary sector figures somewhat larger in Xinjiang than nationally. This is not surprising, given Xinjiang's vast distances relative to population, which boosts the share of GDP deriving from transport, post, and telecommunications.

Extraction played the dominant role in the industrial sector with a 61 percent share. Light manufacturing with nonagricultural inputs and heavy manufacturing held extremely small positions, at 1.6 percent and 4.6 percent, respectively. Xinjiang produced nearly 11.3 percent of China's crude oil in 2000 and 13.0 percent of its natural gas.[22] These shares are projected to rise over the coming decade as capacity expands in Xinjiang and yields decline in mature fields elsewhere in China. Xinjiang also has substantial reserves of coal and such nonferrous metals as copper and nickel. Large mineral deposits and the infrastructure projects now underway to develop them ensure that extractive industries will remain the key to Xinjiang's economic future.

When the central government launched its "Develop the West" (*xibu da kaifa*) initiative in September 2001, it gave a significant boost to the development of infrastructure in Xinjiang.[23] The "west" comprises twelve provincial-level administrative districts, plus the bingtuan separately identified.[24] The premier project for Xinjiang under this initiative is the 4,200-kilometer natural gas pipeline that will extend across the country to a terminus at Shanghai. This project, like oil and gas production in Xinjiang generally, comes under the domain of PetroChina. PetroChina was established as a joint stock company in 1999 with initial public offerings on the New York and Hong Kong stock exchanges, but with the Chinese government retaining majority ownership through the China National Petroleum Corporation.[25] PetroChina sold a 45 percent stake in the Xinjiang pipeline project for $18 billion to a group headed by Royal Dutch Shell, thus making this pipeline China's largest foreign-invested project.[26]

Through PetroChina, the Chinese government has maintained its dominance over the oil and gas industry in Xinjiang. Yet, local interests are also involved. The Xinjiang Uyghur Autonomous Region Petroleum Management Bureau stands out as Xinjiang's largest industrial enterprise in terms of revenue, which reached ¥14.9 billion in 1999. The third- and fourth-ranked en-

Table 6.4

Sectoral Shares, 2000, in Percent of GDP (in percent of industry)

	Xinjiang	China
Primary	21.1	15.9
Secondary	43.0	50.9
Industry, of which:*	30.9	44.3
Light: agricultural inputs	(11.6)	(24.3)
Nonagricultural inputs	(1.6)	(13.2)
Heavy: extractive	(61.0)	(12.4)
Raw materials processing	(21.2)	(24.5)
Manufacturing	(4.6)	(25.7)
Construction	12.1	6.6
Tertiary	35.9	33.2
Transport/Post/Telecom	8.9	5.5
Trade/Catering	8.7	8.2
Total	100.0	100.0

Sources: Xinjiang Uyghur Autonomous Region Bureau of Statistics, *Xinjiang Statistical Yearbook, 2001* (Beijing: China Statistics Press, 2001), pp. 37, 408; and National Bureau of Statistics, *China Statistical Yearbook, 2001* (Beijing: China Statistics Press, 2001), pp. 49, 410.

*For the subsectors of industry, shares are calculated based on a subset of enterprises for which sectoral data are available; this subset accounts for 85.4 percent of all industrial value added for Xinjiang and 64.2 percent for all China.

terprises were also in the oil industry, namely, the Xinjiang Tarim Petroleum Exploration and Development Command Post (¥4.2 billion in revenues) and the Tuha Oil Field Exploration and Development Command Post (¥3.1 billion).[27] Opportunities for private firms to enter the industry are also opening up. According to the *South China Morning Post*, Xinjiang's "richest man," Sun Guangxin, who made his fortune as a property developer, is planning to invest ¥8 billion in a venture to truck liquid natural gas to coastal China, beating the PetroChina pipeline in delivering product to this market.[28]

The Xinjiang government receives tax payments from the central government's operations in the oil and gas industries. The local economy also benefits indirectly from the employment created by the energy industry and from Beijing's support for infrastructure development, plus the multiplier effects that follow from these. Still, profits from the mineral and energy sector in Xinjiang accrue in significant measure to the central government rather than to the region.

The economic ties linking Xinjiang and the central government remain stronger than for other provinces. One reflection of this is the exceptionally high share of investment in capital construction in Xinjiang that originates with the central government, that is, 59.7 percent for Xinjiang versus 32.0 percent for China as a whole in 2000.[29] The same pattern of state domination

Table 6.5

Net Resource Inflows, in Billion ¥ (in percent of GDP)

	(1) GDP	(2) Final Consumption	(3) Capital Formation	(4) Net Inflow (2) + (3) − (1)	(5) Fiscal Subsidy	(6) Foreign Capital*
1981– 1985	40.52	32.43 (80.0)	19.14 (47.2)	11.05 (27.3)	7.49 (18.4)	0.09 (0.2)
1986– 1990	96.17	70.87 (73.7)	48.75 (50.7)	23.45 (24.4)	12.20 (12.6)	0.99 (1.0)
1991– 1995	274.26	164.11 (59.8)	173.58 (63.3)	63.42 (23.1)	16.60 (6.0)	10.84 (4.0)
1996	91.21	57.97 (63.6)	45.70 (50.1)	12.45 (13.6)	5.91 (6.5)	2.21 (2.4)
1997	105.01	64.03 (61.0)	56.49 (53.8)	15.50 (14.8)	6.84 (6.5)	0.72 (0.7)
1998	111.67	67.72 (60.6)	68.58 (61.4)	24.64 (22.1)	8.01 (7.2)	1.34 (1.2)
1999	116.86	74.52 (63.8)	58.16 (49.8)	15.82 (13.5)	9.40 (8.0)	1.16 (1.0)
2000	136.43	89.99 (66.0)	59.07 (43.3)	12.63 (9.3)	11.90 (8.7)	0.16 (0.1)

Sources: Xinjiang Glorious 50 Years, vol. 2 (Urumqi: Xinjiang People's Publishers, 1999), pp. 17, 34, 36, 128, 258; and Xinjiang Uyghur Autonomous Region Bureau of Statistics, *Xinjiang Statistical Yearbook, 2001* (Beijing: China Statistics Press, 2001), pp. 18, 44, 235 (hereafter *XSY 2001*).

*U.S. dollar values are converted to Renminbi at the current exchange rate. See *XSY 2001*, p. 586.

is to be found in the value of gross industrial output: The state share in Xinjiang in 2000 was 77.2 percent while the national figure was only 47.3 percent.[30] Xinjiang has lagged far behind the rest of China in the development of small-scale private industry. In 1999, individually owned firms (*getihu*) accounted for just 6.7 percent of industrial output in Xinjiang, whereas nationally their share reached 18.2 percent.[31]

It is difficult to gauge the extent to which Xinjiang benefits or suffers economically from its strong ties to the central government. A summary measure may be found in the accounting balance between expenditures on final consumption and capital formation, on the one hand, and GDP produced in Xinjiang, on the other hand. The difference equals the net resource inflow from outside the province. Table 6.5 indicates that net inflows to Xinjiang over the last two decades have been huge. Expenditures exceeded

Xinjiang's GDP by ¥12.6 billion in 2000 and by ¥12 billion to ¥19 billion for each year going back to 1993. In 2000, only four provinces—Guizhou, Beijing, Yunnan, and Shaanxi—received larger net transfers; in 1999, only Beijing and Guizhou did; and in 1998, no other province received a larger transfer than Xinjiang.[32] Overall, during the period 1981 to 1995, the transfers amounted to well in excess of 20 percent of GDP. In the late 1990s, though, the size of the transfer relative to GDP declined.

The fifth column of the table shows that only a part of the transfer is explicit in the government budget. The explicit fiscal subsidy has increased in recent years, even as the overall magnitude of the resource transfer has shrunk. Apart from the fiscal subsidy, most transfers take the form of funds received by Xinjiang's state enterprises, either as loans or as budgetary allocations.[33] Foreign capital inflows account for only a tiny component of the overall transfer.

Resource inflows to Xinjiang have supported extremely high ratios of capital formation to GDP, exceeding 50 percent for the most part. By contrast, capital formation rates for China as a whole have been on the order of 35 to 40 percent.[34]

The center's major role in Xinjiang's economy is a natural consequence of the province's enormous oil and gas reserves and the large investments required for exploration, production, and transport to market. The state's major role in agriculture has analogous causes, namely, the investment and managerial demands of irrigating vast tracts of desert and mobilizing the immigrant labor required to bring these tracts of reclaimed land under cultivation. Yet, even beyond the extractive and agricultural sectors, Xinjiang's economy still shows exceptional dominance by the state. The explanation for this must lie not only in the center's active contribution to building industry in Xinjiang but also in the weakness of local entrepreneurial activity. The extent of this problem will emerge more clearly from the following section on employment, particularly the discussion of the relationship between self-employment and ethnicity.

Income Distribution and Employment

Xinjiang differs strikingly from other provinces in its low disparity between rural and urban levels of consumption. Xinjiang's ratio of urban to rural per capita consumption in 2000 was 2.2 versus 3.5 for China as a whole, ranking it twenty-ninth among thirty-one provinces and regions.[35] This relative equality is achieved through a combination of affluence in the rural areas and extremely low living standards in the cities. For rural consumption, Xinjiang ranks near the national mean at twelfth, but for urban consumption it drops to twenty-ninth place.

The explanation for this low urban-rural disparity lies in developmental features particular to Xinjiang. Farming in Xinjiang is relatively large scale, mechanized, and commercially oriented. Cotton accounts for the largest share of sown acreage at about 30 percent, with wheat a close second. Roughly two-thirds of the land now under cultivation was reclaimed only in the 1950s and 1960s.[36] The subsistence farming that characterizes much of China is not the norm in Xinjiang. In 2000, Xinjiang's agricultural output per worker ranked fifth among provinces and was more than double the national average.[37] Also in contrast to the rest of China, a relatively large share of Xinjiang's population resides in urban areas, 50 percent of the total versus 30 percent for China as a whole. Thus, whereas surplus labor in China as a whole is dispersed in the countryside and blocked from migrating to the urban areas, Xinjiang's cities have absorbed more workers in low-productivity jobs.

Although economic disparity between urban and rural populations is exceptionally low in Xinjiang, there exists a strong pattern of disparity related to ethnicity. Han Chinese tend to be concentrated in more economically developed areas, whereas Turkic peoples predominate in poorer regions. Data for 1998 by county on both GDP per capita and the percentage of non-Han people in the population permit a regression estimation of the relationship.[38] The share of population engaged in agriculture is included as a control variable in the regression since one expects GDP per capita to be lower in agricultural counties quite apart from any influence of ethnicity. The sample numbers eighty-two counties of Xinjiang's total eighty-five.[39]

The estimated equation is as follows:

$$GDP\ per\ capita = ¥8531 - ¥44\ (non\text{-}Han\ share) - ¥25\ (agricultural\ share)$$
$$(7.8) \qquad\qquad (14.2)$$

where the numbers in parentheses are standard errors. The t-statistic for the non-Han share coefficient is −5.7, which is significant at the 1 percent level. The agricultural share coefficient is −1.8, which is significant at the 10 percent level. For a given agricultural share in a county's population, every percentage point increase in the non-Han share in population is associated with an expected decrease in GDP per capita of ¥44. For example, take a county with 50 percent of its population in agriculture. If the non-Han share of its population were 25 percent, predicted GDP per capita would be ¥7,306 per year. However, if the non-Han share of the population were 75 percent, predicted GDP per capita would drop to ¥5,106. Because the non-Han population also tends to be more concentrated in agricultural counties, the actual disparity between Han and non-Han localities is greater than reflected in the

Table 6.6

Employment by Ownership Type (in thousands)*

	1995 Xinjiang	2000 Xinjiang	2000 PRC**
Total	6,622	6,725	629,789
	(100.0)	(100.0)	(100.0)
Urban	3,497	3,184	150,166
	(52.8)	(47.3)	(23.8)
State	2,820	2,234	81,018
	80.6	70.2	54.0
Collective	303	156	14,994
	8.7	4.9	10.0
Corp/Share/Joint	15	199	13,406
	0.4	6.3	8.9
Private	68	171	12,679
	1.9	5.4	8.4
Foreign	20	14	6,425
	0.6	0.4	4.3
Self-employed	270	409	21,361
	7.7	12.8	14.2
Rural	3,125	3,541	479,623
	(47.2)	(52.7)	(76.2)
Township/Village	500	806	128,168
	16.0	22.8	26.7
Private	23	52	11,387
	0.7	1.5	2.4
Self-employed	216	198	29,339
	6.9	5.6	6.1
Bingtuan	1,065	926	
	(16.1)	(13.8)	
Self-employed	64	122	
	6.0	13.2	

Sources: National Bureau of Statistics (NBS), *China Statistical Yearbook, 2001* (Beijing: China Statistics Press, 2001), pp. 110–111 (hereafter *CSY 2001*); and NBS, *China Statistical Yearbook, 1996* (Beijing: China Statistics Press, 1996), pp. 90–91.

*Numbers in parentheses indicate percent of total; numbers in italic indicate percent of urban/rural/bingtuan.

**The PRC figures used are sums across provinces. The figure thus derived for total employment is about 10 percent less than the reported national total, and for urban employment the gap is about 30 percent. The yearbook notes that this is due to adjustment "in accordance with the data obtained from the sample surveys on population changes" (*CSY 2001*, p. 107). This adjustment is applied to the total and urban and rural subtotals only and not attributed by ownership category.

ethnicity coefficient alone, although the agriculture-based disparity exists apart from any ethnicity factor.

Reforms shaped earnings and employment patterns to an increasing degree through the late 1990s. The state sector, traditionally the source of the highest wages and benefits, has scaled back while a burgeoning private sector offers a new but uncertain path to riches. Xinjiang's economy began this transition from a more urbanized and state-dominated base than the rest of China and has proceeded with a lag, as shown in table 6.6.

Between 1995 and 2000, the state sector in Xinjiang shed nearly 600,000 jobs, and its share in overall urban employment dropped from 80.6 percent to 70.2 percent. However, this remained well above the state share of urban employment nationally, which stood at 54 percent. Employment in the collective sector also fell, but Xinjiang's share in this sector was always below the national average. In contrast, urban private and self-employment grew rapidly, as did employment in corporate and share-holding forms of business where the latter are often reorganized state enterprises in which the state continues to hold a majority stake. But employment in foreign-invested firms declined and continues to play a minuscule role that contrasts with its more prominent place nationally. The rural economy saw a gain in private non-self-employment but a slight decline in self-employment. Taken together, all forms of private employment in Xinjiang lagged behind national levels.

As with the state sector broadly, the bingtuan saw a radical employment reduction between 1995 and 2000, with 140,000 jobs, or 13 percent of its labor force, cut. This followed prior reductions from a 1992 peak employment of 1.12 million workers.[40] Some of the dismissed workers have returned to home provinces elsewhere; others have gone into retirement or become unemployed, often in the guise of early retirement; and still others have found work in the expanding private sector. Some of the shift to effective private employment has taken place within the bingtuan itself. By 2000, 13.2 percent of the bingtuan labor force was identified as self-employed, with most of these workers having transitioned out of formal bingtuan jobs and others being family members of bingtuan employees.

Han Chinese have disproportionately commandeered the preferred jobs in "staff and worker" (zhigong) positions in state and collective units. This class of employment in 2000 covered 59.9 percent of all nonagricultural jobs and 18.7 percent of agricultural jobs for 36.9 percent of the combined total.[41] The non-Han share in this employment was only 30.1 percent, barely half of its 59.4 percent share in the population.[42] To some extent, this differential might be explained by a lower share for non-Hans in the labor force than in the population due to their higher birth rate and hence younger age profile and to the higher rate of in-migration for working-age Hans. Hans are also more concentrated in urban areas where "staff and worker" employment is generally located. These factors would account, in part, for the lower share of non-Hans in "staff and worker" jobs but not to the extreme observed.

Table 6.7

Self-employment by Ethnicity
(in number of self-employed businesses [*getihu*] per thousand population)

	Han	Non-Han	Uyghur	Hui	Mongol	Kazak	Kyrgyz	Other
Overall	25.33	14.81	15.99	27.48	3.89	2.86	4.25	20.53
Agriculture	0.00	0.01	0.00	0.02	0.00	0.00	0.00	0.01
Extractive	0.01	0.01	0.01	0.56	0.02	0.00	0.00	0.00
Manufacturing	2.79	1.71	2.02	4.13	0.31	0.18	0.38	3.15
Construction	0.07	0.04	0.06	0.01	0.01	0.00	0.00	0.06
Transport/Storage	2.39	0.80	0.82	1.81	0.34	0.15	0.29	1.09
Commerce/ Catering	15.31	10.82	11.42	22.03	2.56	2.42	3.41	13.89
Social Services	4.27	1.29	1.51	1.62	0.60	0.07	0.14	1.92
Other	0.49	0.15	0.15	0.24	0.05	0.03	0.02	0.48

Sources: Li Zhenyang, Li Shengyou, and Zhong Wenyu, *Zou Xiang Quanmian Zhenxing de Xuanze: Xinjiang Geti Siying Jingji Fazhan Yanjiu* (Urumchi: Xinjiang University Press, 1998), pp. 129, 131; and *Xinjiang Glorious 50 Years,* vol. 2 (Urumchi: Xinjiang People's Publishers, 1999), pp. 43–44.

Further underscoring the difficulty experienced by non-Hans in gaining access to more remunerative and prestigious positions, non-Hans fill 46.1 percent of "staff and worker" jobs in local agencies, but only 11 percent of central agency posts.[43]

Increasingly, however, the path to economic success is shifting to outside the state sector. Table 6.7 indicates the wide differences among Xinjiang's ethnic groups with respect to entrepreneurial activity. With the exception of the Hui, minorities are less inclined toward self-employment than Han Chinese. Commerce and catering dominate self-employment generally, but these areas have become special showcases for Hui business acumen. Cultural factors play a role in small-business achievement. And to some extent, success breeds success as access to a network of self-employed family and friends facilitates new start-up businesses. But factors beyond the control of minority groups can also encourage or impede entry into self-employment. Notwithstanding Hui achievements, minorities tend to be more intimidated by the process of securing licenses and approvals and to have greater difficulty obtaining financing.

Official figures on unemployment in China are not very revealing of actual circumstances. Nevertheless, the fact that for Xinjiang the reported figure of 3.8 percent in 2000 exceeded the national figure of 3.1 percent may be suggestive of a problem that is more severe in Xinjiang than elsewhere.[44] China's reported unemployment rates pertain only to the officially registered unemployed. People forced into early retirement or laid off with continued benefits (even benefits that exist only in principle) are not counted among the unemployed, nor are many individuals who are not working and wish to do so but do not register as unemployed. Clearly, then, true unemployment rates are much higher than those officially reported.

In some respects, Xinjiang may be better able to cope with the dislocations of reform than other parts of China. It is already more urbanized than the rest of China and has a more productive agricultural sector; therefore it faces less pent-up pressure to absorb surplus labor from the countryside. It possesses vast mineral and hydrocarbon resources that are still waiting to be fully exploited. Its position on the border of the newly independent states to its west may offer potential for trade growth, especially if transit trade to Europe and the Middle East can be developed. However, prospects will depend on whether these states are willing to liberalize their policies and provide a more hospitable economic environment for transit. The next section addresses these issues.

Foreign Trade and Investment[45]

Beijing's official line on Xinjiang's development strategy makes much of its "locational advantage." Given the complementarity in resource endowments between China and its neighbors in Central Asia, there is great potential for the expansion of trade. Moreover, beyond the opportunities for direct trade, the legacy of the Silk Road conjures up visions of transit trade. Thus far, however, progress in developing regional trade has been erratic and, overall, modest. The main stumbling block has been the reluctance of Xinjiang's principal trade partner, neighboring Kazakstan, to establish supportive policies and institutions. The freight-handling capacity at the rail pass with Kazakstan in 2000 fell short of that achieved in the late Qing dynasty at this border crossing.[46]

Xinjiang's ratio of two-way trade to GDP in 2000 was 15.7 percent. For China as a whole, the ratio was 43.9 percent.[47] Some circumspection is in order in assessing these figures. Besides the usual caveats that apply to Chinese economic statistics, widespread customs evasion in Xinjiang's informal border trade biases its trade ratio downward relative to that of the rest of the country. Estimates for the late 1990s suggest that if such unreported trade were incorporated into the figure, the trade ratio would rise by several percentage points.[48] This still leaves the ratio low by Chinese standards, and even lower by the standards of such heavy trading nations as Indonesia, at 69.2 percent, or South Korea, at 85.7 percent, not to mention the standards of an entrepôt such as Xinjiang aspires to become, like Hong Kong, at 295.1

percent.[49] Even Kazakstan, at 99.2 percent, and Kyrgyzstan, at 83.9 percent, have much higher trade ratios, although most of this trade is with Russia and reflects the legacy of internal specialization in production that characterized the Soviet Union.[50]

Xinjiang borders eight countries: Mongolia, Russia, Kazakstan, Kyrgyzstan, Tajikistan, Afghanistan, Pakistan, and India. Mountainous terrain and harsh climate limit trade along the southern borders. The border with Russia is very short, so that most of Xinjiang's trade with Russia flows indirectly through Kazakstan. The Mongolian border extends at length across northern China, permitting more convenient access than through Xinjiang to China's major economic hubs. Thus, the main focus of Xinjiang's current and potential border trade is on Kazakstan and, to a lesser extent, Kyrgyzstan. According to Chinese customs statistics for 2000, the former accounted for 52.1 percent of Xinjiang's two-way trade and the latter for 7.6 percent. Russia claimed 3.0 percent; Pakistan, India, and Afghanistan together a mere 1.7 percent; Tajikistan, Uzbekistan, and Turkmenistan together 1.0 percent; and Mongolia 0.3 percent. The remaining balance of 34.3 percent was with nonneighboring non-Central Asian countries.[51]

Kyrgyzstan was the first of the former Soviet republics to join the World Trade Organization, testament to its liberal trade orientation. But it is a small country with limited natural resources, and its border crossings with China lie at treacherous elevations prone to extreme cold, heavy snows, and avalanches. Nonetheless, both governments envision joining Kashgar and Jalal-Abad by means of a new railroad line through the Turugart Pass. In June 2001, they joined with Uzbekistan to sign an agreement to construct this line. But the phenomenal cost of building this railroad, at an estimated $3 billion to $5 billion for a 570-km stretch, viewed against the modest projected demand for transport services has led outside analysts to conclude the project is not economically viable.[52] However, the governments of China and Kyrgyzstan evaluate this project according to a different calculus, one that emphasizes the economic development the new rail line might bring to poor border regions. The line would boost Kashgar's role as a trading hub, since it would link that city with the fertile and densely populated Ferghana Valley, which straddles Kyrgyzstan, Uzbekistan, and Tajikistan. It would also tie up with the Karakoram Highway that runs south from Kashgar into Pakistan and provides a connection to the port city of Karachi on the Bay of Bengal. Looking northward, Kyrgyzstan sees the railroad as providing a connection with Siberia through the Altay Shan, yielding a route north that would circumvent Kazakstan.

Would a rail link from Kashgar through Kyrgyzstan to Uzbekistan offer China an alternative route to Europe, one that bypasses the bureaucratic snarl entailed by transit through Kazakstan and Russia? The problem is the Caspian Sea. This can be crossed by unloading cargo onto ships and reloading onto trains on the other side, a cumbersome procedure. The only ways to circumvent the Caspian are either to go south through Turkmenistan and Iran or north through the same countries that impede transit on the existing rail passage. Thus, the Kashgar-Jalal-Abad rail line will probably not compete with the existing "second Eurasian land bridge" that stretches from Lianyungang on the Pacific via Urumchi, Kazakstan, and Russia to Rotterdam on the Atlantic. Completed in 1990, this route has so far failed to provide ready transport between Europe and China due to poor administration. Traded goods that move between Xinjiang and Europe generally ship by sea, connecting to land transport to make the journey across China. Trucks through Central Asia reach Europe more quickly but at a significantly higher cost, again due to poor management.

Most freight that crosses the border by rail at Ala Pass is local, between Kazakstan and China. But management problems are rife even on this scale. China accuses Kazakstan of imposing high and nontransparent taxes and fees on traded goods. It also complains of inspection irregularities, delays at the border crossing, and police interference in railroad affairs. For its part, Kazakstan objects to the high charges that the Chinese Beijing Railway imposes on goods shipped across the Ala-Urumchi link. The Chinese side responds that Kazakstan must provide better disclosure of its pricing standards before lower rates can be negotiated. Besides all the administrative problems in transporting goods by rail between Kazakstan and China, there is also the technical problem presented by differing track gauges, which requires the maintenance of costly equipment for the changing of bogies at the border.

Most goods shipped from Kazakstan to China move by rail, with empty carriages returning. Most goods shipped from China to Kazakstan go by road over the Horgos Pass, with empty trucks returning. Inefficient management may be partly to blame for this situation, but the nature of the goods and transactions involved also provides a reason. China's imports from Kazakstan consist mainly of steel and other metals and oil. Their weight and bulk make rail the most convenient mode of shipping them. China's exports to Kazakstan and thence to other Central Asian republics and Russia consist mainly of apparel, shoes, and other consumer goods that are handled in small lots. Outbound trucking generally operates under Chinese state ownership with transit permitted to interior destinations within and beyond Kazakstan. The exception is that shuttle traders on organized tours are allowed to bring their own trucks into China for return shipping. Inbound cargo must be transferred from private Kazakstan trucks to Chinese trucks at the border.

China's exports of light industrial goods to Central Asia must cater to the ever-changing preferences of the consumer. Trade deals are struck at the Horgos border market and at massive trade complexes in Urumchi and other cities. Through the latter 1990s, some 50,000 "shop" or "shuttle" traders visited Xinjiang each year. Wares from all over China are available in the trade complexes, with suppliers of particular types of products concentrated together to facilitate comparison and selection. Urumchi's Bianjiang Hotel emphasizes wearing apparel and other light consumer goods, and its Hualing Market everything for the home, from construction materials, to furniture and appliances, to all manner of items for daily use. The Hualing Market was built by private Chinese investors. A Hong Kong investor set up a wholesale market for traders in Kashgar, and an investor from China's Zhuhai set up one in Turpan.[53] These are one-stop-shopping installations providing shipping services, customs and commodity inspection, and even hotel accommodation all on site. Venders from all over China exhibit samples and transact business at rented stalls.

Shop trade is generally conducted in U.S. dollar cash. Black market currency trading in Xinjiang long took place with an openness and on a scale not found in the rest of China, although a crackdown in 2001 is blamed in part for a decline in exports in that year.[54] Authorities were so indifferent to the curb market in foreign exchange that a main center of operation was located at the front entrance to the Urumchi branch of the Bank of China. Currency traders even enlisted the services of bank tellers to count money for patrons wary of being cheated. The central government long tolerated Uyghur currency trading even beyond the borders of Xinjiang. Through the 1980s, when black market rates were significantly higher than the official rate, Uyghurs could be seen throughout China offering foreign exchange services. It was so commonplace, in fact, that expatriates referred to these traders as "The Bank of Xinjiang." When queried, Uyghur currency traders would tell customers that the foreign currency was to be used for pilgrimages to Mecca. Following the Renminbi devaluation in 1994, black market prices on the dollar have been only marginally higher than the official rate and street-side currency trading has faded away in most of China. Nonetheless, in Xinjiang the curb market has continued to function actively.

Most shop traders operate on a very small scale. To cover fixed costs and operate profitably, they claim to need a minimum import order of about $6,000 per trip. A high proportion of traders probably operates close to this margin, although at the opposite extreme there are those who deal in the six-figure range. One such successful merchant admitted to declaring only a tenth of his goods to customs authorities, suggesting that official figures on shop trade may greatly understate the reality.

Small-scale traders complain that Kazakstan's overbearing regulations make violation unavoidable. In order to simplify their dealings with officialdom, they rely on trade service companies to make all arrangements. Service companies manage payments—licit and illicit—for visas, trade permits, customs clearance, internal transport, trade law violations, and so forth. By negotiating payoffs collectively on behalf of traders, the service companies gain bargaining power and spread risk. Even so, the overall lack of order and transparency has a very deleterious effect on trade.

Chinese imports from Kazakstan are heavily concentrated in two product areas: metals, which accounted for 76.3 percent of the value of imports in 2000; and crude oil, which accounted for 16.0 percent.[55] Within the metals category, steel was first in value (32.9 percent of the total), followed by copper (22.6 percent) and then aluminum (20.7 percent). Kazakstan has abundant oil and China a burgeoning demand. To meet it, the China National Petroleum Corporation in 1999 paid $320 million for a 60 percent stake in a Kazakstan oil company, Aktobemunaigaz, to gain access to deposits in the Aktobe region. But transportation remains a problem. China currently uses rail transport but has been exploring the possibility of constructing a 3,200-km pipeline from western Kazakstan to Xinjiang. The overall cost for both extraction and the pipeline is estimated at $9.5 billion.[56]

This pipeline project has flagged because the Aktobe fields do not yet yield the volume of oil required to pay for it, while the development of other sources of oil has run into obstacles. Labor unrest, China's failure to meet investment commitments as Kazakstan understood them, and a prevailing mood of suspicion have all hampered the project. Lacking transport, the Chinese have had to sell much of the oil at a loss to a Russian refinery.

The events of September 11, 2001, reshaped the geopolitics of oil transport from Kazakstan. The United States and Kazakstan have signed an agreement to build a pipeline through Azerbaijan and Georgia to the Black Sea.[57] Longer term, there is even talk of a route out through Afghanistan and Pakistan. This breaks Russia's former near-monopoly over the marketing of Kazakstan's oil and weakens China's bargaining position.

Imports to China and exports other than those through shop trade are handled mainly by state trading companies. Only as of 1999 were private companies allowed to conduct foreign trade directly rather than through state trading companies, and even now this privilege is limited to large companies that have secured special approval. However, state trading companies provide their services in a fairly competitive market environment. Several hundred such companies, differentiated by location and product specialty, currently operate in Xinjiang. Still, there is a high degree of market concentration with the two largest of these companies accounting for nearly half of all trade. These are the provincial government's Xinjiang Foreign Trade Group and the bingtuan's principal trading arm, Bingtuan Chalkis. Within the bingtuan itself are many more trading companies that in 2000 together managed exports of $450 million and imports of $303 million, for a combined share in Xinjiang's two-way trade of 33.3 percent.[58]

For the Central Asian republics, trade deficits with China are a source of tension. Such deficits become manifest when shop trade is included in the calculus. The process of post-Soviet industrial restructuring, propelled by the exposure to competition from imports, has caused painful economic dislocations in the region's new states. The sale of mineral resources produces significant foreign exchange earnings for Kazakstan and Turkmenistan but not for Kyrgyzstan and Tajikistan. Whether or not they are endowed with natural resources, however, these states can all raise standards of living and stimulate economic development through trade with China. Indeed, some forms of trade with Xinjiang are symbiotic.

Leather hides and skins are an important export to Xinjiang from Kazakstan, Kyrgyzstan, and Tajikistan, and leather shoes are in turn a major export back from China. As a barrier to the spread of hoof-and-mouth disease, China requires that hides and skins be imported through the Baketu border crossing in Kazakstan, from which the distance to a cleansing facility in Tacheng is just 8 km. The preparation of hides and skins for manufacturing is done in Xinjiang, but most of the production of footwear and apparel takes place in the east of China, where design and workmanship are superior. This industry holds much promise for Xinjiang, given the ready raw material supply and nearby market for its products. However, the border post at Baketu has been especially beset with corruption and in fact was closed down unilaterally by the Kazakstan government for more than a year through 1999.

The new states of Central Asia can use investment inflows rather than exports to finance imports, at least in the short run. In the longer run, they can improve their balance of payments by supporting the development of export- or import-substituting industries. Given its own success in developing light industrial products for the international market, China is in a good position to supply its neighbors with capital goods and technology and has made initial forays in this realm. The food processing industry offers particularly good prospects for investment and the transfer of technology, given Xinjiang's established position in this industry as both producer and exporter. Xinjiang food products sold to Central Asia include instant noodles, granulated sugar, canned beef and tomatoes, fruit juices, and beer and other alcoholic beverages. Xinjiang can ultimately become the supplier of inputs for food processing factories it establishes in Central Asia. One of the largest ventures in this mode is a Chinese-owned tomato sauce factory in Kazakstan. Xinjiang not only provided the machinery but continues to supply the semiprocessed tomato inputs as well. Chinese ventures in Central Asia now number in the hundreds and involve some hundred million dollars of investment capital.[59] In contrast to the high-profile Aktobe oil field project, most of these ventures are small. Incomplete reforms and corruption in the Central Asian states create obstacles for such investment, but Xinjiang businesspeople benefit from affinities of ethnicity and culture to minimize or overcome these obstacles.

China's experience amply demonstrates that exports fueled by foreign investment can drive economic growth. For the nation as a whole, exports of foreign-invested enterprises (FIEs) accounted for 47.9 percent of total exports in 2000.[60] But Xinjiang has not participated in this process. Xinjiang ranks last of thirty-one provinces and regions in the ratio of registered foreign capital of FIEs to GDP. Only 8 percent of Xinjiang's exports were derived from FIEs in 2000. Thus, Xinjiang's efforts to develop exports have benefited little from foreign investors bringing technology and an understanding of global markets.

The most obvious explanation for the lack of foreign investment is that Xinjiang is remote both from the major sources of global investment capital and from the main markets for finished products. Xinjiang's most accessible export markets in Central Asia and Russia do not generate capital outflows to support investment, and third-country investors do not find advantage in producing in China for the Central Asian market. Moreover, both of Xinjiang's main industries—oil and natural gas—are not fully open to foreign investors.

One of the most outstanding FIEs in Xinjiang is the Tian Shan Woolens Company, which got its start in 1981 with an investment of $8 million from Japanese and Hong Kong sources. Tian Shan Woolens expanded rapidly over the years and has been named to the annual list of "China's 500 Best Managed Companies" five times. In 1995, it became a Sino-foreign joint stock company with registered capital of ¥253 million ($30 million). In that year, it produced gross output valued at Rmb 390 million and foreign exchange earnings of $20.28 million. Another successful foreign-invested venture is the Xinjiang Tian Shan Pharmaceuticals Company, Ltd., which uses locally grown licorice root as an input. With investment capital from Japan and Denmark, it has achieved cumulative foreign exchange earnings of hundreds of millions of U.S. dollars. Other major FIEs in Xinjiang are the Xiang Tongyi Food Products Enterprise; the Mei Ke Jia Private Company; the Xinjiang Yida Textile Company, Ltd.; the Urumchi Petrochemical Factory No. 2 Fertilizer Project; and the Tarim Irrigation and Environmental Protection Project.[61]

Foreign direct investment claimed a 66.8 percent share of foreign capital inflows for all of China, but only a 15.1 percent share for Xinjiang.[62] While Xinjiang has benefited little from foreign direct investment, it has relied heavily on foreign loan capital in its development. As a proportion of total foreign capital inflows over the period 1979–2000, loans amounted to just 28.4 percent for China as a whole but reached 87.9 percent for Xinjiang.[63] Foreign loans have funded major infrastructure projects in Xinjiang: the Urumchi-Turfan Highway, the Urumchi-Kuitun Highway, the Urumchi riverbank road, the Tarim Irrigation and Environmental Protection Project, the provincial telephone network construction, the north-south optic cable installation, and the Urumchi airport expansion.[64] Foreign loans have also played a role in the development of social infrastructure through support of projects in education, public health, and technology transfer.

Conclusion

Xinjiang has been pulled along through the broad contours of Chinese economic history over the last century. Yet, it remains an outlier in many respects. Xinjiang ranks at the top of inland provinces in GDP per capita. Still, it has little of the manufacturing base that has spearheaded growth in the rest of China, relying instead on extractive industries to drive its economy. It is much more urban than China generally, and its farms are larger in scale and more mechanized. Rural-urban disparity is narrower than elsewhere in China, but sharp differences in income exist along ethnic lines.

Massive resource transfers from the rest of China have been directed at infrastructure development and minerals extraction. The impact of this on local ethnic populations has been mixed. Better communication and transport facilities confer genuine and broad benefits yet at the same time facilitate Han in-migration. This in turn provides an economic stimulus but gives rise to competition for resources. Construction projects create jobs, yet often these go to Han immigrants rather than local minorities. This occurs in part because locals are not willing to offer their labor at the low wages prevailing and because Han bosses discriminate in favor of workers with whom they share a language and culture. The stimulus from investment inflows coupled with market reforms and the opening of trade have brought entrepreneurial opportunity, but not all ethnic groups have responded equally to this. The Hui have shown a strong propensity for self-employment, but Uyghurs and other groups have not been so inclined. Overall, Xinjiang has lagged behind the rest of China in private-sector development.

Xinjiang has benefited little from foreign investment, and its efforts to develop cross-border trade have brought it up against the erratic and illiberal ways of its key Central Asian neighbor: Kazakstan. Only if and when

Kazakstan develops a more orderly market economy will it greatly enhance Xinjiang's economic prospects.

Viewed from the perspective of coastal China, Xinjiang is extremely distant from the economic heartland and is crisscrossed with forbidding mountains and inhospitable deserts. This image discourages the trade and investment with the West that have so stimulated coastal development in China and even retards close interaction with the rest of China itself. Yet, viewed from a more overarching perspective, Xinjiang stands at the heart of the great Eurasian land mass, at the nexus of the most celebrated trade route in history: the Silk Road. It has the potential to serve as a two-way conduit linking China and Europe, and even the Middle East. Yining on Xinjiang's western border is closer to Warsaw, Poland (4,500 km), than it is to Tokyo, Japan (4,900 km). Development of transit trade routes through Central Asia would not only give Xinjiang better access to European markets but would also enable it to provide trade services for the movement of goods between Europe and all of China.

7

Education and Social Mobility among Minority Populations in Xinjiang

Linda Benson

From the early years of the Chinese Communist Party (CCP) leadership, the immediate aim of educational policy was to create national unity after a half-century of division and to instill a sense of loyalty among minority populations. The ultimate goal of the People's Republic of China's (PRC) educational policy for minority peoples has been to integrate all ethnic groups into a single and unified socialist state. Both of these remain the objectives of minority education today, particularly in border regions like Xinjiang.

From the beginning, however, efforts to provide basic education in Xinjiang faced difficult challenges. During the first years after 1949, the government focused on securing its control over the region. For this purpose, it was willing to leave intact the existing system of separate schools for Xinjiang's ethnic groups. The lack of school buildings, an acute shortage of adequately trained teachers, and the limited availability of text books for all levels made it all but impossible to establish immediately any new regionwide education system.

In addition to these problems, a fundamental issue facing the CCP in Xinjiang, as in other minority regions, was the choice of a language of instruction. In Xinjiang, the numerous languages and four different scripts (Arabic, Chinese, Mongolian, and Cyrillic) not only vastly complicated the task of preparing educational materials and training teachers but also posed political questions. Could national unity still be fostered if each group was to use its own language? Would schools run by educators from local minority groups still provide the same quality of teaching and, more importantly, the same understanding of the region's history and relationship to China as those run by Han Chinese? Would the use of separate languages and schools exacerbate the existing divisions between local Muslims and Han Chinese? Although not articulated in such direct terms, these questions demanded solutions that were politically acceptable in Beijing and culturally acceptable in Xinjiang. Almost half a century later, these issues remain unresolved and continue to frame debates over educational policy in Xinjiang.

As the following discussion of education in Xinjiang will indicate, the Chinese government since 1949 has made considerable headway in its effort to provide elementary education for the vast majority of children of all ethnic groups; progress has also been made in encouraging middle school education, although the percentage of minority students continuing on to middle or high school remains low. Overall, literacy rates have risen, and several minorities in Xinjiang far exceed even the national average in level of education attained by their children.

The government's undeniable successes are tempered by ongoing problems, some of which trace directly to the continued existence of two separate school systems—one for minorities taught in their own languages and one offering instruction only in Chinese. Such a system inevitably gives rise to questions about the relative quality of instruction in minority or *minzu* schools versus Chinese-language schools. Uyghurs and other Muslim peoples link their concern to preserve their cultural and religious identity with the language of instruction in schools. Recent anthropological research suggests that Uyghurs educated in the Chinese-language schools do not attain the same degree of facility in their native language as Uyghurs schooled in their own language. Some intellectuals, therefore, choose to educate their children in the minzu schools. Another reason for choosing Uyghur- over Chinese-language schools has to do with what many deem to be the political indoctrination offered to students from minority groups in the latter, although evidence for this is mainly anecdotal.

The less numerous minority groups of Xinjiang view educational opportunities somewhat differently from the Uyghurs. Thus, the Xibos, Russians, and Tatars not only attain a higher average level of education than the more numerous Uyghurs and Kazaks, but they also exceed the levels of Han Chinese. The reasons for the striking achievement among these groups are not clear. But the following overview of education in the region prior to 1949 and of the evolution of Xinjiang's education system under CCP rule suggests that they may be traced to historical and cultural factors.

Overview of Education in Xinjiang between 1900 and 1949

Chinese sources on the first half of the twentieth century assert that literacy rates among the minority peoples of Xinjiang were very low before 1949. However, some pre-1949 figures suggest that education was available locally for those determined to seek it and that in fact all ethnic groups highly prized it.

At the dawn of the twentieth century, the vast majority of the population was Muslim. Thus, the most common form of education in Xinjiang was that offered through religious schools attached to local mosques. In these traditional *madrassah*, students memorized the Qur'an and learned to read and write the Arabic script. Men and boys who attended these local institutions earned the respect of their communities for their educational attainment, and members of most local-level elites boasted at least a few years of schooling in the urban madrassahs. In the 1920s, some religious schools also began to offer more "modern" subjects, such as mathematics and geography. Local schools that only provided religious education were called in Uyghur "*kona mektep*," while schools offering a partially secular education were referred to as "*yengi mektep.*"

In addition to the new courses being offered at yengi mektep, new secular ideas also made their presence felt outside the school system. Pan-Turkist literature, written in a form of Turkish devised in Istanbul by pan-Turkist intellectuals, began to reach Kashgar by 1915 in the form of pamphlets espousing pan-Turkist and pan-Islamic ideals. This elicited much dismay on the part of the British consul then serving at Kashgar.[1] During World War I and extending to 1922, a school founded in Kashgar by an Ottoman Turk provided Turkish-style education to local Muslims.

Other influences also reached Xinjiang from the outside in the early years of the twentieth century. Although Christian mission schools never played the kind of role in Xinjiang that they did in China proper, Swedish missionaries arrived at the end of the nineteenth century and founded schools offering a European Christian-based curriculum, first at Kashgar, and then at Yengi Hissar and Yarkand. These accepted both boys and girls, and the majority of students were Uyghur. The missionaries also established clinics staffed by Swedish nurses.

The missionaries also brought to Kashgar the first printing press. In 1912, missionaries and employees of the Mission Covenant Church of Sweden (later referred to as the Swedish Mission Society, affiliated with the China Inland Mission) began printing materials in the Arabic and Latin scripts, and some simple materials in Cyrillic. At one point, the press also produced a variety of official forms at the request of the regional government. The Swedish press continued to print both religious and secular materials until 1938, when the mission was forced to close and end all its activities in southern Xinjiang.[2]

The steady growth in secular education at government schools is reflected in the increasing numbers of students and schools in the 1930s and 1940s. A later PRC source acknowledges that in 1937 the total number of primary schools was 215, with 33,045 students.[3] In 1938, the government reported that Xinjiang had 1,540 schools for Uyghurs; together, these schools enrolled 89,804 students. In addition, there were 275 Kazak schools, with a 1938 total enrollment of 14,322 pupils. The government also reported 24 Mongol schools serving 917 pupils, and 1 Hui school with an enrollment of 44 students (possibly low because of the fact that these students could also attend an ordinary Chinese school).[4]

During the war with Japan (1937–1945), additional educational institutes opened, including a school founded in 1941 specifically for Tatar students and a Russian-language school in the Ili River valley. Soviet influence in the westernmost districts of the region increased steadily under the pro-Soviet warlord Sheng Shicai. Sheng, who dominated Xinjiang from 1934 until 1944, promoted education. Partially as a result of his support, secular education became more widely available. By 1942, there were 556 public primary schools with 85,992 students; another 1,883 primary schools taught local minority students who numbered 180,035. Altogether, 266,027 students were enrolled in primary schools in that year. Middle school education also expanded, from three schools teaching 425 students in 1935 to seven with 2,590 students in 1943.[5]

The government of the secessionist state founded at Yining (Gulja) in 1944 also established a number of schools in the area under its control. According to PRC documents, the Eastern Turkistan Republic (ETR) operated 79 elementary schools in its districts, serving 6,200 students. By 1949, the year in which the republic was dissolved, the numbers had increased to 489 elementary schools with 52,719 students, and 30 middle schools with 1,610 students (boys and girls attending separate schools in the latter case). Most likely, none of these students were Chinese, as the latter had fled the three districts under ETR control by 1945. Later, the ETR reportedly founded a school of science and technology in its capital city of Yining, although no details on it are available.

The only tertiary education available in Xinjiang during the Republican period was the Xinjiang College in Urumchi. Foreign residents and visitors to the city did not think highly of the institution and its faculty. Most families with ambitions for their children preferred to send their sons, and a few daughters, elsewhere for further education.

Wealthy families, particularly those with relatives in the Muslim world to the west of Xinjiang, had long sent their sons abroad for university-level education, with the result that a number of the key political and military leaders in the Republican era held university degrees earned in Central Asia and Europe. For example, Mesud Sabiri, of a wealthy Ili River valley Uyghur family, earned a medical degree in Turkey. After returning to Xinjiang, Sabiri founded a school but was soon forced to leave the region due to his involvement in the 1933 ETR. Burhan Shahidi, whom the Nationalist government appointed governor of the region in the late 1940s and who subsequently served as the first governor under the new Communist regime in the 1950s, had studied in Germany. Several leaders of the 1944 ETR, including the charismatic young Ahmet Jan Kasimi, were educated in Soviet Central Asian universities. Young Chinese men and women of elite families also left the region to gain a university education, heading for Chinese cities to the east, a choice also made by a small number of Muslim students.

Generally, however, the political and military turmoil that persisted in the region throughout the first half of the twentieth century prevented the development of a unified school system capable of providing education for the majority of Xinjiang's children. That process began in earnest only after the Communist victory of 1949.

The Xinjiang Education System, 1949–1976

In establishing the regional autonomy system in the 1950s, the PRC gave a certain amount of control over local education to the new autonomous units. However, in Xinjiang the early years were dominated by CCP efforts to secure military control, and only in the mid-1950s did the government foster a regionwide school system.

Education for the Uyghurs and other Muslims in the 1950s was provided in Uyghur-language schools largely modeled on the Soviet school system following a curriculum developed by Uyghur and Russian educators.[6] The basic course of study in these Uyghur-language institutions included four years of elementary education and three years of middle school. None of the schools was coeducational. The 1956 curriculum law required two to three hours of the Chinese language at all schools, that used minority languages as the language of instruction.[7] Teaching materials for most subjects came from neighboring Soviet Central Asian republics and most were in the Cyrillic script, although some texts were also available in Arabic script.

The choice of script for each of Xinjiang's languages was an important matter affecting education at all levels in the 1950s. At that time, a close relationship with the Soviet Union led China to adopt a modified Cyrillic alphabet for its northwestern Muslim minorities, including the Uyghur, Kazak, Kyrgyz, Uzbek, and Tatar. Mongols followed the policy adopted in Inner Mongolia, namely Cyrillic letters with adaptations suitable for Mongolian. These decisions were doubtless driven by politics, but there were practical considerations as well. The proximity of the Soviet republics of Central Asia meant that textbooks and other educational materials could be easily transported from there to Xinjiang, a significant point in an era when the railroad had yet to reach the region (it was extended to Urumchi only in 1962).

But the break in Sino-Soviet relations in 1958 led China to abandon the Cyrillic alphabet in Xinjiang. In its place, Beijing began a short flirtation with the Latin alphabet, which required the preparation of new teaching materials and the wholesale retraining of teachers. Although by 1965 the government claimed great progress toward converting to the new script, the Latin alphabet was never popular with Xinjiang's Muslims, and it does not appear that large amounts of educational materials in the Latin form were ever produced. After the death of Chairman Mao Zedong, the government finally allowed a return to the use of a slightly modified Arabic script (to accommodate Turkic sounds), which remains the official written form for Uyghur and other Muslim minorities' languages.

The small number of Han Chinese in the region during the 1950s were all educated in separate Chinese schools that used course materials prepared in China proper. In 1957, Uyghurs in Urumchi were allowed to attend Chinese-language schools. Some Uyghur parents chose the latter in the hope of ensuring their children's prospects for advancement in the new Chinese-dominated system.[8] In 1958, primary schooling became compulsory, which led to an immediate increase in the number of elementary school enrollments recorded in government reports (see the figures in table 7.1 showing a jump of 239,000 by 1960).

Progress toward universal primary schooling was slower among such nomadic peoples of Xinjiang as the Kazaks and Kyrgyz. As late as 1972, the regional news media noted that the "central task" of educational reform in herding areas was to popularize primary education. In an effort to reach such groups, the government introduced part-time classes and mobile schools that moved with the nomads on their seasonal migrations.[9] This same policy was followed in the Inner Mongolian Autonomous Region in an effort to reach herding families there.

Enrollment in government-run elementary schools rose every year from 1958 through 1966 (see table 7.1). What is not clear from the early statistics on education, however, is the percentage of minorities among the overall student body. Whether or not they were collected, figures on the numbers of minority students were rarely issued in the 1950s. By then, though, many Han Chinese had come to work in the region. Between 1953 and 1964, their numbers had increased from 332,000 to 2,445,000, or about a third of the region's total population. Thus, the increasing numbers do not necessarily attest that Uyghurs and other minority groups rapidly embraced the new educational opportunities.

Advances in providing middle school, high school, and college or university education came more slowly. In 1960, the government reorganized and upgraded the former Xinjiang College, renaming it the University of

Table 7.1

Total Numbers of Schools and Students in Xinjiang

Year	Primary Schools	Students	Secondary Schools	Students
1952	—	307,000	—	16,162
1955	—	365,000	—	28,300
1956	2,000	400,000	71	—
1958	4,434	718,000	110	61,000
1960	4,500	957,000	44	—
1963	3,000	—	360	—
1973	10,051	1,292,000	854	450,000
1975	—	2,000,000	—	—
1983	8,261	1,941,000	2,123	873,657
1984*	8,253	1,962,981	2,143	906,862
1989	9,651**	1,842,100	—	893,200
1991	7,132	1,955,216	2,055	875,162

*Figures are from *Xinjiang de sanshi nian* (Urumchi: Xinjiang People's Press, 1986), p. 569.
**Includes primary and middle schools in 1988.

Xinjiang. In the same period, it established a regional Academy of Social Sciences, which included various research institutes employing both local minority and Han Chinese scholars. But as late as 1964, the number of minority students who had completed any schooling beyond the primary level was only 120,000.[10]

Minority students were also among those attending university classes, although the fact that most teaching and assignments were in Chinese limited their number to those who had mastered that language. In 1965, the Ministry of Education exempted the university's minority applicants from the foreign-language requirement (Han students studied either Russian or English), but they still had to have adequate Chinese-language skills. PRC sources provide few statistics on university graduates for this period, but in 1973 the government reported that a total of 3,700 minority students had graduated from the University of Xinjiang.[11]

Xinjiang's education system shut down during much of the Cultural Revolution period that began in 1966. Zealots from the Red Guards disrupted the economy and attacked religion and minority cultural practices across Xinjiang. Some schools did not resume full operations until after 1976, well after those in other areas in China had reopened. Despite the chaos, however, government reports contend that total enrollment in primary schools grew from 718,000 students in 1958 to 1.2 million by 1973, and in secondary schools from 61,000 students to 450,000 over the same period.[12] Figures for minority students are not given, however, suggesting that the increases may have come from among the Han Chinese who were arriving in dramatically increased numbers during that time.

The Xinjiang Education System in the Reform Era

Following Mao's death in 1976, Xinjiang's educational system once again underwent major changes. Of greatest consequence was a return to the use of the Arabic script for the Turkic and Persian linguistic minorities. This change was most welcomed, but it also brought confusion, suspicions, and resentment. Those educated during the 1950s and 1960s were now literate in a script no longer being taught to their own children. Some minorities came to believe that the shift from Arabic to Cyrillic to Latin and back again to Arabic in 1980 was part of a deliberate effort to divide the generations from each other. In actuality, these changes were driven mainly by China's shifting foreign relations. But the resentment was both real and understandable. The reform era brought the expansion of Xinjiang's educational system at all levels. Beginning in this period, the vast majority of children, even those in remote areas, entered primary school. Adult education began to push the region's high rate of illiteracy downward. But the changes also created new issues for minorities.

The new leadership that came to power after Mao's death acknowledged the need to improve education. In 1985, the national government passed the revised Law of Regional Autonomy, which called on governments in the autonomous regions to eliminate illiteracy, institute compulsory primary education, and, where necessary, expand the use of boarding schools to enable children of herding (nomadic) families or those without a village school to receive a primary education. In an effort to spread Mandarin as the national language,[13] Chinese was to be taught in the upper primary grades. But the new law also encouraged the use of texts and oral instruction in the minority languages. In 1986, the government stipulated nine years of compulsory education, including six years of primary school and three of middle school. Entrance to middle school and to the various types of high schools, including vocational, specialized, and ordinary institutions, required all students, both Han Chinese and minorities, to pass exams, which, in minority areas, constitute one of several obstacles for those wishing to continue their education past the primary level.

Furthermore, in the 1980s schools at all levels began assessing fees. By the 1990s, the fee per semester was 6 yuan in the cities but less in rural areas; fees at the junior secondary level rose to 24 yuan and reached 44 yuan for high school. These amounts seem modest, but they were onerous for many rural families whose incomes remained at roughly half that of urban residents. The financial burden of educating children beyond primary school may have contributed to the drop in numbers of students at the middle school level and beyond that occurred in this period.

While autonomous regions retain the right to establish curricula, the tendency has been toward standardization. Most educational materials for minority classes are direct translations of Chinese-language materials used throughout China.[14] Minority students, however, are required to study the Chinese language, which denies them the option of choosing English or another foreign language as Han Chinese students do. Courses on politics are compulsory for both Han and minorities. In the 1990s, minority students at the college and university level were also required to read the approved history of the Xinjiang region, *Xinjiang difangshi,* and pass an examination on its contents. Uyghur students may question this version of history, which stresses the historical links between Xinjiang and Chinese civilization, but they cannot graduate without passing the examination.[15]

By the end of the 1990s, rising educational levels fed rising expectations, which in turn gave rise to mounting frustrations. Many young Uyghurs complained of the lack of employment opportunities and of discrimination against them by Han Chinese employers. Muslim parents who themselves were educated in the Chinese-language schools (*min kao han*) weighed the relative advantages of that education for their own children. Some intellectuals began to view education in Uyghur-language primary schools (*min kao min*) as preferable, particularly for daughters. For many, however, the choice remains difficult, with urban families still weighing the cultural benefit of education in Uyghur or Kazak against the presumed financial benefit of a Chinese-language education (see table 7.2).

Despite these and other issues attending the process of building an educational system for Xinjiang, the CCP managed to achieve remarkable growth in elementary education. From under 400,000 pupils in 1949, the total school population reached into the millions by the end of the twentieth century (see table 7.1).

In 1990, the national average for years of education was 6.26 years, while the corresponding figure for just minorities was 5.29 years. The national illiteracy rate was just under 22 percent,[16] while fully 31 percent of the total minority population was illiterate. In comparison to both of these national figures, Xinjiang's minority groups have done well, suggesting that the local population has accepted the governmentally orchestrated opportunity for them to educate their children. The single most numerous minority group in Xinjiang, the Uyghurs, exceeded the minority average with 5.43 years of schooling, while the Kazaks did even better, with an average of 6.45 years, thus exceeding the average for all Chinese citizens nationally. The percent-

Table 7.2

Minority Student Population in Xinjiang

	1984	1991
Elementary	1,097,363	1,388,019
Middle School	284,089	353,689
High/Spec School	15,352	24,433
Tertiary	11,200	17,650

Sources: The 1984 figures are from *Xinjiang de sanshi nian* (Urumchi: Xinjiang People's Press, 1986); and the 1991 figures are from *Xinjiang nianjian, 1992* (Urumchi: Xinjiang People's Press, 1992).

age of illiterate Uyghurs in 1990 stood at 26 percent, while Kazak illiteracy was reported as being much lower, a mere 12 percent.[17]

Three Xinjiang minority groups far exceeded the national average in terms of educational level: The Xibo averaged 7.9 years of education and a low illiteracy rate of 6 percent; the Russians averaged 8.53 years, with 7 percent being illiterate; the Tatars exceeded all nationalities, including Han Chinese, with an average of 8.23 years, with only 4.8 percent of the population being illiterate.[18]

In comparison to other minority regions in China, the overall educational attainment in Xinjiang is remarkably high, and the growth in primary school attendance is particularly impressive. Given that many expatriate Uyghurs assert that widespread opposition to Chinese rule continues in Xinjiang, and that Chinese press reports on a long string of incidents suggest active opposition to the Chinese presence, the Xinjiang Turkic peoples' embrace of education appears to present a contradiction. If opposition to Chinese policies is so widespread, then why would so many families entrust their children to an education system that embodies the values and ideology of the Chinese government? Before exploring this seeming contradiction, it is worth examining education at the most local (district) level to gain further insights into how minorities participate in the new system.

Available Chinese statistics give rise to a number of questions. Table 7.3, which indicates the number of students from each major minority group for 1982, provides an overview but does not explain why, for example, the percentage of minority students continuing on to middle school remains relatively low. One factor may be the early withdrawal of girls from elementary school, but crucial figures on the male-female ratios are unavailable. Also, there are no data on attrition or on the number of students who actually complete any given level of education. It is probable that most elementary students from minority groups do not actually complete that level. They may

Table 7.3

Numbers of Minority Students in School, 1982

	Elementary	Lower Secondary	Upper Secondary	University Completed
Uyghur	1,967,410	613,336	208,310	12,676
Hui	1,894,442	1,203,595	458,728	37,709
Mongol	1,163,855	573,875	270,898	18,796
Kazak	351,272	124,781	41,599	2,547
Kyrgyz	38,129	10,533	4,261	302
Xibo	30,589	21,247	9,484	904
Russian	850	824	397	56
Tatar	1,372	842	480	130
Tajik	7,695	2,500	859	65
Uzbek	4,104	2,435	1,276	216

Source: Zhongguo 1982 nian renkou pucha ziliao (Beijing: Zhongguo tongji chubanshe, 1985), p. 240.
Note: These figures include all members of the minority group in China, not only in Xinjiang.

withdraw for financial or other reasons or fail the examination for advancement to the next level.

In an effort to understand this pattern of high elementary enrollments and low middle school numbers of minority pupils, figures for Han Chinese and students at minzu schools were compared in key areas of the region. Table 7.4 presents the results.

These data allow only tentative conclusions because of the lack of detail on school populations at the local level. The usual practice in PRC sources is to cite only two figures: one for the total number of minzu or minority students and one for total enrollment at each educational level. In areas where there are several minorities, however, it is impossible to tell which groups have the higher enrollment. It would also be helpful to know about gender ratios in local-level schools. In predominantly Muslim areas like Kashgar, for example, it would seem probable that more girls than boys withdraw before completing primary education, but these numbers are not known. Despite these limitations, some overall patterns on education at the local level are clear.

One would expect the highest enrollments to be at the elementary level, and such is the case. As summarized in table 7.4, large numbers of minority students enter primary school. Generally speaking, at this level the percentage of minorities attending school matches the percentage of minorities in the district's overall population, a common phenomenon in all official sources reporting on minority education across China. These numbers suggest wide

Table 7.4

Han Chinese and National Minority School Enrollments, Local Level (Selected), 1991

District/Pref./City		Population	%	Elementary	%	Middle	%		% in Middle vs. Elem. School	High School	%
Altay District	Han	221,970	42	22,047	30	11,396	43	Han	38	444*	41
	Min	302,008	48	52,297	70	15,224	57	Min	20	626*	59
Changji-Hui Pref	Han	970,539	74	76,343	61	52,698	77	Han	69	1,815	72
	Min	328,232	26	47,612	38	15,548	22	Min	32	700	28
Hami District	Han	272,311	66	17567	48	14,960	67	Han	85	1,696	64
	Min	142,598	34	19,213	52	7,457	33	Min	39	942	36
Kashgar District	Han	160,500	5	19,855	5	9,639	12	Han	49	262	5
	Min	2,593,600	95	347,745	95	71,261	88	Min	20	4,822	95
Tacheng District	Han	458,416	48	51,677	50	29,343	49	Han	56	—	—
	Min	340,285	42	51,036	50	20,554	41	Min	40	—	—
Turpan District	Han	90,968	19	9,948	17	10,414	100	Han	100	894	46
	Min	357,995	81	57,250	85	13,237	56	Min	23	1,070	54
Ili District	Han	594,800	32	58,200	22	33,800	37	Han	58	1,863	38
	Min	1,239,700	68	192,600	78	58,800	63	Min	31	1,649	62
Yining City	Han	99,592	35	11,589	36	5,842	48	Han	50	—	—
	Min	190,163	65	20,872	64	6,309	52	Min	30	—	—

Source: Xinjiang nianjian, 1992 (Urumchi: Xinjiang People's Press, 1992).

Note: For Urumchi and other major cities, only total numbers were provided for 1991. The same was true of most large and small towns. Yining City, listed above, is an exception.

*Includes all types of high schools in the Altay District.

acceptance of education for both boys and girls. Much greater variation by district can be seen in minority student enrollments in middle schools, where figures from several districts suggest that only one-fifth to one-fourth of minority students continue with their education. Han Chinese students are at least twice as likely as minorities to continue to middle school, regardless of the district in which they live, and in some instances as many as 85 percent of Han students advance to middle school.

Although all districts show relatively low numbers of minorities attending middle school, the drop in attendance varies considerably from district to district. This may be traced to different ethnic mixes or to the degree to which secular education was already accepted prior to 1949. The areas chosen for closer examination include Kashgar, with the highest concentration of Uyghurs; Altay and Tacheng, which have more mixed ethnic populations; and several districts with large Chinese-speaking populations. Figures are also given for the Ili district, the heart of the secessionist movement of the 1940s and the site of the February 1997 incident in which an unknown number of people died.

Education Patterns at the Local Level

Several districts provide good profiles of overall patterns in education. The population of the Turpan district in 1991 was 74.2 percent Uyghur. The only other minority of any substantial number was the Hui, who made up 6.6 percent of the total. Han Chinese constituted nearly 19 percent of the oasis population. In the district's schools, 85 percent of the primary school population were minority, suggesting that virtually all minority children of primary school age enrolled. The pattern in Turpan is unusual at the middle school level, however. While 23 percent of minority primary students continued on with their education, figures for 1991 show that more Han students attended middle school than the number enrolled in elementary school. This is the only district that exhibited such a phenomenon. Presumably, Chinese families moving into the area swelled middle school numbers, but no confirming data are available.

Turpan students who completed middle school could continue on to special technical schools, of which the Turpan district had four, enrolling a total of 1,964 students. Out of the latter group in 1991, 1,070 were classified as minorities.[19] This is about half of the total student population at this level of education, making it appear that the schools serve Han and minority students equally. However, the actual proportion of Han moving on to the highest levels of education is much higher than the corresponding figure for minorities.

Data on the Kashgar district revealed a similar pattern, despite a much higher minority population relative to the Han Chinese. Here, in 1991 the total population of nearly 3 million (excluding State Farm no. 3 and military units in the area, all of which are predominantly Han enterprises) was 92.6 percent Uyghur, making it one of the most concentrated populations of Uyghurs in the entire region. Han Chinese were only 5 percent of the total. The district had 1,119 elementary schools, of which 1,088 were classified as minzu or minority schools. Of the 367,600 children attending these schools, 347,745 or 94.5 percent of the total were minorities, a figure that matches the percentage of Uyghurs in the area. At the middle school level, there were 184 minority schools out of a total of 208, and of the 80,900 students receiving middle school education, 71,261, or 88 percent, were minority. Based on these figures, one can conclude that only 20 percent of minority pupils in primary school go on to secondary school. Despite the concentration of Uyghurs here, this percent is somewhat less than in Turpan. In contrast, figures suggest that nearly half of all Han Chinese primary school pupils are likely to continue on to the next level of education.

Beyond middle school, Kashgar provided further schooling at ten special technical schools, nine of which were classified as minority. Altogether, these trained 4,822 minority students, or 94.8 percent, of the total enrollment of 5,084.[20] It is not clear from the statistics if all of the minority students enrolled at the special high schools originated from the Kashgar area. Furthermore, the very small number of Han attending high schools in Kashgar suggests that many Han Chinese students may be choosing to continue their education elsewhere rather than in this predominantly Uyghur city. Although the number of minorities reaching the upper levels of education is high, there is much room for improvement if the goal is to train Uyghurs in numbers sufficient to guide the process of modernization in the Kashgar area.

A third example is the Ili district, formerly part of the ETR. Unlike Kashgar, with its concentration of Uyghurs, this area on the Ili River has a more diverse ethnic makeup. In addition to Uyghurs, the area is also home to many Kazaks and much of Xinjiang's Kyrgyz population. Here, too, live members of the three nationalities with the highest levels of educational attainment levels in all China: the Xibos, Russians, and Tatars. The Ili district's location on the border with the former Soviet Union also means that the region feels the influence of Central Asian and Russian cultures. And the fact that a secessionist state was centered here in the 1940s further differentiates it from other areas in Xinjiang.

Out of a total district population of just under 2 million in 1994, 66.7 percent were classified as minorities. In that year, there were 775 elementary schools, 424 of which were minzu. These institutions taught 268,054 students, of whom 76 percent were minorities. Of the 172 middle schools, 115 were for minorities; of the 82,505 students at this level, 52,893, or 64 percent, were minorities, a higher than average percentage but less than Kashgar. The percent of minorities in middle school was also relativity high, at 31 percent of the primary school enrollment. Figures for Han Chinese students still show the usual pattern, however, with Chinese still more than twice as likely to continue to middle school as minority students.

In 1994, the Ili district also had four special high school–level training schools with 2,629 students, of whom 1,649, or 62.7 percent, were minorities. The percent of minority teachers in the Ili district was also high: Out of 23,643 teachers and staff, 16,678 (70.5 percent) were classified as minorities. In spite of the relatively large number of minority instructors, the percentage of minority students moving up to middle school is comparable to other areas.

Because of Ili's history as the epicenter of secessionism, minority enrollments in the district's capital city of Yining are of particular interest. Yearbooks indicate that in 1994 the city had a population of nearly 290,000, 65 percent of whom were minority. The city had fifty-nine elementary schools, of which forty-seven were classified as for minorities. These enrolled a total of 32,461 students, of whom 20,872 (64 percent) were minority, fewer than the 76 percent minority students in the district's total schools as a whole. At the middle school were twenty-five schools, eighteen of them minzu, with 6,309 minority students out of the total middle school population of 12,151. Thus, at this level, 51.9 percent of students were minority, again lower than the 64 percent for minorities in the district as a whole. As was true of the district, the number of minority teachers in Yining was relatively high: out of 2,842, 2,004, or 70.5 percent, were minority.[21] Unfortunately, there are no comparable figures for education beyond the middle schools, let alone broken down by ethnic group.

The same pattern is to be found in two districts where Han and minorities are about equal in number. In Altay, where minorities are 48 percent and Han 42 percent, 20 percent of the minorities continue on to the next level, compared to 38 percent of Han. In Tacheng, which is also a rural district, minorities are 42 percent and Han 48 percent. Fully 40 percent of minority students continue on to middle school, but Han students fare better still, with 56 percent entering the next level.

The numbers of minority teachers across the region is high. In each of the areas previously surveyed, minority teachers predominated at the elementary level. The greatest percentage of minority teachers was in Kashgar with 91 percent, but other districts had levels of between 66 and 75 percent minority, except for Tacheng, where the level was a low 52 percent. A large number of minority teachers, however, does not translate into higher numbers of minority students.

Data in table 7.4 support the government's assertion that the vast majority of elementary-age children attend school. However, these figures also show that minorities are less likely to continue with their education beyond elementary level than Han students living in the same district. This situation clearly has implications for the future employment of minorities in better-paying jobs that require a higher level of technical skill or high school–level education.

Teacher Training, Pay, and Conditions

From the earliest years, great efforts were devoted to teacher training for all levels, but the first priority was to staff the elementary schools. As elsewhere in China, large numbers of young people in Xinjiang who completed middle school prior to the reform era were recruited to teach in village and small-town primary schools.

After 1980, the emphasis in teaching training shifted from sheer quantity to raising the qualifications of teachers. In 1990, 72.6 percent of elementary teachers and 45.3 percent of the lower middle school teachers qualified for certification. As a result, recent government reports have asserted that the social standing of teachers in both categories has risen.[22]

Money was also invested in new school buildings and teacher housing during the 1990s. The Xinjiang government announced that between 1985 and 1990 it built 134,000 square meters of new housing units for teachers. Universities and colleges also expanded, adding 370,000 square meters of space. Elementary and middle schools saw the greatest increase, however, with 1.9 million square meters. Teachers' wages also rose at this time, which, the government asserts, improved their social status.[23]

In 1991, the region's teacher training colleges graduated 3,552 new teachers, 1,778 of whom were minorities. Of the total number of graduates, 405 came from China proper while 2,667 were Xinjiang natives. Of these graduates, 3,072 had received financial support from the government, while 480 were self-supporting. Of the self-supporting students, 433 came from inside Xinjiang and 313 were national minorities.

In 1991, the government still assigned graduating teachers to the institutions where they were to work. Of that year's graduates, 75.4 percent were sent to regional, prefectural, and city schools in Xinjiang. Another 180 were assigned to government bureaus in the region, while a small number (1.3 percent) were sent to *neidi* (inner China) to work.[24]

Table 7.5

Educational Expenditures for Selected Areas in 1997
(in millions of yuan)

Guangdong	24,842.9
Jiangsu	18,993.6
Shanghai	12,157.2
Beijing	11,705.9
Anhui	8,061.4
Xinjiang	4,632.6
Guizhou	2,971.9
Hainan	1,639.1
Ningxia	920.7
Tibet	447.9

Source: National Bureau of Statistics, *China Statistical Yearbook, 1999* (Beijing: China Statistics Press, 1999), cited in Robert Perrins, ed., *China: Statistical Yearbook 1999* (New York: Academic International, 2001), p. 257.

In 1993, the government sought to attract more young people to teaching by passing the Law on Teachers, which called for increases in teacher pension plans. Teachers also qualified for special housing allowances and preferential medical treatment. In 2000, the government asserted that the average income for teachers was higher than the average for other professions and that teachers in urban areas enjoyed 8.74 meters of living space, above the average for all urban residents.[25]

Both teachers' pay and working conditions differ dramatically from region to region. In southern Xinjiang, for example, conditions are poor in many small towns and salaries are low. Members of the teaching profession are not thought to make much money, and in the reform era income is a measure of social status. Although no systematic survey on this issue has been conducted, interviews with students in Xinjiang suggest that teaching is very low on the list of career choices. Even students enrolled in teachers colleges choose not to make a career of elementary or middle school teaching.[26]

Ultimately, the recruitment of teachers and hence the quality of education hinge on the amount of money the regional government allots to education. There is much room for improvement in Xinjiang. As illustrated in table 7.5, Xinjiang expenditures on education remain well below many of China's richer provinces, although it is above other minority areas such as Tibet and Ningxia. Whether the government will use some of the income from the sale of Xinjiang's oil and gas to improve education in the region remains an important and unresolved issue.

Boarding Schools

In an effort to provide education to nomadic families and those living in villages with no schools, the government established a number of boarding schools in the 1950s. A Uyghur who boarded in such a school in Kashgar in the 1950s reported that discipline was strict but all expenses were covered by the government and, initially at least, the boarders were well fed. Shortage of funds, however, meant that this student could visit his family only twice during the six years he remained at school.[27] In Kazak areas, many families were reluctant to leave their children at the new state-run institutions.

Boarding schools still existed through the 1990s. In 1991, Xinjiang's Education Department reported 340 boarding schools at the elementary level and 147 at the middle school level, accommodating a total of 126,000 students. No breakdown by ethnicity was given, but presumably the majority came from minority families. As recently as 2000, some families continued to resist efforts to enroll their children in such institutions or withdrew them early from the elementary boarding schools.

Education of Xinjiang Students Elsewhere in China and Abroad

In 1991, eighteen institutes outside of Xinjiang offered special classes for 454 Xinjiang students from minority nationalities. Most of these schools were in north and northwest China, including Lanzhou University, Shanxi Teachers University, and several schools in Xian and Beijing. The smallest number of such enrollments—ten students each—were at Shanghai Medical University and the Beijing Teachers' University.[28]

In 1991, a total of 93 students from Xinjiang were sent abroad for study in Japan, the United States, Russia, Australia, Thailand, the United Kingdom, and Germany. These included both fully enrolled students and those attending short training sessions. Of these, 52 returned to Xinjiang, 8 extended their time of study abroad, and the others chose to emigrate. The same year, 111 self-supporting students also went abroad, studying in the United States, Japan, Russia, and Australia. Figures on the numbers of minority students in any of these categories are not available.

Xinjiang also hosted 22 visiting scholars from institutions in such diverse countries as the United States, the United Kingdom, Russia, Argentina, and Australia. Most came to study languages and the arts. In addition, the region hosted 45 overseas students from a half-dozen different countries, in both the East and West.

Affirmative Action and "Entitlement" Policies for Minorities at the University Level

Beginning in the 1980s, the government sought to enroll minority students in universities in numbers proportionate to, or higher than, their percentage in the overall population. In 1989, for example, the University of Xinjiang enrolled 1,118 new students, of whom 726 (65 percent) were minorities.

By the middle 1990s, however, the university was admitting roughly 50 percent Han and 50 percent minority. Quotas for minority groups were established on the basis of population statistics. Therefore, the largest number of places invariably went to Uyghurs.[29]

Admitted students still had to achieve a minimum score in the university entrance examination before being offered a place. The Chinese version of affirmative action sets the exam scores for Han Chinese and minority students at levels favoring the minorities. In the late 1990s, the Xinjiang Department of Education set a minimum score of 480 for both Han and minority students who graduated from Chinese-language schools. For graduates of Uyghur- and other minority-language schools, however, the minimum score was set at just over 300.

Many Han Chinese resent this policy because it favors minority students. Moreover, since Chinese law allows minority families to have several children but limit Han families to one, Han Chinese argue that the policy gives minority families more chances than their Han counterparts to have a college-educated son or daughter.

Against this, students from the local-language schools who qualify for entrance to colleges or universities within or outside the region must spend an additional year studying Chinese in order to raise their Chinese-language ability to a level adequate for university-level work. As families now pay for their child's university education, this additional year is seen by some as imposing an unfair financial burden. Members of the intelligentsia factor this into their decision on whether to send their children to Chinese- or local-language schools. Clearly, a minority student whose Chinese is already equal to that of a native speaker is at a great advantage in pursuing higher education and also saves a year in tuition cost. On the other hand, study at a native-language school allows entrance into a university with a lower exam score. But the quota system that determines the number of places available to each minority group partially offsets this advantage. Some Uyghur families solve the dilemma by sending their sons to a Chinese-language school and their daughters to a Uyghur-language school, ensuring that their girls can eventually pass on their own language and culture to their own children.

The rising cost of a university education affects both Han and minority students. From around 120 yuan a year in 1990, the average tuition cost rose to 4,500 yuan a year by the end of the decade. In 2000 alone, the cost of university tuition rose 50 percent over the previous year. Considering that the average urban annual income was 5,856 yuan, this is steep indeed.[30] The average cost at the University of Xinjiang was 3,000 yuan a year in the mid-1990s and has continued to climb. University education is thus moving beyond the reach of ordinary urban citizens, and especially of minority students seeking entrance to universities.

The quality of university education is also at risk. During the reform era, pay levels for university professors declined relative to other professions, as did their status. In the 1990s, it was common in Xinjiang for university professors to teach classes at other institutions to make ends meet.[31] Unknown numbers left the profession altogether. Most of those who could afford to remain had several family members employed in the private sector.

Aware of the problems affecting intellectuals, the government instituted a number of changes. Pay increases, improved university housing, and more job opportunities for spouses and children provided some relief. Rules governing change of residence registration were also relaxed, enabling divided families to be reunited. The government reported that in 1990 alone 140,000 dependents of intellectuals, which includes all teachers, changed their registration cards from agricultural to nonagricultural, allowing them to return to Xinjiang's cities.[32] Residence cards were still required in Xinjiang cities in 1996, but in the new economy one could purchase a temporary card for 360 yuan and a permanent residence permit for 15,000 yuan.[33]

Intellectuals also faced new restrictions in the 1990s, when the government reiterated its ban on freedom of expression on certain issues. In 1992, the government banned the works of the popular Uyghur author Abdurehim Otkur, who died in 1995. Authorities placed historian and author Turghun Almas under house arrest in the mid-1990s and strictly monitored his contacts with the public.[34] Thus, gains in housing, pay, and social status for intellectuals were partially offset by continuing restrictions on their intellectual life.

Education of Minority Cadres and Their Changing Social Status

An important task of education has been to train the minority cadre to administer Xinjiang and advance the policies of the CCP there. Because of the shortage of reliable minority cadres in the 1950s, the CCP originally relied on those men and women already involved in local political and military life, despite the fact that some had worked with the Guomindang or had supported the secessionist movements. For example, Burhan, the first governor of the region after 1949, previously served as governor under the Nationalists but was retained during the early years as the Communists secured the area militarily. He was replaced with another pre-1949 personality, Saifudin Aziz. Formerly active in the secessionist movement based in the Ili River valley, Saifudin became concurrently chairman, first secretary, and political commissar of Xinjiang in 1955. Hatewan, a female Kazak appointee to the provincial Nationalist government in the 1940s, accepted an appointment, as did several men of various ethnicities who had filled important roles in the ETR. Notwithstanding these well-placed minority officials, ultimate power in the region remained in the hands of reliable Han Chinese party members, namely Wang Enmao and Wang Zhen. The former held power in the region for most of three decades, while the latter continued to influence events there until his death in 1991.

To ensure a cohort of reliable minorities for visible government posts, the CCP instituted a program of recruitment and training in the 1950s. A number of promising young men were sent to Chinese universities and colleges. Others, who already had some education, were appointed to various governmental posts.

The major vehicles for preparing minority cadres was the Central Institute for Nationalities, which opened in Beijing in 1950, and regional institutes that were founded subsequently. A typical early Uyghur graduate of the Central Institute is Tomur Dawamat, who was elected vice chairman of the standing committee of the Ninth National People's Congress in April 2001. Born in June 1927 at Toksun in southern Xinjiang, he joined the CCP in 1952 and was sent to Beijing soon thereafter. He served in various official capacities in the region before being appointed vice minister of the State Nationalities Affairs Commission, where he served from 1979 to 1985, and then chairman of the Xinjiang government (1985–1994).

Many Muslims in the 1950s and 1960s perceived a "cadre" as one who had "sold out" to the Communists. The fact that successive Chinese governments before 1949 had repeatedly broken promises of fair treatment for the region's Muslim population left residual resentments that carried over to the post-1949 Communist government. The fact that Han-dominated structures—both civil and military—soon emerged as the real power in the region only reinforced the wariness of minority peoples. In the aftermath of the Hundred Flowers campaign, minority cadres who dared to criticize the Communist government's policy on minorities were judged guilty of "local nationalism" and removed from their posts. Despite these political perils, official data indicate that the number of minority cadres (not all of whom were CCP members) rose from 12,841 in 1950 to 62,000 in 1958.[35]

The Cultural Revolution led to a dramatic drop in the number of minority cadres in Xinjiang. From a reported high of 111,500 in 1962 (42,000 of whom were members of the CCP), the number fell to 80,000 by 1975.[36] When the Cultural Revolution finally ended, the new challenge in all minority areas was to rebuild minority cadre numbers.

Between 1978 and 1999, these efforts resulted in an overall increase of minority cadres from 834,000 to 2.8 million.[37] Such substantial increases were reflected in Xinjiang. By 1995, the Xinjiang government reported that 47 percent of all regional cadres, or 269,000, were minorities.[38] Although no figure was given for the number of Xinjiang's minority cadres who were also CCP members, that percentage nationwide was about 33 percent.

Minority enrollments at the Central Institute of Nationalities in Beijing also increased. In the early 1990s, 30 percent of its 3,000 students were minorities. The institute offered four-year degree programs, as well as special programs for minority cadres that ranged from six months to two years. As much of this training was (and still is) at government expense, it offered a chance to study in Beijing as well as to travel within China.

Some Xinjiang minorities seized on these programs as a real opportunity. But as the reform era deepened, cadres, including graduates of these programs, saw their salaries decline relative to salaries in the private sector. The opportunities they had expected often failed to materialize. In response, some minority cadres in Xinjiang used their positions to assist relatives, to pave the way for their own business enterprises, or to generate other types of support. They came to view their jobs as a way of helping fellow minorities benefit from the new economy. By these means, they tried to overcome the charge that they had become mere tools of the Han government.[39]

At the same time, these cadres had to maintain good working relationships with their Han counterparts and also to support policies that often touched on religious matters. For example, they were periodically called on to participate in programs to instruct religious leaders in socialism and to give talks at mosques. Such presentations were unwelcome and heightened resentment against minority cadres.[40] Ambitious cadres are also prompted to assert their atheism publicly and advise young people to spend their time studying science rather than going to the mosque.[41] However, as long as religious believers were prevented from joining the officially atheist CCP, they could only look on their fellow minorities within the party with disdain.

Minority cadres at all levels continue to negotiate their role as non-

Muslim leaders in a predominantly Muslim region. Those who appear to use their positions to help the local populace, as opposed to Han immigrants, are able to maintain some credibility in the eyes of their own ethnic group. Many more are nonetheless viewed as lackeys of the Han Chinese, a perception that carries real risk. Over the last decade, some minority cadres have become targets of local anger, and a number have been killed in violent attacks. Clearly, minority cadres have to balance their ethnic identity with their allegiance to the state in ways that will become increasingly complex as the region's economy and ethnically diverse population continue to expand.

Social Mobility and Patterns of Employment

Since 1949, the link between educational attainment and social status has undergone several shifts. In the early decades of the twentieth century, as the education system accommodated growing numbers of minority students, segments of all minority ethnic groups began to see the new system as offering the possibility of a better life for their children. Reminiscing about the 1950s, Uyghurs speak of a genuine optimism that this time their region would finally receive real autonomy. When the reality failed to meet these expectations, some intellectuals spoke out. As noted earlier, the Hundred Flowers campaign of 1957 led to the arrest of many politically active Uyghurs, including a number of prominent intellectuals, who were given harsh prison sentences, assigned dehumanizing labor, and deprived of the right to write or publish. Among prominent figures sentenced to prison labor camps were the Kazak scholar Nikmet Manjani and the Uyghur writer Zunun Kadir. Although both were later released, the fact that someone like Turghun could remain under house detention as late as 2000 gave reason for other Uyghur intellectuals to exercise caution in expressing their views.

To be classified as an "intellectual" was fraught with peril throughout the 1950s and 1960s. Many minorities, as well as many Han, discovered that it was politically far safer to have the status of "poor peasant." Those who chose to accede to the new Maoist political order had to find a balance between loyalty to the leadership of the CCP and the maintenance of their minority identity. Only through the most adroit accommodations could minority parents secure a job in the state sector that would ensure a reasonable life for their children. Such jobs in the government, schools, or the CCP meant steady pay, housing, health care, and pensions. The route to such jobs and the high social status they brought was through education.

With the passing of the Maoist period, minorities seeking to improve their lives faced new opportunities and new challenges. By 1980, members of the younger generations were, on average, better educated than their parents. Thanks to the popularity of radio and television, young urban residents—even those educated in Uyghur-language schools—now had some familiarity with the Chinese language. Expectations rose as the economy improved.

In the 1990s, the situation in the region changed once more. While state-sector jobs in towns and cities remained secure, and were thus still attractive to some segments of all minority groups, the income from such positions no longer guaranteed the kind of life it once had. Nonetheless, urban life continued to offer more material benefits than rural existence. Families that migrated into the cities in the preceding decades wanted to remain there. Urban areas across Xinjiang expanded as rural minorities migrated there in search of modern amenities. At the same time, the flow of Han migrants into Xinjiang once again increased, offering competition for jobs in Xinjiang's towns and cities, as well as in the farming areas of the major oases. As the economy expanded, competition for posts in government and for lucrative jobs in the private sector also increased.

The reform era also brought back forms of private business proscribed under Mao. Families that had once relied on long-distance trade or small businesses could return to those livelihoods. While these types of work did not provide the security or traditional status to which educated men and women could aspire, those whose family enterprises flourished also saw their social standing rise. A leading example of the Uyghur entrepreneurial spirit is Rebiya Kadir, who used the new trading opportunities to become a multimillionaire. As William C. Clark notes in his account of her rise to economic prominence, she was accorded great respect for her accomplishments and for all she was doing to increase employment opportunities, especially for women.[42] Her arrest in 1999 and subsequent imprisonment have not diminished the public's high regard for her.

If the new economic opportunities have increased the social standing of migrants from Xinjiang's villages, especially those from the south, they have also affected people's perception of social status. Traditionally, Uyghurs accorded the highest social status to scholars and intellectuals. The declining salaries of teachers, professors, and other intellectuals in the 1990s diminished the prestige of these fields. In the new economy, higher status came with higher income. However, to find a job that could enhance one's social standing became a far more complicated matter than it had been in the old society.

By the 1990s, the younger generation at all levels of society came to see the search for employment as a major life issue. Back in the 1950s and 1960s, the limited number of educated Uyghurs and members of other minority groups forced the government to rely on Han Chinese immigrants to fill most posts. As the Xinjiang Production and Construction Corps (Xinjiang shengchan jianshe bingtuan) expanded its role in Xinjiang's economy, there was still less need to resort to local labor. The few available figures suggest that employment of minority "workers and clerks" rose from a low of 40,000 in 1954 to only 106,000 in 1965. Ten years later, the number of such employees reached 160,000.[43] These data confirm that in the Maoist era minorities continued to hold a relatively low number of nonagricultural positions in their Uyghur Autonomous Region.

In the reform era, as the urban minority populations of Xinjiang gained wider access to education, a new class of bilingual men and women began entering the rapidly changing urban labor force. Although little hard data on employment exist, the government reported that 148,000 minorities held "professional and technical" jobs in 1989. By 1995, this figure had risen to 181,000, a modest increase of 33,000 jobs in five years.[44] Such figures support the assertion of young minority workers and Muslims that they continue to fall behind in terms of better-paid employment and that the best positions are reserved for Han Chinese. Anecdotal evidence suggests that in the largest cities, which are deemed the most desirable places to live, active discrimination against Uyghurs and other Muslims does exist. When interviewed, young people commonly complain about the lack of jobs. Many minorities feel that their lack of training in such foreign languages as English or Japanese is but one of many impediments to their securing lucrative posts in the service sector and tourism.

Employment pressure in Xinjiang's cities is expected to increase. As in the rest of China, there is already an enormous gulf between average incomes in the city and in the countryside. In 1995, the average annual income of an urban resident of Xinjiang was 4,252 yuan, while a rural resident earned less than a fourth of that (935.5 yuan).[45] Whether Xinjiang remains stable as its economy enters an ever more rapid phase of expansion will depend in large measure on whether the system can provide educational opportunities and employment for all of Xinjiang's residents, and especially the young.

The Immediate Future

When in 2000 the Chinese government announced plans to intensify development in the northwestern provinces, it once more forced to the surface the question of Beijing's overall strategy for bringing about the "unity of the nationalities" in Xinjiang through minority education and employment. Full details on the government's ambitious plan are not yet available, but the budget announced thus far does not include funds for schools, training centers, or new economic enterprises that might draw on the local non-Han labor pool. On the contrary, most of the money appears earmarked for major construction projects, including roads and highways, pipelines for oil and natural gas, and other infrastructure needed to exploit Xinjiang's natural resources. Neither poverty alleviation in southern Xinjiang nor the improvement of access to basic necessities such as water and housing appears to be a part of this project. Until the government commits major investments to these sectors, the local population will continue to feel justified in its skeptical view of Beijing's goals and plans for their region.

8

A "Land of Borderlands"

Implications of Xinjiang's Trans-border Interactions

Sean R. Roberts

One cannot understand Xinjiang's recent economic, cultural, or political development solely by examining reform processes underway in China. At least as important to Xinjiang's development are the many transnational and cross-border processes in which this region is presently engaged. These interactions are facilitated by geographical, historical, and cultural ties between Xinjiang and its western and southwestern neighbors that, in general, are much stronger than those between Xinjiang and the remainder of China. This chapter provides a brief outline of the extent and impact of these transnational and cross-border processes that, together, have intertwined recent events in Xinjiang with forces from outside China, particularly at Xinjiang's western and southwestern edges. In doing so, the chapter highlights how Xinjiang's recent "opening up" to the world is simultaneously serving both to strengthen the Chinese state's rule of Xinjiang and to provide support to local Muslims who are discontent with that rule.

Roots of Xinjiang's Cross-border Ties

Xinjiang is a land of borderlands. Its major population centers are at the region's edges, while the center of Xinjiang is taken up by the desolate Taklimakan Desert.[1] As both Ludmilla A. Ch'vyr and Justin Rudelson point out, this unique geography has created a situation where each of Xinjiang's oases feels particular cultural influences emanating from its closest cross-border neighbors.[2] As a result, areas in Xinjiang's northeast, such as Urumchi, Turpan, and Hami, have historically had close ties with China proper, but the rest of the region has not. Instead, in Xinjiang's west and south, cultural influences have mostly flowed back and forth between Xinjiang and Muslim regions that lie beyond the borders of the People's Republic of China (PRC) in what is today Pakistan, Afghanistan, and the former Soviet republics of Central Asia.

Historically, this geography has made Xinjiang a tenuous part of China in the modern period and has allowed external political powers to gain extensive access to the region. In the late nineteenth and early twentieth centuries, for example, Xinjiang was a stage for the imperial politics of the "Great Game" between the British and Russian empires, whose influences in the region often overshadowed even that of Xinjiang's Chinese rulers.[3] Not only did Great Britain and Russia exert substantial influence in the area through embassies inside Xinjiang, but they also fostered cross-border ties by supporting trade and interaction between Xinjiang's Muslims and their respective Muslim subjects in the bordering areas of British India and Russian Central Asia.

If British influence in the region waned in the early twentieth century, Russian/Soviet influence reached a peak at that time through the close relationship between the Soviet Union and Xinjiang's warlord leader Sheng Shicai, who became a full-fledged member of the Soviet Communist Party.[4] Andrew D. W. Forbes has gone as far as to assert that, due to this relationship, by 1939 Xinjiang "had become a virtual dependency of the Soviet Union, differing scarcely at all from the neighboring Mongolian People's Republic."[5] While Sheng made a break with the Soviet Union in 1942, Soviet influence remained extensive in the region during the 1940s through the Soviet-sponsored Ili rebellion of 1944 and the establishment of the short-lived Eastern Turkistan Republic (ETR) in Xinjiang's Ili area.[6] Furthermore, while Britain left the region with the establishment of Communist rule in 1949, the Soviets remained a critical force in Xinjiang into the late 1950s, assisting with the publication of books, the building of factories and housing, and the provision of technical assistance.[7] This relationship only ended with the Sino-Soviet diplomatic split in the late 1950s and early 1960s.[8]

This history of cross-border political interaction has also led to the establishment of substantial communities of Muslims from Xinjiang in neighboring countries, thus cultivating continued cross-border cultural and kin relationships that remain important today.[9] In the eighteenth and nineteenth centuries, for example, significant numbers of Uyghur and Kyrgyz adherents to the Afaqiyya Sufi order who once lived in areas around Kashgar fled Qing rule for the Ferghana valley (now in Uzbekistan and Kyrgyzstan).[10] Likewise, beginning in the late nineteenth century, several migrations of Uyghurs, Hui, and Kazaks from China's Yining (Gulja) area to Semirechye in the Russian/Soviet-controlled portion of the Ili River valley laid the basis for what is today a significant population of former Xinjiang residents in Kazakstan and Kyrgyzstan.[11] While the transfer of population from

Xinjiang to Pakistan and Afghanistan has been less significant, various migrations along the mountain passes around the Karakoram have also led to the establishment of Uyghur, Kyrgyz, and Tajik communities in these countries that have their roots in Xinjiang.[12]

During the Sino-Soviet split and the Cultural Revolution, the PRC closed Xinjiang's borders and cut off these external ties. In the 1980s, however, the borders of Xinjiang were reopened and the region's long-held relations with its neighbors renewed. The reopening of these borders has had a profound impact on Xinjiang. While the opening of borders with Mongolia and India to the north and south has increased Xinjiang's external trade and furthered its economic development in the last twenty years, it has been the opening of borders with Pakistan, Afghanistan, and the former Soviet republics of Central Asia that has had the most far-reaching influence on Xinjiang today. Economically, these two border zones have accounted for the majority of Xinjiang's international overland trade; culturally, they have emerged as critical links between the inhabitants of Xinjiang and both the Islamic and Western worlds; and politically, they have become pivotal but contentious areas of support for the independence movement of Uyghurs and other Muslim peoples in Xinjiang.

The Reopening of Borders and Cross-border Travel Today

The reopening of Xinjiang's borders began in the later 1980s, at the peak of the Chinese government's liberalization policies in the region. While numerous traditional routes out of Xinjiang exist, only a few of them have thus far been opened to free travel. The Chinese government has also gone to great lengths to modernize selected routes to allow for maximum efficiency in the shipment of goods. While there are plans for the construction of other modern arteries from Xinjiang to its western and southern neighbors, today four primary border crossings are open to free travel: the Karakoram Highway to Pakistan; the road from Yining to Almaty* in Kazakstan; the railway between Urumchi and Almaty; and the road across the Turugart Pass between Kashgar and Bishkek, Kyrgyzstan.

Chinese engineers constructed the bridges for the dramatic mountain road known as the Karakoram Highway even before the so-called Northern Areas (or Pakistan-controlled Kashmir) had come entirely under Islamabad's control. Begun in 1968, this road initially was envisioned as an important political link between China and the mountainous region of Pakistan's northwest,

---

* Formerly Alma-Ata. The name was changed to Almaty after the fall of the Soviet Union to reflect a more accurate Kazak-language place-name.

thus playing a role in the Cold War competition between Russia and China for influence in South Asia. When the road was opened to travel in 1987, however, its primary purpose had become more economic than political.[13] Today, this border is widely traveled by traders and tourists, but only during the summer and early autumn months when it is passable.[14]

In addition to being a passageway for goods, this road has brought a large number of Pakistanis to Xinjiang and a significant number of Xinjiang Muslims to Pakistan for both short and long stays. Furthermore, since it has become a popular international tourism route, the road has also brought an increasing number of European, American, and Japanese travelers through southern Xinjiang, providing for yet another external influence on the region. Given the difficult terrain and altitude of the mountain passes on this road, it is a very open frontier that is difficult to secure and thus susceptible to the smuggling of contraband. Aside from routes into Pakistan, the location of the Karakoram Highway at the nexus of borders between Tajikistan, Pakistan, China, and Afghanistan facilitates its merger with several other unpaved roads into Tajikistan and Afghanistan that lack significant official cross-border travel as of yet but that are regularly traveled by smugglers.

In contrast to its single border crossing with Pakistan, Xinjiang now has numerous official routes into the former Soviet republics of Central Asia. While eleven official border crossings exist between Xinjiang and Kazakstan, Kyrgyzstan, and Tajikistan, only three of these crossings—Alatau/Dostyk (Kazakstan), Horgos/Khorgus (Kazakstan), and Turugart (Kyrgyzstan)—have been open to significant traffic.[15] In the near future, however, there are plans to increase the number of open border crossings between Xinjiang and its three neighbors to the west, including the construction of a railway that will link Kashgar with Uzbekistan through Kyrgyzstan.[16]

The border crossing at Horgos is positioned at a natural geographic opening between Xinjiang and Kazakstan that follows the Ili River valley. This route has long been a channel for Russian and Soviet influence on Xinjiang, and the city of Almaty, originally called Vernyi, was built in its present location during the nineteenth century in order to access this trade route.[17] When this border crossing reopened to free travel in 1987, it initially served mostly official Sino-Soviet trade and travel in both directions by Uyghurs, Kazaks, Hui, and others with relatives on opposing sides of the border. In the early 1990s, however, this crossing quickly evolved into a bustling site of small-scale commerce for sojourner shuttle traders from both Kazakstan and China, and scores of people crossed back and forth daily bringing consumer goods for resale. While the shuttle trade across this border has slowed down in recent years, it remains a highly traveled route between Xinjiang and Kazakstan.

In 1990, a train link between Kazakstan and Xinjiang at Dostyk was also finished and began service between Almaty and Urumchi through the Zungharian Gate in the Altay region.[18] The construction of this railway had begun during the 1950s, but the Sino-Soviet split delayed its finish for almost thirty years. Today, rail service goes between Urumchi and Almaty in both directions twice a week, and the trains are usually full with travelers, most of whom are shuttle traders from the former Soviet Union who buy their goods in Urumchi. While this is a well-traveled train route, it is also closely monitored by the governments of both China and Kazakstan. Security concerns about the potential military use of this railway have stifled interest in changing the Cold War legacy of different track gauges, and trains must change their wheels at the border before proceeding in either direction.

Finally, Kyrgyzstan has a well-traveled border crossing with southern Xinjiang at Turugart that, like the Karakoram Highway, follows a high-altitude road through a mountain pass. This road was constructed almost exclusively for commerce, and it is only open in the summer.[19] During the summer, however, buses of shuttle traders travel back and forth between Kyrgyzstan and Kashgar five days a week. The tales of American and European travelers who have successfully crossed this border without proper paperwork are indicative of the relative insecure nature of this frontier, which, like the Karakoram Highway, crosses mountain terrain that evades extensive monitoring.[20]

These border crossings with Pakistan and the former Soviet republics of Central Asia provide Xinjiang with extensive access to markets, cultures, and ideas from outside China. Access routes to Kazakstan and Kyrgyzstan are now available from Kashgar, Yining, and Urumchi. Although the only route to Pakistan leaves from Kashgar, the train that now links Kashgar to Urumchi makes travel to and from Pakistan and numerous locations in Xinjiang substantially easier. Together with the increase in political, cultural, and religious liberties in Xinjiang after the end of the Cultural Revolution, this improved access to the outside world has been critical in the recent transformation of Xinjiang.

The Economic Impact of Open Borders

The opening of the borders to Pakistan, Kazakstan, Kyrgyzstan, and Tajikistan has been one of the most important factors in Xinjiang's recent development boom. Trade between Xinjiang and these countries has brought large amounts of capital into this once underdeveloped outpost of the PRC. In 1998, for example, the cross-border trade with Pakistan had a combined import-export value of over $21 million, and trade with Kazakstan and

Kyrgyzstan amounted to over $750 million.[21] These are especially impressive numbers when one takes into account that they do not include the vast amount of goods crossing these borders through shuttle trade and that a significant portion of these unofficially traded goods are never even registered due to the significant corruption at border posts.[22] Furthermore, the cross-border trade in these two frontier zones of Xinjiang appears to be increasing annually.[23] While the goods that come to China from Pakistan and the former Soviet republics of Central Asia are mostly raw materials, those that leave Xinjiang for these other countries are overwhelmingly Chinese consumer goods. The increase of cross-border trade in these two frontier zones, therefore, also fosters the development of new manufacturing and trade industries in Xinjiang.

While this in-flow of capital from the cross-border trade is itself significant, the potential for future profits is even greater, especially with regard to China's economic relationship with the oil-rich countries of Central Asia. As early as 1993, China had expressed interest in Kazakstan's oil and natural gas production and had initiated the idea of a pipeline that could bring oil from Kazakstan's west to China through Xinjiang.[24] While this pipeline has not come to fruition as of yet, in 1997 the Chinese National Petroleum Company (CNPC) won two important tenders for the right to drill oil in the Kazak fields of Uzen and Munai.[25] Furthermore, in 2001 the CNPC cemented a deal with the Royal Dutch/Shell Oil Group to bring this multinational petroleum company into a consortium that will construct a pipeline from Xinjiang to China's east coast.[26] These steps suggest that China's interest in Central Asia's oil and natural gas is long term and strategic and that Xinjiang is envisioned as an important thoroughfare for bringing that oil and gas to the rest of China.

Both the immediate profits of the cross-border trade and the potential future riches associated with China's role in Central Asian oil and gas prospecting have helped to propel Xinjiang's development in recent years, making the region a more attractive destination for potential Han Chinese migrants. While various states in China since the Qing dynasty have encouraged Han Chinese to settle in Xinjiang, this policy has historically had only limited success due to Chinese perceptions of Xinjiang as an uncivilized backwater. To many Han Chinese migrants coming to Xinjiang from elsewhere in the PRC today, however, the region has become a new western frontier and a window to multiple outside markets where fortunes can be made with little or no initial capital. In the context of China's quickly developing capitalism, therefore, Xinjiang has become an increasingly popular destination for Han seeking to improve their socioeconomic status.[27] As part of this in-migration of Han Chinese into Xinjiang in the last decade, the region's urban centers have also been in an almost constant state of construction and development in response to both the present profits of Xinjiang's external trade and the potential fortunes to be made through the region's international commercial trade.[28]

If the economic benefits of the cross-border trade have attracted Han Chinese migrants to Xinjiang, they have also helped to develop a Muslim middle class in the region. Local Muslims in Xinjiang, however, profited more from this trade during its early stages than they do today. In the late 1980s and early 1990s, Uyghurs and Kazaks in particular had the cultural and linguistic skills and kinship ties necessary to navigate the markets of former Soviet Central Asia and Pakistan. As a result, Muslim sojourners from Xinjiang not only became the primary movers of goods to markets directly across the border, but they also were able to use their access to Kazakstan and Kyrgyzstan to become the middlemen in an extensive trade between China and Eastern Europe. It was not uncommon, for example, for petty traders from Xinjiang during this time to leave China through Kazakstan only to travel farther on to markets in places as disparate as Kazan, Moscow, Sophia, Bucharest, and Istanbul. As one Uyghur trader who had traveled this commercial circuit in the late 1980s and early 1990s reported, the presence of Turkish-speaking peoples throughout the Soviet Union and Eastern Europe gave him a particular advantage vis-à-vis others who sought to bring China's inexpensive manufactured goods to these markets. While some traders from southern Xinjiang were able to break into the Pakistani markets as well at this time, the economic benefits of the Karakoram Highway trade were mostly realized through the local sale of products to Pakistani traders who came to Xinjiang on brief purchasing trips.

Gradually throughout the 1990s, however, the role of Xinjiang's Muslim sojourners in the trade with former Soviet Central Asia decreased significantly. Many local industries in Xinjiang began producing cheap clothing and household products for the markets to the west and south of Xinjiang, and many of these companies dealt directly with wholesale buyers in Kazakstan, Kyrgyzstan, and Uzbekistan. As part of this process, industries in Xinjiang organized an annual international trade fair in Urumchi beginning in 1992. The trade taking place at this fair was slightly in excess of $1 million during its first several years; by 1998 it exceeded $5 million, and by 2000 it passed $10 million.[29] At the same time, the demand for better consumer goods in the markets of Central Asia has led to an increase in products coming from the interior of China. Many Central Asian salespeople at the Dordoi market in Bishkek, for example, have recently found that they have more access to legitimate global brand-name products made for the East Asian market by Chinese factories if they bypass Xinjiang entirely and conduct their shopping in Beijing. Since 1999, the demand for these higher-grade Chinese-made goods has increased steadily in Central Asia, reducing demand for the cheaper products that can be found in Xinjiang.[30] Many Pakistani traders are also beginning to adopt this same practice and now use Xinjiang only as a transit point for trading trips to larger cities in eastern China.

While these processes have meant that there are fewer opportunities for Muslim sojourners from Xinjiang in the markets to the immediate west and in Pakistan, many Xinjiang Muslims, and Uyghurs in particular, have continued to seek their fortune by trading in these neighboring states. In doing so, however, Uyghur traders have had to be flexible and ready to change the ways in which they conduct commerce. In the early and mid-1990s, it was not uncommon for Uyghur petty traders from Xinjiang to complete the circuit of Central Asia's wholesale bazaars in the course of several years, moving on to a new market once their goods had become obsolete at another.[31] Since the later 1990s, however, this strategy for small-scale traders from Xinjiang has become less profitable. Many Uyghur traders from Xinjiang say that they were eventually forced to leave every major Central Asian wholesale bazaar by increasing pressure from local mafias and/or police and demands for protection money. Likewise, the difficulty of crossing numerous borders is further complicated by the need to pay multiple bribes. For this reason, one trader smuggled his profits from Uzbekistan through Kazakhstan back to Xinjiang by hiding the money ($10,000) in the core of a melon. He knew that if he declared this money, a large bribe would be levied on him at each border crossing.

By the later 1990s and into the present, therefore, those Uyghur sojourners still trading in Central Asia have adopted a new strategy of specialization and coordination. Now, most Uyghurs trading at Central Asian bazaars work together to concentrate in the sale of a single product, and they operate their sales booths together so as to pool their resources against corrupt police and racketeers. At the Almaty Barakholka bazaar, for example, Uyghurs from Xinjiang now have a virtual monopoly on the sale of cheap polyester and nylon sweat suits, usually counterfeits of well-known brand names such as Addidas, Nike, and Reebok, and they work together in one section of the bazaar. An even more striking example of this trend is seen in Bishkek, where Uyghur traders from Kashgar have established their own bazaar that specializes almost exclusively in cloth. While this sprawling bazaar continues to dominate the Kyrgyzstan market for all types of cloth, it has not escaped the pressure of local organized crime. Despite being financed by Chinese manufacturers from the interior of China, this bazaar was burned down twice under suspicious circumstances at its original location in an old Soviet sports camp. Now, however, it has reopened in a new location with increased security.

While significant numbers of Uyghur and other Muslim men from border cities such as Yining and Kashgar have been able to trade abroad in former Soviet Central Asia and Pakistan, the majority of Muslims from Xinjiang do not have access to such opportunities. There are other ways, however, through which Xinjiang's Muslims are able to profit from the cross-border trade that has developed to the west and southwest since the late-1980s. One means by which Xinjiang Uyghurs, Kazaks, and Hui have made money from the cross-border trade has been to serve as middlemen for Pakistani and Central Asian traders during their buying trips to Xinjiang. This has been well documented by Jay Dautcher, who has studied the middleman role of Uyghurs in the Yining area.[32] The same profession was taking form in the 1990s in Urumchi and Kashgar to accommodate traders from the former Soviet lands of Central Asia and Pakistan, especially those who wished to deal directly with manufacturers who were mostly Han Chinese. Any European-looking visitor to Urumchi's bazaars at this time would recognize these Muslim middlemen by their endless loud greetings of *"brat!"* (the Russian word for "brother") to anybody resembling a shuttle trader from the former Soviet Union. In the later 1990s, however, these means by which local Muslims could profit from the cross-border trade also began to wane. As one Kazakstan Uyghur trader stated in 1997, he had already established direct contact with all of the Han Chinese manufacturers necessary to conduct his trading, and now he no longer needed a middleman to assist him.

Economic benefits of the cross-border trade for Muslim petty traders from Xinjiang have diminished over the last decade. Nonetheless, the wealth accumulated from the early years of the trade has been critical to the emergence of a middle class among Uyghurs and other Muslim peoples in Xinjiang. Some members of this new Muslim middle class have even become extremely wealthy through subsequent investments. Such is the success story of Rebiya Kadir, the Uyghur millionairess who used wealth attained through trade to start several lucrative businesses in Xinjiang.[33] While such success stories are not widespread among Xinjiang's Muslims, the wealth accumulated by those Muslims who were extensively involved in the cross-border trade in the early 1990s did help, at the very least, to develop a variety of minority-owned small businesses in Xinjiang and to provide the capital needed to develop local communities through the building of mosques and other communal institutions.

In general, therefore, the reopening of Xinjiang's external borders has had a profound economic impact on the region, but the beneficiaries of this impact have gradually changed in the last decade. If at first cross-border trade provided local Muslim nationalities in Xinjiang with an important source of revenue that they could invest in their own local communities and institutions, today the benefits of such trade flow mainly to Han Chinese–run businesses and to urban development aimed at the Han population in cities. This situation furthers China's "Develop the West" (*xibu da kaifa*) campaign, but at the expense of the local Turkic peoples. If development projects destroy traditional means of subsistence among local Muslims[34] and if new jobs are increasingly filled by Han immigrants, these developments could have a significantly adverse effect on the local nationalities in Xinjiang. A relatively apolitical Uyghur farmer who lives on the road from Khotan to Yarkand voiced this concern in the summer of 2000 when he recounted that the growing development in the region was putting extreme pressure on his business. He felt that compounding debts would eventually force him to sell his land. As he said with evident despair, "All I want to do is farm, but *they* won't let me."

The Impact of Global Cultural Flows

Muslims of Xinjiang have long had cultural and kin ties with regions bordering China to the west and southwest. With the end of the Cultural Revolution, the local Muslim nationalities of Xinjiang began to reexplore their cultural links with neighboring peoples outside their borders. These cultural links have been reestablished through cross-border trade and the renewal of contacts with family abroad. In focusing on the two most important border regions of Xinjiang, that with Pakistan and Afghanistan and that with the formerly Soviet-ruled countries of Central Asia, two general trends in external cultural influences have emerged.

In both cases, the cultural influences of cross-border contacts do not only reflect historically held cultural ties but also include different global cultural movements that have appeal in the states neighboring Xinjiang. From Pakistan and Afghanistan, the cultural influence has been largely religious and includes exposure to various political movements now popular in the Islamic world. From the independent states of Central Asia, by contrast, the cultural influence has been more Western, secular, and nationalist in character, emerging from the legacy of Soviet rule in those countries and the recent impact of Western development there. Considering Central Asia's growing ties with Europe and the United States, this influence could also be considered to be part of a global neoliberal cultural movement that has grown in reach since the end of the Cold War. While these often contradictory cultural influences have spread throughout Xinjiang, the north has been more influenced by contact with Kazakstan, Kyrgyzstan, and their neighbors while the south has been more influenced by ties with Pakistan.

The Religious Impact of the Reopening of the Pakistan Border

In Xinjiang's Islamic revival since the 1980s, it is difficult to separate external influences from the local retrieval of past practices. That said, the reopening of the border between Pakistan and Xinjiang has undoubtedly influenced the practice of Islam in the region. Pakistani traders in Xinjiang, especially during the early years of the cross-border trade in the late 1980s and early 1990s, often saw it as their duty to provide information about Islam to the local Muslim peoples. For this reason, included among the goods they brought to Xinjiang were women's veils, jewelry with Muslim symbols, posters of Muslim holy sites, copies of the Qur'an, and so on. During the late 1980s and the 1990s, such items quickly found markets in Xinjiang's shops, stands adjoining mosques, and bazaars. Women began wearing veils in areas of southern Xinjiang where nineteenth-century travelers had once remarked on the absence of veils, religious schools were established throughout the region, and many young aspiring imams went to Pakistan to study.

The religious influence of Pakistani traders on the Muslims of Xinjiang seems to have waned after the mid-1990s. This change traces to a clash of cultures. The Pakistani traders were worldlier than the local Xinjiang petty traders, and what was presented as "honest deals" between believers often worked in favor of the guests from the south. Many Pakistani traders also availed themselves of many of the products and services not available in their own Islamic state, including alcohol and prostitutes. These activities have seriously eroded the authority of Pakistani traders as exemplary Muslims, and many Uyghurs in Xinjiang now vilify them as dishonest and immoral.

The impact of Pakistani traders in Xinjiang on the region's religious revival, therefore, has been mixed. In addition to the many alcohol-drinking traders who come each year from Karachi and Islamabad, there are many, particularly from Peshawar and including some Afghan refugees, who arrive with a strong commitment not only to trade but also to provide spiritual guidance to their fellow Muslims in the region. Many Muslims, particularly in Xinjiang's south, have responded positively to these initiatives.

Perhaps more important to the region's Islamic revival than the influence of Pakistan traders on Xinjiang Muslims, however, is the impact on Xinjiang Muslims traveling to Pakistan. Those Xinjiang traders who have spent significant time in Pakistan generally have returned to Xinjiang with an appreciation of the Muslim piety evident in that Islamic state. This has been a factor in the growing role of Islam in Khotan and Kashgar, where veiled women are seen more frequently and more children attend religious schools than in Xinjiang's north.[35] Given the fairly limited nature of the shuttle trade with Pakistan, however, the most significant Pakistani religious influence on Xinjiang has been through the education of Xinjiang's *mullahs* and imams.[36] In the late 1980s, the Chinese government allowed local Muslims to study abroad at *madrassahs* in Islamic countries.[37] Given the close proximity of Xinjiang to Pakistan, a large number of these students went to Pakistan. While the Chinese state has since ceased to support Xinjiang Muslims who wish to study in the madrassahs of Islamic countries, scores of Uyghurs and other Muslims from Xinjiang continue to study in the madrassahs of Pakistan using private means. On returning to Xinjiang, many of these students have been instrumental in promoting a stricter understanding of Islam, but since 1997 the Chinese government has clamped down on this activity.

In general, therefore, the Karakoram Highway has provided Xinjiang with an important window to life in a Muslim state. In southern Xinjiang in particular, where the population is generally poorer than in the north, ideas drawn from the examples of life in Pakistan have gained some popularity.

"Western" Influence from the Former Soviet Union

Both when it was ruled by the Soviet Union and now, when five independent states exist there, the part of Central Asia to Xinjiang's west has consistently served as a testing ground for Western styles of development in the context of Asia. During the first half of the twentieth century, the Western (i.e., Russian) model of socialist development in Soviet Central Asia appealed to many of the educated Muslim nationalists in Xinjiang.[38] While a large number of these educated Muslim nationalists fled to the Soviet Union prior to the closing of the border between Xinjiang and the Soviet Union in 1963, these former representatives of the region's cultural elite continued to command the respect of many in Xinjiang, especially in the north. When Xinjiang's western borders were reopened, therefore, many Xinjiang Muslims, notably Uyghurs, sought to renew their ties with these exiled intellectuals.

This phenomenon has brought Muslim intellectuals in Xinjiang gradually into a closer dialogue with their Uyghur counterparts in Kyrgyzstan, Kazakstan, and Uzbekistan. Westerners who traveled back and forth across the Kazakstan-Xinjiang border throughout the 1990s often found themselves serving as couriers for intellectuals on the two sides who were exchanging reading materials. Beyond the sharing of written sources on local history, language, and culture, these exchanges served as a forum for the sharing of ideas and ideologies. If the ideas initially traveling from former Soviet Central Asia to Xinjiang were mostly founded on Soviet ideology, in recent years they have been more influenced by the liberalism and democracy being promoted in Central Asia under the influence of Europe and the United States.

This subtle cross-border intellectual exchange is bolstered by the experiences of Xinjiang traders who have stayed for extended time periods in the new states in Central Asia. Xinjiang traders in Kazakstan, Kyrgyzstan, and Uzbekistan are exposed to a variety of Western liberal institutions including newly formed local nongovernmental organizations, international development agencies, and multiple political parties (albeit generally ineffective ones in the context of these countries' controlled political climate). Likewise, the mere demographic dynamics of Central Asia expose visitors from Xinjiang to a more multiethnic society where the dominance of a single nationality still exists but is far less pronounced than in China. Furthermore, while many American and European videotapes, computer programs, music tapes, and so on are available in Xinjiang, the access to these hallmark products of Western culture in Central Asia is even more pronounced.

This exposure to Western culture has been humbling for many of Xinjiang's Muslims who have traveled to the former Soviet Union and points farther west. In one essay written by a Uyghur trader from Xinjiang, the author portrays areas outside Xinjiang, former Soviet Central Asia and Turkey in particular, as clean and civilized in contrast to the poor and unclean conditions of his homeland. He ends his essay by calling for the Uyghurs to improve themselves and their homeland so as to be *on par* with the rest of the world. He writes with evident self-deprecation:

> At the beginning of the 90s, we were welcomed warmly with open arms, hugged, kissed, and praised highly by the people of the Commonwealth of Independent States . . . , and in two years we spread our bad smells, forcing them to run away from us in boredom. It is clear that with those qualities of ours we will rot away everywhere in the world in the near future. Let's not do that, and let's cleanse ourselves . . . [and] become real human beings fit for the era [in which we live].[39]

As this passage makes clear, many Xinjiang traders have found in their travels westward that things can be different. A related outcome of this reaction to Western influence has been dissatisfaction with the Chinese model of development and a desire to make concrete changes in Xinjiang. This desire has mostly been evident in Xinjiang Uyghurs' self-improvement movements, such as the Yining *mäshräp* movement aimed at fighting alcoholism and drug abuse and Rebiya Kadir's Thousand Mothers Association promoting the development of women-owned businesses.[40] It has also been reflected, however, in a stronger separatist movement within Xinjiang that would like to end Chinese rule of the region altogether.

The Political Impact of Open Borders

The political impact of the opening of Xinjiang's borders is more difficult to measure than its economic and cultural influence. On the one hand, the exposure of the Uyghurs and other Muslims in Xinjiang to neighboring Muslim sovereign nation-states has increased the hope for the establishment of either a Uyghur or an Eastern Turkistan nation-state. On the other hand, the ability of the Chinese government to use the open frontiers of Xinjiang to make important economic and political alliances with the states that border on the region has ensured that these states do not support any potential Muslim separatist movement within Xinjiang.

Xinjiang's Open Frontier and the Growth of Uyghur Nationalism

As noted earlier, once Xinjiang's Muslims began to travel across the borders of China to conduct trade, they became aware of the possibilities of change in their own homeland. After the fall of the Soviet Union, these possibilities increasingly included the idea of establishing an independent Uyghur nation-state. In Xinjiang by 1994, for example, many Uyghurs were openly stating that there should be a sovereign "Uyghurstan" now that there was an independent Kazakstan, Kyrgyzstan, Uzbekistan, Turkmenistan, and Tajikistan. The desire of the Uyghurs to establish their own sovereign state is, of course, not new, but the independence of the former Soviet Central Asian states brought new hope that this desire would be fulfilled. Furthermore, the Xinjiang Uyghurs' increased interaction with other Central Asians as well as with Pakistanis and Afghanis throughout the 1990s has reinforced this hope.

In Uyghurs' interactions with Afghanis and Pakistanis in the early 1990s, for example, it is likely that they received at least vocal encouragement for their own national independence struggle from the anti-Communist and pan-Muslim political movements within Pakistan that simultaneously supported the Taliban. This would have been especially the case for Uyghurs who were studying at this time in Pakistani madrassahs, many of which included either Afghan Taliban or their supporters as both students and instructors. While there is no evidence that Pakistani political groups have given Uyghur nationalists within Xinjiang any direct monetary or arms support, there has been no lack of moral support. In particular, many Pakistanis have helped to promote the idea of establishing a Muslim state in Xinjiang along the model of either Pakistan or Afghanistan's Taliban regime. These sentiments may also account for the handful of Uyghurs captured by U.S. troops during the U.S. military campaign of 2001–2003 in Afghanistan.[41]

While the idea of establishing a Muslim state has not held much popularity among the majority of Uyghurs, it does have some currency among the Uyghurs of southern Xinjiang. Furthermore, interest in the idea of establishing a Muslim state in Xinjiang has only increased with recent Chinese policies that serve to regulate the practice of Islam in the region.[42] In Kashgar during the summer of 2000, for example, two young students from the local madrassah complained for hours about Chinese policies that restricted Muslim practices including the regulation of the content of sermons in local mosques and the exclusion of people under eighteen from worshipping at those mosques. They pointed out that these were restrictions that did not allow local Muslims to properly worship, constantly drawing examples from Pakistan where the existence of an Islamic state not only did not restrict worship but also helped to facilitate it. Not surprisingly, Xinjiang Uyghurs who have studied in Pakistani madrassahs have voiced similar attitudes, often with even more militancy. Among these young *alims* (Muslim scholars), there is a widely held belief that the Muslim people of Xinjiang can only unify and break away from China through a political movement based on the tenets of Islam.

The political influence emanating from the former Soviet Union, however, has promoted a much different national liberation ideology. In Kazakstan and Kyrgyzstan, in particular, there have emerged numerous Uyghur nationalist organizations, all of which support the establishment of a Uyghur nation-state in Xinjiang. These organizations' visions of a future independent Uyghur state, however, are not based on religious unity or the rule of shari'a law. Rather, the Uyghur nationalist movement among the former Soviet Uyghurs combines socialist ideas about the utility of national liberation in combating colonial exploitation with liberal ideals about human rights and the historical right to sovereignty in one's homeland.

A critical part of the former Soviet Uyghurs' contribution to the nationalist movement inside Xinjiang has been the production of a narrative of Uyghur history that is founded on the Uyghurs' struggle with the Chinese for sovereignty in Xinjiang. While former Soviet Uyghurs have recently examined various periods of the Uyghur national liberation movement's history in print, a significant body of this work has been devoted to the reinterpretation of the history of the short-lived Eastern Turkistan Republic from 1944 to 1949.[43] The Xinjiang Uyghurs' exposure to this history has further fueled Uyghur nationalism in Xinjiang by contradicting the official history of the region offered by the Chinese Communist Party (CCP) and by placing their present independence movement in its historical context.[44]

Furthermore, the Uyghur nationalists in Kazakstan and Kyrgyzstan have published extensive information about the political activities of other Uyghur diaspora groups in Europe and Turkey and have served to distribute these other diaspora groups' literature to Uyghurs from Xinjiang who are trading in their countries. Likewise, Xinjiang diaspora communities elsewhere have sent similar materials to Kazakstan and Kyrgyzstan especially for consumption by Xinjiang Uyghurs living there.[45] These materials have also had a significant effect on the Uyghurs of Xinjiang who have felt empowered by the knowledge that their relatives in exile around the world are advocating for the liberation of Xinjiang from Chinese rule. Finally, Uyghur nationalist groups in Kazakstan and Kyrgyzstan have also worked with Uyghurs from Xinjiang in distributing information to the rest of the world about Chinese human rights abuses in Xinjiang. During the February 1997 riots in Yining, for example, Uyghur nationalist groups in Kazakstan gathered eyewitness accounts of events in Yining from Xinjiang traders in their country and distributed these accounts to the world press both through news conferences and by fax.[46]

Despite the proclamations of Kazakstan's Eastern Turkistan United Revolutionary Front, however, there is no evidence that this group or any other Uyghur group in Kazakstan or Kyrgyzstan has provided arms to Uyghur militants in Xinjiang.[47] In this context, the primary contribution of exiled Uyghur nationalists in the former Soviet Union to any potential Uyghur independence movement inside Xinjiang is that of moral support and international representation. While this contribution has likely helped to bolster the confidence of Uyghur nationalists within Xinjiang today, it is not likely to be decisive in the success or failure of a separatist movement. The CCP, nonetheless, has often blamed Uyghur nationalist activities inside Xinjiang exclusively on such external forces. In addition to official statements accusing unnamed external forces of promoting the separation of Xinjiang from China, the Xinjiang government has even tried to propagate this idea in popular culture through the production of television action shows about Muslim foreign agents masquerading as merchants who have infiltrated Xinjiang.[48]

In general, therefore, cross-border contact has helped to encourage Uyghurs and other Muslims in Xinjiang to resist Chinese rule through two different avenues. One focuses on the aspirations of promoting Islam and a Muslim state, and the other concentrates on using international pressure to advocate for an independent secular Eastern Turkistan or Uyghurstan. While these influences do not create the threat that the Chinese government often suggests, they do provide Xinjiang Muslims who are dissatisfied with Chinese rule with an important source of moral support and ideological guidance that boosts their confidence in resisting Chinese rule.

The Chinese Government's Response and the "Uyghur Card"

In response to these external forces that provide Uyghur nationalists within Xinjiang with moral and ideological support, the Chinese government has actively sought the cooperation of the former Soviet Central Asian states and Pakistan in preventing their respective citizens from promoting Uyghur nationalism inside Xinjiang. As one might expect, the Chinese government has been especially successful in gaining such support through the establishment of strong economic trading relationships and mutual security guarantees with these countries.

Pakistan's relationship with China was long important to both countries as a counterbalance to the Soviet-India alliance during the Cold War. While having a foothold in South Asia in order to counter Soviet influence in the region is no longer important to China, Pakistan sees this friendship as being of continued importance in its competition with India, with whom it has continually been on the brink of war for the last several decades. Furthermore, China has also become an indispensable economic partner for Pakistan, especially following the gradual cooling of U.S.-Pakistani relations during most of the 1990s. While there is no evidence of any official agreement between Pakistan and China requesting that Pakistan prevent the development of any Uyghur nationalist movement on its territory, the actions of the Islamabad government in the later 1990s suggest that at least an informal agreement to this effect exists. As early as the spring of 1997, it was reported that Pakistan had deported thirteen Uyghurs who were studying at local madrassahs to China at the request of the Chinese government, which claimed that the thirteen men were terrorists intent on "splitting" Xinjiang from China.[49] Since this time, there have been several similar reports, some more documented than others, of Pakistan handing Uyghurs in their country over to the Chinese authorities.[50] If these actions do not present enough evidence of Pakistan's pledge to help China curb Uyghur nationalism, President Pervez Musharraf made the country's position clear during his December 2001 trip to China, where he appealed to China's Muslims to support Chinese sovereignty in Xinjiang and openly pledged his country's assistance in stopping "East Turkestan terrorism forces."[51]

China's attempts to enlist the support of the newly independent states of Central Asia in the campaign to suppress Uyghur nationalism have been even better documented. The characteristics of the alliances between China and the Central Asian states, however, have also been more complicated. While the Central Asian states have always officially supported China's efforts to prevent the development of a Uyghur independence movement, there is evidence that unofficially these countries have not always followed Beijing's lead on this issue. In general, for the Central Asian countries, the Uyghur question has become something of a diplomatic card that can be used to gain China's support for these states' own agendas. This "Uyghur card" has become particularly important to these former Soviet states that have retained a deep distrust of China from the experiences of the Sino-Soviet split.

Officially, for example, Kazakstan has always pledged to help China fight Uyghur separatism. Tomur Davamät of the Xinjiang government even notes in his memoirs from a 1993 trip to Central Asia that Nursultan Nazarbaev, the president of Kazakstan, said with authority at that time, "[I]f China stands against separatist movements, we in Kazakstan will also stand against [these same] separatist movements."[52] In reality, however, the Kazakstan government has demonstrated restraint in its dealings with local Uyghur nationalist groups, allowing them to operate, publish newsletters, and hold press conferences despite Chinese demands. While the Kazakstan government also closely monitors Uyghur nationalist activity in its country to ensure that it does not become involved in a militant armed conflict with China, the freedom of expression allowed Uyghurs in Kazakstan is enough to concern the Chinese government. Furthermore, the government of Kyrgyzstan has undertaken a very similar policy.

This situation has led the Chinese to develop a series of security treaties with Kazakstan and other Central Asian states with which it shares a border. These treaties have evolved into a regional body for mutual security in Central Asia that was initially referred to as the Shanghai Five. The Shanghai Five at its inception was a loose alliance between China, Kazakstan, Kyrgyzstan, Tajikistan, and Russia that formed out of a meeting between officials from each country in Shanghai in 1996 during which delegates voiced their respective concerns about security along China's borders with former Soviet states.[53] For the Chinese side, the question of Uyghur separatists using Central Asia as a base for their activities was among the most important issue on this meeting's agenda. Central Asian leaders, by contrast, sought the favor of China as the fastest-growing economy in the world and as a counterbalance to American and European dominance in their region and an ally in their disregard for Western demands that Central Asian governments become more democratic.

Initially, however, mutual suspicions between its members limited the power of the Shanghai Five and its vows to fight Uyghur separatism. This changed significantly in 1999 when several bomb blasts in Uzbekistan's capital of Tashkent, which were apparently targeting Uzbek president Islam Karimov, awoke the Central Asian leaders to the potential of Muslim resistance to their tight control of power. In 2000, Uzbekistan joined this regional security alliance as an observer, and in 2001 this state became its sixth member. At the same time, this loose alliance became further solidified and was renamed the Shanghai Cooperation Organization (SCO).[54] The group's adoption of a more official status and new moniker appears to have been, in part, a conscious effort to counterbalance the power of the Organization for Security and Cooperation in Europe, which has continually levied criticism on its Central Asian members for their lack of democracy. In addition to a more powerful counterbalance to Western influence in the region, however, this reorganization of the alliance demonstrates a real fear on the part of Central Asian leaders of Muslim militants threatening their authority to rule. This fear has also increased since the September 11, 2001, terrorist attacks on the United States, after which the SCO began meeting more regularly and establishing clearer plans for combating terrorism and separatism.[55]

The Central Asian leaders' increased involvement in the SCO suggests that they are playing their Uyghur card in exchange for increased security from external threats and a counterbalance to their critics in the West. Consequently, Central Asian cooperation with Chinese authorities in countering Uyghur separatism has increased since 1999. Already in 1999, for example, Kazakstan extradited two Uyghurs with Chinese citizenship who were under threat of being sentenced to the death penalty for "separatist activity." Ignoring pleas from the United States, European diplomatic missions, and the United Nations High Commissioner for Refugees, all of whom asked it not send these accused "separatists" to their deaths, the Kazakstan government returned them to Chinese authorities without much ceremony. Likewise, more recently Kyrgyzstan's government sentenced a Uyghur with Chinese citizenship to death for "terrorist activity" under suspect circumstances and despite international protest.[56] These clear examples of Central Asian states yielding to China on the Uyghur question are also likely to be replicated in coming years as the SCO plans to open a counterterrorism center in the Uzbekistan capital of Tashkent.[57]

The Chinese government, therefore, has skillfully used its position in Central and South Asia to garner support for its campaigns against Uyghur nationalists. In this sense, it has used the open frontiers of Xinjiang to counter the support for Uyghur nationalism that these same open borders have fostered in neighboring countries. The question, however, remains as to which of these contradictory forces facilitated by the opening of Xinjiang's borders will be stronger in the future: the popular support from abroad that helps to foster Uyghur nationalism or the state alliances that help to suppress it.

Conclusion

In general, the reopening of Xinjiang's borders has been an incredibly important event not only for Xinjiang but also for the entire region of Central Asia. As a result of the cross-border traffic and socioeconomic and political processes created by the opening of these frontiers, two contradictory forces have been unleashed that may be critical to the future of all of Central Asia. On the one hand, Xinjiang's open borders have increased the power of China in Central Asia to such an extent that many in the former Soviet republics of the region fear a gradual Sinification of their own territory, mirroring the large Han Chinese population of Southeast Asia. On the other hand, these open frontiers have renewed the historical ties between Xinjiang and the rest of Central Asia, pulling this tenuously controlled province of the PRC further away from the Chinese state's control. In this context, the future political machinations along Xinjiang's western and southwestern frontiers could be instrumental in determining the future shape of both Central Asia and China.

This situation reflects a conflict that is emerging around the world in our present historical moment of globalization. It is a conflict that is a fairly predictable outcome of open borders and free trade and that highlights one of the central contradictions in the marriage between the powers of centralized statehood and global capitalism. While the opening of borders to commerce is critical to the economic development and, thus, to the strengthening of states, it also opens these states up to external influences that can undermine their authority. The anthropologist Arjun Appadurai characterizes this conflict as follows:

> States find themselves pressed to stay open by the forces of media, technology, and travel that have fueled consumerism throughout the world and have increased the craving, even in the non-Western world, for new commodities and spectacles. On the other hand, these very cravings can be caught up in new ethnoscapes, mediascapes, and, eventually, ideoscapes, such as democracy in China, that the state cannot tolerate as threats to its own control over ideas of nationhood and peoplehood.[58]

In the case of Xinjiang, open borders are obviously critical to the ability of China to develop this area and maintain its stability as an integral part of the Chinese state. At the same time, however, these open borders are helping to foster increased Uyghur nationalism in the region, which seems intent on resisting the authority of the Chinese state and even hopes to eventually separate the region from China altogether.

It seems at present that the Chinese government is banking on the assumption that the power it gains through the economic development associated with open frontiers outweighs the control it loses from external influences. The Chinese state, however, also appears to believe that development alone cannot destroy separatism; it must be accompanied by political control. As one top-ranking official from Xinjiang recently noted, "Neither will the development of economy in Xinjiang destroy the ethnic separatist forces nor will it let those separatist forces give up their separatist activities and dream of independence. . . . Xinjiang must preemptively and aggressively attack and annihilate the *three evil forces*, including the separatists without mercy."[59]

While the development facilitated by Xinjiang's "opening up to the world" could be a positive force in resolving the problems between the Chinese state and the region's Muslim nationalists, mixing development with political control is unlikely to resolve these troubles without grave consequences. Such a policy of attempting to control the impact of Xinjiang's open frontiers is only likely to aggravate the local Muslims' dissatisfaction with Chinese rule. In place of preventing conflict, therefore, it may lead to a more sustained and violent conflict that will not be in the interest of either the Chinese state or the Muslims of Xinjiang.

In this context, one must ask whether the Chinese state's objectives in the Develop the West initiative are to create more opportunities for the local population or to further encourage Han Chinese migration to the region and, through open frontiers, more Han Chinese influence in the rest of Central Asia. If this becomes the eventual result of Xinjiang's open borders, it may not only increase the conflict between local Muslims and Han Chinese, it might also result in the destabilization of the entire region of Central Asia.

Unfortunately, such potential scenarios appear to be far from the attention of the international community given the geopolitical climate following September 11, 2001. While the United States has continued to criticize the Chinese government's violations of the human rights of Muslims in Xinjiang, in August 2002 the U.S. State Department also added a virtually unknown Uyghur political group (Eastern Turkistan Islamic Movement) to its list of international terrorist groups. Likewise, the government of India has increasingly criticized Uyghur separatists and characterized them as terrorists while even suggesting that it might become a member of the SCO.[60] These policies of states outside the region, in turn, appear to be encouraging the former Soviet states of Central Asia to become more suspicious of Uyghur exiles in their own countries. Within the international community, therefore, there is presently little apparent interest in the long-term consequences of the present policies of the Chinese state at Xinjiang's borders.

In order to avoid a potentially disastrous situation in Xinjiang, both the international community and the Chinese government must understand that the future handling of the "opening up" of Xinjiang to the world should involve policies ensuring cultural survival, sustainable development, ethnic power-sharing, and a respect for the integrity of neighboring states. Such an approach requires a long-term vision of the development of Xinjiang and its potentially positive links to Central Asia that focuses on much more than the short-term economic gains of industrial development and the export of consumer goods. This vision must include an understanding of Xinjiang as part of a Central Asian cultural region, regardless of its status within the PRC, and it must involve much more substantial input from the local Muslims of Xinjiang concerning their needs and interests. Only such a plan for the Develop the West campaign will peacefully resolve the problems that the Chinese state faces from Muslim separatists without grave consequences for the stability of Central Asia and prolonged conflict within Xinjiang itself.

Part IV

Costs of Control and Development

9

The Demography of Xinjiang

Stanley W. Toops

How many people are in Xinjiang today? Where are they located, and what changes have occurred over the past decades? What is the regional division of production? These are a few of the questions to be answered in this chapter. First, historical development of the region's population is examined. Next, demographic trends during the twentieth century is discussed. Finally, questions of distribution, ethnicity, migration, and production during the 1990s are considered in closer detail. The overall focus is on the demographic patterns of the past decade, with references to the earlier periods only to elucidate the present.[1]

Data Issues

The primary source for data on the demography of Xinjiang is the *Xinjiang Statistical Yearbook*. The State Statistical Bureau of China produces annual yearbooks for each of China's territorial units (provinces, autonomous regions, and municipalities). These are the best statistical resources available to the researcher. Demographers such as John Aird, Judith Bannister, Dudley L. Poston Jr., and David Yaukey have utilized the State Statistical Bureau publications in their analyses of China population developments. For more than thirty years—between 1949 and the early 1980s—statistical data were an instrument of political propaganda and manipulation or not available at all. In contrast, much of the data from the 1982, 1990, and 2000 censuses are up to international standards. Data from the 1982 and 1990 censuses are readily available.[2] Mapping the statistics produced by the State Statistical Bureau provides an excellent view of the overall pattern of population in Xinjiang. As well, these are the figures used for planning in the People's Republic of China (PRC). The maps produced here convey the population landscape of Xinjiang at the end of the twentieth century. The *Xinjiang Statistical Yearbook* constitutes an invaluable resource for the analysis of regional variations in Xinjiang's overall demographic pattern.[3]

In 1940–1941, the provincial government of Xinjiang made a population survey. The 1930s and 1940s were a complex time for Xinjiang, so there is some concern as to the accuracy of the census. Chang Chih-yi reports the total population in 1941 as 3.7 million.[4] The PRC conducted censuses in 1953, 1964, 1982, 1990, and 2000. With the census in 1953 and thereafter, modern census-taking methods were utilized. The 1953 census included only a few questions and was mainly used to monitor the first Five Year Plan. In 1953, Xinjiang was still being assimilated into the state (e.g., Kashgar was "liberated" in 1952). In 1953, the census mechanism was modeled on the Soviet Union methods. As pointed out by M. Freeberne, the total population for Xinjiang in 1953 was variously reported as between 4.8 and 5.2 million.[5] The 1964 census was in many ways inadequate and the records are poorly organized. Only a part of the collected data was processed. Worse, many of the questionnaires were lost in the Cultural Revolution (1966–1976). The 1960s pose particular difficulties. The Cultural Revolution was a time of such turmoil in Xinjiang, and levels of fertility and mortality and migration patterns are not easily discerned from the census. The 1982, 1990, and 2000 censuses were accomplished according to international standards of demography. In 1982, the population numbered 13.08 million, and in 1990 the total reached 15.16 million. The recent 2000 census registered 18.46 million inhabitants, of whom 40.6 percent were Han and 59.4 percent were minorities, including Uyghurs and Kazaks.[6] Basic issues to consider for the censuses are the degree of minority undercount (an issue also important for the U.S. census) and the numbers of military personnel in the region. Population censuses for provincial-level units do not include military personnel. The complete census results by county for 2000 were not yet available as of this writing. The census is more accurate now, but the political sensitivities of population issues in a region such as Xinjiang are nonetheless very important to the state. The specific results of the 2000 census down to the county level will be a good test of the overall reliability of the census figures for Xinjiang.

History of Xinjiang's Demographics

Referring to chapter 10 on the ecology of Xinjiang, there is a three-part division of Xinjiang (see the map of the Xinjiang Uyghur Autonomous Region located at the front of the book). The northern zone is steppe, primarily inhabited by nomadic peoples such as the Kazaks. The north and south are separated by the Tian Shan (Uyg. Tengri Tagh) range. Settlement in the southern zone is concentrated in the oases of the Tarim basin, which is inhabited by agriculturalist Uyghurs. The eastern zone is focused around the oases of Turpan and Hami (Uyg. Khumul).

The population base of Xinjiang is rooted in the history of migrations into the region from outside. Beginning in 700 BCE, the local population, and in particular the Saka people, was Iranic. From 100 BCE through 200 CE, the Xiongnu and Han empires invaded the region, with the Xiongnu having control north of the Tian Shan and the Han maintaining military colonies in the south. From 200 CE, the Iranic kingdoms of the south were Buddhist. The growth of the Turkic presence in the region began by 700 CE, when the Western Turks, the Karluk, and the Uyghurs held sway. Troops of the Tang dynasty in the region were also mostly of Turkic stock, in this case Eastern Turks. Islam came into the region with the Karluks as they set up the Karakhanid empire in the Turanian basin and Kashgar. The Uyghur empire (800–1200) in Turpan was mainly Buddhist. By the 1200s, the Mongols ruled, and most of the population was by now Turkic. The Chagatai khanate controlled the region from 1227 to 1334 and advanced the conversion of the population to Islam. From the mid-1300s through the 1500s, the Moghulistan successors to the Chagatai ruled. This, too, was a Turkic-Islamic culture. Kazaks entered the north of Xinjiang in the 1500s and the Oirat (Zunghar) Mongols held control over the northern lands in the 1600s.[7]

The Qing (Manchu) dynasty invaded the area in the 1700s. As a result, the Mongols were wiped out in the north, leaving only their name to the Zungharian basin. The Qing rulers brought in Kazaks, Uyghurs, Han, Hui, and Xibos to settle north of the central mountains. This marked the beginning of real Chinese settlement in the region. The Chinese settlers included both Han and Hui, and they were allowed to settle north of the mountains but not in the south. At the same time, the Uyghur population was concentrated mainly in and around the Tarim basin. Qing officials and military personnel also entered Xinjiang in this period, adding elements from the Mongol, Manchu, and Chinese peoples. Although data are imprecise, the Uyghurs in Qing times appear to have accounted for about 62 percent of Xinjiang's population, the Chinese (Han and Hui) constituted about 30 percent, with the remaining 8 percent comprising diverse other minorities (see table 9.1). This basic pattern is roughly similar to today's ratios.[8]

By the end of the Qing era, the distribution of ethnic groups in Xinjiang had taken on a complex character. In the south, Uyghurs predominated in the Tarim region while Uyghurs, Hui, and Han held sway in Turpan. In the north the Kazaks, along with Uyghurs, Hui, and Han, held sway in the Ili River valley, and both Uyghurs and Han inhabited Dihua (renamed "Urumchi" after February 1954) and the surrounding territory. Under the Qing, there were Chinese garrisons and settlers in all of the towns of the region, extending even to Kashgar.

The Qing settlement pattern often resembled a twin-city system, with a Chinese town and a Muslim town positioned next to one another in a re-

Table 9.1

Population of the Western Region (Xinjiang) in the Early 1800s

Ethnic Group	Population	Percent
Uyghur	320,000	62
Chinese	155,000	30
Qing officials	42,000	8
Total	517,000	100

Source: J. Millward, "Historical Perspectives on Contemporary Xinjiang," *Inner Asia* 2, no. 2 (2000): 122–123.

stricted territory. Indeed, that arrangement still prevails in Turpan and Hami today. In other cases such as Dihua, the Chinese inhabited a walled inner city, with the local Muslim population settled in the areas outside the walls. In Urumchi today, the Muslim area is still concentrated to the south of the downtown, outside the old city wall. The wall is gone, but its impact on the distribution of the population groups remains. The sites of former city gates (Beimen, Nanmen, and Ximen) are recalled only through the names of bus stops.[9]

Xinjiang's Population in the Twentieth Century

During the period of the Republic of China, Xinjiang was nominally under the control of the Republican governors or warlords. However, two significant exceptions existed. First, during the 1930s Kashgar and the surrounding area fell under the control of the Turkish-Islamic Republic of Eastern Turkistan. Then, during the 1940s another Eastern Turkistan Republic, or "Three Regions Republic," was formed at the town of Yining (Gulja) in the north. These Three Regions were absorbed into the PRC after it was established in 1949.[10]

Most matters of public policy in Xinjiang were decided by the local warlord governors rather than by the distant central Republican government. The three warlords who ruled in succession—Yang Cengxin, Jin Shuren, and Sheng Shicai—were concerned mainly with the maintenance of their own power rather than the development of Xinjiang. The local government was run to benefit the warlords and, by extension, the small Han Chinese community locally.[11]

In 1940–1941, the provincial government of Xinjiang managed to carry out a census. The 1930s and 1940s were a period of turmoil in most of Xinjiang, so there is ample reason to question the accuracy of any census conducted amid such conditions. Warlord conflicts involving the Kashgar

Table 9.2

Population of Xinjiang in 1941

Ethnic Group	Population	Percent
Uyghur	2,984,000	80.0
Kazak	326,000	8.7
Han	187,000	5.0
Hui	92,000	2.5
Kyrgyz	65,000	1.7
Others	76,000	2.0
Total	3,730,000	100.0

Source: Chang Chih-yi, "Land Utilization and Settlement Possibilities in Sinkiang," *Geographical Review* 39 (1949): 62.

Republic of Eastern Turkistan and the Three Regions Republic, as well as conflicts involving the local Muslim (Uyghur, Kazak, and Hui) and Han communities undoubtedly caused wholesale shifts and transfers of populations, as well as precipitous declines in some areas. Moreover, efforts to resettle Chinese into Xinjiang were carried out at the provincial level during this period. Even though it is certain that these were far less successful than later ventures, their impact is all but impossible to determine from the census data. These and other consequences of the prevailing instability would all have adversely affected the accuracy of the census.[12]

The total population of Xinjiang in 1941 was estimated to be 3.73 million (see table 9.2). Of that number, 80 percent were Uyghur, 8.7 percent Kazak, 5 percent Han, 2.5 percent Hui, and 1.7 percent Kyrgyz. The north was populated mainly by Kazaks, while the south was predominantly Uyghur. The region around Ili had roughly equal amounts of Uyghurs, Hui, and Kazaks, while the city of Urumchi was half Uyghur and half Han.[13]

As indicated earlier, the 1953 census is adequate, the 1964 census is poor, and the 1982, 1990, and 2000 censuses are accurate. The 1953 census documents a population that was 74.7 percent Uyghur, 10 percent Kazak, 6 percent Han, 3 percent Hui, and 1.4 percent Kyrgyz (see table 9.3). The Han and Hui enumerated here had migrated from Gansu during the Republican period.[14] The central government sponsored a large migration of cadres, students, and workers into Xinjiang; also, a large contingent of People's Liberation Army (PLA) and demobilized troops entered the area. The migratory population was mostly Han and primarily male. Female volunteers, many from Hunan and Shandong, were also recruited into Xinjiang to redress the sex-ratio imbalance. Many of these migrants settled in Xinjiang in the 1950s.[15]

In 1954, the Xinjiang Production and Construction Corps (Xinjiang

Table 9.3

Population in Xinjiang, 1953–1990

Ethnic Group	1953	1964	1982	1990
Uyghur	3,640,000	4,021,200	5,995,000	7,195,000
	(74.7%)	(54%)	(45.8%)	(47.5%)
Han	299,000	2,445,400	5,284,000	5,696,000
	(6.1%)	(32.9%)	(40.4%)	(37.6%)
Kazak	492,000	501,400	903,000	1,106,000
	(10.1%)	(6.7%)	(6.9%)	(7.3%)
Hui	150,000	271,100	567,000	682,000
	(3.1%)	(3.6%)	(4.3%)	(4.5%)
Kyrgyz	68,000	69,200	112,000	140,000
	(1.4%)	(0.9%)	(0.9%)	(0.9%)
Others	225,000	133,500	220,500	337,900
	(4.6%)	(1.8%)	(1.7%)	(2.2%)
Total	4,874,000	7,441,800	13,081,500	15,156,900

Sources: Yuan Qingli, "Population Changes in Xinjiang Uighur Autonomous Region (1949–1984)," *Central Asian Survey* 9 (1990): 57; M. Freeberne, "Demographic and Economic Changes in the Sinkiang Uighur Autonomous Region," *Population Studies* 20, no. 1 (1966): 108; and Xinjiang Uyghur Autonomous Region Bureau of Statistics, *Xinjiang Statistical Yearbook, 1996* (Beijing: China Statistics Press, 1996), p. 52.

shengchan jianshe bingtuan) was established. The bingtuan was composed of demobilized PLA troops, demobilized Guomindang (Nationalist) garrisons, volunteers encouraged by the government, and political and criminal prisoners. Through the 1950s and 1960s, many young people from the east were encouraged to move to Xinjiang. By 1955, the bingtuan's workforce numbered over 110,000.[16] During the years of the Great Leap Forward (1958–1960), many eastern youth were rusticated to the frontier and to Xinjiang in particular. In 1959, 800,000 migrants arrived in Xinjiang. There was out-migration as well, as the economy of the eastern regions of China recovered in the early 1960s. In 1961, 500,000 people left Xinjiang to go back east.[17]

One instance of particular note is the Yi-Tar Event in 1962, when some 100,000 to 200,000 Uyghurs and Kazaks decided to leave their home in Ili and Tarbagatay for the neighboring Kazak Soviet Socialist Republic of the Soviet Union. Reasons for the exodus were various, including deteriorating economic conditions in Xinjiang, incoming Han migration, crackdowns on Muslim religious practices, and inducements offered by the Soviet Union. Indeed, many of these Uyghurs and Kazaks had received Soviet passports.[18]

The 1964 census documents a population of 54 percent Uyghur, 33 percent Han, 7 percent Kazak, 4 percent Hui, 1 percent Kyrgyz, and 1 percent "other." Even the sketchy records of the 1964 census register the substantial increase of the Han population since the 1953 census. During the Cultural Revolution, there was no directed campaign of migration into Xinjiang. Nonetheless, by 1967 nearly 1 million youth had moved to Xinjiang, many of these ending up in the bingtuan.[19] Migrants during the Cultural Revolution simply drifted into the region, as household registration in Xinjiang was relatively easy. Poorer rural peasants looked for work in the towns, cities, and state farms of Xinjiang. After the Cultural Revolution in 1977, many rusticated youth, professionals, or retirees left Xinjiang to return to their original provinces. By the early 1980s, though, the new economic policies of openness reversed the flow. Surplus rural labor was henceforth allowed to migrate temporarily without registration. Thanks to this, peasants with skills in construction, carpentry, tailoring, cobbling, driving, or painting have become a floating population, trying their luck in whatever places that offer employment. Many have come to Xinjiang in response to this situation. This floating population is not registered and is therefore not counted in the census.[20]

The 1982 census of the population shows 46 percent Uyghur, 40 percent Han, 7 percent Kazak, 4 percent Hui, and 1 percent Kyrgyz. Thus, the Uyghurs' share of the population had evidently decreased since the previous count while the Han's share had increased. Assuming that these data are accurate, and acknowledging that the fertility rate of the Uyghur population was considerably higher than that of the Han, then this changed ratio can only be explained in terms of a substantial Han migration from elsewhere in China.[21]

The 1990 census documents a population that was 47 percent Uyghur, 38 percent Han, 7 percent Kazak, 4.5 percent Hui, and 1 percent Kyrgyz. The south continued to be populated mainly by Uyghurs with the exception of Bayangol, where many Han were serving in the bingtuan. The Kazak population in the north as of 1990 did not quite constitute a majority, while Ili remained an ethnically diverse area, as it had been since Qing times. In 1990, mainly Han, mostly post-1949 migrants, inhabited the cities of Urumchi, Shihezi, and Karamay. The migrants from the east brought their own culture, customs, and language. *Putonghua* Mandarin became the *lingua franca*, replacing the Gansu dialect spoken by the Han inhabitants at the beginning of the twentieth century.[22] By the mid-1990s, the official state policy was to develop Xinjiang as quickly as possible. This meant that the state facilitated migrants in their search for work, which gave rise to the new floating population that drifted into Xinjiang.

Only a few of the most basic statistics from the 2000 census have as yet been released. Table 9.4 compares the basic data for the 1982, 1990, and 2000 censuses. The 2000 census registered a total population for Xinjiang of 18,462,600, up from 15,156,900 in 1990; this translates into a growth rate of

Table 9.4

Xinjiang Basic Census Data, 1982–2000

	1982	1990	2000
Total Population	13,081,500	15,156,900	18,462,600
Male	6,732,200 (51.5%)	7,823,200 (51.6%)	9,554,900 (51.8%)
Female	6,349,300 (48.5%)	7,333,700 (48.4%)	8,907,700 (48.2%)
Age 0–5	1,867,000 (1.4%)	2,188,500 (14.4%)	1,645,600 (8.9%)
Age 6–14	3,308,500 (25.3%)	2,821,200 (18.6%)	3,396,000 (18.3%)
Age 15–64	7,424,200 (56.8%)	9,554,900 (63%)	12,586,000 (68.1%)
Age 65 and over	481,800 (3.7%)	5,923,000 (3.9%)	835,000 (4.5%)
Han	5,284,000 (40.4%)	5,695,400 (37.6%)	7,497,700 (40.6%)
Minorities	7,797,500 (59.6%)	9,461,500 (62.4%)	10,964,900 (59.4%)
College Education	83,700 (0.6%)	279,800 (1.8%)	949,100 (5.1%)
Senior Secondary	842,800 (6.4%)	1,574,200 (10.4%)	2,231,900 (12.1%)
Junior Secondary	2,286,300 (17.5%)	3,135,100 (20.7%)	5,082,500 (27.5%)
Primary	4,425,700 (33.8%)	5,525,500 (36.5%)	7,006,600 (38%)
Illiterate and Semiliterate	2,653,900 (20.3%)	1,981,100 (13.1%)	1,026,400 (5.6%)

Source: Xinjiang Uyghur Autonomous Region Bureau of Statistics, *Xinjiang Statistical Yearbook, 2001* (Beijing: China Statistics Press, 2001), p. 93.

1.67 percent per year for the 1990s. For 1999, the natural growth rate for Xinjiang was 1.28 percent, while China's overall natural growth rate was 0.88 percent. These rates are low for a developing country and show the success of China's population control policies. However, Xinjiang registered the sixth-highest natural growth rate in all China. The only areas with growth rates higher than Xinjiang are Tibet, Guizhou, Qinghai, Ningxia, and Hainan, all of which are regions that have significant minority populations. In 2000, the Han numbered 7,497,700, or 40.6 percent of the total population. The total for all minorities was 10,964,900, or 59.4 percent of the population. For China as a whole, minorities numbered 8 percent of the population. Only Tibet in 2000 had a higher percentage of minority population than Xinjiang. The sex ratio (male to female) by the same year reached 1.0727, up from 1.0667 in 1990. Xinjiang's sex ratio placed it thirteenth out of thirty-one provinces and regions in China, in short, close to the national average. In 2000, the composition of the population by age was as follows: 27 percent between the ages of zero to fourteen, 68 percent between the ages of fifteen and sixty-four, and a mere 4.5 percent over sixty-five.[23]

The age-dependency ratio is the proportion of the dependent population (children and seniors) as compared to the total population. Xinjiang's age-dependency ratio in 2000 was 48.5 percent, which placed it twenty-first out of thirty-one provinces and regions, or once more close to the national average. Compared to other minority areas, Xinjiang's population ranked seventh out of thirty-one provinces and regions in the rate of literacy among the population over fifteen years of age and was thus above the national average (see chapter 7 for details). According to the 2000 census, 6 percent of the total were either illiterate or semiliterate; 11 percent had some schooling; 38 percent completed elementary school; 28 percent had finished a junior secondary school; 12 percent had graduated from senior secondary school; and a mere 5 percent had attended any kind of institution of higher education. Overall, more than 45 percent of the population had at least a junior secondary school education by 2000.[24]

The data can be analyzed to indicate other possible population totals. For example, if one adds in all those serving in the PLA in Xinjiang (see chapter 5), the total population could be expanded by 100,000.

A particularly important additional calculation would be to include the floating population, that is, the unofficial migrants to the area. This could add up to 15 percent to the total, or approximately 2.8 million. As most of the migrants are Han, their numbers add up to 10.3 million, compared to the total of 10.9 million for minorities. With creative rounding, one could estimate the numbers to show a 50:50 Han–minority distribution. In this scenario, one can state definitely that by 2000 the Han population of Xinjiang outnumbered the Uyghurs.

Alternatively, one could go back to 1941 and assume a constant natural growth rate for the Uyghurs thereafter. In this case, the current population of the Uyghurs would reach over 10 million. However interesting these estimates may be from the standpoint of current polemics, one is on more firm ground to take the official statistics as they are and then determine what those statistics actually mean for Xinjiang.

Population Distribution in the 1990s

Xinjiang's 1998 population of 17.47 million was split between the north and south (see map 9.1). The general population is distributed in two broad belts. The first of these belts runs from east to west through Hami, Turpan, Urumchi, Shihezi, Karamay, and Yining, with an outlier zone in the Altay Shan. This belt connects the major urban centers in the eastern and northern portions of the region. The major centers of population are the Ili district (2.1 million), the Urumchi district (1.5 million), and the Changji district (1.5 million). The northern region embraced by this belt accounts for 52.5 percent of Xinjiang's total population.

The second belt lies in the south and is defined by a series of oases that ring the Tarim basin. Included among these oases are Korla, Kucha, Aksu,

Map 9.1 **Population Distribution in Xinjiang, 1998**

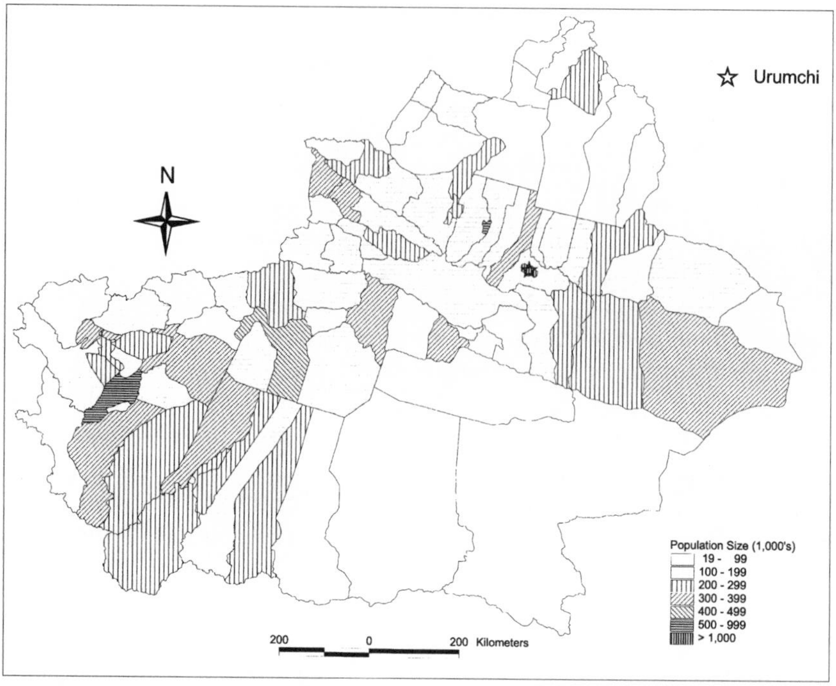

Source: Xinjiang Uyghur Autonomous Region Bureau of Statistics, *Xinjiang Statistical Yearbook, 1998* (Beijing: China Statistics Press, 1998). Map by Huiping Li and Avram G. Primack.

Artush, Kashgar, and Khotan. Of these districts, the most populous are the Kashgar district (3.2 million), the Aksu district (2.0 million), and the Khotan district (1.6 million). Together, this southern belt accounts for 47.5 percent of Xinjiang's population.[25]

Xinjiang has an urban nonagricultural population of 6.2 million (33.75 percent), and China has an urban population of 30.89 percent. The nonagricultural and agricultural urban population of Xinjiang amounts to 53 percent. (Typically, cities in China include substantial agricultural populations.)[26] Xinjiang is thus close to the national average. The high point in the urban demographic landscape of Xinjiang today is Urumchi Municipality, with a population of 1.4 million (see figure 9.1). The next two cities both have less than half Urumchi's population: Shihezi (580,000) and Aksu (500,000). All of the other cites in Xinjiang are in the 150,000 to 400,000 range, with the principal ones being Hami (350,000), Changji (340,00), Yining (330,000), Korla (330,000), Kashgar (310,000), Kuitun (260,000), and

Figure 9.1   **Population of Xinjiang Cities, 1998**

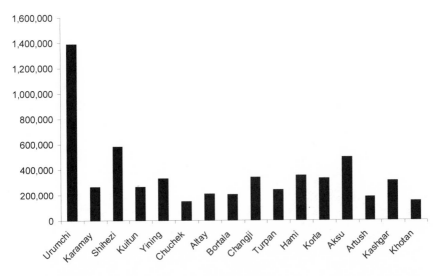

Source: Xinjiang Uyghur Autonomous Region Bureau of Statistics, *Xinjiang Statistical Yearbook, 1999* (Beijing: China Statistics Press, 1999)

Karamay (260,000). Xinjiang's traditional city centers prior to the Qing era were the Ili valley, Kashgar, and Turpan. With the advent of the Qing, Dihua became the region's primary urban center. Along with the expansion of older towns, a number of new cities have also been created, among them Karamay, Shihezi, Kuitun, and Changji. The town of Aksu has also been the recipient of large numbers of new migrants. Two counties are equivalent in size to cities: the Yarkand oasis with 600,000 inhabitants, and the Kucha oasis with 360,000. Both the northern and southern population belts are well represented among the larger cities. Many of the urban centers of Xinjiang are based on modernized agriculture and industry or oil production, with Urumchi, Shihezi, Aksu, Changji, Korla, Kuitun, and Karamay all fitting this description. The traditional urban centers of Yining, Kashgar, and Turpan have been supplanted by these newer urban centers. Thus, one can see that the urban hierarchy of Xinjiang has been transformed by the policies of the PRC.[27]

The size of Xinjiang's population provides only one element of the region's overall demographic picture. The density of population per square kilometer (sq. km) provides an especially revealing insight into the relationship of the people to the land (see map 9.2). Much of Xinjiang is notable for its very low

Map 9.2   **Population Density in Xinjiang, 1998**

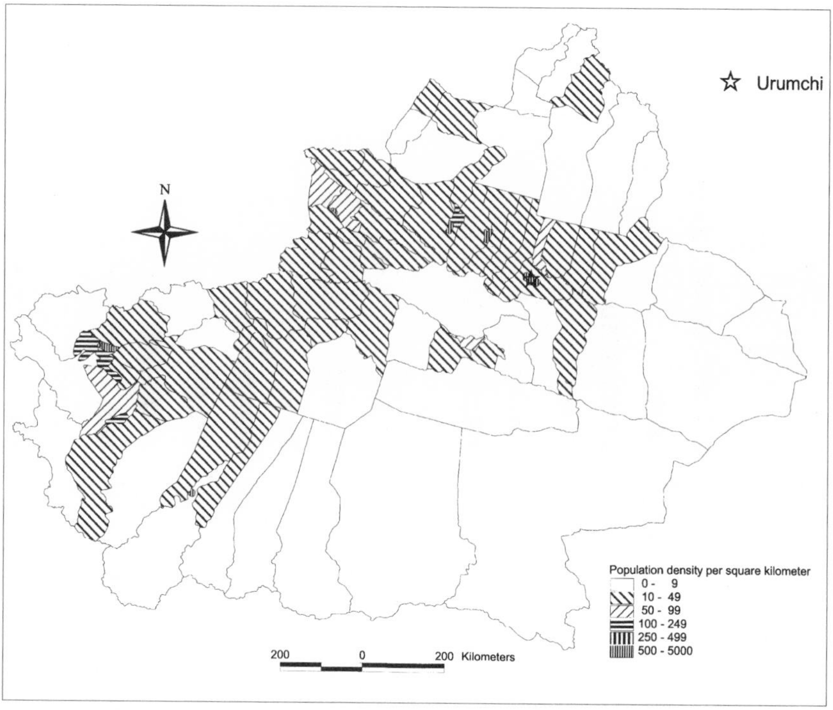

Source: Xinjiang Uyghur Autonomous Region Bureau of Statistics, *Xinjiang Statistical Yearbook, 1998* (Beijing: China Statistics Press, 1998). Map by Huiping Li and Avram G. Primack.

population density. In southern Xinjiang, most of the population is concentrated in a few oasis settlements, while the cities of the north are surrounded by desert. Since much of the land is comprised of either desert or mountain zones, there is little land that is more than marginally suitable for agriculture or grazing. Of Xinjiang's total land area of 1,664,900 sq. km, only 43,500 sq. km are arable. Another 65,600 sq. km are forested, 513,600 sq. km are pastureland, and a staggering 1,042,200 sq. km are wasteland. For all of Xinjiang, only one-third of the land is usable for any sustained economic purpose.[28]

The highest population densities in Xinjiang are recorded in Kashgar, Yining, and the central cities of Korla, Kuitun, Shihezi, and Urumchi. The area surrounding Kashgar and Yining is mainly agricultural, but Korla, Kuitun, Shihezi, and Urumchi are all, to varying degrees, industrial centers.

The natural rate of population increase for Xinjiang in 1999 was 1.28

Map 9.3   **Rate of Natural Population Increase in Xinjiang, 1998**

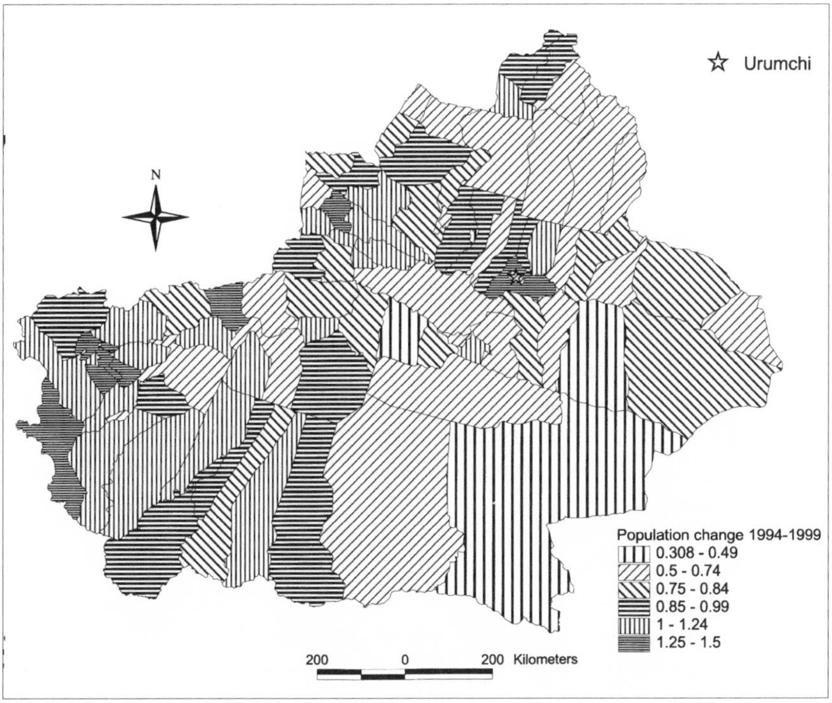

Source: Xinjiang Uyghur Autonomous Region Bureau of Statistics, *Xinjiang Statistical Yearbook, 1999* (Beijing: China Statistics Press, 1999). Map by Huiping Li and Avram G. Primack

percent, which is derived from a crude birthrate of 1.97 percent and a crude death rate of 0.69 percent (see map 9.3). This compares to China's overall rate of natural population increase of 0.87 percent, based on a crude birthrate of 1.52 percent and a crude death rate of 0.65 percent. The region's birthrate has actually increased since 1995, when it was 1.89 percent. Xinjiang's higher birthrate thus accounts for the fact that its rate of population increase is relatively higher than other parts of China. This growth rate results in the annual addition of over 220,000 people to Xinjiang's population.[29]

Especially high levels of natural population growth are seen in the counties of Kashgar (1.5 percent), Khotan (1.6 percent), Yining (1.4 percent), and Urumchi (1.4 percent). Low levels of growth prevail in cities such as Aksu, Kuitun, Shihezi, and Urumchi, as well as in the counties of Shanshan (Pichan), Luntai (Bugur), and Fuhai (Burultokhay). Kashgar and Khotan have high numbers of both births and deaths. Urumchi, Shihezi, Kuitun, Shanshan, and

Aksu all have birthrates below 1 percent. The lowest death rates of 0.25 percent are recorded in Urumchi county and Karamay, Tacheng, and Changji cities. Jiashi (Peyziwat) county of the Kashgar district has the dubious distinction of possessing both the highest birthrate (2.4 percent) and highest death rate (1.2 percent) in all Xinjiang.[30]

These various data permit one to draw the following conclusions. Xinjiang's population is concentrated in particular areas due to the prevalence of deserts and mountains. The population landscape of Xinjiang has been changed with the implementation of official settlement policies promoted by the government in Beijing. There are two belts of population settlement, that is, northern and southern cities, with both of them following transportation linkages. The newly industrialized cities, such as Urumchi, Shihezi, and Korla, have supplanted traditional urban centers, such as Yining, Kashgar, and Turpan. Rural levels of density remain higher in Kashgar and Yining. There is a strong regionalization of natural population increase, with high levels in the south around Kashgar and Khotan, and in the north around Yining and Urumchi county.

Ethnicity in the 1990s

At 46.6 percent of Xinjiang's officially recorded population in 1998, Uyghurs were the most numerous ethnic group in the region (see figure 9.2). By contrast, in the same year Han constituted 38.5 percent of the total, Kazaks were 7.4 percent, Hui were 4.5 percent, and Kyrgyz were 0.9 percent. A mere two years later, the 2000 census reported a striking increase in the Han population, which reached 40.9 percent of the total, compared to a total minority population (including Uyghurs) of 59.9 percent. Since the birthrate among Han is generally quite low, the reported sharp increase in their numbers must be ascribed mainly to Han in-migration.[31]

The ethnic distribution of Xinjiang's population is configured along a north-south divide (see map 9.4 on page 256). Uyghurs predominate numerically in the south, for example, in the Tarim basin, Turpan, and Yining. In addition, there are large pockets of Han throughout the south. For example, there are many Han in Aksu, due to the bingtuan farms there. Bayangol, near Korla and Lop Nor, is also a major Han area. The largest concentration of Han, however, is in Xinjiang's central area, at Urumchi, Shihezi, and Karamay, where they constitute a solid majority. In the northern Altay area, the Kazaks maintain a plurality, with the Han second and the Uyghurs third. In other parts of Ili prefecture, Han are more numerous than either the Kazaks or Uyghurs. The ethnic diversity of the Ili district is reflected in the fact that Han, Uyghurs, and Kazaks are all roughly equal in

Figure 9.2   **Xinjiang Ethnicity, 1998**

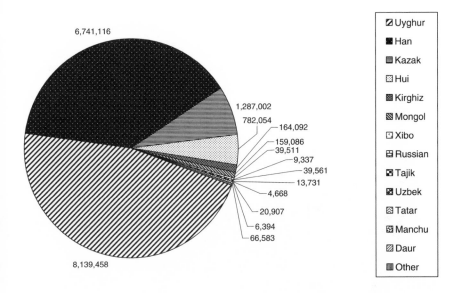

number. Most Hui are located in the major cities, but they maintain a presence among the rural populations of Ili, Changji, Turpan, and Tarbagatay. The smaller ethnic groups are much more regionally focused. The Kyrgyz are to be found mainly in Kizilsu in the south. Two different groups of Mongols inhabit Bayangol and Bortala. The Xibo are to be found in the Ili district's Chapchal county, while the Tajiks are nearly all at Tashkurghan in the Kashgar district. Russians, Manchus, Uzbeks, and Tatars reside in the urban areas of Urumchi and Yining, while the Daur are to be found in Chuchek (Tacheng) (see figure 9.2).[32]

The asymmetrical distribution of Han and minority populations is most evident in the urban areas. Table 9.5 on page 257 profiles the ethnicity of the principal urban centers. Shihezi and Kuitun are essentially Han cities, while Urumchi, Karamay, and Changji are all more than 75 percent Han. Han majorities are present in Chuchek, Altay, Bortala, Hami, Korla, and Aksu. Uyghurs, by comparison, claim majorities in Turpan, Artush, Kashgar, and Khotan, and a plurality in Yining.[33]

Such data explain a bitter piece of black humor that circulates among the Uyghurs. "Look at the map of Xinjiang. Where within Xinjiang is the 'Uyghur autonomous region' to be found?" The Han dominate in the municipalities, the Kazaks have Ili, the Mongols have Bortala and Bayangol, the Hui have Changji, and the Kyrgyz have Kizilsu. This leaves to the Uyghurs only Hami,

Map 9.4 **Ethnic Minority Distribution in Xinjiang, 1998**

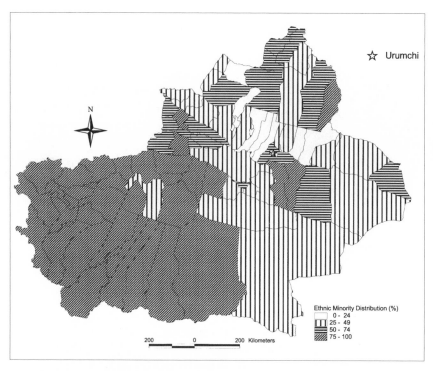

Source: Xinjiang Uyghur Autonomous Region Bureau of Statistics, *Xinjiang Statistical Yearbook, 1998* (Beijing: China Statistics Press, 1998). Map by Huiping Li and Avram G. Primack.

Turpan, Aksu, Kashgar, and Khotan. "It seems that the Uyghurs' 'autonomous region' is to be found only in the wastes of Tarim."

Migration in the 1990s

State policies in the late 1950s and early 1960s encouraged migration into Xinjiang. Ideologically inspired images of heroic migrants opening up vast wastelands and transforming parched deserts into fertile fields inspired many Han Chinese to depart their homes for the northwest. Government officials channeled these zealous migrants to areas such as Shihezi. Most of these migrants were Han from as far afield as Shanghai and Sichuan. Other newcomers were PLA troops who were demobilized in Xinjiang in the early 1950s. The bingtuan after its establishment in 1954 consisted mainly of these demobilized soldiers. From 1954 to 1961, a total of 1.5 million people migrated to Xinjiang, with half a million migrating there in 1959 alone. The

Table 9.5

Xinjiang Urban Ethnicity, 1998

City	Population	Uyghur (%)	Han (%)
Urumchi	1,391,896	13	76
Karamay	263,069	15	77
Shihezi	581,952	11	95
Kuitun	263,942	<1	95
Yining	332,022	48	36
Chuchek	147,546	3	63
Altay	210,302	2	62
Bortala	204,704	16	66
Changji	338,739	3	77
Turpan	242,501	71	21
Hami	352,929	23	69
Korla	331,976	29	67
Aksu	498,937	41	58
Artush	188,224	80	7
Kashgar	311,141	81	18
Khotan	154,352	83	17

Source: Xinjiang Uyghur Autonomous Region Bureau of Statistics, *Xinjiang Statistical Yearbook, 1999* (Beijing: China Statistics Press, 1999), pp. 60–63.

Great Leap Forward was yet another period of tremendous Han influx into Xinjiang.[34]

It is important to note that throughout the period there was migration out of Xinjiang as well. Many Han returned to their homes in China proper after saving enough money on the northwestern frontier. In some years, the flow of returnees was particularly high, as in 1962, for example, when many returned home to Shanghai. In addition, some 100,000 to 200,000 Kazaks crossed the border to Soviet Kazakstan after incidents in Ili and Tarbagatay in 1962. From 1978 to 1982, retired cadres who had served in Xinjiang were allowed to return home in the east, while others were released from exile in Xinjiang where they had been sent during the Cultural Revolution. Youthful offenders from Shanghai who had been exiled in Xinjiang were also allowed to return home during these years.[35]

In 1964, a large contingent of "volunteers" was sent to Xinjiang. This was to be the last major movement of migrants to be fully organized and overseen by the government. Thereafter, people elsewhere in China who were either out of work or in search of a better future simply drifted westward seeking employment in towns and farms. Nearly all lacked authorization and can therefore be considered illegal immigrants. The government either looked the other way or channeled and facilitated a movement of people that it could not readily have stopped and whose presence in Xinjiang, under any circumstances, promoted the policies of the Chinese Communist Party and the state.

Migrating Han peoples moved to Xinjiang along the main transportation routes. In the early 1950s, their principal goals were Hami and Turpan, while in the 1960s they shifted toward Urumchi. It is significant that the rail line had been extended to Hami by 1958 and Urumchi by 1961. In the late 1950s and early 1960s, the migrants' target zone of settlement was extended south to Korla and west to Shihezi, Kuitun, and Karamay, all of which had by then been connected to main railroad lines.

During the 1950s, the Soviet Union had constructed a rail line from the Soviet interior all the way to Zungharian Gate (Uyg., Alatau Pass, Ch. Ala Shankou). But when the Sino-Soviet split occurred in 1961, China elected not to build its part of this connection. By 1992, however, China had extended its rail line to Kazakstan. Immediately, the new inflow of Han migrants began to follow the route of this northern rail line.[36] By 1999, the southern rail line ran all the way to Kashgar. Han migration in the coming years is sure to follow along the tracks of this railroad, as it has all others previously in Xinjiang.

The directions of migration have changed in recent years (see map 9.5). Again, it should be noted that the migration figures listed on map 9.5 tally only those who officially register their households; they do not include the floating population of unofficial migrants. Districts such as Bayangol, Aksu, and Kashgar have seen an increase in population due to migrants from outside Xinjiang. The cities Urumchi, Kuitun, Korla, Aksu, Changji, and Hami and the counties Jinghe (Jing), Yecheng (Kaghilik), and Maigaiti (Makit) have all experienced growing numbers of migrants as well, with the annual numbers going to each ranging in 1998 from 1,000 to 5,000. Most of these new target areas belong to the urban zones of the north, and all of them are now linked to the Chinese heartland by railroads. The focus on Aksu, however, is probably due to the fact that there is already a large bingtuan population there. In a very few cities, one of them being Karamay, the rate of out-migration exceeds the inflow of migrants. This apparent anomaly traces to the circular migration of personnel to and from the oil industry.[37]

Of course, these figures do not include the floating population or those who somehow escaped registration. As indicated earlier, the floating population in China accounts for 10 to 15 percent of the population of many cities. The precise number of migrants in this category for Xinjiang is unknown. Generally, however, the floating population moves through the cities in search of work. Urumchi, Korla, and Aksu all maintain major facilities for people looking for employment and housing. On the street outside the employment

Map 9.5 **Migration in Xinjiang, 1998**

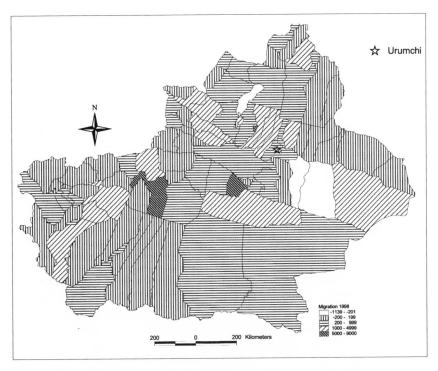

Source: Xinjiang Uyghur Autonomous Region Bureau of Statistics, *Xinjiang Statistical Yearbook, 1998* (Beijing: China Statistics Press, 1998). Map by Huiping Li and Avram G. Primack.

office in downtown Urumchi, one sees lines of such people, many of them skilled construction workers who can command good wages.

Of course, nearly all of the migrants are Han rather than Uyghur or Kazak. Xinjiang's local Uyghurs view these people as illegal migrants who are filling jobs that legitimately belong to them. In contrast, local Han businessmen look on these migrant laborers as an important source of reliable labor. While the presence of Han migrants definitely exacerbates ethnic tensions in Xinjiang, such tensions between local and immigrant labor are not unknown in the rest of China, even when both parties are Han. Thus, in Beijing and Shanghai, immigrants from Sichuan and Zhejiang also encounter resentment and outright hostility from local inhabitants, and especially from those who fear that the migrants might take their jobs.

A second form of migration that is no less dramatic in its scale and consequences is from rural areas to the cities. Large numbers of Xinjiang residents are abandoning the countryside and rural life. Thus, there is much movement into Kashgar from the surrounding countryside. Urumchi is gaining many new residents who arrive not only from the Turpan district but also from the city of Turpan. Indeed, several buses run between Turpan and Urumchi every day. So intensive is this rural-to-urban movement that all of the outlying jurisdictions maintain offices in Urumchi in order to facilitate legal migration to the booming metropolis.

This shift to the city is driven by the quest for better economic prospects, education, and facilities, in short, by dreams of upward mobility. The many educational institutions of all types in Urumchi are a magnet to students from the countryside. Once they have completed their studies, most stay on in the city, secure jobs, and enter the rolls of rural-to-urban migrants. The gap between center and periphery, between Urumchi and the entire countryside and hinterland, is growing rapidly in present-day Xinjiang, with serious implications for the future.[38]

Production in the 1990s

Gross domestic production (GDP) provides a good index of a region's overall economic productivity, while GDP per capita helps define the potential effect of such wealth on the population. As indicated by Calla Wiemer in chapter 6, in 2000 Xinjiang had a GDP per capita that ranked twelfth among China's thirty-one provinces and regions. Those ranking ahead of Xinjiang were all coastal provinces.[39] Xinjiang's status of GDP per capita is due to its relatively smaller population and to its being a center for oil production.

Production in Xinjiang is highly regionalized. Average GDP per capita for the whole region tells part of the story; the rest can be seen in the county-by-county differences in GDP per capita. The productive capacities of Xinjiang are concentrated in three areas. One is the region of Karamay, while a second is the area around Korla at the northern edge of the Tarim basin. The economies of both of these areas are based squarely on oil and gas production and associated industries. The third economic focal point is Urumchi, which ranks somewhat behind both Karamay and Korla. Urumchi's industry is also dominated by petrochemicals, but in addition it includes both light and heavy industries in other sectors (see map 9.6).

Xinjiang's poorer areas as measured in terms of GDP per capita are focused in the south from Khotan to Kashgar, where the economy is dominated by agriculture. Due to the fact that inadequate transportation restricts the flow of farm products to markets, this area is one of the most impoverished zones in all of China. The one area in the Tarim to break out of this mold is Aksu county, which, as has been noted, claims a large number of participants, mainly Han but also Uyghur, in the bingtuan.

Map 9.6 **Per Capita GDP in Xinjiang, 1998**

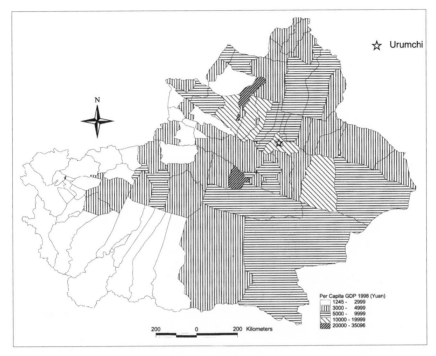

Source: Xinjiang Uyghur Autonomous Region Bureau of Statistics, *Xinjiang Statistical Yearbook, 1998* (Beijing: China Statistics Press, 1998). Map by Huiping Li and Avram G. Primack.

This area also generates far more industrial activity than does either Kashgar or Khotan.[40]

Middle levels of GDP per capita are concentrated in two areas: first, a zone in eastern Xinjiang around Hami, and second, a zone in the far north of Xinjiang. Both of these zones benefit indirectly from the wealth produced by the oil and gas industry centered in Karamay, Korla, and Urumchi. Also, these zones for the most part stretch along the railway lines running east from Gansu across to Kazakstan. On this basis, one can conclude that these regions in the middle levels of GDP per capita are closely related to the emerging urban and industrial worlds of Xinjiang.[41]

How do these three levels of GDP per capita and the geographic zones in which they are centered relate to ethnicity? As we have seen, the lowest levels of GDP per capita are to be found in southern Xinjiang, where the population is mostly Uyghur. The higher levels of GDP per capita are in Karamay, Korla, and Urumchi, all of which have majority Han populations.

The middle levels of GDP per capita are in areas such as Hami and Shanshan, where the population comprises a mixture of Han, Uyghur, and Hui. Thus, it is clear that there is an inverse relationship between the percentage of minority nationalities in a given area and GDP per capita. Overall, Uyghurs are poorer than the Han, with the Hui somewhere in between.

Conclusion

A key factor in demographic analysis is the rate of natural increase of the population. In Xinjiang's case, there has been a steady natural increase among the Uyghurs, while among the Han there has been a corresponding increase due mainly to in-migration. Han make up roughly two-fifths of the officially recorded population of Xinjiang today. Will the level of Han migration increase in the coming years? The volume of migration throughout China has been increasing for some time. But much of this migration is floating or even circular, which means that it is not permanent. The major permanent migrations to Xinjiang in the 1950s and 1960s were all induced by strongly enforced government policies and are now probably an artifact of the past. Overall, the rate of population growth across China is slowing. By contrast, the population growth rate among the Uyghurs has remained at a steady and relatively high level. As the Uyghurs become more urbanized, though, one can expect that their population growth rate will decline.

The processes of urbanization and industrialization in Xinjiang are bringing about the development of a modern workforce in the region. The rural agricultural workforce is also changing, albeit more slowly. Even though more skills and education are required in order to live and prosper in the cities, rural people in Xinjiang are increasingly heading to urban areas. Natural increases in rural populations and improved efficiency in agriculture will gradually create a surplus of agricultural labor. Will that population be able to find work in the city without new skills?

The key variable is, and will be, the flow of population across the region. Han migration has followed the most efficient transportation routes. Now that the railroad has been extended to Kashgar, one can expect a substantial flow of Han migrants into the entire right-of-way from Korla to Kashgar. The Qing had deliberately encouraged Han settlement in the northern Xinjiang during the nineteenth century. The new rail connections opened at the end of the twentieth century will bring more people into southern Xinjiang in the twenty-first century.

The main, and perhaps only, limiting factor is to be found in the availability of water. The oases of the Tarim are already taxing water resources to their limit. In the case of Turpan, the only way to gain access to sufficient amounts of water is to open new wells that tap into an aquifer 100 meters below the surface. That aquifer, however, will last at most from thirty to fifty years. Thus, it is definitely not a permanent solution to Turpan's water problem, let alone Xinjiang's. The addition of more population in Xinjiang, therefore, means that somehow water will have to be brought in from elsewhere.

All of these issues are bound to complicate ethnic relations in Xinjiang. An apt analogy is to be found across the western border in Kazakstan and Uzbekistan. Both countries have populations that include ethnic Russians and Ukrainians, with their percentage in Kazakstan now standing at about 30 percent and in Uzbekistan at about 8 percent. The ancestors of some of these Slavic peoples came to Kazakstan in the 1700s and to Uzbekistan in the 1800s. They are not likely to return to a Russia with which they have had little connection for generations. They will instead become part of the permanent population of the newly independent states. Others migrated to Kazakstan and Uzbekistan only in the 1960s and still maintain close ties to their places of birth. Many, if not most of these, will likely to return to Russia, Ukraine, or Belarus. Indeed, the process of reverse migration from Kazakstan and Uzbekistan was first registered in the census of 1959, fully two generations before those republics gained independence.

Something like this pattern is entirely possible for Han migrants to Xinjiang, regardless of the region's future political status. Many Uyghurs are wary of separatism, preferring instead more subtle forms of resistance to authority.[42] Such pressures will doubtless affect Han migrants to Xinjiang. The continuing process of circular migration that is already evident there suggests it will continue indefinitely into the future.

With the recent relaxation of China's migration policies, Han migrants to Xinjiang have gained the opportunity to vote with their feet. Those Han in Xinjiang who are recent immigrants and who still claim connections with China proper (the *neidi* or "inner area") may well decide to go back. However, such reverse migration would require a strong pull, whether economic, cultural, or political. If the economic incentives to stay in Xinjiang are stronger, then these Han will surely decide to remain and will even be joined by other Han immigrants seeking to improve their prospects in life.

10

The Ecology of Xinjiang

A Focus on Water

Stanley W. Toops

Comprehensive geographic research can illuminate the relative importance of capital and political-economic control in fostering the sustainable use of resources.[1] In Xinjiang, the key ingredient for sustainable development overall is water—the focus of this chapter.

Large-scale groundwater development almost always entails over-exploitation. In arid regions, groundwater cannot be considered as a wholly renewable resource but rather is a one-time resource that will, sooner or later, be "mined out."[2] Injudicious attempts to expand water supplies, without regard to the sustainability of withdrawal, deplete groundwater resources and feed social, political, and environmental instabilities. The mining of groundwater must thus be considered a temporary and often risky expedient.

We know that groundwater is being "mined" at unsustainable rates in both developed and developing countries. But with few exceptions, evidence regarding the impact of this process on natural and human environments is general and anecdotal. Especially in developing countries, the rates of resulting changes in the environment are rarely quantified. And even where hydrologic data are available, the various effects of change are rarely the subject of serious discussion, either with those individuals and organizations responsible for them or with those citizens most directly affected by them.

Regional Divisions within Xinjiang

This chapter focuses on the human dimension of changes in the environment of the Xinjiang Uyghur Autonomous Region. Xinjiang lies in the middle of the Eurasian landmass and consists mostly of intermontane basins and mountain ranges. Much of the population lives in the desert-mountain contact zone, including such oases as Kashgar, Khotan, Turpan, and Urumchi, or in steppe lands such as those around Yining (Gulja) and in the Ili River valley (see map 10.1).

Map 10.1   **Physical Geography of Xinjiang**

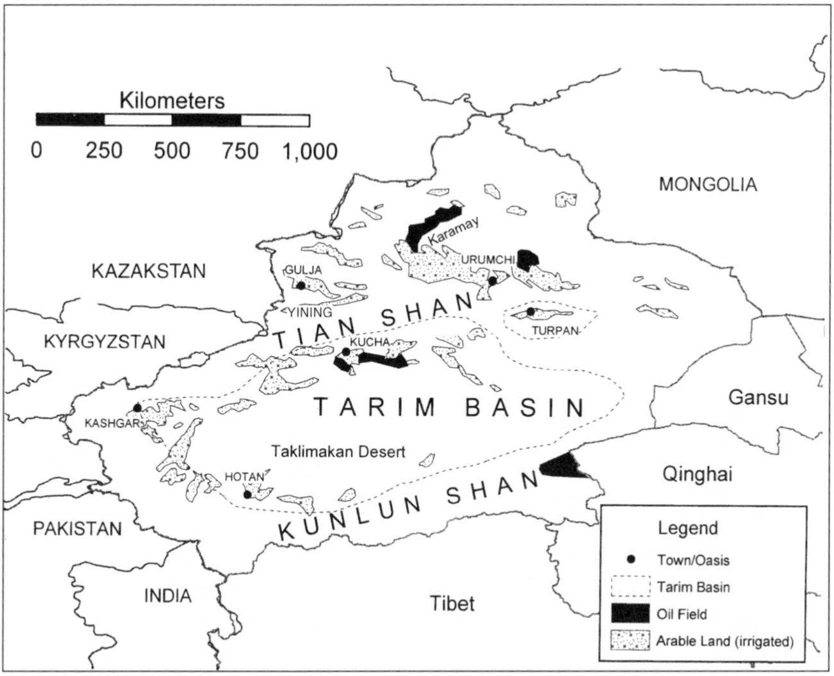

Source: Map by Larry Hargrave and Avram G Primack.

Xinjiang consists of three major geographic regions—south, center, and north—each of which possesses a distinctive ecological character. This regional construct also defines the overall cultural ecology of Xinjiang, identifying the particular productive bases and framework of settlement.[3]

The south is the region surrounding the Tarim basin and covers about half of Xinjiang's total area. In the southernmost part are the Pamirs, which reach to a height of over 6,000 meters. Slightly to the south and east are the Kunlun Shan, several of whose peaks reach 7,000 meters, among them K-2 at 8,611 meters, the world's second-highest peak. In the center of the Tarim basin lies the Taklimakan Desert. The Tian Shan (Uyg. Tengri Tagh) or "Heavenly Mountains," with heights of 5,000 meters, form the northern boundary of this southern zone. These same mountains surrounding Xinjiang's south prevent moisture from reaching the interior. With an average annual precipitation of a mere 20 to 150 millimeters (mm), the region is extremely parched by any measure. Comparatively, few members of the local population engage in industry. Most are instead agriculturalists or traders and are concentrated on oases such as Kashgar and Khotan that are situated on the basin's periphery. Thanks to water coming down from the surrounding mountains as rivers or runoff, these irrigated oases support fruits and vegetables, as well as a large cotton culture at Kashgar. Other resources are notable as well. The Tarim basin is a significant new source of oil and gas for energy-starved China, while minerals abound in the Kunlun Shan and Tian Shan.

Khotan, which lies in the Tarim basin just north of the Kunlun range, epitomizes the fate of human settlements in Xinjiang's south. The very large Khotan oasis, a regional center for agriculture in the southern region, derives its water from rivers flowing from the Kunlun Shan northward into the Tarim basin. Khotan, with some limited industry, has a population of about 150,000, of whom 85 percent are Uyghurs. As a municipality and district seat, it is the local center of governmental activities. While Khotan has an airport, it is not connected to the region's railroad system. And even though Khotan was once a major center of political and economic activity on the old Silk Road, it is now a political backwater, far from the centers of power, and one of the poorest cities in all Xinjiang.[4]

Xinjiang's center lies in a fork of the Tian Shan. Here, the Turpan depression extends to 154 meters below sea level, the second-lowest point on earth. The Turpan and nearby Hami basins are oases that owe their abundant grape arbors and cotton fields to the runoff from the Tian Shan. Temperatures there commonly reach 30 degrees to 40 degrees Celsius (°C) in the summer, and very little rain relieves the heat. For millennia, the traditional system of irrigation was based on underground canals (karez) linking the oases and the mountains. Today, agricultural production depends on wells that are dug deep in order to reach the underlying aquifer. Besides agriculture, this central zone also has some minerals, especially oil, the exploitation of which has had some limited impact on the local economy.[5]

The focus of this zone is Turpan, with a population of about 242,000, of whom 71 percent are Uyghurs. With no nearby rivers, Turpan must rely for its water on traditional karez and wells. Turpan is a local governmental center and is served by the railroad, but as yet it has no airport. Like Khotan, Turpan attained both economic and political eminence while the Silk Road flourished, but nowadays regional power has shifted to the capital at Urumchi, on the highway two hours north of Turpan.[6]

Xinjiang's north is comprised of the Zungharian basin and the Ili River valley, both of which are bounded by the gentle Altay Shan, which reach a maximum altitude of 4,000 meters, and the more imposing Tian Shan. At the center of the Zungharian basin is the Gurbantangut Desert, which is cold and dry throughout the year. By contrast, the Ili River valley, which is separate from the Zungharian basin, is relatively well watered and drains into the Seven River (Yetisu or Semirechye) region of Kazakstan. Siberian air masses influence the climate in the north, producing an average annual precipitation of 150 to 500 mm and temperatures ranging from –40°C in the winter to +25°C in the summer. Sheep, cattle, and horses graze the pasturelands of Zungharia and Ili, while irrigated crops are grown on state farms situated in a band connecting Kuitun, Shihezi, and Urumchi. The Zungharian basin has considerable deposits of oil, especially at Karamay, which in fact means "black oil" in Uyghur. The Altay Shan and Tian Shan both yield mineral and forest products.[7]

A typical settlement of the north is Yining (Gulja). This city of 330,000, of whom 48 percent are Uyghurs, dominates the Ili River valley. In recent times, it has become an economic center serving the entire Ili valley, with its economic life centering on the processing of primary agricultural and animal products. Yining was formerly the headquarters for a succession of nomadic powers, and even today many formerly nomadic Kazaks live in the city. The seat of government for the Ili Kazak Autonomous Prefecture (effectively northern Xinjiang) is at Yining, and even though it boasts an airport, the railroad does not come to the city. While Yining is situated on the periphery of Xinjiang, it maintains many ties westward to Kazakstan, Kyrgyzstan, and Uzbekistan.[8]

Moving from the south through the center and on to the north, one crosses a physical landscape that ranges from the second-highest to the second-lowest point on earth. Thus, the cultural, economic, and political diversity of Xinjiang corresponds to its exceptional physical diversity. Together, these zones embrace an interesting combination of oases, each with its own distinctive population, industries, agriculture, and access to transportation. They provide the context in which any consideration of ecological issues in Xinjiang must be set.

Challenges for Research

The study of water resources must seek to identify those fundamental relations that explain the interactions between human societies and water.[9] Any theoretical framework must enable the researcher to address four interrelated questions. First, what is the impact of regional and national exogenous forces on the exploitation of groundwater? Such exogenous forces include governmental policies, trade, tourism, agricultural development, industry, mining, oil development, population growth, migration, and settlement patterns. Second, what are the impacts of purely local forces (farming, village traditions, sustainable technologies, oasis-centered production, and resource management) on social, economic, and political stability, as well as on the sustainability of agriculture and water usage in Xinjiang? Third, what impacts have these forces had on the use and hydrologic sustainability of groundwater resources (that is, changes in groundwater regimens and in the depth of the water table)? And, fourth, how have these changes impacted the region's socioeconomic systems? These include the beneficial or detrimental effects of the spatial pattern of groundwater withdrawal and aquifer draw-down, and the manner in which the various social and political entities become aware of, and react to, these impacts.

It is important to bear in mind that each of these four components functions as both a cause and effect of every other one. This condition of interaction can be described as "mutual simultaneous shaping."[10] Stated differently, one might ask whether the stress on water resources is purely a *physical* phenomenon (i.e., pertaining to the depth or availability of water), a *social* issue that arises from the community's awareness of the problem, or an *administrative* matter involving the management of water, or some combination of the three. Because such an analysis is conceptually and methodologically grounded in cultural ecology (that is, the interaction between humans and their environment), the inquiry entails both social and environmental science. Considering that the subject is the largest region of China, the answers to these questions are inevitably of great importance.

As economic and social development progress, supplies of surface water are ever more heavily utilized and, in time, overappropriated. As the supply of surface water dwindles, societies increasingly seek to make up the deficit by drawing groundwater to the surface, leading to an exponential increase in the number of mechanized tube wells on the landscape.[11] Then, as more and more groundwater is drawn out, the water table drops. But the process is never uniform. Irrigation schedules vary. If excessive irrigation is used, the water table will decrease. Geological variations in underlying sediments and recharge zones cause groundwater resources in some areas to be shallower and more abundant than in others.

Local farmers and those resource managers, economists, politicians, and village administrators who make up the "elites" may well become aware that a problem exists but typically do not understand the spatial or temporal pattern of the changes that are occurring. Because of this, they are generally unprepared to take the steps necessary to prevent the kind of desiccation that has already been visited on smaller oases in the region or to understand the full impact of change on the ecology, society, or economy of their given oasis or on their territory within an oasis.

Until fairly recently, Chinese policy emphasized the importance of rural life and stressed the need for farmers and rural communities to become self-sufficient so they may better provide for themselves and for the growing urban masses. Such an approach is based on what might be called a "repro-duction" paradigm, the conservation of indigenous land-use systems that maintain cultural identity and historical continuity, in short, a sustainable environment and society. This is to be contrasted with a "development" para-digm emphasizing "commodity production, trade, and industrialization."[12]

As China urbanizes and becomes more fully integrated into regional and global economies, it is undergoing a paradigm shift from "reproduction" to "development." In Xinjiang, this transformation accelerated after 1983, when China launched its campaign to "Develop the Great Northwest."[13] As this occurred, such local forces as farmers, cooperatives, and village elites, and such local practices as traditional sustainable technologies and oasis-cen-tered production and resource management, were being increasingly subor-dinated to, and marginalized by, exogenous forces, whether central governmental policies, migration, tourism, or international business. When this paradigm shift is completed, the availability of the most important re-sources in rural communities, here gauged by changes over time in oasis water tables, will be driven almost entirely by exogenous forces rather than by local activity.

What point has Xinjiang reached on the continuum from local produc-tion to exogenous or national development? Specifically, how far has it progressed from high governmental control to low, and from concern for reproduction and environmental issues to a focus on economic and devel-opmental matters? Geographers seek answers to these developmental ques-tions in a variety of contexts, including the state of market forces, political regulation, biodiversity, and environmental costs. By evaluating these di-verse elements, they seek to gauge the state of sustainable development in a given region.[14]

Sustainable Development in Xinjiang

Chinese officials and scholars have begun to use the concept of sustainable development in examining their country's water problems.[15] This approach is reflected in the document "Agenda 21" that seeks to plot China's course over the new century.[16] In applying the concept of sustainable development to arid northwestern China, the authors of this study claim to promote the rational utilization of water resources while at the same time foster economic growth.[17] However, the fact that the fragile oasis environments of Xinjiang are already focal points for the expansion of production may make it diffi-cult, if not impossible, to achieve both of these ends together.[18] Production has already pressed the environment to the point that many oases in Xinjiang are already in urgent need of programs to control desertification.[19]

The economies of the many cultivated ancient oases of the Tarim basin are relatively underdeveloped. To promote development in the basin, one would have to conserve water in the middle reaches of the Tarim River by limiting the use of water for farmland and focusing instead on forestry and animal husbandry. On the basis of research on sustainable development in Khotan, it is clear that this deeply impoverished area must somehow promote rural industry, control population growth, develop a sustainable energy source, and improve the oasis ecosystem.[20]

Much of the surface water in the basin flows through the Tarim River. However, a catastrophic flood in 1994 damaged the upper and middle reaches of this channel and even today its lower reaches still lack water. The ecological system of the Yarkand and Kashgar Rivers, both of which flow into the Tarim River, has become worse over the past several years due to the progressive salinization of irrigated areas and to overgrazing in the pasturelands.[21]

A number of recent quantitative studies have focused on surface water yields and the impact of development on surface water supplies in the Tarim basin.[22] However, groundwater movements beneath this basin are as yet poorly understood. The quantities of groundwater have been calculated only on the basis of large regions as, for example, north China versus south China, or of such large drainage areas as the Tarim basin as a whole. Even then they are measured only as an element of the runoff from rivers and not in terms of actual aquifer flows.[23] Estimates of recent groundwater depletion exist on a basinwide scale for the northern slope of the Tian Shan: for example, a drop of from 13 to 20 percent between the 1950s and the early 1980s. By contrast, all we know of groundwater changes on the southern slopes of Tian Shan and in the Tarim basin is that the diversion and upstream use of surface runoff, along with the exponential increase in motor-pumped tube wells, have decreased the recharge of groundwater. The water table has declined and the discharge from springs diminished, but by an unquantified amount that has been characterized only as "not by much."[24]

It is not even clear whether the undergroundwater being utilized by pumps is fossil water or an aquifer resource that could regenerate over time.[25] Indeed, the impact of withdrawal on the water table has neither been mapped nor measured for any specific area or community in all of Xinjiang. Neither the causes of change nor its socioeconomic and ecological impacts can be really understood until changes in groundwater are mapped at the scale of individual oases, quantified both spatially and temporally, and reviewed by those local people and organizations most affected by change and responsible for dealing with its consequences.

The economy of this arid quarter of China is expected to develop at an increasing pace in the years to come. Improved transportation will drive this development. The completion of the railroad line between Urumchi and Almaty, Kazakstan, in 1990 and the increases in air traffic between Xinjiang and Europe that have already begun thanks to the completion of Urumchi's new international airport in 1997 are turning Xinjiang into a kind of "continental bridge" linking Europe and Asia. New settlement induced by these developments will lead to even greater claims on water resources and to inevitable shortages.[26] The extension of the railway from Turpan to Kashgar in 1999, projected improvements in road or rail linkages to Kyrgyzstan, Uzbekistan, Russia, and Pakistan, and a mounting flow of foreign tourists along the old Silk Road will bring about further economic development and in turn lure still more migrants into southern Xinjiang.[27] The price of these developments will be ever-greater drains on already scarce groundwater resources.[28]

As places like Khotan and Turpan modernize, the role of handicrafts in the local economic structure will yield to the expanding petrochemical industries.[29] This process is already far advanced in the Zungharian basin of northern Xinjiang. The petrochemical sector is placing heavy demands on the already very scarce water resources of the Tarim and Turpan basins and on the very fragile local ecology.[30] Chinese policy makers are unlikely to allow the country's urgent need for oil and gas to become hostage to what they may perceive as local and parochial ecological concerns.

Migration to Xinjiang from coastal China is already of great local concern, in part because of the pressure that this puts on the water supply.[31] The rise of independent states in neighboring Kazakstan, Kyrgyzstan, and Tajikistan means that water cannot be drawn from those countries without their separate consent, which their governments will have to balance against the mounting demands for water in their own developing economies.[32]

Xinjiang Research Sites

As has been noted, there are few sites in Xinjiang where systematic research on water usage has been conducted to date. Two of them—Turpan and Khotan—have been mentioned. Both are situated along the margin between desert and mountains in the Turpan and Tarim basins. A third site, the Zungharian basin, has also been examined. Together, these provide important insights on the ecological changes taking place today in Xinjiang.

The Tarim basin is an enormous inland depression comprising the Taklimakan Desert and adjacent piedmont slopes of the high Tian Shan to the north and the Kunlun Shan to the south. The annual precipitation here is extremely low, less than 200 mm. In addition, streams fed by melting snow, glaciers, and rainfall in the high mountains carry large volumes of surface runoff to the piedmont plain. From 60 to 80 percent of this runoff penetrates the ground via gravel beds to emerge in springs or to be tapped as groundwater in alluvial fans. This water flowing on to oases becomes the chief source for irrigation and drinking water.[33]

Water is a key to national economic and social development throughout China, but it is the absolute lifeblood of desert regions.[34] With the increase of economic development and population in the arid regions of China, and in Xinjiang in particular, the demand for water from all sectors has been increasing rapidly.[35] Xinjiang's birthrates, in-migration, and rate of economic development are all high, even by China's standards. Its road, rail, and air transport are expanding rapidly, as is the oil and gas industry, with its heavy demand for water.[36] The Ninth Five-Year Plan for 1996–2000 promoted all of these developments as part of its main goal of developing Xinjiang.

All these fundamental changes rest precariously on Xinjiang's limited water supply.[37] Agricultural production is also expanding rapidly, led by large-scale cotton culture in the belt between Turpan and Khotan, where production was expected to grow by more than 60 percent between 1995 and 2000.[38] Cotton production in Xinjiang increaased from 935,000 tons in 1995 to 1,500,000 tons in 2000, an increase of 60 percent.[39] This lucrative crop will never be sustainable at present levels of production. Unless this crop is limited and crop rotation is reintroduced, it will result in large-scale salinization and desertification.[40]

Fully 65 to 90 percent of the Tian Shan snow melt that feeds streams that provide the Tarim basin's surface water flows during the four months between June and September.[41] Thus, the water needed for irrigated agriculture and for such rapidly expanding oil and natural gas fields as those at Tabei and Tazhong must come from aquifers that for most of the year are already grossly overexploited.

One of the announced goals of the recently promulgated "Develop the West" (*xibu da kaifa*) campaign is to achieve "sustainable development." But this cannot be attained without rectifying such long-neglected ecological problems as salinization, the degeneration of natural vegetation, desertification, and the shrinkage of lakes. China can develop the west without addressing these, but such growth will simply not be sustainable.[42]

Planners and academics in Xinjiang speak candidly of the campaign as a way to maintain economic growth.[43] Built on a twin strategy of cotton and oil, however, it is producing ecological effects that will only grow worse unless the next stage of development includes measures to control population, make energy use more efficient, and strengthen the technical capabilities of industry.

In Turpan, Ayding Lake has started to shrink with the usage of the basin's groundwater. Water resources are not rationally utilized. Sustainable development needs to take into consideration the local traditions of the Uyghur population as well as the claims of scientific rationality. Local administration also needs to consider purely local needs and considerations.[44]

Groundwater resources in the oases of Xinjiang have traditionally been exploited by the use of karez, known elsewhere as *qanats, foggara, falaj*, and *khettara*, which are subterranean aqueducts engineered to collect groundwater and direct it to surface canals that water the fields of an oasis. They are visible on the surface by the linear row of earthen mounds piled up around the wells that provide access to the subsurface channel. Since the founding of the "new China" in 1949, these traditional and highly efficient channels have largely been replaced by irrigation stations fed by motor-pumped tube wells, many of which extend deep into the earth. Some 3,300 of these have been installed on the Turpan oasis alone. This has caused the water table in many oases to fall and many karez to dry up.[45]

Serious water shortages have already afflicted many industrial and mining cities, beginning with the capital of Urumchi, which is dependent on already overexploited groundwater. North of Urumchi in Karamay, the center of Xinjiang's oil industry, water shortages are already holding back both oil exploitation and urban development. Water shortages are most common in agriculture regions. China's arid regions equal a quarter of the country's land area, and 86 percent of the water consumed in these quarters is devoted to agriculture. Many crops in the Tarim basin receive only a single application of water each year. As a result, large sections of cultivated lands in the arid northwest are abandoned each year due to the shortage of water.[46]

Similar pressures on resources can be seen in the lives of the Kazaks, who live in and around the Zungharian basin.[47] Most of the seminomadic Kazaks are involved in pastoralism, which they practice both on steppes and in semi-desert regions.[48] Zungharia is also the location of many state farms run by the Xinjiang Production and Construction Corps (Xinjiang shengchan jianshe bingtuan).[49] These agricultural enterprises have been reclaiming land that the Kazaks formerly used for grazing their stock. In recent years, China's market-oriented reforms have allowed the Kazaks to improve their income by increasing the size of their herds. But thanks to the bingtuan, there is less land available for grazing, forcing the herds onto marginal land. This results in overgrazing and erosion.[50]

In spite of China's 1985 Rangeland Law, which tried to switch pastoralists to individual household tenure, collective herding that dates prior to the collectivization of the 1950s still persists.[51] The Kazaks in Altay and Tacheng want to continue their nomadic life and therefore resist the government's efforts to settle them. Even as they seek to do this, however, pollution and acid rain are deteriorating the grasslands on which their existence depends.[52]

Ecological issues also pervade agriculture as practiced in Xinjiang's northern zone. The local inhabitants plant food grains for local consumption, but cash crops such as cotton and especially sugar beets are the mainstays of the local economy. Even though the cost of irrigating these crops is rising, the incomes peasants depend on to pay this cost remain low. Nor do they or local authorities command the resources necessary to offset the rising ecological costs of production.[53]

The scale of ecological degradation is evident also in Yining county, a region of both Han and Uyghur farmers and one of Xinjiang's main suppliers of food grains.[54] Production pressures generated by the economic reforms have given rise to such manifestations of overintensification as excessive use of fertilizers, herbicides, and pesticides, all of which lead to water pollution as well as to erosion. Even though today agriculture is legally in the hands of individual households, most farmers perpetuate the collectivist approach they learned during the period of state farms. As a result, farmers lack the inclination or resources to address the problem as it exists on their land. The only good news in this situation is that, unlike Turpan or Khotan, outright desertification is not a possible result here.

None of these many issues is unique to Xinjiang. Yet, the resulting losses in grain production due to environmental stress are not evenly distributed. Xinjiang, along with such provinces as Gansu, Yunnan, Guizhou, and Shanxi, bear a particularly heavy burden due to the unusually large areas of marginal land that have been brought into production there.[55] In this respect, Xinjiang's agricultural problems resemble those in Uzbekistan and Kazakstan as much, or more, than those existing in most other regions in China.

Nowhere is the negative effect of too many water wells more evident than in the southern oasis of Khotan and the central oasis of Turpan. The internally drained Tarim and Turpan basins are the most arid portions of Xinjiang and the driest of all China's desert regions. What little water is available to Khotan comes from the Kunlun Shan, while Turpan's water flows from the Tian Shan. Together, these oases claim the greatest number of electrically pumped tube wells and the largest area of irrigated land of any desert region of China. This is also where most of the expansion in both irrigated cotton and oil and natural gas production has been occurring and is projected to occur. Hence, these oases are literally on the front line of the ecological crisis in Xinjiang. Their crisis should serve as a bellwether for what might happen in other parts of Xinjiang that today may be more abundantly watered or where water withdrawal and the exploitation of energy resources may not yet be so great.

Even the Zungharian region presents a picture of ecological stress. The growth of settlements at Manass, Shihezi, and Kuitun and the activities of the bingtuan have been accompanied by the intensification of agriculture across the north slope region. Cotton production in these areas requires much water. The Ili River valley is now a major producer of food that also requires much water. Pastoralism continues in the northern Kazak areas but under the conditions of ecological and economic stress noted earlier. A serious crisis may lie further in the future of Zungharia than in Khotan or Turpan, but the differences between them are of degree, not of kind.

It is clear from these observations that the study of local versus exogenous forces in the use of groundwater can provide insights into the political, economic, and cultural dimensions of ecological changes occurring across Xinjiang. Empirical research of this sort can elucidate the implications of China's current policies affecting agriculture and water conservation and place them in a global and comparative context. Such an inquiry gets to the very heart of what is occurring in the ecology of Xinjiang, namely, a collision between highly localized traditional systems and new forms of regional development being driven by powerful national and international forces. Unfortunately, this study is still in its infancy. Nonetheless, it is safe to conclude that unless dramatic changes are made at the levels of both policy and practice, the looming crises that it can already foresee will grow more ominous with the passage of time.

11

Public Health and Social Pathologies in Xinjiang

Jay Dautcher

The importance of public health issues in Xinjiang can hardly be overstated. They affect current social and political dynamics in the region and help define future scenarios of development there. They are a subtle indicator of the state of well-being of all peoples in Xinjiang, but especially of the Uyghurs, since health issues significantly shape the overall relationship of the Uyghur community to the apparatus of state.

Questions of public health cannot be separated from the other economic, political, and cultural concerns dealt with in this book. Rather, they are core elements of all these other issues. This being so, such complex health issues as intravenous drug use or HIV/AIDS transmission cannot be reduced simply to matters of biology or deviant behavior. They are essential components of the overall social environment and, as such, emerge in Xinjiang as sites of contestation among and between different social groups. Thus, among Xinjiang's Uyghurs, health issues take on social meaning as they are refracted through the lens of ethnicity. No wonder, then, that the immediate consequence of the serious health problems facing Xinjiang's diverse population is a rise in ethnic conflict.

Xinjiang's Overall Health Profile

With respect to the usual indicators of health, the population of Xinjiang compares favorably on the whole with many other provincial populations in China. Life expectancy in Xinjiang has risen steadily since 1949, except for a brief period of decline during the years of national famine between 1959 and 1964. While official claims that life expectancy in 1949 was 30 years may be conjectural, it is established that the overall life expectancy at birth in 1999 for Xinjiang's inhabitants was 69.1 years, only marginally lower than the 70.4 years for China nationally.

If average life expectancy in Xinjiang compares favorably to China as a whole, then some groups must be well above the national average, which is in fact the case. Specifically, a sample of the Han Chinese subpopulation (residents of the Xinjiang Production and Construction Corps [XPCC; Xinjiang shengchan jianshe bingtuan]) in this same period reveals that their average life expectancy was a high 75.6 years.[1] By contrast, regional health officials themselves acknowledge that life expectancy rates for Uyghurs are low, in some reports a mere 63 years, far less than for all other ethnic groups in Xinjiang.

Similar disparities between Han Chinese and Uyghurs emerge from data on infant mortality. An apparently reliable 1981 survey indicated 108.1 deaths per 100,000 live births in the region as a whole, far above the national average of 37.3 and the highest in all China. Considering that Uyghur health conditions overall are inferior to those enjoyed by Han residents, then reports that Uyghur infant mortality rates approach 200 deaths per 100,000 live births may be close to accurate.[2]

Various statistical rankings of health place Xinjiang's overall population roughly in the middle of the cluster of inland regions whose economic and social development lags behind the coastal provinces. Available data suggest, further, that both established Han residents and recent Han migrants benefit from higher income levels and better access to health care than do Uyghurs as a group. Surveys indicate that Uyghurs are less likely than Han Chinese to receive adequate health care, and also that they are less inclined to accept available health resources as adequate.[3]

The leading causes of death in most areas of Xinjiang are degenerative afflictions such as cancer and heart disease. Xinjiang people face a greater risk of contracting tuberculosis than do Chinese citizens living elsewhere.[4] Respiratory illnesses are endemic in Xinjiang. This can be attributed to the region's high levels of atmospheric pollution from dust particles made airborne by sandstorms and from factory discharges that persist despite decades of partial solutions.[5] Other environmentally related causes, among them the naturally occurring excesses of fluoride and arsenic in groundwater in some areas and severe iodine deficiency in others, account for a range of other serious public health problems.

The public health field in Xinjiang can undeniably claim certain successes. Efforts to eradicate polio from the region throughout the reform era have made reported cases of that disease extremely rare. Xinjiang also claims one of the lowest rates of reported disability in all of China, at 3.8 persons per 100,000.[6]

Overall, the health of Xinjiang's population compares favorably with health indices in the new Central Asian states across Xinjiang's border. Uyghurs in Xinjiang on average enjoy roughly the same access to health care as their

Turkic brethren in Kazakstan and show similar indices of health.[7] Precise data on the range of conditions obscured by these general indexes are lacking. But considering the broad differential between Han Chinese and Uyghurs, and between Uyghurs in the capital and the rest of the indigenous population, one can assume that the range is wide. It is safe to conclude that Xinjiang Uyghurs living in areas of severe poverty and deprivation face significantly greater difficulties in meeting basic health needs than do their ethnic brethren in more developed parts of Xinjiang and across the border.

Xinjiang's Health Care System

Xinjiang's health care infrastructure has grown considerably in recent decades, but this growth has been uneven, and not all populations in the region are served equally by available resources. Overall, and in spite of recent gains, the current system remains underdeveloped and woefully ill-equipped to meet the region's current needs in both treatment and prevention.

When the People's Republic of China was established, Xinjiang's health care infrastructure was extremely limited. By some reports, in 1949 the entire region claimed only 54 dedicated health care facilities with 696 beds and 348 trained health care workers, or roughly 1 doctor and 8 beds per 50,000 inhabitants. Indicators of infrastructural development rose steadily throughout the period of socialist rule. By the 1990s, Xinjiang had some 4,000 health care facilities, 65,000 hospital beds, and 110,000 trained health care personnel. Throughout the 1990s, approximately 9 percent of government expenditure in Xinjiang was allocated to health care–related costs.[8]

Such quantitative indices do not elucidate the substantial proportion of all facilities that serve specialized (and primarily Han) populations, such as regional soldiers and members of the XPCC and their dependents.[9] Furthermore, those treatment facilities that are accessible to the general population, which include municipal and county-level hospitals and village-level health stations, are concentrated in areas with primarily Han residents. Moreover, they are staffed mainly by Han health care workers who typically speak no minority languages. Both of these factors contribute to a condition of relative neglect for the health care of the Xinjiang's minority groups.

Over the past decade, Xinjiang, along with the rest of China, has seen a large-scale privatization of the health care sector. This has added a further set of serious problems to the existing imbalance of service. First, ethnic Han health workers moonlighting from their jobs in nearby hospitals have set up a multitude of independent (*geti*), for-profit treatment clinics, many of which serve minority communities in urban neighborhoods and rural areas. Such clinics are at best only loosely regulated, and care is essentially unsupervised. A visit to one such clinic in a village outside Yining (Gulja) shortly after it opened its doors in 1992 revealed that all patients were receiving identical treatments of intravenously injected penicillin regardless of their medical complaint. A curtain hanging in a doorway exiting the clinic's single eight-bed treatment room hid from view an adjacent storage room filled with stacked cartons of penicillin ampules, for which patients were charged several times the cost of an equivalent dose at the county hospital. Nor is the supervision of care at larger facilities necessarily better. At one of Yining's largest hospitals in 1996, on-duty doctors privately offered to sell patients boxes of needed pharmaceuticals that they claimed were not stocked by the facility's official pharmacy. The medications offered under this illicit program were clearly marked as expired.

Commitments at home and on the job keep and/or prevent people from traveling even short distances to seek authorized care at more established hospitals, care that may not be readily available in any case, since such facilities are exactly those left understaffed by the same pattern of moonlighting. Patients who do travel in order to receive what they hope will be better care are often disappointed. During the 1990s, Uyghurs in Yining routinely discussed their own health problems and those of friends and family members. They would gladly share stories about those who traveled fourteen hours by bus to Urumchi, spending in several cases more than 10,000 yuan ($1,200) of their savings—substantially more than most Yining middle-class families earned in a year—only to receive a battery of expensive (and for the hospital, profitable) diagnostic tests, but no effective treatment. Hospitals are uniformly concerned to show a profit on their overall operations, leading to an increase in medically unnecessary but profitable ancillary services at the expense of basic treatment. Even more unfortunate are the unrecorded numbers of families who cannot afford to pay the hospitals' expensive admission fees.

One extreme case of denial of care in July 2000 gained notoriety when Xinjiang's principal news organs gave it extensive coverage. In this instance, a severely burned toddler was denied emergency care at four hospitals in a row in Urumchi because the child's father was unable to pay the 20,000-yuan fee those facilities required in cash before they would administer treatment. Shortly after a fifth hospital admitted the child, the patient died.[10] If such a situation could occur in Xinjiang's largest and best-equipped city, it is hard to imagine the difficulties faced in more rural areas, where it is standard procedure to withhold treatment until the receipt of large upfront cash payments.

The situation in preventive health care is, if anything, of even greater concern than the problems in treatment. Throughout the 1990s, efforts to mobilize health care expertise for prevention campaigns relied mainly on the exhortative model of public propaganda developed in the pre-reform period. Medical personnel were stationed in prominent locations along main thoroughfares, in front of banners proclaiming most of the Ministry of Health's most recent directives, and distributed printed pamphlets to passers-by. However, since research on prevention does not include evaluations of such campaigns, the health care system has no reliable means of evaluating their utility and efficacy.

Treatment and prevention of both the physiological and psychological problems arising from drug and alcohol dependence are extremely limited. Most do little more than provide medical supervision of substance withdrawal in a coercive environment. Drug users detained or arrested by police in China are routinely processed by "compulsory detoxification" or "compulsory rehabilitation" centers, where patients undergo supervised withdrawal often under detention in secure prisonlike facilities. In China as a whole through the end of 1997, more drug-dependent persons (210,000) were consigned to labor treatment and rehabilitation centers operated by the Ministry of Justice than were admitted to compulsory detoxification centers (183,000), suggesting that coercive programs remain the dominant approach to substance abuse.[11] Coercive treatment of this sort is also meted out to that small percentage of alcohol-dependent persons whose drinking leads to repeated or serious encounters with the police, as, for example, after multiple incidents of domestic or public disturbance or traffic deaths.

Even in China's most advanced cities, alcohol dependence treatment resources are limited to thirty- to ninety-day residency programs of this kind, which serve less than 1 percent of those in need. Other forms of treatment, such as community- or faith-based programs, are nonexistent. Recent national studies on relapse after treatment for drug and alcohol abuse uniformly report that more than 90 percent return to substance use within sixty days. New treatment paradigms, such as community-based support groups styled after Alcoholics Anonymous and Narcotics Anonymous, are in experimental development in Beijing and Shanghai and will not be widely available even in major cities for at least five to ten years. The structure that such programs have developed successfully in dozens of countries around the world, characterized by self-organized small groups lacking overall leadership, is sufficiently threatening to China's surveillance-minded leaders that some form of direct state supervision will probably need to be accommodated before they will be allowed to expand. Given Xinjiang's especially sensitive social environment, it is by no means obvious that they will ever be permitted there, even on an experimental basis.

The Triple Threat: Alcohol, Drugs, and HIV/AIDS

Three public health issues stand out for their direct bearing on society and political life in Xinjiang. Their centrality arises not only from the severity of their impact on Uyghur communities but also from the degree of attention they have received from Uyghur social activists and Uyghur-language cultural figures. These three issues are, first, widespread alcohol abuse and dependency; second, rising rates of drug use, particularly the smoking and injection of heroin; and, third, the dramatic spread of HIV/AIDS. While each of these problems assumes distinct forms for different regions and for different at-risk populations, a critical commonality is that Uyghur communities all consider them to be issues that Uyghurs must solve for themselves, given that state institutions seem unwilling, uninterested, or incapable of delivering effective programs to address them.

A comprehensive review of the physiological, psychological, and epidemiological dimensions of health issues in Xinjiang is sorely needed but would require more data than are currently available either to foreign analysts or to China's own health researchers.[12] Such a comprehensive study is not needed, however, if the goal is to understand how the most urgent health issues shape attitudes and patterns of response among Uyghur communities. For this purpose, a careful look at these three great issues provides a clear picture, for they have been the main focus of community protest and organization. The model of protest mobilization presented in this chapter applies equally to the entire range of health issues in Xinjiang, including exposure to industrial pollution and concern over the presence of radioactive materials from the Lop Nor nuclear testing range. Understanding this pattern can, moreover, help us to understand the likely future trajectories of a diverse range of health concerns.

Alcohol and drug use have risen sharply in Xinjiang over the past few decades. They reflect the Uyghurs' growing dissatisfaction with their perceived economic disenfranchisement, their social anomie, and the decline in social health generally in Xinjiang's minority communities, particularly among Uyghur adolescents. The following analysis focuses on these two core problems. The third issue—HIV/AIDS—is covered by Justin Rudelson and William Jankowiak in chapter 12.

Alcohol Use in Contemporary Xinjiang

At a joke-telling session recorded in the city of Yining in 1996, a young man told a joke about a guy who arrives late to a drinking party with friends. Because he is late, they cry out:

"Hey man, you're late, that's a fine!" and they pour him three shots of liquor. He drinks the first two, one right after the other, but the third, he spills a little bit on the ground. One of his friends says,

"Hey, you poured liquor on me, another fine!" and pours another three shots. Again he downs the first two, but spills a little bit of the third on his hand.

"You spilled more! Another fine for that," the other guy says, pouring three more shots. Well, the guy can barely get them down, that was three fines, each one three shots, and pretty soon he is totally wasted. He stumbles outside onto the street, and bumps into a cop.

"Hey you!" the cop says. "You're disturbing the peace. I'm going to have to fine you."

"Aw, shut up and pour!"[13]

China has a continuous tradition of alcoholic beverage production dating back to ancient times, and a cultural legacy that associates alcohol connoisseurship with high social status and aesthetic refinement. Together, these factors have helped make the consumption of alcoholic beverages an integral part of social intercourse and ritual celebrations throughout China. However, Islamic social norms long limited the consumption of alcohol in Xinjiang. This did not begin to change until the incursion of outside military troops under the Qing dynasty, first with the Manchu and Solon troops garrisoned in Xinjiang in the 1750s, and later with the Han troops led by Zuo Zongtang who came to put down rebellion in the 1880s. The need to supply soldiers with rations of alcohol undoubtedly prompted the development of local distilling or fermenting operations, which then grew to serve the general local market. Thanks to this, a Uyghur from near Turpan whom a Russian ethnologist interviewed in 1892 acknowledged that "many people, from officials down to the common people, drink alcohol . . . men drink, women drink, and adolescents and children drink. And many people smoke tobacco too. . . . These days there aren't many people who don't smoke."[14]

During the first half of the twentieth century, and from 1949 on through the first three decades of socialist rule, patterns of alcohol consumption among Uyghurs in Xinjiang were constrained by the same economic conditions that limited alcohol consumption elsewhere in China. Low levels of discretionary income among the majority of China's peasants, and low levels of industrial production generally, meant that alcohol was a relatively scarce commodity, enjoyed disproportionately by members of the elite.

Only when the 1979 economic reforms brought rising income did the rate of alcohol consumption in China begin to rise, but then it rose significantly. A nationwide epidemiological survey conducted just before the reforms suggested that alcohol abuse and alcohol dependency (hereafter referred to as problem drinking) were estimated to affect only 0.016 percent of the population during the life span, in other words, only 16 out of every 100,000 persons. By the mid to late 1990s, however, Chinese public health journals were publishing reports on regional and local epidemiological studies that indicated skyrocketing rates of alcohol dependency and abuse in both urban and rural areas. An onslaught of advertisements for beer, wines, and spirits throughout the 1980s and 1990s accompanied steadily rising rates of problem drinking. Women and men of all ages, from adolescents to the elderly, and especially males in their late teens, contributed to problem-drinking rates of 5 to 10 percent. A jump from 16 to as many as 10,000 affected persons per 100,000 in some areas of China translates into an increase of tens of millions of Chinese adults with drinking problems.

Astonishingly, this increase has not yet generated a corresponding expansion in the health care systems devoted to the treatment of alcohol-related problems. The overwhelming majority of persons experiencing drinking-related problems in China will receive no formal treatment in their lifetimes and probably will die unaware that opportunities for treatment exist.

No epidemiological studies have focused on drinking rates in Xinjiang, but the spread of drinking practices is apparent everywhere. Not only do countless products offered by local and national producers of beer, wines, and spirits compete for shoppers' attention on supermarket shelves and in advertisements in all media, but also a range of lottery and promotional giveaway events and activities keep public attention focused on alcoholic products as a basis for entertainment and socializing. Where Uyghur communities have enjoyed relative prosperity in recent decades, such as in Urumchi and in the Ili River valley, areas where Islamic sentiments are arguably weaker than they are in southern Xinjiang, alcohol is routinely and very visibly consumed by men, and less often by women, in private homes, at parks and outdoor venues, and in public restaurants during social gatherings of all kinds.

In spite of the absence of formal epidemiological studies, Uyghurs by the mid-1990s were acutely aware that alcohol abuse and dependency had reached critical levels. The one health issue most often discussed within Uyghur communities visited in this period was the high rate of alcohol use and the negative social consequences—household disruptions, loss of income and productivity, poor marital relations, and domestic violence—of men's drinking. But patterns of interaction in Uyghur society not only created a problem of alcohol abuse, they also gave rise to a promising solution to that problem, a solution that has nonetheless failed up to now because state authorities have repressed it as part of their drive against all forms of local social action initiatives in Xinjiang.

Alcohol in Yining emerged as a social health problem as men struggled to reconcile the contradictions between spiritual and secular dimensions of their everyday lives. In Uyghur neighborhoods (*mëhëllë* or *mahalla*) surrounding Yining, young boys form cohorts with age-peers from their own or adjacent neighborhoods, cohorts that endure as core groups of friends throughout their lives. Most men also involve themselves deeply in the social life of the street and marketplace, where they spend their mornings and afternoons. In the market, additional groupings and networks of friends and colleagues form, for example, among those who share a similar trade, who occupy adjacent stalls in a market, or who exchange information about potential and pending deals. Virtually all men regardless of profession also attend Friday prayers. Since the larger mosques offering Friday prayers usually serve several neighborhoods, this allows men to establish bonds across neighborhood boundaries. Working at times through and at times against these social bonds, male sociality in 1990s Yining tended in one of two directions.

In the first pattern, men participated once or more each week in long drinking parties called *olturax* (pronounced "ole-trash") and may also have attended informal gatherings for smoking hashish, known in the argot of these merchants simply as "goods" (*mal*). Men who attended olturax did so once, twice, even three or more times each week. At these informal gatherings lasting from four to up to eight or more hours, men sat in a circle and took turns drinking 110-proof Chinese *baijiu* spirits from one shared glass or bowl. As they drank, the men would tell jokes and stories to each other, sing songs, play instruments, listen to spontaneous or prerecorded poetry recitations, and generally enjoy each other's company.

Olturax participants argued frequently, and sometimes violently, over whether participants had or had not broken "rules" (*khaidë*) of decorum that applied to conduct during the gathering. If a man spilled his liquor, for example, he was punished by a fine measured in shots of alcohol. When no rules were broken, men congratulated each other on how "prettily" (*qiraylikh*) they had sat together. Regular participation at such events allowed men to establish and maintain their reputations as members of the local community of men; they performed their masculinity for an audience of peers through bodily and emotional comportment, verbal duels, musical performances, and drinking ability. Unfortunately for the participants, and their family members, olturax usually ended only when all present were extremely intoxicated. Strong emotions, sometimes violently expressed, were more the norm than the exception for the end of these marathon drinking sessions.

In the second pattern of male sociality, some Yining men purposefully limited or terminated their participation in olturax in order to avoid the obligation to consume alcohol with the group. These men turned toward Islam more strongly. Instead of praying only on Fridays, they prayed daily, usually once in the morning, though as commitment grew, some of these men began to pray five times a day. For men in this category, associations with Islamic practices such as increased prayer, abstinence from alcohol, and aspirations to complete the hajj pilgrimage were incorporated more deeply into their personal identity and presentation of self in the community, taking the place of secular symbols of masculinity such as an ability to out-drink other men. Instead of attending olturax, men in this latter group were more likely to participate in *mäxräp* (pronounced "mesh-rep") gatherings. Mäxräp are distinguished from olturax in that they have fixed membership, regular (weekly or monthly) meetings, and a more formal repertoire of *dramatis personae* and ritual action. Mäxräp activities involve rules of appropriate behavior, with punishments meted out to rule breakers. In a general sense, this parallels the situation at olturax. At mäxräp, however, pertinent codes of conduct draw not on secular ideals of masculinity but on Islamic ideals of propriety.

Significantly, participants are "punished" and "fined" at mäxräp not only for transgressions occurring during the session itself but also for any infractions against Islamic codes of conduct they may have committed at any time in their everyday lives. If leaders learned of a man's improper conduct—typically consumption of alcohol or use of hashish—they would consult among themselves in full view of all participants and determine the punishment.

When men would talk about their mäxräp activities with a visitor to their homes, they were sure to smile when describing punishments they had witnessed, if not also suffered or inflicted. One form of punishment is called "taking a photo," in which the subject is made to stand outdoors against an earthen wall with his arms raised at his sides. A bucket of water is then thrown at him, leaving his silhouette on the wall behind him. "Giving a baked dumpling" refers to the method by which uncooked dumplings are slapped vigorously against the curved walls of a beehive oven so that they stick and can cook over the coals below. In this punishment, the subject is slapped on one or both sides of the face with the same gesture. "Catching a fish" involves placing an object that does not float, such as a key, in a basin of water several inches deep. The subject must kneel with hands behind his back and then lean over and grab the object in his mouth. Typically, the subject falls helplessly and headfirst into the basin. Such corporal punishments have no lasting effect on the body but are designed to bring men's minds around to the desirability of maintaining group solidarity through proper conduct in daily life. This consensual collective self-policing function made mäxräp an important force for local social control in Yining during the 1990s. It also put mäxräp participants on the state's radar as potentially dangerous activists.

During the spring and summer months of 1995, mäxräp groups came dramatically to the forefront of community activism in Yining. Uyghur men interviewed in this period explained that over the previous months significant numbers of men in their twenties and thirties had decided to end their participation in drinking parties and had joined mäxräp groups whose main purpose, they emphasized, was to provide moral guidance to members. Leaders of dozens of mäxräp groups in and around Yining had initiated a boycott of liquor. Their action was so effective that in the surrounding villages local shops refused to carry liquor on their shelves for fear of community reprisals.

One group of men from Yining, visiting the nearby village of Turpanyüz in this period, set out in search of alcohol for an olturax. None of the many Uyghur-run roadside stands carried alcohol, but the men finally made their purchase at the town's single Han-run store. According to local gossip, it was the effectiveness of the alcohol boycott that so aroused concern in the government that in April officials banned men from participating in mäxräp. Another measure of the boycott's effectiveness is the fact that from July 1995 to August 1996 local liquor factories hired high school students to pass out glossy promotional materials to shoppers and sponsored lotteries and prize giveaways to promote sales.

After the mäxräp were banned, the task of enforcement was assigned to the neighborhood (*mahalla*) Residential Street Committees, which levied a fine of 50 yuan ($6.25) on any man caught participating. When asked about this ban in August, men smiled and admitted that some mäxräp still took place but that many groups had chosen to lay low during the crackdown.

Mäxräp in Yining also organized a boycott of alcohol that was so effective that they gained new visibility as effective social activists. By July 1995, the government took notice and banned them.[15] But mäxräp activities continued underground, despite the ban. Mäxräp participants proceeded to organize and launch a league of sixteen youth soccer teams, gaining access to a suitable playing field. Several days before the season's grand opening tournament, however, local officials cancelled it, announcing that the field would be used instead for military exercises. To reinforce their decision, they immediately sent a number of tanks to occupy the site.[16]

Two days after this announcement, several hundred men at 8:00 AM marched quietly for several blocks along a main street in Yining, past government offices, and then slipped into the surrounding suburban neighborhoods. Chinese Communist Party committees had circulated advance warnings of demonstrations to local work units, giving emergency phone numbers of state security forces and military units. By 10:30 AM, a group of around 700 Uyghur men watched at a main plaza in the center of town as snipers took positions on surrounding rooftops. Paramilitary squads also installed themselves at the city's main intersections, which they had blocked with barbed-wire barriers. Several hundred soldiers armed with assault weapons patrolled the streets on motorcycles and in personnel carriers. Despite the challenge posed by these forces, no violence erupted at any time,[17] and within a few days Yining returned to its previous state of guarded tension.

In the days following the soccer crackdown, Yining's beloved Uyghur-language radio station was compelled to air repeatedly a twenty-minute critique of the "illegal gathering" that had been planned on the soccer field. Nor were propagandistic editorials the only weapon of thought control in the state's arsenal. In February 1997, a large-scale protest on the streets of Yining erupted into a violent confrontation between Uyghur demonstrators and the People's Armed Police Force. According to Uyghur groups in Almaty, Kazakstan, Chinese military forces killed 103 Uyghurs during the initial demonstration.[18] The alleged organizers were arrested, and in the subsequent months, many dozens were executed. Central authorities drew the conclusion that fault for this "instability" lay with lax local officials, and by June of that year the *Xinjiang Daily* reported that 260 local officials had been fired.[19] Then in July, six months after the unrest and subsequent crackdown, Amudun Niyaz, the Uyghur chairman of the Xinjiang Regional People's Congress, made a visit to peasant townships several kilometers from Yining, where he spoke briefly to his media escort, condemning terrorist activity and separatism.

Later that evening, Amudun took part in a mäxräp at a vineyard in Turpan Yuzi Township. Young men and women, dressed in colorful ethnic costumes, sang, danced, and told jokes and stories. Amudun declared:

> Mäxräp is a popular activity among the Uyghurs. However, a handful of national separatists, in order to realize their ulterior motive, have manipulated this recreation to establish illicit ties, using mäxräp as a ground for disseminating speeches, undermining national unity and motherland unification, and for carrying out illegal religious activities. This is absolutely not permissible. We must expose such tricks and conspiracies by refusing to participate in their kind of "mäxräp" and by cracking down on such unlawful activity. Meanwhile, we must actively promote and organize the healthy, traditional mäxräp to enrich the masses' cultural and recreational life and to praise our new life, thereby promoting the advancement of Uyghur culture.[20]

Prior to the 1990s, mäxräp existed as a form of recreation and organization used by Uyghur men throughout Xinjiang to foster community service and promote moral behavior. In the 1990s, these informal and autonomous groups became linked into a loose network of activist associations intent on social and political mobilization.

Strikingly, their first social action was to initiate an alcohol boycott in and around Yining. The boycott succeeded in forcing the removal of alcohol from store shelves only in Yining's environs, but not in the city center. With its hundreds of Han-operated retail outlets and an abundance of Han buyers, even an absolute boycott by Uyghurs could not have prevailed. The boycott was nonetheless widely seen as a successful demonstration of mäxräp groups' power.

Heroin

Heroin, don't smoke it, my dear older brothers
Your lives, don't throw them away, my dear older brothers.
What has it given you, your heroin, except for disaster?
Do not expect any good from it, my dear older brothers.
Your beautiful youth, you only get one chance.
In this world, people cannot blossom on poison.
Heroin has brought mourning to so many homes.
Open your eyes, blind, dear older brothers.[21]

Throughout the 1990s, Uyghur communities grew increasingly concerned over soaring rates of heroin use. Songs attacking heroin addiction were extremely popular among both adolescents and adults during these years and could be heard blaring from stalls in the local markets. Such songs were most often recorded by male performers in their late teens and early twenties, the age when youths, male and female, were increasingly being exposed to heroin use. The song translated above, popularized by a ten-year-old boy, presents a child pleading for his "older brothers" to respect themselves, a message whose power draws on the irony of reversal: In Uyghur society, it is older males who routinely demand signs of deference and respect from their juniors.

In the late nineteenth century, hashish manufactured in Yarkand from local cannabis came to be one of Xinjiang's major export commodities. Records of shipments from Yarkand to India supervised by British agents document tens of thousands of kilograms being exported annually from the late 1800s up through the mid-1930s. Xinjiang officials banned the trade in 1934–1935, but large-scale smuggling continued for decades.[22] The Uyghur man whom N. F. Katanov and Karl Heinrich Menges encountered in 1892 stated, "Originally, our people didn't know what hashish even was. It was only starting around the time of *bëdëwlët* [Yaqub Beg, ca. 1870s] that men and women too began to understand what it was [and to smoke it]."[23] The same informant suggested that smoking opium was also common among those who could afford it.

While little is known about drug use under socialism in the years between 1949 and 1979, it is likely that hashish remained popular among those who could gain access to it. The economic "opening up" of Xinjiang during the 1980s and 1990s enabled young Uyghur men to travel to Guangzhou and the large southern cities, where they may have encountered opium use. It also led to an expansion of overland shipping from the opium-producing areas of Burma to Yunnan Province and from the interior of China to Xinjiang. The use of drugs expanded quickly and steadily. The smoking of opium led to the spread of injection. Informed estimates place the number of intravenous drug users in Xinjiang in 2000 between 80,000 and 100,000. Reported rates of HIV-infection rates among such users ranged from 40 percent in Urumchi to 85 percent in Yining.[24]

How can we understand the social matrix that allowed such a rapid spread of drug use, and what were the consequences for social action among Uyghur communities? In the early 1990s, signs of concern over the consequences of rising drug use were apparent throughout communities in Xinjiang. In Urumchi in the late fall of 1993, for example, several young men working out of a noodle shop adjacent to the Rebiya Kadir department store in Urumchi's Shanxihangzi district began selling what they called heroin to local youths.[25] In the daylight hours, shopkeepers in the area, who contracted with Kadir to sell from stalls in the plaza surrounding her department store, would sip bowls of tea and grumble about the tough-looking youths who wandered about in the evenings after retailers boarded up their stalls. Private guards employed to provide security for the department store and the surrounding plaza reported that petty crime was on the rise. Department store guards occasionally chased away local Uyghur youths found smoking heroin in the infrequently used upper-floor stairwells of the building. Explaining their actions to a visitor a few hours after one such incident, guards remarked that moral outrage had led them to beat up the drug users.

Within a month or two, Kadir decided to take action. An elderly Uyghur calligrapher worked for several days in her office painting in white Uyghur script on red cloth banners an announcement for a campaign to eradicate heroin use among Uyghur youths. Both the color scheme and rhetoric of Kadir's private campaign drew unmistakably on key symbols of state propaganda. What effects, if any, this campaign had on heroin use were unclear. But it did much to stimulate the Uyghur public's eagerness to mount grassroots campaigns against the devastating effects of substance abuse on Uyghur youths.

Shortly after this time, Kadir conceived of and formed the Thousand Mothers Association—modeled explicitly after Mothers against Drunk Driving in the United States—to campaign against heroin use and other ills plaguing Uyghur youths. Kadir's efforts to initiate grassroots antidrug activism unprompted by central directives and unguided by state policy makers and propagandists did not go unnoticed. It is more than likely that their desire to neutralize such independent initiatives was one of the factors that led government officials to impose an eight-year prison sentence on her. Thus, the state exhibited the same unease with a grassroots antidrug campaign that it had shown toward the antialcohol campaigns and alcohol boycotts in the Ili area in the mid-1990s.

At roughly the same time, Kadir's husband, Sidik Rozi Haji, published an editorial in the *Këchlik Gazeti*, Urumchi's leading Uyghur-language newspaper, raising concerns over the rising tide of heroin use. Haji held the position of professor of literary criticism at a second-tier college in Urumchi, and his involvement in writing and publishing activities had established him as a leading intellectual among Urumchi's Uyghurs. In a series of editorials, Haji discussed various social problems, expressing himself in such a way that careful Uyghur readers could easily discern in his words criticism of the state for failing to address the concerns of Uyghur citizens. One of the editorials in that series reads in part:

> Heroin has now spread to 53 counties of our autonomous region. The numbers of those who sell it and smoke it keep multiplying. It has turned into a source of immorality, instability, illegality. Growing numbers of youths set out on a path that ruins their families, parents, relatives. . . . Some of them have died, giving rise to an intense anxiety among our people. Such a tragedy has never before been seen in the history of our autonomous region. . . .
> In former times, because our ethnic group had long come to possess an excellence in terms of knowledge suited to the times, spiritual health, and a nourishing of appropriate religious consciousness, and also outstanding scholars, educators, supporters, and valiant pioneers, even the opium which was at that time circulating among many peoples, indeed among China's interior provinces, was never able to force its way into Uyghur society. . . .
> This was our high, healthy culture.[26]

The editorial invokes the notion that the Uyghur people can lay claim to a magnificent historical legacy, one that Chinese rule in the contemporary era has undermined. For Haji, the glorious past was distinguished both by Uyghurs' "excellence of knowledge" and their "nourishing of appropriate religious consciousness." With this careful combination of phrases, the author elides the distinction between modernizers and religious reformers, eliciting a favorable reading from both intellectuals, for whom scientific knowledge and educational training lead to a better future, and religious progressives, for whom "an appropriate religious consciousness" is the requisite basis for social action. Then Haji takes closer aim at the state:

> In this period of reform and opening, great development has been achieved, but with this serious new problems have appeared, and heroin has now become a menace. The most important reasons for this are:
>
> 1. A portion of our own common people and some foreign smugglers are circulating heroin, creating this disaster.
> 2. The faulty style that has afflicted some of our state organs and the rotten elements serves to protect the smugglers.
> 3. Those in high and low positions, even common people, have been too nonchalant, and relatively concerned discussion on the issue has been insufficient.
>
> The fight against crime by our state judicial organs has only been able to change some of the players: a few criminals are arrested, but a new group of people is able to take their place. *The true eradication or decreasing of [such heroin-related] crime has only been realized by the struggles of the popular masses through related educational practices.*[27]

Here, Haji reinforces the idea that Uyghur-led social entrepreneurship, of the kind enacted by Kadir in her unsanctioned antiheroin campaign, was the only viable means for solving the problems facing Uyghur communities.

The editorial continues with a narrative about China's past in which Haji takes a few jabs at Han Chinese, reminding them—figuratively speaking, of course, since the Uyghur-language newspaper was not read by non-Uyghur speakers—that their own consumption of opium in the nineteenth century earned them "unfortunate names [such as] 'the country of the sick' or 'eastern diseased ones.'" Haji continues, "The Chinese people, enfeebled by invaders and reactionaries, were then bullied by them at will, and it is for this reason, along with a list of other reasons, that the Chinese people were delayed a century in lifting themselves up and gaining their liberation."[28]

Here, China's past is used as an allegory for Uyghurs' present and future. The Uyghur people, enfeebled by heroin and bullied by Han invaders, must lift themselves up physically and spiritually before they can gain their liberation. As he continues, Haji clearly sees an important role for the Uyghur cultural elite in the process, likening the power of their works to the force of a detonating nuclear weapon:

As we all know, even though revolutionary intellectuals like Lu Xun thought that the salvation of the sick bodies of the Chinese people would come from advanced doctoring techniques learned from Western nations, they found that such methods could not be widely implemented. Recognizing the need to first rehabilitate peoples' thinking, they set out to wage their battles with a pen.

Now the popular masses have sufficient knowledge of the dangers of heroin, and they are furious against it. Not long ago two tragedies, *Fog* and *Road of Death*, were performed on the stage, as a response to real problems, and with the widespread excitement they aroused, *they played the role of two nuclear bombs detonated against heroin.* Now heroin circulates in 53 counties, which is 62 percent of our autonomous region's counties and cities. *During the process of reforms, increasing numbers of households are again being left impoverished. If we do not oppose this situation through a people's war we will not be able to secure firmly the results of reforms.*

Now Uyghur youths are joining the ranks of other ethnic groups' youths, more and more frequently they are facing attacks from the "white ghost." With this, Uyghur youths too are now ending up as the "Eastern diseased." Given today's superior conditions and Uyghurs' self-preserved excellence, escape from this disaster is absolutely possible. Those who have been poisoned must make use of their consciousness for self-rescue. Let us actively help judicial organs. Heroin is poisonous. . . . Let all of us, putting our own strengths to the task, *strike hard against heroin.*[29]

In this cultural critique, heroin becomes a device for arguing against Chinese rule in Xinjiang, allowing the editorial expression of sentiments that stand for a larger complex of emotions and arguments, all speaking against the legitimacy of Chinese rule in the region.

How Do State Institutions Address Heroin as a Problem?

In the previous examples centered on alcohol and drug abuse, we have seen that Uyghur communities respond to health concerns with a combination of grassroots mobilization, public advocacy, informal political leadership, and cultural expressions. While these methods have admittedly met with only mixed success in the face of an adversarial state, they nonetheless demonstrate that local groups believe action on their own behalf can be consequential. What, on the other side, can be said of the methods used by state organs to deal with these problems?

The two primary avenues through which state agents address the matter of heroin use are the ongoing "Strike Hard, Maximum Pressure" campaign against criminal activity and a compulsory detoxification for users apprehended by security organs. Neither of these approaches has generated any support among the Uyghur population. The explanation for this lies in part in the fact that such policies are not built on an understanding of the nature of the problem. For instance, an article published by Xin Min, a Han researcher at the Xinjiang Urumchi Compulsory Drug Detoxification Institute, describes a study of 1,281 drug abusers who underwent compulsory detoxification at that institute in 1998. The stated purpose of the study was to "understand the characteristics of drug abuse in Xinjiang district and provide advice on drug control to the government." Demographic information on the subjects included gender, age, occupation, and education level, but the published version of the study gave no information on the subjects' ethnicity. The study concluded that "[t]he main reason of their drug abuse was curiosity and contrary psychology." The at-risk group in this study was defined broadly as "[m]ale, under 30 years old, no proper job, with low educational level, poor psychological diathesis, unhealthy family and social surroundings." Yet, the study ignores ethnicity, despite its clear relevance, indeed primacy, in shaping social dynamics in the region.[30]

Partnerships between Xinjiang health agencies and international nongovernmental organizations (NGOs) can help make the design of research, treatment, and prevention programs better suited to the culturally complex environment of Xinjiang. But it is doubtful that such partnerships alone will change a state apparatus that is ideologically incapable of addressing the root causes of social inequality in the region and the relationship between social injustice and epidemiology, let alone the socially consequential ways those causal relationships are perceived and understood within Uyghur communities.

Conclusion

When Uyghurs narrate their views on contemporary social issues in Xinjiang, they do so by drawing on certain elements of the repertoire of symbols and categories available to them and by rejecting others. If, on the one hand, Uyghurs express dissatisfaction with state policies and demand that the state provide them with equitable access to key resources (e.g., health care, legal institutions, and employment opportunities), this is inherently linked to a claim that says, "We seek to take our place in the Chinese nation." If, on the other hand, large numbers of Uyghurs express the sentiment that the state (through radioactive pollution, heroin trafficking, or the denial of medical services) engages in, encourages, or tolerates campaigns of genocide against them, this frames their situation as one in which there is no meaningful place for them in the Chinese nation. In this case, they see their dilemma as one that can be resolved best by seeking alternate political institutions that can represent their interests in the local and global political arenas.

The local responses to alcohol and drug abuse in Xinjiang described earlier illustrate some of the social and political dimensions of health issues in Xinjiang. These can be summarized as follows. First, numerous health issues in Xinjiang have an important, and potentially critical, impact on the physiological, psychological, and social health of local Turkic populations. Second, these populations increasingly place health concerns at the center of their struggle for social, environmental, and medical equality and justice. Finally, Uyghurs generally, though not exclusively, express their dissatisfaction with the basic health deprivations they endure through idioms of social justice and equality. This manner of articulating social demands has the potential to play an increasingly important role in the institutionalized processes of social action that link Xinjiang with China's center and with a range of governmental and international actors (such as the UN Educational, Scientific, and Cultural Organization and the World Health Organization).

The state's perspective allows it to acknowledge in suitable contexts its recognition that Xinjiang's existing health care facilities are inadequate to meet current needs and to affirm that it is concerned to raise standards for all Xinjiang residents. But the legacy of preferentially allocating resources to the more affluent and socially less threatening Han groups in the region, joined with its support for Han migration into Xinjiang, will continue to undercut whatever positive impact the state's developmental efforts may have on disadvantaged Uyghur populations in the region.

One possible bright spot may be the international NGOs (such as Medecins sans frontieres) that are intensifying their efforts to bring health care programs to Xinjiang. Unfortunately, many legal and administrative barriers to NGO operations in China still exist and especially affect sensitive issues such as HIV/AIDS, prostitution, intravenous drug use and alcoholism. Nonetheless, the gradual and incremental expansion of such programs in the region is likely to make a critical contribution to the mobilization of resources for underserved populations in Xinjiang.

Health concerns are a key factor in the mobilization of protests by Uyghurs in Xinjiang. This point has been elaborated here in regard to just two issues—alcohol and drug abuse—but it appears to be equally relevant to all of the other existing and emergent health care concerns in Xinjiang. For example, the UN Drug Control Program and other monitoring agencies document rapidly rising rates of use of amphetamine-type stimulants in China, including substances such as crystal methamphetamine. Xinjiang's largest at-risk populations are minority youths in cities and towns whose worldview is increasingly defined by a sense of economic disenfranchisement and social disaffection. The predicted rise in China and in Xinjiang in the use of methamphetamine, a drug that is notoriously cheap and easy to produce and transport, threatens to make today's problems seem minor in comparison and may seriously increase the risks faced by all populations and demographic groups in Xinjiang. On the basis of the analysis provided here, there is no question that this and other health issues will only magnify the critical importance of health equity for the success of any program to build long-term stability in the region.

Part V

The Indigenous Response

12

Acculturation and Resistance

Xinjiang Identities in Flux

Justin Rudelson and William Jankowiak

The culture and identity of the Uyghur people of Xinjiang have been shaped by geographic, cultural, and historic interactions with China and surrounding civilizations since the seventh century CE. By the twentieth century, Uyghur identity had evolved in such a way that the Uyghurs can neither acculturate comfortably into China, as Beijing would like, nor effectively resist the Chinese state, as Uyghur nationalists and militants would like.

Factors in Identity Flux: Local, Regional, and National Orientations

Most modern scholars and commentators on Xinjiang dwell on indigenous responses to what is termed the People's Republic's "internal colonization" and exploitation of Xinjiang.[1] Such approaches often fail to examine how Xinjiang's indigenous populations responded even in Qing times to external challenges.[2] The response to externally imposed policies affecting settlement patterns or birth control has been neither passive nor unified. Viewed from the government's perspective, the impact even of such policies as Han immigration on the formation and maintenance of Uyghur identity has been mixed.

To understand the identities of Xinjiang's indigenous peoples and the strategies they have adopted in response to Chinese policies, we must first recognize that these identities are inherently weak and in constant flux. This is especially true for the Uyghurs, who are the largest minority group in the region. This chapter focuses mainly on the Uyghurs and to a small extent on the Huis (known in Xinjiang as "Tungans") and Kazaks. Until there is more systematic field research on the smaller indigenous groups in Xinjiang, one can only conjecture from anecdotal experiences that their responses to Chinese policies in Xinjiang have dovetailed with Uyghur responses.

Three Modes of Response

Since 1949, China has manipulated weaknesses in the Uyghur identity to its advantage by implementing policies that have caused the Uyghurs to respond in ways that divide and weaken the Uyghurs and other indigenous peoples of Xinjiang. The first response is acculturation, that is, adaptation in both its active and passive forms. Uyghurs follow this path when they trust Chinese policies. The second response is one of nonviolent resistance. Uyghur intellectuals who are in the process of acculturating to the urban life in Xinjiang's capital, Urumchi, but who are mistrustful of both the Chinese state and Islamic conservatives in the Uyghur community often respond in nonviolent ways. They produce nationalistic writings and present their own versions of Uyghur history that contradict official government versions. The third response is violent resistance, the tactic favored by secular militants as well as by a small number of Uyghurs who have been placed on the international list of terrorist organizations by the Chinese and American governments.

China's Policy Shifts

Radical fluxes in Chinese policies have dramatically impacted all the peoples of China, including those of Xinjiang. Since 1949, Chinese policies have fluctuated in unconventional phases that have greatly confused Western observers.[3] Rather than pursuing both economic growth and distribution at the same time (that is, the often-employed Western model), China sought to equalize the disparities in its population by focusing first on distribution during the period 1949–1957. This approach involved confiscating landlord properties and privately owned factories and either forcing the wealthy sectors of society to flee or killing them. From 1958 to 1966, the Great Leap Forward collectivized the peasantry and sought to overtake the West's steel production through backyard smelting. Although this growth phase intentionally caused many inequalities to re-emerge in Chinese society and inadvertently led to massive famine, it energized Chinese society in preparation for the movement that would equalize societal disparities: the Cultural Revolution.

Johan Galtung argues that for China to shift gears between distribution and growth cycles, it has had to mobilize the masses or the army, often through turmoil. This offers insights on such otherwise baffling convulsions as the Great Leap Forward, the Cultural Revolution, the rise and fall of the Gang of Four, and even the Tiananmen student movement of 1989. Since 1978, the challenge for the Chinese leadership has been to develop policies that do not require radical shifts in growth and distribution every nine years, but instead facilitate growth and development at the same time, similar to the Western model. Since 1989, it appears that China has indeed met this challenge.

Hard and Soft Policies

It would appear that the Chinese are able to hold two contradictory philosophies or policies at the same time. Thus, it is led by the Chinese Communist Party but pursues an economic strategy that seems completely in line with capitalism. Similarly, in Xinjiang the Chinese government pursues seemingly contradictory "soft" and "hard" measures to undermine Uyghur nationalism. Soft measures are designed to win favor among the Uyghur population and facilitate acculturation into Chinese society. Hard measures are used to clamp down on elements believed to be fostering dissent, advocating independence, or carrying out terrorist strikes.

Beijing's soft policies toward Xinjiang foster regional autonomy and promote affirmative action policies in order to undermine ethnic resistance and sustain Chinese power there. However, Chinese officials have found that such ethnic benefits undermine minority integration into the Chinese nation-state and facilitate nonviolent resistance. From 1985 to 1989, the Chinese government floated another soft policy allowing mosque construction to flourish and even sent hundreds of Uyghur Communist leaders on the hajj to Mecca in order to increase their prestige at the local level. But when this strengthened Islam at the local level, the government employed hard policies to shut down mosques. The government has also supported the writing of Uyghur historical works that openly challenge its own versions but then cracked down on books that were deemed too controversial or nationalistic. China's current "Strike Hard, Maximum Pressure" policy involves both police clampdowns on disaffected Uyghurs and a relaxation of controls on Uyghur society in order to foster Xinjiang's economic development.

In order to govern the indigenous population of Xinjiang, the Chinese state has resorted to policies of ethnic tolerance and intolerance, often simultaneously. Because of the extremely sensitive nature of ethnic relations in Xinjiang, the government often floats new policies as trial balloons, in order to measure the indigenous response. It will then make revisions as necessary or switch to other approaches, even radically different ones. Sometimes such revisions are characterized by extreme fluctuations in policies, reflecting policy fluctuations in Beijing, such as the shift from the Cultural Revolution to reform policies under Deng Xiaoping. The guiding star of all of China's policies in Xinjiang, however, is to acculturate the region's minorities into the Chinese state and integrate the region into China's economy. As in all of

China's autonomous regions, Han immigration is the constant means to achieve this goal.

There is a clear interrelationship between China's hard and soft policies as employed in Xinjiang. Hard policies are used to crush the various forms of resistance that surface during the period that soft policies are emphasized. Soft policies are used to encourage development but only to the degree that Beijing believes it can control the consequences. Often, Beijing will support certain aspects of Uyghur development at the same time it is undermining others. Hard policies slow acculturation by polarizing Uyghurs and Hans. Soft policies tend to accelerate Uyghur acculturation into the Chinese state, but they also provoke violent resistance by Uyghur militants who are set on preventing China's acculturation policies from succeeding.

Factors Weakening Uyghur Identity

Western and Chinese scholars both trace the origin of the Uyghurs to the Uyghur empire (745–840) of northwestern Mongolia. James A. Millward and Peter C. Perdue show in chapter 2 how the term "Uyghur" has had vastly differing meanings throughout its history. Uyghur first referred to a Turkic, steppe, nomadic society practicing shamanism and Manichaeanism in Mongolia. Later, it shifted to become the name for a sedentary oasis society practicing Buddhism, Manichaeanism, and Nestorian Christianity centered in the Turpan region of Xinjiang (844–932). Finally, it became the referent for an elite, primarily Buddhist, Turkic society centered in the Turpan oasis that during the period (932–1450) was known as Uyghuristan. In this instance, the term was used to distinguish Uyghur society from the Islamic Turks living in the west of the region.[4]

After the Buddhist Uyghurs converted to Islam in the fifteenth century, the term "Uyghur" fell into a disuse that lasted into the twentieth century. The Uyghur conceptual construct that was developed then emphasized the comparative homogeneity and timeless qualities of the Xinjiang Turkic oasis dwellers. This conceptualization of ethnicity redefined the Turkic Muslim oasis dwellers as "Uyghur," the first time the ethnic term was used since 1450. While the inclusive definition quickly made the term "Uyghur" readily acceptable to the majority of Xinjiang's Turkic population, it did not provide a strong identity. In fact, it is likely that the Chinese nationalists and Soviets both realized that such an identity had so many cracks and fissures that the newly self-defined Uyghurs would be easy to control.

Because the new ethnic identity was defined in opposition to all dissimilar cultural and linguistic groups, the label "Uyghur" provided a good rallying point. Roughly 95 percent of the indigenous inhabitants were redefined as Uyghurs, and most accepted the term "Uyghur" as representing their perceived ethnicity.

But during the past fifty years, the primary allegiance of Uyghurs has been not to the collective whole of their ethnic group but to their family, clan, and oasis. Although the Uyghur identity gained tremendous strength under Communist rule, presenting Beijing with far more of a challenge than it bargained for, the domestic focus of Uyghur allegiances has made the Uyghur identity fairly weak and easy to control.

Patterns of Response

Xinjiang's geographic legacy works against the program of the Uyghur nationalists.[5] While many of the Uyghurs see themselves as a unified people, for much of their history the populations of Xinjiang's oases were relatively isolated from one another and protective of the distinct local identities that persist to this day. But these divisions also pose a profound challenge to the government's efforts to completely incorporate the autonomous region into China proper. Since 1949, China has adopted various measures to integrate Xinjiang more completely into the Communist nation-state, but none has been notably successful. The Xinjiang oasis cultures have retained their distinctive identities and have remained economically viable entities even in the face of China's hard policies.

Uyghurs in each of the oases of Xinjiang have developed their local identities in response to perceived external threats. For example, the Uyghurs in Kashgar in 950 CE embraced Islam as a means to counter the power of the Uyghur elite in Turpan and align themselves with the Turkic and Muslim peoples to the west.

The new twentieth-century Uyghur identity glossed over a host of internal differences present in the Uyghur oases that many Uyghurs refuse to recognize.[6] According to Nizamdin Yüsüyün, a Uyghur folklorist, there are seven divisions among today's Uyghurs. These include the Dolans, Lopliks, Abdals, Keriyaliks, Kashgarliks, Eastern Uyghurs (Turpan and Hami), and Kuldjaliks or Taranchi (Ili). The Taranchi, "Tillers of the Soil," were oasis Turks and considered a separate ethnic group until 1949, but they are now considered Uyghurs. The Dolans live in the Merkit area near Kashgar. The Lopliks live near Lop Nor in a fishing community. The Abdals are a peripatetic group living in southern Xinjiang who, as Alevi, are considered heterodox Muslims. By not recognizing these significant differences among the Uyghurs themselves and instead insisting on a "primordial" Uyghur unity, many Uyghur intellectuals fail to understand the primary mechanism dividing the Uyghurs, namely, the legacy of division imposed by Xinjiang's geography. More than

Chinese policies, it is instead Xinjiang's geography that must be transcended for the Uyghurs to effectively assert a challenge to the Chinese state.

The practice of oasis and village endogamy (marriage within one's own village) reinforces strong oasis loyalties and limits the development of wide pan-oasis familial ties. Among all the world's Turkic peoples, only the Uyghurs practice oasis and village endogamy that, when combined with long-established trade relationships, has powerfully solidified local oasis identities. More important, it has impeded territorial unification under a single political system and works against the efforts of some Uyghur intellectuals to foster a pan-Uyghur identity and nationalism. It cannot be denied that Xinjiang's geography, along with other factors, thwarts Beijing's own aspirations and policies in the region. But it has a much greater impact on the Uyghurs, for whom time is a more urgently important factor. In all likelihood, the Chinese government can work patiently over the decades and centuries to override the influence of Xinjiang's geography, while the Uyghurs face the possibility of their own people being splintered and atomized in the immediate future.

Qing Legacies and the People's Republic of China Policies

Many policies of the People's Republic of China (PRC) in the area of ethnic relations are remarkably similar to those that had been skillfully and effectively developed under the Qing dynasty (1644–1911).[7] Such policies were organized around local oases rather than regionwide traditions.[8] Chapter 3 indicates how Qing policies also shifted radically between tolerant (soft) and intolerant (hard) approaches and at times even pursued them both simultaneously. Thus, whenever Islam became a force for mobilizing antigovernmental violence, the Qing responded with extreme measures to suppress Islamic expression. And Qing policies were just as effective as Communist ones have been in controlling the indigenous peoples of Xinjiang by leaving little margin for indigenous resistance. Qing officials also encouraged a massive influx of people from China's central and eastern areas, including Manchus, Tungans, and some Hans.[9] Qing officials understood well that the promotion of cultural diversity discouraged pan-ethnic movements from arising in the region.

Urumchi was from Qing times always a government outpost rather than a Uyghur or Turkic Muslim city. The Communists transformed it into a smaller version of the more developed east coast Chinese cities. This process is consistent with the way the PRC has transformed capitals of other autonomous regions (e.g., Huhehot, Lhasa, and Kunming). It also directly recalls the imperial model favored by China's various dynasties, which demonstrated imperial authority and cosmological superiority by redesigning provincial urban sites in the image of Beijing, the imperial capital.

While Qing policies were extremely successful in curtailing sustained pan-ethnic resistance, they were highly unsuccessful in curtailing ethnic unrest in the region. Revolts and spontaneous riots against Qing rule continued right up until the Manchu dynasty's collapse in 1911, and under the Nationalists thereafter. When the Communist army marched into Urumchi in the autumn of 1949, the region was remarkably unintegrated with China proper. The ethnic antagonism that currently exists in Xinjiang is not solely a by-product of Chinese policies in the region, but the inevitable consequence of a dramatic geography that has underpinned the region's nonintegration for millennia.[10]

The PRC government's strategy for managing ethnic borderlands manipulates this legacy of local conflict in order to maximize Beijing's control over the Xinjiang region. To limit pan-Uyghur movements in Xinjiang, the Communist government (like the Qing) has sown conflict between the oasis-dwelling Uyghurs and the Kazaks and other nomadic groups by strengthening the Kazaks' voice in Xinjiang's government. Today, the Kazaks' presence in the Communist government far exceeds their numbers, causing them to be the second most powerful ethnic group in Xinjiang, after the Uyghurs.[11] Officials from Beijing seek out Kazak leaders who are often better educated and more articulate than those selected to represent the Uyghurs. Consequently, Uyghurs tend to have little respect for their representatives, while all of the indigenous peoples of Xinjiang tend to respect Kazak leaders.

Like the Qing, the Communists have had to negotiate, entice, and, in the end, threaten the various ethnic groups who inhabit the region to do their bidding. During the Maoist era, China euphemistically declared Kazak pasturelands "wastelands" and targeted the region for agricultural and industrial development by immigrant Hans, pushing the Kazaks into smaller areas within the region in exchange for political power nearly at parity with the majority Uyghurs. Perceiving that local ethnic groups were often more at odds with one another than they were with the Han migrants and state officials, the government developed a minority management policy, similar to the Qing, that encouraged ethnic diversity over unity—in short, a program of "divide and conquer."[12]

China's Hard Policies in Action

Chinese policies are designed to incorporate Xinjiang into China politically, socially, and economically. China is overriding Xinjiang's geographic and historical divisions in order to integrate the region, within a relatively short time span, more completely and securely into China proper. It is likely that the indigenous population will be unable to effectively resist these efforts. China seeks to incorporate Xinjiang through programs of internal migration and economic development. China's hard policy of settling a massive number of ethnic Hans in Xinjiang has convinced Uyghurs that they must find a way to resist this influx before the sea of Han immigrants fully overwhelms them.

Even though most of the early Han immigrants to Xinjiang during the 1949–1985 period were used by the Chinese state to assert its control of Xinjiang, it must be said that many were idealistic pioneers who came dedicated to working in Xinjiang as a means to build the "motherland" and move beyond their own strained family backgrounds. Others were assigned as worker-soldiers to paramilitary state farms in Xinjiang that helped meet China's mandate for agricultural development and political security in the region. These ethnic Hans were primarily demobilized Communist troops and Nationalist (Guomindang) forces who were ordered to take up positions on the fringe "wasteland" areas, including the areas north and south of the Tian Shan, the steppe lands of Zungharia, and locations along the main transportation routes linking Urumchi with China proper. While such positions were intentionally established not to interfere with local indigenous life, they essentially surrounded indigenous villages and, over time, began to overutilize precious water resources, to the detriment of local agricultural production.

Several previous chapters in this volume describe how these state farms were reorganized into the paramilitary Xinjiang Production and Construction Corps (XPCC; Xinjiang shengchan jianshe bingtuan). The XPCC served as an effective sponge by absorbing those who left or were forced out of China proper. Like those British citizens banished to Australia, many of these Hans truly committed themselves to making a better life in Xinjiang and have come to see themselves as "Xinjiang people." Hans who have lived in Xinjiang for decades insist that they are very different from the Hans in China proper. They believe that by being less tied to traditional family structures, they have taken on the same qualities of openness and expansiveness that characterize the American West and Siberia.

The Chinese government preferred to segregate Han immigrants on land not occupied by Uyghurs or in new towns adjacent to older Uyghur communities. Between 1957 and 1961 and 1964 and 1967, around 2 million Hans moved to Xinjiang and had little contact with the indigenous population. As Stanley W. Toops shows in chapter 9, these settlements often followed newly opened transportation arteries.[13] Although the tide of Han in-migration diminished as the Cultural Revolution died down in Xinjiang in the middle 1970s, it increased in the early 1980s because of natural growth and then once again because of those who came to the region from eastern China as contract workers or for opportunistic short-term jobs— the so-called self-drifter Hans.

During the period 1949–1955, the government implemented a hard policy of persecuting landlords who controlled valuable water rights in the desert oases and distributing their land to the peasantry. In this way, it removed or eliminated many of the educated and powerful elements of local Turkic society and sought to win the support of the masses. The government for the most part refrained from overt acts of cultural suppression, being well aware of how the death of many key leaders of the Eastern Turkistan Republic in a suspicious plane crash in 1949 had engendered widespread animosity toward it. But after establishing the Xinjiang Uyghur Autonomous Region in October 1955, the government felt secure enough to launch hard policies to root out anti-Chinese elements among the minority leadership. In 1957, the China-wide anti-Rightist movement under the deceptive name of the Hundred Flowers movement led to the deaths and incarceration of a great number of indigenous leaders. After the Sino-Soviet split in 1962, some 60,000 to 120,000 Uyghur and Kazak nationals fled to what is today Kazakstan. The Sino-Soviet border was sealed, finally giving China unquestionable control of the Ili–Three Regions area, which had long been a pro-Soviet stronghold.[14]

Uyghurs and Kazaks came under particularly heavy pressure during the Cultural Revolution. Internecine rivalries broke out among Uyghurs within the oases themselves, with those least educated often carrying out the greatest abuses against their own culture. Those minorities who had relatives in the Soviet Union faced struggle sessions and were frequently exposed on trumped-up charges as "spies" by their own neighbors and sent to labor camps for years. The Cultural Revolution's policies on the Xinjiang oases included the abolition of private landholding, the closing of rural bazaars, attacks on Islam, and forcible acculturation and assimilation. All of this engendered among the minorities a profound resentment and antigovernmental distrust that endure to the present.

In 1985, Xinjiang was opened to international trade and tourism and for four years was able to flourish under new soft policies allowing Uyghurs to build mosques, write historical studies of their own people, and reprivatize their land. This had a dramatically positive effect on Xinjiang's economy and Uyghur culture. However, after the Tiananmen protests of 1989, China backtracked on its soft policies that promoted ethnic autonomy. It adopted hard policies that considered all forms of dissent or protest as covert efforts by Islamic fundamentalists to overthrow the government. The unintended consequence of China's hard policies was to produce greater militancy among its Muslim populations, especially the young and nationalistic, as opposed to the particularly devout. Hard policies were, and are, used to "smoke out" Uyghurs advocating independence, plotting armed attacks, or merely showing dissatisfaction with life under Chinese control.

Part of China's difficulty in the wake of Tiananmen and the breakup of the Soviet Union has been the great potential for instability within Central Asia. While China was able to maintain a firm grip on Uyghurs in Xinjiang, it could not prevent Uyghur militant groups across the western border from mounting actions within Xinjiang or Uyghurs from Xinjiang from making their way to Afghanistan for training with the Taliban. As Sean R. Roberts shows in chapter 8, all this changed with the rise of the Shanghai Five, now the Shanghai Cooperation Organization (SCO). This security alliance among China, Russia, Tajikistan, Kyrgyzstan, and Kazakstan (later joined by Uzbekistan) gave China extreme latitude to suppress Xinjiang Uyghur dissent. Its creation radicalized some Uyghurs into terrorist action against Chinese government targets in Xinjiang.

China's Soft Policies in Action

In 1978, following Mao Zedong's death and the rise of Deng, the Chinese government swung back toward policies that were welcomed by the indigenous peoples. It allowed a large number of mosques to be built with private funds while restricting mosque worship to those over eighteen years of age. It also passed laws upholding respect for Muslim food requirements (*halal*) and allowing Muslims time off for religious holidays. Such policies are aimed at undermining antigovernment protests and nationalistic resistance movements.

Chinese officials in Xinjiang are quick to point out that while their policies have sometimes been harsh out of necessity, they have enabled China to maintain control and stability in Xinjiang, in contrast to Soviet policies that led to the collapse of Russian hegemony in Central Asia. Whereas critics decry China's ethnic policies as crude, Beijing itself sees its policy to be one of consensus-building that acknowledges the importance of cultural diversity while blurring the difference between groups. Intentions notwithstanding, this strategy has polarized the indigenous peoples of Xinjiang, dividing them between those who want full autonomy, even independence, and those who prefer integration within the larger Chinese society.

China employs a wide range of methods to incorporate its autonomous regions more fully into China proper. It aids urban economic development and makes large investments in Xinjiang's infrastructure, including roads and communications.[15] It also demanded that Beijing's time zone extends over the whole country, even though Xinjiang is two hours behind the capital. Until the government officially recognized a Xinjiang time zone in 1995, Uyghurs resisted using "Beijing time" by setting their watches and clocks two hours earlier and referring to this as "Xinjiang time." And, above all, the government fosters a migration policy designed to redistribute China's population.

In contrast to many developed countries, the PRC acknowledges and, at least symbolically, recognizes its minority peoples and their cultures as a means of gaining their support. Billboards in China's autonomous regions feature pictures of members of local minority groups. In 1985, public signs on government buildings, along with propaganda posters and office buildings, reversed the order of their bilingual messages, placing Uyghur on top of Mandarin. Ominous posters warning that "The Hans Cannot Succeed without the Minorities, and the Minorities Cannot Succeed without the Hans" gave way to simple exhortations to follow Deng's "Four Modernizations." Television and radio stations began offering a variety of programs in minority languages. As Linda Benson shows in chapter 7, the government also institutionalized an affirmative action policy facilitating talented individuals from minority groups to enter mainstream Chinese society. The same policy of quotas extends to government hiring.

By giving indigenous individuals a stake in the system, the government has been able to dampen nationalistic opposition. Although some minorities claim that minority officials are not willing to defend minority interests or that they have sold out their own people because they have bought into the Han Communist system, most seem willing to defend minority interests from within the political system that continues to reward them rather than from outside it.[16] China has successfully co-opted indigenous elites and stymied resistance movements by valuing individual merit and recognizing ethnic background.

China's simultaneous resort to soft and hard policies in Xinjiang causes some indigenous peoples to accept acculturation and others, at the same time, staunchly to resist it. For all its good intentions, this two-pronged approach has proven to be filled with dangers, yet they are dangers with which the Chinese government appears to be comfortably willing to live. From 1985 to 1989, Beijing's liberal cultural policies raised ethnic awareness and opened a safety valve for religious feelings among Xinjiang's indigenous peoples, particularly the Uyghurs. A very small number of the indigenous population responded to China's strategy of selective toleration and cautious liberalization with infrequent militant bombings, while others made increasing demands for further freedoms and greater autonomy.[17]

China's soft policies are mainly economic in nature, since the government makes the Marxist assumption that economic development will positively reshape the cultural and psychological superstructure of Turkic society. This has proven largely valid, as Uyghurs established international trade ties and improved their standard of living exponentially. Much of the wealth was invested in brick homes that replaced the flimsier mud-brick structures in which Uyghurs traditionally dwelled. But soft cultural policies allowing for improved education for minorities, particularly at the university level, have proven to be a great challenge. Just as universities are a hotbed of political thinking in Western countries, so too are universities for Xinjiang's minorities. The Uyghur female millionaire Rebiya Kadir, who is currently jailed, hired university students to offer classes to high school students in Uyghur history and nationalist thought in her famous seven-floor department store in Urmuchi. The government looked the other way, but only for a time.

The most important impact of the soft policies for the government was in dampening Uyghur animosity toward the large in-migration that started in the late 1980s with the so-called self-drifting Han Chinese to Xinjiang. Officials refuse to prevent this illegal influx, because the government views it as beneficial to China's goals in Xinjiang. Han in-migration to Xinjiang is one of the most serious challenges for the indigenous peoples of Xinjiang, as they are quickly becoming a minority nationality within their "own" territory. Uyghur resistance against the influx generally is passive, often taking the form of verbal attacks, such as jokes and curses, against the government and Hans. The only somewhat effective means to counter this Han inflow over the past three decades has been violent resistance, which has had the effect of scaring some Hans out of their westward adventure.

The central government hopes its project to develop China's poor "great northwest" area, a region that includes Qinghai, Gansu, Tibet, and especially Xinjiang, will accelerate Han population settlement as a force for acculturation and integration. However, this huge planned development project may be unleashing a massive economic and social disaster far greater than it is worth, as it inevitably strengthens the very vectors that will help HIV/AIDS to spread among Xinjiang's Hans, and in a region that already faces an HIV/AIDS crisis of epidemic proportions among its Uyghurs.

Responses to Beijing's Policies: Acculturation

The Chinese government hoped that Communism would provide the vehicle to acculturate the Uyghurs and other Turkic minorities into Chinese society within a few decades. Many Uyghur intellectuals accept this, emphasizing Mandarin language and secular education for Uyghur children in order to allow them to compete fully within Chinese society.[18] The liberal reforms implemented in 1978 and extended to Xinjiang by 1985 enabled minorities to acculturate into Chinese society while at the same time advocating more forcefully for the interests of their own ethnic group. The same was done in southwest China for the Zhuang,[19] the Miao,[20] the Yao,[21] and the Yi[22] peoples. Many ethnic groups were able to reimagine their interests by adopting the government's framework of ethnic rights and privileges. This policy has its inherent risks, as many ethnic minorities have learned that once they acculturate and lose their language, they are highly susceptible to cultural dissolution spurred on by intermarriage with the Hans.

The Uyghurs have the least to fear of all of China's ethnic peoples for they are the most culturally impenetrable. Urban Mandarin-speaking Uyghurs demonstrate a great willingness to associate with Han colleagues, but this openness does not extend to marriage. Unlike the Hans and Huis (Tungans), Hans and Uyghurs practically never marry. This normative restriction can become a source of sexual tension and animosity for Han men whenever they confront the fact that the local population does not consider them suitable marriage partners. For Turkic Muslims, intermarriage between a Han (a nonbeliever) and a Muslim is a fundamental cultural taboo. Those few who do transgress are disowned and their children are never accepted into the larger extended family. Today, intermarriage rates in Xinjiang are so infrequent as to be virtually nonexistent.[23]

The Huis as Acculturation Vectors

The Huis, or non-Turkic Chinese-speaking Muslims, have been an integral part of the political map of Xinjiang since the mid-nineteenth century and form an intermediary position between the Hans and Uyghurs. Uyghurs use the dismissive term *"tawuz"* (watermelon) to refer to the Huis because they wobble between siding with the Hans on some issues and with the Uyghurs on other issues. Some also say that the Huis appear Muslim (green) on the outside and yet are Communist (red) on the inside. Although almost all Turkic Muslims of Xinjiang view the Huis as their adversaries and as allies of the Han Chinese administration, the long history of animosity between the Huis and Uyghurs has been heightened by the fact that the Qing and Republican Chinese authorities utilized Hui troops and officials to dominate the Uyghurs and impose their rule in Xinjiang.[24] Regardless, the Huis are ideal cultural intermediaries since they share Islam with the Uyghurs and the Mandarin language with the Hans.

Many of Xinjiang's Huis are bilingual and live in close proximity to the Uyghurs. Hui teachers of the Mandarin language at Uyghur schools promote an ethos of cultural tolerance and serve as role models of relative social success. They also stress the importance of being loyal citizens of China, China's cultural heritage, and China's role in the world. The Communist government has hoped that the Huis' intermediate status would influence mutual group perceptions and eliminate ethnic tensions, but this has proven only partly true. Although the Uyghurs and Huis are both Muslim, the Huis pray in separate mosques and maintain separate Islamic schools.

The home, mosque, and, to some extent, eating establishments are ethnic borders that are rarely crossed by Uyghurs, Huis, and Hans. These social borders may appear invisible from the outside, but they structure interethnic social, religious, and commercial interactions. Although the Uyghurs will eat at Hui restaurants, they never buy meat from Hui butchers because they mistrust its purity (*halal*). Food preferences are a primary means of demarcating cultural separation between ethnic groups, which is why many Hans refuse to eat in Uyghur restaurants and why Uyghurs refusal to buy Hui meat.

Hans and Uyghurs rarely socialize at each other's homes. Because Hans eat pork, Uyghurs will not eat in their homes. Hans feel self-conscious being in Uyghur homes as they feel their lack of knowledge of Uyghur social customs may offend their hosts. Hans and the Huis often both speak Mandarin dialects, but some Hans fear that because the Huis are Muslims, they might betray the Hans to the Uyghurs. Uyghurs, meanwhile, express this same view about the Huis but in reverse: They fear that the Huis will side with the Hans, with whom they share both language and culture.

While the Huis serving as intermediaries in Xinjiang might not be as effective in acculturating the Uyghurs into Chinese society as the government might hope, they do serve as a model, although one with a difficult history. It took the Huis 700 to 800 years to be fully acculturated into Chinese society. It is likely that the Uyghurs could take even longer. The Huis descend from Persian sailors who came to China beginning in the seventh century and intermarried with Chinese women who converted to Islam. It was not until the Ming dynasty in the fifteenth century that the Chinese government accepted the Huis as Chinese. The Uyghurs will not marry with Hans at all and for the most part will not marry with the Huis.

While rural Uyghurs resist all Sinicization, urban Uyghurs acculturate very quickly. Mandarin-speaking Uyghurs tend to be less religiously active than those less proficient in Mandarin. The ability to speak Mandarin among Uyghurs indicates greater contact with Hans in secular society and Uyghur societal interests away from Islam. Such urban Uyghurs tend to associate more with Han colleagues and have more mixed ethnic friendships than the vast majority of Hans, who prefer to associate only with

Hans.[25] While many urban Uyghurs can speak Mandarin, it is unusual for Hans in Xinjiang to learn the Uyghur language.[26] Uyghurs in Urumchi who speak Mandarin but not their own language are known pejoratively as "the thirteenth minority group."

The dilemma for urban Uyghurs struggling on the front line of acculturation boils down to one issue: education. The decision of whether to send Uyghur children to Mandarin-language or Uyghur-language schools is the most difficult and painful facet of Uyghur acculturation in Xinjiang. Chinese soft policies have allowed Uyghurs an educational choice for their children. Uyghur intellectuals, to a much greater extent than Uyghurs from the merchant and peasant classes, believe that the Uyghur people as a whole will be strengthened by Mandarin-language education. They argue that if Uyghur children are to compete with Hans, in Xinjiang and throughout China, they must master Mandarin Chinese. This challenges them to preserve Uyghur culture and language among their own children while maintaining and developing their ability to compete on a national level. Many Uyghur families respond to this dilemma by sending their sons to Mandarin-language schools and their daughters to Uyghur-language schools. This compromise provides Uyghur sons with the necessary language tools and social experience that will enable them to prosper in Xinjiang's emerging market economy and its unfolding political and social environment. It provides Uyghur daughters the cultural capabilities to pass on Uyghur heritage within their families.

By 1990, cross-border economic links were being renewed. But old rivalries among oasis communities also began to resurface at this time, and these undermined the development of a Xinjiang-wide Uyghur identity.[27] On the other hand, Benson reports that ethnic solidarity appears to be strengthening with the opening of the border to trade.[28] This issue deserves renewed study.

Evidence for weakening oasis identities can be found among the children of educated Uyghur urbanites who have been increasingly intermarrying among themselves and of Uyghur intellectuals living in Urumchi who have been slowly losing their identification with their home oases. The younger urbanites refer to themselves as "Urumchiliks" rather than by the oasis-based terms their parents used.[29]

Nonviolent Resistance

Beijing may seek to ameliorate the impact of Han immigration through soft policies, but this tide of newcomers nonetheless poses the greatest challenge to the indigenous people of Xinjiang since 1949. Between the 1950s and the mid-1980s, this classic hard policy of the government became the single most important force behind the coalescence of modern Uyghur nationalism. Uyghur identity solidified in direct opposition to the Han influx. Until 1985, the government forbade indigenous peoples to voice any criticism or opposition. Only with the soft policies between 1985 and 1989 were Uyghurs allowed to vent their frustration. What followed was an unprecedented outpouring of nonviolent resistance to China's policies and to the ideas the government used to rationalize them.

As China launched its new soft approach in Xinjiang in 1985, many, but by no means all, Uyghurs had already concluded that the Uyghurs, even if united, would never gain control of the region. Instead, they pursued strategies based on their social group or oasis to maximize their place within the Chinese state. Thus, China's hard policies introduced cleavages among the oasis dwellers, while the soft policies served to isolate pan-Uyghur nationalists. At the oasis level, the majority of Uyghurs resisted Chinese policies through nonviolent means. But writings about Uyghur history and national heroes reflected oasis identities more than a regionwide consciousness. Indigenous intellectuals who pushed a regionwide program too hard were treated as pariahs, dismissed from their jobs, or incarcerated.

Strong social cleavages in each oasis made for differences between intellectual, merchant, and peasant notions of Uyghur identity and worked against the creation of a unified pan-oasis Uyghur movement. Many Uyghur intellectuals have come to feel that the peasants are withdrawing into Islamic traditionalism, while the peasants, by contrast, see Islam as intrinsic to their Uyghur ethnic identity. Most intellectuals are anti-Islamic and believe that science and Western education are the only means to bring progress to the Uyghurs. This view finds resonance with China's official doctrines while at the same time greatly upsetting Uyghur peasants who view secular intellectuals as being out of touch with their own people.

In Xinjiang, the three main Turkic social groups—intellectuals, merchants, and peasants—are delineated more by occupation than by family organization, descent, ideology, or commitment to pan-oasis solidarity. Uyghur intellectuals are in the vanguard in resisting official policies that they consider detrimental to Uyghur identity. Because many of them spent years in jail or at hard labor camps, they do not see that violent resistance will lead anywhere. Instead, they challenge the government carefully, pushing to the breaking point and pulling back when necessary. It is a very dangerous game.

Uyghur intellectuals know full well that Uyghurs are not united. What they fail to acknowledge is that Uyghurs have been politically fragmented through most of their history. Hence, they do not focus their attention on the possible causes—geographic, sociological, economic, and political—of this disunity, which in turn vitiates the effectiveness of their efforts to resist detrimental Chinese policies.

To a large extent, the modern identities of Xinjiang's peoples have developed in response to China's current ethnic policies. No matter how vigorously Uyghur intellectuals deny it, "Uyghurness" is a political construct shaped mainly by Chinese policies. Yet, the historical persistence of specific Uyghur cultural traits undeniably imparts strength and viability to the idea.

Disagreements over history in Xinjiang invariably dwell on questions of legitimacy and possession[30] and therefore feed directly into the troubled ethnic relations between Hans and the indigenous peoples.[31] "Uyghurness" is a powerful symbol of cultural reaffirmation coming from the Uyghurs themselves.[32] Against China's claim that the Hans had always lived in Xinjiang while the Uyghurs were outsiders, Uyghurs affirm that they were the original inhabitants and the Hans merely interlopers. Han and Uyghur historians also clash over the inclusive modern definition of Uyghurs as including all oasis-dwelling Turkic Muslims in Xinjiang.[33] China's official version of Xinjiang history relegates Islam to a minor role. This deeply offends pious Uyghur peasants, who aver that Uyghur history began with their acceptance of Islam.

A potent and colorful indigenous challenge to China's version of Xinjiang's past came after Chinese archaeologists discovered desiccated corpses in the Taklimakan Desert in the 1970s.[34] These freeze-dried "Xinjiang mummies," fully clothed in woolen fabrics with felt and leather boots and with hair, eyebrows, and skin intact, were found to be (through carbon dating) 2,000 to 6,000 years old.[35] Western scholars determined through DNA testing that these blond or red-haired people were "Caucasian" in origin, perhaps from the Ukraine region.

Bold Uyghurs immediately claimed these corpses as their ancestors who predated Chinese civilization itself. They argued that these "proto-Uyghurs" and their ancestors were responsible for the very contributions to world civilization of which China is most proud, namely, gunpowder, the compass, paper, and printing. Furthermore, Uyghur historian Turghun Almas asserted that the corpses substantiated Uyghur folklore accounts of the Uyghurs leaving the Tarim basin for the Mongolian steppe when the Tarim basin desiccated 3,000 to 6,000 years ago.[36] This led him to a bold conclusion: If the Jews could reclaim their homeland after 2,000 years, the Uyghurs should be able to regain their homeland after 3,000 to 6,000 years.

The efforts by Chinese authorities to discredit and punish Turghun Almas for this and other historical "errors" are described by Gardner Bovingdon in chapter 14. Suffice it to say that as part of its Strike Hard, Maximum Pressure campaign in 2002, the government demanded that copies of all of Turghun Almas's books still held secretly, along with books by other Uyghur nationalists, be confiscated and burned in pubic bonfires throughout Xinjiang.

China's monumental shift from a socialist economy organized around the work unit (*danwei*) to a market economy has reduced the importance of state employment. This has reduced the government's power to prevent minority officials from openly discussing their grievances against state policies. At the same time, this makes it easier for Han businesses to discriminate against local minorities by hiring cheap migrant Han laborers. Discriminatory hiring practices are bound to increase as the market economy expands, bringing with it an increase in ethnic hostilities between Hans and Uyghurs. Particularly in southern Xinjiang, now served by the new railroad to Kashgar, Uyghur opposition has reached a critical stage. Meanwhile, the Chinese state finds itself unable to prevent the Han majority from asserting its own resentment against indigenous minorities. Should this happen on a large scale, it is bound to push many Uyghurs to become more demonstrative in asserting and defending their interests.

Violent Resistance

While the Uyghur radical resistance movement is fragmented, the Chinese government has claimed that from 1990 to 2001 alone the region was hit by over 200 militant actions, leading to 162 deaths.[37] Uyghur militants attacked police stations, assassinated judges, and demolished communications and electric power infrastructures. They bombed buses, movie theaters, department stores, hotels, markets, and trains and even successfully struck Chinese army bases. Initially, the attacks appeared to be random and limited in scope, focusing especially on the government's policy on religion.[38] But eventually their growing scale and coordination evoked a strong response from the government.

China's Strike Hard, Maximum Pressure policy has spurred violent resistance and posed serious dilemmas to the government. For one thing, resistance is geographically focused. While the government plays up a general Islamic terrorist threat in Xinjiang, anti-Han sentiment is far stronger in Kashgar than elsewhere, mainly in response to the government's own efforts to curtail Islamic practices there. Instead of seeing Islam as a channel through which local Uyghurs are able to express social and political frustrations in a variety of areas, the government chooses to perceive it as the cause of those frustrations, which in turn gives rise to actions that further exacerbate the situation.[39]

The government's clampdown on Islam dates to April 5, 1990, when up to 3,000 Uyghurs were killed in clashes with the Chinese police in the town of Baren near Kashgar. *Newsweek*'s international edition treated the incident as a cover story with the title "The Other China." For the first time since

Tiananmen, troops were airlifted to put down an uprising. Some maintain that the incident was caused by the government's removal of a popular mullah, while others believe it was initiated by Uyghur attacks on government birth control officers. Whatever the case, the Baren affair demonstrated Beijing's fear of Islam as a source and vehicle of resistance.

Religious violence erupted again in 1995 in the southern oasis of Khotan. A large crowd of worshippers at the main mosque spilled into the street, blocking traffic. Uyghurs mistook police efforts to open the street as the arrest of their mullah. A massive revolt against police and troops ensued, during which hundreds were killed and many more imprisoned.

The Chinese government remains convinced that the main causes of religious and ethnic violence were not its own policies but forces operating from beyond its borders, especially in the new states of Central Asia. Barely two months after it established the Shanghai Five organization, China unleashed violent police actions against corruption and illegal activities under the banner of Strike Hard, Maximum Pressure. In Xinjiang, this campaign focused on Uyghur "splittism" or separatism and on "illegal religious activities." This elicited a cycle of protests and bombings across Xinjiang, along with further retaliations. In chapter 11, Jay Dautcher describes the government's 1997 campaign against secular students in Ili, whose sole crime was to have organized a campaign against alcohol abuse. More than 300 perished in the ensuing battle. Between 1997 and 1999, Amnesty International recorded that 210 Uyghurs were executed.

The events in Ili started off a series of increasingly violent actions by Uyghurs. On February 25, 1997 the day of Deng's state funeral, three bombs exploded in Urumchi, killing nine people. On March 7, Uyghur militants blew up a bus in Beijing's busiest shopping district, injuring thirty people. Even as the violence seemed less and less random, no Uyghur militant group took responsibility for these actions. The apparent absence of an organizing center of resistance greatly concerned the Chinese government, for it knew the extent of its vulnerabilities in Xinjiang.

The war against the Taliban and Al-Qaeda in Afghanistan significantly broadened China's Strike Hard, Maximum Pressure campaign in Xinjiang. The Chinese government linked the U.S. war on terrorism with its own antiterrorism campaign in Xinjiang and signed on to assist the war effort.[40] In August 2002, it announced that there were eight Uyghur terrorist forces operating in Xinjiang and throughout China. Judging by their names—the Eastern Turkistan Islamic Movement (ETIM), the Eastern Turkistan Islamic Party, the Eastern Turkistan Islamic Party of Allah, the Islamic Reformist Party "Shock Brigade," and the Islamic Holy Warriors—five have some religious connections. Three others—the Eastern Turkistan

International Movement, the Eastern Turkistan Liberation Organization, and the Uyghur Liberation Organization—appear to have a more secular character.

On August 26, 2002, the U.S. State Department, China, and the United Nations announced that one of the eight Uyghur militant groups, the ETIM, would be placed on the list of international terrorist organizations. Slowly, information about this militant organization came out. The ETIM Uyghur resistance began after the 1990 Baren uprising. Seeing the government's readiness to use force against apparently peaceful students, Uyghur activists from the south of Xinjiang fled to a base at a religious school (*madrassah*) in Pakistan and there founded the ETIM. ETIM fighters dedicated themselves to fighting a "holy war" in Central Asia and to fighting against Chinese invaders. The ETIM's leadership is purported to have had close links to Osama bin Laden and to have sent agents and weapons into Xinjiang beginning in 1998.[41] At least two of the Al-Qaeda fighters captured in Afghanistan and sent to Guantánamo, Cuba, were Uyghurs from the ETIM.

Xinjiang's Endgame

No matter what the Chinese government claims, the greatest immediate threat to Beijing's control of Xinjiang is not Uyghur militancy or terrorism but the HIV/AIDS epidemic that is already spreading there like a whirlwind. HIV/AIDS has already affected the Uyghurs in proportions far exceeding any other ethnic minority in China. HIV/AIDS rates among the Uyghurs are now the highest in China, surpassing Yunnan, which borders on Burma, the source of Xinjiang's heroin. Initially, many Uyghurs smoked heroin, but they began injecting it when the supply began to decrease as a result of the Strike Hard, Maximum Pressure campaign. According to China's Center for Disease Control, about 85 percent of the Uyghur intravenous drug users in Ili, the most secular region of Xinjiang, are HIV positive. The rate in Urumchi is about 40 percent. As of September 2003, there are no methadone clinics or clean-needle exchange programs, and most heroin addicts share needles. HIV/AIDS is becoming the most serious challenge that the Uyghurs have ever faced as a people. As infection rates escalate throughout Xinjiang, it is becoming clear to all Uyghurs, not only to Uyghur nationalists, that the Uyghurs are in a fight for their very survival.

The massive epidemic of HIV/AIDS is undermining the central goals for the region of both the Beijing government and the Uyghurs. The government has placed its hopes in its campaign "Develop the Great Northwest."[42] Even if this did not threaten to overwhelm the region's limited water resources, as Toops in chapter 10 indicates will happen, it will greatly exacerbate the humanitarian and security crises brought on by HIV/AIDS. Up to 2002, the government has viewed HIV/AIDS in Xinjiang as a "Uyghur disease," as indeed it has been. But it will be the very Han people enticed to Xinjiang by the Develop the Great Northwest program—the truck drivers, young pioneer settlers, soldiers, police officers, prostitutes, and government officials, including those most integral to the development scheme—who will now be likely to become infected and pass on the virus.[43] If the Chinese government proceeds with a full-fledged development program in Xinjiang without fundamentally addressing the HIV/AIDS epidemic, it will cause hundreds of thousands of Han as well as Uyghur deaths, especially among the most productive age group, the twenty- to forty-year-olds, as millions of working-age male and female laborers become infected. At the same time, it will throw Uyghurs back on their own communal defenses and hinder their acculturation into Chinese society, which the government so desires.

China's Xinjiang Quandary

The HIV/AIDS crisis will radically affect Xinjiang's economy, stability, and security just as the crisis deeply undermines Uyghur attempts to create a viable future in the region.[44] The Chinese government finds itself in a no-win situation. For decades, most Uyghurs have perceived the Han Chinese as their opponents in the struggle for control of Xinjiang. Now, virtually anything China does to improve relations with Xinjiang's indigenous peoples will provoke resentment. The PRC government is doubtless sincere in its view that the tactic of focusing Han settlers in areas distinct from lands occupied by Uyghurs has enabled the Uyghurs to continue their way of life without Han interference. But nationalistic Uyghurs view the government's policy of settling Hans in the region as a deliberate program of ethnic encirclement and even slow genocide.

Older sources of Uyghur oasis identities and loyalties have strengthened since 1985. But the combined effect of China's accession to the World Trade Organization, the formation of the SCO, the rise of Uyghur militancy, and the HIV/AIDS epidemic in Xinjiang could be to transform Xinjiang's local oasis identities into a larger Xinjiang-wide Uyghur identity. Above all, the HIV/AIDS epidemic in Xinjiang could ultimately derail China's acculturation and incorporation mission in Xinjiang. That same epidemic is certain to be so devastating for the Uyghurs and other indigenous peoples that it overwhelms their battles over identity and turns those battles into a struggle for their communal survival.

13

Islam in Xinjiang

Graham E. Fuller and Jonathan N. Lipman

Apak Khoja and the Fragrant Concubine

Northeast of the great oasis entrepôt of Kashgar, on the edge of the poplar-lined irrigated fields, among the mud-walled village courtyards and new strip malls of shops, lies a complex of old buildings that the guidebooks call "Apak Khoja and Fragrant Concubine Tomb." Its orderly, well-tended flower gardens, preserved and restored facades, and carefully penned explanatory signs—in Chinese, Uyghur, and English—mark it as a significant and government-approved attraction. The main building resembles other Central Asian Sufi tombs in its green tiles, towers, and dome, though it does not appear still to be a site for Sufi rituals as it once was. Inside are arranged over forty coffins, large (male), medium (female), and small (child), each with a trilingual label identifying its occupant as a member of the Khoja family.

The complex also contains a large mosque, where over 2,000 Muslims from neighboring villages gather to hear the Friday sermon and celebrate festivals. A separate building marked as a Qur'anic school shows no signs of current use. The Central Asian–style adobe and plaster of the complex, the garden setting, and the hot desert sun create a calm atmosphere for Chinese and foreign visitors alike, and it has become one of Kashgar's most popular sights.

There the visitor will learn that Apak Khoja was a seventeenth-century leader in the region and that the Fragrant Concubine (Ch. Xiangfei, Uyg. Iparhan), a descendent of the Khoja, had been sent to Beijing to be a consort of the Qing dynasty's great Qianlong emperor (r. 1736–1795, d. 1799). Guides tell stories of the Khoja's devotion to the people's welfare during his service as local chieftain under the Zunghars, Mongols who controlled the area during the seventeenth century. Chinese tourists are also interested in the romantic (and vaguely salacious) tales of the Concubine's journey to Beijing, the emperor's devotion to her (due in part to her mysterious, natural fragrance), and her posthumous return to Kashgar for burial. A cart, conspicuously placed inside the main door of the tomb building, supposedly carried her coffin home. Guides and signs alike proclaim that both the Concubine and the Khoja contributed directly to harmony among China's many nationalities and to the "unity of the motherland," she by mutual love with her master the emperor in Beijing, he by governing justly over Kashgar. Both major figures, and all of the minor occupants of the tomb, are unambiguously identified as "Uyghurs," members of one of China's fifty-six "minority nationalities" (one of ten "Muslim" minorities) and thus of China's great "national family," the Zhonghua minzu.

It is appropriate to begin a discussion of Islam in Xinjiang with this tomb complex because beneath its touristic surface the "Apak Khoja and Fragrant Concubine Tomb" embodies many of the ironies, historical distortions, and contradictions that the literature and present-day residents of the area consistently narrate. For example, many contemporary Uyghurs find Apak Khoja a negative historical figure because during his rule over Kashgar he waged war against the neighboring oasis of Khotan and killed many of its "Uyghur" inhabitants in the name of the Zunghars, a non-Muslim people. His tomb has therefore not recently been an important pilgrimage site for local Muslims. On the other hand, no guide or pamphlet mentions that he was a consequential Sufi, a carrier of revivalist Islam into China proper during several visits to Gansu.[1] His influence in northwestern China led to divisions, feuds, violence, and even anti-Qing rebellion in the eighteenth and nineteenth centuries, about which not a word is mentioned in the sanitized history that is presented at the tomb complex. Chinese-speaking Muslims (Hui) from Gansu often journey to the tomb to pray, for as the teacher of the founder of one of Gansu's largest Sufi orders, the Khoja remains an important saint for its adherents.

In contrast to the romance of Chinese versions, Uyghur stories of the Fragrant Concubine reject all talk of mutual love and nationality unity, insisting instead that she kept herself secretly armed in order to kill the Qianlong emperor in revenge for his invasion and occupation of her homeland and that she refused to allow the consummation of the marriage. The emperor's mother, in this version, finally had Xiangfei murdered in order to protect her son's life and health from the overwhelming desire and danger posed by the Central Asian beauty.[2] No tourist guide mentions the Muslim prohibition on marrying a daughter to a non-Muslim, generally followed with great strictness in Xinjiang. Nor are they likely to discuss the undisputed evidence regarding the burial of the Qianlong emperor's actual Muslim consort, under her palace name of Rongfei, among the Qing imperial graves near Beijing (though that evidence is widely known in Chinese scholarly circles).

Perhaps most telling, no one at the site, or anywhere in Xinjiang, will publicly question the identification of both of these people as Uyghurs, a name that was not current in the seventeenth and eighteenth centuries.[3]

Contemporary arguments, of course, dispute the meanings of the "Uyghurness" of both the Khoja and the Concubine. Defending the inclusion of the entire region within modern China, one Chinese historian wrote, "Xiang Fei and her whole family [presumably including Apak Khoja] made a definite contribution by opposing separatism and protecting nationality harmony and national unity."[4] At the opposite extreme, writing in expatriate publications, Uyghur authors have praised "the heroic Turkic woman who in the year 1760 struggled against the Manchu-Chinese invaders."[5] Clearly, these anachronistic arguments project contemporary social conflicts backward 200 or 300 years. Neither the Chinese nor the Uyghur interpretation mentions the fact that both were Muslims, nor that Islam is still practiced in the complex's large mosque.

Finally, an academic visitor must note the touristic and entertainment side of what was once a serious Islamic shrine. The superimposition of a particular reading of the myth of the Fragrant Concubine onto an Islamic shrine at once trivializes its religious significance and makes it part of a broader and discernible process, what might be termed the "Disneylandization" of Islam and Uyghur culture in China. That is, it has been emasculated, folklorized, prettified, Hanified, and cast into the nationwide museum of safely packaged ethnicity that serves up exoticism and charm to tourists in China but precludes any hint of opposition in the past or present. This process began in the late nineteenth century, when the Apak Khoja tomb (*mazar*) was first combined with imagined memories of the Fragrant Concubine, and the two tombs became firmly joined between 1920 and 1945.[6]

What Is the Problem?

A plethora of questions arise from these contradictions and silences. Clearly, the Khoja and the Concubine are being used, their narratives invented and represented, for contemporary purposes having to do variously with Chinese rule over Xinjiang (reflected backward in Manchu Qing dominion), Uyghur (i.e., local Turki) identity and resistance to Chinese hegemony, and Islam. These elements are inextricably intertwined at every point. No analysis of Islam as a living religion in Xinjiang can be undertaken without considering state sovereignty, state power, and ethnicity.

This chapter describes a number of dilemmas facing Islam as a religious system, its professional personnel, institutions, and lay participants, as well as their comprehension of its tenets and texts. While the following themes have already appeared in earlier chapters in this volume, they bear repeating here for their powerful impact on Islam and Muslims in the autonomous region.

1. *Intermittently contested hegemony over all or part of Xinjiang from China-*

based states for much of the past two and a half centuries. This China-based control, which Chinese nationalist sources call a natural continuation of 2,000 years of Chinese domination over the region, has been termed "colonialism" by Uyghurs in exile and by some Euro-American scholars. Though outside the purview of this chapter to decide, the issue of political legitimacy and power remains crucial for all Muslims in Xinjiang. China-based states and their local officials in Xinjiang have undertaken to control Islam and Muslim behavior, though no pre-1949 government was actually able to constrain the movement of Muslims across frontiers (and later borders). Certainly, the Qing wished to exclude potentially subversive persons and ideas and to restrain indigenous leaders who might have external connections, but they never succeeded in doing so.[7] In contemporary Xinjiang, the power of the state to regulate religion, including Islam, has brought the forces of law and order into direct conflict with Muslims who are trying to live according to the tenets of their faith. Many Muslims have lost their jobs, their freedom, and even their lives in order to be themselves and practice their religion in what they perceive to be their homeland.

2. *Vast migration of Chinese into the region.* As discussed by Stanley W. Toops in chapter 9, the percentage of Uyghurs in the population of Xinjiang has dropped from over 75 percent in 1949 to under 50 percent today, and the demographic center of the region has shifted dramatically, from the southern oases (over 70 percent in 1949) to the northern cities, where more than half of the population now resides. The Han population has grown rapidly during the same period, from under 10 percent to almost 40 percent. Whatever the balance may have been in the more distant past, many Uyghurs today perceive the Hanification of their homeland to be the gravest danger to their religion and culture.

Though Uyghur families are entitled under China's birth control regulations to have one more child than Han families in similar circumstances, this has nowhere allowed the Uyghurs to keep pace with the periodic in-migration of millions of Han (and hundreds of thousands of Hui).[8] A government official in Beijing claimed that many of the Han migrants were seasonal agricultural workers who had no intention of remaining in Xinjiang. A recent Chinese scholarly study, however, notes that the annual growth of the Uyghur population is 2.45 percent, while a Chinese government report gives the growth of Xinjiang's population as a whole as 13 percent. The official Xinhua News Service reported in December 2000 that the state plans major increases in professional personnel throughout western China, including Xinjiang, and there is no indication that this plan means an immediate increase in the number of Uyghur professionals.

It seems very unlikely that the Chinese government will curtail the flow of indigent Chinese into Xinjiang, while the state has positively encouraged Han scientists, engineers, and other professionals to migrate. Though not directly dangerous for Islam, this demographic shift appeared to almost every Uyghur interviewed for this study to be one of the two greatest threats to their culture and society, the other being state control over religion. The presence of vast numbers of non-Muslims (or, in the case of the Hui, non-Uyghurs) in Xinjiang seemed to many of them to guarantee that their children and grandchildren would not be able to practice Islam in what they regard as the traditional way. Most of them worried that their descendants would be drawn away from their ancestral faith by the materialism of Chinese civilization, embodied in its lack of true religion. Only a very small number of them found this a positive or encouraging trend.

3. *Discrimination against religious Muslims.* Many recent articles and most informants described large and small instances of pressure on Muslims not to practice their religion or to engage in any Uyghur custom that might be considered "Islamic."[9] Public-sector employees, for example, may not wear clothing marked as Muslim, including head scarves or coverings for women and the embroidered *doppa* skullcap for Uyghur men. One informant reported that male schoolteachers have been forbidden to grow their mustaches, an important sign of manhood for Uyghurs, and that female students have been expelled from school for wearing overly long skirts and for covering their hair. Chinese Communist Party (CCP) members, of course, may not attend prayers or religious instruction without serious consequences, and the same rule has also been enforced for anyone on the state payroll, except for publicly employed imams.[10] Ordinary believers know that government informers attend prayer services, especially the Friday sermon, and keep a close watch on all religious professionals, so anyone wishing to rise in the state-dominated sectors of society must avoid the mosque and any unseemly contact with Islamic teachers.

4. *Crackdown on "crime," meaning crackdown on Islam.* Because the Euro-American idea of impersonal law is relatively new and almost entirely unpracticed in China, the state has great latitude in determining what is or is not "illegal." China has no functionally independent legislature or judiciary, so the executive departments can act with impunity against any persons or behaviors construed (at any moment) as antisocial or antistate. The "Strike Hard, Maximum Pressure" (Ch. *Yanda*) campaign, begun in the 1990s to cope with skyrocketing crime, in Xinjiang has targeted "separatism" (i.e., Uyghur nationalism) and "illegal religious activities." Elsewhere in China, "illegal religious activities" means primarily the Falungong, but in Xinjiang it means aspects of Islam over which the state functionaries feel they exercise insufficient control.

The forces of law and order have focused their attention on preventing underground religious instruction, on carrying out neighborhood sweeps to catch suspected Uyghur nationalists, and on maintaining surveillance of religious professionals. Their goal is to ensure that imams do not teach Islam to children, do not advocate Islamic "fundamentalism" or radicalism (however the state may define those terms), and do not encourage or create connections between Muslims in China and elsewhere. All of these are defined as "illegal religious activities," and they have been punished, usually with terms in prison. Several informants described small social gatherings in private courtyards interrupted by inquisitive police because a religious professional was present—in one case he was the informant's cousin, paying a family visit. The police squads, usually including Uyghurs, wanted to know what was being discussed, what books were on the table, and what the imam was teaching and to whom.

5. *Employment opportunities and options diminishing for Uyghurs.* This theme pervaded the oral accounts of local residents. The perception of Uyghurs as "backward" (Ch. *luohou*) by virtue of their minority status and Islamic faith definitely biases Han executives and officials against equitable treatment for all citizens. The Chinese state currently promotes the campaign to "Develop the West" (Ch. *xibu da kaifa*) as a national priority. Yet, many Uyghurs, especially religious Muslims, do not see themselves as benefiting from the external investment, enhanced domestic spending, and resource development programs that the central government has initiated to advance this goal. Instead, they tell of Uyghurs who have been denied jobs on the basis of Han managers' preference for Han employees, and they repeat the charge that practicing Muslims cannot find work in the state or state-sponsored sectors of the Xinjiang economy because of the strictures of official atheism.

In such northern Xinjiang cities as Urumchi and Yining (Gulja), members of the Han majority appear to advance more rapidly than similarly qualified Uyghurs, while even in Kashgar many specialized occupations are reserved for the Xinjiang Production and Construction Corps (Ch. Xinjiang shengchan jianshe bingtuan) and other Han-dominated work units. The notion that "minority nationalities" are inherently less intelligent, more backward, and less hardworking than Han, and that this is due in part to their practice of Islam, has great currency in China—to the point that even some prominent leaders of those same "minority nationalities" repeat it. This provides some Han with a convenient explanation for why Uyghurs are not hired for responsible posts or highly skilled professions. Most Uyghurs, of course, do not see themselves as inferior—quite the contrary!—and they desire to retain those aspects of their culture, including Islam and the Uyghur language, that constitute the core of their personal and collective identities. They argue that Islam is not backward or feudal and that their "customs and habits" (Ch. *fengsu xiguan*) mark them as a highly civilized people with a noble history and deep cultural connections with the best traditions of Islamic learning.

With these themes in mind, and the distortions of the Apak Khoja and Fragrant Concubine tomb in the background, let us examine the current state of Islam in the Xinjiang Uyghur Autonomous Region.

Islam in Xinjiang—Description

Islam in Xinjiang has been consistently influenced by the region's proximity to and communication with eastern Central Asia, which it strongly resembles in language, culture, and physical geography. Islam entered Xinjiang from Central Asia in the tenth century, and by the mid-fifteenth century the Turkic speakers of the Tarim basin oases, all the way to Hami, had almost universally converted to Islam. Since then, the oases of the south have remained overwhelmingly Muslim (until the late twentieth century),[11] while the northern cities developed into multicultural centers only under the Qing and Republican governments (the eighteenth to the twentieth century). The Kazaks of the Zungharian basin and the Kyrgyz of the various mountain ranges also converted to Islam.

Even in pre-Islamic times, the Turks of Central Asia were aware of the enticements and dangers of China. In the Orkhon inscriptions, one of the most ancient Turkic texts, a Turk (before Islam had reached the area) wrote:

> The Tabgach [Chinese] who now give us limitless gold, silver, spirits and silk, always employed sweet speech and luxurious valuables to powerfully attract distant peoples. These peoples then settled close by them and thus acquired bad knowledge. But the Tabgach people and their allies could not divert the good and wise peoples and the noble heroes from the true path. If some individuals from the Turks were seduced, whole tribes did not stray.
>
> Having allowed yourselves to be enticed by their sweet words and luxurious valuables, you, O Turkish people, perished in great numbers. Turkish people, when one part of you said, "I wish to settle not only in the south in the Chugai area, but also in the Tyun plains" then evil people there instructed part of the Turkish people, saying, "Whoever lives far from the Tabgach receives bad gifts, but whoever lives close to them receives excellent gifts." With these words they so strongly instructed you. And so you, people, lacking true wisdom and obeying their speech moved in close to them, and so you perished there in great numbers. Therefore, O Turkish

people, when you go to that country, you are on the edge of perdition. But if you remain on Otyuken soil and only send caravans, then you have no woes, and you can live, creating your eternal tribal union. [12]

The coming of Islam deepened the cultural differences between China and the Turkic world. Muslim rulers in Central Asia could not admit any inferiority to the pagan (*kafir*) Tabgach or Khitai, just as no self-respecting Chinese could view the Turks as anything but barbarians. The fifteenth-century Yongle emperor of the Ming dynasty and Shahrukh Bahadur, Tamerlane's son, agreed to correspond as siblings rather than in the unequal language of believer and nonbeliever or of China's tribute system, but neither ever accepted the other's judgment of his own civilization. [13]

It is true that the Turkic-speaking and Islamic culture of today's Xinjiang has interacted with, and been influenced by, Chinese culture to the east for centuries. But until the twentieth century, those influences paled in comparison to others that crossed the mountains and steppe from the Muslim world to the west. During the long Ming period (1368–1644), very little of what is now Xinjiang was actually governed by the Ming state, and only the eastern-most oases—Hami (Qumul) and Turpan—experienced political or cultural pressure from China. [14] After conquering the entire region in the 1750s, the Qing contented themselves with stationing military governors at Yining and garrisons at key points, leaving local government in the hands of Islamic notables until the 1880s. Local culture and religion, too, were left to themselves, provided they did not give rise to antistate sentiments or actions. [15]

Kashgar is closer to Baghdad than to Beijing. Indeed, Xinjiang as a whole has had more ready access to the Turkic and Iranian world, not to mention most of northern India, than to the cultural centers of China proper. Within the region, Kashgar is hundreds of miles more distant from Hami than from Andijan or Kokand, across the mountains in Ferghana, which helps explain why it took almost five centuries for Islam to spread from Kashgar to Hami, whose diplomatic and trade envoys to the Ming court were Buddhists until the 1420s. Indeed, geographic distance may be the most crucial element in our understanding of the *cultural* distance between the Muslim Turkic speakers of the region and the Chinese. Even during the Qing's heyday, when Xinjiang had become an integral part of the empire, few Chinese went there without a heavy heart and the sense that they were going very far from home. In fact, few went voluntarily, and exile to Xinjiang was considered a severe punishment for miscreant officials. [16]

Though the Muslim societies of the region did not experience heavy influence from China before the middle period of the Qing, neither did they ever constitute a single undivided whole in opposition to outsiders. Regardless of who ruled over them, the Islamic peoples of Xinjiang always demonstrated a broad diversity in leadership, politics, and religious practices. Competition between Sufi orders, clan rivalries, and the permanent confrontation of sedentary and nomadic societies divided the region's Muslims from one another, as did their local oasis identities. Further differences arose from their differing commercial orientations, whether toward China, the Kazak steppe, Ferghana, or northern Hindustan.[17] Thus, Uyghur claims to having been a united ethnic group (Uyg. *millet*, Ch. *minzu*) in former times are based more on passion than on evidence. However, despite the various centrifugal forces that divided them from one another, the sedentary Turkic speakers of the Tarim oases did share a common language and culture that differed sharply from the Chinese, and by the mid-fifteenth century all of them had become Sunni Muslims. Over the five centuries since then, this religious bond has constituted a major unifying force within the region, though it has certainly never been sufficient to create political or social unity.

Over the centuries, Xinjiang has witnessed a nearly constant movement of peoples, among them the Zunghars and other Mongols; Turkic peoples including the mountain-dwelling Kyrgyz, Tajiks, and other Iranian speakers; and nomadic or seminomadic Kazaks. This, along with the steady infusion of religious and political influences from the Muslim world, undermined long-term political, religious, and social stability in the oases and on the northern pasturelands.[18] While there is little evidence of a Sunna-Shi'a division in the region, scholars have discovered ample evidence of other forms of conflict, including civil strife, intrigues, fraternal murders, and even wars over the political-religious leadership of the oases and control over the trade routes. All of these purely internal divisions added to the prevailing instability.

Some of the states that ruled parts of what is now Xinjiang before and during the Qing period were Muslim, their rulers often the patrons or even *shaykhs* of Sufi orders, builders of mosques, and protectors of the faith. The various rebellions against Qing rule and against those Muslims who governed in their name, as well as the invasions that took place during the eighteenth and nineteenth centuries, were all led by Muslims and often utilized the vocabulary of jihad.[19] Few of these invaders, however, were motivated by purely religious concerns. Most arose from the khanate of Kokand, in Ferghana, which had powerful economic and political interests in the Tarim oases that impelled them to oppose Qing hegemony there.[20] In the early twentieth century (1933–1934), the Turkish-Islamic Republic of Eastern Turkistan, based in Kashgar and Khotan, proclaimed an Islamic government based on *shari'a*, but it failed to unite Muslims against either the very distant Chinese republic or the more proximate threat of the Soviet Union. In fact, the enemies who brought about its rapid downfall were fellow Muslims—Chinese-speaking Muslim (Hui or Tungan) troops from Gansu—who brutally destroyed the Muslim secessionist movement only a few months after its declaration.[21]

As has been narrated elsewhere in this volume, contemporary Uyghur nationalists place great stock in the history of the second Eastern Turkistan Republic (ETR), which they point to as evidence that their national aspirations and independence movement have a long history. Governing the three westernmost prefectures of northern Xinjiang from 1944 to 1949, this small state has been described both as a successful Turki nationalist and Islamic movement[22] and as a puppet dependency of the Soviet Union.[23] Many of its leaders had studied in modern schools abroad, and only a few were old-fashioned 'ulama. Yet, the proclamations of the ETR emphasized Islam, as well as freedom of religion, among its first principles. As the Communists moved toward victory in the 1945–1949 Chinese civil war, representatives of the ETR flew to Beijing in August 1949 in hopes of negotiating with the country's new leaders. The airplane crashed under suspicious circumstances en route from Alma-Ata (Almaty), and the most charismatic leaders of the Turkish-Islamic nationalist movement perished. Later in 1949, the People's Liberation Army entered Xinjiang and negotiated a settlement that liquidated the ETR and incorporated all of Xinjiang into the newly formed People's Republic of China.

This brief chapter can only state, not solve, the problem of sovereignty for the Muslim peoples of Xinjiang: Can Chinese rule over what many Muslims perceive to be their territory *ever* be legitimate? By what processes of legitimation have states based elsewhere been able to rule Xinjiang for much of the past two millennia? Twentieth-century Chinese scholars have assiduously pressed their claim that the Qing empire at its height constituted *what China has always been* and that all the peoples therein must therefore be integral, inseparable parts of the Chinese national family. To support this claim, they have cited archaeological arcana and trotted out "willing" members of the "minority nationalities" to agree with them.[24]

Opposing this view, local nationalists, primarily Uyghurs, argue that "Chinese" (or Manchu) rule over the region has been a short-lived phenomenon, colonial in its essence, always opposed by local people in the name of religion and freedom. Islamists, of course, argue that non-Muslim rule over Muslims can never be legitimate and that the Uyghurs must therefore struggle for independence and the formation of a Muslim state. As will be shown shortly, the Chinese state has succeeded in completely silencing these antistate Islamic voices in Xinjiang. Like all struggles over sovereignty—Tibet, Palestine, Kurdistan, Chechnya, Northern Ireland,

South Africa, among many others—this one may be framed in terms of history, but its life is very much in the present.

Two actual historic events dominate the current struggle over Islam in Xinjiang: the end of the Maoist period and the subsequent policies of reform sponsored by Deng Xiaoping and his successors in Beijing; and the collapse of the Soviet Union, followed by the establishment of independent states (Kazakstan, Kyrgyzstan, Tajikistan, Uzbekistan, and Turkmenistan) in adjoining parts of Central Asia. The opening of China to foreign influences and foreign trade has been focused in the burgeoning modern cities of the eastern littoral, with their orientations toward Japan, the United States, and Europe. The great historic events noted earlier might, under different circumstances, have brought about a concomitant opening of China to the Muslim cultures of Central Asia and the Middle East, but that has not come to pass.

In the 1980s and early 1990s, increasing numbers of Muslims from all over China—Uyghurs, Hui, Kazaks, and more—went on the pilgrimage (hajj) to Mecca, deepening their perceptions of the Muslim world and joining them with the various discourses of Islamic modernity and antimodernity. Some discovered Islam's potential as a political force for resistance to authority.[25] Muslim students from China went to Muslim countries to study languages, science, and religion, and they returned to become teachers, businessmen, and religious professionals. Missionary (*da'wa*) groups from such countries as Malaysia and Pakistan visited Muslim communities in China proper. Each was intent on persuading them of the rectitude of their particular version of Islam or of the power of political Islam as each was practicing it. The Karakoram Highway from Pakistan to Kashgar, improved roads over the passes from the Tarim to Ferghana, and the new highway and railroad from Xinjiang to Kazakstan allowed unprecedented exchange across frontiers previously closed to all but caravans. A number of Xinjiang cities, including Urumchi, Kashgar, and Yining, now have airports with regular service to international as well as domestic destinations.

Unlike the east coast's opening to Europe, the United States, and Japan, however, this external connection to China's west has caused a negative reaction among officials in Beijing and the provincial capital. Though eager for the power and wealth that China's burgeoning economy could generate through diplomacy and trade with Central and South Asia, China's government has consistently limited, or even forbidden, trans-border interaction from Xinjiang by Muslim "minority nationalities." Since the early 1990s, the ominous phrases "separatism and splittism" and "illegal religious activity" have dominated state discourse in the region. To prevent these "crimes," the state has imposed more stringent police controls on Islam than anything attempted since the end of the Cultural Revolution.[26] A Beijing official assured us that

"Xinjiang is different from other places in China. Islam is administered much more strictly there than elsewhere." He used the term "*guan*" for "administer," with its additional meaning of "supervised, watched." As subjects of this "administration," a number of Xinjiang Muslim informants compared their situation unfavorably to that of Tibetans. "At least the Tibetans have the Dalai Lama and Hollywood to create international pressure to protect them from state attacks on their religion. We have nothing like that." Several of our Uyghur informants longed for a Uyghur version of the Dalai Lama—a prestigious and powerful religious figure living in exile—who could plead their cause before the court of world opinion.

Travelers in Xinjiang with access to local languages report a prevailing mood of fear. Religious professionals fear the constant surveillance of the state, while ordinary Muslims fear the social, economic, or judicial consequences of participation in religious activity. Uyghurs fear the loss of their religious or cultural identity, and non-Uyghurs fear "Uyghur" or "Muslim" violence. A Beijing professor reported that even scholars avoid the "sensitive" (Ch. *min'gan*) subject of religion in order not to transgress the state's politically touchy vision of Islam. A survey of recent Chinese publications reveals that the story of Islam in Xinjiang, in book after book, officially ends in 1949. Of the subsequent half-century, one finds only antiseptic descriptions of "Uyghur customs and habits." Absent is any narrative or discussion of recent history, for example, of the excesses of the Cultural Revolution, the revival of Sufism, or the recent development of Wahhabism.[27] True, reports, even book-length studies, on these topics exist, but their circulation is strictly limited to trusted scholars and concerned officials of the state.

Due to the prevailing fear and the ubiquitous "administration" of the state, actual religious practice in Xinjiang has a closed, hermetic character that makes it relatively inaccessible to outsiders, who can do little to describe the religious life of ordinary Muslims beyond noting its obvious similarities to Muslim practices elsewhere in Central Asia. However, some areas are indirectly available even to foreign observers.

Mosques and Neighborhoods

Mosques tend to be segregated not by religious factions or Sufi orders, as is often the case in Muslim regions elsewhere in China, but by ethnicity. The split between Uyghur and Hui mosques is especially pronounced, even in architecture. The latter tend toward the Chinese-temple style that was popular in Qing and Republican times. Hui mosques are usually associated with the former native place of the neighborhood's Hui (e.g., the Great Shaanxi Mosque in Urumchi). In contrast, many of the Uyghur mosques strongly resemble those of oases in Central Asia—adobe exterior walls, tile, domes, and short, broad-based minaret towers. The Uyghur Friday and holiday mosques are often open-air, with broad courtyards shaded by poplars and large unwalled terraces for the rows of worshippers. Hui do not frequent Uyghur mosques and vice versa. Indeed, while the Chinese-speaking Hui can associate more freely with the non-Muslim Han Chinese, their relations with Uyghurs are defined by neighborhood segregation, personal prejudice, and general mistrust. Uyghur informants called the Hui "more Chinese than Muslim," and Hui informants referred to Uyghurs as "backward and feudal-minded."

Muslim Leadership

Lacking a unitary religious center, the universal community of Islam, the *umma*, has long been divided and subdivided into local congregational entities, each with its own leadership. Men possessing Islamic learning and high moral character are held to qualify as 'ulama, and it is they who lead the congregation in prayer, give sermons on Friday, and present an authoritative voice on questions of religion, law, morality, and every other aspect of human life. They teach the children, beginning with their Arabic letters and their first Qur'anic verses, and they train the next generation of scholars and leaders to succeed to their learning. Such men often hold the highest and most respected status that a Muslim community can give. In Sufi communities, the shaykh has an even greater weight of responsibility, for he holds the key to the *baraka* (religious charisma) from God and to the *tariqa* (mystical path), which leads to unity with the Divine. Through common loyalty to himself and his particular religious path, he can also connect communities with one another, which helps explain why many secular states (including China) have long viewed Sufi organizations as potentially subversive and untrustworthy.

In post-1949 China, state controls on Islam and official hostility to religion in general have altered the condition of the 'ulama in Uyghur society. Islam is branded a reactionary ideology and feudal throwback, at best a backward aspect of human society doomed to wither with progress and the advance of science. Atheism is proclaimed as public doctrine, and Han Chinese culture as the most advanced of all cultures. This means that Islam and its religious professionals must perforce be regarded as inferior to, or at least less enlightened than, secular intellectuals, and Uyghurs as a group must strive to catch up with the progressive Han. Numerous ordinary aspects of Muslim observance, such as abstinence from pork, endogamy (marriage within one's own religion), and daily prayer, have at times been judged bizarre, antisocial, or even illegal, especially during the Cultural Revolution.

Given these views, the 'ulama should long since have lost their place at the head of Uyghur society, replaced by Uyghurs who have assimilated into Chinese society—mastered the Chinese language, achieved public recognition, and become professionals, officials, intellectuals, or celebrities—all without reference to Islam. Such people do exist, but do they enjoy the respect and confidence of the rest of Uyghur society? Most Uyghurs still live in villages, where few acculturated Uyghurs reside. In the rural areas, religious leaders remain the core of community solidarity, and the mosque remains the central institution.

Some nonreligious leaders do enjoy a measure of respect (combined with fear and occasional hostility). Among these are Uyghurs who have succeeded within the party and state apparatus, whether locally, in Urumchi, or even in Beijing. They can exert great power in Xinjiang through their connections inside the establishment. They can protect their relatives, friends, and allies from official harassment, soften (though rarely eradicate) government policies that discriminate against Uyghurs, and mediate in conflicts that arise between Uyghurs and non-Uyghurs. But such people gain the right to represent their "minority nationality" in the councils of power only at the price of repudiating any connection to Islam and embracing instead a secular Sinocentrism.[28] The 'ulama therefore remain as a layer of local or (in a few cases) regional leaders, uneasily positioned between ordinary Uyghurs who retain a personal connection to Islam and the secular establishment.

The 'ulama's Islamic training, however, and both their public spoken and written explanations of Islam now fall under state control. There is only one officially sanctioned *madrassah* for training religious professionals in all of Xinjiang, the Institute for the Study of Islamic Texts (Yisilanjiao Jingxueyuan) in Urumchi. All members of its faculty are government employees, and its curriculum is established by the Islamic Association of China (Zhongguo Yisilanjiao Xiehui), a government-funded national religious association headquartered in Beijing. Only graduates of this seminary can become official imams in the region. Their status as religious leaders also places them under the special surveillance of local law enforcement and "religious affairs" officials. Ordinary Muslims are well aware of the terrible pressure under which their imams function and know that they must conform to the state's policies and pronouncements on all issues in order to keep their jobs and their freedom. Because of this, the Muslim public rarely blames its imams for what might otherwise be perceived as craven conformity.

One hears occasional murmurs that some 'ulama practiced quiet resistance, obviously in secret, doing their limited best to transmit a less state-constrained Islam to their congregants. Certainly, many of the Uyghurs we met continued to have respect for men who become Islamically knowledgeable people. The photographers who take souvenir pictures of tourists in the great square facing the Idgah Mosque in Kashgar all have attractive glossy photos of local imams, bearded and turbanned, in their display cases. "They are our leaders," said one older Uyghur photographer in thickly accented Chinese, "and they prove that Kashgar can produce notable men of religion." However, Uyghur activists stabbed an imam of that same mosque, presumably because he had betrayed the Uyghur cause by maintaining too intimate a relationship to state power or too brazen an adherence to state doctrine.

All imams in major Friday and holiday mosques are state employees, but small neighborhood mosques may have religious leaders who are not on the public payroll. They are chosen by the community, visitors are told, for their moral character and Islamic learning rather than any formal credential. But state informers attend their sermons, too, and the police carefully monitor their religious activities. In Kashgar or in Urumchi's Uyghur section, where seemingly every lane and alleyway has its mosque, the local imams remain respected figures. But their independence, judgment on religious affairs, and even their physical movements are closely circumscribed by an often hostile government.

Language

Until the twentieth century, the majority of the Turkic speakers of Xinjiang, like most human beings, were monoglot and illiterate. If they learned to read and/or write, they did so in Arabic and Persian in the madrassah. The *jadid* movement, emanating from Kazan and Central Asia in the late nineteenth century, advocated study of modern languages, including Russian and Turkish, as part of a modern Islamic education. Until the 1950s, however, only a few elite local people in Xinjiang had learned Chinese, Russian, English, or any other international language.

In recent decades, this has changed radically. Uyghurs are now required to learn some Chinese in school, and most of them look on knowledge of Chinese as the sine qua non for secular advancement. This does not stop many from resenting the imposition of what they perceive to be a colonial language on their culture.[29]

Debates over how to educate Uyghur children resonate in the mosques and private religious spaces of Xinjiang. This question inevitably involves Islam as an element of identity that is intimately bound up with the Uyghur language. People wonder how their children can carry on Islamic tradition without a firm grounding in what constitutes for them the Islamic language, namely Uyghur. They ask whether children educated entirely in the Chinese-language curriculum, the so-called *min kao Han* students, can still in any meaningful way remain either Uyghur or Muslim. Many such Uyghurs, even highly educated and successful ones, speak the Uyghur language poorly; some cannot read it at all. Oriented entirely toward the Chinese world in which they were educated, they tend to be completely detached from religious life.

All of this leaves a sour impression on Uyghur nationalists. It is revealing that such people often prefer to communicate with Chinese-speaking foreigners through English. Such visitors may even be cautioned not to use Chinese in the vicinity of a mosque, lest it generate mistrust among the Muslims, even though the guests are obviously not Chinese.

Today, works translated from Turkic, Persian, and Arabic originals are available to anyone who reads Chinese, thanks to a large academic establishment working specially to produce them. The reality is dawning on many Uyghurs that their language and culture might soon become superfluous for public discourse. At a time when Chinese are pouring into the region and when Chinese speakers already control corporations and public work units, those Uyghurs who speak Chinese poorly or not at all face drastically diminished prospects of doing business outside of Uyghur neighborhoods and villages. Yet, as noted earlier, the state has recently discouraged Uyghurs from learning English, denying them one of the best tickets to social and economic advancement. Even Uyghur-language education now takes place in an atmosphere hostile to Islam. The daughters who are often chosen to carry on the Uyghur language and culture must remove their head scarves and shorten their long skirts, that is, violate their religion's fundamental notions of female modesty, in order to attend public schools.

Religious Education

The state now strictly enforces rules against religious instruction or even mosque attendance by any children under eighteen. Posted over the door of almost every large or small mosque is a sign in Uyghur forbidding entrance to minors. This deprives many young people of the grounding in community and values that Islam has conventionally fostered in Xinjiang. This gives rise to a process of deculturalization. Persuaded by the larger culture around them that distance from Islam represents progress and modernity, some Uyghurs have ceased to practice their ancestral religion, substituting the secular ideology of the Chinese state or that of Kemalist secularism. Thus, a successful Uyghur employed by the provincial government drew on phrases from the government's own manuals on "minority nationalities" to describe Islam as a repository of outdated customs and habits rather than as a living religion. This man informed us that he has not given his daughter an Islamic education, and we heard them talk to one another in Uyghur mixed with Chinese. For her part, the daughter already speaks Chinese with an impeccable accent and commands a rich vocabulary. Her father encourages her also to master English, despite obstacles, so that she might someday study abroad.

As is often the case in colonial situations, however, Islam and Islamic education in Xinjiang have become a means for resisting state power and are likely to grow in that role. Many families teach their children to pray at home. One cosmopolitan English speaker confessed that his wife and young son pray five times daily at home, though he himself never does; he wondered aloud how he was going to prevent the child from revealing his religious practice once he begins school. One also hears oblique references to underground religious schools and tales of courageous imams who visit families in the guise of social interaction and teach the children to pray, which the police endeavor to prevent by raids and surprise visits.

Some of the resistance to state power in Xinjiang comes from small and secretive Islamist groups that receive encouragement, and some say funding, from external Islamic sources. The Taliban of Afghanistan (before late 2001), the Hizb al-Tahrir in Kyrgyzstan, the Islamic Movement of Uzbekistan, and the Jama'at-i Islami of Pakistan are all mentioned as helping to advance Islamic education and organization in Xinjiang.[30] Such learning often carries an overtly antistate, or at least anti-Chinese, message and has therefore been proscribed and harshly repressed by the government. Uyghur nationalists outside of China, many of whom are resolutely secular, praise the Islamist activists as allies in the struggle against Chinese rule, while the Chinese state excoriates them as separatists, terrorists, and perpetrators of "illegal religious activities." It seems safe to predict that Islamic education, whether "legitimate" through the state's madrassah or underground, will continue to be a powerful weapon of identity for Uyghurs and a major bone of contention between elements of the Uyghur community and the Chinese state. We were not able to obtain any information about the current existence or practices of Sufi orders, which were once so powerful in Xinjiang, except that one informant knew of a Sufi group that continues to meet despite strict supervision by the government.

Religious Observance

Foreign visitors to Xinjiang are unable to carry out systematic surveys of mosque attendance and must content themselves with anecdotal evidence on Islamic observance. Every Uyghur village and neighborhood has a local mosque, and, as is usually the case in Muslim societies, older men respond most consistently to the call to prayer. In Xinjiang, the call to prayer is usually chanted unamplified from minarets and second-story windows rather than being broadcast through loudspeakers, as is commonly done throughout the Muslim world and in Hui communities elsewhere in China. Evidently, the state has imposed strict controls on even this most quotidian of Islamic activities.

Outside the city centers, in suburbs and villages, one sees young men at work, alone or in small groups, taking breaks to pray at the proper times despite the low volume of the call to prayer. The early afternoon prayer, the most popular of the day, drew dozens or even hundreds of men of all ages to large urban mosques, nor is there any shortage of worshippers in the lanes and market alleyways of Urumchi and Kashgar. Thousands of men attend the Friday sermons at the Idgah Mosque, at the mosque in the Apak Khoja tomb complex, and at other large centers. On festivals, they said, tens of thousands of men and women crowd the squares and streets outside each important mosque, sometimes requiring the police to close the area to traffic. This vast increase in attendance at festival prayers may also be seen in the Hui areas of China, such as in Xining or Lanzhou, where major mosques might have to accommodate tens of thousands of worshippers.[31]

Other Islamic practices continue to be followed by most Uyghurs. In fact, some non-Muslims in Xinjiang have learned to be sensitive to Muslim dietary regulations. Non-Muslim friends or colleagues might point out that "this is Muslim food" or "this is Han food" in order to allow Muslims to adhere to their faith. Some Uyghurs refuse to eat food prepared by non-Muslims, or even by Hui, on the grounds that they are ignorant of the Islamic dietary rules. Others have adapted to Chinese society even to the extent of eating forbidden foods on occasion, when etiquette requires participation in a non-Muslim banquet or meal, and alcohol consumption among Uyghurs has become a major social problem, despite Islam's strict prohibition.[32] The state-controlled electronic media also play a role in propagandizing secular (i.e., Chinese) versions of rationality. One of Xinjiang's Chinese-language television channels recently aired a program on the development of the ham industry, which showed Uyghurs being taken on a tour of ham-processing facilities, a documentary that must have been utterly offensive to any Muslim viewer. Given the importance of eating as social cement in the larger society, a Muslim clearly must compromise to some extent in order to be successful outside of Uyghur communities.

The Ramadan fast provides a rich opportunity for Muslims and the Chinese state to test each other's resolve. Throughout the month of Ramadan, Muslims around the world must fast from sunrise to sunset, a particular hardship when Ramadan falls during the long days of summer. In China, religious professionals and privately employed Muslims may, of course, fast as they please and eat after sunset and before sunrise, as religion and custom dictate. But one hears many reports of government employees, teachers, cadres, and especially schoolchildren being offered specially prepared meals during the days of Ramadan to thwart their desire to fast in favor of their desire to conform and to continue in their current jobs or studies. As one Uyghur observed, "They would never ordinarily prepare meals for the children or employees, but during Ramadan they made a special point of it, so as to prevent Uyghurs from fasting." Employees and students who refuse such meals might be subjected to ridicule or even lose their positions. Thus, individual Uyghurs had to decide, often on the spur of the moment (and at a very young age), whether to continue to fast as their religion demands or to bow to the pressure and eat, thereby validating the Chinese state's demand that backward-looking Islam give way to rationality and nutritional science. In addition, the police often visit the large gatherings of Muslims who eat together in the evening dark or the gray of dawn during Ramadan in order to ensure that children under eighteen are not being given religious instruction and to observe who might be fasting, in defiance of CCP and state regulations.

Islam, Ethnicity, and Uyghur Identity

The place of Islam in Uyghur life cannot be assessed without examining its crucial role as an integral part of Uyghur identity as it has evolved historically. The concept of identity in any culture is a notoriously slippery one, involving shifting political, social, cultural, historical, and psychological elements. According to one Western scholar, Uyghurs today can identify their ethnicity in terms of no fewer than five separate components, with varying degrees of salience for specific individuals in particular circumstances. Thus, a "Uyghur" can be variously a Uyghur; a Muslim; a Turk who is part of a greater Turkic world and a speaker of a Turkic language; a resident of a specific oasis town, which has its own special local culture (e.g., Kashgar, Turpan, and Aksu); and a citizen of China, however unsought this status might be.[33] For Uyghurs, as for all individuals, precisely which aspect of identity comes to the immediate fore, and when, depends on the issue at hand and the social context.

Islamic identity among Turkic speakers in today's Xinjiang region is far older than the ethnic concept of "Uyghur" itself. This is not unusual. Across most of the Muslim world in the many centuries preceding the rise of modern nation-states, Muslims saw themselves both as Muslims and as residents of a city or distinctive region and, if asked, would so identify themselves. Language (and its associated literary culture) was not a "national" issue but represented simply a facet of one's community and culture. But the salience of particular aspects of identity is intensified by the arrival or presence of "others" (in this case, the Han Chinese) who do not share that identity. Thus, the people who came to see themselves as Uyghurs took Islamic identity for granted during their long and intricate historical interaction with other Muslim peoples to their north and west. On Xinjiang's eastern frontiers, however, Islamic identity played a crucial role due to the prolonged encounter with China, which possessed an altogether different culture, language, and religion.

In the eyes of many Uyghurs today, the vast migration of Han Chinese into Xinjiang represents the single greatest threat to their religion and national culture, if not to their very existence as a people. To meet this challenge, they aim to strengthen their own national identity by emphasizing those ethnic, linguistic, cultural, and religious characteristics that distinguish them from the Han Chinese. Mosque attendance on Friday, for example, is consciously recognized as a means of reinforcing the distinctiveness of the Uyghur community from the dominant Han population and the Chinese state. That state, as noted earlier, demands openly expressed atheism and abandonment of Islamic practice as requirements for those seeking public education or civil service jobs in the province. This creates a terrible dilemma for ambitious and upwardly mobile Uyghurs.

Yet, we should not conclude that Islam is actually the *source* of Uyghur confrontation with the Han Chinese or the Chinese state. It is instructive here to compare the Uyghurs' situation with that of the Hui, the 9 to 10 million Chinese-speaking Muslims who, according to Chinese ethnic policy and current self-image, constitute a distinct national minority by virtue of their descent from foreign Muslims, their Islamic religion, and their shared history.[34] The Hui are broadly scattered across China, with particular concentrations just to the east of Xinjiang—that is, in Gansu, Qinghai, and Ningxia—and in Yunnan Province. Because the Hui do not appear to have separatist ambitions, their Islamic practice constitutes a lesser threat to the state and has therefore not been so closely controlled since 1978.[35] Unlike the Hui, the Uyghurs are distinct from the Han not only in religion but also in language, culture, and historical experience.[36] Their identity has been forged especially through close geographic and cultural proximity to Central Asia. Thus, it is not Islam alone but rather a complex of identity components, of which Islam is one, that strengthens many Uyghurs' desire for independence from Han control and domination.

In considering the role of Islam in the Uyghur national struggle, a significant contradiction emerges. Historically, intellectuals have constituted the leadership of nearly all separatist, secessionist, or irredentist movements.

Yet, Uyghur intellectuals are reportedly far less inclined than other Uyghurs to identify Islam as a key part of their personal identity. Indeed, many Uyghur intellectuals downplay the Islamic aspect of their national quest for an independent state. As in other parts of the Muslim world, they argue that Islam "has stifled modernization and made the Uyghurs passive; they maintain a Marxist view of Islam as an opiate of the masses."[37] Some have also been influenced by the extreme secularism of the Kemalist movement in Turkey, which views religion as a retrogressive force.

From another perspective, the Uyghur nationalist intellectuals living in the West (primarily in Germany and the United States) today have every reason to minimize the centrality of Islam in their nationalist movement out of fear that the Chinese government will exploit any invocation of Islam. In the wake of the events of September 11, 2001, it was relatively easy for the Chinese government to persuade the U.S. government to condemn a minor splinter group of the Uyghur nationalist movement as a "terrorist organization." Beijing claims that the Chinese state is struggling against the spread of radical Islam, a tactic used by the Russian government with some effect in justifying its massive violence against the Chechens. Indeed, nearly all besieged authoritarian regimes facing political opposition by Muslims routinely (and darkly) invoke "Wahhabi" or "fundamentalist" influence as the source of the threat to otherwise happy and peaceable people. Given Euro-American suspicions about Islam and Muslims, this tactic has solid chances of success. Knowing this, expatriate Uyghur nationalists consider it prudent to mute the Islamic component of their personal and collective identities.

The perception of Uyghur intellectuals (especially those of the diaspora), of the negative features of an "impassive Islam," ignores an important dimension of contemporary political Islam as it is evolving in much of the Muslim world. In many Muslim countries, Islam is today a major, if not the central, vehicle for the mass political expression of opposition. One sees this most starkly where Islam combines with national liberation movements of Muslim peoples against non-Muslim rule. Examples range all across Eurasia: Palestinians against Israeli Jewish rule, Bosnian and Kosovar Muslims against Serbian Orthodox rule, Chechens against Russian Orthodox (or Communist) rule, Kashmiris against Hindu rule, and Moros in the Philippines against Christian rule.

Uyghur resistance to Han rule—whether we see that rule as Communist, neo-Confucian, post-Buddhist, or simply Chinese—conforms to this pattern. In each of these cases, Islam powerfully reinforces the nationalist movement by investing essentially secular nationalism with religious overtones and emotional content of more universal character. Yet, so far this phenomenon has scarcely been manifested on the Xinjiang scene. The key question is, Will it increase as we might predict? Or have the Chinese draconian policies made it nearly impossible for a widespread Islamist-based opposition movement to emerge?

Beijing's strict controls on field research in Xinjiang make it difficult to gauge precisely the role of Islam in fueling the nationalist movement among the Uyghurs. One can only note that very few Uyghurs openly reject the role of Islam in helping define and strengthen their national identity. Instead, they make explicit reference to the importance of Islamic practice and mosque attendance on Fridays in reinforcing Uyghur national identity, culture, and even social discipline. Islam, and associated practices (such as the *mäshräp* age-cohort meetings that were revived a few years ago and then repressed), are cited as the Uyghurs' best defenses against alcoholism, drug addiction, domestic violence, and the many other "modern" ills that plague their communities.

Nearly all Uyghur nationalists readily acknowledged the importance of Islam in the national struggle. For precisely that reason, Beijing forbids mosque attendance by youths under eighteen years of age and tries to restrict participation in the pilgrimage to Mecca and other overt forms of religious expression. Indeed, from the regime's point of view there can be no "good Islam" in Xinjiang unless it is focused strictly on the narrowest details of religious practice. Least of all can it allow any searching inquiry into the place of a world religion in defining local community life and the values of its members.

The events of September 11, 2001—explicitly carried out in the name of an Islamic struggle—intensified Islam's salience in the perception of terrorism by governments around the world. Since that pivotal date, the American government has perceived most aspects of international relations through the sole optic of the war against terrorism. At the same time, nearly all governments facing any kind of political problems with either Muslim minorities or Islamist political groups have taken advantage of the war on terrorism to proclaim their particular antagonists to be part of the Islamic terrorist problem. This tactic has been used by Israel, Russia, the Philippines, Egypt, Algeria, Tunisia, India, and, of course, China, among others. The war on terrorism immediately gave Beijing an advantage in Xinjiang, both during and after the U.S. overthrow of the Taliban in Afghanistan, where allied forces captured a number of Uyghur militants who were receiving either religious education or guerrilla-terrorist training. We have little reliable information about Uyghur association with the Taliban or Al-Qaeda. But the discovery of Uyghur citizens of China in Pakistani fundamentalist madrassahs and in Afghan training camps radically altered the official U.S. view of the Uyghur struggle. Since then, Washington has become much more sympathetic to Beijing's charges of widespread "separatism and splittism" and to the Strike Hard, Maximum Pressure campaign against them, though American representatives continue to insist publicly that Beijing not use the war on terrorism as an excuse to suppress the Uyghurs.

The facts and numbers of Uyghurs captured in Afghanistan vary from account to account, but the exact figures matter less than the implication of the figures for Beijing and Washington. As early as 1999, a Chinese academic specialist on Xinjiang, Wang Jianmin of the Nationalities University in Beijing, had estimated that as many as 10,000 Uyghurs had traveled to Pakistan for religious schooling and "military training." In May 2002, the Chinese government claimed that over 1,000 Uyghurs had been trained in Taliban camps and that many of them had returned to Xinjiang to participate in the separatist struggle. Beijing also claimed that approximately 20 Uyghurs were killed by U.S. forces in Afghanistan and that some 300 Uyghurs had been captured. One Uyghur is believed to have been in U.S. custody and under interrogation in Guantánamo, Cuba.[38] Hundreds of other Uyghurs reportedly fled from Afghanistan to northern Pakistan during the U.S. attack. In June 2002, the Chinese military attaché in Washington reported that his government had identified some 400 Uyghurs as fighters in Afghanistan. In November 2001, the Chinese Foreign Ministry stated that the Uyghurs in Afghanistan "have been trained by the international terrorists. So the fight against separatists in Xinjiang is part of the fight by the world against terrorism." Without presenting any concrete evidence, the ministry also claimed that financial and other support to internal Uyghur separatists came from abroad.[39] Furthermore, Amnesty International claimed that Chinese security forces, as part of Beijing's domestic "antiterrorist campaign," had arrested "tens of thousands" of Uyghurs in Xinjiang since September 11, 2001.[40]

In its struggle against Uyghur nationalism, China has also sought to reinvigorate the Shanghai Cooperation Organization (SCO). As noted elsewhere in this volume, the SCO, founded in 2000, brought together China, Russia, Kazakstan, Tajikistan, Kyrgyzstan, and later Uzbekistan in a united front aimed at suppressing "terrorism" in the region, especially armed violence or resistance in the name of Islam. To stimulate this cooperation in the wake of September 11, 2001, Foreign Ministry spokesman Zhu Bangzao on November 14, 2001, presented his colleagues with a list of ten organizations based in Afghanistan, elsewhere in Central Asia, and in Xinjiang itself that he said were employing armed force to end Chinese rule over the region.[41] Beijing had initially sought to develop the SCO in such a way as to enable it to play a key strategic role in Central Asian security affairs. But the arrival of U.S. forces in Central Asia in the autumn of 2001 to conduct antiterrorist operations suddenly threatened this initiative. The fact that American and European forces were granted semipermanent basing rights in Uzbekistan, Kyrgyzstan, and Tajikistan carried serious geopolitical implications for China's own goal of becoming the major voice in the region's security affairs. Currently, it is impossible to predict how successfully China will be able to invoke the SCO in competition with direct U.S. military presence in the same region to the same end.

Although Beijing and Washington agreed to closer bilateral cooperation in December 2001, when Washington established a Federal Bureau of Investigation office in Beijing to facilitate coordination of the war against terrorism, significant differences soon emerged between the two sides on the Uyghur issue. General Francis Taylor, the top U.S. envoy on counterterrorism, stated that the United States would not repatriate to China any Uyghurs who had been captured in Afghanistan during the anti-Taliban campaign. At the same time, he indicated that there were "sharp differences over China's labeling of terrorists in the Muslim Northwest" and that Washington did not deem the Uyghur nationalists to be terrorists.[42] This position, while seeming to contradict other statements from Washington, reflected long-standing U.S. concerns over China's record on human rights issues, especially in matters of religious freedom.

The Uyghurs' prospects took a significant turn for the worse in August 2002, when the U.S. State Department designated a heretofore little-known Uyghur group, the Eastern Turkistan Islamic Movement (ETIM), as a "terrorist organization." Washington claimed to have evidence that the ETIM had planned a strike against the U.S. embassy in Kyrgyzstan. The United States accused the ETIM of working with Osama bin Ladin's Al-Qaeda network and said it was believed to be responsible for over 200 acts of terrorism in China—the same figure that China had claimed earlier, but in connection with several Uyghur organizations, not just the shadowy ETIM. Hasan Mahsum, the ETIM's leader in exile, denied any organizational or financial links with Al-Qaeda, although he stated that some individual members might have independently fought with bin Ladin.[43]

Uyghur groups in exile considered this U.S. declaration to be catastrophic for their cause. They claimed that while the United States may have limited its designation of terrorism to the ETIM, an organization scarcely known even to scholars, the reality was that the Chinese case against the Uyghurs would now gain international legitimacy. Thereafter, China would in effect have carte blanche to designate all Uyghur nationalist or independence movements as "terrorist." Uyghur spokesmen abroad spoke bitterly of the U.S. decision, stating that the only state in the world in which they could place their faith for fair treatment and sympathy had betrayed the Uyghurs, leaving them without any ally or friend capable of defending them against

Chinese determination to crush their aspirations.[44] Independent observers writing in the U.S. press suspected that the change in U.S. policy was based on relatively flimsy evidence and, more importantly, that it was part of a process of mutual concessions between the two countries designed by Washington to gain Beijing's support for the broader war against terror. In any case, September 11, 2001, and its aftermath struck a hard blow to the Uyghur national cause.

Conclusions and Prognoses

Islam is likely to play an increasing role in the Uyghur nationalist movement in the future. The intensity of the nationalist movement will inevitably increase, for it is nourished by the single dominant and sinister reality for all Uyghurs—relentless, massive, and unceasing in-migration of Han Chinese that threatens virtually every aspect of the Uyghurs' communal existence across Xinjiang. Under these conditions, we believe Islam will serve to reinforce nationalist feeling and community identity and solidarity, compelling even secular Uyghur intellectuals to recognize its power, though probably not to become Islamists themselves.

The attacks of September 11, 2001, and the subsequent global U.S. war on terrorism raised suspicions about the Uyghur movement's possible ties with terrorism and Islamic radicalism, thereby weakening and isolating it internationally. If the various Uyghur groups seeking self-determination now find the door for a sympathetic hearing closed to them outside of China, and especially in Europe and the United States, they will lose whatever incentive they may have once had to act with moderation. Islam might then become yet more attractive as a vehicle for the expression of Uyghur nationalism and separatism. This does not mean that all Uyghur forms of Islam will necessarily grow more radical. Rather, it means that radical Islamic elements both within Xinjiang and abroad will sympathize more keenly with the Uyghur cause as one among many grievances of oppressed Muslims around the world. Lacking other international allies, some Uyghurs will ally themselves with those elements.

Surveillance and suppression of religion by the Chinese state have the paradoxical effect of strengthening the central role of Islam in Uyghur life. When a Beijing official spoke of "administering" religion, he in fact articulated an approach that places Islamic activism squarely in opposition to national and provincial power. Indeed, Islam and the Uyghur language are the only two factors—apart from Han in-migration and Beijing's apparently indiscriminate oppression—that can strengthen Uyghur communal solidarity across the province. It is also probable that further Han in-migration into Xinjiang will have a negative impact on the livelihood of the Uyghur agricultural classes, which up to now have been relatively untouched by Han influence. Because Islamic practice and identity are still strong among Uyghur farmers, in-migration will help bring about a fusion of Islamic and nationalist sentiment in the villages. However, the dispersion of Uyghur villages over Xinjiang's vast area and the powerful coercive capacity of the state will render it extremely difficult to mobilize and lead such a movement.

Bringing a comparative perspective to bear on these developments, it is hard to ignore the experiences of Palestinians, Chechens, Kashmiris, and other Muslims who, under increasing pressure from non-Muslim states, have merged their causes ever more closely with Islam and have grown more violent and radical in the process. There is no reason to believe that Xinjiang will not follow this pattern. Yet, to hypothesize that the Islamic factor in Uyghur nationalism is likely to increase says nothing about its potential for success. Islam can strengthen the intensity and fervor of the resistance movement, but that does not mean the resistance movement will produce positive results, especially in the face of what we view as overwhelming national instruments of repression.

Given the complexity of the problem and the paucity of information available, no one can predict the course of future developments in Xinjiang with any certainty. However, one can examine some of the variables likely to affect the role of Islam in the future and some of the alternative strategies or possible outcomes that individual Uyghurs are likely to embrace.

Absorption into China

The experience of Inner Mongolia powerfully reinforces the Uyghur fear that their national existence is under a direct threat. Pessimists go so far as to say that Inner Mongolia represents the Uyghur future. In those parts of Mongolia ruled by China, the local Mongol population has been reduced to a minority of less than 20 percent. In the process, it has ceded nearly all supralocal control to Han Chinese. What Mongols see as their traditional ways of life are coming to an end, except as theater and museum pieces, performed primarily for tourists. Though artificially maintained by the minzu system of the Chinese government, the Mongols inside China may functionally disappear as a distinct ethnic group within a few generations.

A small percentage of Uyghurs may be content with the prospect of being fully absorbed into a Han-dominated province. Members of this small group— educated in Chinese, Chinese speaking in their daily lives, eschewing literacy in Uyghur, and secular in outlook—believe that the Han constitute the de facto dominant power in the country and offer a more advanced and developed model of society to which Uyghurs must accommodate themselves or perish. This strategy places greatest value on successful integration and even assimilation into Han life and views the preservation of a distinct Uyghur identity as a minimal concern compared to the broader challenges of modernization. Whether in religious or cultural terms, Islam is nearly irrelevant to this group, except to the extent that it is perceived as a constraint on Uyghur progress toward Han-style modernity.

Uyghur Autonomy

A second and much more widespread Uyghur strategy advocates a higher degree of Uyghur political autonomy within China. This option considers the preservation of Uyghur culture and language and of Islam to be a key goal and an absolute good in itself. Uyghurs who adhere to this position aim at establishing genuine ethnic autonomy in what is today only nominally a Uyghur "Autonomous Region" (Ch. *zizhiqu*). They view most of Xinjiang as the homeland of a people whose national characteristics must be preserved and protected. One of their primary objectives lies in ending the massive inmigration of Han Chinese and encouraging the departure of low-skilled (called "low-quality") Han, retaining only those Han with high-level professional qualifications who could assist the development of the region under the direction of indigenous leaders. In this scheme, Islam is perceived as an essential part of Uyghur identity and a valuable force for reforming Uyghur society and mobilizing Uyghurs to protect Xinjiang from Han domination. Eying the model of the *jadidist* (or reform-minded modernist) Islam popular in Central Asia at the end of the nineteenth century, Uyghurs choosing this option believe that imams and other religious officials must be broadly educated in secular knowledge as well as in religion. Indeed, they advocate both religious and secular education for all members of the Uyghur community, so that Xinjiang can develop its own indigenous, ethnically conscious professional classes.

In its avoidance of any demands for outright independence, this strategy offers the most moderate form of systematic resistance to contemporary Chinese state policies. Islam plays a central role here, but its role does not include declaring armed jihad against the state. However moderate, this approach nonetheless directly confronts the reality (though not the rhetoric) of Beijing's present policies. The central and provincial authorities have scant interest or motivation in adjusting their strategy of promoting Han domination of the region. In their view, this is progressing relatively smoothly except for the violent outbreaks of "splittism and illegal religious activity" that, they insist, must be confronted directly with further repression.

For many moderate Uyghur nationalists, Islam alone can provide a moral framework capable of controlling the many ills thrust on them by rapid modernization and centralized control. Unchecked, these ills will lead to further social disintegration, alcohol and drug problems, domestic violence, sexual laxity, AIDS, and despair.[45] Many of these social evils can be seen as forms of escape born of frustration, as coping mechanisms in an environment that offers little hope. The more young people respond to anomie by turning to drugs and alcohol, the more Islam appears to be the only antidote, the sole moral force that can combat these evils and restore social vitality.

Uyghur Independence

A third Uyghur strategy aims at outright independence and is willing to use violence to achieve it. A recent, highly selective, and imprecise poll of opinion among the Uyghur diaspora in Central Asia reports that a high proportion of exiled Uyghurs see independence as the only legitimate goal. But so far, the Chinese state has responded with overwhelming repression to crush any overt expression of this sentiment. Nonetheless, there are consistent reports of ongoing low-level violence across the region. Largely anecdotal evidence gathered in a tightly controlled province where all such information is suppressed indicates that some of the actions by armed groups are carried out in the name of Islam. There has been very little reporting on these events in China, primarily because of their extreme sensitivity and the state's desire to do nothing that might encourage further separatist sentiment. As is customary in China, violent events appear in the public press only after they have been "solved"—that is, after the perpetrators have been apprehended and, in most cases, executed and after responsible state officials have been cashiered or demoted.

It is all but impossible for an outsider to distinguish between "secular" and "Islamic" resistance groups. Religion may well play a key part in the nationalist identity of some rebels who nonetheless do not act in the name of Islam. Spotty information indicates that Uyghurs regard some of those killed by the state in the national struggle as religious martyrs for Islam (*shahid*). As such, their funerals may merit a benediction, at least in secret, from appropriate religious leaders.[46] Those whom Uyghurs consider to have perished in the national resistance struggle may be considered martyrs, though this would probably not be extended to other forms of antistate or antisocial activity, whether drug smuggling or other conventional crimes.

The logistics of armed struggle and the specifics of contact with radical Islamic groups abroad have proved impenetrable to outside investigation. Since the violent incidents of 1997, centered in Yining, the Chinese government is reluctant to grant Uyghurs passports for travel abroad for any reason, whether education, trade, tourism, or pilgrimage. Officials expressed concern that foreign travel will infect Uyghurs with extreme nationalist and Islamist ideas and that they will return to Xinjiang radicalized. Numerous reports have appeared on the Internet of Uyghur radicals participating in Islamist struggles in Chechnya, Afghanistan, and Kashmir.

To address this, Beijing's foreign policies are now designed in part to pressure its neighbors to suppress Uyghur political activity on their territory. The governments of Pakistan, Kazakstan, and Kyrgyzstan have all deported Uyghurs engaged in political or jihadist activities. Returned to China, these people face almost certain death. While some claim that weapons can still be smuggled into Xinjiang across its long borders, the Chinese government has markedly increased its vigilance and interdictive capacities since September 11, 2001. Today, China often identifies and arrests visitors whom it deems to be promoting religious activism among the Uyghurs. It is fair to conclude that the increased effectiveness of the Chinese government in Xinjiang has made armed jihadist activity increasingly difficult.

Yet, the resulting sense of desperation can itself stimulate resistance in Xinjiang. At present, Beijing does not publicly acknowledge even the possibility of Uyghur collective action, preferring instead to demonize "a tiny minority of splittists" or "small numbers of illegal religious activists." But it is quite possible that larger numbers of Uyghurs will begin to respond to what they perceive as colonial repression and an existential threat with a ferocity and tenacity that others might call "irrational." The insurrections in Palestine and Chechnya, for example, have continued and grown, even in the face of crushing losses and massive state violence.

The Chinese state has shown in Tibet that it is quite willing to ride roughshod over humanitarian concerns, public opinion, and external pressures to neutralize separatist movements. But if the separatist struggle in Xinjiang grows, and if violence connected with it becomes more popular and spontaneous, it will increasingly attract public attention outside of China. The movement could then assume a more overtly Islamic character as leaders seek to call forth a popular jihad or *intifada* against Beijing. It is, of course, impossible to judge how the international community would respond to such developments.

The role of the Muslim clergy in Xinjiang is likely to become increasingly untenable. Assassinations of "pro-Chinese clergy," presumably by Uyghur nationalists, are regularly reported.[47] As the situation grows more polarized, Uyghur activists and even the general population might repudiate those Uyghur imams whom they perceive to be serving Beijing rather than Islam or the Uyghur cause. Assassinations arising from such sentiments will further polarize the religious situation, leaving little room for moderation as imams and laypeople alike are forced to choose between the state and the nationalist movement. Under these circumstances, the state could come to view Islam per se as an unvarnished enemy. Increased state repression of clerics may drive many of them toward the Uyghur nationalist cause.

An alternative scenario would predict the state's successful co-optation of a substantial portion of the clergy, as occurred in the former Soviet Union. This would undercut the legitimacy of "official" Islam in the eyes of the laity precisely because of its association with state power. In many countries, such a process has led to the emergence of a potent Islamist opposition as much against a "co-opted 'ulama" as against the state.

Because of the growing publicity they have received abroad, conditions in Xinjiang have already begun to affect China's external relations. This trend will certainly continue, as a new generation of leaders in Beijing grows more sensitive to China's image abroad. They know full well that the high-profile public campaigns of the Tibetans, led by the Dalai Lama, have constrained China's ability to deal as roughly with Tibet as it would like. Uyghurs are not blind to this reality. While they lack a substantial international movement or a leader of international stature like the Dalai Lama, Uyghurs in Xinjiang are quick to cite the relevance of the Tibetan model to their own project.

"Irrational" resistance and violence can extract a significant price from Beijing and limit its freedom of action. Ironically, however, the more effective Islamist ideology becomes in strengthening the national Uyghur struggle, the greater its potential for alienating European, American, and even Asian sympathizers, who might also fear a wave of "Islamic radicalism" sweeping across the region. Beijing will certainly play this card to the full. Ultimately, then, internal resistance in Xinjiang would have to be violent, dramatic, widespread, intense, prolonged, and internationally visible before the Uyghurs could even begin to affect China's policies in the province. Given Beijing's stated willingness to "seize a thousand to obtain one," resistance of this sort might well prove so costly in Uyghur lives that they themselves reject it.

Variables Determining the Future Role of Political Islam in Xinjiang

As Uyghurs come to perceive they have literally no way out, the situation in Xinjiang will likely move toward more explosive confrontations. Han domination is likely to increase with time, and there is little that the Uyghurs themselves can do to change their situation within the province. However, some developments outside Uyghur control could possibly change the situation in Xinjiang. While these events are of low probability, their potential impact would be great:

1. *Weakening of central power in China.* The transition from Communist rule to non-Communist rule was deeply destabilizing in the Soviet, Yugoslav, and Ethiopian cases, particularly concerning ethnic issues. Despite China's impressive record of economic growth in the recent era of economic liberalization, major political, social, and economic problems remain, and they could become explosive, especially if the CCP's centralized authority is weakened or delegitimized. Under such conditions, weakened central control could break down, opening the way for regional forces, especially in Xinjiang, to assert themselves against the state, in the classic pattern of the breakup of Chinese dynastic regimes.

2. *Significant internal democratization in China.* Either through the severe weakening of the state as already described or as part of a broader process of peaceful transition to less authoritarian rule, the Uyghurs in Xinjiang could attain more genuine autonomy, especially if Beijing acknowledges this as the price for preserving the territorial integrity of China. Such a process would sharply reduce the likelihood of a radical Islamic resistance movement succeeding in the province.

3. *Increased external Muslim aid to the Uyghurs.* Since September 11, 2001, and the U.S. declaration of global war on terrorism, this scenario is relatively improbable. China has already moved dramatically to forestall this eventuality through the SCO and in cooperation with Washington, symbolized by the U.S. branding of the ETIM as a terrorist organization. All of the SCO member states share a deep fear of Islamic radicalism and are unlikely to countenance, let alone encourage, Islamist resistance among the Uyghurs. Nonetheless, each of these states also has reason to be wary of China's growing power in the region, and historically all have reason to fear Chinese expansionism. The possibility of heightened tensions between Central Asian states and China in the future thus cannot be ruled out. However, Uyghurs in Xinjiang claim to have given up any hope of Islamic intervention in the province or aid from Muslim countries to Uyghur nationalist organizations.

Should any Muslim state or coalition of states, whether in Central Asia or in the Middle East, begin to exhibit greater tolerance toward the political activities of the Uyghur diaspora, it could affect the ability of the Uyghur external opposition, secular and religious, to infiltrate Xinjiang more effectively. More dramatically, a charismatic Uyghur leader could emerge abroad who could speak in both the name of Islam and Uyghur aspirations, advocate the Uyghur cause abroad, and stimulate the resistance movement inside Xinjiang.

Domestically, we see no potential allies for Uyghurs or the Islamic cause. The Hui are structurally in competition with the Uyghurs and will not assist them in any separatist activity. The possibility cannot be excluded that Hui voices, especially in higher councils in Beijing, could, under the right circumstances, help ameliorate some of the harsher pressures on Islam and the Uyghurs and encourage a more enlightened policy—including one that might encourage Beijing to limit Han migration to sensitive areas of the province. At the moment, however, prospects for this are minimal. Should the Chinese government move toward political liberalization, the possibility of cooperation among Muslim minorities (*minzu*) would increase. Other Muslims in Xinjiang—Kazaks, Tajiks, Kyrgyz, and so on—are currently competitive with Uyghurs, and it is unlikely that they would prefer Uyghur rule to the current Chinese domination.

For some years, Pakistan and Afghanistan were key centers of religious education and training for Uyghurs abroad. Since the U.S. overthrow of the Taliban, Afghanistan no longer has a government supportive of guerrilla training camps or radical Islamic doctrines. At the highest levels of government, Pakistan is likewise quite committed to the war on terrorism, but outside the military and political classes of Pakistani society, radical Islamic thinking and rhetoric are still as strong as ever and command considerable domestic resources. If radical Islamists strengthen their role in Pakistan's political life and use that platform to lend support to Muslim resistance in Kashmir and Xinjiang, it could greatly complicate the problem for Beijing and raise the level of Islamist engagement in the province. The Chinese state, however, has shown itself quite willing to close borders and to forgo even lucrative foreign trade if domestic stability or territorial integrity is at stake.

Overall, then, prospects for the near-term amelioration of the Uyghurs' plight are minimal. But neither Islamist nor secular separatist movements can be entirely dismissed in a volatile region where Islamist resistance organizations are functioning underground and where the political, economic, and social conditions of local Uyghurs could degenerate quickly. China itself faces an uncertain transitional period in domestic politics as well as in international relations. Russia has a long history of influence in Xinjiang, including Soviet support for the ETR of the 1940s, and Russian ties with China could certainly deteriorate in the decade ahead if Russians give free rein to their fear of China's growing power and of China's potential threat to an empty Russian Siberia. In such a case, Moscow could also affect Chinese relations with Central Asia, resulting in far greater tolerance for Uyghur nationalist, if not Islamist, activity in states bordering Xinjiang.

Finally, in the unlikely event that Beijing's policies take an increasingly radical and aggressive turn, weakening its economic ties with Europe and the United States and expanding its regional military power, the Euro-American powers might seek to weaken China's advance by lending some external support to the Uyghur opposition in Xinjiang, as has consistently been done in Tibet. Many Uyghurs devoutly desire this. They see Europe (especially Germany) and the United States as their sole allies in the world. But the logistics of a potential containment of China are far more complex in Central Asia, and, as has been pointed out earlier, European and American powers have been extremely wary of direct aid to Islamist movements except in the one case of Afghan resistance to the Soviet invasion. The fact that the Taliban regime arose in the wake of massive aid to Islamist opponents of the Red Army is bound to make the West extremely wary of supporting the Uyghur nationalist movement if there were a serious prospect of a radical Uyghur Islamist movement coming to the fore in the process. The events of September 11, 2001, will certainly prevent the United States from becoming a source of aid for any Islamist movement, especially one reputed to have had links to the Taliban and Al-Qaeda.

In sum, the salience of Islam in the nationalist movement among Uyghurs is destined to grow, but the movement faces formidable odds in achieving the kind of autonomy or independence to which so many Uyghurs aspire. Their religion, social life, education, and culture have fallen under the control of a Chinese nation-state that has the power to neutralize or eliminate their national aspirations and force on the Uyghurs an acculturative process that is oriented exclusively toward the east. To circumscribe the scope of Islamic life in Xinjiang, Beijing has had to construct a large, intrusive, and doubtless expensive apparatus of control. But there is no evidence that the state intends to ease its strictures on religious professionals, on religious education, or on religious practice. For the foreseeable future, Uyghurs will have to comply or resist in an environment that makes their practice of Islam potentially dangerous.

14

Contested Histories

Gardner Bovingdon
with contributions by Nabijan Tursun

Chapters 2 and 3 narrate the history of the region known today as Xinjiang. This chapter will analyze what became of that history in the hands of official Chinese historians, on the one hand, and Uyghur nationalist historians on the other. The party-state has long relied on official histories to justify its political and military control over Xinjiang, vindicate Han immigration there, and inspire confidence in its economic policies. Since the early 1990s, texts on Xinjiang history have been studied by students from middle school through the university. Conversely, Uyghur nationalist histories have provided a charter for Uyghur identity, underscored the centrality of Islam in Uyghur life, and offered Uyghurs both precedent and warrant for their resistance to Chinese rule.

All written history is partial. Political history is ineluctably so, and within that category nationalist history is perhaps the most prone to manipulation. Historical works produced by official Chinese historians and Uyghur nationalists are fundamentally incompatible, because their purposes are opposed. Uyghur intellectuals are waging a desperate struggle to prove that Uyghurs constitute a nation and that that nation can rightfully claim the territory of Xinjiang as its homeland. Historians writing for the Chinese state labor to deny both claims, asserting instead that Uyghurs belong to the Chinese nation and Xinjiang to the territory of China. Writers in each camp claim to have resolved long-standing disputes by revealing definitive historical truths. Instead, they demonstrate the wisdom of the Roman proverb that no one should be judge in his or her own case. The powers of the two sides as judges of each other are grossly mismatched: Whereas Uyghurs can only protest that Chinese historians spread lies, Chinese Communist Party (CCP) officials can accuse Uyghur historians of subversion and declare their works illegal. The Uyghurs' political weakness and their stubborn resistance to the party's ideological claims have made history one of the hottest zones of contention in Xinjiang.

Nationalist History

Nationalist histories from around the world share certain basic features or organizing principles. Despite the objective modernity of nations, nationalists invariably contend that their nations are ancient, tracing their origins into deep antiquity. They often back-date the incorporation of peripheral territories into the core, thus reducing the heterogeneous and conflictual past of modern states to a unilinear narrative of national becoming. As Prasenjit Duara points out, single-stranded narratives intentionally suppress evidence of historical alternatives.[1] They write competing narratives out of history.

The last few decades have witnessed the emergence of many groups that reject their incorporation into contemporary nations. To justify and to gain support for their resistance, these groups have produced alternative histories of their own. Seamus Deane argues that such groups are bound to replicate the "totalizing strategies" of the nationalisms they oppose, which leads to homogenized and often quite similar results.[2] In the case at hand, histories written by Uyghur nationalists depict a starkly different past from that found in official Chinese histories, yet the structures and narrative strategies of the opposed texts strikingly recall each other.

Uyghur intellectuals have aimed to show that Uyghurs arrived in today's Xinjiang a very long time ago and are therefore indigenous. Being such, and having founded a series of independent states there, they can legitimately claim the land today. Official Han historians have also sought to link people and land, specifically by denying the connections claimed by Uyghurs. They assert that in ancient times "the" Chinese state claimed the land, and the Chinese nation the people, and neither has ever relinquished these claims. To support their claim to Xinjiang as an ancient part of China, they assert that Uyghurs migrated to the region only in the ninth century.

The language in which each side writes its history helps define its audience and reception. Very few Hans read Uyghur and many Uyghurs cannot or will not read Mandarin. Where official histories have been intended to reach Uyghurs as well as Hans, translators have been called into service. In order to read the offending texts of Uyghur nationalist historians, high officials and many Han historians often rely on hastily prepared Mandarin translations.

Readers respond not only to the language but also to the authors. If the impromptu history lessons served up to foreign visitors by taxi drivers, students, and janitors are any gauge, Hans tend to believe the government-sponsored histories, while nearly all Uyghurs deeply mistrust the official accounts. Precisely because Uyghurs assume the government intentionally spreads misinformation, they are predisposed to believe Uyghur authors whose writings differ dramatically from the official version. When the party publicly repudiated the works of a famous Uyghur author in 1991, Uyghurs generally took this as a sign that he had revealed uncomfortable truths. Furthermore, while the government insists that all peoples in China are equal, official histories depict Uyghurs as lagging behind Hans culturally and economically. It is no surprise that Uyghurs eagerly consume histories that endow them with a splendid past and novels that help them imagine how independent statehood would improve their lives.

The official histories' claim that Xinjiang has "always been part of China" is intended to quell the foolish Uyghur idea that it might ever become independent. Officials also hope to kill the widespread notion that Xinjiang was once independent, which many Uyghurs take as moral justification for opposing CCP control. What is more, in asserting that Xinjiang has always been home to multiple nations (*minzu*), they directly challenge Uyghurs' view that Xinjiang belongs uniquely to them.[3]

Official histories press on Hans the congenial idea that since Xinjiang is and always has been a part of the "national" territory, separatists have no case. The claim that Hans have occupied Xinjiang since antiquity[4] is served up to Hans in such a way as to justify their immigration, even as it is intended to silence Uyghurs' objections.

In launching the reform era in 1978, Deng Xiaoping proposed to open China to the world after decades of isolation. Since then, the government has prepared books and articles on Xinjiang history with international audiences in mind.[5] These histories claim that China's sovereignty over Xinjiang not only is ancient but antedates the founding of all contemporary states. The histories imply that any state or international organization that contemplates challenging China's grip on the territory should first inspect its own past. Indeed, so important does the party-state consider historiography to its dealings with the international community that it has fostered a special institute in Beijing, the Center for Research on the History and Geography of China's Frontiers.[6] Scholars at that institute have played central roles in developing and disseminating the conceptions of history that are the subject of this chapter.

Historiographic Strategies

While official and Uyghur nationalist histories share features in common, they also differ in important ways. We can best understand the significance of these differences, and also gain an appreciation for the systematic distortions both versions introduce, by considering each in turn.

Without exception, official histories written after 1949 are China-centered. The focus of the narrative is the central plains of East Asia, and particularly the regions of the Yellow and Yangtze Rivers. This is true not only of "national" histories but also of "local" histories. Not surprisingly, the latter universally begin by referring to China and to the place of the locality (or non-Han people) in China. Histories of Xinjiang or the Uyghurs are necessarily histories of the periphery.

Official histories also share a hybrid interpretive frame that might be called "Marxism-nationalism,"[7] which mixes components from Karl Marx with ideas from later Soviet interpreters. They make use of Marx's analysis of social formations to argue that Hans had achieved an advanced level of civilization before the 1949 Revolution, while Uyghurs and other non-Hans lagged far behind.[8] They intentionally interpret all violent clashes before 1949 as class rather than ethnic conflicts, insisting that they pitted "the people of various nationalities" against elites, also composed of "various nationalities."[9] Official historians also follow Marx in identifying "objective historical trends." But where Marx focused on falling wages and growing working-class consciousness, Chinese historians writing on Xinjiang instead discern a general trend of unification (*tongyi*). Unification has been the dominant theme (*zhuliu*) of Chinese history, the authors agree, while division (*fenge* or *fenlie*) has been at most a minor theme. Thus, attempts to divide the country by setting up an independent regime in Xinjiang were not merely morally reprehensible; they went against the historical tide (*niliu*) and were therefore objectively bound to fail. The same judgment is naturally intended to apply to contemporary separatists.

From Vladimir Lenin, Chinese historians have absorbed a concern with imperialism as the inevitable result of unbridled global capitalism. The aftermath of the Opium Wars and the stealthy seizure of territory by tsarist Russia demonstrated that China was a victim of imperialism by the Great Powers. This slow baptismal experience cleansed China, figuratively speaking, of its own imperial past or, put another way, indemnified it against claims that it was itself an imperialist power.[10] For these historians, China's throwing off the yoke of "semicolonialism" between 1911 and 1949 granted all "Chinese" a single one-time exercise of the right of self-determination.[11]

Finally, party historians used Joseph Stalin's theories of ethnogenesis and ethnic differentiation to justify a policy of "divide and conquer" in Xinjiang. Official ethnologists determined that the various Turkic-speaking peoples of Xinjiang belonged not to a single *ethnie*, nationality, or minzu—which might have favored the development of pan-Turkism—but to five (Uyghur, Kazak, Kyrgyz, Uzbek, and Tatar). With this in hand, historians projected these discrete identities onto the past and turned out carefully distinct histories for each group.[12]

Official histories also depend on tendentious interpretation of key terms and events. The texts illustrate that this occurred in both the reading and the writing of history. In using the canonical twenty-four Chinese histories as sources, historians have interpreted each military protectorate (*duhufu*) in what is today Xinjiang, from the Han dynasty through the Ming, as proof that the region was part of the respective dynasty's territory. Authors have adduced chronicles of "tribute" by peripheral peoples and grants by central plains dynasts of official titles to local potentates as further proof that the peoples recognized dynastic authority.[13]

It is an article of faith among official historians that each successive dynasty was "China," or rather a more or less faithful approximation of a Platonic ideal of "China," which just happened to be based on the Qing at its greatest territorial extent.[14] It is but a short step from this to positing a timeless Xinjiang that remained an "inseparable part of China" from the Han forward, in other words, for the past 2,000 years. Though a particular work might note, for instance, that the Ming only managed to revive the military post in Qumul (Hami), and then only for a short time, the thesis of inseparability remains unchanged.

Having established that unification is the main trend of history, authors then depict all territorial increases as unifications (*tongyi*), never as conquests (*zhengfu*) or annexations (*tunbing*). As one historian recently put it, "China's basic territory was not acquired through aggression" but rather "opened up over thousands of years by the ancestors of China's various peoples (*minzu*)."[15] Terms implying military conquest were reserved for the actions of foreign empires, such as the British and the Russian, when they wrested territory from the Qing.

Reacting to this official history, Uyghur historians have devised a contrasting set of interpretations. They have "recentered" the historiography of the Uyghurs in Central Asia. In their narratives, the Uyghur homeland is the center, while China is the periphery. While China's official nationalists consider today's Xinjiang part of the historical "western regions," Uyghur nationalists widely refer to it as Central Asia or "Eastern Turkistan."

Uyghur historians, too, depend on a hybrid interpretive frame, but theirs comprises Uyghur nationalism and pan-Turkism by turns. Where official Chinese historiography retroactively designates all polities on the territory of the People's Republic of China (PRC) as parts of "China's history," Uyghur historians retroactively designate most Central Asian polities as Uyghur. Thus, the famous writer Turghun Almas claims as "our ancestors and blood brothers (*qan-qerindaš*)" the Oghuz, Hun Tengriqut, European Hun, White Hun, Kök Turk, Orkhon, Idiqut, Karakhanid, Ghaznavid, Seljuk, Khwarazm, and Sa'idi (Yarkand) khanates.[16]

Like the Chinese historians, the Uyghurs also resort to far-fetched interpretations. For instance, Turghun Almas asserts that the several-thousand-year-old mummies, as described in chapter 12 in this volume, were Uyghurs. His reasoning is based on an improbable syllogism: (1) The earliest Uyghurs practiced shamanism; (2) the orientation of the buried suggests that they were shamanists; (3) ergo, the mummies were Uyghur.[17] In like fashion, the Uyghur archaeologist, linguist, and philologist Qurban Wäli affects to find "Uyghur" words written in Sogdian or Kharosthi scripts several thousand years ago. That a particular word is Uyghur, rather than a Sogdian word later absorbed into Uyghur, as more scrupulous linguists would claim, proves that the Uyghurs and their language were already present in Xinjiang.

All of these interpretive stratagems and selective distortions are clearly evident in historical writings since 1949, as Han and Uyghur historians have vied to interpret the past authoritatively. But the roots of the story lead back well before 1949.

Historical Writings before 1949

By comparing postrevolutionary histories to those written in the Republican era (1911–1949), one clearly sees how the rise of the CCP affected writings on Xinjiang. As shown in chapter 3, during the Republican era a series of autocratic governors ruled Xinjiang as a virtual fiefdom. In 1936, Zeng Wenwu, a graduate in political science from Central (later Nanjing) University, published a three-volume history titled *A History of China's Management of the Western Regions*.[18] The first two volumes chronicle the "management" of the region by dynasties ranging from the Han to the Qing, while the third volume conspicuously fails to describe Republican-era policies as "management." Zeng worries that misrule by Chinese governors and Russian scheming might result in China's once again losing control of the western regions. The foreword to the book bluntly notes that the "Song and Ming lost the Western Regions" and that the Qing "once again brought [Xinjiang] into China's territory."[19] In sum, he acknowledges that the central plains dynasties' control over the western regions was at best sporadic. At the same time, as a nationalist, Zeng argues that the succession of the central plains states constituted a single uninterrupted "China."

Only months after the book's publication, the writer Li Xin heaped scorn on Zeng's interpretative liberties in a review published in the prominent journal *New Asia*. He particularly disagrees with Zeng's assumption that the Chinese nation could claim the Mongol Yuan conquests. If this is so, then why not also arrogate the exploits of the Xiongnu and Tujue (two notorious enemies of the central plains dynasties)? "Why, if in the future some other nation should conquer China, then its military accomplishments shall be the glory of our people too!"[20] Without saying so explicitly, Li hints that future Chinese historians might write of the brilliant exploits of the Japanese empire as if they, too, were Chinese accomplishments.

Both Zeng's history and Li's response illustrate that Chinese authors in the Republican era could think critically about the state's claims to peripheral territories and could have their views published. Discussions of the history of Xinjiang's peoples enjoyed broad freedoms as well. Notably, in 1932 the Hui author and Foreign Affairs Bureau adviser Wang Zengshan referred to Xinjiang as "Eastern Turkistan" in *New Asia;* the same author wrote in 1944 that Uyghurs were direct descendents of the notorious Tujue.[21] After 1949, the CCP forbid the publication of such ideas, and even any discussion of them. From then on, top leaders in Beijing laid down a firm line for historical writings and equally firm punishments for heterodoxy. Uyghur scholars in the Soviet Union could write with a relatively free hand about Uyghur history, but from 1949 to 1980 their counterparts in Xinjiang faced a stark choice between orthodoxy and silence.[22]

The History of Xinjiang in the People's Republic of China

After gaining control of Xinjiang in late 1949, party officials sought to outflank Uyghurs advocating their own state by co-opting local elites. But by 1957 it was clear that popular aspirations for independence had not disappeared. On instructions from Beijing, officials waged a campaign against "local nationalism," which condemned Uyghurs pursuing independence as enemies of the people. For months, local newspapers carried revelations about nefarious plots that the party had foiled. Each article would carefully note that the party's actions enjoyed the full support of the people. The media soon announced that "local nationalists" were advancing specious historical arguments in their quest to "split the motherland." The first broadside against local nationalists that appealed to history appeared in 1958. In that year, an ordinary citizen wrote to the *Xinjiang Daily* complaining about the disloyalty of secessionists and observing that "[h]istorically, Xinjiang was an inseparable constituent part of our motherland."[23] In a sense, this claim was unobjectionable. One might pick a date, for instance, of the establishment of Xinjiang province in 1884, after which Chinese governors controlled most of the region. But party officials wanted to claim a far earlier date. In 1959, the national journal *Nationalities Research* carried an article on Xinjiang history that began, "Xinjiang has since ancient times been an inseparable part of the motherland."[24] This formulation[25] soon became the obligatory first line of any published history of Xinjiang.

Three political initiatives shaped the production of official histories of

Xinjiang and the Uyghurs. First, in the early 1950s the CCP leadership dispatched ethnologists to investigate—and then institutionalize—the identities of various non-Han groups throughout the country. Among the researchers' duties was the collection of materials for a history of each group. Then, when Mao Zedong announced the Great Leap Forward in 1958, ethnologists and historians were given a year to prepare histories of every non-Han group to celebrate the tenth anniversary of the PRC's founding.[26] But the chaos unleashed by the Great Leap Forward quickly swallowed this massive collective project. And when the Cultural Revolution broke out in 1966, all writings on subnational history became suspect.

Only after Deng Xiaoping announced the reform era did historians dare to write, and publishers issue, histories of peripheral regions and non-Han peoples. Many of the first books published in the 1980s had originally been prepared in the late 1950s. The fate of one such work illustrates the efforts to reshape history after the long hiatus. Its careful alteration provides a window onto the enterprise of historical revision in Xinjiang.

Back in the mid-1950s, the esteemed and prolific historian Feng Jiasheng had coedited *Brief Compilation of Historical Materials on the Uyghurs*. The two-volume manuscript was limited to internal circulation in 1956,[27] but two years later the first volume was revised and offered to the public. In 1981, the whole was revised yet again and published. Three years later, a review in an internal circulation journal provided the inside story of that revision. Liu Ge, the author of the review and a junior researcher at the Xinjiang Academy of Social Sciences, surveys with satisfaction the series of changes that, she claims, make the text more accurate.

In fact, these changes bring the text into line with the CCP's needs. Where the original work notes that the Uyghurs "formed a great independent khanate of their own" in the eighth century, Liu is pleased to find that the new version adds "but finally they became part of the Tang's Hanhai protectorate." Elsewhere, where the original text describes the Qing's annexation (*hebing*) of Xinjiang, the revised version "corrected this to read 'unification (*tongyi*).'" Liu also notes with approval that where the original describes Uyghur states as "feudal countries (*fengjian guojia*)," the new edition changes this to "local regimes (*difang zhengquan*)."[28]

Each of these changes served contemporary political needs. The first transformed what might have been interpreted as the ultimate independence of a Uyghur state into a temporary condition that cleared the way for subordination to the Tang (which, as noted in chapter 3, was itself temporary and partial). In the second case, where the term "annexation" might suggest military colonization, the term "unification" implied instead the fulfillment of a prior destiny. Britain and tsarist Russia had built empires through conquest, but the Qing merely reunited the fragments of a once and future China.[29] The third alteration erased the implication that Uyghurs had ever established independent countries, transforming historical states with a few strokes of the pen into mere local extensions of central plains authority.[30] In the first and third cases, the revisions captured "loose threads" in Uyghur history and rewove them firmly into the narrative of Chinese history. Nowhere in the article does Liu ponder why a team of respected historians might have chosen the original language, or who induced them to alter it for the revised edition. Though Liu focuses entirely on political matters, she never raises the issue of the influence of politics on historiography. For evidence of that, one must look elsewhere.

The History of the Uyghurs

> The Uyghur nation (*minzu*) is not a branch on the great tree of the "Turki nation"; the Uyghur nation is a branch on the great tree of the Chinese nation (*zhonghua minzu*). Turcology is not a pure academic problem; it contains within it a political problem. . . . We must search for historical and contemporary materials and continue to write articles on national solidarity.[31]

Wang Enmao was not unqualified to address Xinjiang's most prestigious social science research institute. The former first party secretary of the Xinjiang CCP, he was in 1986 vice chair of China's national political association and head of the autonomous region's advisory committee. He had immense political experience and, while head of Xinjiang, was widely respected for enacting moderate and successful policies. The one qualification he lacked was any kind of historical training. This scene crystallizes the peculiarities of historical research and writing in Xinjiang: a former soldier and political commissar, sixty years distant from his modest formal schooling, lecturing a room full of academic researchers on ethnological pruning and grafting.

At the time Wang lectured the assembled scholars in Urumchi, several large-scale histories were in process. Two of the three belonged to the familiar socialist category of "history by committee." A large team had been at work since 1979 on the multivolume *Concise History of Xinjiang*; the third and final volume (which naturally ended in 1949) had been sent to press in January 1986 and would be published in late 1987. Xinjiang Academy of Social Sciences scholar Liu Zhixiao had published the first volume of his projected three-volume *History of the Uyghurs* in 1985, and in 1986 he began working on the second.[32] Though Liu was the sole author, each of his manuscripts was reviewed by a committee consisting of scholars and party officials.[33] Liu's massive history announced in its introduction that "modern Uyghur history is a constituent part of modern Chinese history" and never deviated from that line.[34] During fieldwork in 1989, Justin Rudelson learned that Liu's 1985 history was "widely criticized by Uyghur intellectuals" and was among the works that had stimulated them to produce their own versions of Uyghur history.[35]

But the most hotly contested history in the genre was the *Concise History of the Uyghurs*. The Uyghur history was surely one of the most protracted projects and most-revised collaborative works ever undertaken in the PRC: First prepared in manuscript form by 1961, the massive work was finally published almost thirty years later, in 1989.

Between 1981 and 1983, a team of three authors produced a revamped version of the manuscript. In January 1983, the autonomous region's party committee convened a large symposium of Hans and Uyghurs to discuss the manuscript in Beijing. The conclusion of the symposium was that the already much fussed-over book "needed yet another revision."[36]

We know from the roster of participants that Turghun Almas, by far the most prolific and independent-minded Uyghur historian of the day, was among the Uyghurs present, alongside several dozen Han scholars and officials. One can imagine Turghun and others arguing strenuously for a less Sinocentric version of history and being voted down. At two subsequent Urumchi symposia convened to discuss the book in 1985 and 1987, Turghun was conspicuously absent. Nor did he attend what appears to have been four months of meetings between December 1987 and April 1988 to determine the shape of the final manuscript. Allowed to speak his mind in the mid-1980s, Turghun was not welcome thereafter, nor presumably was anyone else who strongly objected to the emerging history. We can understand Turghun's work of the late 1980s as his angry response to a debate from which he was excluded. It is easy enough to see what he and others found irksome. In the fifteen-page chapter subsection on the Orkhon khanate[37]—a subject to which Turghun would devote 256 pages—the *Concise History* notes that "[f]ollowing the development of cooperative political, economic, military, and cultural relations, the advanced productive technology and culture of the Hans had a fairly sizable impact on Uyghur (*Huigu*) culture. This was especially the case with each [Han] princess given in marriage, who would bring with her a great number of Han carpenters and a retinue of attendants."[38]

It is hard to choose which is more offensive: the assumption that Han culture was superior to Uyghur culture, or the notion that that superiority was reflected even in the skills of house builders and cooks.

Another official work published in 1987 announces with disarming candor what was going on. The single-volume chrestomathy of historical materials pertaining to Xinjiang declares on its first page that it "does not contain all of Xinjiang history; it condenses the history which illustrates that Xinjiang has since ancient times been a part of China's territory."[39] The choice of words concealed precisely what the method conceals: The authors omitted not only materials irrelevant to the claim but also any that vitiated that claim. In short, they *suppressed* all sources that could harm their case.

Like the other official volumes, this one did not record the many clear examples of deep hatred between indigenous inhabitants and officials or immigrants from the central plains. It glossed over the many strong states that had ruled the region quite apart from, and often in opposition to, central plains dynasties. The authors of the volume read Chinese sources too credulously as reliable records of "Chinese" power and influence in the region. Were it not for the timing of the volume, one might attribute the editorial committee's selectivity to incompetence or unfamiliarity with the materials. It emerged in the late stages of the protracted dispute over the *Concise History of the Uyghurs*, at the midpoint of Turghun's furious writing spree. This was misprision with a purpose.

The Uyghur Response

Between 1983 and 1989, Turghun launched an assault on the historiographic mainstream with a series of articles and three major books. He begins his best-known volume, *The Uyghurs*, with a powerful sentence quite unlike anything written in China for decades, "One must state definitively: the motherland of the Uyghurs is Central Asia."[40] The book is the culmination of his historiographic mission, providing a richly detailed narrative of the Uyghur "nation" in history.

Beginning with the bald assertion that the Uyghur homeland is Central Asia, Turghun adopts the same peremptory tone as his party-sponsored counterparts. He is not proposing a thesis for consideration but insisting that it is the only correct view. Where official history had described Uyghurs forming from other groups, assimilating still others, and migrating to their present location over a long period, Turghun posits Uyghurs as a transhistorical entity—again, in Duara's words, "a self-same, national subject evolving through time."[41] Furthermore, far from being itinerant over centuries as official histories asserted, he insists that the Uyghurs had a definite homeland. Finally, that homeland was defined not in terms of contemporary international boundaries but in the language of historical geography. In a single sentence, he establishes the Uyghurs as a stateless nation and specifies the territory to which they could legitimately lay claim.

Turghun's title is a misnomer: The book is by no means a history only of those who understood themselves to be "Uyghurs." He claims for Uyghurs all empires built by Turkic-speaking peoples in Inner Asia. All of them, he purred, "founded great, powerful, rich, and civilized states; all founded splendid cultures; all made inextinguishable contributions to human historical progress and culture."[42]

To anyone versed in official PRC histories of the region, these lines are at once eerily familiar and strange. The word "China" is nowhere mentioned in this narrative. And yet, Turghun uses the exact phrases favored by Chinese historians to describe the achievements of the Chinese nation (*Zhonghua minzu*): The talk of civilization, of splendid culture, and of contributions to progress could have been lifted directly from CCP propagandists' briefs. The strange (and entirely intentional) twist is that where the Chinese histories credited these contributions to the "collective struggle of the people of various nationalities," he limits them to "Uyghurs and their blood brothers." Party historians rightly read this as an open provocation.

But he is not finished bragging. Turghun grows even more grandiose, claiming, "Not only was Central Asia the motherland of the Uyghurs from earliest times. It was perhaps one of world culture's most ancient, most celebrated golden cradles. No wonder the historian Morgan said that 'the key to world culture is buried in the Tarim Basin. When that key is found, the secrets of world culture will be revealed.'"[43]

Turghun's *Uyghurs* offers historical revisionism with a vengeance. Not only does he implicitly deny any political association between Uyghurs and China before the seventeenth century, he challenges Chinese bragging rights to being one of a very few birthplaces of culture on earth.

Though Turghun would later be singled out for opprobrium, he was by no means the only Uyghur author claiming for Uyghurs a far longer history than that depicted in official accounts. Qurban Wäli published a slim volume of selected essays titled *Our Historical Scripts*. The title is arresting, since the "our" implicitly marks out the boundaries of the community: speakers and readers of Uyghur. In the preface to his book, Qurban notes that his research on writing systems invalidates several "incorrect assumptions" concerning Uyghur history: "I concluded that Uyghurs had not emerged only with the appearance of the name 'Uyghur' in historical texts; rather, they had been a constant presence throughout the course of Xinjiang's several thousand years of history and were one of the principal nations (*millät*) that had created Central Asian civilization."[44]

On the basis of fifth-century wood strips on which are written "Uyghur" words in Sogdian script, Qurban argues that Uyghurs must have inhabited Xinjiang from that time or earlier. This evidence, he asserts, refutes the persistent "popular opinion" that Uyghurs had migrated from the Orkhon valley

to Xinjiang in 840 CE and brought their writing system with them, and that
"'[b]efore then there were no Uyghurs in Xinjiang.' . . . This kind of incorrect perspective persists like an 'inexpungible thesis,' having taken a place in
the sphere of historiography, in school books, and in dictionaries."[45]

He expresses confidence that the pernicious thesis—"inexpungible" because it was the watchword of official history—will slowly disappear under
the weight of this new evidence. Subsequent chapters assert that "our ancestors" lived in Urumchi 3,000 to 4,000 years ago and that Uyghur dance had
a history of at least 4,000 years.[46]

As these authors labored to write history they insisted was factual, the
poet and novelist Abdurehim Otkur took advantage of the cultural openness
of the reform era to publish two historical novels about events in Qumul
early in the century: *Tracks* (1985) and *The Awakening Land, part I* (1987).[47]
He began the first novel with an eponymous poem:

We were young when we set out on our long journey,
and now our children are old enough to ride.
We were few when we began our difficult quest,
and yet they called us a caravan, when we laid our prints in the sand.
We left our tracks in the wasteland, and on many hills;
many lions went graveless in the desolate regions.
Yet do not say graveless! Among the willows in reddening wilds,
our graves were covered in flowers, in spring, at dawn.
Our footprints remain, our dreams, everything, over those distances.
Let the winds blow, let the sands roll. Our prints will not be buried.
Though the horses be starving, our caravan never stopped on the road;
and they will find those traces one day, either our children,
or our children's children.[48]

Published at the beginning of a novel set in the 1920s, the poem served as
an anthem to an earlier, officially sanctioned struggle against Guomindang
oppressors. The transition from past to present to future tense—"they will
find those traces"—was located safely in the past. Because the journey seemed
to have been completed by the novel's end, the censors allowed it to be published. But Uyghurs clipped out the poem and printed it by itself on posters,
made it the frontispiece of magazines, or even scrawled it on building walls.
Stripped from the historical setting of the novel, the poem referred to a still
unfinished journey toward Uyghur independence.[49] The winds and sands were
taken to represent CCP efforts to erase the legacy of Uyghur resistance. The
starving horses evoked both the poor peasants of southern Xinjiang and the
isolated activists still at work for the cause. And the language of a "long

journey" that maintained its forward momentum despite all obstacles certainly conjured an image contrary to party depictions of terrorists as doomed to fail. Rudelson calls Abdurehim's novels "well-disguised nationalistic literature."[50] Abdurehim enjoyed a wide audience among literate Uyghurs, as indicated for instance by the fact that his 1985 novel went into a fourth printing in 1996, bringing the total run to 68,000 copies.

The authors cited earlier were by no means the only Uyghur historians to take advantage of the new atmosphere of openness. Imin Tursun, Haji Nurhaji, Ibrahim Muttehi, Mirsultan Osman, Haji Yaqup, and the prolific Abdušükür Muhämmät'imin all published scholarly work that met an enthusiastic readership. Many of these authors had cherished an interest in historiography even while spending years in jail and relished the opportunity to write, as their audience did to read, history not prompted exclusively by state-serving goals.

While these texts were rolling off the presses, the political atmosphere was changing yet again. At the end of the 1980s, political events abroad, in Beijing, and in Xinjiang shocked officialdom and drastically reduced the CCP's tolerance for intellectual challenges of the kind Turghun and Qurban had launched. The Tiananmen student movement of 1989 and the Eastern European "velvet revolutions" rattled the Party Central Committee in Beijing, the mounting crisis in the Soviet Union added to its alarm, and the secession of Central Asian states would later induce near panic. In Xinjiang, the Baren uprising in April 1990 (described more fully in chapter 12) led the party leadership to conclude matters were badly out of control and to respond with both military and political initiatives. People's Liberation Army troops moved in to dissuade others who might have followed the example of Baren from doing so. Party officials quickly turned their attention to the ideological front. As hard-liners railed against the chaos unleashed by the reform era, the leadership concluded that it was time to rein in popular discourse. The attack on Turghun was one of the first signs of this return to strict control.

Though several Uyghur authors had challenged historical orthodoxy, only Turghun came in for direct criticism in February 1991. Over seven days, a long series of officials and scholars presented papers attacking Turghun's many errors of fact and interpretation: how he had fabricated an episode of climate change, misinterpreted crucial political terms, and ignored evidence that Xinjiang and the Uyghurs had long been part of China. All agreed that Turghun was seeking to "provide a historical basis for separatism." They identified him as an acolyte of Mämtimin Bughra, a former emir and opponent of CCP rule who had been hounded out of the country and later wrote his extremely nationalist *The History of Eastern Turkistan* from exile in Afghanistan.[51] As soon as the party became aware of Mämtimin's text, it was banned in China, but according to Turghun's accusers, it had circulated in *samizdat;* the heterodoxies served up in *The Uyghurs* struck the critics as nothing but rewarmed versions of Mämtimin's abominable ideas.[52] It is no small irony that Mämtimin had done the first systematic research in China on the Karakhanid khanate, employing Persian, Arabic, and Turkish sources, as well as works by European and Russian historians, to which Chinese scholars, limited by language, had had no access. The Chinese historians who forty years later criticized Turghun are rumored still to make use of Mämtimin's research even as they publicly revile it.[53]

The party's next challenge was to involve the public in repudiating Turghun's unacceptable views. In April 1991, the *Xinjiang Daily* carried a seven-part, 70,000-character essay titled "A List of One Hundred Historical Errors in the Three Books including *Uyghurs.*" Officials also organized 186 "reporting activities" in Urumchi and southern Xinjiang, where speakers condemned the "errors" in Turghun's work and thereby "contributed actively to the generally good situation of stability and development in Xinjiang."[54]

But the response did not stop there. The government made it illegal to sell Turghun's works and ordered citizens to surrender their copies. Officials made sweeps of the markets and staged public book burnings. Work units conducted criticisms of Turghun's ideas and demanded that employees submit written critiques of their own.[55] But if officials had hoped through this campaign to convince Uyghurs that Turghun was wrong, they hoped in vain. The immediate consequence was that the price for copies of his works skyrocketed to five, even ten times the original. The official ban lent the books a cachet that made them compulsory reading for a broad segment of Uyghur society. These factors, combined with the density and length of Turghun's books, led to a predictable result. Many who wished to read them, but could not, settled instead for summaries by those who had. Turghun's histories were reduced to a few simple claims, such as that Uyghurs had a history of 6,000 years and that they had founded numerous independent states. These were, of course, precisely the claims the party hoped to suppress. More galling still, the sudden independence of the Central Asian states in 1991 lent these ideas even greater salience. Kazakstan and the other territories had until recently seemed "inseparable parts" of the Soviet Union; now they were nation-states and the Soviet Union had ceased to exist.

Despairing of eliminating Turghun's influence through censorship and other defensive maneuvers, officials embarked on a new historiographic offensive, focusing at once on the captive audience of students. Early in 1992, a team of faculty from Xinjiang University and Xinjiang Normal University issued the textbook *Local History of Xinjiang* in both Mandarin and Uyghur editions. The fundamental point made by the *Local History*, discernible from the title alone, was that Xinjiang was a *region* within China. Xinjiang's history was derivative of China's. Immensely detailed, the book pressed the point by pursuing three themes throughout. First, it traced relations between "Xinjiang" and the central plains states from dynasty to dynasty, suggesting in each section that events in the imperial court materially affected those in the western regions. Second, the narrative insistently identified links even during the periods when "China" was fragmented or too weak to project power west of the central river basins. Third, it stressed the positive effects of protracted periods of *Pax Sinica* on cultural development and economic growth.[56] The book was immediately made the text for a course in Xinjiang's history, as discussed in chapter 7, and declared compulsory for all postsecondary students in the region. Four years later, it was supplemented by a study guide. This guide boiled the original text down even further and attempted to ensure that students missed none of the principal arguments by asking leading questions at the end of each chapter.[57]

Clearly worried that even younger students were being swayed by improper ideas, the party commissioned a simpler version of the text for high school students, and then for middle school students a radically streamlined version that reduced Xinjiang history to "thirty-six questions" and their corresponding correct answers.[58] The authors of the latter text claimed to have been prompted by questions middle school students asked their teachers about Xinjiang history. Some of the questions, they found, "implied misunderstanding or lack of understanding, some betrayed fuzzy perspectives, but some indicated a problem of skewed thinking." To alleviate misunderstanding and rectify deviant thoughts, the authors presented their thin question-and-answer volume in the form of a catechism.[59]

Where Turghun, Qurban, and others had presented an independent Uyghur past worthy of collective pride, the new orthodox histories reduced the Uyghurs' roles to bit parts in the grand drama of Chinese history. To Abdurehim's novels that revived past struggles and hinted that they might not be finished, official textbooks juxtaposed a rigid story stressing ad nauseam that Xinjiang had always been, and would always be, part of China. Interviews with Uyghur students in 1996 and 1997 indicated how badly the government's campaign had misfired. Far from converting Uyghur students to orthodoxy, these works provoked scorn. One Uyghur graduate student, spying the book on a foreign researcher's shelf, scolded him for purchasing it. "There is nothing of use in this book at all," she said dismissively. "We only read it to prepare for the test, and then throw it into the garbage."[60]

Xinjiang History at the Turn of the Millennium

Faced by a spate of bombings and collective uprisings in various parts of Xinjiang in the late 1990s, the party leadership drew two conclusions: Uyghurs persisted in rejecting the official version of the past, and their aspirations for the future diverged widely from the party's plans for them. Officials were also increasingly concerned that Islam might further stimulate antistate sentiments. Other chapters in this volume describe administrative, economic, demographic, and military policies aimed at stemming Uyghur discontent and reducing its relevance. Let us here consider the latest official initiatives governing the writing of history.

The party has not relaxed its vigilance toward heterodox histories. An author at the Xinjiang Academy of Social Sciences recently set forth the official position on how to handle dissenting materials. It reads as a blunt acknowledgment of the party's inability to prevent the influx of "subversive" historiography from the several states in Central Asia where dissident Uyghur intellectuals are active: "[A]s for those people who use the bully pulpit to distort Xinjiang's history . . . we must handle them firmly and absolutely cannot let them off with a slap on the wrist. At the same time, we must strengthen our work of monitoring television, radio, news, publishers, and customs offices, preventing reactionary texts and audiovisual media from entering our Region, firmly employing effective methods to block and to withstand all kinds of infiltration from abroad."[61]

Despite this call for renewed vigor in policing the borders and the presses, the noted Uyghur author Zordun Sabir managed to publish a vast three-volume historical novel titled *Motherland.*[62] Its theme is the movement that established the Eastern Turkistan Republic (ETR; 1944–1949) in Ili. Zordun had long been a member in good standing of the literary establishment, and his historical theme had been judged safe since Mao himself had declared the "Ili revolution" a component part of the Communist revolution. Yet, the work that made it past the censors after numerous revisions still contained passages describing Turkic contempt for Hans and depicting the ETR as a fully functioning state. Numerous Uyghurs indicated their keen delight at reading Zordun's published novel. Predictably, the government promptly banned the work. Interviews in the summer of 2002 indicated that the work continued to circulate widely even after the official proscription. One well-educated informant said, "I stayed up two whole days reading the novel. I was so excited! Never before had I heard that we once founded an independent country, and so recently!"[63] The work could be found for sale in numerous shops, hidden out of sight of prying eyes, for only a slight markup over the original price. Salespeople expressed no reservations about selling the book, even to a foreigner.

In sum, the ban on Zordun's book proved ineffectual. Meanwhile, the party did not abandon more draconian tactics for purging other works considered pernicious. In the summer of 2001, officials staged a major book burning in Kashgar. There, they cast to the flames the works of the young novelist and historian Abduwali Ali, as well as some by Turghun that had not previously been destroyed.[64]

But suppressing bad ideas was only part of the battle. Officials and historians still faced the need to persuade ordinary people to learn the proper version of history. Wang Binghua, the former head of the Xinjiang Museum and the Archaeology Research Institute and a powerful figure among historians in the region, abjectly admitted during a recent group interview that "history is something that needs to be instilled in people . . . but if they don't want to read it, there's nothing you can do." Xinjiang Propaganda Bureau vice chair Shao Qiang, also present at the interview, pointed out that the bureau was "recommending" three new works on the history of Xinjiang in answer to Jiang Zemin's call to "correctly propagandize Xinjiang history." The party group secretary at Xinjiang People's Press added that presses were touting these works as "a practical move" in the fight against Uyghur separatism. But as the reporter who conducted the interview observed, campaigns by the Propaganda Bureau might provoke revulsion rather than interest among members of the public.[65]

A visitor returning to Xinjiang in 2002 after five years' absence was startled at the explosion in the number of historical works, themes, and authors available at any bookstore. There were now more scholarly studies, more tiny propaganda volumes, and more popular histories than ever before. And in Uyghur bookstores, shelves that had once held three or four grubby volumes translated from Chinese originals now groaned with dozens of books unmistakably penned by Uyghur authors, including four by the young scholar Äsät Suläyman, and a number of volumes from the corpus of the revered late historian Abdušükür Muhämmät'imin. While they refrained from explicitly challenging orthodoxy, these histories limned a long and distinguished history for the Uyghurs.[66]

Concern about the long-running historiographic dispute had plainly reached the highest levels of the party. Historian Ling Jun observes that "comrade Jiang Zemin has made important speeches on questions concerning Xinjiang history in various venues" urging scholars to "systematically research and correctly propagandize Xinjiang's history." Ling argues that answering Jiang's call requires three steps: first, a new crop of "properly trained" historians who are thoroughly imbued with Marxism; second, systematic histories that "get the story right"—in this case meaning telling the story exactly as the state wants it, without regard for the niceties of historical fact; and third, popular histories that tell the "right stories" in a form palatable to most people.[67]

A volume published by the Arts and Photography Press, *A Hundred Questions about Xinjiang History*, met this need perfectly.[68] Like the previous catechisms, it presented short vignettes prompted by a series of questions. The brief narratives, full of colorful historical figures and references to exotic local culture, covered all the familiar themes from the neolithic through the Republican period in a mere 150 pages. In many ways, it resembled works produced in the late 1980s and early 1990s, but it also contained something new. Sprinkled throughout the text were stylized line drawings of "native" chieftains kowtowing before upright Confucian officials, the latter with their arms joined in a fist pledging benevolent rule.[69] The drawings, done in the style of socialist realism, leaven the text and graphically illustrate, in a memorable and grossly simplified fashion, the long loyalty of the locals to the central plains dynasties and their struggle for liberation from class exploitation (see illustrations 14.1 and 14.2).

The editor who conceived the book insisted in an interview that "the government did not put me up to this. I came up with the idea on my own." She was nevertheless gratified when officials proposed that the press digest the volume into a less expensive textbook version. The result satisfied both parties. The CCP could offer the schools a dynamic, simplified primer on Xinjiang history that pupils might even enjoy reading, while the press derived considerable benefit as well. Where the original version had been printed in an edition of 5,000, the primer quickly went into six printings, for a total of nearly half a million volumes.[70]

Bookstore shelves gave evidence of another clever new strategy. In hopes of interesting adults repelled by drab, didactic texts, officials sponsored a new series titled "literary works on Xinjiang's key historical topics." Party propagandists almost certainly absorbed this tactic from Uyghurs. The works of Zordun, Abdurehim, and other Uyghur authors had demonstrated how effectively fiction could lodge a particular historical interpretation in readers' minds.

The first book in the series was a novel about how the Guomindang military went over to the Communist side in 1949. Its preface declared the hopes of the committee that planned the series. Since written history is useless if unread, the committee has sought authors to write works people will choose to read: "using literature to represent Xinjiang . . . has a special lasting appeal and invites people's interest." For the reader who might be curious about how authors manage the line between "fact" and "art," they explain that the books in the series "reflect Xinjiang's history, but they are written not as histories but as literary work." Finally, they note that every topic and detail

Illustration 14.1   **People of the Western Regions Beg Ban Chao to Stay On**

Source: Ji Dachun, ed., *Xinjiang Lishi Baiwen* (A hundred questions about Xinjiang history), Lishi Shang De Xinjiang Huitu Congshu (The ilustrated book series on Xinjiang in history) (Urumchi: Xinjiang meishu sheying chubanshe, 1997), p. 23.

has been chosen strategically. The committee strove to "select a set of Xinjiang's most significant historical themes, to create a set of literary works of different types including biographies of key people, novels, and full-length reportage, and to bequeath them to the broad readership."[71]

Officials and propagandists clearly hope that this new genre will attract a broad readership willing to absorb historical precepts in this form. It is surely no accident that the first title chronicles the CCP's creation of "facts on the ground" near the end of the revolution rather than events of the more distant past.

Conclusion

This chapter has analyzed an enduring struggle over history that is also a battle over the future of Xinjiang and the Uyghurs. The two sides in the contest command vastly unequal resources. The party-state has devoted much

Illustration 14.2   **Cang Ci, Protector of the Silk Route Trade**

Source: Ji Dachun, ed., *Xinjiang Lishi Baiwen* (A hundred questions about Xinjiang history), Lishi Shang De Xinjiang Huitu Congshu (The illustrated book series on Xinjiang in history) (Urumchi: Xinjiang meishu sheying chubanshe, 1997), p. 23.

money and time to the research and writing of history. It has inculcated in generations of Han scholars a sense of obligation to both party and nation. It has cultivated loyal officials and scholars among Uyghurs and other non-Hans. It has encouraged and rewarded those who sculpt histories of Xinjiang and the Uyghurs to match Beijing's political specifications. Party officials have lavished funds and other inducements on publishers and media organs to get them to disseminate the official versions of history. Finally, the party has used its control over schools to establish courses at every level to promulgate its view of the past. Because Hans overwhelmingly accept the official version of history, the party's efforts with that population must be judged an unqualified success.

Uyghur intellectuals, with far fewer resources and under severe political limitations, have produced a major body of work, though one with the same totalizing aims and characteristic distortions as its official counterpart. The works of Turghun and Qurban directly challenge the tenets of official orthodoxy by reconstructing an ancient, independent, and continuous history for the Uyghurs. Historical novels by Abdurehim and Zordun capture the political conflicts between Uyghurs and Hans in vivid prose, slyly articulating Uyghur aspirations for independence in ways that initially eluded censors but struck Uyghur readers with satisfying immediacy. When officials sought to halt the dissemination of these works and stop the publication of unnamed others, it only increased Uyghurs' eagerness to acquire and read them. The government's attempts to stamp out the offending ideas simply confirmed Uyghurs' conviction that they must be true. Official machinations have not only failed to inculcate among Uyghurs the "correct" ideas about history, they have done the opposite. The government's efforts with this population have largely failed.

Party officials in Beijing daily underscore the importance of opening China to the world and opening the minds of Chinese citizens to modern ideas, in the service of China's quest for wealth and power. But even as Xinjiang's borders have opened, *apparatchiks* in Beijing and Urumchi still propose to seal the region hermetically against harmful foreign ideas and to blanket the media with a single vision of the past—all, ironically, also in the name of Xinjiang's development. As the other chapters in this volume demonstrate, Uyghurs contend with the party in various spheres; the "contest of histories" is only one campaign in the larger battle. The party is least likely to win this campaign for Uyghur minds. Officials cannot afford to abandon it as long as Uyghurs carry weight in Chinese politics. Sadly, if past immigration policies are a prologue, how Uyghurs view their own past may grow ever less important as Hans come to form the majority population in the region.

15

Responses to Chinese Rule

Patterns of Cooperation and Opposition

Dru C. Gladney

In the summer of 2002, both the United States and the United Nations supported China's claim that an organization known as the Eastern Turkistan Islamic Movement (ETIM) should be recognized as an international terrorist organization.[1] It is important to note, however, that China makes little distinction between separatists, terrorists, and civil rights activists—whether they are Uyghurs, Tibetans, Taiwanese, or Falungong Buddhists. One person's terrorist may be another's freedom fighter. Are the restive Uyghurs of Xinjiang terrorists, separatists, or freedom fighters? How can the incidents of recent years be seen in terms of patterns of cooperation and opposition to Chinese rule in the region?

After denying the problem for decades and stressing instead China's "national unity," official reports and the state-run media began in early 2001 to detail terrorist activities in the region officially known as the Xinjiang Uyghur Autonomous Region (XUAR).[2] Prior to the release of the "White Paper on Xinjiang Uyghur Autonomous Region" by the Chinese State Council and the subsequent media reports, the term "Eastern Turkistan" was not allowed to be used in the official media, and anyone found using the term or referring to Xinjiang as Eastern Turkistan could be arrested, even though this is the term most often used to refer to the region by Uyghurs and other Turkic-speaking people outside China. Concerning the northwestern part of the XUAR, the Chinese State Council and the official media reported on the ongoing series of incidents of terrorism and separatism since the large riot in Ili of February 1997, with multiple crackdowns and arrests that have rounded up thousands of terrorist suspects, large weapons caches, and printed documents allegedly outlining future public acts of violence.[3] Amnesty International claims that these round-ups led to hurried public trials and immediate, summary executions of possibly thousands of locals. One estimate suggests that in a country known for its frequent executions, Xinjiang had the highest number, averaging 1.8 per week, most of them Uyghurs.[4] In his April 16, 2002, speech to the

UN High Commission in Geneva, Enver Can, the president of the East Turkistan (Uyghuristan) National Congress (ETNC; www.eastturkistan.com) based in Munich, claimed that in the two years, between 1997 and 1999, 210 death sentences were recorded.[5] Since September 11, 2001, claims have been made that arrests and executions have increased, but there is little accurate documentation in support of this claim. The Uyghur service of Radio Free Asia (RFA) recently announced that in January 2002, 350 suspected Uyghur separatists were rounded up in Xinjiang.[6]

The nationwide campaign known as "Strike Hard, Maximum Pressure," launched in 1997, called for China to erect a "great wall of steel" against separatists in Xinjiang. Troop movements in connection with this campaign were reportedly the largest since the suppression of the large Akto insurrection in April 1990—the first major uprising that initiated a series of unrelated and sporadic protests.[7] Alleged incursions into Xinjiang by Taliban fighters from Afghanistan via the narrow Wakhan Corridor caused serious concern in Beijing. As Yitzhak Shichor shows in chapter 5, beginning at least one month prior to the September 11 attack, the Chinese government increased security forces in the area and conducted large military exercises there. Under U.S. and Chinese pressure, Pakistan returned to China one Uyghur activist, who was apprehended among hundreds of Taliban detainees, which follows a pattern of repatriations of suspected Uyghur separatists from Kazakstan, Kyrgyzstan, and Uzbekistan.[8]

International campaigns for Uyghur rights and possible independence have become increasingly vocal and well organized, especially on the Internet. Repeated public appeals have been made to Abdulahat Abdurixit, the Uyghur people's government chairman of Xinjiang in Urumchi. International human rights organizations increasingly include Uyghur indigenous voices from the expatriate Uyghur community. Notably, the 1995 elected chair of the Unrepresented Nations and People's Organization based in the Hague is a Uyghur, Erkin Aliptékin, the son of the separatist leader Eysa (Isa) Yusuf Aliptékin, who is buried in Istanbul where there is a park dedicated to his memory.[9] Serving primarily an audience of expatriate Uyghurs, at least twenty-five international organizations and websites based in Amsterdam, Munich, Istanbul, Melbourne, Washington, D.C., and New York are working for the independence of Eastern Turkistan. Following September 11, 2001, the vast majority of these organizations disclaimed any support for violence or terrorism and pressed ever more vigorously for a peaceful resolution of ongoing conflicts in the region. Nevertheless, the growing influence of "cyber-separatism" is of increasing concern to Chinese authorities, who see it as further evidence supportive of their claim that Uyghurs pose a genuine domestic and international threat as terrorists.

The core question is whether and how local responses to Chinese rule have changed since the events of September 11, 2001. It is clear that the so-called separatist activities focusing on Xinjiang are certainly not new. The Istanbul-based groups championing independence for Xinjiang have existed since the 1950s. In Soviet times, Uyghurs in the Soviet Union's Central Asian republics were well organized and received tremendous support from Moscow for their verbal attacks on China's policies in Xinjiang. And the establishment of independent states in neighboring parts of Central Asia after the collapse of the Soviet Union in 1991 led many to hope and plan for a similarly independent Uyghuristan in Xinjiang. The expansion of China's market policies have been accompanied by numerous if limited separatist actions. And the opening of six overland border gateways from Xinjiang and the opening of the trans-Eurasian railway, accompanied by China's campaign to "Develop the Great Northwest," have caused no diminution of such activity. The Chinese government itself, in a landmark 1999 white paper, admitted serious economic shortfalls in Xinjiang despite large investments extending over half a century, "The Chinese government is well aware of the fact that . . . central and western China where most minority people live, lags far behind the eastern coastal areas in development."[10] In light of all this, it is clear that Beijing has chosen to utilize the international campaign against terrorism to resolve a vexing internal problem in Xinjiang.

In previous years, China denied any serious social or political problems in Xinjiang and followed the old Soviet "divide-and-rule" strategy, which sought to limit all references to Turkistan or even Turcology that might link the Uyghurs, Kazaks, and other Turkic-speaking minorities to broader pan-Turkic movements. Since early 2001, however, impelled by the desire to gain international support for its domestic war on terrorism, China's Foreign Ministry and the *People's Daily* have documented, as discussed earlier, an ongoing series of incidents of terrorism and separatism that occurred since the large Ili riot of February 1997, including multiple crackdowns and the arrest of thousands of terrorist suspects, the discovery of large caches of weapons, and the exposure of printed documents allegedly outlining future public acts of violence. In June 2002, under U.S. and Chinese pressure, Pakistan returned one Uyghur activist to China, who was apprehended among hundreds of Taliban detainees, which follows a pattern of repatriations of suspected Uyghur terrorists in Central Asia. This detainee was supposedly one of several hundred Uyghurs who were arrested while fighting with the Taliban, six of whom were placed in the detention facility at Guantánamo Bay, Cuba.[11] That there are now large groups of militant Uyghur Muslims fighting abroad, that the Chinese government feels compelled to publicize separatist actions both within and outside Xinjiang, and that it has launched large-scale campaigns to suppress potential terrorists all indicate clearly how fundamentally the indigenous response to Chinese rule in Xinjiang has changed dramatically in the last twenty years. At the same time, whether because of China's increasingly harsh crackdowns or in spite of them, there have been fewer reports of civil unrest or terrorist activities since the peak in the late 1990s. This suggests yet another shift in the pattern of opposition to Chinese rule in the region.

Loyalty, Voice, or Exit?

The Princeton economist Albert O. Hirschman describes the options of a constituency as loyalty, voice, or exit.[12] Hirschman applies his theory to institutions and states in decline, while this volume argues that China's presence in Xinjiang has anything but declined. Nevertheless, it could be argued that for many Uyghurs in Xinjiang, where their relative numbers and influence have declined precipitously over the most recent fifty years of Chinese rule, loyalty, voice, and exit are indeed the main options open to them. It was clear that most Xinjiang residents welcomed the end of the Cultural Revolution as a respite from the harsh treatment that minorities and religious practitioners had received between 1966 and 1976. They had suffered during the twenty years of restrictions on religion and discrimination against religious practitioners that had begun in 1958 with the "Religious System Reform" campaign.[13] When Deng Xiaoping liberalized the marketplace, cultural and religious practice also flourished, leading to the revival of religious education in the region, as Linda Benson notes in chapter 7. During this period, scores of mosques in Xinjiang were built or reopened, young men were allowed to pursue Islamic training to become imams, and pilgrimages to Mecca were resumed. Indeed, many residents of Xinjiang, Uyghurs included, strongly support the Deng reforms as they have been continued under Jiang Zemin and now Hu Juntao. As loyal citizens, they acknowledge the dramatic economic and social progress that has been achieved since the end of the Cultural Revolution and generally share the government's vision of a modernized, developed Xinjiang. Working not only in the state sector as cadres, teachers, production corps farmers, and factory workers but also in the growing private sector in private and semiprivate small businesses, these supporters of the state's development program are disinclined to listen to any criticism of state policies, especially from disgruntled minorities or outsiders.

Given the lack of public polling or uncensored media in the region, it is difficult to ascertain if these supporters of Beijing's policies are a silent majority or a tiny minority. Nevertheless, the Deng reform era in general can be characterized as a period of heightened loyalty to the state and new-found optimism after the previous twenty years of internal chaos and repression. To many, the recent period recalls the years of relative progress and loyalty to the regime that followed Xinjiang's incorporation into the People's Republic of China and the establishment of the Xinjiang Uyghur Autonomous Region.

However, in the late 1980s and mid-1990s, this period of relative loyalty gave way to increasing expressions of what Hirschman terms "voice," not only among Uyghurs but also among a wide cross-section of Xinjiang residents who felt the northwest was not keeping pace with the rapid development of the rest of the country. Many Uyghurs were particularly disappointed that the independence of the former Central Asian republics of the Soviet Union in 1991 did not lead to independence or at least increased autonomy in their own autonomous region. Throughout the early and middle 1990s, increasing expressions of "voice," ranging from university protests to greater ethnic and civil unrest, demonstrated these concerns. Alternative histories and stories of Uyghur heroes and origins proliferated, and these differed radically from what was presented in the official Chinese texts, as Gardner Bovingdon shows in chapter 14. Whether or not there had been earlier smaller and unreported expressions of "voice" in the past, the mid-1990s witnessed an ever-growing number of public expressions of contrary views and dissatisfaction with state policies in Xinjiang.

The 1990s period of voiced opposition began with the report of a major uprising in Akto County, near Kashgar, in April 1990. Official reports claimed that this was nothing less than an "armed counterrevolutionary rebellion." The People's Liberation Army (PLA) suppressed it, with twenty-two deaths.[14] In 1995, the People's Armed Police Force (PAPF) reported finding a large cache of weapons, and in May 1996, a Xinjiang People's Political Consultative Conference official was assassinated. Both were blamed on supposed "Eastern Turkistan" terrorists.[15]

In the spring of 1996, the *Xinjiang Daily* reported that five serious social eruptions had occurred in the region since February 1996. In the ensuing crackdown 2,773 terrorist suspects, 6,000 pounds of explosives, and 31,000 rounds of ammunition were rounded up. Overseas Uyghur groups claimed that the actual number arrested surpassed 10,000 and that more than 1,000 had been killed.[16] The largest protest, which took place between February 2 and 8, 1996, was sparked by a Chinese raid on an evening mäshräp cultural meeting, where young Uyghur men and women had gathered to pray, sing religious and folk songs, and feast.[17] Protests against the arrests led to 120 deaths and over 2,500 arrests. On February 12, the local press reported that a train had been bombed and derailed, possibly by people angered by the arrests. The government claimed at once that this action had been coordinated by the United Revolutionary Front, based in Kazakstan.[18] On February 25, following the uprising and crackdown in Ili and the same day as Deng's memorial speech, bombs exploded simultaneously on three buses in downtown Urumchi. This obviously well-organized action led to twenty civilian deaths and scores of injuries, including some Uyghurs. In reprisal, the government executed eight Uyghurs allegedly responsible for the bombings.[19] The Almaty-based United Revolutionary Front, led by Yusupbek (Modan) Mukhlisi, denied all responsibility for the bombings.[20]

Later that spring, the United Revolutionary Front claimed responsibility for the bombing of a police building in Urumchi that was meant to disrupt antiseparatist security measures.[21] Then the violence came to Beijing. On March 7 and then again on the following day, two separate bombs exploded on public buses in the capitol.[22] The first bomb in the Xidan district claimed three lives with ten injured, while the second bomb killed two. The bombs were timed to take place during the Chinese National People's Congress and were widely attributed to Uyghur separatists, though this has never been independently verified and no group has ever claimed responsibility.[23] On May 29, 1996, knife-wielding Uyghur militants stabbed the progovernment *mullah* of Kashgar's Idgah mosque, Arunkhanji, and his son. Earlier, on May 27, there was an attack on a senior government official, and in September of the same year six Uyghur government officials were killed by other Uyghurs in Yecheng.

The Ili uprising on February 7, 1997, and the subsequent bombings in Urumchi and Beijing were heavily covered by the world's media.[24] This distinguishes the late 1990s events from ongoing problems in the region in the mid-1980s, which received little media coverage. One report suggested that throughout late 1997 and early 1998 violence was widespread in Xinjiang, from "the wanton killing of Han people," to assassination attempts on police, to various bomb blasts in the southern Tarim region. All were blamed on Xinjiang separatists, yet not one Uyghur organization or individual claimed credit for any of these incidents.[25] In addition, at least two major incidents in Xinjiang were initially widely believed to have been carried out by Uyghur separatists but later on were found to be completely unrelated: first, the poisoning of elementary school children in Ili on May 8, 1998, and, second, the explosion of radioactive material in downtown Urumchi. The latter was eventually found to have been due to army soldiers' mishandling of weaponry.[26] Many Uyghurs in the diaspora point to these accusations as proof that many crimes have been falsely blamed on Uyghur separatists. Indeed, many hold that the these highly publicized incidents were deliberately instigated by government saboteurs in order to justify further official crackdowns in the region.

In the late 1990s, the government struck back with a host of arrests and new policy announcements. In the spring of 1998, the National People's Congress passed a New Criminal Law that redefined "counterrevolutionary" crimes as "crimes against the state," which were punishable by severe prison terms or even execution. Included in "crimes against the state" were any actions considered to involve "ethnic discrimination" or "stirring up anti-ethnic sentiment."[27] Many human rights activists have argued that this was a thinly veiled attempt to criminalize "political" actions by transforming them into other violations, thus preserving China's ability to claim that it holds "no political prisoners." Since any minority activity could be regarded as stirring "antiethnic sentiment," activists are concerned that the New Criminal Law will be easily turned against them.

The Strike Hard, Maximum Pressure campaign, launched in Beijing in April 1997, was originally intended to clamp down on crime and corruption, but it also included severe restrictions on the practice of religion.[28] This sustained campaign, according to an April 1999 report by Amnesty International, led since 1997 to 210 capital sentences and the execution of 190 Uyghurs.[29]

The 1997 riot in Ili, described by Justin Rudelson and William Jankowiak in chapter 12, marked the apex of the Uyghurs. A marked decline in Xinjiang civil unrest and so-called separatist events set in thereafter, perhaps because of the government's harsh crackdown and arrest of prominent Uyghur activists.

For all the tensions and frequent reports of terrorist acts, very few attacks have been aimed at civilians or even the civilian economy of the region. Most confirmed incidents have been directed against Han Chinese security forces or against Uyghur Muslims perceived to be collaborating too closely with the Chinese government. A further possible assault directed against a governmental target was the bombing of a missile base reported by a Taiwan news agency in early 1999 but later denied by Chinese government officials.[30] Exceptions include attacks on Han Chinese immigrants, the reported bombing of a Xinjiang train on February 12, 1997, and an attack on a power station in Hejing on July 10, 1999,[31] as well as the two Beijing bus bombings mentioned earlier.

Examining all incidents of civil unrest, assassinations, and bombings in China since 1990, very few can be definitely traced to Uyghur separatist groups or events in Xinjiang. One unpublished report revealed that of 140 publicly reported "terrorist" incidents in China between 1990 and 2000, only 25 can be connected to separatists or political causes of any sort, and of these only 17 can be connected either to Xinjiang or to Uyghur separatists. The vast majority of incidents apparently arise not from separatist sentiment but from more general forms of alienation.[32]

On August 11, 1999, Rebiya Kadir, a well-known Uyghur businesswoman who had been a delegate to the United Nation's 1995 Beijing International Women's Conference, met with a delegation from the U.S. Congressional Research Service. She was promptly arrested for "revealing state secrets."[33] Human rights activists claim that she merely gave the guests clippings from the official news media that she wanted them to deliver to her husband, who was in exile in Washington, D.C. After reviewing her case, Amnesty International concluded that the evidence was insufficient for her to be detained, let alone arrested, and launched an international campaign in the spring of 2002. It also designated Kadir as their "detainee of the month" in hopes of publicizing her plight and gaining her release.[34]

Most analysts agree that China is not vulnerable to the same ethnic separatism that split the former Soviet Union. But few doubt that should China fall apart, it would divide, like the Soviet Union, along centuries-old ethnic, linguistic, regional, and cultural fault lines.[35] Anwar Yusuf, the president of the Eastern Turkistan National Freedom Center in Washington, D.C., argues that a political breakup would probably occur in a manner that "would make Kosovo look like a birthday party." Despite the possibility of bloodshed, Yusuf indicated that his Eastern Turkistan National Freedom Center nonetheless supported the call for a free and independent Xinjiang.[36] On June 4, 1999, Yusuf met with President Bill Clinton to press for fuller support for the Uyghur cause.[37] Subsequent Uyghur organizations sought to pressure the George W. Bush administration, with varying degrees of success. Now, many fear that Sino-U.S. cooperation in the war against terrorism will end American support for Uyghur human rights issues.

Since the high point of expressions of "voice" and of ethnic violence in the late 1990s, the number and scale of incidents have gradually declined. Documented separatist incidents in Xinjiang have dropped off dramatically since the late 1990s. In July 2002, Philip Pan reported that local Xinjiang security officials were able to cite only three relatively minor occurrences.[38] More important, although scarcely noted by observers, and despite the many instances of ethnic and civil unrest in the region, not one significant terrorist attack against any strategic infrastructural target (oil refinery, pipeline, railroad, dam, or bridge) has ever been convincingly documented. Nor has even one incident, whether within Xinjiang or abroad, been convincingly traced to any international Uyghur or Islamic organization.

Visitors to the region have increasingly reported a sense of disillusionment and disappointment among Uyghur activists. One acquaintance mentioned to me in late August 2001, "We've given up on independence, we just want to emigrate." Loyalty and voice, for many young Uyghurs, have turned to exit.

Cyber-separatism: Virtual Voices of the Uyghur Opposition

Whether because of Chinese restrictions on public protest and the existence of a state-controlled media or because of the deleterious effect of China's decade-long war on domestic terrorism documented in this chapter, very few critical Uyghur voices can be heard today in Xinjiang itself, and certainly not in public. Though silenced within China, Uyghur voices can still be heard on the Internet.* Interestingly, only by exercising Hirschman's "exit" alternative can Uyghur oppositional voices continue to be heard. On the Internet, the international campaign for Uyghur rights and independence has become increasingly vocal and well organized. Serving mainly an expatriate Uyghur audience, at least twenty-five international organizations and websites are now devoted to the independence of "Eastern Turkistan." These are based in Amsterdam, Munich, Istanbul, Melbourne, Washington, D.C., and New York.

Estimates differ widely on the number of Uyghurs living outside of China in the diaspora. As Sean R. Roberts notes in chapter 8, the Uyghurs in Central Asia are often undercounted by the official censuses, especially since 1991. Shichor estimates that approximately 500,000 Uyghurs live abroad, or 5 to 6 percent of the total world Uyghur population.[39] Uyghur websites claim dramatically higher numbers for Uyghurs, ranging up to 25 million inside Xinjiang and up to 10 million in the diaspora.[40]

Although the United Nations and the U.S. government have agreed with China that at least one international organization, the ETIM, is a Uyghur-sponsored terrorist organization, the vast majority of the Eastern Turkistan independence and information organizations emphatically disavow violence. Supported largely by Uyghur émigrés who left China prior to the Communist takeover in 1949, these organizations maintain a plethora of websites and activities. Although not all organizations advocate independence or separatism, the vast majority of them press for radical change. They report in detail on human rights violations, environmental degradation, and economic injustices and offer their readers alternative histories of the region. Some offer mainly news and information, while others are politically active advocacy sites. Nearly all of them, whether focusing on information or advocacy, are sharply critical of Chinese policies in Xinjiang.

Key informational websites that mainly provide Uyghur- and Xinjiang-related news and analyses include the *Turkistan Newsletter* (Turkistan-N) maintained by Mehmet Tutuncu of SOTA (www.euronet.nl/users/sota/Turkistan.html), the

---

*Unless otherwise noted, all the websites cited in the following pages were accessed on 10 May 2002.

Open Society Institute (www.erasianet.org/), the Uyghur Information Agency (www.uyghurinfo.com/), and the virtual library of the Australian National University–based Eastern Turkistan WWW VL (www.ccs.uky.edu/~rakhim/ et.html). An increasing number of scholars are building websites that feature their own work on Xinjiang and provide links to other sites and organizations engaged in similar research and educational activities pertaining to the region. One of the best sites in this genre is that maintained by Nathan Light of the University of Toledo (www.utoledo.edu/~nlight), which not only includes most of his dissertation and useful articles on Uyghur history, music, and culture but also directs readers to other links to the region. While there is a plethora of Internet sites and Web links to Xinjiang and Uyghur human rights issues, there is as yet no central site that is regularly updated. Information on Uyghur organizations and Internet sites has been gathered by the Uyghur American Association (www.uyghuramerican.org/). An interactive question-and-answer site with a "Special Report: Uyghur Muslim Separatists" can be found at the Virtual Information Center (www.vic-info.org/), which is an open-source organization funded by the U.S. Commander in Chief, Pacific Command.

Even though Xinjiang has often been treated under the rubric of Chinese rather than Central Asian studies, a growing number of Central Asian–related sites contain information and discussion of events in Xinjiang. For example, see the Central Asia–Caucasus Institute's Central Asia–Caucasus Analyst (www.cacianalyst.org), edited by Svante Cornell. Harvard's Forum for Central Asian Studies (www.fas.harvard.edu/~centasia), which is run by John Schoeberlein, maintains the Central Asian Studies World Wide Website (www. fas.harvard.edu/~casww/) and the listserv CentralAsia-L (www.fas.harvard. edu/~casww/CASWW_CentralAsia-L.html) that frequently reports on Xinjiang-related issues. The informational website For Democracy, Human Rights, Peace and Freedom for Uzbekistan and Central Asia (www.uzbekistanerk.org/) provides links to Uyghur and East Turkistan sites. In addition, Silk Road sites increasingly focus on the Uyghur issue. For example, The Silk Road Foundation (http://silk-road.com/toc/index.html) is a general informational site for Central Asia, with sections on Xinjiang and a links page to other Uyghur issues. Interestingly, a NOVA/PBS website (www.pbs.org/wgbh/nova/chinamum/taklamakan.html) reports on the Taklimakan mummies, an issue exploited by Chinese and Uyghurs alike to establish claims of territorial history, and offers ongoing reports on research on the mummies' ethnicity.

While most of these sites do not claim to take a position on the issue of Uyghur independence in Xinjiang, most tend to report information that is supportive of Uyghur claims against the Chinese state. An example is the GeoNative "informational site" (www.geocities.com/athens/9479/

uyghur.html), maintained by the Basque activist Luistxo Fernandez, who seeks to report "objectively" on minority peoples less represented in the world press. Yet, his site, which provides a useful chart on English-Uyghur-Chinese transliterated place-names, contains the statement, "Chinese colonization by Han people is a threat to native peoples."[41] Abdulrakhim Aitbayev's Page (www.ccs.uky.edu/~rakhim/et.html) is another so-called informational website that reports on Chinese police action in various areas of Xinjiang and also provides links to other sites and articles that are generally critical of China.

An important addition to the list of "informational sites" is the site maintained by the RFA as part of its regular broadcasts to Xinjiang and surrounding regions that are reportedly beamed from transmitters in Tajikistan and Kyrgyzstan (www.rfa.org/service/index.html?service=uyg). According to its site, the RFA broadcasts news and information to Asian listeners who lack regular access to "full and balanced reporting" in their domestic media. Through its broadcasts and call-in programs, the RFA aims to fill what is regarded as a "critical gap" in the news reporting for people in certain regions of Asia. Created by Congress in 1994 and incorporated in 1996, the RFA currently broadcasts in Burmese, Cantonese, Khmer, Korean, Lao, Mandarin, the Wu dialect, Vietnamese, Tibetan (Uke, Amdo, and Kham), and Uyghur. Although the service declares its commitment to the highest standards of journalism and aims to exemplify accuracy, balance, and fairness in its editorial content, local governments have often complained that it is biased in favor of groups critical to the regimes in power. The Chinese government regularly blocks the Uyghur service, criticizing it for carrying stories supportive of so-called separatists and especially for reporting on the Kadir case. Despite cooperation between the United States and China in the war on terrorism, the site continues its regular broadcasting. When Dolkun Kamberi, the Uyghur director of the service, was asked if the increased Sino-U.S. cooperation on terrorism and the labeling of the ETIM as an international Uyghur terrorist group had led to any restriction on RFA's funding or broadcast content, he reported that no changes had been requested or had occurred. Uyghur listeners to the program, however, have complained that the site no longer criticizes China as strongly or frequently for its treatment of Uyghurs in Xinjiang.

Funding for the informational sites is generally traceable to academic organizations, advertising, and subscriptions. It is much harder to establish the sources of funding for the advocacy sites. While most sites are supported primarily by subscribers, advertising, and small donations from Uyghurs and other Muslims outside of China who are sympathetic to the Uyghur cause, there is no evidence that the organizations and the sites they sponsor have ever benefited from subventions from any government. Other than the U.S. government, which supports the RFA's Uyghur service, no foreign government provides support for the dissemination of information related to Uyghur human rights issues. However, many Uyghur organizations in the past have claimed sympathy and tacit official support from officials in Turkey, Saudi Arabia, Iran, Australia, Germany, France, Holland, and Canada.

Advocacy sites that openly seek international support for Uyghur- and Xinjiang-related causes take a strong and critical stance against Chinese rule in Xinjiang. They claim to give voice to a "silent majority" of Uyghurs in Xinjiang and abroad who advocate radical political reform, if not outright independence, in the region. These sites include one maintained by the International Taklamakan Human Rights Association (ITHRA; www.taklamakan. org), which contains links to several other websites concerned with East Turkistan, Uyghurs, and Uyghuristan. Another is run by the Uyghur American Association, whose website contains links to articles and websites concerning issues of human rights and territorial freedom of Uyghurs in Xinjiang and lists twenty-two other organizations around the world that do not have websites. Yet another is maintained by the ETNC.

Citizens against Communist Chinese Propaganda (www.caccp.org/), an outspoken U.S.-based site that bills itself as counterpropaganda, has one page titled "Free East Turkistan!" Based in Florida and led by its founder, Jack Churchward, the group Free East Turkistan originally made a name for itself through a series of protests against the Chinese-owned and -operated theme park Splendid China, located in Kissimmee, Florida. The organization found the park's minireplicas of mosques and the Potala Palace to be denigrating to Uyghurs and Tibetans.[42] The Uyghur Human Rights Coalition (www.uyghurs.org) is another website reporting human rights abuses against Uyghurs in China and containing links to articles and other sites. KIVILCIM (www.kivilcim.org and www.doguturkistan.net) is an East Turkistan information website that issues its calls for Xinjiang's independence in the Uyghur language.

Other advocacy sites include the East Turkistan Information Center (www.uygur.org), the East Turkistan National Freedom Center (www. uyghur.org), and other more popular sites including ITHRA, the Alachua Freenet (www.afn.org), and the ETNC. As most of these sites are cross-linked, they often repeat and pass along information contained on other sites.

The number of more or less well-known Uyghur advocacy organizations grew to nearly twenty in the late 1990s, but they seem to have declined in number, membership, and activities since September 2001.[43] In the United States, one of the most active information and advocacy groups is the Uyghur

American Association, which has been chaired by Alim Seytoff and Turdi Hajji.[44] Founded like many advocacy groups in the late 1990s, it supports public lectures and organizes demonstrations to raise public awareness regarding Uyghur and Xinjiang issues. The Uyghur Human Rights Coalition, directed by Kathy Polias and located near the Georgetown University campus, tracks human rights issues and has organized several demonstrations and conferences in the Washington, D.C., area, especially pushing for the release of Kadir.[45] The East Turkistan National Freedom Center, whose leader is Anwar Yusuf, made a clear stand for an independent Eastern Turkistan in his personal meeting with President Clinton on June 4, 1999, the tenth anniversary of the Tiananmen Square massacre. Yusuf stated in a personal communication to me that he has no fear of launching a civil war in the region.[46] One of the earliest Uyghur advocacy organizations established in the United States in 1996 is ITHRA. Under its president Ablajan Layli Namen Barat, it maintains the active listserv UYGHUR-L, as well as the listserv SMONGOL-L, which covers events in Inner Mongolia.

In Europe, most of the Uyghur organizations are concentrated in Munich, where there is the largest number of Uyghur émigrés. These groups include the ETNC; the East Turkistan Union in Europe led by Asgar Can; the Eastern Turkistan Information Center led by Abduljelil Karakash, which publishes the online journal *The World Uyghur Network News;* and the World Uyghur Youth Congress (www.uyghurinfo.com) chaired by Dolqun Isa. In Holland, there is the Uyghur Netherlands Democratic Union led by Bahtiyar Semsiddin, and the Uyghur House chaired by Shahelil. In Belgium, there is the Uyghur Youth Union chaired by Sedullam and the Belgium Uyghur Association chaired by Sultan Ehmet. In Stockholm, one finds the Eastern Turkistan Association chaired by Faruk Sadikov, while in London there is the Uygur Youth Union UK chaired by Enver Bugda. In Moscow, there is the Uyghur Association chaired by Serip Haje. Turkey-based organizations include the East Turkistan Foundation led by Mehmet Riza Bekin in Istanbul, the Eastern Turkistan Solidarity Foundation (also in Istanbul) led by Sayit Taranci, and the Eastern Turkistan Culture and Solidarity Association led by Abubekir Turksoy in Kayseri. Canada claims the Canadian Uyghur Association chaired by Mehmetjan Tohti in Toronto. In Australia, there is the Australian Turkistan Association chaired by Ahmet Igamberdi in Melbourne.

Meanwhile, in Kazakstan several organizations based in Almaty are listed on the Internet, but they are difficult to contact on the ground, as they have met with recent governmental sanctions. These include the Nozugum Foundation, the Kazakstan Regional Uyghur (Ittipak) Organization chaired by Khahriman Gojamberdie, the Uyghuristan Freedom Association chaired by Sabit Abdurahman, the Kazakstan Uyghur Unity

(Ittipak) Association chaired by Sheripjan Nadirov, and the Uyghur Youth Union in Kazakstan chaired by Abdurexit Turdeyev. In nearby Kyrgyzstan, one finds in Bishkek the Kyrgyzstan Uyghur Unity (Ittipak) Association chaired by Rozimehmet Abdulnbakiev and the Bishkek Human Rights Committee chaired by Tursun Islam.

While these are the main organizations listed on the Internet, many of them are no longer accessible, and there are several other smaller organizations that remain unlisted.

It is difficult to assess the audience for these websites and organizations, as they are all blocked in China, and mostly inaccessible in Central Asia due to either inadequate Internet access or the high costs of getting on the Web. Many Uyghurs one meets in China and in Central Asia have never heard of most of these sites. Interestingly, even government officials in Xinjiang who profess an interest in gaining access to the information provided on these sites also report that they have no means of accessing them. It is clear that Uyghurs in the Western diaspora, particularly in Europe, Turkey, the United States, Canada, and Australia, are frequent readers and contributors to these sites. In addition, events in the region since September 11, 2001, have led an increasing number of journalists and interested observers of the region to begin visiting the sites more regularly. A cursory monitoring of these sites reveals very little that can be associated with militant or radical Islam, and almost no calls for an Islamic jihad against the Chinese state. As noted earlier, their main concern is to document the Uyghurs' plight under Chinese rule in Xinjiang, as opposed to their glorious independent past.

It is also important to note that few Chinese inside or outside China have visited these sites, so they are quite unaware of the alternative histories available there. Although several sites issue materials in Turkish and Uyghur, there is not one in the Chinese language. Like all Internet groups, the public for these sites is a self-selected audience and rarely reaches beyond those who are already interested in, and supportive of, the agenda promoted there.

Financial support for these organizations and websites comes mostly from private individuals, foundations, and subscriptions (though these are rare). It has been reported that wealthy Uyghur patrons in Saudi Arabia and Turkey have provided financial support to these organizations. Yet, there is no publicly available information on these purported donors. Many Uyghurs who migrated to Saudi Arabia and Turkey in the 1930s and 1940s became successful in construction and the restaurant business and were thus in a good position to support Uyghur causes. In a personal interview, Anwar Yusuf, the president of the Washington-based East Turkistan National Freedom Center, claimed that he had received substantial support from patrons in Saudi Arabia, but by the late 1990s funding had begun to dry up due to the proliferation of organizations and waning interest in the Uyghur cause.[47] Uyghurs who migrated to Central Asia and the West in ever greater numbers during the last two decades generally remain poorer than the earlier émigrés to the Middle East. This is starting to change, however, as they and their children become more well established in the United States, Canada, Europe, and Australia.

Although most of these websites have limited funding and circulation, they should not be dismissed as forming merely a "virtual community" that has no substantial impact on events within Xinjiang. These websites serve as an important source of information not available in the official Chinese media. Indeed, some scholars have begun to argue that Internet sites like these often help to sway public opinion by virtue of their widespread availability and alternative reporting of important events.[48] There is an emerging consensus that Internet sites have altered the way information is circulated and opinions are formed. Perhaps more importantly, scholars have concluded that the "virtual communities" formed by Internet websites establish links and connections that can lead to broader social interactions and coalitions of a kind that can affect political and socioeconomic events. For example, it has been shown that social movements in East Timor, Aceh, Chechnya, and Bosnia have all gained strong support through Internet communities, which have provided not only a broader range of information but also a large amount of financial assistance.[49] Even though "cyber-separatism" would never on its own be able to unseat a local government, it is clear that it can link like-minded individuals and raise their consciousness on issues that are inaccessible to the general public. For an isolated region such as Xinjiang, and the widely dispersed Uyghur diaspora, the Internet has already proven to be a significant force and is likely to become more so in the future. It has helped shape the way the world views the region, and the Chinese state must eventually respond to the issues it brings to the fore.

It is clear that there are more than just Internet organizations involved in separatist activities in and around Xinjiang. As noted earlier, the United Nations in October 2002 designated the ETIM as an international terrorist organization responsible for domestic and international terrorist acts, which China claimed included a bombing of the Chinese consulate in Istanbul and the assassination of Chinese officials in Bishkek and of Uyghur officials in Kashgar thought to be collaborating with Chinese officialdom.[50] However, neither China nor the United States presented convincing public evidence to link the ETIM organization with the specific incidents described.[51]

In 2001, the U.S. State Department released a report that documented several separatist and terrorist groups operating inside the region and abroad that call for an independent Xinjiang.[52] The list included the United Revolutionary Front of Eastern Turkistan, whose leader, Yusupbek Mukhlisi, claims to have 30 armed units with "20 million" Uyghurs primed for an uprising; the Home of East Turkistan Youth, with a reported 2,000 members and said to be linked with Hamas; the Free Turkistan Movement, whose leader Abdul Kasim is said to have led the 1990 Baren uprising that is discussed in chapters 12 and 14; the Organization for the Liberation of Uyghuristan, whose leader, Ashir Vakhidi, is said to be committed to fighting Chinese "occupation" of the "Uyghur homeland"; and the so-called Wolves of Lop Nor, who have claimed responsibility for various bombings and uprisings. The State Department report claims that all of these groups have tenuous links with Al-Qaeda, the Taliban, the Hizb-ut-Tahrir (Islamic Revival), and the Tableeghi Jamaat. A Chinese report issued in early 2002 spoke of several of these groups but failed to mention the ETIM. It came as a surprise, therefore, when at the conclusion of his August 2002 visit to Beijing, Deputy Secretary of State Richard L. Armitage identified the ETIM as a leading international terrorist group.[53] At the time, very few people, including activists deeply engaged in working for an independent East Turkistan, had ever heard of the ETIM.[54] Even the U.S. military did not seem to be aware of the group's existence. A "Special Report: Uyghur Muslim Separatists" issued in 2001 by the Virtual Information Center in Honolulu, which is in turn funded by the Pacific Asia Command, not only did not mention the ETIM but also concluded regarding separatist violence in Xinjiang that there is "no single identifiable group but there is violent opposition coordinated and possibly conducted by exiled groups and organizations within Xinjiang."[55]

The main criticism raised by those critical of this designation is that, with so many identified groups, it has not been made clear why the ETIM was singled out, unless it was for the political purpose of strengthening Sino-U.S. relations. Calling them "scapegoat terrorists," the *Oxford Analytica* report on the ETIM issue concluded that the ETIM and other groups are only a "dubious threat" and had been used as an excuse for increased repression.[56] Interestingly, Mukhlisi's United Revolutionary Front was not included with the ETIM, despite its frequent claims of responsibility for violent acts in Xinjiang, such as the 1997 train derailment and police station bombings.[57] At the same time, several Uyghurs have complained that although there have been many reported violent protests and terrorist bombings in Tibet, they do not see the United States ever siding with China in condemning a Tibetan independence organization as terrorist.[58] Despite international protests, on January 27, 2002, China executed a Tibetan monk found guilty of lethal bombings in Tibet.[59] Many feel that it is only due to the fact that they are Muslims that one Uyghur group has been singled out as being a terrorist organization. The real issue for this chapter, however, is that despite the designation of the ETIM, there are indeed active Uyghur-related activist groups that support terrorism but that have never been directly implicated in any specific incident.

Following Armitage's announcement and the State Department's report, the Chinese State Council issued its own report on January 21, 2002, charging that between 1990 and 2001 Uyghur separatist groups "were responsible for over 200 terrorist incidents in Xinjiang" that resulted in the deaths of 162 people and injuries to 440 others. The report, "Eastern Turkistan Terrorist Forces Cannot Get Away with Impunity," also dismissed allegations that Beijing had used the U.S.-led war on terror as a pretext to crack down on Uyghurs. The report condemned numerous Uyghur groups by name, including Mehmet Emin Hazret's Eastern Turkistan Liberation Organization (ETLO), the ETIM, the Islamic Reformist Party "Shock Brigade," the Eastern Turkistan Islamic Party, the Eastern Turkistan Opposition Party, the Eastern Turkistan Islamic Party of Allah, the Uyghur Liberation Organization, the Islamic Holy Warriors, and the Eastern Turkistan International Committee.

An Internet search of many of these organizations and their backgrounds reveals little, if any, information. In addition, neither these organizations nor the many Internet news and information organizations discussed earlier have claimed responsibility for any specific action, though many are clearly sympathetic to actions they regard as challenging Chinese rule in the region. Interestingly, there seems to be very little support among these groups for radical Islam. A search for the term "jihad" (holy war) among the various websites and news postings turns up almost no use of the term, let alone calls for a religious war against the Chinese. As Rudelson and Jankowiak note in chapter 12, many Uyghur nationalists are quite secular in their orientation; they would overthrow Chinese rule in Xinjiang in the name of Uyghur sovereignty and human rights rather than in the name of religion. Uyghur expatriates in the United States, Canada, Turkey, and Europe tend to be quite religious, yet they rarely call for a jihad against the Chinese. Again, their concerns are more related to historical claims on their ancestral lands, Chinese mistreatment of the Uyghur population, and a desire to return home to a "free Eastern Turkistan." A Uyghur family in Toronto maintains a deeply religious life that it claims was impossible in China. Disavowing violence, the family's Ramadan prayer was for a free "Uyghuristan" where their relatives could be free to practice religion. In Istanbul, the Uyghur community is quite active in the mosques in Zeytinburnu and Tuzla and strongly advocates a "liberated Eastern Turkistan." But a frequent visitor to these communities since 1993 never once heard them call for a jihad against the Chinese government, even in its most mild sense that John Esposito has described as "defensive jihad," or protecting Islam from persecution.[60]

To repeat, since September 11, 2001, very few groups have publicly advocated terror against the Chinese state and most have denied any involvement in terrorist activities, though some express sympathy for them. A case in point is the ETLO, led by the secretive Hazret. In a January 24, 2003, telephone interview with the Uyghur service of the RFA, Hazret admitted the possible need to establish a military wing of his organization that would target Chinese interests, but he denied any prior terrorist activities or association with the ETIM. "We have not been and will not be involved in any kind of terrorist action inside or outside China," Hazret declared. "But the Chinese government's brutality in Eastern Turkistan may have forced some individuals to resort to violence." Hazret, a former screenwriter from Xinjiang who in his forties migrated to Turkey, denied any connection between his organization and Al-Qaeda or Osama bin Laden. Nevertheless, he did see the increasing need for a military action against Chinese rule in the region: "Our principal goal is to achieve independence for Eastern Turkistan by peaceful means. But to show our enemies and friends our determination on the Eastern Turkistan issue, we view a military wing as inevitable. . . . The Chinese people are not our enemy. Our problem is with the Chinese government, which violates the human rights of the Uyghur people." Once again, he made no reference to Islamic jihad or religious nationalism but emphasized instead human rights violations and Uyghur claims on Eastern Turkistan.[61]

In 2001, China ratified the International Covenant on Economic, Social, and Cultural Rights. Article 1 says, "All peoples have the right of self-determination. By virtue of that right they freely determine their political status and freely pursue their economic, social and cultural development." Article 2 reads, "All peoples may, for their own ends, freely dispose of their natural wealth and resources without prejudice to any obligations arising out of international economic co-operation, based on the principle of mutual benefit, and international law. In no case may a people be deprived of its own means of subsistence." China continues to quibble with the definition of "people," but its assent to this and other conventions has given grounds for high-ranking human rights advocates to voice their criticism of China. Chinese authorities are clearly concerned over increasing international attention to its treatment of minority and dissident peoples. But with Xinjiang being the last Muslim region under Communism, China's large trade contracts with Middle Eastern Muslim nations, and five predominantly Muslim nations on its western borders, China has concerns that go beyond international criticism of its record on human rights.

China's Uyghur separatists are small in number, poorly equipped, loosely linked, and vastly outgunned by the PLA and PAPF. And though sometimes disgruntled over the abuse of their own rights and other forms of mistreatment, China's nine other official Muslim minorities generally do not support

Uyghur separatism. The enmity between Uyghur and Hui (Tungan) in the region is noted in chapters 12 and 13. Few Hui support an independent Xinjiang, and the 1 million Kazaks in Xinjiang would probably have little voice in an independent "Uyghuristan." Local support for separatist activities in Xinjiang and other border regions is ambiguous at best, given their relative prosperity compared to neighboring Tajikistan, Kyrgyzstan, Pakistan, and especially Afghanistan. Memories of mass starvation and widespread destruction during the Sino-Japanese war and the civil war in the first half of the twentieth century are still strong in Xinjiang, as are memories of bloody intra-Muslim and Sino-Muslim conflicts, not to mention the chaotic horrors of the Cultural Revolution.

Many local activists stop short of calls for complete independence and focus instead on environmental degradation, nuclear testing, the absence of religious freedom, overtaxation, and recently imposed limits on childbearing. Many ethnic leaders are asking that the five autonomous regions currently led by Han Chinese first party secretaries controlled by Beijing be replaced with locally chosen leaders and that the "real" autonomy promised by Chinese law be granted them. Interestingly, freedom of religion does not seem to be a key issue, even though, as Graham E. Fuller and Jonathan N. Lipman note in chapter 13, recent visitors to the region report an increase in restrictions against mosque attendance by youth, students, and government officials. In addition, Islamic extremism does not as yet appear to have widespread appeal, especially among urban, educated Uyghurs, as Fuller and Lipman also note. However, the government has consistently rounded up any Uyghurs suspected of being too religious, especially those identified as Sufis or the so-called Wahhabis (a euphemism in the region for strict Muslims, rather than an organized Islamic school).

However, all the periodic roundups, detentions, and public condemnations of terrorism and separatism have not erased the problem but have forced it underground, or at least out of the public's eye, and increased the possibility of alienating Uyghur Muslims even further from mainstream Chinese society. It was widely reported that during the 2001 Asia Pacific Economic Cooperation meetings in Beijing, Uyghur travelers were not allowed to stay in hotels in the city and were often prevented from boarding public buses due to the government's fear of terrorism.

The history of Sino-Muslim relations in Xinjiang, as James A. Millward and Nabijan Tursun document in chapter 3, has been one of relative peace, broken by enormous social and political disruptions fostered by both internal and external crises. The relative quiet of the most recent two or three years does not indicate that the ongoing problems of the region have been resolved or that opposition has dissolved. Local opposition to Chinese rule in Xinjiang has not reached the level of Chechen opposition to Russian rule or the Intifada in Palestine. Like the Basque separatists of the Euskadi Ta Askatasuna in Spain or the former Irish Republican Army in Ireland and England, the Uyghur movement may continue to erupt unexpectedly, bringing limited but violent moments of terror and resistance. And just as these oppositional movements have persisted in Europe, the Uyghur problem in Xinjiang will not readily go away. The Chinese government acknowledges the problem of Uyghur dissent and resistance and recognizes that it extends to members of an active diaspora. But to acknowledge it is not to resolve it, let alone to achieve integration and development in a region where the majority of the population is ethnically distinct and devoutly Muslim. How does a government integrate a strongly religious minority (be it Muslim, Tibetan, Christian, or Buddhist) into a Marxist-capitalist system? China's policy of economic incentives coupled with harsh repression of dissent has failed so far to solve this issue.

Local Responses and Chinese Rule: Prospects for Change

It is important to note here that other border regions with large minority populations, such as Yunnan, Guizhou, Guangxi (with 16 million Zhuang), Hainan, and even the Ningxia Hui Autonomous Region, have not had any reported separatist or terrorist activities. Thus, the problems in Xinjiang and the oppositional voices of mostly Uyghur groups stand out all the more sharply.

Could Xinjiang survive economically were it independent? The problems facing an independent Xinjiang would be much greater than those of an independent Tibet. Not only are Xinjiang's infrastructure and economy more closely integrated with the rest of China than are Tibet's, but the Uyghur part of the population is less than half of the total and primarily located in the south, where there is less industry and natural resources, except for oil. Without substantial investments, which would be less likely in an independent Xinjiang, Tarim oil and energy resources will not become a viable source of independent wealth.

The history of poor relations among the three main Muslim groups in Xinjiang—Uyghurs, Kazaks, and Hui—suggests that in the event of independence, conflicts among Muslims would be as great as those between Muslims and Han Chinese. Most local residents concede that independence would lead to significant clashes between these groups along ethnic, religious, urban-rural, and territorial lines.

Under such circumstances, many Xinjiang Han would naturally seek to return to the interior of China, since Russia and Mongolia would be in no position to receive them. But there would be few places for them to go, since the bordering provinces of Gansu and Qinghai would be just as disrupted, and Tibet would not be an option.

Nor would it be any easier for Uyghurs seeking to flee. Most would likely move south, since the north would be dominated by Han Chinese and Kazakstan and Kyrgyzstan would not be open to them. That would leave only the southern routes. But neither Tajikistan nor Afghanistan would be likely to receive them, Pakistan would think twice about admitting any more refugees, while India would surely not wish to add to its Muslim population. Conversations in Xinjiang with local residents, Muslim and Han alike, made it clear that these facts are well understood there. Most think that in a worst-case scenario, they would have no alternative but to stay and fight.

Clearly, China needs a new approach to resolve tensions in Xinjiang; neither Marxist nor Keynesian economic development strategies have addressed the basic social problem of the region. The Develop the West campaign described by Calla Wiemer in chapter 6 has slowed considerably since September 2001, and revenue from tourism in Xinjiang has also plummeted. The state's investment plan has done little or nothing to resolve ongoing ethnic problems in the region, mainly because they arise from a number of complex causes besides poverty. Although organized resistance and violent actions have declined sharply since their high point in the late 1990s, it is clear that tensions remain and the problems underlying them are unresolved. Some travelers to the region report no obvious incidents of protest or dissent, but those who stray from the group, speak local languages, or have long-term friendships or relatives in the region report very different experiences.[62] It is clear that tensions will continue to simmer below the surface. In a *Foreign Affairs* article, Chien-Peng Chung of the Singaporean Institute of Defense and Strategic Studies called for immediate political changes in Xinjiang in order to avoid a further deterioration in ethnic relations.[63]

China is a sovereign state, and like all modern nations in the era of globalization, it faces tremendous challenges. In Xinjiang, it must address issues of Han migration, economic imbalances, ethnic unrest, and cyber-separatism. The future of this vastly important region, which Owen Lattimore once called the "pivot of Asia," depends on China's response to these challenges. The stakes are high. As S. Frederick Starr argues in his introduction to this volume, since September 11, 2001, the entire region has once again become pivotal to the rest of the world. The sources of discontent for Uyghur opposition groups, as *Oxford Analytica* outlines, remain today what they have been for generations: massive unrestricted Han migration to the region, a dramatically expanding gap between the wealthy and mainly Uyghur poor, decreasing educational opportunities in the modern sector for poorer residents, higher mortality rates among Uyghurs, increased restrictions on religious and cultural practices, unresolved health problems arising from nuclear testing in the region, and a burgeoning HIV/AIDS epidemic.[64] Economic stimuli through the Develop the Great Northwest campaign and continued affirmative action for minorities have done little to resolve these ongoing tensions. Indeed, as Zheng Yongnian's study of Chinese nationalism concludes, by increasing the gap between the rich and the poor, the majority and the minority, the reform policies and market economy have themselves exacerbated interethnic tensions and fostered increased ethnic nationalisms.[65] A *Jane's Intelligence Digest* report concludes, "All the indications are that China faces a major increase in Uyghur militancy."[66]

In the past ten years, China's opening to the outside world has meant much for Uyghurs, who may now easily travel along the Karakoram Highway to Pakistan, through the Ili River valley into Kazakstan, or by several Civil Aviation Administration of China flights to Istanbul from Urumchi. The number of Uyghur pilgrims on the hajj to Mecca increased by 300 per annum for several years, although the figure has declined somewhat since September 2001 due to tighter border controls. These contacts have allowed Uyghurs to see themselves as participants in the broader Islamic *Umma*, while at the same time being Muslim citizens of the Chinese nation-state. Groups of Uyghurs returning from the hajj tell of a greater sense of affinity with their own as one people than with the other multiethnic members of the international Islamic community. State-promoted tourism by foreign Muslims to Muslim areas in China also affects Uyghurs' sense of identity. Urumchi, a largely Han city constructed in the last fifty years, is undergoing an Islamic face-lift with the official endorsement of Central Asian and Islamic architecture. Many visiting foreign Muslim dignitaries are impressed by this, while other foreigners respond to the traditional dances and costumes by which the ethnicity of Uyghurs and other minorities are portrayed in Chinese and foreign travel brochures.

A Japanese tourist recently crossed the Karakoram Range from Pakistan by bicycle in search of the "real" Uyghurs who, a government travel brochure assured him, could only be found in Kashgar. Kashgaris have no difficulty casting themselves as the repositories of unspoiled "Uyghur" traditions, however anomalous that may be, and on this basis eagerly encourage tourists to spend money in their city. The very notion of a "real Uyghur" confirms that in one sense Uyghur nationalists have succeeded and teamed up with tourism agencies. Uyghurs believe they have a 6,000-year cultural and physical history in Xinjiang, of which they are not likely to let go. China's nationality policies have not lessened local people's attachment to the land or their commitment to what they have embraced as their history. Unless new policies are developed and applied, diverse streams of Uyghur opposition may coalesce in such a way as to offer a growing resistance to Chinese control in Xinjiang.

Notes

Notes to Chapter 1

1. Nikolay M. Przhevalsky, *Ot Kuldzhi do Tian-Shan* (Moscow: Gos.izd-vo geograficheskoi literatury, 1947); Peter Sandberg, ed., *C. G. Mannerheimin Valokuvia Aasian-Matkalta, 1906–1908* (Helsinki: Otava, 1990); and Harrison E. Salisbury, *The New Emperors: China in the Era of Mao and Deng* (New York: Avon, 1993).

2. Owen Lattimore, *Pivot of Asia: Sinkiang and the Inner Asian Frontiers of China and Russia* (Boston: Little, Brown, 1950), p. 3.

3. Ferdinand von Richthoven, *China, Ergebnisse eigener Reisen und darauf gegruendeter Studien*, 5 vols. (Berlin: D. Reimer, 1877–1912).

4. *The Economist,* 19 June 1999, p. 69.

5. Justin Jon Rudelson, *Oasis Identities: Uyghur Nationalism along China's Silk Road* (New York: Columbia University Press, 1997).

6. Olivier Roy, *The New Central Asia: The Creation of Nations* (New York: New York University Press, 2000), chapters 4–6.

7. RAND, personal and official communication, RAND Corporation research, 2003.

8. David S. G. Goodman, *China's Provinces in Reform: Class, Community, and Political Culture* (London: Routledge, 1997).

Notes to Chapter 2

1. Henry Yule's *Cathay and the Way Thither,* 4 vols., rev. ed., ed. Henri Cordier (London: Hakluyt Society, 1913–1914) and Cordier's notes in this revised edition are foundational works in this endeavor.

2. PRC materials use the spelling "Uigur"; some Western-language sources use this or "Uighur." Technically, the romanization "Uyghur" best corresponds to the Uyghur language in its modified Arabic script and is preferred by many Uyghurs. We thus use this spelling in this book.

3. See Richard C. Foltz, *Religions of the Silk Road: Overland Trade and Cultural Exchange from Antiquity to the Fifteenth Century* (New York: St. Martin's, 1999); Edward H. Schafer, *The Golden Peaches of Samarkand* (Berkeley: University of California Press, 1963); and Susan Whitfield, *Life along the Silk Road* (Berkeley: University of California Press, 1999).

4. Owen Lattimore, *Inner Asian Frontiers of China* (1940; reprint, Hong Kong: Oxford University Press, 1988); Sechin Jagchid, *Peace, War, and Trade along the Great Wall: Nomadic-Chinese Interaction through Two Millennia* (Bloomington: Indiana University Press, 1989); and Thomas J. Barfield, *The Perilous Frontier: Nomadic Empires and China* (Oxford: Basil Blackwell, 1989).

5. Elizabeth Wayland Barber, *The Mummies of Ürümchi* (New York: Norton, 1999), chapter 4; and Nicola Di Cosmo, "Ancient Xinjiang between Central Asia and China," *Anthropology and Archaeology of Eurasia* (Spring 1996): 87–101.

6. Nicola Di Cosmo, "China on the Eve of the Historical Period," in *The Cambridge History of Ancient China: From the Origins of Civilization to 221 B.C.,* ed. Michael Loewe and Edward Shaughnessy (Cambridge: Cambridge University Press, 1999), pp. 941–944; and Barber, *Mummies of Ürümchi,* pp. 33–34.

7. Though many scholars believe the Yuezhi formed the principal ethnic element in the Kushans, this question has not been fully resolved. In any case, the administrative language of the Kushan empire was no longer Tokharian, but eastern Iranian, generally written in Greek script. See Peter B. Golden, *An Introduction to the History of the Turkic Peoples* (Wiesbaden: Otto Harrassowitz, 1992), pp. 55–56.

8. A. K. Narain, "Indo-Europeans in Inner Asia," in *The Cambridge History of Early Inner Asia,* ed. Dennis Sinor (Cambridge: Cambridge University Press, 1990), pp. 151–176.

9. The first Indo-Europeans were in Greece around 2000 BCE, but the pottery of the Gansu region shows a continuous local development, distinct from elsewhere in China, from 2500 to 250 BCE, when it links with the historical Yuezhi. Tokharian, moreover, most resembles Hittite, which was the earliest offshoot of the Indo-European family.

10. The Xiongnu were probably Turkic speaking "or at least contained Turkic-speaking elements." Yet, some of them at least were Europoid in appearance. See Golden, *Introduction to the History of the Turkic Peoples,* p. 57.

11. A.F.P. Hulsewé and M.A.N. Loewe, *China in Central Asia: The Early Stage: 125 B.C.–A.D. 23* (Leiden: Brill, 1979), p. 49.

12. The Hephthalites appear in Greek and Chinese sources under a variety of different names: Avar, Var, Hua, and Hyōn (Hun), in addition to Hephthalite and its variants. See Dennis Sinor, "The Establishment and Dissolution of the Türk Empire," in *The Cambridge History of Early Inner Asia,* ed. Dennis Sinor (Cambridge: Cambridge University Press, 1990), p. 301.

13. William Samolin, *East Turkestan to the Twelfth Century* (The Hague: Mouton, 1964), pp. 52–58.

14. For a detailed account of the multilateral military struggles in Central Asia in this period, see Christopher I. Beckwith, *The Tibetan Empire in Central Asia: A History of the Struggle for Great Power among Tibetans, Turks, Arabs and Chinese during the Early Middle Ages* (Princeton, N.J.: Princeton University Press, 1987).

15. Quantities of documents detailing Tang period household census, land registration, and labor service have been gathered from the Turpan region by Western, Japanese, and Chinese archaeologists. See Tatsuro Yamamoto and Yoshikazu Dohi, eds., *Tun-huang and Turfan Documents Concerning Social and Economic History,* part II, *Census Registers,* 2 vols. (Tokyo: Tōyō Bunko, 1984–1985).

16. Xue Zongzheng, Ma Guorong, and Tian Weijiang, eds., *Zhongguo Xinjiang gudai shehui shenghuo shi* (Social history of ancient Xinjiang) (Urumchi: Xinjiang renmin, 1997), pp. 327–334, 337–340.

17. Note that originally this term included neither the Tarim basin nor Zungharia. Today, it is sometimes used by Uyghur nationalists as a name for the independent state they wish create in the entirety of the Xinjiang region.

18. Beckwith, *Tibetan Empire in Central Asia,* pp. 155–172; Golden, *Introduction to the History of the Turkic Peoples,* pp. 163–164; Colin Mackerras, "The Uighurs," in *The Cambridge History of Early Inner Asia,* ed. Dennis Sinor (Cambridge: Cambridge University Press, 1990), pp. 317–342; and Xue, Ma, and Tian, *Zhongguo Xinjiang,* pp. 325–326.

19. The precise origins of the Karakhanids are complex and disputed. Component tribes probably included the Yaghma, Chighil, and Tukhsi, as well as remnant Türgesh and the Karluk. Principal scholarship on the question is by W. Barthold, "History of Semireche" in *Four Studies on the History of Central Asia*, Trans. Vladimir and Tatiana Minorsky (Leiden: E.J. Brill, 1956–62), and his entry "Karluk" in *Encyclopaedia of Islam*, 1st ed. I follow Golden, *Introduction to the History of the Turkic Peoples*, pp. 214–216, and Peter B. Golden, "The Karakhanids and Early Islam," in *The Cambridge History of Early Inner Asia*, ed. Dennis Sinor (Cambridge: Cambridge University Press, 1990), pp. 348–351, with additional reference to Chinese sources in Samolin, *East Turkestan to the Twelfth Century*, pp. 76–85. There is another explanation that equates the Islamized Turks of the Karakhanid dynasty with the Toquz Oghuz and thus with the Uyghurs; this has political ramifications today, as discussed later on. The standard dates of the Karakhanid dynasty mask the fact that the Kara Khitay became their overlords beginning in 1125.

20. Dughlat Mirza Muhammad Haidar, *A History of the Moghuls of Central Asia, Being the Tarikh-i-Rashidi of Mirza Muhammad Haidar, Dughlat*, ed. N. Elias and trans. E. Denison Ross (1895; reprint, New York: Barnes and Noble, 1972), p. 287n1; see also W. Barthold, *Turkestan down to the Mongol Invasion*, 3rd ed., trans. Tatiana Minorsky (1900; reprint, London: Luzac, 1968), p. 254, who is an agnostic on the question, and Golden, *Introduction to the History of the Turkic Peoples*, pp. 198–199, 201, where may be found specific references to the Islamic geographers who provide the primary evidence for this interpretation. Compare M. Louis Hambis et al., *L'Asie Centrale: histoire et civilization* (Paris: l'Imprimerie nationale, 1977), p. 24.

21. Turkic and Mongolian are major divisions of the Altayic language family; early speakers of each were centered on what is today Outer Mongolia. To say that the Khitan were speakers of Mongolian is a bit anachronistic, as at this point the Mongols were but one of several tribes speaking Mongolian. The name "Mongolian" is of course applied retroactively to the language branch, as it is to the lands centered on the Orkhon region.

22. Yu Taishan, ed., *Xiyu tongshi* (Survey history of the western regions) (Zhengzhou: Zhongzhou guji chubanshe, 1996), p. 309.

23. Karl A. Wittfogel and Chia-sheng Feng, "Appendix V: Qarâ-Khitâi," in *History of Chinese Society: Liao, Transactions of the American Philosophical Society*, vol. 36 (Philadelphia: American Philosophical Society, 1949), pp. 807–1125; Yu Taishan and Ji Zongan, *Xiliao shilu, Yelü Dashi yanjiu* (Historical discussions of the Western Liao, research on Yelü Dashi) (Urumchi: Xinjiang renmin chubanshe, 1996).

24. Thomas T. Allsen, "The Yüan Dynasty and the Uighurs of Turfan in the 13th Century," in *China among Equals: The Middle Kingdom and Its Neighbors, 10th-14th Centuries*, ed. Morris Rossabi (Berkeley: University of California Press, 1983), pp. 247–248.

25. The sources are mutually contradictory on whether Uyghuristan was included in the Chagatai *ulus* or not. Juvaini, who wrote most completely and closest in time to the post–Genghis Khan dispensation of uluses, implies that the Uyghur iduqqut initially reigned in his own right, directly subordinate to the Great Khan. Later, Uyghuristan was subsumed within the Chaghatai khanate. See Allsen, "Yüan Dynasty," pp. 248–250.

26. Allsen, "Yüan Dynasty," pp. 254–261.

27. A speaker at a forum entitled "China's Emergence in Central Asia: Security, Diplomatic and Economic Interests," held at the Center for Strategic and International Studies in Washington, D.C., repeated this misconception as recently as Febru-

ary 5, 2003, in an address devoted to the historical background of China's Central Asia policy.

28. For example, see the passage, "That the latter Chaghataid princes of Beshbaliq and Turpan repeatedly sought to present *gong* to the Ming court shows us, first, that they saw themselves as Ming vassals [*fanshu*], a member of the Chinese nation [*zhonghua minzu*], and second, that at the same time economically they were mutually inseparable [from China]." See Su Beihai and Huang Jianhua, *Hami, Tulufan Weiwuer wang lishi* (History of the Uyghur kings of Hami and Turfan) (Urumchi: Xinjiang Daxue chubanshe, 1993), p. 154. The Jesuit traveler Bento De Goes witnessed the organization of such a China-bound caravan by the khan in Yarkand in 1603. See C., Wessels, S.J., *Early Jesuit Travellers in Central Asia, 1603–1721* (The Hague: Martinus Nijhoff, 1924), p. 25.

29. Joseph Fletcher, "The Naqshbandiyya in Northwest China," in *Studies on Chinese and Islamic Central Asia,* Variorum Collected Studies Series, by Joseph Fletcher, ed. Beatrice Forbes Manz (Aldershot: Variorum, 1995), pp. 1–45; and Henry G. Schwarz, "The Khwâjas of Eastern Turkestan," *Central Asiatic Journal* 20, no. 4 (1976): 266–296.

30. Yuan Wei, *Shengwuji* (Beijing: Zhonghua shuju, 1984), p. 156.

31. For further information on this conquest period, see Peter C. Perdue, *China Marches West: The Qing Conquest of Central Eurasia, 1680–1760* (Cambridge, Mass.: Harvard University Press, forthcoming).

32. For example, see Molla Musa Sairami, *Tarixi Eminie* (History of peace), ed. Mehemet Zunun (Urumchi: Shinjang xelq neshriyati, 1988). The heroine is known in Chinese as Xiangfei, the fragrant concubine. See James A. Millward, "A Uyghur Muslim in Qianlong's Court: The Meanings of the Fragrant Concubine," *Journal of Asian Studies* 53, no. 2 (May 1994).

33. Perdue, *China Marches West.*

34. Joseph Fletcher, "The Heyday of the Ch'ing Order in Mongolia, Sinkiang, and Tibet," in *The Cambridge History of China,* vol. 10, *Late Ch'ing, 1800–1911,* part I, ed. John K. Fairbank (Cambridge: Cambridge University Press, 1978), p. 375.

Notes to Chapter 3

1. For a more thorough survey of the period covered in this chapter, see James A. Millward, *Xinjiang: A History of Chinese Turkistan* (London: Hurst, forthcoming 2005).

2. Liu Jintang, *Liu xiang le gong zougao* (Memorials of Liu Jintang), vol. 3 (1898; reprint with an introduction by Wu Fengpei, *Zhongguo wenxian shanben chushu* Series, Beijing [?]: Shumu wenxian chubanshe, 1986), p. 44b; and Miao Pusheng, *Boke zhidu* (The Beg system) (Urumchi: Xinjiang renmin chubanshe, 1995), p. 74.

3. Li Hongzhang, *Li wen zhong gong quanji* (Collected letters of Li Hongzhang), 17, cited in Kataoka Kazutada, *Shinchō Shinkyō tōji kenkyū* (Researches on Qing dynasty rule in Xinjiang) (Tokyo: Yū San Kaku, 1991), pp. 133, 146n16.

4. Kataoka, *Shinchō Shinkyō,* pp. 135–136.

5. Hamada Masami, "La Transmission du mouvement nationalist au Turkestan oriental (Xinjiang)," *Central Asian Survey* 9, no. 1 (1978): 28–29; and Zuo Zongtang, *Zuo wen xiang gong quanji, 1888–1897* (Complete collected works of Zuo Zongtang, 1888–1897) (Taipei: Wenhai chubanshe, 1968), zougao, 56, pp. 22b–25a, "Banli Xinjiang shanhou shiyi," quote from p. 22b.

6. Hua Li, *Qingdai Xinjiang nongye kaifa shi* (History of the Qing period agricultural opening of Xinjiang), Bianjiang shidi congshu, no. 5 (Harbin: Heilongjian jiaoyu chubanshe, 1994), pp. 215–218, citing Tao Mo, *Tao le su gong zouyi*, 2, pp. 9–10, and 3, pp. 10–11.

7. The previous section on provincehood and late Qing policies is based largely on Kataoka, *Shinchō Shinkyō*. Regarding the migration of Uyghurs to eastern and northern Xinjiang in the late nineteenth century, Uyghur inhabitants of these areas today and Uyghur intellectuals regard this as a return to Uyghur lands, contending that Zuo's conquest had cleansed the area of sizeable numbers of Uyghurs. According to the Korean scholar Kim Ho-dong's account, however, it was mainly Tungans who bore the brunt of the Qing reconquest in the Urumchi area. Qing dynasty records of the eighteenth and early nineteenth centuries indicate concentrations of Uyghur population in Turpan and Hami, but not in Urumchi and the string of new settlements north of that city. See Kim Ho-Dong, *Holy War in China: The Muslim Rebellion and State in Chinese Central Asia, 1864–1877* (Stanford, Calif.: Stanford University Press, 2003).

8. See David Bello, "Opium in Xinjiang and Beyond," in *Opium Regimes: China, Britain and Japan, 1839–1952,* ed. Timothy Brook and Bob Tadashi (Berkeley: University of California Press, 2000), pp. 127–151.

9. Zeng Wenwu, *Zhongguo jingying Xiyu shi* (History of China's management of the western regions) (1936; reprint, Urumchi: Xinjiang Weiwu'er zizhiqu zongbian shi, 1986), p. 532.

10. Kataoka, *Shinchō Shinkyō,* pp. 348–356; and Andrew D. W. Forbes, *Warlords and Muslims in Chinese Central Asia: A Political History of Republican Xinjiang, 1911–1949* (Cambridge: Cambridge University Press, 1986), pp. 11–13.

11. Aitchen Wu, *Turkestan Tumult* (London: Methuen, 1940; reprint, Hong Kong: Oxford University Press, 1984), p. 38 (page citations are to the reprint edition); and Owen Lattimore, *Pivot of Asia: Sinkiang and the Inner Asian Frontiers of China and Russia* (Boston: Little, Brown, 1950), pp. 52–64.

12. This story appears in several sources; the most colorful English account is in Aitchen Wu, *Turkestan Tumult,* pp. 43–44.

13. Olivier Roy, *The New Central Asia: The Creation of Nations* (New York: New York University Press, 2000), pp. 39–40.

14. Chen Chao, "Fan Yisilanzhuyi, Fan Tujuezhuyi zai Xinjiangde zaoqi chuanbo yu Yang Zengxin de duice," in *Fan Yisilanzhuyi, Fan Tujue Zhuyi Yanjiu Lunwenji,* ed. Yang Faren (Urumchi: N.p., 1993), p. 44; and Zeng Wenwu, *Zhongguo jingying Xiyu shi,* p. 605.

15. Bai Zhensheng and Koibuchi Shinichi, eds., *Xinjiang xiandai zhengzhi shehui shilue* (Brief history of contemporary Xinjiang political and social history) (Beijing: Zhonguo shehui kexue yuan chubanshe, 1992), pp. 122–124; Lattimore, *Pivot of Asia,* pp. 58–59; and Forbes, *Warlords and Muslims.*

16. Forbes, *Warlords and Muslims,* pp. 28–29; Lattimore, *Pivot of Asia,* p. 59; Li Sheng, *Xinjiang dui Su (E) Maoyi shi 1600–1900* (A history of Xinjiang's trade with the Soviet Union [Russia], 1600–1990) (Urumchi: Xinjiang renmin chubanshe, 1993), p. 324, cited in Linda Benson and Ingvar Svanberg, *China's Last Nomads: The History and Culture of China's Kazaks* (Armonk, N.Y.: Sharpe, 1998), p. 64; and Chen Huisheng, *Minguo Xinjiang shi* (History of Xinjiang in the Chinese Republican period) (Urumchi: Xinjiang renmin chubanshe, 1999), pp. 189–200.

17. Shirip Hushtar, "Musabayow we uning soda karxanisi" (Musabayow and his corporation), in *Hüseyniye rohi: Teklimakandiki oyghinish* (The Hüseyn Musabayow

Spirit: Awakening of the Taklimakan), ed. Seypidin Ezizi et al. (Urumchi: Shinjang Xelq Neshiryati, 2000), pp. 210–215.

18. Yalqun Rozi and Mirehmet Seyit, *Memtili Ependi* (Mr. Memtili) (Urumchi: Shinjang Uniwersiteti Neshiryati, 1997), pp. 20–23; and Chen Chao, "Fan Yisilanzhuyi, Fan Tujuezhuyi," pp. 40–42.

19. Yi-bu-la-yin Mu-yi-ti (Ibrahim Muhiti), "Huiyi qimeng yundong de xianquzhe, Mai-he-su-ti Mu-yi-ti" (Remembering a leader in the enlightenment movement, Mahsud Muhiti), in *Xinjiang wenshi ziliao xuanji,* vol. 13 (Urumchi: Xinjiang renmin chubanshe, 1985 [Chinese edition]), pp. 91–96.

20. Altishahr means "six cities," that is, those of the western Tarim basin.

21. M. Rozibaqiyev, *Uyghur helqining Munewer Perzendi* (Educated son of the Uyghur people) (Alma-Ata: Qazaqistan Neshiryati, 1987), pp. 33–34; and M. Kabirov, *Istoria Uygurov Sovetskogo Kazahstana* (History of the Uyghurs in Soviet Kazakstan) (Alma-Ata: N.p., 1968), pp. 130–170.

22. Xie Bin, *Xinjiang youji* (Record of Xinjiang travels) (1925; reprint in *Minguo congshu* [Republican period collectanea] 2 bian, no. 87 [lishi, dili lei], Shanghai: Shanghai shudian, 1990), pp. 78, 80.

23. Forbes, *Warlords and Muslims,* pp. 42–46; and Chen Huisheng, *Minguo Xinjiang shi,* pp. 248–249.

24. Abdurehim Otkur, *Oyghanghan Zimin* (The awakened land), 2 vols. (Urumchi: Shinjang Xelq Neshiryati, 1986, 1994), vol. 1, pp. 130–190.

25. See especially Forbes, *Warlords and Muslims;* and Aitchen Wu, *Turkestan Tumult.*

26. Bay Aziz (Bai-ai-ze-zi), "Tulupan nongmin baodong," in *Ma Zhongying zai Xinjiang* (Ma Zhongying in Xinjiang), Xinjiang wenshi ziliao, no. 26 (Urumchi: Xinjiang renmin chubanshe, 1994), pp. 55–60; and Shinmen Yasushi, "'Higashi Torukusitan kyōwakoku' (1933–34 nen) ni kansuru ichi kōsatsu" (An inquiry into the Eastern Turkestan Republic of 1933–34), Ajia-Afurika gengo bunka kenkyū (30th anniversary commemorative number 1), nos. 46–47 (Tokyo: gaigokugo daigaku Ajia-Afurika gengo bunka kenkyujo, 1994), pp. 5–6.

27. Lars-Eric Nyman, *Great Britain and Chinese, Russian and Japanese Interests in Sinkiang, 1918–1934* (Stockholm: Esselte Studium, 1977), pp. 75, 78.

28. Muhemmed Imin Bughra, *Sherqi Turkistan Tarixi* (History of Eastern Turkistan) (Kabul: N.p., 1940; reprint, Ankara: N.p., 1998), p. 395 (page citations are to the reprint edition). On Abduhaliq Uyghur, see Justin Jon Rudelson, *Oasis Identities: Uyghur Nationalism along China's Silk Road* (New York: Columbia University Press, 1997), pp. 145–153.

29. Shinmen, "'Higashi Torukusitan kyōwakoku,'" p. 6. The best-known English-language account of this period, Forbes's *Warlords and Muslims,* depicts Bughra and the Khotan emirate as fanatical Islamist conservative (pp. 83–87). However, in his own history, published in 1940, Bughra stresses nationalistic, not religious, goals— including the establishment of a new educational system for the Khotan government (an item in the jadidist agenda). His book neither preaches pan-Islamism nor advocates Islamic jihad. See Bughra, *Sherqi Turkistan Tarixi,* pp. 462–464, 468. However, neither was the Khotan government a secular regime: It issued coins inscribed with "Hoten Jumhuryeti Islamiye" (Khotan Islamic Republic).

30. Shinmen, "'Higashi Torukusitan kyōwakoku'"; and Abduqadir Haji, "1933– 1937 Yilighiche Qeshqer, Xoten, Aqsularda bolup otken weqeler" (Events of 1931– 1937 in Kashgar, Khotan and Aksu), *Shinjang Tarixi Materyalliri* (Xinjiang historical

materials), no. 17 (Urumchi: Shinjang Xelq Neshiryati, 1986), pp. 60–62.

31. People's Republic of China State Council Information Office, "East Turkistan Separatists Will Not Get Away with Impunity," English version; white paper released January 21, 2002, downloaded from www.china.org.cn (accessed 25 January 2002); see also Forbes, *Warlords and Muslims,* pp. 83–89 et passim.

32. Shinmen, "'Higashi Torukusitan kyōwakoku'"; Abduqadir, "1933–1937 Yilighiche Qeshqer, Xoten, Aqsularda bolup otken weqeler," pp. 60–62; and Chen Huisheng, *Minguo Xinjiang shi,* p. 283.

33. Nabijan Tursun, personal interview with Gholamidin Pahta.

34. P. Aptekar, "Ot zheltorossii do vostochno-turkestanskoi respubliki" (From Yellow Russia to Eastern Turkestan Republic), www.narod.ru (accessed 16 October 2001) and http://rkka.vif2.ru/oper/sinc/sinc (accessed 5 November 2001).

35. Shinmen, "'Higashi Torukusitan kyōwakoku,'" p. 38, citing Muhämmät Imin Qurban, "Qeshqer tarixidiki Féwral paciesi," in *Shinjang Tarix Matiriyalliri,* vol. 12 (Urumchi: Shinjang Helq Neshriyati, 1983), pp. 167–181.

36. Tang Yongcai, ed., *Ma Zhongying zai Xinjiang* (Ma Zhongying in Xinjiang). *Xinjiang wenshi ziliao,* no. 26 (Urumchi: Xinjiang renmin chubanshe, 1994). The solution to the puzzle of Ma Zhongying's disappearance into the Soviet Union awaits a researcher in the Soviet archives.

37. Rudelson, *Oasis Identities,* p. 149.

38. One opponent was Muhemmed Imin Bughra. See Linda Benson, *The Ili Rebellion: The Moslem Challenge to Chinese Authority in Xinjiang, 1944–1949* (Armonk, N.Y.: Sharpe, 1990), p. 31.

39. A. Narenbayev, "Uygursikie misliteli" (Uygur thinkers), in *Glavnaia Kirgizskaia Ensiklopediia* (Bishkek: N.p., 1995), pp. 61–70; and Iliyev Exmet, "1937–1938 yillardiki weqeler" (Events of 1937–1938), in *Yengi Hayat* (Almaty), 15 February 1997.

40. Benson, *Ili Rebellion,* p. 28; Forbes, *Warlords and Muslims,* pp. 157–162; and Lattimore, *Pivot of Asia,* p. 74. Allen Whiting interviewed Sheng in Taiwan and reprints Sheng's own account of these events in Allen S. Whiting and Sheng Shih-ts'ai, *Sinkiang: Pawn or Pivot?* (East Lansing: Michigan State University Press, 1958).

41. Whiting and Sheng, *Sinkiang,* p. 98; Lattimore, *Pivot of Asia,* pp. 79, 83–84, 106; Benson, *Ili Rebellion,* pp. 38–39; and Chen Huisheng, *Minguo Xinjiang shi,* p. 381.

42. Benson, *Ili Rebellion,* p. 36; Chen Huisheng, *Minguo Xinjiang shi,* p. 385; Forbes, *Warlords and Muslims,* pp. 163–170; and David Wang, *Under the Soviet Shadow: The Yining Incident, Ethnic Conflicts and International Rivalry in Xinjiang, 1944–1949* (Hong Kong: Chinese University Press, 1999), pp. 89–90.

43. Benson, *Ili Rebellion,* pp. 36–37, 62; Chen Huisheng, *Minguo Xinjiang shi,* pp. 384–385, 388; and Lattimore, *Pivot of Asia,* p. 156.

44. The U.S. consular report is cited in Benson, *Ili Rebellion,* p. 45.

45. Abdurup Mehsum, former cabinet member of the ETR, interview by Nabijan Tursun, Almaty, November 2001 and November 2002; Aytogan Yunichi, Tatar colonel in ETR forces, interview by Nabijan Tursun, Almaty, January 2003; and Esiet Teyipov, editor-in-chief of the ETR paper *The People's Voice,* interview by Nabijan Tursun, Almaty, November 2001.

46. The following account of the second ETR and coalition government period is drawn from Benson, *Ili Rebellion;* Forbes, *Warlords and Muslims;* Roostam Sadri, "The Islamic Republic of Eastern Turkestan: A Commemorative Review," *Institute of*

Muslim Minority Affairs 5, no. 2 (July 1984): 294–319; and Wang, *Under the Soviet Shadow.* Millward, *Xinjiang,* chapter 4, contains a synthetic account more detailed than what is presented here.

47. Both Forbes (*Warlords and Muslims,* pp. 193–195) and Wang (*Under the Soviet Shadow,* pp. 69–70) link the halt of the ETR offensive with these treaties.

48. In *Xinjiang Ribao* (Urumchi), 14 August 1947, cited in Forbes, *Warlords and Muslims,* pp. 199–200.

49. For full biographies of these men, see Linda Benson, "Uygur Politicians of the 1940s: Mehmet Emin Bugra, Isa Yusuf Alptekin and Mesut Sabri," *Central Asia Survey* 10, no. 4 (1991): 87–113.

50. Chen Yanqi, "Xinjiang Sanqu geming zhengfu jingji gongzuo shuping" (Description and evaluation of the economic work of the government of the Three Districts revolution), in *Zhongguo Weiwuer lishi wenhua yanjiu luncong* (Collected research articles on Chinese Uyghur history and culture), ed. Liu Zhixiao, no. 1 (Urumchi: Xinjiang renmin chubanshe, 1998); Benson, *Ili Rebellion,* pp. 144–151 (the U.S. consular report of Robert Ward is cited p. 149n83); and Seypullayuf Seydulla, "Shanliq Seipe" (Pleasant leaf), *Shinjang Tarixi Materyalliri* (Shinjang Xelq Neshiryati), no. 41 (1999): 50–63. For a negative assessment of the Ili regime's social and economic achievements, see Wang, *Under the Soviet Shadow,* pp. 321–336.

51. Ted Gup, *Book of Honor: Covert Lives and Classified Deaths at the CIA* (New York: Doubleday, 2000), chapter 1.

52. Sadri, "Islamic Republic of Eastern Turkestan"; Forbes, *Warlords and Muslims,* pp. 221–223; Chen Huisheng, *Minguo Xinjiang shi,* p. 443; and Seypidin Ezizi, *Omur Dastani* (Poetry of life) (Beijing: Milletler neshriyati, 1991), p. 467.

53. Sadri, "Islamic Republic of Eastern Turkestan," p. 313; Wahidi Hashir et al., "Masud Ependi Heqqide Heqiqet" (The truth about Mr. Masud Sabiri), *Yengi Hayat* (Almaty), 21 September 1991, pp. 3, 5, 7, 10, 12, 14, 17, 19. On the Sino-Soviet joint-stock companies in Xinjiang, see Forbes, *Warlords and Muslims,* p. 226; and Donald H. McMillen, *Chinese Communist Power and Policy in Xinjiang, 1949–1977* (Boulder, Colo.: Westview, 1979), pp. 34–35.

54. McMillen, *Chinese Communist Power,* pp. 131–136. On collectivization of the Kazaks in Xinjiang, see Benson and Svanberg, *China's Last Nomads,* pp. 113–116, 134–135. Note that in the Soviet Union, "Sovietization" of Kazaks likewise involved a continuation of clan structures under new names. See Roy, *New Central Asia.*

55. This section on Islam is based on Wang Jianping, "Islam in Kashgar in the 1950s" (unpublished manuscript).

56. On Xinjiang's bingtuan and population figures listed here, see McMillen, *Chinese Communist Power,* pp. 56–57, 61–66; James D. Seymour, "Xinjiang's Production and Construction Corps, and the Sinification of Eastern Turkestan," *Inner Asia* 2, no. 2 (2000): 171–193; Lynn T. White, "The Road to Urumchi: Approved Institutions in Search of Attainable Goals during Pre-1968 Rustication from Shanghai," *China Quarterly,* no. 79 (September 1979): 481–510; and Zhao Yuzheng, *Xinjiang tunken* (Xinjiang land reclamation) (Urumchi: Xinjiang renmin chubanshe, 1991), p. 332.

57. Statements to this effect appear in the 1931 Chinese "Soviet" constitution, Mao Zedong's 1935 "Resolution on Current Political Situation and Party Tasks," and his 1936 "Declaration of the Soviet Central Government to the Muslim People." See Walker Connor, *The National Question in Marxist-Leninist Theory and Strategy* (Princeton, N.J.: Princeton University Press, 1984), p. 81. Our thanks for this reference to Gardner Bovingdon, who also discusses the issue in Gardner Bovingdon,

"Strangers in Their Own Land: The Politics of Uyghur Identity in Chinese Central Asia" (Ph.D. diss., Cornell University, 2002).

58. Zhu Peimin, *Ershi shiji Xinjiang shi yanjiu* (Research on Xinjiang's twentieth-century history) (Urumchi: Xinjiang renmin chubanshe, 2000), p. 335.

59. Benson and Svanberg, *China's Last Nomads,* pp. 95–100; June Teufel Dreyer, *China's Forty Million: Minority Nationalities and National Integration in the People's Republic of China* (Cambridge, Mass.: Harvard University Press, 1976), pp. 95–98, 104–106; Colin Mackerras, *China's Minorities: Integration and Modernization in the Twentieth Century* (Hong Kong: Oxford University Press, 1994), pp. 141–143; and McMillen, *Chinese Communist Power,* pp. 44, 68–69.

60. McMillen, *Chinese Communist Power,* pp. 86–88.

61. Ibid., pp. 92–94, 117; Benson and Svanberg, *China's Last Nomads,* p. 136; and Zhu, *Ershi shiji,* p. 335.

62. Sadri, "Islamic Republic of Eastern Turkestan," p. 315; and Zhu, *Ershi shiji,* pp. 351–352.

63. Zhu, *Ershi shiji,* pp. 280–281, 290, 293–295. Zhu argues that that most serious famine incident, in Bai county, was due not to absolute shortages but to local officials refusing for political reasons to release stockpiled grain.

64. Benson and Svanberg, *China's Last Nomads,* pp. 117, table 4.2, 136; see also George Moseley, *A Sino-Soviet Cultural Frontier: The Ili Kazak Autonomous Chou* (Cambridge, Mass.: East Asian Research Center, Harvard University, 1966).

65. Wang Enmao, cited in Moseley, *Sino-Soviet Cultural Frontier,* p. 77, see also pp. 105–106; McMillen, *Chinese Communist Power,* pp. 122–123, 138–143; and Zhu, *Ershi shiji,* pp. 285–289.

66. Benson and Svanberg, *China's Last Nomads,* p. 104; McMillen, *Chinese Communist Power,* pp. 122–123, 157–162; Moseley, *Sino-Soviet Cultural Frontier,* pp. 108–109; and Zhao Yuzheng, *Xinjiang tunken,* pp. 212–213.

67. McMillen, *Chinese Communist Power,* pp. 48, 96, 149–150.

68. McMillen, in *Chinese Communist Power,* provides a detailed account of political and military aspects of Cultural Revolution in the Han areas of Xinjiang; see also Dreyer, *China's Forty Millions,* p. 214; Seymour, "Xinjiang's Production and Construction Corps," pp. 175–181; and Zhu, *Ershi shiji,* pp. 310–316.

69. Zhu, *Ershi shiji,* pp. 314–316.

70. Seymour, "Xinjiang's Production and Construction Corps," pp. 181–182.

71. An *Economist* obituary (21 April 2001) eulogizes Wang Enmao's career in Xinjiang.

72. Zhu, *Ershi shiji,* p. 323.

73. Li Ze et al., "Xinjiang minzu fenliezhuyi yanjiu" (Research on separatism among Xinjiang nationalities), in *Fanysilanzhuyi, fantujuezhuyi yanjiu* (Research on pan-Islamism and pan-Turkism) (n.p., n.d.), pp. 209–210 (this manuscript circulates in photocopy form outside of China).

74. McMillen, *Chinese Communist Power,* p. 298.

75. Mackerras, *China's Minorities,* p. 152.

Notes to Chapter 4

1. Morris Rossabi, "Muslim and Central Asian Revolts," in *From Ming to Ch'ing,* ed. Jonathan D. Spence and John E. Wills Jr. (New Haven, Conn.: Yale University Press, 1979).

2. The best "Uyghur nationalist" retelling of this unbroken descent from Karakoram is in the document "Brief History of the Uyghurs," originating from the Eastern Turkestani Union in Europe, www.geocites.com/CapitolHill/1730/buh.html (accessed 10 May 2002). For a recent review and critique, including historical evidence for the multiethnic background of the contemporary Uyghurs, see Dru C. Gladney, "Ethnogenesis and Ethnic Identity in China: Considering the Uygurs and Kazaks," in *The Bronze Age and Early Iron Age People of Eastern Central Asia*, vol. 2, ed. Victor Mair (Washington, D.C.: Institute for the Study of Man, 1998), pp. 812–834. For a discussion of the recent archaeological evidence derived from DNA dating of the desiccated corpses of Xinjiang, see Victor Mair, introduction to *The Bronze Age and Early Iron Age People of Eastern Central Asia*, vol. 2, ed. Victor Mair, pp. 1–40.

3. Joseph Fletcher, "China and Central Asia, 1368–1884," in *The Chinese World Order*, ed. John K. Fairbank (Cambridge, Mass.: Harvard University Press, 1968), p. 364n96.

4. The best discussion of the politics and importance of Xinjiang during this period is that of an eyewitness and participant, Owen Lattimore, in his *Pivot of Asia: Sinkiang and the Inner Asian Frontiers of China and Russia* (Boston: Little, Brown, 1950).

5. Linda Benson, *The Ili Rebellion: The Moslem Challenge to Chinese Authority in Xinjiang, 1944–1949* (Armonk, N.Y.: Sharpe, 1990).

6. Andrew D. W. Forbes, *Warlords and Muslims in Chinese Central Asia* (Cambridge: Cambridge University Press, 1986).

7. Justin Jon Rudelson, *Oasis Identities: Uighur Nationalism along China's Silk Road* (New York: Columbia University Press, 1998), p. 8. For Uyghur ethnogenesis, see also Jack Chen, *The Sinkiang Story* (New York: Macmillan, 1977), p. 57; and Dru C. Gladney, "The Ethnogenesis of the Uighur," *Central Asian Survey* 9, no. 1 (1990): 1–28.

8. For more information on the State Ethnic Affairs Commission, see Dru C. Gladney, *Muslim Chinese* (Cambridge, Mass.: Harvard University Press, 1996), pp. 261–288; June Dreyer, *China's Forty Million: Minority Nationalities and National Integration in the People's Republic of China* (Cambridge, Mass.: Harvard University Press, 1976), pp. 95–96; and Barry Sautman, "Legal Reform and Minority Rights in China," in *Handbook of Global Legal Policy*, ed. Stuart Nagel (New York: Marcel Dekker, 1999), pp. 49–80. Note that in the late 1990s the State Commission changed the English translation of its name from "State Commission for Nationality Affairs" to the "State Ethnic Affairs Commission," reflecting evolving debates in China about the translation of the term "minzu" into English and state policy toward minorities; see Gladney, *Muslim Chinese*, pp. 84–87.

9. The debate over the translation and meaning of "minzu" has become an intellectual industry in and of itself. See Prasenjit Duara, *Rescuing History from the Nation* (Chicago: University of Chicago Press, 1995); and Gladney, *Muslim Chinese*, pp. 6–20.

10. Forbes, *Warlords and Muslims*, pp. 157–159.

11. Mao Zedong, "Appeal of the Central Government to the Muslims," *Tou-cheng* 1–3, no. 105 (12 July, 1936): 1–3.

12. Edgar Snow, *Red Star over China* (New York: Grove, 1938), p. 320.

13. Sautman, "Legal Reform and Minority Rights in China," pp. 49–80.

14. Walker Connor, *The National Question in Marxist-Leninist Theory and Strategy* (Princeton, N.J.: Princeton University Press, 1984), p. 89.

15. Dreyer, *China's Forty Million,* p. 17.

16. Connor, *National Question,* p. 89.

17. Ibid., p. 38.

18. Claude Lefort, *The Political Forms of Modern Society: Bureaucracy, Democracy, and Totalitarianism,* ed. Roger B. Thompson (Cambridge: Polity, 1986), pp. 279–280.

19. Benson argues persuasively that the so-called peaceful liberation was anything but peaceful and the 100,000 or so troops under the Guomindang at the time gave the local people no choice but to "invite" the PLA in to "liberate" Xinjiang. They really had no choice in the matter. See Linda Benson, "Peaceful Liberation of Xinjiang Region" (paper presented to the annual meeting of the Association of Asian Studies, 20 March 1998).

20. The best account of the Uyghur diaspora in Central Asia, their memories of migration, and their longing for a separate Uyghur homeland is contained in the video documentary by Sean R. Roberts, *Waiting for Uighurstan* (Los Angeles: University of Southern California, Center for Visual Anthropology, 1996), filmstrip.

21. Rym Brahimi, "Russia, China, and Central Asian Leaders Pledge to Fight Terrorism, Drug Smuggling," CNN News Service, 25 August 1999, www.uygur.org/ enorg/wunn99/990825e.html (accessed 10 May 2002).

22. "Kasakistan Government Deport Political Refugees to China," Eastern Turkistan Information Center (Munich), 15 June 1999, www.uygur.org/enorg/reports99/ 990615.html (accessed 10 May 2002).

23. Dru Gladney, *Ethnic Identity in China* (New York: Wadsworth, 1998), pp. 20–25.

24. Ma Weiliang, quoted in Judith Banister, *China's Changing Population* (Stanford, Calif.: Stanford University Press, 1987), pp. 315–316.

25. For China's minority integration program, see Colin Mackerras, *China's Minorities: Integration and Modernization in the Twentieth Century* (Hong Kong: Oxford University Press, 1994).

26. Forbes, *Warlords and Muslims,* pp. 56–90.

27. See the discussion of population numbers in "Population of Eastern Turkistan: The Population in Local Records," Eastern Turkistan Information Center (Munich), n.d., www.uygur.org/enorg/turkistan/nopus.html (accessed 10 May 2002). A useful guide with tables and breakdowns is found in "How Has the Population Distribution Changed in Eastern Turkestan since 1949?" International Taklamakan Human Rights Association, n.d., www.taklamakan.org/uighur-L/et_faq_pl.html (accessed 15 May 2002), where it is reported that the Xinjiang Uyghur population declined from 75 percent in 1949 to 48 percent in 1990. The problem with these statistics is that the first reliable total population count in the region did not take place until 1982, with all earlier estimates highly suspect, according to the authoritative study by Banister, *China's Changing Population.*

28. The late Uyghur historian Ibrahim Muti'i in an unpublished 1989 paper provides an excellent historical synopsis of the role of the Central Asian Islamic Madrassah in traditional Uyghur education. Muti'i argues that it was the madrassah, more than religious or cultural continuities, that most tied the Uyghur into Central Asian traditions. See Ibrahim Muti'i, conversation with author, May 1989.

29. James P. Dorian, Brett Wigdortz, and Dru Gladney, "Central Asia and Xinjiang, China: Emerging Energy, Economic, and Ethnic Relations," *Central Asian Survey* 16, no. 4 (1997): 469.

30. Ibid., pp. 461–486.

31. See Keith Bradsher, "China Wrestles with Dependence on Foreign Oil," *International Herald Tribune,* 4 September 2002, p. 1.

32. Ahmed Rashid and Trish Saywell, "Beijing Gusher: China Pays Hugely to Bag Energy Supplies Abroad," 26 February 1998, cited in Turkistan News and Information Network, [TURKISTAN-N] TN 3 (10 June 1999): 135.

33. Ahmet Türköz, interview with the author, Istanbul, 7 April 1997.

34. Dorian, Wigdortz, and Gladney, "Central Asia and Xinjiang, China," p. 480.

Notes to Chapter 5

1. I would like to acknowledge the assistance of Itamar Livni, Ran Shauli, Ofer Ben-Zvi, and Zhang Hongbo, for which I am grateful.

2. *South China Morning Post,* 26 September 2001; and Associated Press of Pakistan, *News Summary,* 27 September 2001, pp. 5–6, www.pak.gov.pk/public/news/app/app27_sep.htm#10 (accessed 29 September 2001). Some reports said that four or even ten divisions have been transferred from Urumchi to Tashkurghan, where the number of troops suddenly doubled. While there is no doubt that reinforcements have been rushed to the border area, the numbers are much overstated.

3. Report from Oliver August, in *Turkistan Newsletter,* 28 September 2001. In addition to crack People's Armed Police Force troops sent from Urumchi, demolition, telecommunication, and civil crime experts from Beijing have reportedly arrived in Kashgar to deal with potential terrorist acts and to train local policemen. See http://news.creaders.net/newreader.php?idx=78851 (accessed 25 September 2001).

4. Erik Eckholm, "China Seeks World Support in Fight with Its Muslim Separatists," *New York Times,* 12 October 2001; see also Amnesty International Press Release, ASA 17/032/2001, *News Service,* no. 181, 11 October 2001.

5. See http://ofind.sina.com.tw/cgi-bin/news/mkNews.cgi?ID=4092545&Loc=TW (accessed 24 October 2001); see also in ID=4156293&Loc=TW and ID=4156597&Loc=TW (accessed 8 November 2001).

6. *Washington Times,* 3 August 2001; *Financial Times,* 15 August 2001; and *Jiefangjun Bao* (Liberation Army Daily), 2 August 2001, http://news.creaders.net/newsreader.php?idx=17299 (accessed 30 September 2001). More data and photographs are at www.pladaily.com.cn, 14 September 2001 (accessed 30 September 2001); and Uighur Information Agency, 26 August 2001, based on www.cmilitary.com (accessed 20 September 2001).

7. Eastern Turkistan Information Center report, 3 September 2000, www.uygur.org/spark/archiv/2/7/7.html (accessed 20 September 2001).

8. Xinjiang's territory equals that of France, Germany, the United Kingdom, Italy, and Spain combined.

9. The MUCD (*junshi danwei daihao*) are five-digit numbers assigned to units of regimental level and above. In October 2000, this system was changed. All MUCD numbers in this chapter reflect the older system. See Dennis J. Blasko, "PLA Ground Forces: Moving toward a Smaller, More Rapidly Deployable, Modern Combined Arms Force," in *The People's Liberation Army as Organization: Reference Volume,* ed. James C. Mulvenon and Andrew N. D. Yang (Santa Barbara, Calif.: RAND, 2002), p. 326.

10. You Ji, *The Armed Forces of China* (St. Leonards, Australia: Allen and Unwin, 1999), pp. 31–37; and Yitzhak Shichor, "Demobilisation: The Dialectics of PLA Troop Reduction," *China Quarterly,* no. 146 (June 1996): 336–359.

15

11. See www.webspawner.com/users/andrewkc/, 9 June 2001 (accessed 13 June 2001); and www.china-defense.com/orbat/pla_div_list_rev34/lanzhou_mr.html (accessed 30 July 2001).

12. Constructed in 1965, the Hotan Airfield has three mountain-cave sheds, with each housing seven MiGs. See Chao Chia, *A Perspective Review of the Maoist Regime's Rearmament and War Preparations* (Taipei: World Anti-Communist League, China Chapter, 1970). According to IATA Airport Codes, there are at least eleven airports in Xinjiang: Korla (KRL), Kashgar (KHG), Yining (YIN), Hotan (HTN), Aksu (AKU), Urumchi (URC), Hami (AMI), Karamay (KRY), Kuqa (KCA), Qiemo (IQM), and Tiwu (YIW). While these are civilian airports, they are most probably also being used by the military.

13. Ken Allen, "PLA Air Force Organization," in *The People's Liberation Army as Organization: Reference Volume,* ed. James C. Mulvenon and Andrew N. D. Yang (Santa Barbara, Calif.: RAND, 2002), p. 448.

14. Jiao Ran and Xu Junfeng, "A Great Feat and a World Wonder," *Xinhua* (Beijing), 18 August 1996.

15. "The World Bank and the Chinese Military," www.laogai.org/reports/worldbank.htm (accessed 7 September 2001). All the examples given in this source reinforce the conclusion that the XPCC has indeed been involved in internal security and border control missions, yet never as a regular military force.

16. James D. Seymour, "Xinjiang's Production and Construction Corps, and the Sinification of Eastern Turkestan," *Inner Asia,* no. 2 (2000): 182–183.

17. Tai Ming Cheung, "Guarding China's Domestic Front Line: The People's Armed Police and China's Stability," *China Quarterly,* no. 146 (June 1996): 532; and Murray Scot Tanner, "The Institutional Lessons of Disaster: Reorganizing the People's Armed Police after Tiananmen," in *The People's Liberation Army as Organization: Reference Volume,* ed. James C. Mulvenon and Andrew N. D. Yang (Santa Barbara, Calif.: RAND, 2002), pp. 587–635.

18. For example, following the disturbances in Yining in February 1997, Beijing allegedly sent five PLA and PAPF divisions, altogether 50,000 to 60,000 troops, from Lanzhou to Xinjiang. See *Ping Kuo Jih Pao* (Hong Kong), 19 April 1997; and *The World Uyghur Network News (WUNN),* no. 35 (23 April 1997): 4–5.

19. David D. Wang, *Under the Soviet Shadow: The Yining Incident, Ethnic Conflicts and International Rivalry in Xinjiang, 1944–1949* (Hong Kong: Chinese University Press, 1999).

20. Linda Benson, quoted by Thomas Laird, *Into Tibet: The CIA's First Atomic Spy and His Secret Expedition to Lhasa* (New York: Grove, 2002), p. 148. This is the most comprehensive study of these attempts. See also NSC 37/8, 6 October 1949, *Documents of the National Security Council,* Film 438, Reel 1; Thomas J. Christensen, *Useful Adversaries: Grand Strategy, Domestic Mobilization, and Sino-American Conflict, 1947–1958* (Princeton, N.J.: Princeton University Press, 1996), p. 106; and "Draft Report by the National Security Council on Supplementary Measures with Respect to Formosa," *Foreign Relations of the United States, 1949,* Vol. 9, *Far East: China* (Washington, D.C.: U.S. Government Printing Office, 1974), pp. 291–292. For Chinese documents, see Zhang Yuxi and Zhu Bian, comps., *Xinjiang Pingpan Jiaofei* (The suppression of bandits and rebels in Xinjiang) (Urumchi: Xinjiang renmin chubanshe, 2000).

21. William W. Whitson, with Chen-hsia Huang, *The Chinese High Command: A History of Communist Military Politics, 1927–71* (London: Macmillan, 1973), chart A, B, map 2.

22. A recent visit to Xinjiang demonstrated yet again that, despite the extensive construction of railroads and highways (e.g., the Urumchi-Kuitun Highway), Xinjiang's transportation infrastructure is still quite backward.

23. Whitson, *Chinese High Command,* pp. 367, 466–468.

24. This and the following are based on *Dangdai Zhongguo Jundui de Junshi Gongzuo* (China today: The military affairs of the Chinese army), vol. 2 (Beijing: Zhongguo shehui kexue chubanshe, 1989), pp. 38–45.

25. Donald H. McMillen, "The Urumqi Military Region: Defense and Security in China's West," *Asian Survey* 22, no. 8 (August 1982): 729n9.

26. Ngok Lee, *China's Defence Modernisation and Military Leadership* (Sydney: Australian National University Press, 1989), pp. 159–160, 267.

27. *Directory of People's Republic of China Military Personalities* (n.p., October 1999), pp. 130–131.

28. Jack Chen, *The Sinkiang Story* (New York: Macmillan, 1977), pp. 267–268, 319.

29. Lee Fu-hsiang, "The Turkic-Moslem Problem in Sinkiang: A Case Study of the Chinese Communists Nationality Policy" (Ph.D. diss., Rutgers University, 1973), p. 230.

30. J. Malcolm Mackintosh, "The Soviet Generals' View of China in the 1960s," in *Sino-Soviet Military Relations,* ed. Raymond L. Garthoff (New York: Praeger, 1966), p. 184.

31. Lee, "Turkic-Moslem Problem in Sinkiang," p. 231nn172–173.

32. Central Intelligence Agency, "Military Forces along the Sino-Soviet Border," *Intelligence Memorandum,* SR IM 70–5 (January 1970), Top Secret (declassified and sanitized), p. 5.

33. Harry Gelman, *The Soviet Far East Buildup and Soviet Risk-Taking against China* (Santa Monica, Calif.: RAND, August 1982), pp. 66–67.

34. Whitson, *Chinese High Command,* pp. 490–491, 605n64; and International Institute of Strategic Studies, *The Military Balance, 1970–1971* (London: Institute for Strategic Studies, 1970).

35. Harvey Nelsen, "Military Forces in the Cultural Revolution," *China Quarterly,* no. 51 (July–September 1972): 444–447.

36. Gerald Segal, *Defending China* (Oxford: Oxford University Press, 1985), p. 219.

37. Under wartime conditions or facing Sino-Soviet military deterioration, this high command could also include the Central Asian Military District. See Gelman, *Soviet Far East Buildup,* pp. 76–77.

38. Neville Maxwell, *India's China War* (Harmondsworth: Penguin, 1972), pp. 209–215, 247.

39. Jeffrey Richelson, *The Wizards of Langley: Inside the CIA's Directorate of Science and Technology* (Boulder, Colo.: Westview, 2001), p. 94.

40. A. Doak Barnett, *China's Far West: Four Decades of Change* (Boulder, Colo.: Westview, 1993), pp. 354, 617.

41. For the most recent and updated discussion, see Li Danhui, "A Historical Examination of the Origin of the 1962 I-Ta [Ili-Tacheng] Incident Supported by Materials from Archives in Xinjiang, China," *Social Sciences in China* 22, no. 3 (Autumn 2001): 140–161; see also O. B. Borisov and B. T. Koloskov, *Soviet-Chinese Relations, 1945–1970* (Bloomington: Indiana University Press, 1975), p. 222; and Allen S. Whiting, *The Chinese Calculus of Deterrence: India and Indochina* (Ann Arbor: University of Michigan Press, 1975), p. 32.

42. The most comprehensive and recent study is S.C.M. Paine, *Imperial Rivals: China, Russia, and Their Disputed Frontier* (Armonk, N.Y.: Sharpe, 1996); see also Denis J. Doolin, *Territorial Claims in the Sino-Soviet Conflict: Documents and Analysis*, Hoover Institution Studies, no. 7 (Stanford, Calif.: Hoover Institution Press, 1965); and Pi Ying-hsien, "China's Boundary Issues with the Former Soviet Union," *Issues and Studies* (July 1992): 63–75.

43. Melvin Gurtov and Byong-Moo Hwang, *China under Threat: The Politics of Strategy and Diplomacy* (Baltimore, Md.: Johns Hopkins University Press, 1980), pp. 126–127; Whiting, *Chinese Calculus of Deterrence*, p. 33; and Borisov and Koloskov, *Soviet-Chinese Relations*, p. 223.

44. David Armstrong, "The Soviet Union," in *Chinese Defence Policy*, ed. Gerald Segal and William T. Tow (London: Macmillan, 1984), pp. 188, 190.

45. Whiting, *Chinese Calculus of Deterrence*, p. 190.

46. *Dangdai, Zhongguo de Xinjiang* (China today: Xinjiang) (Beijing: Dangdai zhongguo chubanshe, 1991), p. 785.

47. A recent visit to the Horgos Pass between Xinjiang and Kazakstan showed that except for the border station itself, the entire border remains unmarked, and certainly unfenced, to this very day.

48. Gurtov and Hwang, *China under Threat*, pp. 214–215.

49. Whiting, *Chinese Calculus of Deterrence*, p. 239.

50. Christian F. Ostermann, "East German Documents on the Border Conflict, 1969," in the Cold War International History Project, *Bulletin*, nos. 6–7 ("Cold War in Asia) www.gwu.edu/~nsarchiv/CWIHP/b6–7a13.htm (accessed 24 July 2001).

51. Allen S. Whiting, "Sino-Soviet Hostilities and Implications for U.S. Policy," 16 August 1969, top secret report to Henry Kissinger, pp. 3–5 (National Archives, E.D. 12958, declassified 24 May 2001). This argument is duly repeated by Kissinger in his *White House Years* (Boston: Little, Brown, 1979), p. 177.

52. Central Intelligence Agency, "Military Forces along the Sino-Soviet Border," pp. 2–3; Armstrong, "Soviet Union," p. 181; and Segal, *Defending China*, pp. 178, 181. The Soviet threat was made public for the first time by Victor Louis in the *London Evening News*, 16 September 1969. Quoting "well informed sources in Moscow," he said that the Soviets prefer to use rockets instead of manpower in dealing with border issues and that "Russian nuclear installations are aimed at Chinese nuclear facilities." The Soviets, he added, have a "plan to launch an air attack on Lop Nor."

53. Gelman, *Soviet Far East Buildup*, p. 22.

54. White House, "Memorandum of Conversation," Top Secret/Sensitive, Exclusively Eyes-Only (declassified), in www.gwu.edu/~nsarchiv/nsa/publications/DOC_readers/kissinger/nixonzhou (accessed 22 July 2001).

55. *New York Times*, 30 September 1979; *Daily Telegraph*, 17 April 1979; and Gelman, *Soviet Far East Buildup*, pp. 98–103.

56. On the contradictory claims to this region, see Dorothy Woodman, *Himalayan Frontiers: A Political Review of British, Chinese, Indian and Russian Rivalries* (London: Barrie and Rockliff, Cresset Press, 1969).

57. John W. Garver, *Protracted Contest: Sino-Indian Rivalry in the Twentieth Century* (Seattle: University of Washington Press, 2001), p. 89.

58. John Gittings, *The Role of the Chinese Army* (London: Oxford University Press, 1967), pp. 38–40; Gurtov and Hwang, *China under Threat*, pp. 116–117, 144; McMillen, "Urumqi Military Region," p. 707; and Maxwell, *India's China War*, p. 82.

412   NOTES TO PAGES 142–147

59. Gurtov and Hwang, *China under Threat,* pp. 138–139, 142.

60. Whitson, *Chinese High Command,* pp. 487–489.

61. Yaacov Vertzberger, *The Enduring Entente: Sino-Pakistani Relations 1960–1980* (Washington, D.C.: Center for Strategic and International Studies, Georgetown University, and Praeger, 1983), pp. 9, 24.

62. Woodman, *Himalayan Frontiers,* pp. 306–307.

63. Yaacov Y. I. Vertzberger, *Misperceptions in Foreign Policymaking: The Sino-Indian Conflict, 1959–1962* (Boulder, Colo.: Westview, 1984), pp. 28, 112.

64. John Pomfret, "Separatists Defy Chinese Crackdown: Persistent Islamic Movement May Have Help from Abroad," *Washington Post,* 26 January 2000.

65. This and the next paragraph are based on the following sources: "Chinese Uighur Militants Killed in Kashmir: Report," *Times of India,* 22 February 2001; *WUNN,* no. 105 (6 December 2000), www.uygur.org/wunn00/2000/0612_1.htm (accessed 18 August 2001); Editorial, "The Chinese Way," *Hindustan Times,* 8 July 1999; and Rohit Bhan, "ISI Training Chinese Youth on Pakistan-Afghanistan Border," *Indian Express,* 7 May 1998.

66. Julie R. Sirrs, "Report on Foreign POWs Held by the Anti-Taliban Forces," October 1999, www.afghanradio.com/azadi.html (accessed 13 May 2001).

67. M. Ehsan Ahrari, "China, Pakistan, and the 'Taliban' Syndrome,'" *Asian Survey* 40, no. 4 (April 2000): 658–671.

68. *WUNN,* no. 53 (26 August 1997): 6–8.

69. *The Muslim* (Islamabad), 2 November 1998; and "Situation of Uyghurs in Pakistan Deteriorates," *WUNN,* no. 92 (18 December 1998): 8–9.

70. "Sino-Pakistani Relations: An 'All-Weather Friendship,'" *Spotlight on Regional Affairs* 20, no. 5 (May 2001): 11, www.irs.org.pk/spotlight/Pak-China%20Relations.htm (accessed 23 September 2001).

71. The following discussion is based on Laird, *Into Tibet.*

72. *China Today: Defence Science and Technology,* vol. 1 (Beijing: National Defence Industry Press, 1993), pp. 180–181 (hereafter *CTDST*); and John Wilson Lewis and Xue Litai, *China Builds the Bomb* (Stanford, Calif.: Stanford University Press, 1988), pp. 78n13, 268.

73. See www.laogai.org/hdbook/xinjiang.htm (accessed 21 July 2001); and James D. Seymour and Richard Anderson, *New Ghosts, Old Ghosts: Prisons and Labor Reform Camps in China* (Armonk, N.Y.: Sharpe, 1999), pp. 107–109; see also Richelson, *Wizards of Langley,* p. 55.

74. *CTDST,* pp. 205–208; and Lewis, *China Builds the Bomb,* pp. 175–177.

75. Though the possibility of attacking China's nuclear facilities was raised in Washington immediately after the first explosion, as well as a few months before, the potential target was fissionable material production facilities rather than testing facilities, such as Lop Nur. See G. W. Rathjens, U.S. Arms Control and Disarmament Agency, "Destruction of Chinese Nuclear Weapons Capabilities," 14 December 1964, Top Secret (declassified), www.gwu.edu/~nsarchiv/NSAEBB/NSAEBB1/nhch6_1.htm (accessed 24 July 2001).

76. Lewis, *China Builds the Bomb,* pp. 203–206.

77. See www.fas.org/nuke/guide/china/facility/malan.htm (accessed 6 June 2001).

78. According to a report originating in China, "a guided missile base" about 10 km from Korla was attacked, probably by Uyghur militants. See *China News Analysis* (Ankara), 26 February 1999, cited in Foreign Broadcast Information Service, *Daily Report: China,* no. 228, 27 February 1999 (hereafter FBIS-CHI).

79. *CTDST,* pp. 288, 297.

80. Richelson, *Wizards of Langley,* pp. 93, 136. The device was later swept away by an avalanche.

81. *South China Morning Post,* 8 June 2000; and "Failed DF-31 Test," *Washington Times,* 4 January 2002.

82. *CTDST,* photo 87.

83. Ibid., pp. 384–385.

84. See C. P. Skrine and Pamela Nightingale, *Macartney at Kashgar: New Light on British, Chinese, and Russian Activities in Sinkiang, 1890–1918* (Oxford: Oxford University Press, 1987); and Peter Hopkirk, *Setting the East Ablaze: On Secret Service in Bolshevik Asia* (Oxford: Oxford University Press, 1984).

85. Roger Faligot and Rémi Kauffer, *The Chinese Secret Service* (London: Headline, 1990), pp. 111–118 passim.

86. See www.fas.org/irp/world/china/facilities/index.html (accessed 16 August 2001).

87. *New York Times,* 8 December 1980, and 19 June 1981.

88. Richelson, *Wizards of Langley,* pp. 216–218; and John K. Cooley, *Unholy Wars: Afghanistan, America and International Terrorism* (London: Pluto, 1999), pp. 68–69.

89. Charles Smith, "Our Pact with Nuclear Danger," *Worldnet Daily,* 4 May 1999, www.worldnetdaily.com/news/article.asp?20511 (accessed 8 February 2001); Charles Smith, "The Information Vacuum Cleaner: National Security Agency Casts Wide Net of Global Surveillance," *Worldnet Daily,* 9 April 2000, www.worldnetdaily.com/news/article.asp?20603 (accessed 8 February 2001); and Lee, *China's Defence Modernisation,* pp. 171–172, which is based on Jeffrey Richelson, "Monitoring the Soviet Military," *Arms Control Today* 16, no. 7 (October 1986): 14–16, and *Washington Post,* 18 June 1981, p. 34.

90. Conversation with Antonio Chiang, Deputy Secretary-General, National Security Council (Taiwan), Tel Aviv, 5 March 2002.

91. Bill Gertz and Rowan Scarborough, "Inside the Ring: China Eavesdropping," *Washington Times,* 5 May 2000, p. A10, quoted by Desmond Ball, "China and Information Warfare (IW): Signals Intelligence (SIGINT), Electronic Warfare (EW) and Cyber-Warfare" (paper presented to the Asian Security Conference, New Delhi, January 27–29, 2003).

92. James Mann, *About Face: A History of America's Curious Relationship with China, from Nixon to Clinton* (New York: Vintage, 2000), pp. 136–139.

93. Nicholas Eftimiades, *Chinese Intelligence Operations* (Annapolis, Md.: Naval Institute Press, 1994), pp. 100–102.

94. Donald W. Klein and Ann B. Clark, *Biographic Dictionary of Chinese Communism, 1921–1965,* vol. 2 (Cambridge, Mass.: Harvard University Press, 1971), pp. 892–893.

95. On Wang Enmao, see Klein and Clark, *Biographic Dictionary of Chinese Communism,* pp. 902–904; and Donald H. McMillen, "Xinjiang and Wang Enmao: New Directions in Power, Policy and Integration?" *China Quarterly,* no. 99 (September 1984): 569–593.

96. Much of this information is based on Red Guard documents in "Cultural Revolution in Sinkiang," American Consulate General Hong Kong, *Current Background,* no. 855 (17 June 1968): 1–19.

97. Much of this information is based on "Collection of Documents Concerning the Great Proletarian Cultural Revolution," *Current Background,* no. 852 (6 May 1968).

98. Whitson, *Chinese High Command,* p. 119.

99. *Current Background,* no. 852, pp. 54–56.

100. Quoted by Thomas W. Robinson, "Chou En-lai and the Cultural Revolution," in *The Cultural Revolution in China,* ed. Thomas W. Robinson (Berkeley: University of California Press, 1971), p. 229.

101. *Current Background,* no. 852, pp. 68–70; see also Whitson, *Chinese High Command,* p. 383.

102. Harvey W. Nelsen, *The Chinese Military System: An Organizational Study of the Chinese People's Liberation Army* (Boulder, Colo.: Westview, 1977), pp. 161, 244n21; and *Current Background,* no. 855, pp. 9–11.

103. Whitson, *Chinese High Command,* p. 119.

104. Ibid., pp. 102, 509–510; and Gurtov and Hwang, *China under Threat,* pp. 196–197.

105. Whitson, *Chinese High Command,* pp. 122, 297; and Jürgen Domes, "The Role of the Military in the Formation of Revolutionary Committees, 1967–68," *China Quarterly,* no. 44 (October–December 1970): 141.

106. It is ironical that Xiao Hua, who now underscored the primacy of party ideology and politics, had been condemned by the Red Guards during the Cultural Revolution for opposing Xinjiang radicalism, supporting the conservatives, withholding information sent by Xinjiang radicals to the CMC, and being "the black back-stage boss of Wang En-mao." See *Current Background,* no. 855, pp. 12, 19.

107. Lee, *China's Defence Modernisation,* pp. 220, 239–241.

108. This section draws heavily from Yitzhak Shichor, "Pacifying the West: Confidence-Building Measures between China and Central Asia," in *Globalization of Civil-Military Relations: Democratization, Reform and Security,* ed. Michael Popa (Bucharest: Encyclopedica Publishing House, 2002), pp. 239–258.

109. British Broadcast Corporation, *Summary of World Broadcasts: Far East,* no. 2092 (hereafter BBC-SWB FE); ITAR-TASS, 3 September 1994; and *Xinhua* (Beijing) and BBC-SWB FE/2440, 19 October 1995.

110. Robert Cutler, "Redrawing the Architecture of Central Asian Security," *Central Asia-Caucasus Analyst,* 27 February 2002.

111. For the full text, see the Henry L. Stimson Center, Confidence-Building Measures Project, www.stimson.org/cbm/china/crplus.htm (accessed 21 October 2001).

112. Based on news agencies reports. See www-ibru.dur.ac.uk/cgi-bin/data.pl (accessed 24 September 2001).

113. *Xinhua* (Beijing), 10 November 1999, in FBIS-CHI-1999–1144.

114. Radio Free Europe/Radio Liberty (hereafter RFE/RL), *Newsline,* part 2, 7 July 1998, and 11 March 1999; *Xinhua* (Beijing), 4 November 1998, in FBIS-CHI-1998–308; and *Interfax* (Moscow), 3 February 1999, in FBIS-SOV-99–034.

115. ITAR-TASS, 11–13 August 1999, in FBIS-SOV-1999–0811, and FBIS-CHI-1999–0813.

116. RFE/RL (Dushanbe), 20 May 2002; *Daily Report on Russia and the Former Soviet Republics* (hereafter DRRFSR), 21 May 2002, p. 4; and *Turkistan Newsletter,* 30 May 2002.

117. "Chinese Border Controversy," *Central Asia Monitor,* no. 4 (2001): 37; Alisher Khamidov, "Dispute over China-Kyrgyz Border Demarcation Pits President vs. Parliament," *Eurasia Insight,* 12 July 2001; and Igor Grebenschikov, "China Nibbles Away at Kyrgyz Border," *Reporting Central Asia,* no. 58 (11 July 2001).

118. Quoted in Grebenschikov, "China Nibbles Away at Kyrgyz Border."

119. Dmitri Plesanov, "Kyrgyz Border Pact with China Stirs Tension in Bishkek," *Eurasianet,* 26 May 2002; and "Kyrgyz Border," *Turkistan Newsletter,* 30 May 2002; see also *DRRFSR,* 15 May 2002, p. 4, and 20 May 2002, p. 4. Although sharply criticizing the prime minister, President Akaev rejected his resignation.

120. Eftimiades, *Chinese Intelligence Operations,* pp. 100–102; Faligot and Kauffer, *Chinese Secret Service,* p. 440; Lillian Craig Harris, "China's Support of People's War in the 1980s," in *China and the Third World: Champion or Challenger?* ed. Lillian Craig Harris and Robert L. Worden (Dover: Auburn House, 1986), pp. 132–133; and Ahmad Lutfi, "Blowback: China and the Afghan Arabs," *Issues and Studies* 37, no. 1 (January–February 2001): 202–204.

121. The following paragraph is based on Ahmed Rashid, "The Taliban: Exporting Extremism," *Foreign Affairs* 78, no. 6 (November–December 1999): 22–35; see also Ahmed Rashid and Faizabad, "Afghanistan: Heart of Darkness," *Far Eastern Economic Review,* 5 August 1999, p. 8.

122. *The Guardian* (London), 3 September 1998; Ahmed Rashid and Susan V. Laurence, "Joining the Jihad," *Far Eastern Economic Review,* 7 September 2000; and Judith Miller, "Holy Warriors: Killing for the Glory of God, in a Land Far from Home," *New York Times,* 16 January 2001.

123. Calum MacLeod, "China-Taliban Deal Signed on Attack Day," *Washington Times,* 14 September 2001. The story was firmly denied by China as "groundless." See *Xinhua* (Beijing), 25 December 2001.

124. Waheguru Pal Singh and Jing-Dong Yuan, "Cooperative Monitoring for Confidence Building: A Case Study of the Sino-Indian Border Area," Cooperative Monitoring Center, Occasional Paper, no. 13 (August 1999), www.cmc.sandia.gov/Links/about/papers/SAND98–0505–13/ (accessed 23 September 2001).

125. BBC News Online, 3 April 2000.

126. Atul Aneja, "Renewed India-China Border Talks to Cover New Sectors," *The Hindu,* 13 August 2001, p. 13, in FBIS-CHI-2001–0813, 14 August 2001.

127. Franz Schurmann, "Of Hegemons and Straps: Today, U.S. Superpower; Tomorrow, World Empire," *San Francisco Chronicle,* 17 February 2002, p. D8; see also Ariel Cohen, "Regional Powers in Central Asia Grapple with Expanding U.S. Military Presence," *Eurasianet,* 18 February 2002.

Notes to Chapter 6

1. For a vivid firsthand account of a 1935 journey, see Peter Fleming, *News from Tartary: A Journey from Peking to Kashmir* (Los Angeles: Tarcher, 1936).

2. For an argument that in localities where ethnic minorities have participated more fully in economic development there is a greater sense of affinity with the PRC, see Justin Jon Rudelson, *Oasis Identities: Uyghur Nationalism along China's Silk Road* (New York: Columbia University Press, 1997).

3. National Bureau of Statistics (NBS), *China Statistical Yearbook, 2001* (Beijing: China Statistics Press, 2001), p. 52 (hereafter *CSY 2001*). China's official statistics are subject to unknown and potentially serious margins of error that some analysts suspect have increased since the late 1990s. For an assessment, see Thomas G. Rawski and Wei Xiao, "Roundtable on Chinese Economic Statistics Introduction," and related papers, in *China Economic Review* 12, no. 4 (2001): 298–398. Despite this caveat, the overall patterns of development and the contrasts between

Xinjiang and the rest of China that the NBS statistics are used to illuminate in this chapter are so pronounced as to hold up credibly, in my view, even given suspected margins of error.

4. Xinjiang Uyghur Autonomous Region Bureau of Statistics (XBS), *Xinjiang Tongji Nianjian, 2001* (Xinjiang statistical yearbook, 2001) (Beijing: China Statistics Press, 2001), p. 38 (hereafter *XSY 2001*).

5. The lower per capita growth rate in Xinjiang in the latter period occurred in the context of a widening gap between population growth rates in Xinjiang and China as a whole. The per annum population growth rates implicit in reported growth rates for GDP and per capita GDP are 1.2 percent for China and 2.0 percent for Xinjiang. Population growth rates derived from census data diverge even more at 1.0 percent for China and 2.2 percent for Xinjiang. See *CSY 2001*, p. 91; and *XSY 2001*, p. 93.

6. *CSY 2001*, p. 59.

7. This section on Qing and Republican economic development draws on Wang Shuanqian, *Zou xiang 21 Shiji de Xinjiang* (Xinjiang moving toward the twenty-first century) (Urumchi: Xinjiang People's Publishing House, 1999), chapters 1–3.

8. Wang, *Zou xiang 21 Shiji de Xinjiang,* p. 50.

9. Ibid., p. 63.

10. Ibid., pp. 34–36.

11. Ibid., p. 66.

12. Ibid., pp. 51–52.

13. Ibid., p. 61.

14. Martin R. Norins, *Gateway to Asia: Sinkiang, Frontier of the Chinese Far West* (New York: John Day, 1944), p. 146.

15. Wang, *Zou xiang 21 Shiji de Xinjiang,* p. 39.

16. Ibid., pp. 64–66.

17. *Xinjiang Glorious 50 Years,* vol. 2 (Urumchi: Xinjiang People's Publishers, 1999), p. 357.

18. Ibid., p. 50; and *50 Years of New China: The Volume of Xinjiang Production and Construction Group* (Beijing: China Statistics Press, 1999), pp. 328–329.

19. This section on reform and opening in Xinjiang relies on Shao Qiang and Wang Shuanqian, eds., *Xinjiang Gaige Kaifang 20 Nian* (Xinjiang's twenty years of reform and opening) (Urumchi: Xinjiang People's Publishers, 1998).

20. *Xinhua* (Beijing), 21 March 2002, www.drcnet.com.cn/ (accessed 24 May 2002), author's translation.

21. *Xinhua* (Beijing), 6 November 2001, www.drcnet.com.cn/ (accessed 24 May 2002).

22. *CSY 2001*, p. 453.

23. State Council, "Suggestions on the Implementing of Policies and Measures Pertaining to the Development of the Western Region," 29 September 2001, www.chinawest.gov.cn/english/asp/start.asp?id=c (accessed 8 June 2002).

24. These are Chongqing Municipality, Guizhou Province, Sichuan Province, Yunnan Province, the Tibet Autonomous Region, Shaanxi Province, Gansu Province, the Ningxia Hui Autonomous Region, Qinghai Province, the Xinjiang Uygur Autonomous Region (the XPCC is listed separately), the Inner Mongolia Autonomous Region, and the Guangxi Zhuang Autonomous Region.

25. See www.petrochina.com.cn/english/gsjs/gsjs.htm (accessed 9 June 2002); and www.ethicalconsumer.org/magazine/corpwatch/petrochina.htm (accessed 9 June 2002).

26. See www.europe.cnn.com/2002/BUSINESS/asia/06/28/hk.petrochina/ (accessed 9 June 2002).

27. XBS, *Xinjiang Tongji Nianjian, 2000* (Xinjiang statistical yearbook, 2000) (Beijing: China Statistics Press, 2000), p. 495 (hereafter *XSY 2000*). Xinjiang's second-ranked industrial enterprise in 1999, the China Petroleum Urumchi Petrochemical Factory (revenue ¥5.5 billion), was also connected to the oil industry.

28. *South China Morning Post*, 5 April 2002; see www.gasandoil.com/goc/news/nts22281.htm (accessed 9 June 2002).

29. *CSY 2001*, p. 164.

30. *XSY 2001*, p. 399, and *CSY 2001*, p. 401, respectively. State-owned enterprises have undergone widespread transformation in recent years to become limited liability companies or joint stock corporations but with the state retaining a majority ownership position. The figures in the text refer to the combined shares of traditional state enterprises and state-controlled companies. Traditional state enterprises accounted for 23.5 percent nationally and 24.4 percent in Xinjiang of gross industrial output value in 2000.

31. *XSY 2000*, p. 361, and NBS, *China Statistical Yearbook, 2000* (Beijing: China Statistics Press, 2000), p. 409 (hereafter *CSY 2000*), respectively. *Getihu* industrial output value is not reported for 2000 for China as a whole, which may be a sign of the difficulty of collecting reliable data for this ownership type. For Xinjiang, the share reported for 2000 is 6.2 percent (*XSY 2001*, p. 399), actually down slightly from 1999.

32. *CSY 2001*, p. 63, *CSY 2000*, p. 67, and NBS, *China Statistical Yearbook, 1999* (Beijing: China Statistics Press, 1999), p. 69, respectively.

33. During the period 1979 to 1996, Xinjiang obtained 57.6 percent of its economic construction funding from three sources: foreign capital, central government direct inputs to enterprises, and extra-budgetary funds, most of which were extra-budgetary funds for state enterprises under central administration. Only 4.12 percent of funds for economic construction were reportedly from the local government budget. See Shao and Wang, *Xinjiang Gaige Kaifang 20 Nian*, p. 198.

34. *CSY 2001*, p. 61.

35. Ibid., p. 66. The national figures are for 1999 as no 2000 figures are published. See *CSY 2000*, p. 70.

36. *Xinjiang Glorious 50 Years*, p. 172.

37. *CSY 2001*, pp. 364, 366.

38. *Xinjiang Glorious 50 Years*, pp. 411–510. Not all provincial GDP is attributable at the county level, so county per capita GDP values lie generally below the provincial per capita GDP value.

39. The sample of eighty-two counties captured a population of 14.62 million out of Xinjiang's 17.47 million. One county is excluded from the sample due to missing data (Hetian City, Hetian Prefecture [*Xinjiang Glorious 50 Years*, p. 503]). Two counties are excluded because the impact of oil production on GDP in these localities is so large that it distorts the results. These are Ku'erqin City, Bayangolin Mongol Autonomous Prefecture (p. 465) and Shanshan County, Turfan Prefecture (p. 417). Furthermore, some population is excluded because it resides in areas not under county-level jurisdiction. Of particular note is the oil-producing prefecture-level Kelamayi City (p. 413), which has jurisdiction over four townships but no intermediate counties. Average per capita GDP for the sample is only ¥3,755 in 1998 prices. This reflects adjustment from 1990 price data using the price deflator of 1.58 implicit in reported current and constant price GDP figures for Xinjiang. This figure is much lower than

the reported average per capita GDP for Xinjiang in 1998 of ¥6,229. Even reintroducing the oil-producing localities into the calculation results in an overall GDP per capita of only ¥4,028. The gap is presumably explained by GDP produced in Xinjiang that is not attributable by county. Income actually received per person might differ substantially from GDP per capita on a county-by-county basis. Nevertheless, the negative connection between minority share in population and GDP per capita is so strong that one must suspect the pattern carries over to household income per capita.

40. *50 Years of New China: The Volume of the Bingtuan* (Beijing: China Statistics Press, 1999), p. 328.

41. *XSY 2001*, pp. 128, 133–135.

42. Ibid., pp. 130, 193.

43. *XSY 2000*, pp. 121–122.

44. *CSY 2001*, p. 107; and *XSY 2001*, p. 145.

45. This section draws on consulting work undertaken by the author for the Asian Development Bank and reported in two internal documents: "PRC Trade with Central Asia," prepared under Technical Assistance Project no. 5760, 5 January 2000, and "Regional Economic Cooperation in Central Asia (Phase II)," prepared under Technical Assistance Project no. 5818–REG, 22 November 1999.

46. Wang Haiyan, "Hasakesitan Yu Zhongguo Xinjiang de Diyuan Jingji Hezuo" (Regional economic cooperation of Kazakstan and Xinjiang, China), *Xinjiang Shehui Kexue* (Xinjiang Social Science) 1 (2002): 45–50.

47. *CSY 2001*, pp. 49, 56, 599, 600.

48. Wiemer, "Regional Economic Cooperation in Central Asia (Phase II)."

49. Technically, in considering Xinjiang's role as an entrepôt, rather than making use of trade data by source of exports and destination of imports, as is the case here, one would want to make use of data for Xinjiang as a trade administrative unit. Chinese data sources provide such figures, but they reflect even smaller trade engagement than the source-destination figures. In any case, the distinction is probably not well preserved in compiling the statistics.

50. See www.worldbank.org/data/countrydata/countrydata.html#DataProfile (accessed 26 May 2002).

51. *XSY 2001*, pp. 629–631.

52. This is the conclusion reached in studies done for the Asian Development Bank and the Transport Corridor Europe Caucasus Asia (TRACECA), a Programme of the European Commission. For a report on the TRACECA study, see www.traceca.org/tracecaf.htm (accessed 26 May 2002).

53. Wu Caixia and Chen Guo'an, "West International Trade Center, East Central Enterprises," *Xinhua* (Beijing) [in Chinese], 24 January 2002, www.drcnet.com.cn/DrcNet/AreaView/AreaView_index.asp (accessed 24 May 2002).

54. Yu Miao, "Reasons for Slide in Xinjiang Exports and What to Do about It," Xinjiang People's Broadcasting Station [in Chinese], 6 November 2001, www.drcnet.com.cn/DrcNet/AreaView/AreaView_index.asp (accessed 22 May 2002).

55. Customs Administration printout.

56. World Press Review Online, www.worldpress.org/specials/pp/china.htm (accessed 16 March 2002); Michael Lelyveld, "Kazakstan: Oil Pipeline to China a Victim of Diplomatic Dispute," www.rferl.org/nca/features/2001/09/19092001115328.asp (accessed 16 March 2002); and Lola Gulomova, *Caspian Brief No. 19* (Washington, D.C.: Cornell Caspian Consulting, August 2001), www.cornellcaspian.com/pub/19_0108Kazak-China.htm (accessed 16 March 2002).

57. Alexander Nemets and Thomas Torda, "Eastern Cinderella, a Broken Web and the Turkish Card, Part I," 2 January 2002, www.newsmax.com/archives/articles/2002/1/2/161158.shtml (accessed 16 March 2002).

58. Xinjiang Production and Construction Group, *Xinjiang Production and Construction Group Statistical Yearbook, 2001* (Beijing: China Statistics Press, 2001), p. 369.

59. Wang, *Zou xiang 21 Shiji de Xinjiang,* p. 412.

60. *CSY 2001,* pp. 600–601.

61. Wang, *Zou xiang 21 Shiji de Xinjiang,* pp. 411–412.

62. *CSY 2001,* p. 618, describes other foreign investment as follows: "It includes the total value of stock shares in foreign currencies issued by enterprises at domestic or foreign stock exchanges . . . , rent payable for the imported equipment through international leasing arrangement, cost of imported equipment, technology and materials provided by foreign counterparts in compensation trade and processing and assembly trade."

63. *CSY 2001,* p. 602; *Xinjiang Glorious 50 Years,* p. 258; and *XSY 2001,* p. 633.

64. Wang, *Zou xiang 21 Shiji de Xinjiang,* p. 408.

Notes to Chapter 7

1. Jacob M. Landau, *Pan-Turkism: From Irredentism to Cooperation* (Bloomington: Indiana University Press, 1995), pp. 53–54. Landau cites various British consul reports of the period. In an effort to prevent such notions taking root, the first Republican-era governor, Yang Cengxin, sought to control all printed matter, but without much success.

2. For a partial account of the press, and for a list of all its many publications, see Gunnar Jarring, *Prints from Kashghar* (Istanbul: Swedish Research Institute in Istanbul, 1991).

3. Colin Mackerras, *China's Minority Cultures* (New York: Longman, 1995), pp. 44–45, citing Fu Xiruo, "Lun Xinjiang sheng jiaoyu," in *Xibei minzu zongjiao shiliao wenzhai (Xinjiang fence),* vol. 2, comp. Gansu Provincial Library Bibliography Department (Lanzhou, Gansu: Gansu sheng tushuguan, 1985), p. 952.

4. L. Benson and I. Svanberg, *China's Last Nomads: The History and Culture of China's Kazaks* (Armonk, N.Y.: Sharpe, 1998), p. 176.

5. Mackerras, *China's Minority Cultures,* p. 44.

6. William C. Clark, "Convergence or Divergence: Uighur Family Change in Urumqi" (Ph.D. diss., University of Washington, 1999), p. 144.

7. H. C. Taussig, "One Sixth of China," *Eastern World* 10, no. 12 (December 1956): 15.

8. Clark, "Convergence or Divergence," p. 145.

9. *Xinhua* (Beijing), 8 February 1974, translated in *Survey of China Mainland Press* 5556 (1974), p. 65 (hereafter *SCMP*).

10. *Xinhua* (Beijing), 25 February 1964, translated in *SCMP,* 3168 (1964), p. 17.

11. *Xinhua* (Beijing), 24 December 1973, translated in *SCMP* 5528 (1973), p. 25.

12. The 1958 figures are from *Xinhua* (Beijing), 28 August 1958; the 1973 figures are from *Renmin Ribao,* 20 July 1973.

13. The full text of the new law is in Katherine Kaup, *Creating the Zhuang: Ethnic Politics in China* (London: Rienner, 2000), pp. 183–197.

14. In his research on the Yi people of Yunnan, Martin Schoenhals notes that texts

and curriculum at Yi schools were identical to materials used in Chinese schools. See Martin Schoenhals, "Education and Ethnicity among the Liangshan Yi," in *Perspectives on the Yi of Southwest China,* ed. Stevan Harrell (Berkeley: University of California Press, 2001), p. 241. Mackerras offers the same observation, noting that this practice was widespread in minority areas he visited in 1990–1994. See Mackerras, *China's Minority Cultures,* p. 136.

15. Personal communication with university and college students, as well as faculty, in 1996.

16. *Zhongguo renkou tongji nianjian, 1994* (China population statistics yearbook, 1994) (Beijing: China Statistical Press, 1994), p. 397.

17. Ibid., p. 397.

18. Ibid.

19. *Xinjiang nianjian, 1991* (Xinjiang yearbook, 1991) (Urumchi: Xinjiang People's Press, 1991), pp. 473–474.

20. Ibid., p. 502.

21. Figures are from *Xinjiang nianjian, 1995* (Urumchi: Xinjiang People's Press, 1995), pp. 400–402.

22. Ibid., p. 359.

23. Foreign Broadcast Information Service-China, 4 December 1990, 90–233, p. 54 (hereafter FBIS-CHI).

24. *Xinjiang nianjian, 1991,* p. 360.

25. *Beijing Xinhua* (English service), 11 September 2000, cited in Robert John Perrins, ed., *China: Facts and Figures Annual Handbook,* vol. 26. (New York: Academic International, 2001), p. 283.

26. See Clark, "Convergence or Divergence," pp. 158–159. I found the same to be true of students I met in the mid-1990s.

27. Ibid., p. 112.

28. *Xinjiang nianjian, 1991,* p. 362.

29. Clark, "Convergence or Divergence," p. 165.

30. *Beijing Xinhua Press* [in English], 18 October 2000, reprinted in Perrins, *China,* pp. 283–284.

31. Clark, "Convergence or Divergence," p. 158.

32. FBIS-CHI-1990–233, 4 December 1990, p. 54.

33. Clark, "Convergence or Divergence," p. 86.

34. On both men, see comments in Justin Jon Rudelson, *Oasis Identities: Uyghur Nationalism along China's Silk Road* (New York: Columbia University Press, 1997), pp. 157, 163–165.

35. *Xinhua* (Beijing), 27 June 1958.

36. Ibid., 1 October 1975.

37. BBC Monitoring Service, 21 July 2000.

38. FBIS-CHI-1995–201, 18 October 1995, p. 87.

39. Clark, "Convergence or Divergence," p. 114.

40. FBIS translation of "PRC Steps Up Religious Management in Xinjiang," *Xinjiang Ribao,* 3 October 2001.

41. "China Hoping Development of West Will Dampen Xinjiang Separatism," *Agence France Presse* (Urumchi), 21 August 2000, quoting Nur Bakri, the mayor of Urumchi.

42. Clark, "Convergence or Divergence," pp. 191–192.

43. Number for 1954 from *Central Asian Review* 4, no. 4 (1956): 442; for 1975, FBIS, 23 April 1975.

44. For the 1989 figure, see FBIS-CHI-1990–078, 23 April 1990, p. 65; for the 1995 figure, see FBIS-CHI-1995–201, 18 October 1995, p. 84.

45. FBIS-CHI-1995–201, 18 October 1995, p. 84.

Notes to Chapter 8

1. For a more extensive description of this geography, see Stanley W. Toops, chapter 10 in this volume.

2. See Ludmilla A. Ch'vyr, *Uigury Vostochnogo Turkestana i sosednie narody v kontse XIX- nachale XX v.* (The Uyghurs of Eastern Turkistan and neighboring peoples in the end of the 19th and beginning of the 20th centuries) (Moskva: "Nauka," 1990); and Justin Rudelson, *Oasis Identities: Uyghur Nationalism along China's Silk Road* (New York: Columbia University Press, 1997).

3. Great Britain had significant access to the region through what is now the northern frontier of Pakistan, and Russia accessed the region mostly through the north via the Ili River valley.

4. Allen S. Whiting and General Sheng Shih-Ts'ai, *Sinkiang: Pawn or Pivot?* (East Lansing: Michigan State University Press, 1958), p. 68.

5. Andrew D. W. Forbes, *Warlords and Muslims in Chinese Central Asia: A Political History of Republican Sinkiang, 1911–49* (Cambridge: Cambridge University Press, 1986), p. 152. For more on the extensive influence of the Soviet Union in Xinjiang during the 1930s, see Valery Barmin, *SSSR i Sin'tszyan, 1918–1941* (The USSR and Xinjiang, 1918–1941) (Barnaul: Izdat BGPU, 1998).

6. It has long been assumed that the Soviet Union played a central role in the establishment of the ETR, but recent research in the Russian archives by the Russian historian Valery Barmin has proven that Soviet involvement was very extensive and decisive. See Valery Barmin, *Sin'tszyan v Sovetsko-Kitayskikh otnosheniyakh, 1941–1949* (Xinjiang in Soviet-Chinese relations, 1941–1949) (Barnaul: Izdat BGPU, 1999). For more on this period of Xinjiang's history, see James A. Millward and Nabijan Tursun, chapter 3 of this volume.

7. See Sean R. Roberts, "Uyghur Neighborhoods and Nationalisms in the Former Sino-Soviet Borderland: An Historical Ethnography of a Stateless Nation on the Margins of Modernity" (Ph.D. diss., University of Southern California, 2003), chapter 5. For more discussion of Soviet assistance during this period, see Calla Wiemer, chapter 6 of this volume.

8. In traveling from the Soviet Union to Xinjiang in 1990, I was surprised at the legacy of Soviet influence in the region despite the years of the Sino-Soviet split and the Cultural Revolution. Not only were a large number of the modern buildings in the area obviously built on Soviet models (and likely with Soviet assistance), but Uyghurs continued to use Russian terminology rather than Mandarin words to refer to many products of modern technology (e.g., cars, airplanes, and factories).

9. For more on the importance of such cross-border relationships to the development and expression of Uyghur nationalism, see Sean R. Roberts, "The Uighurs of the Kazakstan Borderlands: Migration and the Nation," *Nationalities Papers* 26, no. 3 (1998): 511–530.

10. Writing in 1858, Chokan Valikhanov noted that approximately 200 family members of the Afaqiyya lineage lived in Kokand and Margelan; roughly 50,000 families of Kashgar émigrés and supporters of the Afaqiyya Khojas (known locally as "Taghliklar") lived in the villages surrounding Andijan, Shakhri-khan, and Karasu;

and an entire village of Afaqiyya followers from Kashgar numbering about 56,000 was located on the outskirts of Tashkent in an area known as Yangi-Shaar. See Chokan Valikhanov, *Izbrannye proizvedeniya* (Selected works) (Alma-Ata: Kaz. gos. izdat. khudozhestvennoi literatury, 1952), p. 523.

11. The largest of these migrations took place in the early 1880s after a ten-year Russian occupation of the Yining (Gulja) area in Xinjiang. Official Russian Imperial statistics from this time note that 9,752 Taranchi families, or 45,373 individuals, along with 1,147 Dungan (Hui) families, numbering 4,682 individuals, came to Russian territory from the Yining area in the early 1880s. See *Zapiski o pereselenii Kul'dzhinskikh osedlykh musul'man v Semirechinskuyu oblast' sostavlena 10 Iyunya 1884 g., g. Vernyi* (Notes on the migration of Yining's settled Muslims to the Semirechye Oblast compiled on June 10, 1884, City of Verniy) (Verniy: Handwritten Manuscript Fund of the National Library of Kazakstan, no. 63, 1884), p. 119. In addition, approximately 20,000 Kazaks migrated, bringing the total to some 70,000 people who had immigrated from Xinjiang to Russian territory. See Yu. Baranova, "K Voprosu o pereselenii musul'manskogo naseleniya iz Iliiskogo kraya v Semirech'e v 1881–1883 gg." (Toward an understanding of the migration of the Muslim population from the Ili region to Semirechye in 1881–1883), in *Trudy sektora vostokovedenii Akademii Nauka Kazakskoi SSR* (Alma-Ata: Tom I, 1959), p. 51.

12. The largest migration of Muslims from Xinjiang to Afghanistan and Pakistan was likely in 1949 when many local anti-Communists fled the region on hearing of the establishment of Chinese Communist rule in the north of Xinjiang. Many of these Xinjiang Muslim refugees eventually migrated farther west to Turkey.

13. This border crossing was officially opened to travel in May 1986. See Dru C. Gladney, "Transnational Islam and Uighur National Identity: Salaman Rushdie, Sino-Muslim Missile Deals, and the Trans-Eurasian Railway," *Central Asian Survey* 11, no. 3 (1992): 5.

14. It is also probably used by illegal travelers and smugglers in the winter months and springtime when the pass is officially closed.

15. Witt Raczka, "Xinjiang and Its Central Asian Borderlands," *Central Asian Survey* 17, no. 3 (1998): 391–392.

16. For more on this railroad, see Calla Wiemer, chapter 6 in this volume.

17. S. Dzhusupbekov, *Gorod Vernyi: stranitsy istorii* (The city of Verniy: Pages of history) (Alma-Ata:1980), p. 16.

18. Gladney, "Transnational Islam and Uighur National Identity," p. 5.

19. Like the crossing on the Karakoram Highway with Pakistan, however, it is likely that this pass is utilized by illegal travelers and smugglers during the months it is officially closed.

20. One traveler even told me that he had found a way to bicycle around the border post, but he returned after realizing that he did not want to leave China without an entry stamp.

21. *Shinjang Yilnamisi, 1999* (Xinjiang yearbook, 1999) (Urumchi: Shinjang Khälq Näshriyati, 1999), pp. 585–586.

22. One report commissioned by the Asian Development Bank, for example, stated that $300 million would be a conservative estimate for the value of shuttle trade leaving Xinjiang for former Soviet Central Asia in 1998, but it also states that the figure could very easily be twice that. See Calla Wiemer, "PRC Trade with Central Asia: Final Report," *Asian Development Bank,* 5 January 2000, p. 6.

23. For a table of cross-border trade figures between Xinjiang and former Soviet Central Asia for the years 1992–1996, see James Dorian, Brett Wigdortz, and Dru Gladney, "Central Asia and Xinjiang, China: Emerging Energy, Economic, and Ethnic Relations," *Central Asian Survey* 16, no. 4 (1997): 477. It should also be noted that Wiemer, in chapter 6, points out that a decrease in trade with Kazakstan and Kyrgyzstan occurred in 2001 due to new customs regulations that were instituted in Kazakstan. Still, it is doubtful that this will cause problems for traders in the long term.

24. Vitalii Khlyupin, *Geopoliticheskii treugol'nik: Kazakstan-Kitai-Rossiya proshloe i nastoyaschee pogranichnoi problemy* (Geopolitical triangle: Kazakstan-China-Russia, past and present border problems) (Washington, D.C.: International Eurasian Institute for Economic and Political Research, 1999), p. 116. Dorian, Wigdortz, and Gladney note that the Chinese interest in Kazakstan's oil stems from a recognition of China's limited energy reserves in the context of its vastly expanding economy. See Dorian, Wigdortz, and Gladney, "Central Asia and Xinjiang, China," pp. 467–472.

25. Khlyupin, *Geopoliticheskii treugol'nik,* p. 118.

26. See *Agence France Presse,* 15 January 2002; see also Wiemer, chapter 6.

27. For a more extensive discussion of this phenomenon, see Stanley W. Toops, chapter 9 in this volume.

28. In visiting three separate Xinjiang cities (Yining [Gulja], Urumchi, and Kashgar) on four different occasions between 1990 and 2000 (1990, 1994, 1997, and 2000), I have been amazed at the pace of development in each of these urban spaces. While Urumchi is expected to be a center of development as the capital of Xinjiang, these other regional centers that have traditionally been Muslim cities have also surprisingly grown, particularly during the second half of the 1990s. In addition to increasing numbers of high-rise buildings housing businesses and hotels, both Yining and Kashgar now have large four-lane highways leading into the cities.

29. For more on the Urumchi International Trade Fair, see its official website, www.urumqifair.com (accessed 23 September 2003).

30. However, there are now instances of Chinese goods being sent from the interior of China to large trade halls in Xinjiang's cities explicitly for the purpose of reaching the former Soviet market. See Wiemer, chapter 6.

31. This circuit includes the Barakholka bazaar in Almaty, the Hippodrome in Tashkent, and the Dordoi bazaar in Bishkek.

32. Jay Dautcher, "Down a Narrow Road: The Poetics and Politics of Uyghur Identity" (Ph.D. diss., University of California, Berkeley, 2000).

33. Rebiya Kadir was long upheld by the Chinese Communist Party as an example of a successful Muslim businesswoman. Due to the vocal stance of her husband, who is a prominent Uyghur writer now in exile in the United States, and her charitable support of families in Yining who had lost members during and after the 1997 riots, however, she was placed under house arrest in 1997 and stripped of her position on the People's Advisory Board to China's Parliament. See *BBC World News Asia and Pacific,* 12 March 1998. Furthermore, in August 1999 she was arrested en route to meet with a U.S. congressional research team that was examining human rights abuses in Xinjiang. Subsequently, she was sentenced to eight years in prison in March 2000 for allegedly planning to hand over state secrets to a foreign state. See *Resolution on China's Rabiya Kadeer,* 106th Cong., 2nd sess., Senate Confirmation Resolution 81, 3 May 2000.

34. For a more developed discussion of the dangers of the present development practices and policies in Xinjiang and the potential consequences for the environment and local inhabitants, see Toops, chapter 10.

35. This influence appears to be particularly strong in Khotan, perhaps due to the already strict Muslim orientation of the population there. The majority of women wearing Pakistani veils in Xinjiang, for example, are from Khotan, and this area has been the most accepting in the region of the radical Muslim ideas that are popular in many of Pakistan's madrassahs.

36. For more on the religious education of Uyghurs in Pakistan, see Graham E. Fuller and Jonathan N. Lipman, chapter 13 in this volume.

37. See Gladney, "Transnational Islam and Uighur National Identity," pp. 5–6.

38. See Roberts, "Uyghur Neighborhoods and Nationalisms," chapter 5.

39. Omär, "Greetings from a Far Away Borderland" (unpublished essay, 1993), p. 40. This essay was given to me by my colleague Bill Clarke, who had it translated into English while in Xinjiang.

40. For more on the Yining mäshräp movement, see Sean R. Roberts, "Locality, Islam, and National Culture in a Changing Borderlands: The Revival of the Mashrap Ritual among Young Uighur Men in the Ili Valley," *Central Asian Survey* 17, no. 4 (1998): 673–700. For more on the Thousand Mothers Association, see *Chinese News Digest,* 13 March 2000.

41. See Reuters, 6 December 2001. In monitoring information released about these captures in the press, Jonathan N. Lipman estimates the total number of Uyghurs discovered fighting with the Taliban and Al-Qaeda to be eleven. Jonathan N. Lipman, conversation with the author, Washington, D.C., March 2002. It should also be noted that the United States has refused to extradite these prisoners to China despite official requests from the PRC government. See Reuters, 11 December 2001.

42. For more on recent Chinese government crackdowns on Muslim religious observation in Xinjiang, see Fuller and Lipman, chapter 13.

43. For example, see Abduräup Ibrahimiy, "Shärqiy Turkstan Inqilavidin Bäzi Khatirilär" (Some memories from the Eastern Turkistan revolution), *Uyghur Avazi* (The Uyghur Voice), 15 October 1994; Vasiljan, "Oz Nami Bilän Atayli" (Let's call it by our own name), *Yengi Hayat* (New Life), 22 October 1994; and Sabit Uyghuriy, *Shärqiy Türkstan Inqilavi Toghrisida* (About the Eastern Turkistan revolution) (Almaty: N.p., 2000).

44. For a more extensive discussion of the production of Uyghur history within Xinjiang and the PRC as a whole, see Gardner Bovingdon, chapter 14 in this volume.

45. For an article published in Kazakstan about the worldwide Uyghur political movement, see Dolqun Yasen, "Vakalätsiz Millätlär Täshkilati vä Shärqiy Türkstan Mäsilisi" (The Organization for Unrepresented Nations and the Eastern Turkistan question), *Uighur Avazi* (The Uyghur Voice), 15 April 1995. Some of the publications of other Uyghur diaspora groups that have circulated among local and Xinjiang Uyghurs in Kazakstan include the reprinted version of Uyghur exile Muhämmäd Imin Buhra's anti-Chinese history of Eastern Turkistan (Muhämmäd Imin Buhra, *Shärqiy Türkistan Tarikhi* [Eastern Turkistan history] [Ankara: Bayak Mat. San ve Tic. Ltd. Sti, 1999]) and a passionate political treatise written by a recent arrival to Turkey from Xinjiang calling for the mobilization of Uyghurs to gain independence of their homeland (Äzimät, *Mustäqilliq Kürishi* [The struggle for independence] [Istanbul: Kasim, 1997]).

46. See Roberts, "Uyghur Neighborhoods and Nationalisms," introduction.

47. The Eastern Turkistan United Revolutionary Front has claimed that it supports

militant and armed revolutionary cells inside Xinjiang. See Dewardric L. McNeal, "China's Relations with Central Asian States and Problems with Terrorism," *CRS Report for Congress,* 17 December 2001, p. 11. Given that this group's primary members are a seventy-seven-year-old exile from Xinjiang and his son and that the group was initially created in the 1970s likely with the assistance of the Soviet KGB for propaganda purposes, these claims are highly unlikely.

48. During the 1990s, two such television series were produced, and they have focused on Uyghur exiles from Pakistan and the former Soviet Union, respectively, as the foreign agents seeking to infiltrate Xinjiang and influence the local inhabitants. See *Asiyadiki Kulanggu* (Asia's shadow) (Urumchi: Shinjang Televiziasi, 1990); and *Tutqun Qilinghan Qachqun* (The deserter who was taken prisoner) (Urumchi: Shinjang Televiziasi, 1997).

49. See Huji Tudi, "Uyghur-Pakistan Relations," *Turkistan Newsletter,* 14 December 2000.

50. See *Daily Pioneer,* 5 April 2000; and Anwar Iqbal, "Pakistan Detains Two U.S. Nationals," *Washington Times,* 18 June 2002.

51. See Ahmad Faruqui, "China Card Could Yet Trump Musharraf," *Asia Times,* 25 May 2002.

52. Tomur Davamät, *Dostliq Säpiri: Ottura Asiyadiki Bäsh Dölätkä Ziyarät* (Friendship journey: A trip to Central Asia's five states) (Beijing: Millätlär Näshiriyati, 1996), p. 198.

53. Tamora Vidaillet, "Central Asian Grouping to Seek Revival in China," Reuters, 6 January 2002.

54. Uzbekistan's inclusion in the alliance in 2001 was also significant in that it represented a reorientation of the group's joint interests to address the issues of Muslim fundamentalism and terrorist activity in Central Asia.

55. See Vidaillet, "Central Asian Grouping to Seek Revival in China"; David R. Sands, "China Counters U.S. Influence," *Washington Times,* 11 January 2002; and Sean L. Yom, "Conflict Profile: Uighur Muslims in Xinjiang," *The Self-Determination Organization,* 14 December 2001.

56. *Radio Free Europe/Radio Liberty,* 29 November 2001.

57. See John Pomfret, "In Its Own Neighborhood, China Emerges as Leader," *Washington Post,* 18 October 2001.

58. Arjun Appadurai, *Modernity at Large* (Minneapolis: University of Minnesota Press, 1997), p. 40.

59. "The Annihilation of Separatist Forces Is Xinjiang's First Priority," Uyghur Information Agency, 15 January 2003.

60. For more on the Indian government's recent stance toward Uyghur nationalists, see B. Ramam, "U.S. and Terrorism in Xinjiang," South Asian Analyst Group, Paper no. 499, 24 July 2002, www.saag.org/papers5/paper499.html (accessed 23 September 2003).

Notes to Chapter 9

Thanks to Avram Primack and Huiping Li for helping me with the maps, S. Frederick Starr for his editing, and Justin Rudelson for introducing me to this project.

1. S. Toops, "China: A Geographic Preface," in *Understanding Contemporary China,* ed. R. Gamer (Boulder, Colo.: Rienner, 1999), pp. 11–27.

2. J. Aird, "Population Studies and Population Policy in China," *Population and Development Review* 8, no. 2 (1982): 267–297; Judith Bannister, *China's Changing Population* (Stanford, Calif.: Stanford University Press, 1987); and Dudley L. Poston Jr. and David Yaukey, eds., *The Population of Modern China* (New York: Plenum Press, 1992).

3. C. Pannell and L. Ma, "Urban Transition and Interstate Relations in a Dynamic Post-Soviet Borderland: The Xinjiang Uygur Autonomous Region of China," *Post-Soviet Geography and Economics* 38, no. 4 (1997): 206–229.

4. Chang Chih-yi, "Land Utilization and Settlement Possibilities in Sinkiang," *Geographical Review* 39 (1949): 57–75.

5. M. Freeberne, "Demographic and Economic Changes in the Sinkiang Uighur Autonomous Region," *Population Studies* 20, no. 1 (1966): 103–124.

6. Yuan Qingli, "Population Changes in Xinjiang Uighur Autonomous Region (1949–1984)," *Central Asian Survey* 9 (1990): 49–73; Pannell and Ma, "Urban Transition and Interstate Relations," p. 212; and Xinjiang Uyghur Autonomous Region Bureau of Statistics (XBS), *Xinjiang Tongji Nianjian, 2001* (Xinjiang statistical yearbook, 2001) (Beijing: China Statistics Press, 2001) (hereafter *XSY 2001*).

7. S. Toops, "The Population Landscape of Xinjiang/East Turkistan," *Inner Asia* 2, no. 2 (2000): 155–170; and Owen Lattimore, *The Inner Asian Frontiers of China* (London: Oxford University Press, 1940).

8. J. Millward, "Historical Perspectives on Contemporary Xinjiang," *Inner Asia* 2, no. 2 (2000): 121–136.

9. P. Gaubatz, *Beyond the Great Wall: Urban Form and Transformation on the Chinese Frontiers* (Stanford, Calif.: Stanford University Press, 1996).

10. Linda Benson, *The Ili Rebellion: The Moslem Challenge to Chinese Authority in Xinjiang, 1944–1949* (Armonk, N.Y.: Sharpe, 1990).

11. Linda Benson and Ingvar Svanberg, *China's Last Nomads: The History and Culture of China's Kazaks* (Armonk, N.Y.: Sharpe, 1998).

12. Chang, "Land Utilization and Settlement," p. 62.

13. Ibid.

14. Freeberne, "Demographic and Economic Changes," p. 108.

15. Yuan, "Population Changes in Xinjiang."

16. J. Seymour, "Xinjiang's Production and Construction Corps, and the Sinification of Eastern Turkestan," *Inner Asia* 2, no. 2 (2000): 171–193.

17. Yuan, "Population Changes in Xinjiang," p. 62.

18. Benson and Svanberg, *China's Last Nomads,* p. 137.

19. Seymour, "Xinjiang's Production and Construction Corps," p. 174.

20. Yuan, "Population Changes in Xinjiang," p. 63.

21. XBS, *Xinjiang Tongji Nianjian, 1996* (Xinjiang statistical yearbook, 1996) (Beijing: China Statistics Press, 1996) (hereafter *XSY 1996*).

22. Ibid., p. 52.

23. *XSY 2001*, p. 93.

24. Ibid.; and State Statistical Bureau, *Zhongguo Tongji Nianjian, 2000* (China statistical yearbook, 2000) (Beijing: China Statistics Press, 2000) (hereafter *CSY 2000*).

25. XBS, *Xinjiang Tongji Nianjian, 1998* (Xinjiang statistical yearbook, 1998) (Beijing: China Statistics Press, 1998).

26. *XSY 2001*, pp. 95, 117; and *CSY 2000*, p. 95.

27. XBS, *Xinjiang Tongji Nianjian, 1999* (Xinjiang statistical yearbook, 1999) (Beijing: China Statistics Press, 1999) (hereafter *XSY 1999*), pp. 67–69.

28. Ibid., p. 5.
29. Toops, "Population Landscape of Xinjiang/East Turkistan," pp. 160–161; *CSY 2000*, p. 96; and XBS, *Xinjiang Tongji Nianjian, 2000* (Xinjiang statistical yearbook, 2000) (Beijing: China Statistics Press, 2000) (hereafter *XSY 2000*).
30. Ibid., p. 70.
31. *XSY 2001*, p. 93; and *XSY 1999*, pp. 67–69.
32. *XSY 2001*, pp. 108–113.
33. Ibid.
34. Yuan, "Population Changes in Xinjiang," pp. 61–63; and Freeberne, "Demographic and Economic Changes," pp. 105–107.
35. Yuan, "Population Changes in Xinjiang," p. 63; and Benson and Svanberg, *China's Last Nomads*, p. 137.
36. S. Toops, "Trade between Xinjiang and Central Asia," in *Xinjiang in the Twentieth Century: Historical, Anthropological, and Geographical Perspectives*, Occasional Paper no. 65, ed. L. Benson, J. Rudelson, and S. Toops (Washington, D.C.: Woodrow Wilson Center, Asia Program, 1994), pp. 18–35.
37. *XSY 2001*, pp. 120–122.
38. Toops, "Population Landscape of Xinjiang/East Turkistan," p. 167.
39. *CSY 2000*, p. 60.
40. *XSY 1999*, pp. 40–41.
41. Ibid.
42. S. Toops, "Xinjiang (Eastern Turkistan): Names, Regions, Landscapes, Future(s)," in *Changing China* , ed. C. Hsieh (Boulder, Colo.: Westview, 2003), pp. 411–421.

Notes to Chapter 10

My thanks to Dr. Avram Primack, Huiping Li, and Larry Hargrave for producing the maps. The assistance of Dale R. Lightfoot, Abduwali, and Hamit is greatly appreciated. Thanks to S. Frederick Starr for his editing and to Justin Rudelson for introducing me to this project.
1. Thomas J. Wilbanks, "'Sustainable Development' in Geographic Perspective," *Annals of the Association of American Geographers* 84, no. 4 (1994): 541–556.
2. S. Mandel and Z. L. Shiftan, *Groundwater Resources: Investigation and Development* (New York: Academic Press, 1981).
3. Owen Lattimore, *Inner Asian Frontiers of China* (London: Oxford University Press, 1940); and Chang Chih-yi, "Land Utilization and Settlement Possibilities in Sinkiang," *The Geographical Review* 39, no. 1 (1949): 57–75.
4. Xinjiang Uyghur Autonomous Region Bureau of Statistics (XBS), *Xinjiang Tongji Nianjian, 2000* (Xinjiang statistical yearbook, 2000) (Beijing: China Statistics Press, 2000) (hereafter *XSY 2000*).
5. Xie Xiangfang, ed., *Xinjiang Weiwuer Zizhiqu Jingji Dili* (Xinjiang Uyghur Autonomous Region Economic Geography) (Beijing: Xinhua Press, 1991).
6. *XSY 2000*.
7. Xie, *Xinjiang Weiwuer Zizhiqu Jingji Dili, 1991*
8. *XSY 2000*.
9. Graham A. Tobin et al., "Water Resources," in *Geography in America,* ed. Gary L. Gaile and Cort J. Wilmott (Columbus, Ohio: Merrill, 1989).

10. Yvonna S. Lincoln and Egon G. Guba, *Naturalistic Inquiry* (Beverly Hills, Calif.: Sage, 1985).

11. Dale R. Lightfoot, "Moroccan Khettara: Traditional Irrigation and Progressive Desiccation," *Geoforum* 27, no. 2 (1996): 261–273; and Dale R. Lightfoot. "Syrian Qanat Romani: History, Ecology, Abandonment," *Journal of Arid Environments* 33, no. 3 (1996): 321–336.

12. T. Hoppe, "An Essay on Reproduction: The Example of Xinjiang Uighur Autonomous Region," in *Learning from China?* ed. B. Glaeser (London: Allen and Unwin, 1987), pp. 56–84.

13. Hoppe, "Essay on Reproduction."

14. Wilbanks, "'Sustainable Development.'"

15. Zhang Qishun and Zhang Xiao, "Water Issues and Sustainable Social Development in China," *Water International* 20 (1995): 122–128.

16. Xu Jinfa, "China's 21st Century Agenda and Sustainable Development in Northwest China," *Ganhan Dili* (Arid Land Geography) 19, no. 1 (1996): 85–89.

17. Zhang Yangsheng, "Thoughts on Sustainable Development in the Arid Areas of Northwest China," *Ganhan Dili* (Arid Land Geography) 19, no. 1 (1996): 27–31.

18. Gao Zhigang, "Preliminary Study on Some Issues of Sustainable Development in Xinjiang's Oases," *Ganhan Dili* (Arid Land Geography) 19, no. 1 (1996): 85–89; Ma Junjie, "On Basic Problems of Regional Sustainable Development Study in Northwest China," *Ganhan Dili* (Arid Land Geography) 19, no. 1 (1996): 64–67; and Wang Shuji, "Arid Environment and Human Production Activity in the Turpan Basin," *Geographical Symposium of Arid Zone (Beijing)* 4 (1995): 28–34.

19. Han Delin, "Strengthen the Research and Construction of Oases in China," *Ganhan Dili* (Arid Land Geography) 19, no. 1 (1996): 43–47.

20. Sun Rongzhang, "Some Strategic Problems of the Agricultural Development of the Tarim Basin," *Geographical Symposium of Arid Zone (Beijing)* 1 (1989): 33–43; Sun Rongzhang, "Agricultural Development and Management in the Khotan Area of Xinjiang," *Zhongguo Ganhan Yanjiu* (Chinese Journal of Arid Land Research) 7, no. 4 (1995): 323–332; and Sun Rongzhang et al., "The Utilization of Water Resources of the Tarim River and the Distribution of Agriculture Production," *Geographical Symposium of Arid Zone (Beijing)* 1 (1989): 24–43.

21. Sun Wanzhong et al., "The Changes and Administration of the Ecological Environment in the Oases of the Yarkant and Kashgar River Basin," *Ganhan Dili* (Arid Land Geography) 11, no. 2 (1988): 31–35; and Cheng Zhengcai, "A Catastrophic Flood and Some Related Problems in the Tarim River in 1994," *Ganhan Dili* (Arid Land Geography) 18, no. 2 (1995): 8–16.

22. Tang Qicheng, "Development and Utilization of Water Resources in the Desert Areas of Northwestern China," *Zhongguo Ganhan Yanjiu* (Chinese Journal of Arid Land Research) 4, no. 4 (1991): 283–294; Chen Hesheng, "Problems of Water Resource Utilization in Northwestern China," *Zhongguo Ganhan Yanjiu* (Chinese Journal of Arid Land Research) 4, no. 4 (1991): 273–282; Richard W. Reeves, Charles F. Hutchinson, and John W. Olsen, "Agricultural Development in China's Arid West: Variations in Some Familiar Themes," in *Agricultural Reform and Development in China: Achievements, Current Status, and Future Outlook,* ed. T. C. Tso (Beltsville, Md.: Ideals, 1990), pp. 339–350; Zhao Songqiao, *Physical Geography of China* (New York: Wiley, 1986); Wei Zhongyi and Tang Qicheng, "The Hydrological Effect of Water Resources Development and Its Changes on Utilization Models in the Arid Zone of Northwest China," *Zhongguo Ganhan Yanjiu* (Chinese Journal of Arid Land

Research) 2, no. 1 (1989): 45–52; and You Pingda, "Surface Water Resources and Runoff Composition in the Tarim River Basin," *Ganhan Dili* (Arid Land Geography) 18, no. 2 (1995): 29–35.

23. Chen Mengxiang and Zuhuang Cai, "Groundwater Resources and Hydro-environmental Problems in China," *Episodes* 18, no. 1 (1995): 66–68; Tang, "Development and Utilization of Water Resources"; and Wei and Tang, "Hydrological Effect."

24. Wei and Tang, "Hydrological Effect."

25. T. Hoppe, "Observations on Uygur Land Use in Turpan County, Xinjiang: A Preliminary Report on Fieldwork in Summer 1985," *Central Asiatic Journal* 31, nos. 3–4 (1987): 224–251.

26. Hao Yuling and Lu Xin, "Water Environment and Sustainable Development along the Belt of Xinjiang Section of the New Eurasian Continental Bridge," *Ganhan Dili* (Arid Land Geography) 19, no. 1 (1996): 21–26; and Tang, "Development and Utilization of Water Resources."

27. S. Toops, "Trade between Xinjiang and Central Asia," in *Xinjiang in the Twentieth Century: Historical, Anthropological, and Geographical Perspectives,* Occasional Paper, no. 65, ed. L. Benson, J. Rudelson, and S. Toops (Washington, D.C.: Woodrow Wilson Center, Asia Program, 1994), pp. 18–35.

28. S. Toops. "Tourism in Xinjiang, China," *Journal of Cultural Geography* 12, no. 2 (1992): 19–34; and Stanley Toops, "Tourism in Xinjiang: Practice and Place," in *Tourism in China,* ed. A. Lew and L. Yu (Boulder, Colo.: Westview, 1995), pp. 179–202.

29. S. Toops, "Xinjiang's Handicraft Industry," *Annals of Tourism Research* 20, no. 1 (1993): pp. 88–106.

30. Zhao Hongbin and Jiao Peixin, "Study on Interrelated Countermeasures of Water Resource Utilization and Petroleum Industry Development in Xinjiang," *Ganhan Dili* (Arid Land Geography) 18, no. 3 (1995): 15–19.

31. T. Cannon, "National Minorities and the Internal Frontier," in *China's Regional Development,* ed. D. Goodman (New York: Routledge, 1989), pp. 57–76; K. Griffin, "Rural Development in an Arid Region: Xinjiang," *Third World Quarterly* 8, no. 3 (1986): 978–1001; D. H. McMillen, *Chinese Communist Power and Policy in Xinjiang, 1949–1977* (Boulder, Colo.: Westview, 1979); and D. H. McMillen, "Xinjiang and the Production and Construction Corps: A Han Organization in a Non-Han Region," *Australian Journal of Chinese Affairs* 6 (1981): 65–96.

32. Gaye Christoffersen, "Xinjiang and the Great Islamic Circle: The Impact of Transnational Forces on Chinese Regional Economic Planning," *China Quarterly* 133 (1993): 130–151; Lillian Craig Harris, "Xinjiang, Central Asia, and the Implications for China's Policy in the Islamic World," *China Quarterly* 133 (1993): 111–129; and S. Toops, "Recent Uygur Leaders of Xinjiang," *Central Asian Survey* 11, no. 2 (1992): 77–99.

33. Chen Hesheng, "Problems on Water Resource Utilization in Northwestern China," *Zhongguo Ganhan Yanjiu* (Chinese Journal of Arid Land Research) 4, no. 4 (1991): 273–282; Wei and Tang, "Hydrological Effect"; and Chen and Zuhuang, "Groundwater Resources and Hydro-environmental Problems."

34. Tang Yijian and Zhang Shen, "Economic Development and Water-Related Environmental Problems in China," *Chinese Geography and Environment* 3, no. 3 (1990): 82–98; Tang, "Development and Utilization of Water Resources"; and Zhang and Zhang, "Water Issues."

35. Tang, "Development and Utilization of Water Resources"; Chen Hesheng, "Prob-

lems of Water Resource Utilization"; Reeves et al., "Agricultural Development in China's Arid West"; and Wei and Tang, "Hydrological Effect."

36. P. S. Triolo and C. Hegadorn, "China's Wild West," *The China Business Review* (March–April 1996): 41–46.

37. Reeves et al., "Agricultural Development in China's Arid West."

38. Triolo and Hegadorn, "China's Wild West."

39. Xinjiang Uyghur Autonomous Region Bureau of Statistics (XBS), *Xinjiang Tongji Nianjian, 2001* (Xinjiang statistical yearbook, 2001) (Beijing: China Statistics Press, 2001).

40. Pan Xuebiao, "Analysis on the Temporal and Spatial Change of Cotton Production in Xinjang Based on GIS," *Ganhan Dili* (Arid Land Geography) 23, no. 3 (2000): 199–206.

41. Reeves et al., "Agricultural Development in China's Arid West."

42. Fan Zili et al., "Problems, Protection and Improvement of Ecological Environment in Xinjiang," *Ganhan Dili* (Arid Land Geography) 23, no. 4 (2000): 298–303.

43. H. Tursun et al., "Some Thoughts about the Regional Economic Development in Xinjiang in the 21st Century," *Ganhan Dili* (Arid Land Geography) 23, no. 1 (2000): 49–54; and H. Tursun et al., "Great Exploitation of the West and Some Thoughts of the Great Development Strategy of Xinjiang," *Ganhan Dili* (Arid Land Geography) 23, no. 3 (2000): 193–198.

44. Ma Yanlin, "Study on the Index System of Appraising Sustainable Agricultural and Rural Development (SARD) in Arid Area—A Case Study of Turpan Oasis, Xinjiang," *Ganhan Dili* (Arid Land Geography) 23, no. 3 (2000): 252–258.

45. Song Yi, "Changes in China's Agriculture," *Beijing Review* 34, no. 40 (1991): 17–21; and Hoppe, "Observations on Uygur Land Use."

46. Tang, "Development and Utilization of Water Resources"; Zhang and Zhang, "Water Issues"; and Wei and Tang, "Hydrological Effect."

47. Linda Benson and Ingvar Svanberg, *China's Last Nomads: The History and Culture of China's Kazaks* (Armonk, N.Y.: Sharpe, 1998).

48. Tsui Yenhu, "The Development of Social Organizations in the Pastoral Areas of North Xinjiang and Their Relationship with the Environment," *Culture and Environment in Inner Asia* 2 (1996): 205–230.

49. J. Seymour, "Xinjiang's Production and Construction Corps and the Sinification of Eastern Turkestan," *Inner Asia* 2, no. 2 (2000): 171–194.

50. B. Hamann, "Impacts of the Reform Policy on Kazak Pastoral Farming in China," *Geographische Zeitschrift* 87, no. 1 (1999): 46–53.

51. T. Banks, "Property Rights and the Environment in Pastoral China," *Development and Change* 32, no. 4 (2001): 717–740.

52. Benson and Svanberg, *China's Last Nomads.*

53. B. Nizam, "Grain Balance and Recent Trends in Grain Production in Xinjiang Uighur Autonomous Region, China," *Science Reports of the Tohoku University,* Series A, 74, no. 1 (2000): 115–148.

54. B. Nizam, "Spatial Structure of Agriculture and Its Changes in Xinjiang Uighur Autonomous Region, China," *Science Reports of the Tohoku University,* Series 7: Geography, 50, no. 2 (2001): 115–148.

55. S. Rozelle, G. Veeck, and J. Huang, "The Impact of Environmental Degradation on Grain Production in China, 1975–1990," *Economic Geography* 73, no. 1 (1997): 44–66.

Notes to Chapter 11

1. Data supporting this discussion are taken from the UN Development Program (UNDP), www.undp.org (accessed 23 October 2002); Li F. et al., "Study on the Life Expectancy of Residents in Xinjiang Production and Construction Group, from 1997 to 1999," *Zhonghua liuxing bingxue zazhi* 23 (2002): 194–197; and Tom Korski, "Uygurs' Lives Shorter Than Most Other Parts of Region," *South China Morning Post,* 3 February 1998.

2. Dudley L. Poston Jr., "Social and Economic Development and the Fertility Transitions in Mainland China and Taiwan," *Population and Development Review* 26 supplement (2000): 40–60; and "Eastern Turkestanis Condemn Chinese Nuclear Test," *World Tibet Network News,* 8 October 1994, www.tibet.ca/wtnarchive/1994/10/8_1.html (accessed 8 October 2003).

3. For example, see the 2002 study in which Uyghurs ranked health care as their primary concern relating to development issues. Analysis of the results of this questionnaire are broken down at the township level in *SAI Survey Section Report One—XUAR* (July 2002), which is available at UNDP, www.unchina.org/undp/documents/partners/English/Xinjiang.pdf (accessed 8 October 2003).

4. See Wang X. and You X., "An Analysis of the Uneven Prevalence of Tuberculosis in Various Areas and Regions in China," *Zhonghua liuxing bingxue zazhi* 15, no. 4 (1994): 195–198, available online in the PubMed database at PMID: 7834700 (accessed 8 October 2003).

5. For more on the consequences of environmental degradation in Xinjiang, see Stanley W. Toops, chapter 10 in this volume.

6. See Japan International Cooperation Agency Planning and Evaluation Department, *Country Profile on Disability—PRC* (March 2002).

7. Such a generalization emerges from review of materials such as the UNDP human development reports for Kazakstan. A finer-grained comparison would require analysis of the effects of rising mortality rates and declining health care in 1990s Kazakstan during its own social transitions under market reform.

8. Deng Kezhong, "Bianhua juda de xinjiang weisheng shiye" (Xinjiang health care sector in transformation), in *Xinjiang jingji yu shehui fazhan gaishu,* ed. Jin Yunhui (Urumchi: Xinjiang renmin chubanshe, 1993), pp. 154–156; and XUAR People's Government, *Xinjiang nianjian, 1995* (Xinjiang yearbook, 1995) (Urumchi: Renmin chubanshe, 1996), pp. 338–345.

9. For example, see Deng, "Bianhua juda de xinjiang weisheng shiye." Expenditure figures are taken from table 5 of Government of Australia and the Government of the People's Republic of China, *XUAR-PRC HIV/AIDS Prevention and Care Project* (2000), p. 22, prepared for submission to the Australian Agency for International Development.

10. For a discussion of articles appearing in *People's Daily* and *China Youth Daily,* see Antoaneta Bezlova, "Health System Ill Due to Market Reforms," IPS Wire Service Report, 18 August 2000, www.hartford-hwp.com/archives/55/350.html (accessed 8 October 2003).

11. UN Office on Drugs and Crime, *UNDCP China Country Profile* (June 2000), www.unodc.un.or.th/material/document/2000-7.pdf (accessed 8 October 2003).

12. What limited information exists is even more limited in its circulation. For example, in the early 1990s I was able briefly to inspect a newly published volume on

economic development in Urumchi that mapped and listed all the sources of industrial pollution in that city and the surrounding region; the volume was labeled classified (*baomi*), one grade more restricted than documents marked for internal circulation (*neibu*). Such materials cannot be circulated freely among Han and Uyghur scholars in Xinjiang and are even more sensitive for foreign researchers.

13. Muhtar Hesam, joke-telling session recorded by the author, Yining, 1996.

14. N. F. Katanov and Karl Heinrich Menges, *Volkskundliche Texte aus Ost-Türkistan* (1933; reprinted, Leipzig: Zentralantiquariat der Deutschen Demokratischen Republik, 1976), pp. 46–47 (translated from the Uyghur by the author).

15. Artoush Kumul cites Jean Baptiste Naudet in support of his claim that the groups were banned in August. See Artoush Kumul, "Le 'Separatisme' Ouïgour au XXe Siècle: Histoire et Actualité," *Cahiers d'études sur la Méditerranée orientale et le monde turco-iranien* 25 (1998): 83–91; and Jean Baptiste Naudet, "Quand la Chine écrasa la révolte des Ouïgours du Xinjiang," *Le Monde,* 23 May 1997. In early August, informants who were Yining residents reported that fines of 50 yuan per person were being levied for anyone who continued to participate and that such fines had been instituted since early April.

16. For more on this, see Jay Dautcher, "Reading Out of Print: Popular Culture, Protests, and the Politics of Religion on China's Northwest Frontier," in *China Beyond the Headlines: A Global Dialogue on the Search for China's Future,* ed. Timothy Weston and Lionel Jensen (Boulder, Colo.: Rowman and Littlefield, 2000), pp. 273–294.

17. A larger number of alleged mäxräp leaders were detained for a few days after the protest, but only four young men were kept in detention, where they remained for more than three months; this was according to the brother of one of the detained men.

18. See "Uighur Emigres Warn Central Asia of Conflict," *BBC—Summary of World Broadcasts,* 6 November 1997.

19. Benjamin Kang Lim, "China Fires Officials in Muslim Region Crackdown," Reuters News Service, 26 June 1997.

20. The phrase "'Determined efforts must be made to eliminate "vermin" and eradicate poisonous weeds,' says Amudun Niyaz during inspection of Ili prefecture" (*Xinjiang ribao* [Xinjiang Daily], 28 July 1997, p. 1) appears as "Xinjiang Official Says 'Poisonous Weed' Separatists Must Be Eliminated," *BBC—Summary of World Broadcasts,* 13 August 1997.

21. Popular song performed by Abdukhahar on a Uyghur-language radio in Yining (Gulja) in 1996.

22. For example, see "The Surprising Extinction of the Charas Trade," *ODCCP—Bulletin on Narcotics* 1 (1953), www.odccp.org/odccp/bulletin/bulletin_1953–01–01_1_page002.html (accessed 26 October 2000).

23. Katanov and Menges, *Volkskundliche Texte aus Ost-Türkistan,* pp. 46–47.

24. See *XUAR-PRC HIV/AIDS Prevention and Care Project* (2000).

25. I was living in the Shanxihangzi area throughout this period and was present at discussions on the topic that took place among local merchants and store security personnel, but I cannot state with certainty whether the drugs sold were opium or heroin.

26. Sidik Rozi Haji, "Hro'ingha kharshi küchlük hujum khilayli" (Let's strike hard against heroin), *Urumchi Këchlik Gazeti,* 30 May 1994, p. 1 (translation from Uyghur by the author).

27. Haji, "Hro'ingha kharshi küchlük hujum khilayli," p. XX, emphasis added.

28. Ibid.

29. Ibid., emphasis added.

30. Xin Min, "Analysis of Drug Abuse in Wulumuqi," *Zhongguo ayowu yilaixing zazhi* (Chinese Journal of Drug Dependence) 10, no. 1 (2001), www.nidd.ac.cn/English/journal/2001/2001–1/contents.htm#xin (accessed 8 October 2003).

Notes to Chapter 12

1. For example, see Gaye Christoffersen, "Xinjiang and the Great Islamic Circle: The Impact of Transnational Forces on Chinese Regional Economic Planning," *China Quarterly* 133 (March 1993): 130–151; Lillian Craig Harris, "Xinjiang, Central Asia and the Implications for China's Policy in the Islamic World," *China Quarterly* 133 (March 1993): 111–129; and Jane Macartney, "China to Build Steel Great Wall against Separatism," Reuters News Service, 4 June 1996.

2. Justin Jon Rudelson, *Oasis Identities: Uyghur Nationalism along China's Silk Road* (New York: Columbia University Press, 1997).

3. Johan Galtung illuminates the twists and turns in Chinese policies over the past fifty years in "China's Path to Development," in *Learning from China? Development and Environment in Third World Countries*, ed. Bernhard Glaeser (London: Allen and Unwin, 1983).

4. Rudelson, *Oasis Identities*, p. 6.

5. The southern Tarim basin region from Yarkand to Keriya was most influenced by Indian culture; the western Turkistan region of the Ferghana valley, including the Andijan, Kokand, and Osh, influenced Kashgar toward Kucha; the northwestern Zungharian basin was oriented to the Semirechye (Seven Rivers) region, today's Kazakstan and parts of western Central Asia; and eastern Xinjiang, including Turpan and Hami (and Urumchi), was tied to China.

6. Cultural awareness is strongest among Uyghurs living around the Tarim basin, the region known as Altä-shähär, or "six cities," for the six historically major oases of the Tarim basin (i.e., Khotan, Yarkand, Kashgar, Uch-Turpan, Yangi-Hissar, and Aksu). The Turkic dialects spoken in Xinjiang are mutually intelligible to one degree or another.

7. James A. Millward, phone conversation with the author, 7 July 1995.

8. Jonathan N. Lipman, phone conversation with the author, 23 January 1997.

9. See Joseph Fletcher, "The Heyday of the Ch'ing Order in Mongolia, Sinkiang, and Tibet," in *The Cambridge History of China*, vol. 10, *Late Ch'ing 1800–1911*, part I, ed. John K. Fairbank (Cambridge: Cambridge University Press, 1978), pp. 351–408.

10. C. P. Skrine, *Chinese Central Asia* (Boston: Houghton Mifflin, 1926); and Rudelson, *Oasis Identities*, p. 41.

11. Linda Benson and Ingvar Svanberg, "The Kazaks in Xinjiang," in *The Kazaks of China: Essays on an Ethnic Minority*, Acta Universitatis Upsaliensis, Studia Multiethnica Upsaliensia no. 5, ed. Linda Benson and Ingvar Svanberg (Uppsala, Sweden: Uppsala University Center for Multiethnic Research, 1988), pp. 1–106.

12. Akira Haneda, "Introduction: The Problems of Turkicization and Islamization of East Turkistan," *Acta Asiatica* 34 (1978): 1–21; and Joseph Fletcher, "Ch'ing Inner Asia," in *The Cambridge History of China*, vol. 10, *Late Ch'ing 1800–1911*, part I, ed. John K. Fairbank (Cambridge: Cambridge University Press, 1978), pp. 35–106.

13. Donald H. McMillen, *Chinese Communist Power and Policy in Xinjiang, 1949–77* (Boulder, Colo.: Westview, 1979), p. 175.

14. Ibid., p. 123.

15. Ji Ping, "Frontier Migration and Ethnic Assimilation: A Case of Xinjiang Uygur Autonomous Region of China" (Ph.D. diss., Brown University, 1990), pp. 200–201.

16. See Mette Halskov Hansen, *Lessons in Being Chinese* (Seattle: University of Washington Press, 1999); William Jankowiak, *Sex, Death and Hierarchy in a Chinese City* (New York: Columbia University Press, 1993); P. K. Kaup, *Ethnic Politics in China* (Boulder, Colo.: Rienner, 2000); and Martin Schoenhals, "Education and Ethnicity among the Liangshan Yi," in *Perspectives on the Yi of Southwest China,* ed. Stevan Harrell (Berkeley: University of California Press, 2001), pp. 238–255.

17. Donald H. McMillen, "Xinjiang and Wang En Mao: New Directions in Power, Policy and Integration." *China Quarterly* 99 (1984): 579.

18. Rudelson, *Oasis Identities,* p. 117.

19. Kaup, *Ethnic Politics in China.*

20. L. Schein, *Minority Rules* (Durham, N.C.: Duke University Press, 2000).

21. R. Litzinger, *Yao* (Durham, N.C.: Duke University Press, 2000).

22. Schoenhals, "Education and Ethnicity among the Liangshan Yi."

23. Rudelson, *Oasis Identities;* Ping, "Frontier Migration and Ethnic Assimilation," p. 194; and William C. Clark, "Convergence or Divergence: Uighur Family Change in Urumchi" (Ph.D. diss., University of Washington, 1999), p. 99.

24. Andrew D. W. Forbes, *Warlords and Muslims in Chinese Central Asia: A Political History of Republican Sinkiang, 1911–1949* (Cambridge: Cambridge University Press, 1986).

25. Ping, "Frontier Migration and Ethnic Assimilation," p. 194.

26. Ibid.

27. Rudelson, *Oasis Identities.*

28. Linda Benson, phone conversation with the author, 18 March 1996.

29. Clark, "Convergence or Divergence," p. 100.

30. B. Williams, "Nationalism, Traditionalism, and the Problem of Cultural Inauthenticity," in *Nationalist Ideologies and the Production of National Cultures,* ed. Richard Fox (Washington, D.C.: American Ethnological Society Monograph Series no. 2, 1991), pp. 112–129; D. Lowenthal, *The Past Is a Foreign Country* (Cambridge: Cambridge University Press, 1985); and Schein, *Minority Rules.*

31. Rudelson, *Oasis Identities,* pp. 167–175.

32. Ibid., p. 6.

33. Ibid., pp. 137–165.

34. Thomas B. Allen, "The Silk Road's Lost World," *National Geographic* 189, no. 3 (1996): 44–51; and Geng Shimin, "Recent Chinese Research in Turkic Studies," *Central Asian Survey* 1, no. 1 (1982): 109–116.

35. Evan Hadingham, "The Mummies of Xinjiang," *Discover* (April 1994): 68–77.

36. Rudelson, *Oasis Identities,* pp. 157–159.

37. Charles Hutzler, "Trade Is China's Carrot to Muslim Separatists," *Wall Street Journal,* 21 September 2001.

38. Ibid.

39. Nicolas Becquelin, "Xinjiang in the Nineties," *China Journal* 44 (July 2001).

40. "China Also Harmed by Separatist-Minded Eastern Turkistan Terrorists," *People's Daily,* 10 October 2001; and Erik Eckholm, "China Seeks World Support in Fight with Its Muslim Separatists," *New York Times,* 12 October 2001.

41. "Chinese Police Eager and Ready to Step Up Fight against Terrorism," *Agence France-Presse,* 21 September 2002.

42. "Jiang Calls for Pushing Forward 'Develop the West' Campaign," *People's Daily,* 2 April 2002; Guo Li, "Wu Yi Inspects Xinjiang 2–8 September, Urges Xinjiang to Expedite Economic Growth," *Xinhua* (Beijing), 9 September 2002; and "Wu Bangguo Makes Inspection Tour of Xinjiang, Qinghai," *Xinhua* (Beijing), 4 September 2002.

43. "HIV/AIDS: China's Titanic Peril: China's Response to AIDS—2001 Status and Analysis," *UNAIDS* (2001).

44. Zeng Yi and Wu Zunyou, "Control of AIDS Epidemic in China," *Bulletin of the Chinese Academy of Sciences* 2 (2001): 6.

Notes to Chapter 13

We are grateful to the many informants who spoke with us in Beijing and in Xinjiang, sometimes at considerable risk to themselves. Given current conditions in Xinjiang, we must be extremely circumspect about identifying our interlocutors, and the reader should be aware that we have altered identities in order to protect those who provided us with information and opinions.

1. In his memoirs, a Gansu Muslim teacher narrates an oral history of Apak Khoja (whom the Chinese-speaking Muslims call Hidayat Allah) teaching the *Maktubat* of Sirhindi, one of the most important Sufi revivalist texts, to his Sino-Muslim disciples. See Anonymous, ed., *Long Ahong* (Linxia: Gansu sheng Linxia shi Mingde Qingzhensi, 1996), p. 21.

2. James Millward, "A Uyghur Muslim in Qianlong's Court: The Meanings of the Fragrant Concubine," *Journal of Asian Studies* 53, no. 2 (1994): 427–458.

3. Justin Rudelson and William Jankowiak, in chapter 12 in this volume, among others, narrate the evolution of "Uyghur" as a twentieth-century ethnonym for the sedentary oasis-dwelling Turks of Xinjiang.

4. Millward, "Uyghur Muslim," p. 447.

5. Ibid., p. 450.

6. Dru Gladney, "Representing Nationality in China: Refiguring Majority/Minority Identities," *Journal of Asian Studies* 53, no. 1 (1994): 92–123. The timing of this evolution indicates that it is not simply a project of the CCP but one more deeply embedded in the enterprise of Chinese modernism.

7. In Qing times, this suspicion was particularly focused on the khanate of Kokand, which, until its destruction by the Russian empire, constantly tested the Qing's patience and defenses by its engagement in the Kashgar region. See Laura Newby, "The Begs of Xinjiang: Between Two Worlds," *Bulletin of the School of Oriental and African Studies* 61, no. 2 (1998): 278–297.

8. In earlier periods, the government of the PRC sponsored rapid expansion of the Xinjiang Production and Construction Corps (Ch. Xinjiang shengchan jianshe bingtuan), but beginning in the early 1980s the Han were attracted to Xinjiang for economic opportunity (primarily in agriculture and construction) and migrated of their own accord. See Toops, chapter 9 in this volume. Scholars disagree on the rates of increase, and some argue that the Han-Uyghur ratio declined in the 1990s. For example, see Barry Sautman, "Is Xinjiang an Internal Colony?" *Inner Asia* 2, no. 2 (2000): 239–271. The Chinese-speaking Muslims or Hui, called "Tungan" unofficially in Xinjiang, constitute an important intermediate group all over China. See Rudelson and Jankowiak, chapter 12.

9. Here, we must note the habit, common among both Uyghurs and non-Uyghurs in Xinjiang, of conflating "Uyghur" with "Muslim." That is, a Uyghur hat is a Muslim hat, and anything true of Muslims-in-general must be true of Uyghurs. Though clearly inaccurate, such perceptions color a myriad of social, political, economic, and intellectual interactions.

10. One informant told us of an imam at an important urban mosque who is not only a state employee but also a member of the CCP. When we asked if members of the community could accept such an imam as a religious leader, he said, in Chinese, that "they have an opinion of him" (Ch. *dui ta you yijian*), implying community disapproval, but would not discuss the matter any further. In other parts of China, Hui members of the CCP may attend mosque, even go on the pilgrimage to Mecca, without significant penalty, but "Xinjiang is different."

11. As noted in several previous chapters, massive Han migration into the region has changed this demographic balance. One informant claimed that Aksu and Korla, two oases on the northern edge of the Tarim basin (in southern Xinjiang), are now Han-majority towns. Whether it is true or not, the claim represents what many Uyghurs think is happening to what they perceive as their homeland.

12. S. E. Malov, *Pamyatniki Drevnetyurkskoi Pis'mennosti* (Moscow: Publishing House of the Academy of Sciences of the USSR, 1951), pp. 34–35.

13. Joseph Fletcher, "China and Central Asia, 1369–1884," in *The Chinese World Order: Traditional China's Foreign Relations,* ed. John K. Fairbank (Cambridge, Mass.: Harvard University Press, 1978), pp. 206–224.

14. Morris Rossabi, "Ming China and Turfan, 1406–1517," *Central Asiatic Journal* 16, no. 3 (1972): 206–225.

15. James Millward, *Beyond the Pass: Economy, Ethnicity, and Empire in Qing Central Asia, 1759–1864* (Stanford, Calif.: Stanford University Press, 1998); and Newby, "Begs of Xinjiang."

16. Joanna Waley-Cohen, *Exile in Mid-Qing China: Banishment to Xinjiang, 1758–1820* (New Haven, Conn.: Yale University Press, 1991).

17. Justin Jon Rudelson, *Oasis Identities: Uyghur Nationalism along China's Silk Road* (New York: Columbia University Press, 1997).

18. See chapters 3 and 4 in this volume.

19. Joseph Fletcher, "Ch'ing Inner Asia c. 1800" and "The Heyday of the Ch'ing Order in Mongolia, Sinkiang, and Tibet," in *The Cambridge History of China,* vol. 10, *Late Ch'ing, 1800–1911,* part I, ed. John K. Fairbank (Cambridge: Cambridge University Press, 1978).

20. Newby is completing a book on Qing-Kokand relations that will explain the diverse motivations—political, religious, economic, and personal/familial—for Kokandi engagement in Qing Xinjiang.

21. Andrew D. W. Forbes, *Warlords and Muslims in Chinese Central Asia: A Political History of Republican Sinkiang, 1911–1949* (Cambridge: Cambridge University Press, 1986).

22. Linda Benson, *The Ili Rebellion: The Moslem Challenge to Chinese Authority in Xinjiang, 1944–1949* (Armonk, N.Y.: Sharpe, 1990).

23. Sean R. Roberts, chapter 8 in this volume, citing newly available Soviet sources, inclines to the latter view, as does Forbes, *Warlords and Muslims.*

24. We place "willing" in quotation marks here because the Chinese state has multiple means to compel public agreement not only with its policies but also with its definitions of reality. For a fascinating discussion of the relationship or disjuncture

between public and private discourses in China, see Perry Link, *Evening Chats in Beijing: Probing China's Predicament* (New York: Norton, 1992), especially the introduction.

25. From the beginning, this opening was funded, in part, by Saudi Arabia in the interests of drawing Muslim citizens of China (of whatever minzu) into the worldwide Islamic sphere. The Saudi government still sponsors some hundreds of pilgrimage trips per year by citizens of China.

26. The famous case of businesswoman Rebiya Kadir, arrested for sending newspaper clippings to her husband in the United States and planning to talk to American legislators, illustrates the state's power of definition inherent in the term "illegal religious activities." Part of the indictment against Kadir included the charge that she allowed or even encouraged illegal religious schools to operate in her large office building in downtown Urumchi's Uyghur quarter. She is currently serving an eight-year sentence in prison for this and other offenses.

27. Gardner Bovingdon, "Strangers in Their Own Land: The Politics of Uyghur Identity in Chinese Central Asia" (Ph.D. diss., Cornell University, 2002), cites a few exceptional publications, all of them for internal consumption only (Ch. *neibu faxing*), which do touch on these sensitive religious issues. We were able to find only hints of the continuity of Sufi rituals and must acknowledge the complexity or even inappropriateness of the term "Wahhabism," but it is used in Xinjiang to mean the "foreign" (non-Uyghur) Islamic revivalism emanating from Saudi Arabia.

28. A number of informants and scholars have called into question even the possibility of "representation" by these acculturated "minority nationalities." Several Uyghur friends scoffed at the notion that such officials (included in the ubiquitous "they" of the state) could or would ever do anything for "us."

29. The debates over the ascendancy of French, English, and Portuguese in sub-Saharan Africa carry some of the same power and ambiguity.

30. None mentioned the "Eastern Turkistan Islamic Movement" recently branded as a terrorist organization by the American government. Hizb al-Tahrir does seek a Central Asian Muslim state but has publicly repudiated violence.

31. In his dissertation, Bovingdon argues that the publicly funded reconstruction of the previously extensive great square outside the Idgah Mosque in Kashgar, much of which is now taken up with a fenced-in flower garden and obnoxiously loud clock tower (which plays an American folk song on the hour), expresses the Chinese state's desire that worshippers should have a harder time attending and hearing public prayer services and sermons at holiday times.

32. See Jay Dautcher, chapter 11 in this volume.

33. See Rudelson, *Oasis Identities,* pp. 117–120. Neither we nor Rudelson would argue that these are the *sole* components of any Uyghur's identity. Quite the contrary, variables including gender, family or lineage affiliation, socioeconomic status, educational status, neighborhood, and many more also come into play in any individual's description of self.

34. Like all ethnic identities, Hui-ness has powerful imagined components, and it has received strong stimulation and support from the Chinese state. Some Uyghurs, and a few courageous Hui, told us that the Hui "are not really a minzu," noting their strong resemblance to Han and their demographic scattering all over the Chinese culture area. Others note that the "identification" (or creation) of ten separate Muslim minzu by the Chinese state has served a very convenient "divide and conquer" function. See Jonathan N. Lipman, *Familiar Strangers: A History of Muslims in North-*

west China (Seattle: University of Washington Press, 1997); and Jonathan N. Lipman, "White Hats, Oil Cakes, and Common Blood: The Huizu in the Contemporary Chinese State," in *Governing China's Multiethnic Frontiers,* ed. Morris Rossabi (Seattle: University of Washington Press, forthcoming).

35. Scholars differ as to the importance of religion in this preservation. Some see it as an essential component of Hui identity, while others argue that the Hui are an ethnic, not a religious, minority and thus will be preserved by the Chinese state's correct minzu policies and by their own inherent (genetically determined) Hui-ness, whatever becomes of Islam among them. The latter position, of course, conforms more closely to the views of the Han leadership.

36. The ethnic, that is, genetic, distinction of Hui from other Chinese remains a complex and conflicted issue. Though most Hui do not question their own putative descent from foreign, that is, Persian or Arab, Muslims, a great deal of intermarriage must have occurred during the early centuries when only male Muslims traveled to China to sojourn. Uyghurs, on the other hand, do not doubt the "Chineseness" of the Hui and often express mistrust and suspicion of this particular group of coreligionists.

37. Rudelson, *Oasis Identities,* p. 136.

38. "Beijing Slakes the Fires of Ethnic Tension in Xinjiang," *Businessweek,* 29 May 2002.

39. "China Increases Anti-terror Efforts," Associated Press, 14 November 2001.

40. It is rarely made clear in these various government, nongovernmental organization, and journalistic reports whether the Uyghurs in question came directly from China or from the substantial Uyghur diaspora in Central Asia.

41. David Murphy, "Uyghurs: No Afghanistan," Review Publishing Company Limited (Hong Kong), 29 November 2001 (info@mail.uyghurinfo.com).

42. "Uighurs Taken in Afghanistan Must Be Returned—China," Reuters (Beijing), 11 December 2001.

43. Philip P. Pan, "U.S. Warns of Plot by Group in W. China," *Washington Post,* 29 August 2002.

44. Erkin Dolat, "The US Has Justified Chinese Persecution of the Uyghur People," Uyghur Information Agency, 27 August 2002, as reported in *Turkistan Newsletter,* 31 August 2002 (sota@wanadoo.nl).

45. In a number of recent reports on the rapid spread of HIV/AIDS in China, Xinjiang has been mentioned as a particular trouble spot, in part because of the ready availability of heroin in the region (shipped in from both the Golden Triangle and Afghanistan). See Dautcher, chapter 11, and Rudelson and Jankowiak, chapter 12.

46. Since the authorities dispose of the bodies of victims of state violence, such benediction might have to take place at considerable remove in distance and time from the actual burial.

47. For example, see "Seven Pro-Chinese Imams Killed," Associated Press, 17 September 1997.

Notes to Chapter 14

1. Prasenjit Duara, *Rescuing History from the Nation: Questioning Narratives of Modern China* (Chicago: University of Chicago Press, 1995).

2. Seamus Deane, introduction to *Nationalism, Colonialism, and Literature,* ed. Seamus Deane et al. (Minneapolis: University of Minnesota Press, 1990).

3. Because the term *"minzu"* is used to mean both "nation" and "nationality" (in the sense of the Russian term *"narodnost"*) and because the dispute between Uyghurs and the Chinese party-state hinges precisely on which sense is appropriate, there is no satisfactory English translation for the term. I render it here as "nation" throughout, though in other writings I prefer to leave it untranslated. For a further discussion, see Gardner Bovingdon, "Strangers in Their Own Land: The Politics of Uyghur Identity in Chinese Central Asia" (Ph.D. diss., Cornell University, 2002); see also Dru C. Gladney, chapter 4 in this volume, especially note 9.

4. Uradyn Erden Bulag observes that Han citizens and officials in the early 1990s "began to claim that they are also indigenous in the autonomous regions, . . . perhaps more indigenous than the Mongols." See Uradyn Erden Bulag, "Ethnic Resistance with Socialist Characteristics," in *Chinese Society: Change, Conflict and Resistance,* ed. Elizabeth J. Perry and Mark Selden (London: Routledge, 2000), pp. 191–192.

5. For example, in its January 21, 2002, document claiming that the CCP's battle with Uyghur separatists was part of the global "war on terror," the Chinese State Council elected to begin the text with a lengthy rehearsal of China's historical claims to Xinjiang. See www.peopledaily.com.cn/GB/shizheng/3586/20020121/652705.html (accessed 10 February 2002).

6. The official English translation of the institute's name, Zhongguo bianjiang shidi yanjiu zhongxin, is Center of China's Borderland History and Geography Research. I generally follow James A. Millward in translating the term *"bianjiang"* as "frontier." See James A. Millward, "New Perspectives on the Qing Frontier," in *Remapping China: Fissures in Historical Terrain,* ed. Gail Hershatter et al. (Stanford, Calif.: Stanford University Press, 1996).

7. Walker Connor's thorough and comparative study of nationalism in socialist states remains the standard reference. See Walker Connor, *The National Question in Marxist-Leninist Theory and Strategy* (Princeton, N.J.: Princeton University Press, 1984). Albert Feuerwerker saw quite early on that CCP historiography alloyed nationalism to Marxism. See Albert Feuerwerker, "China's History in Marxian Dress," in *History in Communist China,* ed. Albert Feuerwerker (Cambridge, Mass.: MIT Press, 1968), p. 23.

8. Gladney points out that Marx and Friedrich Engels adopted this stage theory of human evolution from American anthropologist Lewis Henry Morgan. See Dru Gladney, *Muslim Chinese: Ethnic Nationalism in the People's Republic* (Cambridge, Mass.: Harvard University Press, 1991), pp. 72–74.

9. A scholar of Soviet historiography observed that the value of the term "the people" lay in "its flexibility. . . . [T]he Soviet spokesman can maneuver the term almost arbitrarily." See Lowell Tillett, *The Great Friendship: Soviet Historians on the Non-Russian Nationalities* (Chapel Hill: University of North Carolina Press, 1969), p. 8. Sinologists have spotted similar patterns in Chinese official discourse. See A. Doak Barnett, *China on the Eve of Communist Takeover* (New York: Praeger, 1963); and Michael Schoenhals, *"Non-People" in the People's Republic of China: A Chronicle of Terminological Ambiguity,* Indiana East Asian Working Papers Series on Language and Politics in Modern China (Indianapolis: Indiana University East Asian Studies Center, December 20, 1997, www.easc.indiana.edu/Pages/Easc/working_papers/framed_4A_PEOPL.htm (accessed 7 July 1998).

10. William T. Rowe reminds us that "[c]enturies before the Chinese empire assumed its celebrated role as victim of incorporation into a Western-dominated 'world

system,' it was an established master at imperial domination of peripheral lands and peoples." See William T. Rowe, "Education and Empire in Southwest China: Ch'en Hung-Mou in Yunnan, 1733–38," in *Education in Late Imperial China, 1600–1900,* ed. Benjamin A. Elman and Alexander Woodside (Berkeley: University of California Press, 1994), p. 417; see also Peter C. Perdue, "Comparing Empires: Manchu Colonialism," *The International History Review* 20, no. 2 (1998).

11. For a discussion of the idea that self-determination can only be exercised once by each polity and then loses its force, see Alexis Heraclides, *The Self-Determination of Minorities in International Politics* (London: Frank Cass, 1991).

12. On the drawing up and institutionalization of these distinct categories, and particularly on the revival of the ethnonym "Uyghur," see Joseph Fletcher, "China and Central Asia, 1368–1884," in *The Chinese World Order: Traditional China's Foreign Relations,* ed. John King Fairbank (Cambridge, Mass.: Harvard University Press, 1968); Dru Gladney, "The Ethnogenesis of the Uighur," *Central Asian Survey* 9, no. 1 (1990); Justin Jon Rudelson, *Oasis Identities: Uyghur Nationalism along China's Silk Road* (New York: Columbia University Press, 1997); and Bovingdon, "Strangers in Their Own Land."

13. For critiques of the concept of tribute, see, inter alia, Fletcher, "China and Central Asia"; and James L. Hevia, *Cherishing Men from Afar: Qing Guest Ritual and the Macartney Embassy of 1793* (Durham, N.C.: Duke University Press, 1995).

14. The respected historian Tan Qixiang of Fudan University headed the editorial committee that compiled the first historical atlas of China published after the revolution, in 1955. In a 1981 lecture (published a decade later), he explained how the committee had arrived at the novel idea that "the dynasties and China cannot be equated . . . in the entire span of history only the Qing equalled China. . . . In any period prior to the Qing, China included two more polities; we absolutely cannot say that this polity was China, that one was not." Tan and the committee proposed this startling metaphysical proposition, so patently advantageous to the geopolitical interests of the PRC, as the only possible stance for "new China's historians." See Tan Qixiang, "Lishi Shang De Zhongguo He Zhongguo Lidai Jiangyu" (Historical China and China's territory in successive eras), *Zhongguo bianjiang shidi yanjiu,* no. 1 (1991): 34, 41.

15. Ma Manli, ed., *Zhongguo Xibei Bianjiang Fazhan Shi Yanjiu* (Research on the history of the development of China's northwestern frontiers) (Ha'erbin: Heilongjiang jiaoyu chubanshe, 2001), pp. 7, 11. For further discussion of the strategic use of the words "unify" and "reunify" by nationalists, see Eugen Weber, *Peasants into Frenchmen: The Modernization of Rural France, 1870–1914* (Stanford, Calif.: Stanford University Press, 1976), p. 95.

16. Turghun Almas, *Uyghurlar* (The Uyghurs) (Urumchi: Šinjang yašlar-ösmürlär näšriyati, 1989), p. 4.

17. For more examples of this kind of reasoning, see Bovingdon, "Strangers in Their Own Land," pp. 179–238. For a thorough, if occasionally sensationalist, account of the mummies' discovery and analysis, see J. P. Mallory and Victor H. Mair, *The Tarim Mummies: Ancient China and the Mystery of the Earliest Peoples from the West* (New York: Thames and Hudson, 2000).

18. Zeng Wenwu, *Zhongguo Jingying Xiyu Shi* (A history of China's management of the western regions) (Urumchi: Xinjiang Weiwu'er Zizhiqu Difangzhi Zongbianshi, 1986).

19. Ibid., p. 295 and passim.

20. Li Xin, "Ping 'Zhongguo Jingying Xiyu Shi'" (A review of "A history of China's

management of the western regions"), *Tianjin yi shi bao-du shu zhoukan,* 10 December 1936.

21. Wang Zengshan, "Dong Tu'erqisitan Gu Kucha Yi Dai Zhi Wenming" (The civilization of the area around ancient Kucha in Eastern Turkistan), *Xin Yaxiya* 4, no. 6 (1932); and Wang Zengshan, "Xinjiang Yu Tu'erqi" (Xinjiang and Turkey), *A'ertai,* 15 January 1944.

22. Uyghurs in the Soviet Union began earning doctorates in Uyghur history in the 1930s—Ershidin Hidayetov, the author of "Uyghur Uprisings for National Liberation" and "Questions Concerning Uyghur Literature and History," was one of the earliest—and their numbers increased in ensuing decades. The first Uyghurs to receive doctorates in the same subject in China emerged only in the late 1990s. To be sure, training Uyghurs to produce histories critical of Chinese claims to Central Asia was not without political interest for the Soviet government. See Ershidin Hidayetov, *Uyghur Ädäbiyat Wä Tarikh Mäsililiri* (Questions concerning Uyghur literature and history) (Alma-Ata: Qazaq Eli jurnilining näšriyati,1948); and Ershidin Hidayetov, "Uyghur Milli Azadliq Qozghilangliri" (Uyghur uprisings for national liberation), *Šärq häqiqiti,* no. 2 (1942). For more on Chinese histories before and after 1949, see Gardner Bovingdon, "The History of the History of Xinjiang," *Twentieth Century China* 26, no. 2 (2001).

23. Ma Huaiyi, "Zuguo Bu Rong Fenlie" (The motherland cannot be split apart), *Xinjiang Ribao,* 18 May 1958.

24. "*Xinjiang zi gu yilai jiushi zuguo bu ke fenge de yi bu fen.*" See Zhang Dongyue, "Guanyu Xinjiang Lishi De Ji Ge Wenti" (A few problems concerning the history of Xinjiang), *Minzu Yanjiu,* no. 6 (1959): 14. Work on other contested territories, such as Tibet and Taiwan, has adopted similar phrasing. See Cui Zhiqing, *Taiwan Shi Zhongguo Lingtu Buke Fenge De Yi Bu Fen* (Taiwan is an inseparable part of China's territory) (Beijing: Renmin chubanshe, 2001); and Xizang shehui kexueyuan, ed., *Xizang Difang Shi Zhongguo Buke Fenge De Yi Bu Fen* (The Tibet region is an inseparable part of China) (Lhasa: Xizang renmin chubanshe, 1986).

25. On the use of formulations (*tifa*), or officially set phrases, see Michael Schoenhals, *Doing Things with Words in Chinese Politics: Five Studies,* China Research Monograph Series, vol. 41 (Berkeley: Institute of East Asian Studies, University of California, 1992), pp. 6–29.

26. For more on the fate of these histories, see Ralph A. Litzinger, "Making Histories: Contending Conceptions of the Yao Past," in *Cultural Encounters on China's Ethnic Frontiers,* ed. Stevan Harrell (Seattle: University of Washington Press, 1995).

27. As the term implies, internal circulation (*neibu*) texts were distributed to a limited readership, generally to officials and specialists. Works might be limited to internal circulation because their subject matter was deemed sensitive, because their conclusions were provisional, or because officials were concerned about their possible social effects.

28. Examples are drawn from Liu Ge, "'Weiwu'erzu Shiliao Jianbian' Xin Jiu Liangge Banben De Bijiao" (A comparison of the new and old editions of "A brief compilation of historical materials on the Uyghurs") *Xinjiang tushuguan xuehui huikan* 1 (1984): 79.

29. Tillett notes that Soviet historians used terms like "*prisoedinenie,*" which suggests a fusion of equals, to euphemize the military conquest of territories by the tsarist empire. See Tillett, *Great Friendship,* pp. 331–332.

30. For further evidence of this curious stance, consider the astonishing statement

of the Nanjing University historian Wei Liangtao, "[N]o matter whether Uyghurs' historical political entities were independent or not, they were all khanates and dynasties in Chinese history." See Wei Liangtao, "Guanyu Weiwu'erzu Lishi Bianzuanxue De Ruogan Wenti" (A few questions concerning the discipline of compiling a Uyghur history), *Xinjiang Daxue Xuebao (zhexue shehui kexue ban)*, no. 3 (1984): 32.

31. Wang Enmao, speaking to scholars at Xinjiang Academy of Social Sciences in 1986, quoted in Wang Shuanqian, ed., *Xinjiang Shehui Kexueyuan 20 Nian* (Twenty years of the Xinjiang Academy of Social Sciences) (Urumchi: Xinjiang Renmin Chubanshe, 2000), p. 208. The problem of translating the term *"minzu"* is once again apparent. See note 3.

32. For details about the writing process from the afterword to the second volume, see Liu Zhixiao, *Weiwu'erzu Lishi-Zhong Bian* (The history of the Uyghurs), vol. 2 (Beijing: Zhongguo shehui kexue chubanshe, 1996), pp. 881–882. Liu died in 1999 before he could complete the third volume. See Liu Zhixiao, *Weiwu'erzu Lishi-Shang Bian* (The history of the Uyghurs), vol. 1 (Beijing: Minzu chubanshe, 1985).

33. Liu, *Weiwu'erzu Lishi-Zhong Bian,* 882.

34. Ibid., introduction.

35. Rudelson, *Oasis Identities,* p. 184n15.

36. "Weiwu'erzu jianshi" bianxiezu, ed., *Weiwu'erzu Jianshi* (A concise history of the Uyghurs), Zhongguo Shaoshu Minzu Jianshi Congshu (Series of Brief Histories of China's Minority Minzu) (Urumchi: Xinjiang renmin chubanshe, 1991), p. 407.

37. The empire of the eastern branch of the Kök Turks ruled much of today's Mongolia and northeast Xinjiang from 640 to the mid-eighth century, at which point the Uyghur empire began. See Svat Soucek, *A History of Inner Asia* (Cambridge: Cambridge University Press, 2000), chapter 2.

38. "Weiwu'erzu jianshi" bianxiezu, *Weiwu'erzu Jianshi,* p. 40.

39. Xinjiang shehui kexueyuan lishi yanjiusuo, ed., *Xinjiang Difang Lishi Ziliao Xuanji* (Selected materials on the local history of Xinjiang) (Beijing: Renmin chubanshe, 1987), p. 1.

40. Turghun, *Uyghurlar,* p. 1.

41. Duara, *Rescuing History from the Nation,* p. 4.

42. Turghun, *Uyghurlar,* p. 4.

43. Ibid.

44. Qurban Wäli, *Bizning Tarikhiy Yeziqlirimiz* (Our historical scripts) (Urumchi: Šinjang yašlar-ösmürlär näšriyati, 1988), pp. 1–2.

45. Ibid., p. 8.

46. Ibid., pp. 178, 236.

47. Abdurehim Ötkür, *Iz* (Tracks) (Urumchi: Šinjang khälq näšriyati, 1985); and Abdurehim Ötkür, *The Awakening Land, part I* (Urumchi: Šinjang khälq näšriyati,1987). He published the second part of *Awakening Land* in 1994.

48. Abdurehim, *Iz,* p. 1.

49. Rudelson makes a similar point. See Rudelson, *Oasis Identities,* pp. 32, 163–165.

50. Ibid., p. 163.

51. Mehmet Emin (Mämtimin) Bughra, *Šärqi Türkistan Tarikhi* (The history of Eastern Turkistan) (Srinagar: Bruka Parlis Basmakhanesi, 1946).

52. These criticisms are drawn from the various articles in Feng Dazhen, ed., *"Weiwu'er Ren" Deng San Ben Shu Wenti Taolunhui Lunwenji* (Collection of papers from the symposium on the three books including "The Uyghurs") (Urumchi: Xinjiang

renmin chubanshe, 1992). Most of the articles were included in Uyghur translation in an internal circulation text Uyghur college students were required to study. See Šinjang dašösi partkom täšwiqat bölümi, ed., *"Uyghurlar" Qatarliq Üc Kitab Mäsilisi Häqqidiki Muhakimä Yighinining Ilmiy Maqaliliridin Tallanma* (Selection of scholarly articles from the symposium on the problem of the three books including "The Uyghurs") (Urumchi: Neibu, 1991). For a more extensive analysis of the criticisms, see Bovingdon, "Strangers in Their Own Land."

53. A 1993 historical survey of pan-Turkism and pan-Islamism written by Ji Dachun and others refers to a mimeographed Chinese translation of Mämtimin's work circulated in 1959. See Ji Dachun et al., "Fan Yisilan Zhuyi, Fan Tujue Zhuyi Zai Xinjiang Chuanbo De Lishi Kaocha" (A historical investigation of the dissemination of pan-Islamism and pan-Turkism in Xinjiang), *Zhongguo bianjiang shidi yanjiu baogao*, nos. 3–4 (1993): 19.

54. Wang, *Xinjiang Shehui Kexueyuan 20 Nian*, p. 16.

55. Bovingdon, "Strangers in Their Own Land," pp. 218–220.

56. XUAR jiaoyu weiyuanhui gaoxiao lishi jiaocai bianxiezu, ed., *Xinjiang Difang Shi-Shiyong Ben* (A local history of Xinjiang–trial edition) (Wulumuqi: Xinjiang daxue, 1992).

57. Li Sheng and Wu Fuhuan, eds., *Xinjiang Difang Shi Xuexi Zhidao* (A local history of Xinjiang—a study guide) (Wulumuqim: Xinjiang daxue chubanshe, 1996).

58. Mämtimin Tursun and Wu Fukhuän (Wu Fuhuan), eds., *Šinjang Tarikhidiki Bäzi Mäsililär Toghrisida So'al Jawablar* (Questions and answers concerning some issues in Xinjiang's history) (Urumchi: Šinjang Dašösi näšriyati, 1992); and Wu Fuhuan and Maimaitiyiming Tu'ersun (Mämtimin Tursun), eds., *Xinjiang Lishi 36 Wen* (36 questions about Xinjiang's history) (Urumchi: Xinjiang daxue chubanshe, 1992).

59. Mämtimin and Wu, *Šinjang Tarikhidiki Bäzi Mäsililär Toghrisida So'al Jawablar*, p. 67.

60. Author's field notes, summer 1997.

61. Ling Jun, "Xitong Yanjiu He Zhengque Xuanchuan Xinjiang De Lishi Wei Zizhiqu Wending He Fazhan Fuwu" (Systematically researching and correctly propagandizing Xinjiang's history serves the stability and development of the autonomous region), *Xinjiang Shehui Kexue* 6 (2001): 78.

62. Zordun Sabir, *Ana Yurt* (Motherland), 3 vols., 2nd ed. (Urumchi: Šinjang yašlar-ösmürlär näšriyati, 2000).

63. Author's field notes, summer 2002.

64. Ibid.

65. Material drawn from Zhu Youke, "Lishi Huati: Chuban Yu Fuzai" (A historical topic: Publishing and burdens), *Xinjiang jingji bao*, 20 March 1999, www.unn.com.cn/GB/channe1445/1686/2486/2487/200109/14/105906.html (accessed 15 April 2002).

66. Other Uyghur historians have faced greater challenges in publishing their work. Tokhti Muzart, who did advanced research in Japan, was jailed in 1998 for "stealing state secrets." Nabijan Tursun, who received a doctorate in history in Moscow, was unable to publish his memoir-cum-historical essay "Moscow Impressions" (previously serialized in several journals) in book form despite its having been selected by Uyghur scholars as one of the "one hundred best Uyghur literary works of the twentieth century." He has published several historiographic works in Russian in Moscow. See the Bibliographic Guide to Xinjiang for further reading.

67. Ling, "Xitong Yanjiu He Zhengque Xuanchuan Xinjiang De Lishi Wei Zizhiqu Wending He Fazhan Fuwu."

68. Ji Dachun, ed., *Xinjiang Lishi Baiwen* (A hundred questions about Xinjiang history), Lishi Shang De Xinjiang Huitu Congshu (The illustrated book series on Xinjiang in history) (Urumchi: Xinjiang meishu sheying chubanshe, 1997).

69. Ibid., pp. 23, 27, 81.

70. Interview with the author, Urumchi, summer 2002.

71. Li Baosheng, *Xinjiang 1949 Guomindang Xinjiang Zhujun 9/25 Qiyi Jishi* (Xinjiang 1949: The true story of the September 25 uprising of the Guomindang occupying forces), Xinjiang Zhongda Lishi Ticai Wenxue Congshu (Literary Series on Major Themes in Xinjiang History) (Beijing: Zuojia chubanshe, 1998), pp. 1–2.

Notes to Chapter 15

1. Erik Eckholm, "U.S. Labeling of Group in China as Terrorist Is Criticized," *New York Times,* 13 September 2002, p. 1.

2. Chinese State Council, "White Paper on History and Development of Xinjiang," Beijing, 26 May 2003; and "China Also Harmed by Separatist-Minded Eastern Turkistan Terrorists," *People's Daily,* 10 October 2001.

3. Rym Brahimi, "Russia, China, and Central Asian Leaders Pledge to Fight Terrorism, Drug Smuggling," CNN News Service, 25 August 1999, www.uygur.org/enorg/wunn99/990825e.html (accessed 12 May 2002).

4. "People's Republic of China: Gross Violations of Human Rights in the Xinjiang Uyghur Autonomous Region," Amnesty International, 21 April 1999, p. 24.

5. Enver Can, speech to the UN High Commission on Human Rights, Geneva, Fifty-eighth sess., Item 11, 16 April 2002. In his speech, Can claimed to represent the Transnational Radical Party.

6. "Separatist Leader Vows to Target Chinese Government," Radio Free Asia, Uyghur Service, 24 January 2003, www.rfa.org/service/index.html?service=uyg (accessed10 May 2002).

7. Charles Hutzler, "Trade Is China's Carrot to Muslim Separatists," *Wall Street Journal,* 21 September 2001.

8. Erik Eckholm and Craig S. Smith, "Fearing Unrest, China Pressures Muslim Group," *New York Times,* 5 October 2001; and Pamela Pun, "Separatists Trained in Afghanistan, Says Official," *The Standard,* 22 October 2001, http://hk-imail.singtao.com/inews/public/article_v.cfm?articleid=30156&intcatid=2 (accessed 10 May 2002).

9. See the writings by Erkin Aliptékin, which also present alternative histories of the Uyghurs. Erkin Aliptékin, *Uygur Türkleri* (The Uyghur Turks) (Istanbul: Bogaziçi Yaygnlari, 1978); and "Xinjiang a Time Bomb Waiting to Explode," *South China Morning Post* (Hong Kong), 29 May 2002. For Aliptékin's involvement with the Unrecognized Nations and Peoples Organization in The Hague, see its website www.unpo.org/member/eturk.html (accessed 10 May 2002).

10. Information Office of the State Council of the People's Republic of China, "National Minority Policies and Its Practice in China," Beijing, 1999, p. 50; see also the Law of the People's Republic of China on Regional National Autonomy (1984), with full text of "National Minorities and Its Practice in China," Beijing, 28 September 1999, www.China.org.cn (accessed 10 May 2002). For poverty in the region, specifically among Uyghurs, see Calla Wiemer, chapter 6 in this volume; and Bruce Gilley, "'Uyghurs Need Not Apply,'" *Far Eastern Economic Review,* 28 August 2001.

11. "Uyghur Separatist Sentenced to Death," Reuters, 18 October 2001; Craig S. Smith, "Fearing Unrest, China Pressures Muslim Group," New York Times, 5 October 2001; and Pun, "Separatists Trained in Afghanistan, Says Official."

12. Albert O. Hirschman, Exit, Voice, and Loyalty: Responses to Decline in Firms, Organizations, and States (Cambridge, Mass.: Harvard University Press, 1970).

13. See Dru C. Gladney, Muslim Chinese: Ethnic Nationalism in the People's Republic (Cambridge, Mass.: Harvard University Press, 1996), pp. 122–130.

14. See discussions of this event, which had only sketchy reports, by Colin Mackerras, The New Cambridge Handbook of Contemporary China (Cambridge: Cambridge University Press, 2001), p. 38; and Michael Dillon, Xinjiang: Ethnicity, Separatism, and Control in Chinese Central Asia (Durham, N.C.: University of Durham Press, 1995), p. 26.

15. Reported in Dewardic L. McNeal, "China's Relations with Central Asian States and Problems with Terrorism," U.S. Department of State, Congressional Research Service Report, 2001, http://fpc.state.gov/documents/organization/7945.pdf (accessed 10 May 2002).

16. Xinjiang Daily, 9 April 1997, cited in People's Republic of China: Gross Violation of Human Rights in the Xinjiang Uyghur Autonomous Region (London: Amnesty International, 1999); and Xinjiang Daily, 21 July 1997, cited in Reuters (Beijing), 26 June 1997.

17. See Ildiko Beller-Hann, "Making the Oil Fragrant: Dealings with the Supernatural among the Uyghurs in Xinjiang," Asian Ethnicity 2, no.1 (2001): 9–23; see also Nathan Light, "Slippery Paths: The Performance and Canonization of Turkic Literature and Uyghur Muqam Song in Islam and Modernity" (Ph.D. diss., Indiana University, Bloomington, 1998), as well as his website on Uyghur and Turkic culture and art, www.utoledo.edu/~nlight/mainpage.htm (accessed 10 May 2002).

18. "Xinjiang Uygurs Blast Railway in Retaliation; Lanzhou Train Derails, Casualties Unknown," Ping Kuo Jih Pao (Hong Kong), 17 February 1997, Foreign Broadcast Information Service (FBIS) FTS19970505001156.

19. "Five 'Counterrevolutionaries' Executed for Bomb Explosions," Xinjiang Ribao (Urumchi), 31 May 1995, p. 1, FBIS, FTS19970417001417; "Xinjiang Government Worker Says Four Killed in Urumchi Blasts," Voice of Russia World Service (Moscow), 26 February 1997, FBIS, FTS19970513001178; and "Further on Bomb Explosions in Xinjiang," Agence France Presse (Hong Kong), 26 February 1997, FBIS, FTS19970513001179.

20. Pamela Pun, "Officials Say No Links Found between Separatists, Bombing," Hong Kong Standard (Hong Kong), 11 March 1997, p. 8, FBIS, FTS19970311000056.

21. "Exile Group Claims Bomb Blast in Xinjiang," Agence France Presse (Hong Kong), 1 March 1997, FBIS, FTS19970513001183.

22. Tung-chou Kuang, "Zhongnanhai Holds Emergency Meeting to Discuss Explosion Case, Mayor Says It Was a Political Incident in Retaliation against Society," Sing Tao Jih Pao (Hong Kong), 9 March 1997, p. A1, FBIS, FTS19970310000201; "Cracking Down on Separatist Organizations to Become Central Topic of Discussion at NPC, CPPCC Sessions," Ping Kuo Jih Pao (Hong Kong), 3 March 1998, p. A20, FBIS, FTS19980303000089; and "Radio Reports Bomb Blasts in Beijing, Guangzhou," Broadcasting Corporation of China News Network (Taipei), 9 March 1997, FBIS, FTS19970309000422.

23. See "A Bomb in Beijing," The Economist, 13 March 1997; and Patrick E. Tyler, "Chinese Muslims Recount Their Days of Terror," New York Times, 10 Novem-

446 NOTES TO PAGES 380–385

ber 1996, p. 3. Note that many Uyghurs in the diaspora believe that the bombs were set by Chinese authorities in order to justify a crackdown on Uyghurs in Xinjiang. See "Tao Siju Says No Evidence Shows Xinjiang People Commit Crime," *Ming Pao* (Hong Kong), 11 March 1997, p. A15, FBIS, FTS19970311000034.

24. "China Fears for Its Wild West," *The Economist,* 13 November 1997.

25. "Cracking Down on Separatist Organizations."

26. On the poisonings, see "Chinese Doctors Poisoned 150 Children," Eastern Turkistan Information Center, 15 May 1998; and "China Executes Woman for Fatal Child Poisonings," *Deutsche Presse-Agentur,* 19 January 1999. On the radioactive detonation, said to be due to the sale of dated weaponry by one PLA unit to another based in Guyuan, Ningxia, see Zhao Yu, "Defying Hazard in Five Days of Relentless Pursuit, Police Crack Smuggled Radioactive Case," *Xinjiang Ribao* (Urumchi), 11 November 1998, p. 1, FBIS, FTS19981130001784.

27. "People's Republic of China," p. 21.

28. *Xinjiang Daily,* 21 July 1997, cited in Reuters (Beijing), 26 June 1997; see also Nicolas Becquelin, "Xinjiang in the Nineties," *China Journal,* no. 44 (July 2001).

29. "People's Republic of China."

30. "Report Says Missile Base in Xinjiang Attacked," *Taiwan Central News Agency,* 27 February 1999, FBIS, FTS19990228000905; and "CPPCC Member Denies Reports on Missile Base Bombing," *Ta Kung Pao* (Hong Kong), 4 March 1999, p. A12, FBIS, FTS19990304000211.

31. "Power Station in Xinjiang Blown Up," *Cheng Ming* (Hong Kong), 1 August 1999, p. 29, FBIS, FTS19990803000414.

32. Unpublished report.

33. Ian Johnson, "China Arrests Noted Businesswoman in Crackdown in Muslim Region," *Wall Street Journal,* 18 August 1999.

34. See "Amnesty International, Library, China: Women's Rights Action 2000—Arbitrary Detention of Rebiya Kadeer—a Women's Human Rights Defender and Prisoner of Conscience," AI Index: ASA 17/04/00, http://web.amnesty.org/802568F7005C4453/0/08216A2C1385F107802568790040AB71?Open (accessed 10 May 2002).

35. Dru C. Gladney, "China's Ethnic Reawakening," *Asia Pacific Issues,* no. 18 (1995): 1–8.

36. Anwar Yusuf, interview by the author, Washington, D.C., 14 April 1999.

37. *Turkistan News and Information Network,* Press Release, 8 June 1999.

38. Philip Pan, "In China's West, Ethnic Strife Becomes 'Terrorism,'" *Washington Post,* 14 July 2002, p. A4.

39. See Yitzhak Shichor, "Virtual Transnationalism: Uygur Communities in Europe and the Quest for Eastern Turkistan Independence" (unpublished paper, 2002).

40. For example, see www.uyghur.org (accessed 10 May 2002), which is supported by Yusuf, who has suggested there are up to 25 million Uyghurs worldwide. Shichor, based on information from Enver Can in Munich, estimates there are about 500 Uyghurs in Germany (mostly in Munich), 500 in Belgium (mostly from Central Asia), 200 in Sweden (mostly from Kazakstan), 40 in England, 35 in Switzerland, 30 in Holland, and 10 in Norway. See Shichor, "Virtual Transnationalism." In addition, there are an estimated 10,000 Uyghurs in Turkey, 1,000 in the United States, 500 in Canada, and 200 in Australia (mostly in Melbourne).

41. See www.geocities.com/athens/9479/Uyghur.html (accessed 10 May 2002). The entire paragraph reads, "Area: 1.6 million sq. km. Population: 14 million (1990

census), Uyghurs: 7.2 million (official), 14–30 million (estimates by the Uyghur organizations abroad). Capital: Urumchi. The Sinkiang-Uyghur Autonomous Region in China (*Xinjiang Uygur Zizhiqu* in Chinese) is also known under the names Eastern Turkistan or Chinese Turkistan. Uyghur people prefer Uyghuristan. It is inhabited by the Uyghurs also known under names Uyghur, Uigur, Uygur, Weiwuer, Sart, Taranchi, Kashgarlik. The other native peoples are *Kazak, Uzbek, Kyrgyz, Tajik, Tatar.* Chinese colonization by Han people is a threat for the native peoples."

42. For a comparative study of the role of theme parks in ethnic identity construction in China and the United States, see Dru Gladney, "Theme Parks and Path Dependency: Comparing the Polynesian Cultural Center and the China Ethnic Cultural Park," in *Chinese Ethnology: Practice and Theory* (Taipei: Academia Sinica, forthcoming).

43. A list of some of the international Uyghur and East Turkistan organizations can be found at http://uyghuramerican.org/Uyghurorganiz.html (accessed 10 May 2002) and www.uygur.org/adres/uygur_organization.htm (accessed 10 May 2002).

44. See their website introduction, "The Uyghur American Association was established on 23 May 1998 in Washington, DC at the First Uyghur American Congress. The growing Uyghur community in the United States created a need for a unified Uyghur organization to serve the needs of the community here and to represent the collective voice of the Uyghurs in East Turkistan." See Uyghur American Association, http://uyghuramerican.org/ (accessed 10 May 2002).

45. See their organizational statement, "The Uyghur Human Rights Coalition (UHRC) is a 501(c)(3) nonprofit dedicated to educating Americans, particularly university students, about the Chinese government's human rights violations against the Uyghur people of the Xinjiang Uyghur Autonomous Region of China (known to the Uyghurs as East Turkistan). Through its educational efforts, the UHRC strives to build a broad base of support for the Uyghur people's struggle to obtain democratic freedoms and self-determination and to protect their culture and environment." See Uyghur Human Rights Coalition, www.uyghurs.org (accessed 10 May 2002).

46. Anwar Yusuf, e-mail to the author, 14 March 2002, "I also said to you that China is afraid of civil war with the people of Xinjiang, and which is why China always brutally crush [*sic*] the every effort of the Uyghur Muslims which advocates independence for Xinjiang. In short, I said that it would be the most joyful event for the people of Xinjiang if China would disintegrate as his communist neighbor Soviet Union did. I said that the people of Xinjiang did not have fear of widespread civil disorder. The people of Xinjiang have fought against the Chinese for over two hundred years without any fear. Why are they supposed to fear a civil war? As a representative for those brave Uyghur Muslims, I and my organization Eastern Turkistan National Freedom Center do support a free and independent Xinjiang, and that is exactly what I told President Clinton when I met with him on 4 June 1999."

47. Yusuf, interview.

48. For studies of the influence of the Internet in influencing wider public opinion in Asia, see Zaheer Baber, ed., "The Internet and Social Change in Asia and Beyond," *Asian Journal of Social Science* 30, no 2 (2002).

49. For studies related to the Internet's role in building community and mobilizing support for specific causes, see Derek Foster, "Community and Identity in the Electronic Village," in *Internet Culture*, ed. David Porter (New York, Routledge, 1997); Steven G. Jones, "The Internet and Its Social Landscape," in *Virtual Culture: Identity and Community in Cybersociety*, ed. Steven G. Jones (London: Sage, 1997); Tim Jordan, *Cyberpower: The Culture and Politics of Cyberspace and the Internet* (Lon-

don: Routledge, 1999); Douglas Rushkoff, *Cyberia: Life in the Trenches of Hyperspace* (New York: Harper Collins, 1994); and Mark A. Smith and Peter Kollock, eds., *Communities in Cyberspace* (London: Routledge, 1999).

50. The ETIM is a shadowy group known only to be previously active in Afghanistan and founded in the mid-1990s by Hassan Mahsum. Mahsum had served three years in a labor camp in Xinjiang where he recruited other Uyghurs, including his number three leader, Rashid, who was captured with the Taliban and returned to China in the spring of 2001. See Charles Hutzler, "China-Iraq Policy Is Risky for U.S.," *Asian Wall Street Journal,* 10 September 2001.

51. "China Also Harmed by Separatist-Minded Eastern Turkistan Terrorists," *People's Daily,* 10 October 2001; Eckholm, "U.S. Labeling of Group in China as Terrorist Is Criticized"; and Charles Hutzler, "U.S. Gesture to China Raises Crackdown Fears," *Wall Street Journal,* 13 September 2002.

52. Dewardic L. McNeal, "China's Relations with Central Asian States and Problems with Terrorism," in *Congressional Research Service Report* (Washington, D.C.: U.S. Department of State, 2001); see also Scott Fogden, "Writing Insecurity: The PRC's Push to Modernize China and the Politics of Uyghur Identity" (master's thesis, University of Wales, Aberystwyth, 2002).

53. Deputy Secretary of State Richard L. Armitage, "Conclusion of China Visit," Press Conference, Beijing, China, U.S. Department of State, 26 August 2002.

54. For example, Mehmet Hazret, in a recent interview (see following discussion), claimed he had never heard of the ETIM; "I hadn't even heard of ETIM until the Chinese government mentioned its name in a report in January 2002," he said. "But I knew the leaders of this group whom the report mentioned. For many years, they were in Chinese prisons for political reasons, and they escaped from China. We don't have any organizational relations with them because politically we don't share the same goals. But I cannot believe they carried out any terrorist attacks as the Chinese authorities say they did, because they themselves are victims of Chinese state terrorism." See "Separatist Leader Vows to Target Chinese Government."

55. See a "Special Report: Uyghur Muslim Separatists," Virtual Information Center, 28 September 2001, p. 6, www.vic-info.org (accessed 10 May 2002).

56. See "China: China Increases Suppression in Xinjiang," *Oxford Analytica,* 20 December 2002. The report concludes, "Distinguishing between genuine counterterrorism and repression of minority rights is difficult and the Uyghur case points to a lack of international guidelines for doing so. In any case, Chinese policies, not foreign-sponsored terrorism, are the cause of Uyghur unrest. China's development and control policy in Xinjiang is unlikely to stabilize the region as long as development benefits remain so unevenly distributed."

57. "Exile Group Claims Bomb Blast in Xinjiang."

58. Bombings in Tibet and other "terrorist acts" have been frequently reported in the press. For example, see "Explosion Hits Tibet's Capital after China Announces New Regional Leader," *Agence France Presse* (Hong Kong), 9 November 2000, FBIS, CPP20001109000079; "London Organization-Migrants' Shops Bombed in Tibet," *Agence France Presse* (Hong Kong), 27 December 1996, FBIS, FTS19970409001372; "Tibet Blames Dalai Lama for Bombing in Lhasa," Tibet People's Radio Network (Lhasa), 27 December 1996, FBIS, FTS19970409001370; Kang Che, "Bomb Explodes in Lhasa, Local Authorities Offer Reward for Capture of Criminals," *Ta Kung Pao* (Hong Kong), 30 December 1996, FBIS, FTS19970409001371; and "Suspect

Detained for Bomb Attack on Tibetan Clinic," *Agence France Presse* (Hong Kong), 14 January 1999, FBIS, FTS19990114000015.

59. See John Pomfret, "China Executes Tibetan Monk for Alleged Bombings," *Washington Post Foreign Service,* 28 January 2003. The RFA reported that the government is silencing any reporting on the execution, www.rfa.org/service/article.html?service=can&encoding=2&id=98250 (accessed 10 May 2002).

60. For a discussion of the various meanings of "jihad" in Islam, see John L. Esposito, *Unholy War: Terror in the Name of Islam* (Oxford: Oxford University Press, 2002), pp. 26–35. For studies among Uyghur and other Turkic communities in Istanbul, see Dru C. Gladney, "Relational Alterity: Constructing Dungan (Hui), Uygur, and Kazak Identities across China, Central Asia, and Turkey," *History and Anthropology* 9, no. 2 (1996): 445–477; and Ingvar Svanberg, *Kazak Refugees in Turkey: A Study of Cultural Persistence and Social Change* (Stockholm: Almqvist and Wiksell International, 1999).

61. "Separatist Leader Vows to Target Chinese Government."

62. Pan notes that during his summer 2002 visit no one revealed to him a recent assassination attempt in Yining until he was able to meet privately with a Uyghur resident. See Pan, "In China's West, Ethnic Strife Becomes 'Terrorism,'" p. A4.

63. Chien-Peng Chung, "China's 'War on Terror': September 11 and Uyghur Separatism," *Foreign Affairs* (July–August 2002): 8.

64. See "China: China Increases Suppression in Xinjiang," *Oxford Analytica,* 20 December 2002. The report notes, "Uyghur desire for self-rule has been strengthened by the political climate in Central Asia, a heightened sense of Islamic cultural and ethnic identity across the new republics, the support of Islamic groups in the new republics and the radicalizing effect of the war in Afghanistan."

65. Zheng Yongnian states, "Reform policies [in China] have led to the rise of ethnic consciousness and thus the emergence of ethnic nationalism as exemplified in Tibet. . . . The aim of Chinese nationalism is to pursue national power and wealth through domestic development." See Zheng Yongnian, *Discovering Chinese Nationalism in China* (Cambridge: Cambridge University Press, 1999), pp. 35, 147.

66. "China's Growing Problem with Xinjiang," *Janes Intelligence Digest,* 13 June 2000, www.janes.com/regional_news/asia_pacific/news/jid/jid000613_1_n.shtml (accessed 10 May 2002).

Bibliographic Guide to Xinjiang

Chapter 2
Political and Cultural History of the Xinjiang Region
through the Late Nineteenth Century
James A. Millward and Peter C. Perdue

On the famous mummies, see J. P. Mallory and Victor H. Mair, *The Tarim Mummies: Ancient China and the Mystery of the Earliest Peoples from the West* (New York: Thames and Hudson, 2000); and Elizabeth Wayland Barber, *The Mummies of Ürümchi* (New York: Norton, 1999). For the early imperial period, see Christopher I. Beckwith, *The Tibetan Empire in Central Asia* (Princeton, N.J.: Princeton University Press, 1993); Peter B. Golden, *An Introduction to the History of the Turkic Peoples: Ethnogenesis and State-Formation in Medieval and Early Modern Eurasia and the Middle East* (Wiesbaden: Harassowitz, 1992); and Thomas T. Allsen, "The Yuan Dynasty and the Uighurs of Turfan in the 13th Century," in *China among Equals: The Middle Kingdom and Its Neighbors, 10th–14th Centuries*, ed. Morris Rossabi (Berkeley: University of California Press, 1983), pp. 243–280.

For the Ming, see Morris Rossabi, *China and Inner Asia: From 1368 to the Present Day* (New York: Pica, 1975); and "Ming China and Turfan, 1406–1517," *Central Asiatic Journal* 16, no. 3 (1972). For a discussion linking Ming-Qing issues with contemporary developments, see Peter C. Perdue, "Bringing Xinjiang into the Fold: The Ming-Qing Era," in *La Chine et son Occident* (China and Its Western Frontier), ed François Godement (Paris: Centre Asie Ifri, 2002), pp. 81–110.

For the Qing period, the best short overview is still the chapters by Joseph Fletcher, "Ch'ing Inner Asia c. 1800" and "The Heyday of the Ch'ing Order in Mongolia, Sinkiang, and Tibet," in *The Cambridge History of China*, vol. 10, *Late Ch'ing, 1800–1911*, part I, ed. John K. Fairbank (Cambridge: Cambridge University Press, 1978), pp. 35–106, 351–408. Peter C. Perdue, *China Marches West: The Qing Conquest of Central Eurasia, 1600–1800* (Cambridge, Mass.: Harvard University Press, 2003), discusses the wars that brought Xinjiang into the empire. James A. Millward, *Beyond the Pass:*

Economy, Ethnicity, and Empire in Qing Central Asia, 1759–1864 (Stanford, Calif.: Stanford University Press, 1998), analyzes Qing incorporation of Xinjiang. Joanna Waley-Cohen, *Exile in Mid-Qing China: Banishment to Xinjiang, 1758–1820* (New Haven, Conn.: Yale University Press, 1991), discusses the exile colonies.

Chapter 3
Political History and Strategies of Control, 1884–1978
James A. Millward and Nabijan Tursun

For general surveys, see Zeng Wenwu, *Zhongguo jingying Xiyu shi* (History of China's management of the western regions) (1936; reprint, Urumchi: Xinjiang Weiwu'er zizhiqu zongbian shi, 1986); Chen Huisheng, *Minguo Xinjiang shi* (History of Xinjiang in the Chinese Republican period) (Urumchi: Xinjiang renmin chubanshe, 1999), covers 1911 to 1949; and Zhu Peimin, *Ershi shiji Xinjiang shi yanjiu* (Research on Xinjiang's twentieth-century history) (Urumchi: Xinjiang renmin chubanshe, 2000), is the only People's Republic of China (PRC) book on the post-1949 period and represents a first draft of an official line. For a rare but important Uyghur perspective, see Muhemmed Imin Bughra, *Sherqi Turkistan Tarixi* (History of Eastern Turkistan) (Kabul: N.p., 1940; reprint, Ankara: N.p., 1998).

Kim Ho-dong, *Holy War in China: The Muslim Rebellion and State in Chinese Central Asia, 1864–1877* (Stanford, Calif.: Stanford University Press, 2003), revises our understanding of Yaqub Beg and the character of the Qing reconquest of Xinjiang. The best work on the period from Zuo Zongtang's reconquest to the 1911 revolution is in Japanese: Kataoka Kazutada, *Shinchō Shinkyō tōji kenkyū* (Researches on Qing dynasty rule in Xinjiang) (Tokyo: Yū San Kaku, 1991). On the 1920s through the 1940s, see Andrew D. W. Forbes, *Warlords and Muslims in Chinese Central Asia: A Political History of Republican Xinjiang, 1911–1949* (Cambridge: Cambridge University Press, 1986). Shinmen Yashushi's "'Higashi Torukusitan kyōwakoku' (1933–34 nen) ni kansuru ichi kōsatsu" (An inquiry into the Eastern Turkistan Republic 1933–34), *Ajia-Afurika gengo bunka kenkyū*, nos. 46–47 (1994), and other works revise these errors on the basis of Uyghur and other sources. Linda Benson, *The Ili Rebellion: The Moslem Challenge to Chinese Authority in Xinjiang, 1944–1949* (Armonk, N.Y.: Sharpe, 1990), provides an account of the second Eastern Turkistan Republic in northern Xinjiang. David Wang's *Under the Soviet Shadow: The Yining Incident, Ethnic Conflicts and International Rivalry in Xinjiang, 1944–1949* (Hong Kong: Chinese University Press, 1999), resembles PRC histories in its overall outlook. For PRC-period

Xinjiang, the only history in English is Donald H. McMillen, *Chinese Communist Power and Policy in Xinjiang, 1949–1977* (Boulder, Colo.: Westview, 1979). James A. Millward's *Xinjiang: A History of Chinese Turkistan* (London: Hurst, forthcoming 2005) surveys the long durée of all Xinjiang history.

Chapter 4
The Chinese Program of Development and Control, 1978–2001
Dru C. Gladney

For an overview of human rights and Chinese rule in Xinjiang, see the comprehensive Amnesty International report "People's Republic of China: Gross Violations of Human Rights in the Xinjiang Uyghur Autonomous Region," Amnesty International (London), 21 April 1999. Gardner Bovingdon's "Can Wolves Too Be Descendants of the Dragon? Uyghur Resistance to Chinese Nationbuilding" (Ph.D. diss., Cornell University, 2001) is the best recent analysis of the challenges of Chinese rule in Xinjiang; see also the excellent analysis by Nicolas Becquelin, "Xinjiang in the Nineties," *China Journal*, no. 44 (July 2001): 23–38. For a survey of Chinese policy toward minorities, see Colin Mackerras, *China's Minorities: Integration and Modernization in the Twentieth Century* (Hong Kong: Oxford University Press, 1994). For current energy and development issues related to Chinese rule, see James P. Dorian, Brett Wigdortz, and Dru Gladney, "Central Asia and Xinjiang, China: Emerging Energy, Economic, and Ethnic Relations," *Central Asian Survey* 16, no. 4 (1997): 461–486; and Dru C. Gladney, "China's Interests in Central Asia: Energy and Ethnicity," in *Energy and Conflict in Central Asia and the Caucasus*, ed. Robert Ebel and Rajan Menon (Lanham, Md.: Rowman and Littlefield, 2002), pp. 209–223. An excellent recent treatment of Chinese rule and Uyghur religious practice is found in Ildiko Beller-Hann, "Making the Oil Fragrant: Dealings with the Supernatural among the Uyghurs in Xinjiang," *Asian Ethnicity* 2, no.1 (2001): 9–23. An earlier treatment of Uyghur identity under Chinese rule in the 1980s and 1990s can be found in Dru C. Gladney, "The Ethnogenesis of the Uyghur," *Central Asian Survey* 9, no. 1 (1990): 1–28.

Chapter 5
The Great Wall of Steel: Military and Strategy in Xinjiang
Yitzhak Shichor

Among the few articles on the Chinese military in Xinjiang is Donald H. McMillen, "The Urumqi Military Region: Defense and Security in China's West," *Asian Survey* 22, no. 8 (August 1982). Pieces of information on the military in Xinjiang can be gleaned from such general works as *Dangdai Zhongguo Jundui de Junshi Gongzuo* (China today: The military affairs of the Chinese army) (Beijing: Zhongguo shehui kexue chubanshe, 1989); William W. Whitson, with Chen-hsia Huang, *The Chinese High Command: A History of Communist Military Politics, 1927–71* (London: Macmillan, 1973); and You Ji, *The Armed Forces of China* (St. Leonards, Australia: Allen and Unwin, 1999).

On the consolidation of Chinese rule in Xinjiang, see Zhonggong Xinjiang Weiwuer Zizhiqu Weiyuanhui Dangshi Yanjiushi (Xinjiang-Uyghur Autonomous Region Chinese Communist Party History Research Office), comp., *Xinjiang Jiefang* (Xinjiang's liberation) (Urumchi: Xinjiang xinhua shudian, 1999). On the military involvement in Xinjiang's economy, see James D. Seymour, "Xinjiang's Production and Construction Corps, and the Sinification of Eastern Turkestan," *Inner Asia*, no. 2 (2000).

For occasional discussions of Xinjiang's strategic situation, see Allen S. Whiting, *The Chinese Calculus of Deterrence: India and Indochina* (Ann Arbor: University of Michigan Press, 1975); Melvin Gurtov and Byong-Moo Hwang, *China under Threat: The Politics of Strategy and Diplomacy* (Baltimore, Md.: Johns Hopkins University Press, 1980); John W. Garver, *Protracted Contest: Sino-Indian Rivalry in the Twentieth Century* (Seattle: University of Washington Press, 2001); O. B. Borisov and B. T. Koloskov, *Soviet-Chinese Relations, 1945–1970* (Bloomington: Indiana University Press, 1975); Harry Gelman, *The Soviet Far East Buildup and Soviet Risk-Taking against China* (Santa Monica, Calif.: RAND, August 1982); and Yaacov Vertzberger, *The Enduring Entente: Sino-Pakistani Relations 1960–1980*, The Washington Papers, no. 95 (New York: Praeger, 1983).

Chapter 6
The Economy of Xinjiang
Calla Wiemer

China's National Bureau of Statistics and its subordinate, the Xinjiang Uyghur Autonomous Region Bureau of Statistics, put out annual yearbooks (*China Statistical Yearbook*; *Xinjiang Statistical Yearbook*; and *Xinjiang Production and Construction Group Statistical Yearbook*), as well as occasional historical compendia (*Xinjiang Glorious 50 Years* and *50 Years of New China: The Volume of Xinjiang Production and Construction Group*) that report economic statistics. Provincial trade data are to be found in the Customs General Administration publication *China Monthly Exports and Imports*. The Development Research Center of the State Council, www.drcnet.com.cn (accessed 24 May 2002), maintains a website containing up-to-date regional economic news. A well-researched comprehensive treatment of the Xinjiang economy in Chinese has been compiled by the Xinjiang Academy of Social Sciences: Wang Shuanqian, ed., *Zou xiang 21 Shiji de Xinjiang* (Xinjiang moving toward the 21st century) (Urumchi: Xinjiang People's Publishing House, 1999).

Chapter 7
Education and Social Mobility among
Minority Populations in Xinjiang
Linda Benson

For the contemporary period, primary sources include the Xinjiang yearbooks (*Xinjiang Nianjian*), Xinhua press reports, and daily translations from the Chinese media published by the U.S. government's Foreign Broadcast International Service, China service. Together, these provide official data on education, although some kinds of information are either not collected or not made available, for example, on the ratio of males to females. Information on policy is found in some of these publications as well as in general English-language works on minorities. For an overview of policy since 1949, see Colin Mackerras, *China's Minority Cultures* (New York: Longman/St. Martin's, 1995); Thomas Heberer, *China and Its National Minorities: Autonomy or Assimilation* (Armonk, N.Y.: Sharpe, 1989); and June Teufel Dreyer, *China's Forty Millions: Minority Nationalities and National Integration in the People's Republic of China* (Cambridge, Mass.: Harvard University Press, 1976).

Comparative material for this chapter is drawn from studies of specific minority populations in China. See especially Dru Gladney, *Muslim Chinese: Ethnic Nationalism in the People's Republic* (Cambridge, Mass.: Harvard University Press, 1991); Stevan Harrell, ed., *Perspectives on the Yi of Southwest China* (Seattle: University of Washington Press, 2001); Jonathan N. Lipman, *Familiar Strangers: A History of Muslims in Northwest China* (Seattle: University of Washington Press, 1997); Charles McKhann, "The Nazi and the Nationalities Question," in *Cultural Encounters on China's Ethnic Frontiers*, ed. Stevan Harrell (Seattle: University of Washington Press, 1995), pp. 39–62; Katherine Kaup, *Creating the Zhuang: Ethnic Politics in China* (London: Rienner, 2000); and Ralph Litzinger, *Other Chinas: The Yao and the Politics of National Belonging* (Durham, N.C.: Duke University Press, 2001). Of particular importance for this chapter is the recent research by William C. Clark, whose ten years of experience living in Urumchi and Yining brought him remarkable access to those urban Uyghur communities. See William C. Clark, "Convergence or Divergence: Uighur Family Change in Urumqi" (Ph.D. diss., University of Washington, Seattle, 1999).

Chapter 8
A "Land of Borderlands": Implications of Xinjiang's Trans-border Interactions
Sean R. Roberts

Zhao Yueyao's master's thesis is one of the only longer works that examines Xinjiang's recent "reopening" to Central Asia, "Xinjiang and Central Asia: Ethno-religious, Political, and Economic Interactions" (master's thesis, Florida International University, 1993). Articles on this subject include Dru Gladney, "Transnational Islam and Uighur National Identity: Salaman Rushdie, Sino-Muslim Missile Deals, and the Trans-Eurasian Railway," *Central Asian Survey* 11, no. 3 (1992): 1–21; Justin Rudelson, "The Uighurs in the Future of Central Asia," *Nationalities Papers* 22, no. 2 (1994): 291–308; James Dorian, Brett Wigdortz, and Dru Gladney, "Central Asia and Xinjiang, China: Emerging Energy, Economic, and Ethnic Relations," *Central Asian Survey* 16, no. 4 (1997): 461–486; and Will Raczka, "Xinjiang and Its Central Asian Borderlands," *Central Asian Survey* 17, no. 3 (1998): 373–407.

Russian-language sources that provide more in-depth analysis of the socioeconomic and political processes at Xinjiang's borders include Konstantin Syroezhkin, "Kitai i Tsentral'naia Aziia: politicheskie otnoshenie i torgovo-ekonomicheskoe partnerstvo," *Kazakstan-spektr: analiticheskie issledovaniia* 1–2 (1997): 109; and Vitalii Khliupin, *Geopoliticheskii treugol'nik: Kazakstan-Kitai-Rossiia proshloe i nastoiaschee pogranichnoi problemy* (Washington, D.C.: International Eurasian Institute for Economic and Political Research, 1999).

Finally, my own work looks at the subject from the perspective of the cross-border Uyghur community between Central Asia and Xinjiang. See Sean R. Roberts, "Uyghur Neighborhoods and Nationalisms in the Former Sino-Soviet Borderland: An Historical Ethnography of a Stateless Nation on the Margins of Modernity" (Ph.D. diss., University of Southern California, 2003); Sean R. Roberts, "Toasting the Nation: Negotiating Stateless Nationalism in Transnational Ritual Space," *The Journal of Ritual Studies* 18, no. 2 (2004); Sean R. Roberts, "Locality, Islam, and National Culture in a Changing Borderlands: The Revival of the Mäshräp Ritual among Young Uighur Men in the Ili Valley," *Central Asian Survey* 17, no. 4 (1998): 673–700; Sean R. Roberts, "The Uighurs of the Kazakstan Borderlands: Migration and the Nation," *Nationalities Papers* 26, 3 (1998): 511–530; and Sean R. Roberts, *Waiting for Uighurstan* (Los Angeles: University of Southern California, Center for Visual Anthropology, 1996), video.

Chapter 9
The Demography of Xinjiang
Stanley W. Toops

To understand the changing demography of China, one should start with Judith Bannister, *China's Changing Population* (Stanford, Calif.: Stanford University Press, 1987); and Dudley L. Poston Jr. and David Yaukey, eds., *The Population of Modern China* (New York: Plenum, 1992). The best introduction to the historical geography of the area remains Owen Lattimore, *Inner Asian Frontiers of China* (London: Oxford University Press, 1940). For Xinjiang's demography, see, in chronological order, Chang Chih-yi, "Land Utilization and Settlement Possibilities in Sinkiang," *Geographical Review* 39 (1949): 57–75; M. Freeberne, "Demographic and Economic Changes in the Sinkiang Uighur Autonomous Region," *Population Studies* 20, no. 1 (1966): 103–124; Yuan Qingli, "Population Changes in Xinjiang Uighur Autonomous Region (1949–1984)," *Central Asian Survey* 9 (1990): 49–73; C. Pannell and L. Ma, "Urban Transition and Interstate Relations in a Dynamic Post-Soviet Borderland: The Xinjiang Uygur Autonomous Region of China," *Post-Soviet Geography and Economics* 38, no. 4 (1997): 206–229; and S. Toops, "The Population Landscape of Xinjiang/East Turkistan," *Inner Asia* 2, no. 2 (2000): 155–170. *Inner Asia* 2, no. 2 (2000) profiles Xinjiang history, economy, demography, colonization, ethnicity, and nationalism. A close reading of Chinese publications such as *Xinjiang Statistical Yearbook* will also prove fruitful.

Chapter 10
The Ecology of Xinjiang: A Focus on Water
Stanley W. Toops

Useful Chinese sources on Xinjiang's ecology are found in Xie Xiangfang, ed., *Xinjiang Weiwuer Zizhiqu Jingji Dili* (Xinjiang Uyghur Autonomous Region economic geography) (Beijing: Xinhua Press, 1991); and in various editions of *Ganhan Dili* (Arid land geography) produced by the Xinjiang Academy of Sciences.

The best overall historical geography of the area's environment remains Owen Lattimore, *Inner Asian Frontiers of China* (London: Oxford University Press, 1940). Another geographer, T. Hoope, has two valuable works, "An Essay on Reproduction: The Example of Xinjiang Uighur Autonomous Region," in *Learning from China?* ed. B. Glaeser (London: Allen and Unwin, 1987), pp. 56–84; and "Observations on Uygur Land Use in Turpan County, Xinjiang: A Preliminary Report on Fieldwork in Summer 1985," *Central Asiatic Journal* 31, nos. 3–4 (1987): 224–251.

Chapter 11
Public Health and Social Pathologies in Xinjiang
Jay Dautcher

On China's health care system during the Maoist era, see Joseph R. Quinn, ed., *Medicine and Public Health in the People's Republic of China*, DHEW Publication No. (NIH) 73–67 (Washington, D.C.: John E. Fogarty International Center for Advanced Study in the Health Sciences, 1973); and Marilynn M. Rosenthal, *Health Care in the People's Republic of China* (Boulder, Colo.: Westview, 1987). On changes in the health care system between 1979 and the present, see Yanzhong Huang, "The Paradoxical Transition in China's Health System," *Harvard Health Policy Review* 3, no. 1 (Spring 2002); and Mei-ling Wang, "The Impact of WTO Membership on China's Healthcare System: A Political Analysis," *Harvard Health Policy Review* 3, no. 2 (Fall 2002). The Xinjiang Uyghur Autonomous Region–PRC HIV/AIDS Prevention and Care Project is available at www.ausaid.gov.au/publications/pdf/hivprevention_china_pdd.pdf and presents information from field researchers not yet available in published journals.

Chinese-language sources include the summaries on health care that appear in the yearbook released by the Xinjiang Uyghur Autonomous Region People's Government, *Xinjiang nianjian* (Urumchi: Renmin chubanshe, Year[s]); see also *Xinjiang yi xue yuan xue bao*, also known as *Acta Academiae Medicinae Xinjiang* (Journal of Xinjiang Medical College), which provides information on a wide range of health issues in the region.

Among Uyghur-language materials, Sidiq Rahmat and Mukhtar Mamut Muhammidi, eds., in *Mäshhur Uyghur tevipliri* (Famous Uyghur physicians) (Kashgar: Uyghur Näshriyatim, 1997), offer a review of Uyghur traditional medical practice, accompanied by a valuable bibliography.

Chapter 12
Acculturation and Resistance: Xinjiang Identities in Flux
Justin Rudelson and William Jankowiak

This chapter examines various modes of acculturation and resistance through the path-breaking model developed by Johan Galtung in his chapter "China's Path to Development," in *Learning from China? Development and Environment in Third World Countries*, ed. Bernhard Glaeser (London: Allen and Unwin, 1983). This model was combined with Justin Rudelson's approach to studying the flux of multiple Uyghur identities in his *Oasis Identities: Uyghur Nationalism along China's Silk Road* (New York: Columbia University Press, 1997). Besides some research that has been made available through dissertations, there are few studies on ethnic identity change in Xinjiang besides Rudelson's. These include Ji Ping, "Frontier Migration and Ethnic Assimilation: A Case of Xinjiang Uygur Autonomous Region of China" (Ph.D. diss., Brown University, 1990); and William C. Clark, "Convergence or Divergence: Uighur Family Change in Urumqi" (Ph.D. diss., University of Washington, 1997).

The chapter also draws from many other studies of non-Xinjiang ethnic minority identity in China that focus on China's acculturation efforts on individuals, involving China's promotion of talented minorities, and minority efforts at cultural resistance. Several notable works include William Jankowiak, *Sex, Death and Hierarchy in a Chinese City* (New York: Columbia University Press, 1993); Stevan Harrell, ed., *Perspectives on the Yi of Southwest China* (Berkeley: University of California Press, 2001); Mette Halskov Hansen, *Lessons in Being Chinese* (Seattle: University of Washington Press, 1999); P. K. Kaup, *Ethnic Politics in China* (Boulder, Colo.: Rienner, 2000); L. Schein, *Minority Rules* (Durham, N.C.: Duke University Press, 2000); R. Litzinger, *Yao* (Durham, N.C.: Duke University Press, 2000); and Martin Schoenhals, "Education and Ethnicity among the Liangshan Yi," in *Perspectives on the Yi of Southwest China*, ed. Stevan Harrell (Berkeley: University of California Press, 2001).

Chapter 13
Islam in Xinjiang
Graham E. Fuller and Jonathan N. Lipman

The bibliographical resources on Islam in Xinjiang are scattered and often difficult to find. There is no single-volume monograph on the subject in English, though many articles have been published in scholarly journals. The monographs by James A. Millward, Linda Benson, Andrew D. W. Forbes, and Joanna Waley-Cohen, among others cited in our notes, should certainly be consulted for material on Islam. For the eighteenth and nineteenth centuries, the work of the late Joseph Fletcher remains fundamental, "Ch'ing Inner Asia c. 1800" and "The Heyday of the Ch'ing Order in Mongolia, Sinkiang, and Tibet," in *The Cambridge History of China*, vol. 10, *Late Ch'ing, 1800–1911*, part I, ed. John K. Fairbank (Cambridge: Cambridge University Press, 1978). Other essays may be found in Joseph Fletcher, *Studies on Chinese and Islamic Inner Asia*, Variorum Collected Studies Series, ed. Beatrice Forbes Manz (London: Variorum, 1995). For a more recent analysis of Muslim leadership in Qing Xinjiang, see Laura Newby, "The Begs of Xinjiang: Between Two Worlds," *Bulletin of the School of Oriental and African Studies* 61, no. 2 (1998): 278–297. To contrast the situation of Uygurs in Xinjiang with that of the Hui elsewhere in China, see Jonathan N. Lipman, "White Hats, Oil Cakes, and Common Blood: The Huizu in the Contemporary Chinese State," in *Governing China's Multiethnic Frontiers*, ed. Morris Rossabi (Seattle: University of Washington Press, forthcoming).

The histories of Islam in Xinjiang published in China are far more detailed and comprehensive, but they must necessarily conform to the line of the Chinese government, including its conceptions of "minority nationality" and the eternal solidarity of all of China's peoples. As a result, they often indulge in serious historical distortion, and their accounts all end in 1949. They nonetheless contain valuable data. In Chinese, see Zhongguo Xinjiang diqu Yisilan jiao shi bian xie zu, *Zhongguo Xinjiang diqu Yisilan jiao shi* (Urumchi: Xinjiang renmin, 2000); and in Uyghur, see Haji Nurhaji and Chen Guoguang, *Shinjang Islam tarikhi* (Beijing: Millatlar Nashriyati, 1995).

Chapter 14
Contested Histories
Gardner Bovingdon, with contributions by Nabijan Tursun

To date, very little has been written in English on nationalist historiography in Xinjiang. Justin Rudelson has written two of the first focused accounts, "Uighur Historiography and Uighur Ethnic Nationalism," in *Ethnicity, Minorities, and Cultural Encounters*, ed. Ingvar Svanberg (Uppsala, Sweden: Centre for Multiethnic Research, Uppsala University, 1991); and *Oasis Identities: Uyghur Nationalism along China's Silk Road* (New York: Columbia University Press, 1997), chapter 6. Gardner Bovingdon, "The History of the History of Xinjiang," *Twentieth Century China* 26, no. 2 (2001), compares the Chinese historiography of the region before and after the 1949 revolution.

Liu Ge and Huang Xianyang provide an index of both source texts and historiography in Chinese in *Xiyu Shidi Lunwen Ziliao Suoyin* (An index of papers and materials on the history and geography of the western regions) (Urumchi: Xinjiang renmin chubanshe, 1988). For an index of historiography in Uyghur, see Räkhimä Osman and Khalidä Šarakhman, *Uyghur Tarikhigha A'it Maqalilar Katalogi* (Catalog of articles concerning Uyghur history) (Urumchi: Šinjang khälq näšriyati, 1993). For two scholarly studies in Russian, see Nabijan Tursun, *Voprosy etnogeneza Uigurov v Kitaiskoi istoriografii* (The problem of Uyghur ethnogenesis in Chinese historiography) (Moscow: Izdatelstvo "Turkestan," 1997); and Nabijan Tursun, *Voprosy politicheskoi istorii Uigurov v Kitaiskoi istoriografii* (Questions concerning the political history of the Uyghurs in Chinese historiography) (Moscow: Izdatelstvo "Turkestan," 1998).

Articles by Igor de Rachewiltz, Corradini, and Stary in *The East and the Meaning of History* (Rome: Bardi Editore, 1994) analyze Chinese revisions of the history of Mongols and Manchus. For studies of the politicization of historiography in China more generally, see Prasenjit Duara, *Rescuing History from the Nation: Questioning Narratives of Modern China* (Chicago: University of Chicago Press, 1995); Albert Feuerwerker, ed., *History in Communist China* (Cambridge, Mass.: MIT Press, 1968); and Jonathan Unger, ed., *Using the Past to Serve the Present* (Armonk, N.Y.: Sharpe, 1993).

Chapter 15
Responses to Chinese Rule: Patterns of
Cooperation and Opposition
Dru C. Gladney

For a recent assessment of China's participation in the U.S.-led war on terrorism, see Chien-Peng Chung, "China's 'War on Terror': September 11 and Uighur Separatism," *Foreign Affairs* (July–August 2002). The analytical approach adopted in this chapter can be found in Albert O. Hirschman, *Exit, Voice, and Loyalty: Responses to Decline in Firms, Organizations, and States* (Cambridge, Mass.: Harvard University Press, 1972). There is a plethora of Internet sites and Web links to Xinjiang and Uyghur human rights issues, but there is no central site that is regularly updated. Information on Uyghur organizations and Internet sites has been gathered by the Uyghur American Association, www.uyghuramerican.org (accessed 10 May 2002). An interactive question-and-answer site with a "Special Report: Uyghur Muslim Separatists" can be found at the Virtual Information Center, www.vic-info.org (accessed Virtual Information Center), which is an open-source organization funded by the U.S. Commander in Chief, Pacific Command.

An excellent example of a Uyghur nationalist view of Uyghur history can be found in Eastern Turkestani Union in Europe, "Brief History of the Uyghers," n.d., www.geocities.com/CapitolHill/1730/buh.html (accessed 10 May 2002). For indigenous responses to educational issues, see Dru C. Gladney, "Making Muslims in China: Education, Islamicization, and Representation," in *China's National Minority Education: Culture, Schooling, and Development*, ed. Gerard A. Postiglione (New York: Garland, 1999). For a discussion of minority rights in Chinese law, see Barry Sautman, "Legal Reform and Minority Rights in China," in *Handbook of Global Legal Policy*, ed. Stuart Nagel (New York: Marcel Dekker, 1999), pp. 49–80.

Contributors

Linda Benson is a professor of history and international studies at Oakland University, Rochester, Michigan. She holds a master's in philosophy from Hong Kong University and a doctorate from the University of Leeds (UK). In addition to publishing numerous book chapters and articles on modern Xinjiang, she is the author of several books, including *The Ili Rebellion: The Moslem Challenge to Chinese Authority in Xinjiang, 1944–1949* (1990), *China's Last Nomads: The History and Culture of China's Kazaks* (1998), and most recently, *China Since 1949* (2002). Benson is currently completing a study of Western women travelers in northwest China during the early twentieth century.

Gardner Bovingdon received a bachelor's in politics from Princeton University and a master's and doctorate in government from Cornell University. He conducted twenty-two months of research in Xinjiang between 1994 and 2002. His significant publications include articles on historiography and popular resistance in *Twentieth Century China* (2001) and *Modern China* (2002), as well as a chapter on regional autonomy in the volume *Governing China's Multiethnic Frontiers* (forthcoming). Bovingdon is currently working on two monographic projects, one on the political contest between the Chinese government and Uyghurs, and the other on nationalist historiography in China. He has previously taught political science at Yale and Washington Universities and currently teaches in the Department of Central Eurasian Studies at Indiana University.

Jay Dautcher received his doctorate in social-cultural anthropology from the University of California, Berkeley, in 1999. After postdoctoral research at Harvard University and the University of California, Berkeley, he joined the University of Pennsylvania faculty as an assistant professor of anthropology and folklore. Dautcher's book *Down a Narrow Road: Uighur Society in Northwest China* (forthcoming) portrays the impact of economic development and Islamic revitalization on community life among ethnic Uyghurs in Xinjiang. He has received support from the National Science Foundation, the Social Science Research Council, the MacArthur Foundation, the Mellon Foundation, and the Committee for Scholarly Communication with China. Dautcher is currently conducting ethnographic research on alcohol consumption in China and examining new drinking activities and the practices of actors in institutional networks of beverage marketing, beverage regulation, and alcoholism treatment, which shape the social field of drinking.

Graham E. Fuller was a former vice chairman of the Central Intelligence Agency's National Intelligence Council where he was responsible for all long-range global forecasting. He served twenty years in the U.S. Foreign Service, spending seventeen years abroad in the Muslim world and Hong Kong. He speaks Russian, Turkish, Arabic, and Chinese. He was a senior political scientist at RAND Corporation for twelve years. Since then, he has traveled extensively in the Muslim world, including Xinjiang, doing research on Islamist movements. Fuller has written a large number of studies and numerous books on the interrelationships of politics, ethnicity, and religion in the Muslim world, including a RAND study on "The New Geopolitics of Central Asia" (1992). His books include *The Democracy Trap: Perils of the Post–Cold War World* (1991), *The Center of the Universe: The Geopolitics of Iran* (1991), *Turkey's New Geopolitics: From the Balkans to Western China* (1993), *Turkey's Kurdish Question* (1995), and *The Arab Shi'a: The Forgotten Muslims* (1999). His latest book is *The Future of Political Islam* (2003).

Dru C. Gladney is a professor in the Asian Studies and Anthropology departments at the University of Hawaii, Manoa. A cultural anthropologist, he has conducted fieldwork among Muslims in China for over twenty years, visiting Xinjiang every year since 1985. Gladney has been a Fulbright Research Scholar twice to China and Turkey, and he has authored over fifty academic articles and chapters, as well as the books *Muslim Chinese: Ethnic Nationalism in the People's Republic* (1996), *Ethnic Identity in China: The Making of a Muslim Minority Nationality* (1998), and *Dislocating China: Muslims, Minorities, and Other Sub-altern Subjects* (2003). His research languages include Mandarin Chinese, Turkish, Uyghur, Kazak, Russian, and French.

William Jankowiak is a professor of anthropology at the University of Nevada, Las Vegas. He is the author of *Sex, Death and Hierarchy in a Chinese City: An Anthropological Account* (1993) and editor of *Romantic Passion: A Universal Experience?* (1995) and (with Dan Bradburd) *Stimulating Trade: Drugs, Labor and Expansion* (2003). In addition to numerous academic publications on Chinese society and cross-cultural topics, Jankowiak has written for *The World and I* and *Natural History.* His current research projects include an ethnography of a Mormon polygamous community and a restudy of Huhehot, Inner Mongolia.

Jonathan N. Lipman is a professor of history at Mount Holyoke College, where he has taught since 1977. A specialist on Islam and Muslims in China, he is the author of *Familiar Strangers: A History of Muslims in Northwest China* (1997) and of numerous articles and book chapters, as well as translations from Chinese and Japanese sources. Research for this chapter was supported in part by the National Endowment for the Humanities.

James A. Millward (bachelor's from Harvard University in 1982; master's from the School of Oriental and African Studies, University of London, in 1985; and doctorate from Stanford University in 1993) is an associate professor of intersocietal history at the Edmund Walsh School of Foreign Service, Georgetown University, where he teaches world and Asian history. His research focuses on the modern history of Chinese frontiers with Inner and Central Asia, including Mongolia, Tibet, and especially Xinjiang. He has lived and traveled extensively in China and throughout the Xinjiang region. Millward's other publications include *Beyond the Pass: Economy, Ethnicity and Empire in Qing Central Asia, 1759–1864* (1998) and *Xinjiang: A History of Chinese Turkestan* (forthcoming). He is also the coeditor of *New Qing Imperial History: The Manchu Summer Palace at Chengde* (forthcoming).

Peter C. Perdue is the T. T. and Wei Fong Chao Professor of Asian Civilizations and a professor of history at the Massachusetts Institute of Technology. His publications include *Exhausting the Earth: State and Peasant in Hunan, 1500–1850 A.D.* (1987), "Military Mobilization in Seventeenth- and Eighteenth-Century China, Russia, and Mongolia" (1996), "Boundaries, Maps, and Movement: Chinese, Russian, and Mongolian Empires in Early Modern Central Eurasia" (1998), and "China in the Early Modern World: Shortcuts, Myths and Realities" (1999). Perdue's current interests focus on environmental change, ethnicity, and the relationship between long-term economic change and military conquest in the Chinese and Russian empires. His forthcoming book, *China Marches West: The Qing Conquest of Central Eurasia, 1600–1800,* offers an integrated account of the Chinese and Russian conquest of Siberia and Central Eurasia in the seventeenth and eighteenth centuries.

Sean R. Roberts is a social anthropologist doing research on the Uyghur communities of both Xinjiang and former Soviet Central Asia. He has spent over six years in Central Asia and has made several trips to Xinjiang during that time. In 1996, he produced a one-hour-long documentary about the Uyghur community of Kazakstan entitled *Waiting for Uighurstan*. He is also the author of several articles on the Uyghur community of the Xinjiang-Kazakstan borderland. His dissertation, which was defended at the University of Southern California in 2003, is entitled "Uyghur Neighborhoods and Nationalisms in the Former Sino-Soviet Borderland: An Historical Ethnography of a Stateless Nation on the Margins of Modernity." Roberts presently lives in Almaty, Kazakstan, where he manages programs focused on democratic reform, human rights, and independent media for the U.S. Agency for International Development. Roberts is fluent in the Uyghur, Russian, and Uzbek languages and is learning Kyrgyz.

Justin Rudelson is the first anthropologist to conduct fieldwork in Xinjiang, China, research conducted in 1984–85 and in 1989–90 that resulted in his book *Oasis Identities: Uyghur Nationalism along China's Silk Road* (1997). He conducted his undergraduate work in Asian studies at Dartmouth College and received his master's (1988) and doctorate (1992) in anthropology from Harvard University. Rudelson taught anthropology and Asian studies at Tulane University and later served as the deputy director of the Central Asia–Caucasus Institute of the Johns Hopkins University–SAIS and as the executive director of the Institute for Global Chinese Affairs at the University of Maryland. He is head of the Mandarin language program at Suffield Academy in Connecticut.

Yitzhak Shichor is a professor of political science and East Asian studies at the University of Haifa and a senior research fellow at the Harry S. Truman Research Institute for the Advancement of Peace, Hebrew University of Jerusalem. He is a former Michael William Lipson Chair in Chinese studies, dean of students at the Hebrew University, and provost of the Tel-Hai Academic College; his research and publications cover China's military modernization and defense conversion, Middle East policy and arms transfers, international energy policy, Sino-Uyghur relations and the Uyghur diaspora, and the Eastern Turkistan independence movement.

S. Frederick Starr is the founding chairman of the Central Asia–Caucasus Institute at Johns Hopkins University's Nitze School of Advanced International Studies. Starr has been involved in Turkic studies since spending several years doing archaeological work at Gordium in Turkey and mapping ancient roads across Anatolia. He serves as a rector pro tem of the University of Central Asia, a private, secular, and coeducational institution of higher education serving the region's most remote mountain regions. Prior to that, he served as president of the Aspen Institute, president of Oberlin College, and vice president of Tulane University. He was the founding director of the Kennan Institute for Advanced Russian Studies at the Wilson Center in Washington. He has written or edited twenty-one books and several hundred articles, most recently on conflicts in mountain regions and on economic developments in Central Asia.

Stanley W. Toops is an associate professor of geography and international studies at Miami University in Oxford, Ohio. He received his master's (1983) and doctorate (1990) in geography at the University of Washington, Seattle, each on minority regions of China (Yunnan and Xinjiang). He has made over fifteen research trips to Xinjiang since 1985, when he studied Uyghur at Xinjiang University. Besides his work on the geography of China, Toops has written a number of articles on Xinjiang that have appeared in journals such as *Inner Asia, Central Asian Survey, Central Asiatic Journal, Annals of Tourism Research*, and *Journal of Cultural Geography* and in books such as the edited volumes *Tourism in China* (1995) and *Changing China* (2003).

Nabijan Tursun was born in East Turkistan, received his bachelor's from the Central University for Nationalities, served as assistant professor at Xinjiang University, and later studied Chaghatay and Persian in Beijing as a visiting scholar. He received his master's in Uyghur history from Xinjiang University and his doctorate from the Institute for Oriental Studies of the Russian Academy of Sciences, shortly after which he was named a member of the Russian Orientalists' Society. From 1996 to 1998, he was an associate professor in the Department of Uyghur Language and Literature of the Kyrgyzstan State University. Tursun has published three books and over a hundred articles on Uyghur and Central Asian history, culture, and politics. He has also published a novel, short stories, and other literary works. Tursun speaks and writes Uyghur, Mandarin, Russian, English, Kyrgyz, Uzbek, Turkish, and other Turkic languages. He now works as an independent scholar.

Calla Wiemer took up freelance consulting on the Chinese economy in 1997 after spending thirteen years on the University of Hawaii economics faculty. She has advised the Asian Development Bank on China's economic relations with Central Asia, examining Xinjiang's border trade in this capacity. Having embarked on a China career with dissertation research at Nanjing University in 1981 for a doctorate at the University of Wisconsin, Wiemer's study of China spans the reform era.

Index

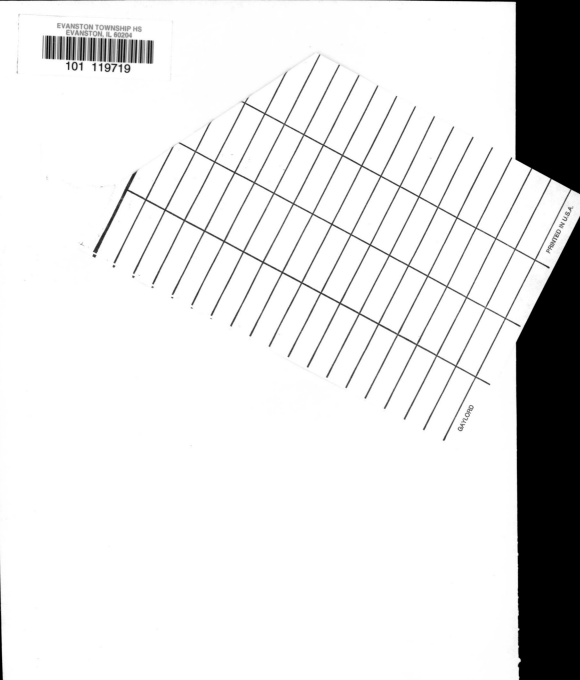

GAYLORD

PRINTED IN U.S.A.